THE MODERNIST PAPERS

THE MODERNIST PAPERS

FREDRIC JAMESON

Published in India by ABS Publishers & Distributors,
E-9, Jungpura Ext., New Delhi - 110014 (INDIA)

First Published by Verso 2007

For information, address : Verso, 6, Meard Street, London, WIFOEG, United Kingdom.

First Indian Edition, September 2007

Reprinted by arrangement with Verso, U.K.

International Standard Book Number : 978-81-905832-0-6

A Catalogue record for this book is available from British Library.

This reprint edition is a complete reproduction
of the U.K. Edition specially authorized, by the
original publisher, Verso U.K. for publication and Sale in South Asia.

Printed in India at Vishal Binding House, B-15, Sector-65, Noida.

In memory of Claudio Guillén

Contents

PART FIVE

PART SIX

PART SEVEN

Introduction

The coherence of any serious and extended engagement with cultural experience depends on a productive coordination between contingency and theory; between chance encounters and an intellectual project. It is true that we always try to resolve this tension one way or the other, by philosophically confirming the aleatory nature of the experience, or subsuming the personal under a theoretical meaning. But the vitality of the engagement depends on keeping the tension alive. In practice, this probably means the construction of a Gestalt which can be read either way; as a comment on the text or as the illustration of a theory; and despite the desirability of performing both these operations at once and together, either will ultimately lead us back to history itself, to the history of the text fully as much as to the history of the theory.

This makes for a good deal of heterogeneity, both in the literary texts examined here, and in the variety of theoretical contexts tried out over a thirty-year period. I like to think that, faced with an alternation of written and spoken materials, some of them overwritten and others rhetorically amplified, this very unevenness will prove to be a relief for the reader. As for the repetitions, I would be more disturbed by their absence than the reader might be; for good or ill, the dialectic requires you to say everything simultaneously whether you think you can or not; and that inevitably means that you cannot avoid certain topics just because you have dealt with them elsewhere. One has never definitively dealt with them; but be reassured—the situations from which such topics emerge have modified their appearance dramatically from the Eisenhower era to the age of globalization.

But it is not only the theoretical reference points (Sartre, Hegel, Deleuze, Greimas, Lukács, Althusser, Adorno, etc.) that may seem eclectic or, even worse, to obey the more suspicious laws of intellectual fashion. The literary texts might also be taken to form some personal canon, if not indeed a constellation of more universal validity. But that is to reckon without absences and omissions which are themselves accidental, however much I regret them. Only Japan seemed called upon to stand for the non-Western—

indeed, I might even say, the non-European—world; which scarcely documents my own personal debts to Latin America, to North Africa, or to China. As far as my private formation is concerned, indeed, I would have to be puzzled by the absence of Pound or Faulkner, or indeed of virtually the entirety of the French modern tradition with which I have been affiliated. To be sure, there are sometimes professional explanations for such gaps: some of the texts discussed in this collection are here because I taught them in classes and seminars; but just as often works and writers equally important to me are missing precisely because I taught them so often.

Still, these assurances and apologies will do little to assuage the doubts of readers who assume that these analyses, particularly since they are meant to accompany my *A Singular Modernity* as a kind of source-book, were all designed to illustrate this or that component of a theory of the modern. But *A Singular Modernity* was thought through later than most of the essays in this book, and its theorization of modernism was reluctant and provisional, and organized around Luhmann's notion of an intensifying differentiation of the elements and levels of the social world. An earlier version, or Platonic myth, told the story in terms of the cultural consequences of the spread of reification around the globe.[1] (Inasmuch as I understand Lukács's notion of reification as including Weberian rationalization within itself, this figure to be sure is itself closely related to Luhmann's.) The essays collected in the present volume, however, also deploy other interpretive codes: the fragmentation of the reading public, the incompatibility between Third and First World perspectives, the loss of a Utopian language (or the attempt to reinvent one), the internal limits on the representability of a specific historical content, the pressure of a new sense of space on linguistic and narrative structures, the tension between private languages and classification schemes, that between the revolutionary instant and the construction of narrative time, the emergence of a non-universalizable sensory or bodily datum, and so forth. These codes or interpretive frames are no doubt all interrelated, but their conceptual languages send us in different directions, which are far from converging.

Yet even if these essays are read, much against my own philosophical and stylistic convictions, as examples of such theories, even if they somehow dramatize "historicism"—a word I have never wanted to repudiate, and which Joan Copjec usefully encapsulates as "the reduction of society [and presumably also of its cultural products] to its indwelling network of relations of power and knowledge"[2]—that was never the way I saw it. I don't even mind the implication that these discussions perpetuate that old opposition of base and superstructure which now so long ago Raymond Williams (along with many others) told us to abandon. I will say some more about oppositions in a moment, but I want to insist at this point that, even if base and superstructure were still relevant, my conception of their relationship or even their interrelationship would not all be one of reflexion or replication. It is rather one of situation and response, and of the creativity of the various superstructures with respect to a national and socio-economic, infrastructural situation which is "not of their own making." To be sure, the nature of that infrastructural situation can be reconstructed from the response, from the attempt to resolve its contradictions or to escape its death grip, as well as from the constraints imposed on that "socially symbolic act" in virtue of its reference to that specific historical situation and not some other one.

There is, however, another argument that might be made in support of "historicist reductionism," if that is what you still want to call it. It is this: that in the pre-theoretical atmosphere of the Anglo-American 1950s and early 1960s, in the context of the subjectivism and psychologism of the then United States (leaving Britain out of it), in a society in which everything is "reduced" in advance to the private and the personal,[3] any insistence on the public, the economic, the political, any injunction to "include history," has the value of an expansion of the meaning of cultural texts and not their reduction, and of an enlargement of their resonance, an increase of their complexity and the number of their symbolic levels, an enrichment in the contexts in which a given act or symbolic gesture or expression is situated and understood.

It is worth insisting further on the philosophical originality of the idea of the situation which is at stake here. If indeed, as theory argues, we process the data of reality through a certain number of conceptual categories—an epistemological model pioneered by Kant, as we shall see—then we should add the familiar reminder, not only that such categories are historical, and subject to modification, but also that one of the signal historical modifications they have undergone in modern times is the shift from a substantive or thing-organized categorical system—through which the outside world is grasped as so many items or static substances—to a new set of process-organized categories whose multiple versions can be identified throughout contemporary philosophy. What is less often observed is the central role—under whatever terminology—of the category of the "situation",[4] as a way of constructing the dynamic of human activity: it is because we organize the data of a given present into a situation to which we are compelled to respond in some way, even if the response is inaction or the passive reception of affect, that we can reconstruct and reinterpret such interactions in terms of acts and of praxis. Such reconstruction is by no means an easy or commonsensical matter when we have to deal with works of art; but it will become an essential feature of what has come to be called the critique of representation, as we shall see in a moment.

Still, this supposedly new antithesis of action in situation—whatever its debt to Heidegger's supposedly equally innovative conception of being-in-the-world—may still be thought to fall prey to the oldest false problem in the book, the oldest ideological trap, which is that of the opposition between subject and object, for Heidegger himself the very *fons et origo* of everything degraded about modernity (and indeed it was this fundamental misconception that he himself influentially named "representation" in the first place).[5] Is not the proposed notion of the situation—which can itself perhaps be seen as an attempt illicitly to smuggle back in the older and even more disreputable opposition of base and superstructure touched on above —just such another helpless reinvention of the subject–object dichotomy?

This is the point at which I am tempted to insert an apologia of the binary opposition as such, or even a celebration of its structuralist rediscovery, which has always seemed to me a milestone on the road towards a reinvention of the dialectic. The rediscovery was of course an ambiguous one: for Lévi-Strauss the demonstration of the central role of opposition in all of our conceptual constructions already pointed in two directions. On the one hand, it could seem to call for precisely the kind of celebration I have proposed here; on the other, it suggested that the deeper vocation of any meaningful critique of ideas or ideologies should then lie in the detection (and extirpation) of just such binary oppositions, which can be taken to be the primal form of ideology as such.

In fact, one can endorse both these programs, provided they do not lead us back to some German-idealist notion of the transcendental and indeterminate identity that precedes all oppositions (what Hegel, in a damaging attack on Schelling, famously called "the night in which all cows are grey"[6]). Another version of the same caution is to be found in Sartre's approving recollection of the warning of one of his teachers: "everything begins with the cogito, provided you can get out of it." Certainly the search for oppositions is nothing but a mechanical or additive procedure if one is not intent from the outset on somehow getting out of their initial closure or double-bind (particularly if one is forewarned that the facile declaration of self-consciousness or reflexivity does not in itself solve anything).

So this is the sense in which everything begins with the binary opposition, provided some strategy is devised to get out of it; to transcend it in unexpected ways that have nothing to do with that old but still influential caricature of the dialectic which is supposed to conclude with a "synthesis" of the thesis and antithesis of which the binary opposition is alleged to consist. How one gets out of the binary opposition can, however, never be predicted in advance; the solutions are always concrete and unique to a specific historical or formal situation, itself always unique.

But if the problems are always as unique as the solutions, how can this view lead to any useful statement about method? Indeed, maybe each so-called binary opposition is itself so unique as to forfeit its own classification under such a conceptual category as Opposition in the first place? Then, of course, not only does the theoretical scaffolding I have been constructing here fall to the ground, but also the critique of the ideological nature of oppositions falls with it (and drags Heidegger's initial diagnosis of representation as such down along with it into inconsequentiality).

The prospects change somewhat when we understand that getting out of binary oppositions may often mean, not so much doing away with them, as multiplying them and using the initial ideological starting point as the beginning of a more complicated construction which is at the same time a more complex diagnosis. I will take as an example of this procedure another opposition, one as hotly denounced as any of those we have already mentioned—unsurprisingly, insofar as it is intimately related to all of them—but one perhaps more immediately relevant to the literary operations of the essays in the present book; and that is the traditional opposition that relates form to content.

For has it not been said that the absolute historicism I endorse here and elsewhere in my work (the term is Gramsci's characterization of Marxism) is also an absolute formalism? It will in any case shortly become evident even to the casual reader that there is a good deal of talk about form throughout these pages (and in discussions of modernism more generally). Would it not be the duty of any serious Marxist criticism to denounce such formalisms and to revindicate the claims of content as such on the discussions of modernist texts? To be sure; but modern twentieth-century history abounds in horrible object lessons in the ways this should not be done, so perhaps here too some serious retheorization is in order.

Everyone understands that to emphasize either one of these terms—form or content—in the absence of the other one will lead to results that are distorted and unhelpful (however much they may be suggestive for future work and reelaboration). As a bad word, *formalism* is often restricted to designating an emphasis on pure form as such, in the absence of any content: but we reach history again here when we come upon moments, like that of Flaubert, in which form production takes as its very aim and end the elimination of content as such.[7] The exclusionary emphasis on content, meanwhile, is inevitably and insensibly transformed into a prescription for this or that specific type of content, a prescription for which form is transparent and unproblematic, but whose failures (and occasional successes) might well tend to reawaken some productive sense of the ways in which form is a precondition for content just as content is a precondition of form.

I have felt, here and throughout, that the opposition between form and content is only to be overcome (that is to say, made productive) by complicating it, and not by doing away with one of its terms. Is this to say that there reemerges here that old pseudo-Hegelian mirage that has been mentioned above, in which the truth lies somewhere in between, and form and content finally meet in some new kind of synthesis (which is of course none other than the work of art itself)? Not quite: yet it is in the insistence on holding to a dual perspective for each of our binary terms that we may well find a more satisfactory answer, and that dual perspective may well look like not one, but a series of partial syntheses.

At any rate, the answer consists in seeing the binary opposition between form and content as a four-term set of positions rather than a simple dualism, and I borrow an oversimplified and vulgarized model for these possibilities from Hjelmslev's linguistics,[8] which alongside the purer versions of a form-oriented perspective ("the form of the form") and a content-oriented one ("the content of the content") adds in two new ones, which result from taking the point of view of each on the realities under consideration. We thereby reach the new terms he designated as the "content of the form" and the "form of the content" respectively, and once our stereotypical views of form and content have been sufficiently startled and rebuked, if not challenged, by the addition of the new entities, we will be in a better position to evaluate the possibilities this ancient dualism still has to offer. We can make the possibilities visible by seeing both form and content—the horizontal phenomena—from the perspectives of the same categories, now operating as vertical designators respectively:

	form	content
CONTENT	form of content	content of content
FORM	form of form	content of form

As a practical matter, each of these combinations or perspectives will project a type of literary criticism that has its own validity as well as its own internal limitations; while at some outside boundary, slipping from description into prescription, each will seem to posit a specific aesthetic and a program for writers to follow. I will suggest that such prescriptions are illegitimate, as the extremes of their Cold War versions will now testify: a stereotypical social realism on the one hand and a tiresome linguistic formalism, full of irony, paradox, and autoreferentiality, on the other. The essays in this book certainly presuppose the symptomatic value of a given aesthetic realization for any judgement or interpretation of its historical moment and situation; but the works have to come first. We cannot do without projections of the future in practical political life, but we do not have to prognosticate the future of art, something art always does for itself in a twofold way: first, by way of the artist's own laboratory of forms in which the latter are tested for their continuing productivity; and then by way of the personal taste and aesthetic inclinations and intuitions with which our own historical experience endows us as connoisseurs and consumers. In any case, nothing in the present volume is to be construed as prescription, for the excellent reason that the texts under consideration here owe their existence to conditions and situations of modernism that are no longer ours today.

Returning to the fourfold possibilities with which any presupposition of the terminology of form and content seems to provide us, I will try briefly to characterize the most familiar results of each. An emphasis on the content of content is inevitably a referential operation, in which we attempt to identify the social and historical realities in which the text comes into being and which it presumably designates. I take it that there can be no serious disagreement with the assumption that the text comes into being in some kind of real world, and also that its language, however fictional the project, has to manipulate a period language assumed to have its own referentiality. Maybe there will not even be much disagreement about the desirability for the reader to have some knowledge of the historical situation, however general, and also to have some lexicological background in the history of the meaning of the relevant words (of what Conrad means by the word "imperialism," for example: see essay 7).

Where problems set in might have been predicted on the basis of our model: for it specifies that this particular term or element—the content of content—does not yet have a form or in other words is by definition inexpressible and unfigurable. The dilemma may best be conveyed by the way in which Freud had to confront it when hypothesizing the various avatars of desire: all very well and good to see them as so many substitutes for and representations of the mother, but then what is the mother a representation of? The infant, in other words (and by literal definition), precedes all possibilities of figuration and representability and must imply a stage in which the drives are experienced immediately, that is to say, without the mediation of the various representational and figural systems. But that stage would have to remain purely hypothetical, since we have no way of thinking or theorizing it.[9]

Is not something like this the situation we find ourselves in when we seek to posit some objective version of the historical situation or the social reality in question in a given text? Nowhere is this dilemma quite so dramatic as with that undoubted reality which is social class. No one has ever seen a social class or experienced one immediately: social classes meanwhile define themselves only in moments of great social crisis and intensity. To that degree, any attempt to characterize class as it were over the heads of preexisting forms and languages runs into the problem of Kant's thing-in-itself, whose reality it is as necessary to posit as it is impossible to express or describe. The language we generally use to convey the referents at stake in what is generally designated as a "context" is the language and the figuration of historians and sociologists, and it is no less figural, no less a "form," for all the authority of their disciplines. So it is that no one doubts that there was an aristocracy in Dickens's time, and that it entertained complicated and historically distinctive relationships with the other classes and with an emergent capitalism; but few have been willing to take Dickens's caricatures of aristocrats at face value. His idiosyncratic personal figuration of this class, in other words, but also the seemingly objective figuration of the social scientists, both gradually lead us on from the perspective of the content of a content towards the possibility of a new perspective on the latter's form.

Indeed, the form of the content can be said to encompass everything called ideology in the most comprehensive acceptation of the word. The aristocracy exists, as a thing-in-itself; but it can only be evoked for all practical purposes by way of some preexisting representation of the aristocracy as a social class, and that representation is bound to be ideological and to have its own history as an ideology (or as an element of a social ideology). Dickens has his own passionate conviction about how his social order functions and what it does to people, as well as the role played in it by the aristocratic drones themselves; it is a picture in which only education and philanthropy seem able to offer some small measure of positive activity. Yet the clearly ideological nature of this social representation should not lead us to believe that the social representations of the historians and social scientists (very much including the Marxists themselves) are any less ideological.

This literary situation is not so very different, then, from the philosophical situation Kant faced at the very beginnings of theoretical modernity, when, having come to the realization that all of our seemingly concrete experiences were somehow subjective ones, and conveyed our own experiences of reality rather than anything bearing on the reality of the things-in-themselves, he deduced the existence in the mind of operative categories and forms which organized those experiences. In literature, the things-in-themselves are the social and historical realities, but also the inner psychic realities, with which the literary text tries desperately to come to terms; the ideologies constitute that enlarged set of categories that necessarily process and organize the intensities of that formless content and seek to produce representations of it. Kant's powerful compromise, then, suggests that in literary criticism, as well, we cannot do without these two initial moments of the form–content position, and must always acknowledge the claims these first two perspectives inevitably have on us.

But the very disgust with which we have found ourselves confronting the asphyxiating hold this Kantian situation has on us—the existence of unrepresentable referents, the inescapable interposition of ideology between ourselves and those realities—suggests what may be a new step in the process and a new issue from that impasse. For the omnipresence of ideological mediation may also encourage us in wondering, as Flaubert did, whether something new and different is not to be achieved by an unparalleled new effort to silence the voices of ideology altogether, by isolating the pure forms of their representations and substituting the play of those formal categories for an older or now traditional representation of content.

Here clearly we have begun to pass over into the perspective of form on itself, of a formalistic production of form; and also into the historical moment designated as modernism, in which the ideological forms of an older content are somehow neutralized and bracketed by an abstraction that seeks to retain only from them their purely formal structures, now deployed in a kind of autonomy. How this process works and the variety of texts it proves able to generate is a matter for the examination of the individual modernisms themselves. But the characterization of the general process I have suggested makes it at least minimally clear that the term "formalism" is not necessarily to be grasped negatively. To be sure, we may wish to insist that such a process of abstraction can never really be completed without emerging into what must ultimately fail to be a completely non-representational language (Khlebnikov) or visuality (Malevich), or into nonsense (but with all the resonance of Deleuze's use of the word). Formalism must therefore necessarily fail; we cannot escape our being-in-the-world, even by way of its formalizing negations. Yet the attempt to escape that world's ideologies must also be faithfully registered, and counted as a Utopian one.

With such an acknowledgment, that the pure forms still bear the traces and the marks of the content they sought to extinguish, we find that we have already entered the fourth of our perspectives, that of the content of the form itself.[10] Indeed, the very implication that each of the three preceding moments constitutes a certain kind of perspective itself dialectically presupposes this fourth one, from which their insufficiencies could alone be registered. This is not a vicious circle, I think, because the new one is also the only perspective from which the usefulness and indeed the indispensability of the other three could be appreciated. It also constitutes the only productive coordination of the opposition between form and content that does not seek to reduce one term to the other, or to posit illicit syntheses and equally illicit volatilizations of an opposition whose tensions need to be preserved at the same time that we become aware of how philosophically incompatible each of these terms is with respect to the other one. There is thus a way in which the notion of the content of the form stands as a philosophical and dialectical solution to the initial binary dilemma, and as a theoretical transcendence of Kant's version of the problem: something that cannot be pursued any further here.

Yet it does seem worth adding that this whole form–content issue is neither a purely local, aesthetic problem, nor an equally local and technical philosophical one, but arises over and over again in a variety of contemporary contexts. We need only dwell a little longer on the word "content"—a characterization that from one standpoint has become as opprobrious as its counterpart—to appreciate the vaster resonance of an impasse in which "content-oriented" is as contemptuous a judgement as purely "formalistic." Content, however, seems a more proletarian and underclass kind of designation, invoking the *miserabilisme* and the *nostalgie de la boue* of some naturalist rummaging around in alleyways (naturalism being preeminently that aesthetic obsessed with content as such, or so the modernist stereotype has it): whereas formalism strikes us as some more idealist and ethereal matter, involving etiquette and good taste, grooming, keeping the proper forms, and so on (a kind of "content" closer to Henry James than to Zola?). In fact, formalism was always the professional deformation of academics and intellectuals, inasmuch as the truly bourgeois and middle-class reply to any aesthetic of content was always one of humanism and meaning (the human condition, the meaning of life, the eternal verities, or the pop-psychological caricatures of existentialism).

At any rate, one also sees from time to time, perhaps as a result of the influence of an essentially demotic Marxism or mass-cultural communism, a different kind of expression or *Redewendung* in serious political discussions, namely the observation that this or that position "had no content," or more precisely, "had no political content"; as when, in response to all conceivable social problems, "free elections" are called for as the inevitable knee-jerk solution, in complete indifference to the specific content of the situation in question, of the forces at play, their organizational development, and the historical specificity of the local dilemma itself. (Or perhaps one should rather qualify this phrase as "in apparent indifference," inasmuch as in reality there are no "purely formalistic" political proposals or positions in the first place, no program or panacea that does not have—as its own "content"—an ideological character and function.) At any rate, the evocation of content in this situation always stands for a Brechtian estrangement-effect, a defamiliarization that asks us to imagine what a real political proposal or program, one that had real content, might be.

Understood in this way, it is clear that the diagnosis of a position "without content" not only spans a variety of fields but may even characterize the foundation of whole disciplines in their own right. One may adduce, for example, the vanity of ethics and ethical reflections, a kind of introspective hairsplitting about intention and possibility, sincerity and imperfect realization, which always begins by bracketing the genuine historical or social content of the ethical dilemma. Thus, current debate about capital punishment, and even more pertinently about the deplorable US innovation of calling for the testimony of the victims during the sentencing procedure, pointedly omits the pre-history of vengeance and retribution as such: should it not be the business of the tribe as such, of the collectivity (in which case it is bound to be interminable and a never-ending cycle), or on the other hand the decision of a single wronged individual (something only conceivable in an already atomized and individualized social order), both options then presumably canceled by the ethos of a Christianity that calls for the other cheek? But these are scarcely ethical issues, but rather so many concrete and incompatible historical situations. That a more sophisticated philosophical ethics knows as much and seeks to draw the historical situation itself back into the ethical decision (should I not resist the norms of my own society?) is not a solution but the very diagnosis and symptom, less of the dilemma itself than of the very framework of the philosophical subfield in question: for by the time ethics has subsumed historical content, it has already become something else, namely politics.

So it is that the problem of content and form largely transcend their merely aesthetic reference and in the long run come to haunt all the corners and closets of the social itself. Indeed, was not communism itself an attempt to endow a purely formalistic and Kantian Second International socialism with genuine content? And is not the current debate on difference, multiculturalism and natural or international law—a debate generally staged in the form of the incommensurability of universality and singularity—itself a renewed and heightened rehearsal of just this one, between content and form?

Barthes long ago complained of the ritualistic invocation on the Left of the magic formula of the "concrete"; but what was this ideal if not the longing for a squaring of the circle in which form was finally at one with a content that had become pure form? (The language of the aesthetic version of all this lapsed back into Hegelianism with its invocation of the "concrete universal.") We do not, today, have to be reminded of the limits of political, social, or economic projections: but the problem of content may well be helpful in helping us map the internal or structural limits of artistic modernism itself, in which the very effort to transform the last shreds of content into pure form—whether in garden-variety autoreferentiality or the overweening project of the Book of the World—obeys the same desperate impulse. What used to be called the Absolute is the very name for this ultimate mirage of the identity of form and content, and modernism comes into being as a quest for that Absolute.

Utopia is another name for the persistence of that Absolute, in a social system which is either pure content—the infinite contingency of an endless collection of commodities—or pure form—in the abstractions of finance and the sheer relationality of the exchange system. But it is also, if you like, a name for the failure of their identification with each other, which is why the essays in this book tend to move back and forth between a focus on the form of the content—in the limits of a specific historical situation and its contradictions—and focus on the content of the form, or in other words the possibilities for figuration or representation. Even this alienation, however, ought to put us in a position to hold to the gap itself, to the difference that relates: it also makes up an important part of the story here, which runs from Baudelaire (or at least from the Third Republic) up to the immediate post-World War Two era.

Killingworth, July 2006

Notes

1 *A Singular Modernity* (London, 2002) pp. 141–60; and *Postmodernism, or, The Cultural Logic of Late Capitalism* (Durham and London, 1990), pp. 95–6.

2 Joan Copjec, *Read My Desire* (Cambridge MA, 1994), p. 6.

3 Since Hannah Arendt is back in vogue, the reference might well be to her notion of the tendential privatization of the public and in particular of politics. See *The Human Condition* (Chicago, 1958), pp. 50–8.

4 It is a category apparently invented by Karl Jaspers (in *Psychologie der Weltanschauungen* [Berlin, 1925]), and then less developed in Heidegger than in Sartre; see *Being and Nothingness* (New York, 1963). Even Sartre, however, develops his conception of the situation ontologically or metaphysically, rather than foregrounding it as a category in the broader sense proposed here.

5 See Martin Heidegger, "Die Zeit des Weltbildes," in *Holzwege* (Frankfurt, 1950). English trans. J. Young and K. Haynes, "The Age of the World View," in *Off the Beaten Track* (Cambridge, 2002).

6 Hegel, "Preface", *Phenomenology of Spirit,* trans. A.V. Miller (Oxford, 1979), p. 9.

7 Gustave Flaubert, *Correspondence II* (Paris, 1980), p. 31:

> "Ce qui me semble beau, ce que je voudrais faire, c'est un livre sur rien, un livre sans attaché extérieure, qui se tiendrait de lui-même par la force interne de son style, comme la terre sans être soutenue se tient en l'air, un livre qui n'aurait presque pas de sujet ou du moins où le sujet serait presque invisible, si cela se peut. Les oeuvres les plus belles sont celles où il y a le moins de matière; plus l'expression se rapproche de la pensée, plus le mot colle dessus et disparaît, plus c'est beau." A Louise Colet, 16 janvier 1852.
>
> "What seems beautiful to me, what I should like to write, is a book about nothing, a book dependent on nothing external, which would hold up on its own by the internal strength of its style, just as the earth, with no support, holds up in the air; a book which would have almost no subject, or at least in which the subject would be almost invisible, if such a thing is possible. The finest works are those that contain the least matter." Letter to Louise Colet, 16 January 1852

8 Louis Hjelmslev, *Prolegomena to a Theory of Language* (Madison, 1963). I have collapsed Hjelmslev's more complicated permutation scheme, which coordinates the two sets of opposites—expression/content and form/substance—into a formula putting the single (traditional) one to work on itself.

9 See, for a review of the debate, Jean Laplanche and Jean-Bertrand Pontalis, "The Vorstellungsrepräsentaz or Representational Representative," in *The Language of Psychoanalysis* (London, 1973).

10 *The Content of the Form* is, of course, the title of a relevant work of Hayden White (Baltimore, 1987).

ONE

1

The Poetics of Totality

Just as the adventure of something recognizable as postmodernity has seemed to offer a chance, and indeed to impose an obligation, to rethink "modernism" in some new way—as ideology fully as much as a set of canonical works which do not vanish but are now lent more classical or historical status—so also, and for related reasons, the very analysis of these now peculiar works or classics has become technically more difficult. We must see them in double or stereoptic focus, as works that are at one and the same time bearers of a whole ideology of the modern; works that, by virtue of being rereadable in new ways, can also be thought to contain the elements of at least a few postmodern features (which we must then be careful not to exaggerate or deform into full postmodernity, thereby illicitly rewriting such authors as precursors of the postmodern). Finally, we must make an assumption that problematizes the very work of textual analysis itself—namely, the presupposition that the works we have canonized as the classics of modernism are in fact not successes, but failures. It is a presupposition that is required for any successful dereification of these now institutionalized texts. Philosophically, it is no doubt related to a deeper assumption in much of modern philosophy (openly thematized in Sartre's posthumously published ethics, for example) that only failure makes possible human experience as such, where success binds and alienates us more securely and inextricably into an external world of things (and not least of money and business and the market, so that failure as an ethos is linked to capitalism itself as a system). Finally, an aesthetics of failure is built into the works themselves, at least those whose awareness of their own aims is more lucid and reflexive and has not required the blind and productive self-deception of ideologies of myth and expression in order impossibly to come into being.

There would be many ways of approaching this necessary presupposition of failure in any reconsideration of modernism. Barthes's famous pronouncement (in *Le Degré zéro de l'écriture*) is one of those:

> the greatest modern works linger as long as possible, in a sort of miraculous stasis, on the threshold of Literature, in this anticipatory state in which the breadth of life is given, deployed but not yet destroyed, by this crowning phase, an order of signs.[1]

Barthes does not only have in mind here everything paralyzing about the institution of literature as such (which in the United States essentially takes the form of the university curriculum), but above all the great fact of personal style as it removes the individual text from immediacy and converts it into a mere example of some imaginary essence (signed Faulkner, Stevens or whatever). The text thus wishes desperately to escape from this condition of a mere example; it does not wish to be yet another characteristic Faulkner or Stevens, but something far more immediate and impersonal; but it cannot do this by way of depersonalization, since what we now know as style was itself the desperate set of conditions by which a Faulkner or a Stevens managed to speak and to say something—anything—in the first place. These "modern" writers were therefore condemned to the invention and elaboration of what Barthes called "a system of signs," whose full and definitive realization then at once necessarily spelled the failure of their very enterprise, since it signaled the moment in which that very system triumphantly mastered its content, became a frozen mannerism, and objectified the contextuality and the intentions which, in all kinds of fluid and unformed, inchoate and uncreated ways, drove them in the direction of such elaboration in the first place. "Winner loses," to adapt a famous slogan of Sartre in much the same spirit (and which derives from some of the same experiences of the dilemmas of the construction of Literature and the literary in post-World War Two France).

But there is a paradoxical corollary of this particular version of the imperative to fail, and that is the requirement that the writers in question not merely attempt to succeed, but also believe success is somehow possible. Yet their capacity to do so, and to sustain a vision of the concrete possibility of genuine aesthetic construction under conditions of modernity, would also surely stand as a symptom of some deeper lack of insight and intelligence into the conditions that make modern art impossible in the first place. So these winners lose in yet another way, by virtue of the very self-deceptions they constitutionally require to sustain the hubris that can alone sustain their projects (in a combination of the mystifications and the enabling energies Marx thought he could identify in the most productive moments of revolutionary praxis as well, at least when those were approached by middle-class groups driven into innovation by forces beyond their control and intent).

Still, a few works even more peculiar than these constitutively self-defeating and unconsciously self-undermining objects which are the conventional classics of the modern do seem to exist: William Carlos Williams's *Paterson* is then signally one of those, a modern epic that knows in its deepest structural impulses—unlike its great models in the pocket epics of Pound and Eliot, and in ways quite unlike the naïveté of cognate efforts like Hart Crane's *Bridge*—that it must not succeed, that its conditions of realization depend on a fundamental success in failing, at the same time that it must not embody any kind of will to failure either, in the conventional psychology of the inferiority complex or in the willful self-crippling of the accident-prone or the writer's block.

Yet there are other ways of describing this peculiar structure of the modern situation, so often celebrated in terms of the new and innovation and analogized by comparisons with scientific discovery (something from which Williams's poem is scarcely exempt, as witness the appearance of Madame Curie in the second section of the fourth book and the celebration of the "LUMINOUS!" "gist," explicitly identified both with poetic invention and with economic productivity). Clearly, this conception of innovation is ideologically complicitous with the whole teleological theory of the modern itself, which naturally enough emerged from the category of perpetual innovation as its sequel and after-image.

Adorno has, however, reformulated the drive to innovation in what seems to me both a more plausible and also a more useful form, in terms of taboos and negatives: what drives modernism to innovate is not some vision of the future or the new, but rather the deep conviction that certain forms and expressions, procedures and techniques, can no longer be used, are worn out or stigmatized by their associations with a past that has become conventionality or kitsch, and must be creatively avoided. Such taboos then produce a desperate situation in which the nature of the innovation, to continue to use such language, is not traced or given in advance; rather, what emerges then determines the form by which the blocks and taboos of the next generation will be governed (and, in this sense, postmodernity and its pluralisms have been seen as a final turn of the screw in which it seems to be just such taboos and negative restrictions that have themselves become taboo). But this way of formulating the modern situation then suggests a mode of analysis and presentation in which something like the opposite of the great Stevens litany in "Notes Towards a Supreme Fiction" ("It must be abstract, it must change, it must give pleasure") can be productively deployed. In what follows, then, I will try to map out *Paterson* by way of the things and forms it is under an obligation to avoid, hoping thereby to avoid at least some of the reification implicit in the conventional positive lists of strong features and realized aspects.

That all of these features are ultimately formulable in terms of language itself, however, is clearly the ultimate "modernist" presupposition in

Williams and one that cannot be interpreted away: comparisons with other objects—

> That the poem,
> the most perfect rock and temple, the highest
> falls, in clouds of gauzy spray, should be
> so rivaled (etc., 80/80[2])

—are not so significant as the still relatively classical or neoclassical way of conceiving of "the poem" in the first place (as "a column; a reply to Greek and Latin with the bare hands" [2/2]). The rivalry is with History and death, the beast in the jungle (22–3/22: "were we near enough its stinking breath / would fell us. The temple upon / the rock is its brother"): but the fundamental conception is still that of the great modern work whose prototype is literary or poetic (although not necessarily any longer epic in the old classical sense), and whose fundamental theory (and ideology) will therefore be thematized in terms of literary language (as in the most basic program-statements from the Formalists and Proust all the way to the New Criticism, and passing by way of the most visionary avant-gardes, which must still—witness surrealism!—struggle to reconcile a linguistic conception of the cultural process with experiential data that are more and more visual). At the same time, the conception of a supreme work or Book of the World brings with it a rather different kind of dialectic of the universal and the particular which will be examined separately later on.

Language remains, however, at the very center of an essentially modernist "system of the fine arts," and it is in terms of its unique properties that the other arts, as they approach the intensities of a properly modern realization and transformation, will be celebrated—it being understood that the very conception of something like language as "unique", as having "properties" in the first place and as though it were a thing that could be compared or not to other "things," is itself the modernist ideology in question here. For example, Williams's conventional image of the poem as a temple—in other words, as a centering power around which both city space and collective activity are organized—reappears significantly in Heidegger's cognate *Origin of the Work of Art,*[3] where as an example it follows the purely visual image of Van Gogh's painting of the "peasant shoes," and of Mörike's exclusively imagistic poem on the Roman fountain, which the philosopher seems to use as a specifically visual illustration, so that the fact of the derivation of the emblematic structure of the fountain from a verbal or linguistic object seems relatively secondary and inconsequential or accidental. Heidegger's temple then follows hard on the shoes, which, immobile, seem to hold concentrated within themselves the years of treading drudgery and movement through the fields of the putative "peasant woman," and on the fountain, whose movement is at one with its rest ("und fliesst und ruht"): the temple will then be cast in the role of what, most immobile of all and at the very motionless center of what moves around it, is also the very locus of the most prodigious of all tensions and oppositions, a place of perpetual struggle and the gap or rift in which *world* and *earth* threaten to tug each other apart. It is appropriate to juxtapose Heidegger's evocation of the temple and Wallace Stevens's quintessential "Anecdote of the Jar,"—not only to appreciate the way in which the endowment with form suddenly brings movement and activity into being where none existed before (after the jar, the "wilderness" moves, rises, sprawls, etc.), but also to compare a work which, like Heidegger's text, produces an aesthetic, with Williams's very different mode of operation in which that aesthetic is deployed in desperate, contradictory, unrealizable ways, yielding a production of a language of an altogether different type. That Stevens's lyric is a kind of fable—that (like all of Stevens) it turns essentially on the attempt to express and characterize, even to analyze, the aesthetic as such—would not particularly distance his text from the self-referentiality present in all modernism, and present in a very distinctive way in the epic of Williams (where to define and celebrate America is at one and the same time to identify a specifically American language as such, so that the poem's form is here also its content).

But what is crucial about these operations, and in particular about the sequence of Heidegger's illustrations, to which we now return, is the way in which these quintessentially physical and non-verbal materials should lead climactically into a celebration of art as Language which nonetheless strikes the reader, if not as an afterthought, then at least as a form of supplementarity not structurally unlike Kant's addition of the sublime to his account of beauty. That "as the setting-into-work of truth, art is poetry" is no doubt enlarged and qualified by the more general meaning of the German "Dichtung" (although it could be argued that the modernist celebrations of Language and the poetic in the Anglo-American tradition aim essentially to expand those English terms into a direction as large and suggestive as the untranslatable German equivalent). But the crucial point here is that, at whatever extreme point of the modernist aesthetic, language as such emerges as the fundamental point of reference, whether we have to do with manifestos of painting and the visual or theories of music or architecture. The movement of Heidegger's own text, not noticeably alert to words or syntax in any recognizably critical or exegetic fashion, is thus characteristic in the way in which, without any particular preparation, Language necessarily has the last word.

My working assumption is then that in the postmodern this commitment to language has disappeared: the predominance of the visual and the spatial creates a situation of a very different kind in which there is no longer any particular advantage gained by referring such phenomena back to the ways words and sentences function; the great Utopian idea of a purification of language, a recreation of its deeper communal or collective function, a purging of everything instrumental or commercial in it, seems to have faded away without a trace, as though in the society of the spectacle and of the electronic media what had unexpectedly been discovered was the boundless capacity for language itself to be reified and commodified, and the utterly unanticipated fact that, far from offering a power that can resist cliché and doxa, language itself turns out to be the very source of such degradation in the first place. This is not to posit some Hegelian "end of poetry," but rather to underscore the shift in the very function of poetry in some postmodern "system of the fine arts": leaving aside the new syncretisms of the media and the emergence of composite arts, installations, and mixed media, one can also observe, for example in the Language Poets, the emergence of new aims for poetry (which they now redefine as anti-representational and non-humanist) in a kind of analytic decomposition of alienated commercial language from the inside, rather than in the speculative leap into a Utopian and radically other type of language which was in one way or another the impulse of all the moderns.

2. Modernism and Language

This is not to say that a modernist poetic vocation need posit the achievement of such Utopian language, but only that it must affirm it as a coordinate and a frame of reference, as Williams does in the italic motto to *Paterson* to be found across from its poetic Preface already quoted. Otherwise, the absence of the Utopian language will do just as well and, given the peculiarly absent–present dialectic in the very idea of Utopia as such, can be uniquely inscribed here (as in so many other characteristic American works) in the very failure of an American language itself, its silences, its incoherencies and inarticulate outcries, its awkwardness and un-European clumsiness and lack of rhetorical grace or elegance—all of these features can at one and the same time signify what is exceptional about the American experience and also what is both modernist and Utopian about Williams's own project, which uniquely never seeks to substitute itself and its own linguistic capacities (as both Whitman and Stevens might be seen very differently as doing) for the inability of Americans to speak (and to speak a language uniquely and recognizably American, rather than English):

> A false language. A true. A false language pouring—a
> language (misunderstood) pouring (misinterpreted) without
> dignity, without minister, crashing upon a stone ear. (15/15)

At once, in these first pages, two anecdotes emerge which become charged with symbolic significance in this respect: the deaths of Mrs Cumming and of Sam Patch, both of whom fall from the cataract, Patch's disappearance as a stunt gone wrong, that of Mrs Cumming (the wife of the "minister" in the preceding quote) as an accident, if not a suicide, and including the supplementary symbolic significance of the frustration of American women's lives:

> Patch leaped but Mrs. Cumming shrieked
> and fell—(20/20)

But both accidents are somehow, by virtue of the waterfall itself conceived as a kind of infinite murmur of language and expression, associated with a failure to speak. This seemingly arbitrary figural link is made with extraordinary delicacy in Williams's prose account of the Patch episode, where the very movement of the falling body is read as a form of expression or rather a wavering, a hesitation, the failure of effective language itself:

> On the day the crowds were gathered on all sides. He appeared and made a short speech as he was wont to do. A speech! What could he say that he must leap so desperately to complete it? And plunged toward the stream below. But instead of descending with a plummet-like fall his body wavered in the air—Speech had failed him. He was confused. The word had been drained of its meaning. There's no mistake in Sam Patch. He struck the water on his side and disappeared. (17/16)

We will see shortly that it is crucial for the way this poem must function that such episodes not be read as symbols, nor even thematically. But they prepare more overtly thematic outbursts, such as the fundamental modernist one:

> The language, the language
>   fails them.
> They do not know the words
>   or have not
> the courage to use them (11/11)

At the same time, these social consequences of the language thematic are also inflected in the direction of poetic technique, where, beyond the more conventional modern insistence on innovation, they take the form of the invention of specifically new kinds of meter—

>   unless there is
> a new mind there cannot be a new
> line (50/50)[4]

—a preoccupation then ingeniously referred back to the social in the appended note on "lame or limping" iambics which concludes Book I and underscores a connection between some of the features of this verse and a social marginality to be discussed later.

Yet in all this emphasis on the poetic, so easily assimilable to a more conventional ideology of the modern, a certain democratic depersonalization in Williams, reinforced by the collage method of his various documents and inserted letters, does away with the more charismatic temptation to endow the poet with a seer-like or prophetic, vatic function, and indeed returns us to something of a situation beyond subject and object, very much in the spirit of Heidegger's nostalgia for the pre-Socratics:

> The province of the poem is the world.
> When the sun rises, it rises in the poem
> and when it sets darkness comes down
> and the poem is dark. (99/100)

It is a serenity subtly different from the hyperaestheticism of other classical modernisms, such as is to be found in Mallarmé's famous injunction that "everything in the world exists in order to end up in the Book"; and this despite the guild-driven professionalism of the fateful term ("the poem"), redolent of the in-group winks of a New Critical academic tradition. Here Williams seems to deploy the larger framing apparatus of an epic (already considerably liberated by Pound's new form) in order to sketch in something like an element (as in "the watery element"), a whole enveloping space, which renders the articulating categories of individual subject and object unnecessary, if not redundant.

In this (following Heidegger), the larger conception of space or field resembles that of the Dao or the "Feldweg," not so much because it mimics the latter's ritual movement and rhythm, as simply because (like the Eastern category of landscape itself) it projects a larger intelligible canvas than the dramatistic events that are transacted between individuals, to use Kenneth Burke's terms. This is why questions about narrative point of view, which necessarily recur in prose narrative where they must, however ingeniously, be resolved, can here triumphantly be evaded or neutralized: and this particular formal evasion would seem ultimately more successful than what happens in *The Waste Land*, where completion is achieved by way of a partial return to the existential and the phenomenological—the poem finally coming to rest under the sign of the destiny of an individual and the categories of individual salvation—or in *The Cantos*, where the immense length and burden of reference finally dissolve the multiple provisional frameworks altogether. For what is called "point of view" is the ultimate challenge to literary form production posed by the content of an individualized and subjectified social life: the references above (the invocation of Heidegger, for instance) should not be allowed to minimize the enormous difficulties confronted by any attempt to escape point of view—one cannot simply drop the categories of subject and object by the taking of a thought; nor can one abandon the "epistemological" because one has read Rorty and finds the argument persuasive. Even if contemporary categories of subjectivity (with their now considerable Cartesian heritage and genealogy) are unsatisfactory, they cannot simply be abandoned; nor does the announcement that the subject is henceforth "decentered" necessarily make it so.

3. Allegory

It is a situation, then, in which all solutions are necessarily *ad hoc*; and Williams's takes place on two levels, one as what the Formalists called a "motivation of the device," the other on the level of allegorical construction. The conventional analogies to Williams's particular motivation of the device in *Paterson* can be explained by the difficulties confronted in modern society by any attempt to convey the variety of social life and experience distributed among the various social classes—or even, if you prefer to think about it that way, to get some personal sense of that variety by way of one's own experience, since even the imperative to imagine the radical difference of the life of other classes needs itself to be motivated, let alone furnished with the elements of a solution. Thus, a social and narrative role must somehow be discovered in which the protagonist's possibility to enter various realms of social life—to visit the private spaces of the very rich fully as much as to pass through the most terrifying flophouses and spaces of extreme misery—is somehow motivated and made plausible. In popular fiction, of course, this role is very precisely that of the private detective: whence the immense formal success of this particular solution to the "point of view" problem, a success that has made the detective story form virtually hegemonic in recent years as a vehicle for social commentary (despite the obvious and increasing historical problems with it, and in particular the question of whether there exist private detectives as such at all anymore or whether they have not been replaced by institutional forms of surveillance, beginning with the police themselves).[5]

In Dr Williams's case, of course, the solution now becomes clear: it is the old-fashioned medical practitioner who is supremely able to compete with the private detective insofar as he also necessarily visits and confronts people from all walks of life and hears a virtually endless stream of American social material and anecdote. That, unlike the detective story, this variant is ideologically burdened with a populist temptation in the very form can be witnessed by the related practice of Céline, in *Journey to the End of the Night* (see below); but even Williams's own populism serves as a useful ideological shock absorber here, where, emerging from the immense Left force-field of the 1930s, *Paterson* escapes the humiliating apostasies of the Cold War period, which are contemporaneous with the setting in place of the very ideology of aesthetic modernism in the US, and can plausibly continue to sustain a progressive and Left-oriented vision (including some Pound-modified economics—"the radium's the credit" [182/181]) after the "end of ideology" and without the immense effort required to "become" Marxist in this period (one recalls Eliot's comments on Blake's labors to construct his own private ideological framework[6]).

That Williams paid for this particular "motivation of the device" with his own life, that is to say, with his whole life (as a professional physician), will be surprising only to those who underestimate the implications of the Russian concept, in which, very much as already in Mallarmé, life and art are inextricably intertwined and the resultant "price"—which Williams himself consciously and deliberately chose to pay—seems great only if you imagine that the resultant formal possibilities are not worth paying for. That this somehow reintroduces the tabooed biographical material back into the aesthetic heart of North American modernism in ways henceforth considered illicit by its legislative wing in the New Criticism—is the reader, for example, required to know that Williams was a family doctor? do we really evaluate the various episodes of *Paterson* with this fact in mind, and allow the writer to get away with bits of social material that we would not let pass in the case of mere non-medical invention?—is, I think, a problem that would arise only within a "point of view" framework. Williams's transubjective dissolution of that and of the subjective categories as such blurs the old legal boundary line between the textual and the biographical; and this is all the more the case in a book in which documentary material renders whatever is fictional unrecognizable as such, and which thereby transcends and cancels the very category of the fictive itself, opening up the text to investments greater and other than those that obtain for the overtly fictional narrative.

But the possibilities remotivated by Williams's career are then as we have suggested redoubled and enlarged on another structural level altogether by the emergence of a second, more properly allegorical framework, derived, no doubt, initially from Joycean mythography. This begins on the first page of Book I—"Paterson lies in the valley under the Passaic Falls" (6/6)—where "lie" however designates an enormous human body, the "spent waters" of the Falls "forming the outline of his back." The entire city is then grasped as a single man, accompanied in more shadowy and fantasmatic fashion by an equally allegorical "woman," if not several:

A man like a city and a woman like a flower
—who are in love. Two women. Three women,
Innumerable women, each like a flower. But
only one man—like a city. (7/7)

Sometimes, however, the woman is the mountain:

The Park's her head, carved, above the Falls, by the quiet
river. (8/8)

And in this form "she" also has an allegorical, universalizing relationship to the various (female) individuals who people her space:

All these
and more—shining, struggling flies
caught in the meshes of Her hair, of whom
there can be no complaint, fast in
the invisible net—from the back country,
half awakened—all desiring. (192/191)

There is a Sister Carrie note to this evocation of the women from the back country ("Not one, / to escape, not one" [192/191]), who gradually drift down into the small city to live out their frustrations and unsatisfied desires (sometimes, as at the very beginning of the final book, finding their way across the meadows into Manhattan itself). But more often the women are viewed from the point of view of the Man, whose wives or lovers they are (the most notorious evocation being:

a *Geographic* picture, the 9 women
of some African chief semi-naked
astraddle a log, an official log
to be presumed, heads left. [13/13])

The imbalance is the classic patriarchal one, in which allegorical Man represents himself as an individual (with various lovers, wives, etc. [see page 192/191]), as well as everyone (male and female) within the city, while the allegorical Woman only represents herself (and the various women in the city). The question of whether *Paterson* is then an exclusively male epic, or whether, as a modernist work, it participates in the gender exclusivity with which a feminist postmodernism has taxed the modern movement as a whole, is scarcely an idle one. That the poem faithfully represents the imbalance of its own historical period, and that it also marks that imbalance structurally by way of the visible deconstruction of this allegory, may not be a particularly satisfying defense; but women's voices play a very special role in this work, as we shall see below (and "interrupt" it in a very different way than does Molly Bloom's voice in an in any case fictional and narrative monologue in *Ulysses*), while the figures of "marriage" and "divorce" are also dealt with in technically unique and reflexive ways that prevent them, as we shall see shortly, from becoming themes.

At any rate, the allegorical elements in *Paterson* have the role of "shifters" of a rather different kind than the expanding and contracting personages of *Finnegans Wake*, who enlarge to historical dimensions and cultural relativity and then shrink again to the existential proportions of the "realistic" characters of a modern Dublin city-scape: in *Paterson*, to be sure, the archaic, mythic and antediluvian dimension is sounded in the evocation of the "giants" themselves (whose "delineaments" in fact give the title of Book I as a whole):

> the giants
> who have died in the past and have
> returned to those scenes unsatisfied
> and who is not unsatisfied, the
> silent, Singac the rock-shoulder
> emerging from the rocks. (etc., 25/24)

But in this sense the giants fold back into the earth and the primal landscape itself and thus link up with a very different dimension of the poem, about which their outrageous figurality asserts that it is both present and not to be known or represented: America is a telluric or chthonic reality which is also, from the inescapable standpoint of a debased commercial modernity, a meretricious figment of the poetic imagination—no ultimate "ground of Being" ever to be glimpsed beneath the macadam of the parking lots or the 1930s fragility of a still classical downtown. The giants thus "derealize" themselves as an impossible allusion to what, even if a fact, is untrue: to what is fantastical in the bad poetic sense: a *via negativa* in which something is kept alive by virtue of the untruthfulness of the very form itself—this being, as we shall see, the fundamental ontological "strategy" of *Paterson* as a whole.

But this also holds for the allegorical or characterological level, where "the giants" also designate some formal evocation of an ur- or primal American race, whether Indian or settler-colonial—also a vain and meaningless gesture, since that primal History always recedes as a kind of bad infinity, ever preceding whatever can earliest be imagined, at the same time that it participates in the paradoxical unrepresentability of all American history in this book so full of historical materials and of an incessant reinvocation of multiple American pasts. Knowing that the giants do not exist then also expresses our deeper unconscious certainty that the American past does not exist either.

Nor does "Mr Paterson" exist; yet his existence as a supreme allegorical structure and framework is one of the fundamental tentative and multiple enabling figures of this poem, whose characters are not versions of him (as in Joyce), but rather figments of his imagination:

> Eternally asleep,
> his dreams walk about the city where he persists
> incognito. (6/6)

This peculiar allegory is therefore more closely affiliated to arithmetic and multiplication than to the rather different philosophical category of universals and their particulars: approaching "Mr Paterson," grasping the city as an "untotalizable totality" (Sartre) means

> rolling
> up the sum, by defective means (3/3)

—adding up the sheer numbers and multiplicities of individuals. The clumsiness of the naïve mathematical figure is somehow more truthful than Eliot's more poetic and Baudelairian vision of the masses themselves—"Unreal city! city full of dreams!" etc.—who, in *The Waste Land*, certainly yield a vision, but from what privileged point of view?—let alone the historic multitudes presupposed but rarely enough envisioned by Pound. The American small town is not mythic or poetic in any of these senses (nor is New Jersey to be sentimentalized *à la* Sherwood Anderson): the fact that the figure does not work and one cannot imagine how to go about "adding up" separate people or separate lives—that unworkable fact is itself the poetic datum at stake here, and it is underscored and reemphasized again and again by remarkable figural structures which equally do not work either:

> Say it! No ideas but in things. Mr.
> Paterson has gone away
> to rest and write. Inside the bus one sees
> his thoughts sitting and standing. His
> thoughts alight and scatter—
>
> Who are these people (how complex
> the mathematic) among whom I see myself
> in the regularly ordered plateglass of
> his thoughts, glimmering before shoes and bicycles?
> They walk incommunicado, the
> equation is beyond solution, yet
> its sense is clear—that they may live
> his thought is listed in the Telephone
> Directory—(9/9–10).

How individual people, including the physician–poet himself, could be ideas or figments of some more comprehensive consciousness or Absolute Spirit is what this passage asks us to imagine and forestalls at the same time: it offers the example of what we may call figural literalization, a kind of analytic device or interpretive estrangement effect, whereby the deeper hidden figuration of a given way of thinking is brought to the surface like a watermark by a thoroughgoing working through of its most literal effects and consequences. Most frequently, such figural literalization has been used on religious concepts, which clearly enough become vividly incoherent when developed in absolutely literal or literalizing ways. One thinks, for example, of the "death of the antique gods" in Flaubert's *Temptation of Saint Anthony*, where the long historical decay of belief and practice related to the classical pantheon is dramatized by the etiolation of individual gods, Jupiter physically weakening, Minerva growing as "weak as a woman," Diana putting on mourning and committing ritual suicide. Literalization of this kind does not destroy the figure; it rather resituates it on another level on which it continues as a narrative of a different sort: the figure is now not undermined as a mystification, but rather foregrounded in its essential structure *qua* historical fact as such, where it continues a different kind of existence, one that does not imply the existence, alongside the figure, of literal or prosaic, exact representation, but rather the permanence and inescapability of figuration itself. Thus, the empty character, or characterological function, of "Mr. Paterson" circulates through the poem, having affairs:

> Oh Paterson!   Oh married man!
> He is the city of cheap hotels and private
>   entrances,   of taxis at the door, the car
> standing in the rain hour after hour by
> the roadhouse entrance. (154/154)

or relaxing on a Sunday:

> And so among the rest he drives
> in his new car out to the suburbs, out
> by the rhubarb farm. (etc., 38/37)

Yet this distance which is inscribed in the allegorical figure is itself an echo of a constitutive distance in the structure of the poem as a whole, if not of all significant works we call modern—namely a kind of necessary gap between the conception of the work and its line-by-line execution. It is a gap of which the very title of *Ulysses* is supremely emblematic, naming a program which can be incidentally referred to in passing, but which subsists in its own being and floats above the text according to some different and incommensurable logic. This Idea of the work, which must somehow always remain at a distance from it, does not stand as a universal to a particular text which it subsumes (any more than does the allegorical figure of Paterson who "contains multitudes" in so un-Whitmanesque a sense). This incommensurability, which already Coleridge prophetically began to theorize in his distinction between Fancy and Imagination, is perhaps the consequence of the abandonment of the classical genre system, but more evidently still a compensation for the decay of the unities, which were hitherto in neoclassical times always available in order to allow the temporal dispersal of a theater play or even novel (*Tom Jones*) to be reassembled in the mind as a single object one could possess all at once. Now, however, the idea of the work, its conception, drifts apart from its impossible execution, occupying different spaces of the writer's or the intellectual's activities, dissociating itself as well from the fact of sheer duration—allowing the work either to expand or contract, to reach lengths of mammoth and even monstrous proportions, as in the endless melody of Wagnerian opera or Mahler's symphonic movements, or shortening to the instants of expressionist music or minimalisms of all kinds—since henceforth the sheer time, or dimensions, of the work are unrelated to the Idea of which it is no longer exactly the execution, but, as it were, the latter's marker, its reminder or place-holder. The invention of the Idea then sometimes enters the work as sheer content, as above all in that moment at the beginning of the *Ring* in which Wotan, "wie von einem grossen Gedanken ergriffen, sehr entschlossen," suddenly conceives of the plan to create a race of Walsungen to recover the ring, in other words, conceives of the idea of the *Ring* itself as a plot, at some point in which it would be frivolous to say that Wotan has become a representation of Wagner himself (let alone vice versa), but in which some last spark of reflexivity crosses the gap between the whole and the part (before decaying into the self-indulgence of garden-variety autoreferentiality as a modernist convention).

4. Number

But this distance also defines the Idea as a new kind of form, even though the category of form only determines the title after the fact as something ungeneric (if not generic in a new way) which has to be named nominalistically as something deriving from *The Cantos*—the pocket epic, say—or from *Ulysses*—the single-day book. Here, indeed, it is as with Wittgenstein's notion of family resemblances: whatever the distant allusions of these new *ad hoc* named forms to the older ones (remanence of epic theory in so many of them, recrudescence of marginal notes as in Frye's and Bakhtin's evocation of Menippean satire), they represent a new way of giving body to the universal–particular dialectic within the modern, and in a certain fashion themselves resist abstraction, becoming visible only by concrete comparisons which show up precisely that family likeness which must otherwise escape abstract conceptuality. We think Los Angeles is unique, until an experience of Houston, otherwise an utterly different city space with very different libidinal associations and investments, creates a pause in which it seems possible that some new and as yet unclassified urban species exists, of which we now know two distantly related species, but for which a simple abstract or classificatory term like "sun-belt city" is abusive, among other things because it represses the very process of discovery involved. Those who come to Schelling after Hegel may have a similar experience in a different order of things, where suddenly many of the speculative peculiarities only associated with the canonical or classic dialectic thinker prove instead to be features and traits of a whole disposition of thought and system-building in this period. The problem is then not to argue some seminal and liberating enablement of the first *Cantos* as a predecessor of everything from Eliot to Olsen and Zukofsky, taking in *The Bridge* and McAdams in passing, but rather, first to understand how it was the formal idea of the *Cantos* that played this fundamental role as detonator, rather than anything in the lines of the poem, or even its content, let alone Pound's own idiosyncratic style and tastes—although to be sure the more literal responses to the Idea involved an unconscious or slavish mimicry of all those things. But this is an idea of form which it is not particularly easy to abstract or to name—miniature epic only does so in a summary and exclusionary or definitional way insofar as it decisively removes these works from any conventional conception of lyric poetry or even of poetry itself in general.

The analogous problems of definition with respect to *Ulysses*, although they must mark something like an overall time frame which is the acknowledgement not of a return to the classical unities, but rather of the new unity of the single day and night in modern urban experience (a unity then otherwise underscored in Freud's remarkable observation that everything in the dream must somehow pass through the figuration and associational filter of events from the previous day—or even from the waking period after the last moment of previous sleep)—the real definitional problems emerge with the fact that it is not even this temporal material in Joyce, but rather its organizational composition into distinct and separate semi-autonomous chapters—an imperative so strong as to propel each of the later chapters into a style unmistakably its own and thereby divided from the others as by language itself—that is somehow the key and the essential thread.[7]

So here also it is not the "inclusion of history" in Pound—although it is the sign of that reduction of the individual subject we have spoken of earlier in connection with Williams, its documentary materials also allowing the dispersal of all the fictional and fictive categories that keep that conventional narrative subject in place (in the novel, for instance)—which is the fundamental discovery: but rather something to do with the separation of the Books, Cantos, Parts—that is to say, with the *ad hoc* positing of a certain unity within the terrific piling up and mixture of those units. They are units too vast, or rather they contain varieties of sentences, references, facts, tones, too numerous to be organized by the mind into any single unity (not even the narrative and temporal ones of Joyce). The words *collage, montage, ideogram, constellation* are then results, and in that sense are as unsatisfactory as they are indispensable. What happens then is that these enormous units tend to become related to each other externally: something formalized by Eliot's mythological names for his five sections, but perhaps more satisfactorily realized by Williams's four titles which do not cohere in any narrative way or project some secret narrative (or mythological) reunification. But then what needs to be noted is the way in which the sheer fact of number rises up as a secret clue to the concreteness of the work's interrelationship, something paradoxical in the light of the abstract quantitativeness of number as such and only suspiciously recompensated in the mysticisms of number theory and numerology. (Even Pound's "first XXX Cantos" bore the telltale mark of sheer number, and later dealings with the Cantos have always had to reify the numerical division of the batches of publication ...) But in Eliot and in Williams, it is as though some earlier cultural meaning of number—let us say, the conventional division of the symphony into four movements—came back into play in a residual suggestion that has nothing to do with music and its history and evolutions but rather merely in the conviction that a division into four or five sections has its own immanent meaning: immanence is surely then the crucial feature here, for it forbids the expression of any more abstract formulation and suggests that what we call meaning (whatever it is we call meaning) is here to be grasped only in the sheer experience of these differences and interrelationships between the four or five parts (Eliot's supplementary fifth part, the Phlebus section, is as markedly deviational as some of Mahler's "extra" movements), has an intelligibility within itself on its own terms. (And this is why some of us resist the canonicity of Williams's Fifth Book, which would tend to open *Paterson* up into the endless work-in-progress diaries of Pound, Olsen and Zukovsky; whereas the fact of the four books seems somehow as monumental and irrevocable as the Joyce/Viconian cycle, to which it is of course distantly related: "Then headed inland, followed by the dog" [203/202], where the spatial cycle no doubt begins all over again, without however the dissolution in the sea—"the sea is not our home" [202/200].) In fact, I believe that this process of producing the Idea is itself inscribed in the poem in the form of the grasshopper episode, from Book II:

When! from before his feet, half tripping,
picking a way, there starts
                    a flight of empurpled wings! (47/47)

We need, incidentally, not merely a study of Williams's punctuation (above all, the mysterious spaced period as a pause for breath in the uniquely patterned irregularities of the free verse "new line"), but more importantly some disquisition on the philosophy of the exclamation point in Williams, which supremely marks our non-metaphorical attention to the present instant of time and its excitements and threatens to tear through the fabric of syntax as a prose relationship ever reemergent within the worldly fabric of the project and experience. The grasshopper (later glimpsed in reified objectal form as pre-Columbian artifact in the Chapultepec museum—the Aztec name means "grasshopper hill") is the supreme embodiment of that to which the transcendental or poetic exclamation point must be applied: it is a specificity in the present which is briefly but supremely at one with the universal, or the Idea of the work itself—

AND a grasshopper of red basalt, boot-long,
tumbles from the core of his mind (47/47)

—something like the opposite of the library of Book III, in which all the old Ideas and dead "presents" are stored up in dust unless they are seized upon by sheer conflagration: reading as consumption in fire and destruction that leaves nothing of the text behind, or reading which somehow "in a fever heat, / cheeks burning . loaning blood / to the past" (101/101), manages to reawaken the fire that burns in all the dead moments of past history and their written traces. But here the fire is the absolute of the Idea that seizes upon the particular, where in the moment of inception—the moment of the emergence of the Modern—it is the particular which "tumbling" out of items of the empirical present has disclosed itself as the Idea of the work itself.

It seems to me, then, that it would be desirable to reverse the order of generic abstraction for the modern, and to attempt to grasp these named yet nameless forms first as concrete meanings in their own right. Thus Williams's four books are somehow a concept, they or it has some relationship to other modern concepts such as Eliot's, for example, but Williams's is susceptible to philosophical interpretation in its own right as a specific object or conceptual phenomenon, any attempt to reclassify it in older generic terms before proceeding somehow reversing the priorities and the deeper logic of the thing itself.

5. Taboos

However this may be, that external order then surely replicates itself inside of the four books, which are divided into three sections each, the musical associations then becoming even more insistent as we move down into smaller and more manageable units (but those associations must in that case be resisted even more energetically), until, finally, within each of the three individual component parts we face the abrupt changes in tone and matter consistent with the streaming of the poetic text itself. I want to argue that it is not (it is rarely) the substance of any particular moment of this streaming which is of any great significance: that is to say, many anecdotes are told, many moments of expression are registered, which lodge in the mind and the memory: but none of those has ultimate significance in itself, for imperative reasons which will be examined in a moment. None of them has aesthetic significance either (if that is a separate thing from the former), since what is aesthetic here—and what is significant as well—is rather the shifts and modulations between all these disparate materials. It would be too facile to say that everything here lies in the blanks and gaps between the poetic episodes, and in fact I think, faced with a poem of this length which one must continue to read and whose pages must be incessantly turned, that is not at all the case: far from silence, Paterson projects the spectacle of a deafening blast of voices and sounds

> in which a falls unseen
> tumbles and rights itself
> and refalls—and does not cease, falling
> and refalling with a roar, a reverberation
> not of the falls but of its rumor
> unabated (96/97)

It is therefore not in moments of rest or stillness that *Paterson* can be said to do something unique, but rather in the ceaseless transitions and modulations, whose fundamental effects surely turn on the distance between the various materials. It would take a well-programmed computer to tabulate the variety of these specific shifts (as one understands has been done in some forms of "advanced" twelve-tone music), but it is certainly possible to make a few general remarks which go further than the obvious law (discovered by the surrealists in another connection altogether) that the effects are proportionally greater and more interesting in proportion as the materials involved are distant, and perhaps also—and here the reference would not be the surrealists' definition of the image, but rather Yvor Winters's analysis of free verse laws of prosody (very much based on Williams's own "new line" itself)—that the number and multiplicity of the shifts is also a crucial requirement in this aesthetic. What can perhaps be said negatively—and here we return to a few suggestions that have been made about technical concepts earlier—is that the modulation must not always be understood in a signifying way, after the order of the montage or even of the ideogram.

It is certain that such ideogrammatic moments exist in this poem, in which disparate materials are appealed to convey a certain non-abstract idea. Such is for example the wondrous moment in which, after some seemingly unrelated remarks on Chaucer's failure to innovate in prosody, and then after the decisive moment in which Madame Curie returns to the studio at night and finds the first trace of radium—

LUMINOUS!

—suddenly an astonishing modulation brings a set of prosaic sentences before us:

> On Friday, the twelfth of October, we anchored before the land and made ready to go ashore [...] During that time I walked among the trees which was the most beautiful thing which I had ever known (178/177)

—where at once Columbus and the discovery of radium are combined into a powerful ideogram of poetic and economic innovation in the modern: "THE GIST" (185/184), etc.

But this is not, I think, the fundamental moment in *Paterson* and is indeed inconsistent with its deeper logic, since for once an idea is projected rather than dealt with negatively. To be sure, these Poundian moments are ones of great secondary construction: the elaboration of the great modern levels or homologies in which art, science, economics, personal life are all somehow momentarily combined in a Utopian schematic (if not a vision). Yet, as has already been observed, the notion of innovation (with its privileged form in the innovation in poetic language or the line) is the fundamental mark of modernist ideology, so that it is scarcely surprising that it is at just such moments of an essentially ideological affirmation that we should find Williams reverting to a more conventional practice of the ideogram or the conceptual montage.

A rather different use of the modulation is to be found in what I will call the pure forms or flourishes of narrativity as such and in the abstract, something like narrative ornamentation, most strikingly registered, of course, at the very close of the poem, where the lines

> This is the blast
> the eternal close
> the spiral
> the final somersault
> the end (204/202)

turn closure itself into something of an arabesque or a paraphon.

Still, it is important to realize that they refer to the execution of John Johnson on Garrett Mountain on April 30 1850, after a particularly gruesome murder which has been fed to us in anecdotal pieces and details throughout the work (see 72/72 and 198/197), and which thus has the function of undermining our deeper belief in narrative logic in the first place and in closure itself. For this figure asks us to wonder whether it is not a rather trivial habit of the human mind to think that death (execution, etc.) is the most accessible trope for closure or ending: and thereby to ask ourselves whether we really have a proper category for such formal conclusion in the first place (the alternative, immediately preceding the execution, was the cyclical one of the return of man and dog back from the sea into the hinterland—a different kind of figure which cannot be substituted for the other one exactly, but is thereby equally distanced and underscored as sheer figuration, rather than as some ontological form or movement in reality itself). What is happening here, however, is that shards of narrativity are being abstracted from these anecdotal materials which come to function as new narrative components in their own right and as the possible building blocks of new kinds of meta-narrative constructions (and to the degree to which Eisenstein sometimes also sounds as though he means that in his descriptions of montage, rather than as defining the latter simply as a form of concrete conceptuality, the deliberate allusion to Eisenstein [58] is as formally relevant as those to Pound himself).

For a kind of textbook demonstration of this new construction which wishes to be purely formal movement rather than narrative of even a collective actantial variety, one may, for example, examine the series of components that make up the conclusion of Part III of Book II, which notoriously concludes with the accusatory and depressed letters of Williams's erstwhile woman writer protégée: a kind of emotional low point of the poem, but which begins that concluding movement—as with the endless reprises that sketch a beginning conclusion to a Mahler symphonic movement—with the opening page of that last section: "the descent beckons" (77/78, reference to the seasons), then "the pouring water" (79/79), the failure of the poem and the words "dangling, about whom / the water weaves its strands" (81). Not unexpectedly then, there follows the reprise of the great fall over the edge of Mrs Cumming, and on to the prose letter which documents both the failure of Williams's relationship to the woman's demands and the failure of her own poetry. Here it is something like "descent" itself in all its senses, spatial and physical fully as much as figurative, emotional, historical, that is the object of representation, consisting not so much in an idea or concept as in some purer form of movement which would take all these diverse materials as its composite embodiment.

6. On Thematic Contamination

Yet beginnings and endings are notoriously easy movements to embody, and in order to get some clearer sense of what goes on between them, what the actual substance of the poem might be said to be, we need now to turn back to the question of the individual components. Many of these obviously involve history; a good many of them also deploy this or that aspect of the physical landscape of the Paterson region; and we will come to both these dimensions of content later on. What is now wanted is some closer examination of the anti-substantive or process-oriented treatment of these materials as they succeed each other in the textual stream. But this now requires us to return to the notion of modernist taboos, as *Paterson* noticeably allows us to disengage and demonstrate the operation of these negative formal commandments. We have in fact begun to grasp how these operate already in the preceding examples: for much depends on our seeing how the Columbus montage, as striking and beautiful as it may be, stands out like something of a foreign body and runs counter to the very spirit of the poem (and also to that of its official poetic ideology, which we have not yet mentioned). A first negative taboo can thus be formulated as excluding conceptual montage as such, or rather—since in the case of a poem that takes as its province a complex industrial society where concepts can scarcely be omitted as part of the essential social raw material—at least as blocking the signifying effect such conceptual montages—expended or unanticipated—might have.

The spirit of such aesthetic taboos might perhaps best be illustrated by the deeper reason for being of the inventions of Schoenberg's twelve-tone system, which forbids the return of any single note of the scale until all others have been traversed, for one excellent reason: namely, that even the most local and episodic dwelling on a single note rather than the others might threaten to restore a kind of general if provisional tonal center. If one thinks of the "meaning" of the Columbus montage in that way, as momentarily giving the epic a thematic meaning, and making it over into a work whose deeper message is that—innovation—and therefore: only that! it becomes possible to appreciate an otherwise seemingly self-defeating logic in which this particular signifying constellation is to be avoided, forestalled, neutralized or undermined as constituting an unwanted consonance (and paradoxically, the fact that "dissonance" is itself one of the motifs of the material surrounding this passage scarcely helps the passage evade this particular pitfall, which is that of poetic "success").

The formal abstraction that was examined next (descent and fall, closure, culmination and conclusion) would seem to present fewer problems in this respect, but in that case their threats lie elsewhere: in the production of a series of pure movements and arabesques, of a visual formalism of a relatively empty and vacuous kind. In fact, we will see that this particular danger is handled—while the advantages of its formal dynamics are retained—by way of a very special conception of the physical elements that lead us on into other dimensions of the work.

But the ban on meaning—or, better still, its suspension, the effort to dissolve it as soon as it begins to constitute itself, the appropriation of its components in the service of other kinds of processes once they have become even fitfully identified—is a stylistic or micrological form of that Barthesian description of the attempt of the modern to avoid reification (which has been quoted earlier) and takes the multiple form of a taboo on figural language, on symbols, on themes, on "great style" or achieved poetic language, and even on coherent narrative itself (something we have already been able to identify in the neutralization of "point of view" in another context). That Williams was notoriously (and uniquely) hostile to metaphor as everybody's "hallmark of genius" from Aristotle to Proust perhaps needs no further argument: this being his particular way of dealing not merely with the general guilt of culture in modern times for contemporary intellectuals, but also of associating that stigmatized culture with the remnants of Europe and its traditions of Literature and High Art with capital letters.

Yet this literality, however desirable, does not yet exist; it cannot simply be chosen and preferred to ornament and the trappings of poetic convention, and then put to use "with the bare hands." Rather, as with the free verse pattern, it must be disengaged within the line where attention to temporal and prosodic patterns, to be sure, displaces the relatively more spatial attention to metaphor and image and tends to undermine the ceaseless reformations of these visual figures. But it is precisely that ceaseless tireless reformation of the figure within all language and thought which poses the most urgent problem for such an aesthetic, which can remain unproblematical only within the narrow and frustrating limits of the historical framework of "Imagism," as the latter sealed itself off from conceptuality and figural relationship by the discipline of small forms in time and the iron modesty of isolated perceptions taken one by one.

Otherwise, the relational necessarily generates a web of figures whose growth and destiny lie in the emergence of the metaphoric itself, along with themes, meanings and symbols: to preclude it from the outset is literally suicidal and a way of preventing thought and thinking from coming into being at all—something even more tragic where we have to do with a sterile American reality barren of thought and lacking even the ossified remnants of the dead thoughts and linguistic figures of an older European culture. So from any impression of this social impoverishment, figures of speech arise:

> Life is sweet
> they say: the language!
> —the language
> is divorced from their minds,
> the language . . . the language! (12/12)

It is a harmless enough turn of phrase, in any case applied to something (language) that has no substantial or thing-like existence and can in any case only be evoked or discussed figuratively. How many other ways can we imagine to convey the haplessness of minds unable to express themselves and from whom that expressive power is somehow distant, or separated, if not unlearned or unappropriated? But the figure has its own life:

> a bud forever green,
> tight-curled, upon the pavement, perfect
> in juice and substance but divorced, divorced
> from its fellows, fallen low— (18/17)

Now a kind of self-critique of imagism sets in which the very separation of the perfect image ("like a flower") from the ecology of context is thematized as the rather ridiculous pathos of a bud fallen off a stalk (so that this passage, like the previous one, leads us back to the ideology of the modern and can at least initially be considered as a momentary meditation on art itself and its verbal destiny). The predicate, too, when it comes, is if anything less metaphorical than in the previous usage, conventionalized into the merest figure of speech, as when one says of anything that it is "divorced" from its context. Yet it is that very conventionality that now frees the word up for the most unacceptable further developments—as in the hectoring voice which now immediately follows on this one:

> Divorce is
> the sign of knowledge in our time,
> divorce! divorce!

And the trick is turned, irrevocable: "divorce" has suddenly become an official theme of the poem, at once retroactively generating its opposite number, marriage (which can now be seen immediately to have followed on the earlier mention, with the African chief's wives, on page 13, and to be replicated as a "theme" virtually everywhere later on). This "thematic meaning", then, clearly enough has expansive and contaminatory power and gradually enlarges to include the very structure of the poem itself, where the allegorical problem of the contradiction between the universality of "Mr. Paterson" and his gender, the spatial requirement to hold a second place open for the allegory of the woman lying beside him above the Falls, now also takes its place within the nascent system. At length, then, the other dramatic highpoints—the bitter correspondence from "C." (as the "woman scorned", who awakens all the stereotypical or archetypal masculine fear of the devouring mate) and the "pastoral" interlude of the crippled poetess and her nurse (with its lesbian overtones)—also range themselves within a thematics that has taken over the entire work. But this thematic expansion, which could easily be transformed into a feminist reading and critique of Williams's epic (despite the fact that he has himself inscribed it in the work), clearly also undermines the formal claim of the poem to be a totality and to be about everything, rather than just "something in particular": it is this neo-epic vocation (or ambition or pretension) that must resist a reduction to specific themes and the subsequent "meanings" they produce.

This is why there must be a way of reversing the figurative process, which tends otherwise to formalize itself in the production of just such official "themes" (and as the word suggests, in doing so to turn the work into mere Literature). The rapid shifts in materials, the collaging of other documents and voices, along with their preoccupations and equally nascent themes, constitutes a basic "technique" for doing this, and clearly enough, the faster and more numerous such shifts and changes in direction, the more surely will the mind be diverted from this temporary fixation or obsession ... for, with respect to an aesthetic of totality, this kind of thematization, not to speak of outright symbolization, or even conceptual reification, may be seen as just such a pathology, an attempt to hold fast morbidly to a single figure—

> spitted on fixed concepts like
> roasting hogs (etc., 32/32)

But there can also be other ways of reversing the process of figuration, a little like Hamilton's grand schemes for Paterson and for the national economy:

> The bird, the eagle, made himself
> small—to creep into the hinged egg
> until therein he disappeared, all
> but one leg (etc., 73/73)

Such is for example the moment in which the poet, idly scraping about inside his ear with a hairpin (30/29), finds that object transmogrified and metamorphosed

> to the magnificence of imagined delights
> where he would probe
>
> as into the pupil of an eye
> as through a hoople of fire, and emerge
> sheathed in a robe
>
> streaming with light. (etc., 31/30)

It is not clear whether this magnified snapshot of the moment of poetic inspiration, seen from the diminishing perspective of a purely subjective and individual point of view, reduces the "magnificent" language to triviality by way of its association with the hairpin or on the contrary continues to perform that transformation of everyday life that it has been the function of modernism at least since Joyce to assume: in either case figuration has itself been estranged and shorn of its legitimacy as "poetic language."

The logical consequence of these new poetic taboos is then the exclusion of realized poetic language as such—not merely the foreclosure of individual style and the very category of personal or private style as such, fundamental in almost all the great works of modern literature (whose result, if not their intent, has been to create the signature and the uniquely recognizable private signed world)—something Williams achieves not only by way of his non-fictionality and also his multiple insertion of documents of all kinds (not, after all, very much like Dos Passos), but above all by a peculiarly immediate relationship to the American language which somehow precedes the formation of Literature and of the "literary" as such.

But this means eschewing the great moments literature has sometimes been able to achieve, the great effects of style, Houseman's bristling and tingling, the "sublime" in all the various modern senses: and it accounts therefore equally for the presence in Williams's compendious epic of an outright bad poetry—

> Here's to the baby,
> may it thrive! (etc., 193/192, but see also the doggerel on pp. 68/68, 160/159–60)

Bad poetry and doggerel are the sign, not only of misguided aesthetics and popular kitsch, but even more fundamentally of the longing of the inarticulate to capture and express unique existential moments for which they have no language: so that in just such moments of failed verse—which are then narratively realized in the failures of "C."[8] and above all in the bad poetry of the crippled heiress of Book IV (with her attempt mythically to convert the rocks of the East River into the sheep of her pastoral [152–3/151–2; 161/160–1])—the dialectic of Williams's own poem is itself implicitly concentrated: in order to succeed it must fail, only the impossibility of language can convey the dilemmas of an American language that has not yet come into being.

7. Against Abstraction

But the intent to fail is not a very satisfactory starting point, calculated pre-eminently to self-defeat and to paralyze the process from the outset. The ideological origin of Williams's aesthetic surely lies elsewhere, and the source of his fruitful taboos on symbol, theme, meaning, and style can be found in a much more familiar place (which we have already anticipated in our mention of Imagism as a movement). It is none other than the familiar slogan

> Say it, no ideas but in things (6/6; and also 174/173)

Leave aside the question whether this injunction itself is not more like an idea than a thing: it shapes the fundamental taboo that drives invention forward here and is at the same time so consistent with contemporary attitudes that it is desirable to take some distance for a moment or two, with a view towards estranging such an odd commandment and situating it more historically.

The underlying feeling surely has something to do with the conviction that things and their experience are somehow more trustworthy than mere ideas, which are in one way or another the locus of sheer opinion and mere ideology, and perhaps also the locus of untrustworthy individuation as well: the unarticulated conviction that abstraction is bad and the concrete—however you define it—always more desirable or preferable; that what can be grasped by the senses (even though via the medium of language) is more tangible and thing-like than the associations left open by the vagueness of conceptual language; and so on and so forth. These attitudes, which powerfully motivate the purgation of the Victorian poetic traditions in Williams's youth by the Hulmean choice of the imagistic and of the objectified, can also be identified as a reconfiguration of the standard ideology of philosophical empiricism, and of many of the dominant Anglo-American forms of anti-intellectualism. (Nor is it pointless to explore what may be our own inner contradictions in finding the poetic face of these attitudes more appealing than the philosophical one.)

Williams's poetic is surely extraordinarily consonant with the modern in general in its suspicion of the multiplicity of intellectual codes, that (as Barthes and Sartre taught us) mark complicity with this or that group or intellectual or professional caste in our society, or with this or that fundamental ideology: Williams's refusal of what he calls "ideas" is seen from this perspective as a Utopian aspiration to classlessness and to a democratic universality only available by way of shared things rather than of the learned appropriation of their representations.

But it is no less profoundly anti-intellectual for all that, and to it may be opposed Adorno's cultural diagnosis of the universal positivism of modern society, which he interprets in a twofold way as heightened instrumentalism and the technological appropriation and domination of the world and other people, and also as a calculated strategy for the neutralization of intellectual distance and negativity, the stigmatization as unscientific and superstitious of anything conceptual, let alone dialectical, which might result in a dangerously critical position from which the existent order could be judged. Adorno's conception of the decline of negativity and critical thinking (which was if anything reinforced by his experience in exile in America during the years Williams worked on *Paterson*) stands thus in the sharpest contrast to the radicality of the North-American epic—work in a form utterly unfamiliar to the continental Europeans (unless the distant kinship with Benjamin's intellectual aesthetic and his practice of the "constellation" in the Arcades project be pursued). The fact that "theory" is released as powerfully from Williams's montages and ideograms as Benjamin wished it to be from his own constellations does nothing to resolve this particular contradiction, which it may be desirable to think about in terms of the homeopathic, of the therapeutic application of the very poison—positivism, anti-intellectualism—that is to be treated in the first place.

At any rate, this poetic strategy, which forces the work into elaborate detours around abstractions and conceptuality as such, can now be seen to have its kinship with other, pre-modern thought patterns that have played a significant role in nineteenth- and twentieth-century philosophy. Lévi-Strauss's notion of "pensée sauvage" or what might better be translated as "perceptual science", a thinking of tribal peoples which, independently of scientific abstraction, must convey its findings by way of the materials of perception themselves, the leaves and the landscapes of indigenous medical and natural knowledge, is surely the most influential contemporary model of a thinking that is forced to seek the necessary distances of abstraction within the concrete itself. Lévi-Strauss is necessarily ambiguous about this stage of human intellection, whose kinship with "structuralism" he affirms at the same time that he celebrates the Western science which can alone bring it to light and theorize its originality: Levi-Strauss's scornful refusal of any characterization of nostalgia for these cultures is matched only by the implicit affirmation of the superiority of the concrete thinking of what will come to be called "structuralism" over the more abstract forms of Western thought and philosophy from which it triumphantly liberates itself. There is therefore a whole philosophy of history implicit in this stance on abstraction, which alerts us to features in Williams we might otherwise overlook. But it is in Hegel that an even more suggestive version of this conception of a thinking before or beyond mere abstraction is to be found.

For Hegel, indeed, the thinking of non-Western traditions (more precisely, of non-Western religions and religious cultures) is very precisely characterized by their failure to achieve abstraction, that is to say, to attain what he calls the work of the concept. In his *Aesthetics* this immense stage is named as that of the Symbolic, as opposed to the intellectual or conceptual immanence of the Classical, in which both philosophy and the sculpture of the pure human form emerge, or to the modernism of the Romantic, or of Christian civilization, in which the predominance of the idea over matter and the world is secured and extended. The Symbolic, by contrast, is a moment in which matter predominates, and intellectual and conceptual impulses seek vainly to realize themselves through a material which has no abstract dimensions (this is also then, oddly, for Hegel the moment of the "sublime," which so many other thinkers from Kant himself onwards identify rather with the modern period). In its most fully realized form, the Egyptian, there emerges then in the Symbolic the hieroglyphs of a kind of material dialectic, in which, as in the following characterization of Osiris, the "symbol" fails to constitute itself and allegorically passes back and forth into various equally concrete versions of itself, from human being to river, from the sun to living beings themselves:

> The parallelism of the course of human life with the Nile, the Sun and Osiris, is not to be regarded as a mere allegory—as if the principle of birth, of increase in strength, of the culmination of vigor and fertility, of decline and weakness, exhibited itself in these different phenomena, in an equal or similar way; but in this variety imagination conceived only *one subject*, one vitality. This unity is, however, quite abstract: the heterogeneous element shows itself therein as pressing and urging, and in a confusion which sharply contrasts with Greek perspicuity. Osiris represents the Nile and the Sun: Sun and Nile are, on the other hand, symbols of human life—each one is signification and symbol at the same time; the symbol is changed into signification, and this latter becomes symbol of that symbol, which itself then becomes signification. None of these phases of existence is a Type without being at the same time a Signification; each is both; the one is explained by the other. Thus there arises one pregnant conception, composed of many conceptions, in which each fundamental nodus retains its individuality, so that they are not resolved into a general idea. The general idea—the thought itself, which forms the bond of analogy—does not present itself to the consciousness purely and freely as such, but remains concealed as an internal connection.

> We have a consolidated individuality, combining various phenomenal aspects; and which on the one hand is fanciful, on account of the combination of apparently disparate material, but on the other hand internally and essentially connected, because these various appearances are a particular prosaic matter of fact.[9]

But it is a process that has to mark itself as such, so that as what Hegel calls "symbol" and "signification" ceaselessly change places and substitute for one another without finding appeasement in "the general idea" or the Concept, the *Begriff*, in the same way the materiality of each of these moments comes to stand for itself and emblematize itself, being marked at once as allegory and as the imperfection of representation. This is something like a perpetual reflexivity, which oddly replicates the modern by failure rather than by achievement, in which the symbolic material is perpetually forced to designate itself as it reinvests in the "things" in which it both comes to expression and fails to express itself.

8. The Elements

But Williams's allegorical framework precludes the kind of movement Hegel describes in his analysis of the Osiris figure, for it already designates and identifies the allegorical structure in advance and as such—thus disqualifying either the giants or the larger Paterson figure for internal movement and differentiation of this kind. Thus, in a scientific age, symbolic investment must sink to the most seemingly disinvested materials themselves, to what appears as utterly devoid of conceptual content, namely the natural elements which are both the most impoverished and the most concrete things. Even the idea of "natural elements"—the four great material components of the universe in earth, air, fire, and water—betrays a rather archaic form of thinking more consistent with Heidegger, no doubt, than with the modern (but already industrially decaying) American land- and city-scape; or with Williams's acute documentary time-sense, his intense feeling that the past is a voluminous and contingent archive, and that what we call the deep past or the well of time is simply the always-already, the retroactive illusion of a preceding moment, multiplying mirages behind itself (the Giants).

Earth is in fact the most problematical of these elements, appearing in its own person as it were only in the rockdrill of page 139 (139), which lists the various subsoils from red sandstone all the way down to shaly sandstone at 2,100 feet: yet it is no surprise that earth resists direct perception, that it withdraws into itself whenever we attempt to confront it thus without mediation:

> A stone presses downwards and manifests its heaviness. But while this heaviness exerts an opposing pressure it denies to us any penetration into it. If we attempt such penetration by breaking open the rock, it still does not display in its fragments something inward that has been disclosed. The stone has merely withdrawn again into the same dull pressure and bulk of its fragments. If we try to lay hold of this in another way by placing the stone on a scales, we merely bring its heaviness into the form of a calculated weight. This perhaps very precise determination of the stone remains a number but the weight has escaped us. (H673/43)

It seems possible that—at least in Williams's poem—the capacity of the elements to reveal or deconceal themselves may be variable, and that fire happens and water appears in very different ways from those in which earth and air somehow conceal themselves from us. But this earth is not nature either in the older sense, and the wonderfully nostalgic evocation of the backcountry in the closing pages of *Paterson* ("There was an old wooden bridge to Manchester," [196/195]) is an effect that derives less from sheer matter than from the categorical opposition between city and country: Williams's backcountry is therefore not earth so much as it is the countryside (not yet the suburb) of a city, social rather than natural, and a human construct rather than the revelation of Being.

But if earth can only reveal itself by indirection, then it seems plausible to suggest that it makes its presence felt here essentially by way of topology and geography. Garrett Mountain, the emplacement of the park and the Falls, the downtown and the streets that lead out of it, the unseen presence of Manhattan in the distance—all these essentially relational positions remind us of what the city itself attempts to conceal or to consign to an essentially modern and urban forgetfulness, namely that we are still inhabiting and moving about the non-human space of an undomesticated, not yet even American earth.

It is an awareness we can only attain, however, in the presence of the urban: and this is the deeper truth of Heidegger's great idea that earth and world mutually deconceal and reveal each other by way of their struggle and their opposition:

> Soldier, there is a war between the mind and the sky.

However, in Heidegger, the possibility of this mutual deconcealment—"world worlds [Welt *weltet*, (H671/41)] and is something that *is* to a greater degree than the tangible and perceptible realm in which we believe ourselves to be at home"—passes through the work itself, as we shall see shortly, because it is in the work that the essential incompatibility of world and earth is staged and reexperienced. At that point—where "the work discloses a world", (H671/40) and "the work lets the earth be an earth" (H673/43)—it becomes clear that there is a fundamental incommensurability between these two dimensions, which could be translated perhaps as Matter and History respectively, at the risk of losing the kind of estrangement Heidegger's language is designed to enact. Contingency is the result of their intersection—the fact of unique bodies given over to genetically coded diseases, the accidents of terrain and of natural disaster, in bitter conflict with the assertion of life destinies and collective projects: it is as though earth and world, matter and history, were two absolutely distinct languages into which data must be translated completely, without either retaining a trace of its former existence in the other realm, without anything showing of the deeper underground channels or ontological relations between what are obviously mere "aspects" of the same being. Many are the forms this particular opposition has taken in the history of thought, but almost all of them have been influenced by a will to overcome it and to produce something like a unified field theory *avant la lettre* in which the data of the human and the historical, or of praxis, can be fully recoded in the language of nature or vice versa. These impossible resolutions can then be seen as generating the various idealisms on the one hand (whose paradigmatic German-idealist version takes the form of the postulate whereby consciousness brings the outside world and the being of things into being by fiat) and the various materialisms on the other (whose classical form lies in the positivist dream of locating the source of consciousness in the fibers of the brain itself). Alongside these irrepressible attempts to overcome the gap or rift between earth and world by identifying and thereby reducing the one to the other (in a multitude of different versions), there can also be said to be the unconscious acceptance of their coexistence in all the various traditional models of the relationship between subject and object (or mind and body), where the problem is somehow taken for granted in a reified form that both replicates and occults it all at once. The originality of Heidegger's "solution" here is to suggest that it is only by intensifying the incompatibility between earth and world that something is achieved: that, since no resolution of this opposition is conceivable, what is desirable is an awareness of the contradiction so intense as to sharpen our simultaneous life in both dimensions all at once: for Heidegger, this is what the authentic work of art is called upon to do (but it seems to be possible for him in other domains as well, as we shall see later):

> In setting up a world and in setting forth the earth, the work is an instigation of the struggle. But this does not happen in order that the work should settle and put an end to the strife in an insipid agreement, but in order that the strife should remain a strife. (H675/46–47)

This is then what *Paterson* seems to confirm in the way in which it is the indirection of the topology and of the contingent history of the urban agglomeration that somehow gives the inhuman earth beneath Paterson to be felt; while it is at the same time by way of the material elements that the social community, with its perpetually repressed pasts, is brought into view as a world:

> world is the ever un-objective realm that shelters us as long as the paths of birth and death, blessing and curse, keep us exposed to being. Wherever the essential decisions of our history are made, are taken up and abandoned by us, mistaken and reexamined, there the world worlds [*weltet*]. (H671/41)

But even as has been said, the being of water and of fire have a rather different mode of revelation in this poem about a river and a waterfall, which also, in its third book, "The Library", tries to think its archival past in terms of a conflagration as immense and catastrophic, as world-historical, as that of the library of Alexandria. Still, the spirit of indirection, the refusal of immediacy, are registered in the more intense forms of appearance of water, which are not so much to be found in the movement of the waterfall as rather in the sogginess of the terrain of the fire after rain:

> If it were only fertile. Rather a sort of muck, a detritus,
> in this case—a pustular scum, a decay, a choking
> lifelessness—that leaves the soil clogged after it (140/140)

But in this powerfully sensory evocation of the humid that "fouls the mind," we can also grasp the way in which Williams wills and chooses the "dissociation of sensibility," since surely in some sense these remains of the library and the culturally conserved past are his equivalent of Pound's hell in the *Cantos*, and offer a vivid example of how the material components of *Paterson* are deliberately arrested on their way to meaning and sheer "symbolism." This notion of cultural degradation is then held away from its sensory realization in the "muck" as though locked into a different component of the mind altogether with which it fails to communicate as completely as world fails to communicate with earth.

In fact, it is here as though water can come to expression only by its contamination with fire; elsewhere, the evocation of subterranean canals and sewers marks the requirement that water come to representation only by way of earth itself (in the more limited, physical sense of land or dirt):

> There is a drumming of submerged
> engines, a beat of propellers.
> The ears are water. The feet
> listen. Boney fish bearing lights
> stalk the eyes (etc., 129/129)

And of course, even and above all in the waterfall itself water is manifested by way of air:

> they coalesce now
> glass-smooth with their swiftness,
> quiet or seem to quiet as at the close
> they leap to the conclusion and
> fall, fall in air! as if
> floating, relieved of their weight,
> split apart, ribbons; dazed, drunk
> with the catastrophe of the descent
> floating unsupported
> to hit the rocks (etc., 8/8)

So also with fire, which needs the element of air for its representation, thereby itself furnishing the representation of air itself, otherwise intangible and invisible. Thus, for example, the grand movement of the updraft that offers

> the awesome sight of a tin roof (1880)
> entire, half a block long, lifted like a
> skirt, held by the fire—to rise at last,
> almost with a sigh, rise and float, float
> upon the flares as upon a sweet breeze,
> and majestically drift off, riding the air,
> sliding
> upon the air, easily and away under
> the frizzled elms that seem to bend under
> it, clearing the railroad tracks to fall
> upon the roofs beyond (etc., 121–2/122)

These combined elements then (as in the present instance) frequently embody a kind of abstract movement that is transferable, as the downward movement of the Falls is replicated in this horrific movement of the burning roof landing, and both these movements are anticipated by the end of the previous section in which the riding of hawks on the updraft looking down upon the cityscape is imitated by the downward movement of the reader in the library who once again looks down

> Searching among books; the mind elsewhere
> looking down
> Seeking. (112/112)

There results an inventory of concrete but abstract movements that greatly exceed the simple ones of Heidegger's Roman fountain and his Greek temple (or Wallace Stevens's jar), but are perhaps not different in nature from those, which essentially represent the way in which perception must capture the play of elements in Earth.

What it is most crucial to grasp, however, is the way in which Williams's four elements—as perception then separates them out once again from each other as ultimate building blocks of the universe—are the raw materials of the poem in as literal a sense as is possible for "letters" or "literature" which cannot physically incorporate the physical as such (unlike "the luster and gleam of the stone" of the temple—H669/38). The poem is to be thought of as a gigantic material collage, upon which, alongside the varied documentation of Paterson's "world" in the form of letters, newspaper clippings, and personal reminiscences, there are also pasted, in person, the elements themselves: water laid alongside fire, air added in alongside earth—a veritable "concrete" work of art in the musical sense of the term, in which the raw sensory constituents or component parts of the physical world are grossly appropriated into the aesthetic construction, and circulated "with the bare hands" throughout the other materials. No other modern work has so consequently aspired to this reduction to the physical (which is quite different from the contemporary or postmodern reduction to the body as such): it does not make for vulgar materialism in any obvious sense but also marks the distance of "civilization" from matter by the equally necessary failure of the effort, since *Paterson* cannot bring water and fire before us in any immediate let alone sensory fashion.

9. Including History

As for "world," however, its historicity is first of all as indirect as these elements of "earth" are mediate: the city of Paterson means any number of "significant" historic events, from the American revolution and Hamilton's scheme for a national manufactory to the great IWW strike reported by John Reed just before World War One (and this overt form of "politics" is sustained throughout the poem by Williams's Poundian-economic reflections on credit on the one hand, and the various intermittent mob scenes on the other [see, for example, p. 46]). But unlike Lukács's representational conception of the historical novel, this material is present only by allusion or association: as with the conventional actants of narratology, here also neither a positive nor a negative hero is desirable, so that the formal contradictions or antinomies characteristic of 1930s political art are also at one stroke displaced. (The positive hero had the disadvantage of idealizing the class subject in ways that masked problems of organization and consciousness; the negative hero had the effect of victimizing the same subject and producing "defeatism"; and it can be shown that this particular unacceptable alternative continues to characterize the political literature of the new social movements and in particular to dog both feminism and a Black political literature.) But the world-historical figures are also trivialized, when not banished to the wings altogether: General Washington appears in order to visit Peter the Dwarf in a newspaper *fait divers* (10/10), but John Reed and Big Bill Haywood do not appear in person at all. (Still, a certain narrative interest is sustained by optional character lines, as witness the late reappearance, in Book Four [193] of this same Peter the Dwarf, whose skull was rediscovered in 1885.) In a formal or allegorical way, therefore, one might argue that Lukács's intuition in *The Historical Novel* was not wrong after all, and could be transferred to anecdote and raw material in such a way that the distance of the more "noble" or serious world-historical anecdotes (involving the great figures and names) guarantees the historical efficacity of the absolutely average or trivial daily-life ones, as when, in a characteristic clipping from the year 1878, Special Officer Goodridge fires at the mink (49/49). Indeed, this historicization of kitsch and also of daily life—the two standing to each other in the US as something like form to content or consciousness to situation or raw material—is one of the fundamental operations of the poem, which is in this respect aesthetically the reverse or the inverse of the great prose constructions of Williams's *In the American Grain*, as the latter set out to invent a non-personal, elevated, but perhaps also non-literary style (whose relations with pastiche and parody remain to be worked out) for the officially great, named moments of our history, from the "conquest of Mexico" to Lincoln.

But the distancing from official history and its named characters is the formal side of a more fundamental social attitude, not unrelated to the dominant populism of the period, and which I hesitate to characterize by way of the otherwise accurate word "marginality" (which has specific and rather different contemporary associations in the politics of the new social movements, for example, that are clearly inapplicable and anachronistic). But the language of margins and of the distance from the center—both socially and geographically—is very appropriate indeed for this particular poem, which can only glimpse New York City in the distance across the New Jersey meadows—

> higher than the spires, higher
> even than the office towers, from oozy fields
> abandoned to grey beds of dead grass (6/7)

—a feeling only reconfirmed by the reverse-shot setting of the Manhattan apartment in Book IV. Finally, then, the more appropriate language for this more traditional "decentering" is probably the more equally traditional one of the capital and the provinces, all the more so since Williams's locale strips the experience of provinciality of all possible nostalgia or regionalism and gives it to us in a virtually pure state.

Paterson reconfirms, then, the intuition that a certain modernism is deeply interrelated with the experience of provinciality as such, whether on a world scale (in which it is somehow even the sophisticated and world-weary ancient cities, like Alexandria and Lisbon, that feel themselves as distant from the centers of true historical or commercial power), or culturally, in the case of the United States itself or the other Americas as they confront the dominant European culture post-colonially and prove to be the true forcing houses of aesthetic modernism (Rubén Darío, Pound and Eliot), or internally, where the provincial towns and regions yearn for the freedom of the great city and produce a new kind of art in compensation for that longing, an art whose formal freedom simulates the moral and sexual freedoms of the metropolis, an art whose abstraction has no little to do with the abstractions of the urban, as Simmel describes those in "Metropolis and Mental Life", but whose portable forms also somehow rebuke all claims of centrality on the part of the hegemonic inhabitants of whatever national privileged space.

It is this fundamental spatial provincialism that then finds itself inscribed, not merely in *Paterson*'s social position and ideologies, but in the social raw material of the poem, which, even when working-class-based, sees its subjects—immigrants, lower-class people in the park on Sunday, black girls, women—from the angle and optic of the doctor's office rather than the sociological survey. As between class, race and gender, it is surely the last which is the most pronounced, but all are somehow subject to the Lukács principle that the truth of such categories is best surprised mediately and by indirection rather than by official representation. The changes rung on the social motif range from outright teratology (as in the case of Peter the Dwarf, already mentioned, in whom some essential deformation and monstrosity of the American experience in general is expressed) to sexual "flagrancy" (59/59) and general disreputability and lack of bourgeois respectability—

> among
> the working classes SOME sort
> of breakdown
> has occurred (etc., 51/51)—

all the way to medical pathos—

a great belly
that no longer laughs but mourns
with its expressionless black navel love's
deceit . (28/27)

What it is necessary to observe is that this kind of social "marginality" does not produce a populist ideological effect, even though it clearly issues from populism in politics and in the situation of this historical period. Williams's indirection—but also, as we shall see in a moment, his new emphasis on daily life—is able to neutralize his populist elements *qua* ideology, to forestall their inevitable re-formation into outright ideology: it is a neutralization that is then to be ranged alongside the processes mentioned earlier which operate to prevent or to forestall meaning-formation in general and thematic reification in particular.

If women's frustration (as expressed above all in the great letter sequence from C.) is the dominant vehicle for this social material, its quintessential symbolic markers are, on the contrary, an obsession my students were astonished to find throughout this particular poem, but which, once noticed, proves to be omnipresent and inescapable, namely dogs: dogs of all shapes and forms, from the noble animals sacrificed in the Kinte Kaye (132/132) to mongrels running through the park, and then on to the pathos of the genuine pets ("you had him killed on me" [131/131], "your dog *is* going to have puppies" [54/53]). Few great modern works can have been so insistently punctuated by the presence of non-symbolic animals, whose literal existence is somehow beneath the level of attention of Literature itself, while they can only be converted into meanings either by way of kitsch sentimentalism or a highly exaggerated and improbable symbolism that would scarcely escape kitsch either at its outer limit (but in film one can think of the mangy dog Death in *Los Olvidados*). Are there dogs in Proust or in Musil? I doubt it; and while one can imagine a Rilke dog with a little effort (and it is true that Thomas Mann, archburgher, wrote *Herr and Hund*), it is hard to imagine man's best friend lurking through either infernal or paradisal spaces in T.S. Eliot[10] or the most influential pages of Valéry's verse. This may, however, constitute a judgement on them, to the degree to which in Williams the dog is the very marker of the *Alltag, la vie quotidienne*, or daily life as such: that new content produced in the twentieth century as a theory by phenomenological sociology (and then above all by Henri Lefebvre), and in real life by the urban turn and democratization, the passage from an overestimation of great figures and political history to greater appreciation of the social in its thick dimensionalities. (Meanwhile, the relationship between the public/private ratio and this virtual invention of daily life in modern society, and thereby in modernist literature, can be historically evaluated by its tendential disappearance in the postmodern, where daily life has expanded to become everything, and has thereby disappeared into the omnipresent images of mass culture.)

Dogs are then very specifically the markers of the public realm in Williams, of a daily real life which it is the task of his new epic form to render, just as it is the task of his new line, his free verse, to handle its reified language. This daily life is meanwhile neither fact nor fiction, so to speak: kitsch is its cultural expression, especially in the United States, but the documentation by way of kitsch (newspaper clippings of a *Reader's Digest* kind) merely designates the existence of daily life as so many symptoms. But Williams's epic is also able to avoid the oppressive dangers of fictionality of modern novelistic narrative as such: the reification into the existential, in which, for example, the fundamental anonymity of these experiences is necessarily subjectified and then thematized as an existential "anonymity"—a special destiny of a named character whose "personal" experience it rigorously is: even Joyce is not altogether exempt from this ideology inherent in his form. One may compare the requirement that Stephen observe the dog on the beach in chapter 3 of *Ulysses*, with the reprise of this motif on the very last page of *Paterson* (203/202) when the man and his dog turn mythologically inland: fiction brings with it subjectivity, as has been argued earlier; but *Paterson* as an epic form is able to render the subject/object category intermittent, and thereby to give a more authentic feeling for anonymity than the philosophers of authenticity themselves.

All of which is finally dependent on the matter of epic form itself, on the capacities of the "poem that includes history"; and it must therefore be to this that we turn in conclusion. Here the mark of historicity is called contingency: "The last wolf was killed near the Weisse Huis in the year 1723" (97/97)—it is the mark of the radically singular, as that is unveiled by the axis of history itself passing through and transversing innumerable private lives and enormous quantities of unevaluated documents. Contingency of this epic kind then can only result from the intersection of both axes, since History in any official or unitary form is unrepresentable (the old modes of chronicle or world-historical figure being worse than unsatisfactory), while the individual data can develop no relations with each other unless they are formally prepared and conditioned: such preparation is scarcely what is now meant by the ugly word "contextualization," since any one of these documents can have multiple contexts of study and none of those can be officially preferred by Williams except at the risk of thematizing his material and conveying a thesis about it. What is rather done to this mass of anecdotes, trivial and significant, is to place them in the element of History itself, as potential bearers of witness, without any preconditions as to what in fact they may end up expressing or documenting. They are assembled and brought into a space lit by the focus on history, in which everything they contain of implicit historicity can be released. It would be tempting to think of them as the voices of history, as some vast heteroglossia that echoes down out of the historical time of this particular place: except that, as we have seen, *Paterson* is not a place but the absence of place, and these American lives and experiences are also the absence of voice, the failure of subjects to reconstitute themselves, the lack of even those multiple subjectivities that could alone sustain and subtend the Bakhtinian vision of a kind of spiritual democracy. Williams remains more than modern in his conviction that these are not voices but written documents, and that even what is not yet written must by himself be typed out in order to reach any persistence of being.

Contingency is in one way or another the greatest formal conquest of the modern (or Poundian, miniature) epic, and transcends anything possible in the remarkable apparatus of the modern novel itself (but see Sartre's *Nausea* for an effort intellectually and novelistically to recontain contingency within that apparatus). The holding on to a passing moment of time—

> L'ombre d'un grand oiseau me passe sur la face—

the registration of the ephemerality of a present of the past that seemed, in its time and moment, an absolute—

> The thaws came early that year, and again we crossed the Po—

these are more authentic conquests of the temporal than anything elegiac since they offer no consolation and show time eating away at the event, rather than the event's monumental conquest of the ephemeral and the transitory. The epic form then reaches out to touch its limits at two extremes of its construction: the one is clearly the message of the Poundian ideogram itself, here formulated (above all in Book IV) as the homology of the gist (radium)—credit—and the poetic innovation: a modernist telos culminating, as Pound recommended, in economics. Hamilton (73–4) is no doubt the John Adams and Confucius of this more American version of the *Cantos*, although it is not always easy to see how Williams thinks of the inventor of the National Bank (evil!) and the planner of the abortive National Manufactury (good?): perhaps it is this very indeterminability of Williams's economic thoughts as opposed to Pound's only too clear ones that marks a formal advantage, since in *Paterson* the requirement to "include economics" is more purely foregrounded, without content, than in the Poundian schemes. Social credit in the latter characterizes a specific politics and ideology, whereas Hamilton is folded back into the anecdotal past as a failure among others; while "credit" in Williams is as general as value itself.

As for the other end point in which the epic is somehow grounded, it may be seen in the very realm of violence which saves the materials of this work from an only too American sentimentalism and kitsch—those materials being redeemed by the omnipresence of an atmosphere of violent death which sometimes seems to turn the great fire of Book III into something of a decorative and aesthetic affair. We have said that the poem undoes its own formal temptation to project the archaic. But violence and death in *Paterson* more generally can be seen as something like an intersection between mortality and history, earth and world. What lies just beyond the boundary of the American epic is then something not archaic exactly in any mythological sense, yet alien to the American realities which will shortly take dominion and develop across this geography: it is, already, acknowledged in a very different way in *In the American Grain*, the preceding culture and mode of production, that of a Native American society itself stamped out by a violence only too vividly recorded in the pages of *Paterson.* What falls outside American society is then the way in which the Indians themselves confront such ultimate violence which necessarily defeats and destroys them: the ritual of the Kinte Kaye, the dance that defies death itself and execution whose intermittent sounds (102/102–3) not only punctuate the epic at crucial moments and restore to the record a fearful history of domination and imperialism, but also in a deeper sense accompany the poem and subtend its movement like a great dirge, an expressive music not available in white North American culture, a stance in the face of death not available to the inhabitants of Paterson, but whose memory the poem preserves in some other place and time as its own secular history unfolds.

(*1993*)

Notes

1 Roland Barthes, *Writing Degree Zero* (New York, 1968), p. 39.

2 William Carlos Williams, *Paterson* (New York, 1963); page references within the text are to this edition first, and next to the new annotated *Paterson*, ed. Christopher MacGown (New York, 1992); thus here, 80/80. I should add that I here consider the four books as the completed poem and the fifth as an afterthought that weakens its previous form for reasons mentioned later on in the text.

3 References in the text are marked H, followed by page numbers, first to the English translation in *Philosophies of Art and Beauty*, ed. A. Hofstadter and R. Kuhns (New York, 1964) and then to the German text, *Der Ursprung des Kunstwerkes* (Stuttgart, 1960).

4 See Allen Ginsberg's reflections on Williams's "new line" in *Paterson*, pp. 174–5/172/174. It is also worth mentioning here Yvor Winters's fundamental deduction, from Williams's and his own early practice, of the basic laws of so-called "free verse," in *In Defense of Reason* (Athens OH, 1987).

5 I have discussed all this further, for the detective story, in my two-part essay, "On Raymond Chandler" (in *Southern Review*, no. 6 (1970), pp. 624–50) and for the medical doctor, in "Céline and Innocence" (*South Atlantic Quarterly* 93.2, Spring, 1994), see below.

6 T.S. Eliot, *Selected Essays* (New York, 1950), p. 279.

7 See the essays on Joyce below, and also, for the overlapping system of internal systems, that on *The Magic Mountain*.

8 For a record of Williams's exchanges with Marcia Nardi, see *The Last Word*, ed. Elizabeth Murrie O'Neill (Iowa City, 1994).

9 G.W. Hegel, *The Philosophy of History* (New York, 1956), p. 209. I discuss a comparable attempt, in Adorno, to defamiliarize both by exchanging natural history for human history, in *Late Marxism: Adorno, or, the Persistence of the Dialectic* (London and New York, 1990).

10 Cats are a nobler animal.

2

Céline and Innocence

I want to say something about fascism and sentimentalism, or perhaps I had better say, about anti-Semitism and sentimentalism. It will not be yet another theory of anti-Semitism, of which we have many—the most noteworthy in my own tradition being summed up by August Bebel's contemptuous observation that anti-Semitism was the socialism of the stupid. But Céline was not stupid, and it may be worth following this up a little more closely.

Actually, I will begin that closer look by drawing back across a certain distance, and taking the roundabout road of the matter of the profession of Dr Destouches, an issue which will also serve to juxtapose Céline with yet another American writer, namely, Dr William Carlos Williams (though no mutual influence need be asserted).

I want to link the fact of medical practice to the problem of narrative by way of some of the doctrines of the Russian Formalists. One of the most dramatic interpretive moves of modern times was indeed the proposition, which we owe mainly to Viktor Shklovsky, that the character of Don Quixote (about the significance of which so much ink has been shed) was not to be seen as a character at all in any anthropomorphic sense, but rather as what the Formalists came to call a "motivation of the device." This is to say that Cervantes—one of the great practitioners of the Renaissance art-novella—had collected a number of stories and anecdotes for which he required a "frame": the peripatetic figure of the Knight of the Rueful Countenance then offered itself as a convenient string or thread upon which all those narrative beads could somehow be linked together. "Don Quixote" is then simply the name for this string, for this narrative scaffolding or "device": and the psychology with which it was necessary to endow the figure in order to "motivate" or make plausible the sequence of stories and episodes produces the "effect" of an *actant* or even a character, who can then be interpreted and further analyzed to their hearts' content by successive generations of critics and commentators.

The medical doctor can be seen to play an analogous structural role in certain North American literary works: but this is the point where I have to stress the way in which my eventual comparison (not exactly of Williams with Céline) will be significantly limited by the radical difference of French social space and the organization of the French class system from their American equivalents. For in the horizontal distribution of US social space, literature has always confronted an intractable problem: namely, how to motivate plausible narrative intersections among people from widely different walks of life, from utterly unrelated zones in the urban landscape, and from different classes—a problem the "picaro" once solved for a different kind of European society.

One of the genuinely time-honored and successful "motivations of the device" in this respect, at least for modern American society, has been the private detective: the figure who has not merely the right, but also the professional obligation, to penetrate such sealed and disparate social spaces, to visit the rich as well as the unemployed, to listen to the voices of workers as well as those of bureaucrats and politicians. The detective story thus became an extraordinary vehicle for the mapping of social space, a precision instrument for its X-ray and its surgical exploration; and it continues to offer a privileged instrument for just such cognitive mapping in our own period, when it has burst the generic confinement of its specialized paperback, or "pulp," form and has spread out to colonize other mass-cultural genres, most notably, the "major novel" or "best-seller."

But there is a price to pay for this particular narrative apparatus: the gap that necessarily and structurally persists between the detective, as a vehicle for knowledge and an instrument of perception and social exploration, as an epistemological device, and the "people," the characters who are his objects of study, and whose relationships are the content of this particular formal process. The detective, even today, is not quite the same kind of person as his or her (today very much her!) clients and sources, targets and suspects: semiotics teaches that the enunciated is to be distinguished from the enunciation, while the Formalists had already posited a fundamental difference between the plot line or story (*fabula*) and its emplotment (*sjuzet*). The reader, to be sure, rides roughshod over both these levels, not, however, without some vague preconscious sense that the status of the detective (who returns, in the series, and is often, at least in the classical detective story, marked by personal eccentricities and obsessions, from the violin to orchids) is somehow not exactly the same as the status of these mortal, ephemeral figures who will vanish into nothingness once their tale is told, or, rather, solved. There is thus here something like a secondary form problem that follows closely on the heels of the first one: for the latter, that "motivation of the device" called the detective now demands that its traces be papered over, and the narrative-ontological gap between form and content, between detective and "characters," be somehow obliterated. We will see that Céline's novels, or at least *Voyage au bout de la nuit*, are not exempt from this particular dilemma.

But first we must return to medicine and satisfy ourselves that under certain circumstances, and particularly in American social space, the physician can fill some of the same narrative and epistemological functions as the private detective and can similarly offer a vehicle for the cognitive mapping of American society. Or at least the general practitioner could, when he still made house calls. At any rate, Dr Williams's experience as a "médecin des pauvres," not unlike Dr Destouches's, afforded him an unusual source of raw material, not generally available to the run-of-the-mill writer of stories and novels. Even more than that, however, it also suggested a unique structural framework for his poem *Paterson*, which I think I am not alone in believing to be (after Whitman) our great national poem, the only US national epic.

For now that "motivation of the device" which is the medical doctor is available to serve as one optional frame (among several others) for generating what in the epic context it would be improper to call point-of-view or narrative consciousness: that is to say, the impossible totalizing gaze of the allegorical hero "Mr. Paterson," who includes the more limited gaze of Dr Williams along with the rest of the city's population:

> Mr.
> Paterson has gone away
> to rest and write. Inside the bus one sees
> his thoughts sitting and standing. His
> thoughts alight and scatter—
> Who are these people (how complex
> the mathematic) among whom I see myself
> in the regularly ordered plateglass of
> his thoughts, glimmering before shoes and bicycles?[1]

The epic secures depersonalization by virtue of this totalizing, allegorical distance from each of the individual lives it contains:

> —that they may live
> his thought is listed in the Telephone
> Directory—

The detective story meanwhile vouches for its objectivity by the difference in status of its observer, who by definition does not share the interests and the passions of the characters he observes.

In the absence of generic convention, however, something within the protagonist must underwrite his epistemological soundness: in Céline, this will be the essential *innocence* of Ferdinand, something that surely comes as the first shock for readers of the great novels, that initial quality of the reading that, little by little, comes to determine our fundamental relationship to things in Céline, to dictate the successive bursts of astonishment, to pose our distance from the people we see gesticulating in front of us, one by one. This "point of view" is not exactly the now-familiar one of the "decentered subject," nor is its depersonalization pathologically neutral (as, say, in Platonov): but it does not judge, and it seems worthwhile in this context to recall that (along with Flaubert) Céline served as the central exhibit and horrible object lesson for Wayne Booth's classic defense of stable ironies (in *The Rhetoric of Fiction*), and for his attack on nihilism and relativism in modern literature, positions which fail to make moral judgements.

What the *naif* ends up observing will always in one way or another be the agitation of other people, their senseless and spasmodic reactions to what are not yet understood to be passions: these spectacles range from the furies of isolated individuals to their predictable fusion in the St Vitus' dance of whole groups, a movement which itself secures a certain recurrent evolution in these chapters, a repetitive rhythm which is, however, not exactly narrative. The content of such observations also retains something of the structure of the detective story by way of the inexplicability of the behavior thus contemplated: the Formalists' famous "defamiliarization effect" has here all the wide-eyed nonparticipation of a Candide in what everyone else considers to be "natural" and all too human. What sharpens the puzzle and calls for investigation and explanation is the way in which these passions, which the others evidently feel to be normal enough and an inescapable part of their human condition, seem to tend, by way of a well-nigh natural and gravitational process, toward the victimization of other people. In an idiosyncratic and unrecognizable fashion, Céline recapitulates the period doxa about the crowd itself, the revolutionary "mob," irredeemably irrational and bloodthirsty, unruly and unpredictable, aroused only at society's peril.

"Frenzy" is the word for this perpetually fascinating event, this inescapable end toward which all individual passion tends. Its motivation, its immediate pretext or social content, is unimportant: what counts is the form itself, replicated again and again in the frenzy with which a collectivity pursues its manias and of which modern warfare is only the absolute formalization:

> Il existe pour le pauvre en ce monde deux grandes manières de crever, soit par l'indifférence absolue de vos semblables en temps de paix, ou par la passion homicide des mêmes en la guerre venue. S'ils se mettent à penser à vous, c'est à votre torture qu'ils songent aussitôt les autres, et rien qu'à ça. On ne les intéresse que saignants, les salauds!

> A poor man in this world can be done to death in two main ways, by the absolute indifference of his fellows in peacetime or by their homicidal mania when there's a war. When other people start thinking about you, it's to figure out how to torture you, that and nothing else. The bastards want to see you bleeding, otherwise they're not interested![2]

Patriotism is only the most peculiar and incomprehensible species of such collective frenzy—as witness the professional attentions of Dr Bestombes (who in this instance illustrates the way in which the outside medical observer can become an ordinary human being, just like everyone else):

> Sans façon, empoignant familièrement l'épaule de l'un de nous, le secouant paternellement, la voix réconfortante, il nous traça les règles et le plus court chemin pour aller gaillardement et au plus tot encore nous refaire casser la gueule.
>
> D'où qu'ils provinssent décidément, ils ne pensaient qu'à cela. On aurait dit que ça leur faisait du bien. C'était le nouveau vice.

> Taking one of us by the shoulders and shaking him with paternal familiarity, he explained the regulations in a comforting tone and indicated the quickest and surest way of getting ourselves sent back to the front to be lambasted some more.
>
> Wherever they came from, no two ways about it, that was their only thought. It seemed to give them a kick. It was the new vice.[3]

This is indeed the category and the diagnosis all at once: frenzy is the vice to which human beings are addicted; the collectivity is virtually an agglomeration of "vicieux," without regard for the content of the agitation, which is a mere pretext and which can convulse the swarm of the colonized equally well, pressing into Lieutenant Grappa's courtroom to have themselves whipped, fully as much as the lynch mob of patriots intent on sending Bardamu back to the front.

These are the great moments of an essentially comic writer, who has more affinities with Chaplin than with most novelists, since it is technically a matter of some difficulty for written narrative to encompass collective explosions of this kind. Formally, therefore, Céline's capacity to write the collective is an achievement of the greatest significance for literary history. Yet the first point one would want to make about it is that it is not yet narrative: at worst, what can happen (from the narrative point of view, that is) is a cumulative yet monotonous rhythm whereby various obsessed individuals stimulate each other into an uncontrollable collective outburst; at best, the process acquires a certain reciprocity, and the observer-narrator is finally impelled to respond to this contagious spectacle with an explosion in his own right, an attack of delirium in which the bounds of conscious rationality are burst with unpredictable results that generally end up in unconsciousness. (My impression is that these seizures are even more frequent in *Mort à crédit* than in *Voyage*.)

Given this contagion of frenzy and delirium, another feature of the characteristic rhythm of Céline's chapters becomes comprehensible—the pause or withdrawal, the attempt to find shelter, rest, silence, and to put a certain minimal distance between the convalescent and other people in general. Whence the desirability of spaces like the hospital, "où l'on pouvait se sentir un peu oublié, à l'abri des hommes du dehors, des chefs" ("where you could feel forgotten, safe from the people outside, the bosses").[4] It is an interesting reversal on the profession's conventional motivation: now the doctor has every incentive to be sheltered within the hospital like a patient.

But nothing narrative can come of this structure: the women with whom Ferdinand sketches out a conventional love story (with the possible exception of Molly) all end up as cheerleaders of the mob. The even rarer moments in which collective frenzy is concentrated in a single gigantic figure—one thinks above all of the Courtial of *Mort à crédit*—at best allow the detective or observer position to modulate into a filial one; what can alone cross this gap is feeling, an immense pity that can scarcely motivate further action: a *misérabilisme* or populism that may be said to constitute the first temptation, the first sentimentalism, of the "médecin des pauvres."

This is why, in my view, Céline is something like a *faux romancier*: his antecedents are not to be found in any of the novelists of the tradition, not even in Zola, but rather in the different, if equally glorious, French *moralistes*: for it is there, if anywhere, in the language of their lapidary formulations, that we encounter diagnoses of human frenzy and folly, of the unruliness of the human "passions"—an "anatomy" that seems roughly comparable to what Céline was intent on dramatizing. Psychology is not the best word for this particular focus, which seeks to arrest and to eternalize what is depressingly repetitive about the convulsions of human nature; it is at any rate a different kind of focus from the attention to the empirical, the contingent, and the ephemeral of the great nineteenth-century novelists. If it is true, as Gide once observed, that La Rochefoucauld's maxims are in reality potential miniature novels, then Céline is there to show what particular structures would have to be invented to endow them with novelistic momentum.

Yet those same structures—that gap that forbids narrative in Céline—are also clearly enough the deeper source of his modernism: for the representation of this eternal return of an obsessional human nature demands an extraordinary invention and exercise of language; a breathless catalogue of vices and a frenzied accumulation of epithets; the delirious, self-perpetuating diatribes and tirades that call each other into existence, that can alone fill the narrative void, and that then place Céline at the side of Proust rather than Balzac.

But, like the isolation of the doctor (or the detective), the non-narrative is intolerable at any great length: an intolerability that may go a certain distance toward explaining—after the instructive reversal of a remarkable version of scapegoating in his own manner (on Bardamu's unhappy boat trip to Africa)—why Céline might have been tempted to invent a genuine narrative (something I think he never does in his novels) and to create a villain to account for the existence of so much suffering and misery. This is, I suppose, what is often called artistic integrity: Céline's respect, in the written works, for the limits of the form that alone made his writing possible in the first place. Within those limits, indeed, there could be no villains, since human beings are all by definition maniacs, and are thereby exonerated in advance, by virtue of the misery of human nature itself.

Sentimentalism, however, is the giving in to the temptation to turn all that into causality and "real-life" narrative; when Dr Destouches gives in, as conventionally and stereotypically as any other classical petit-bourgeois, and identifies the Jews and the Bolsheviks as the ultimate sources of all suffering and evil, then we have left the novels of Céline behind, and returned to history and its quite different ideological pathologies.

(1994)

Notes

1 William Carlos Williams, *Paterson* (New York, 1963), 1: p. 9.
2 Louis-Ferdinand Céline, *Voyage au bout de la nuit* (Paris, 1981 [1932]), p. 82; *Journey to the End of the Night*, trans. Ralph Manheim (New York. 1983), p. 68.
3 Céline, *Voyage*, p. 86; *Journey*, p. 71.
4 Céline, *Voyage*, p. 145; *Journey*, p. 124.

TWO

3

Form Production in *The Magic Mountain*

1. Reading as Content

Adventure stories obey a principle of saturation in which time and space are to be as full as possible, something conventionally indexed by the exhaustion of the protagonist, and analogized by the saturation of the scene itself, by great heat or heavy rain, elements through which all action must fray its path laboriously, like the friction of a satellite reentering the earth's atmosphere. The bonus for the reader lies probably not so much in the reenacted spectacle of difficulty itself, as rather in the Utopian glimpse of a human time every moment of which is redeemed by human meaning, or, if you prefer, from which the dead zones of boredom and habit have miraculously been banished. Yet as Benjamin put it, "boredom is the dream bird that hatches the egg of experience";[1] empty time is the condition for filled time, or at least for our possibility of perceiving it in the first place; and no doubt the first empty time in question here is simply that of the reader of adventure stories in the first place, whose leisure strangely inverts the overstrenuous exertions of the hero, the one acting as a foil to the other, every daring climb up the cliff's surface producing its harvest in the contented yawning and stretching of what comes to be called relaxation or entertainment (a concept that blocks further thinking and should probably at this point be bracketed or suspended altogether).

What is even more interesting is to find traces of just such empty times within the mass-cultural work itself, inscriptions of the reading process there where we have been mainly taught to observe the absence of self-consciousness or reflexivity. Thus Martin Beck is able to seize a few moments from his harried schedule, clear the overtime away, send the family on a weekend trip, and in the clearing of this empty space and time organize his leisure decisively:

> Among other things he bought a bottle of Grönstedts Monopole cognac and six strong beers. Then he devoted the rest of Saturday to putting down the deck of

> the model of the *Cutty Sark*, which he had not had time to touch for several weeks. For dinner he ate cold meatballs, fish roe and Camembert on pumpernickel bread, and he drank two beers. He also drank some coffee and cognac and watched an old American gangster film on television. Then he got his bed ready and lay in the bathtub reading Raymond Chandler's *The Lady in the Lake*, every now and again taking a sip of cognac which he had placed within reach on the toilet seat.[2]

Neither the notion of the busman's holiday (it is the very title of a novel by Dorothy Sayers) nor that of the hobby are particularly startling when we have to do with detectives; policemen, to be sure, are likely to want to have more prosaic hobbies than those of the most famous and eccentric private detectives (who notoriously cultivate their orchids, play the violin, and take cocaine). But the sailing ship is itself the very marker and epitome of adventure as such, and the model a pretext for the deployment of that space which it was surely physically the most intolerable to cross long day after day and yet which counts as the most exciting thing to read about. Nor does the *mise en abîme* of Americanism seem to mean much in the context of the satiric realism of this triumphantly Swedish procedural. Still, it is worth asking ourselves why even the insert of Beck's leisure adds to our enjoyment of his more general drudgery and harassment, and whether this particular self-designation of the mass-cultural product cannot be added to all those Brechtian and reflexive features that Jane Feuer, against all doxa, found to throng thick and fast in so characteristically commercial a genre as the Hollywood musical.[3]

Perhaps the "high cultural" text has to be more circumspect about such references: I remember a moment in Zola's novel of the Franco-Prussian war—a form to be sure itself poised on the very brink of modern mass culture and already bristling with all those "techniques" we have mentioned for the filling of space and time and the systematic physical exhaustion of the characters—a wondrous moment in which the soldier "en perm" revels in a whiteness one is tempted to compare with that of the page itself:

> dans la joie de la nappe très blanche, ravi du vin blanc qui étincelait dans son verre, Maurice mangea deux oeufs à la coque, avec une gourmandise qu'il ne se connaissait pas ...[4]

The gourmandise in reality solicits its equivalent in the reader: reading is itself this furlough—Hegel's (and Queneau's) "dimanche de la vie"—which then allows for a contemplative proxy enjoyment of what can otherwise scarcely be imagined to be enjoyable, down to the smallest details (the smell of the trenches, the permanent wetness of the socks, the well-nigh vertiginous want of sleep) of a content that must, not by accident but virtually by definition, be the very opposite of enjoyable.

Whatever the paradoxical deferment structure of human reality to which writing as such corresponds, of which it may furnish an emblem or a reactualization, we must accustom ourselves to thinking of reading as an altogether unnatural act (Mallarmé says "une pratique de désespoir"): and indeed something of this monstrous artificiality is captured in the concomitant deconstructive account of a reading which always necessarily breaks down and fails of an achieved meaning it must then ideologically claim to have triumphantly achieved and completed. Here, however, in these examples of the use of reading in figuration, it may be preferable to recall Freud's interpretation of the capacity of money to serve as a vehicle for symbolic meaning: "In later years ... the interest in money makes its appearance as a new interest which had been absent in childhood."[5] He goes on to explain that it is this adult belatedness and novelty of the theme that "makes it easier for the early impulsion [the interest in feces] ... to be carried over to the newly emerging aim." It is as though such adult preoccupations remained essentially unoccupied by libido in the form of childhood desires (the desires of the stages of the maturing organism): historically new "aims" or "interests" (to use Freud's expressions), which can then be perceived to be artificial in the sense in which they correspond to developing "civilization" (or capitalism), rather than to the familial structure of older, more organic societies, and which can therefore also be seen to have something in common with each other (the earliest form of writing has indeed been associated with processes of accounting, if not with money itself), now offer themselves as figures to be invested with very different kinds of unconscious content. The new figures are in other words available for symbolization in much freer ways than the infantile desires themselves identified more literally. Nor does it matter much that Freud himself binds money as such back ever more tightly into symbolization, and stresses a seemingly more absolute link between money and the anal stage; what interests us here is rather the floating nature of the other adult theme—that of reading—particularly when it is reincorporated into a text itself ostentatiously written to be read.

But, as our preceding account may have suggested (with its less than acceptable language of the organic and the natural), certain kinds of guilt attach to these new experiences or phenomena that have no childhood equivalence. That of money (complicated, to be sure, by the reintegration of this theme into the complex of childhood desires described by Freud) is related to the class system itself; that of reading, and the leisure and instruction it implies, is mediated by the more general guilt of culture which also emerges from class society. It would seem likely that societies in which both money and reading are still reduced and relatively marginal activities tend to feel less guilt about their structural inequalities (I'm thinking of Aristotle's views of the "good life" and of slavery).

At any rate the guilt of culture, the guilt associated with leisure and with reading and negotiated in rather different and more complex ways when it is a question of the guilt of instruction or "cultural capital," is not likely to find itself brandished with abandon by those modern works that seek ever more intensely to engage and simultaneously to escape their own guilty complicity with culture as such. They do so most often by separating high art from culture in general, and by assigning some uniquely transcultural value to the former (a value which can range from the political to the philosophical or the religious).

It is therefore not as surprising as it ought to be that, in the works of intellectuals in whose lives reading has taken up a disproportionate percentage of their waking time, reading plays so little role. Few are the novels—and they stand out sharply as sports and oddities: Flaubert's *Bouvard et Pécuchet*, for example—whose pages are given over generously with an account of the main characters' reading experiences; and when a book does exceptionally play a role, it generally *stands for something else* (as Freud put it when recounting the theories of that lone tribe that had developed a sexual interpretation of dreams, with the logical exception of dreams having a specifically sexual content).

All the more remarkable, then, is the complacency with which Thomas Mann exhibits the scholarly activities of Hans Castorp, who "had ordered certain books from home, some of them bearing on his profession ... But these volumes now lay neglected in favour of other textbooks belonging to a quite different field, an interest in which had seized upon the young man: anatomy, physiology, biology, works in German, French and English, sent up to the Berghof by the book-dealer in the village."[6] To be sure, it may be noted that Mann displaces and inflects the conventional stereotype of an intellectual's reading in two different ways: first, by insisting on the physicality of the volumes and on everything opaque and thing-like implied by the foreign languages (and the technical or scientific languages, at that!) in which they are printed. This way Borges lies: a materiality of the book itself substitutes a thematics of objects, collections, and manias or obsessions for the evaluation of an activity. But in a second and more basic way it is the very non-intellectuality of Hans Castorp himself (this very ordinary young man, as Mann never tires of insisting) which, by turning the act of reading into an unusual event, something inhabitual and out of the ordinary, makes it over into a figure that would seem to demand interpretation. Still, we must note with some satisfaction that Hans Castorp's starting point retains some distant kinship with Martin Beck's hobby, even though the principal business of his native city, as well as his own chosen profession motivate and naturalize the choice of *Ocean Steamships* as the one volume to accompany the more high-literary traveler on his three-week holiday.

But it should not be thought, by analogy with the Freudian account of money, that the experience of reading, carefully isolated in this way, set off and defamiliarized, will in Thomas Mann be reconverted into a specialized symbolic meaning of some kind: rather, it remains in *The Magic Mountain* the occasion for the possibility of a perpetual reflexivity of experience as such. Identified as the essential or fundamental feature of art—something which is not obvious from the start, for the modernist alternatives include language, absence, the image, libido—reading, since by definition we are always in it, offers the permanent possibility of analogical demonstration, of the reality we can always reach out and touch (like Martin Beck's cognac): the analogon, to use Sartre's technical expression for that remnant of a somewhat more external reality which the mind is able to compare with its own idea, as though reminding itself of the fact of externality itself—more on the order of comparing notes than of pinching yourself, and probably some primitive starting point, some elementary mental operation, in an ascending ladder of Hegelian or phenomenological forms of self-consciousness.

This means, however, that it is not so much reading itself whose significance we need to determine, but rather that with which it is thus, virtually without distance, compared. To call that more fundamental construction art or the monad would be premature; to describe it as the meaning of *Der Zauberberg* is perhaps more acceptable at this stage, although that really tells us nothing. To identify what is "modernist" in Thomas Mann here, in this process of substituting a primary experience indissociable from the book or work itself for its representational contents—for its "narrative," which is simply the pretext for the deployment of that more concrete reality of the experience of reading, and of extended, indeed dilated, reading time—is structurally accurate, provided we add to this canonization the ambiguity of its popular success, which tends to draw Mann's work in general from the high modern over into the middlebrow category, and which can at this point be accounted for by the relative naiveté of this very systematic utilization of reading itself, tending as it does to mobilize some mid-cult pride in getting through long and difficult books, staying the course, and carrying off a more advanced reading certificate.[7]

But it would be wrong to think that reading is here a particularly abstract or elite starting point, or even a rarefied and specialized experience: for in order to be foregrounded as such, and to become audible as the very ground bass of our time with these pages, the body must be awakened as a participant in the process, indeed the only participant. Like Hans on his balcony—

> And in the evening, when the almost full moon appeared, the world, enchanted, turned magical. There reigned far and wide the scintillation of crystal, the glitter of diamond ... etc.
>
> (LP267, W271, D380)

—and note that the night-time shadows cast by the moonlight are something like the mimetic objects of representation in the Zauberberg itself (as in Plato's cave)—all this must now be interiorized, so that it is understood that the body itself is the inner sky of this work: the starry heavens depicted in the passage just quoted (which were for Kant the very epitome of Law) must now be somehow recreated with the muted energies and hum of the body at rest, reading.

2. The Blushing Monad

That all modern writing tends in one way or another towards the sensory can abundantly be documented, beginning with Flaubert and Baudelaire; but it is within this very modern "tradition" (if the word is not a misnomer) that Thomas Mann's style has an originality all of its own and a distinctiveness that demands biographical explanation no doubt, but also its specific place in the history of form. For this language practice systematically betrays, and I may even say sets out to betray (as its inner logic), a wide-ranging affinity for the symptom as such, for a symptomatology that is at one and the same time the detection of the most minute symptoms and their expression, which is to say their complacent encouragement, an incitement of these minute bodily and perceptual tics and stirrings to unfold and to develop. Who says "symptom" obviously always means the body in some fundamental sense; for even a paranoid alertness to clues in the outside world—and nothing is less alien to Thomas Mann than just such moments when his characters read dimly ominous omens (the snub-nosed man on the cemetery wall in *Death in Venice*)—is at one with a bodily stance, the furtive gaze, a certain way of welcoming the world's events and judging them. Yet equally clearly the symptom is a game we play with ourselves, insofar as it comes into being as a substitute for desire and a way of outsmarting the latter. Complacency then itself, as an instrument of ever greater consciousness, has something louche about it, and may be said to exhibit Thomas Mann's decadent side (something he himself was only too complacent about reveling in), for it seems to offer a peculiar misreading of the Freudian ethos ("wo es war ...") in which not stoic heroism but rather a giving in seems recommended, a laisser-aller approximating the dangers of Circe's island ("You will be going on all fours—already you are inclining toward your forward extremities, and presently you will begin to grunt—have a care!" [LP247, W243, D347]). Indeed, this ambiguity can stand as a first demonstration of Mann's specific dialectic: its paradoxes are only apparent, for clearly enough it is the peculiarity of repression that is responsible for a situation in which being able to let yourself go is an active conquest, in which laisser-aller is heroic: the discipline of free association itself, in Freud, marks the visible official version of this duality of a passivity which is activity, a weakness which is strength, not to say an evil that is also good—like disease itself? or living organic matter? or the air of Davos?

Yet it is clearly enough only at the price of affirming and encouraging just such symptomal complacency, and of developing a specific style of awareness of the body in which perception consists in a narcissistic and hypochondriac flattering of the organism's velleities, that Mann's style is possible. Its effects do not consist in those specifically writerly and expressive moments that he shares professionally with the other great modern writers, scriptable moments of *le mot juste*, which produce sentences as such, sentences which are events ("man lies die Flachkelche klingen und leert das erste Glas auf einen Zug, elektrisierte sich den Magen mit dem eiskalten, duftigen Geprickel" [LP570, W561, D810]). Indeed, there are occasional refusals of the gambit, and not merely in the let-down of Mann's characterizations of music here and in *Doktor Faustus*, which do not rise linguistically to the occasion like comparable moments in Proust or Joyce. One must also reckon in the deeper repudiation of a certain conception of physical experience as such as an object of writing and expression or mimesis: as with those "assurances, given, not during that reported conversation in the French tongue, but in a later interval, wordless to our ears, during which we have elected to intermit the flow of our story along the stream of time, and let time flow on pure and free of any content whatever" (P347, W342, D347). But this omission of sexuality must surely distinguish the sensory dimension in Mann from a more widespread reduction to the body that can be observed elsewhere in the various modernist languages; and must thereby distinguish his conception of linguistic expression from the more mimetic one of the task set for language and writing, a painterly job to do, in which the artist posits model or object over against himself as the task of representation. Here, in the symptom, what is crucial is not the outline of the object or the feeling itself, but its aftereffects in the organism, the tremors of a feeling that, as yet unidentified or named, is still properly inhuman or non-human, provoking an oscillation of judgement back and forth between positive and negative, so that only its emergence from the non-feeling of repression itself can be freshly registered, as it were in an estrangement-effect whose peculiarity would consist in the absence of any habituated or familiar perception to begin with:

> Yet whether the pilgrim air the stranger wore kindled his fantasy or whether some other physical or psychical influence came in play, he could not tell; but he felt the most surprising consciousness of a widening of inward barriers, a kind of vaulting unrest, a youthfully ardent thirst for distant scenes—a feeling so lively and so new, or at least so long ago outgrown and forgot, that he stood there rooted to the spot, his eyes on the ground and his hands clasped behind him, exploring these

> sentiments of his, their bearing and scope. True, what he felt was no more than a longing to travel; yet coming upon him with such suddenness and passion as to resemble a seizure, almost a hallucination.[8]

Yet *The Magic Mountain* is if anything more ambitious than this, since it aims at nothing less than the explicitation of the very structures that accounted for such repression-emergence in the first place. In traditional representation, bodiliness was an event that we observed via the Geiger counters of the sentences; here it is given in advance in the very nature of the reading process, in which the body consents to withdraw from the world as such and to close in on itself. Now it is a question therefore of the exploration of its capacities in a kind of a *priori* way, of a demonstration (in the laboratory situation of Hans's simplicity and simple-mindedness) of the more general ways in which reading can drink the blood of the body as it were ("you are but a guest here, like Odysseus in the kingdom of the shades?" [LP57, W56, D78]) and borrow the latter's concreteness in order to endow itself with density.

The crucial physical feature is then in this sense body-warmth, particularly as that reveals itself in the flush or in outright blushing: these experiences are still informal and quotidian enough, unmelodramatic and one would like to say unofficial, to serve as the liaison between Hans's story and our own situation. They can still make the link, and even a memory of a flushed face (whether from exertion or feeling) can, by virtue of the fact that it has itself lingered, be pressed into service as a *hyle* or matter (stuffing or filling) of the first genuine event on which the narrative itself dwells, namely the persistence of Hans's flushed face, like a timid and inconsequential, yet telltale, muted, secondary declaration of independence of his body itself from its master: "My face burns so," he tells us, "it is really unpleasant" (LP10, W10, D13), but like any symptom, this first appearance is natural enough, given the fatigue of the long train journey and cold wind outside, not to speak of the altitude. Yet this detail persists, as an annoyance:

> Here Hans Castorp remarked with surprise that the flush which had mounted in his freshly shaven cheek did not subside, nor its accompanying warmth: his face glowed with the same dry heat as on the evening before. He had got free of it in sleep, but the blush had made it set in again. (LP40, W39, D54)

The reference is to his reaction to the telltale scandalous sounds of the couple next door (itself a detail that functions in the more paranoid way of the *Death in Venice* external visual omen, it being understood that the symptom in this larger sense includes both—the telltale displacement or spot/stain, and the telltale physical reaction, as aberrant as one likes); but these reactions continue to multiply, many of them equally motivated: as by the enormous meals therapeutically ingested five times a day by the patients, which Hans Castorp supplements with a beer for breakfast. The beer, the scandal, the chill air outside—all supply the cloak of a motivation for a generalized physical reaction in excess of that and on its way to a certain autonomy: the body, as Hans Castorp observed with jocularity, pursuing a "munterer Betrieb" in its own right: "leading a very active existence all on its own account, growing hair and nails and doing a lively business in the physical and chemical line ..." (LP71, W69, D98; although the reference here is to the active afterlife of the dead body).

To be sure, in some prosaic sense these signals simply foretell Hans Castorp's discovery that he is himself mildly infected by tuberculosis (unless, indeed, as Settembrini warns, this "infection" is the result of the fear propaganda waged by the officials of the sanatorium itself, and, beyond them, by extension, by the unenlightened and superstitious governments and traditions against which it is his mission in life, as a Voltairean philosopher, to wage war). But on the sensory level of Thomas Mann's sentences (and of the special kind of addiction that must necessarily attach us, as with Proust in a very different way, to the reading of these endless pages) this is overdetermined, and the fever condition gradually constructed by such hints and symptoms is also at one with the construction of the reading body, with its monadization and neutralization of external stimuli.

With this, to be sure, we have struck the fundamental motif of all modern aesthetics as such: that specification of the work of art in terms of withdrawal and contemplation, of which Kant's remarkable deduction of a "purposiveness without purpose" is only one possible formulation among many.[9] Its other version, the conception of a specific autonomy of the aesthetic, has seemed to offer a more positive characterization, while any number of theorizations of the way in which what is merely symbolic or virtual can be said to elude the categories of action or praxis also stress this peculiar suspension. Leibniz's notion of the monad, which was invoked in passing above, was a favorite figure of Adorno's, who observes somewhere that whatever its validity as a solution to the technical philosophical problem for which it was devised, the idea unwittingly theorizes art itself with prescience. It was of course the characterization of the monad as windowless that has captivated other readers as well, clearly offering a dramatic reformulation of the standard theory about the work's "purposelessness," "autonomy," "purely symbolic character," and the like.

But three other features of Leibniz's odd new concept need to be mentioned before we reach the one most relevant to Thomas Mann's novel. For one thing, the notion of the monad posits a simultaneity of just slightly alternate worlds, each one organized around the neighboring substance or existent (and which range all the way downwards into the being of things, the barely perceptible, slow dull sentience—Leibniz calls it "perception"—of stones and inanimate objects). Here the characterization of windowlessness takes on a more striking meaning: it is not that we cannot look outside, but that our own world does not have immediate access onto other worlds. But this is now something that characterizes the multiplicity of the works of art.

As for the more conventional notion of what is outside, the second point to be made is that that is already included in the monad itself, which is thus the entire world, but from a specific "standpoint" (from the standpoint of the plants nearby, or that of neighboring animals, humans or granite outcroppings, that same entire world is just slightly modified and arrives with sometimes feebler resonance). In aesthetic terms, this involves a restatement of doctrines that attempt to formulate the work's context as somehow implicit and inherent in the text itself, and as a kind of eco-system that forms it and whose traces it carries within itself. (Adorno's formulation of history as the content of the monad is a particularly strong version of this idea, which can be rewritten as the irrelevance of the opposition of intrinsic and extrinsic to the work itself, in which, in however mediated a fashion, everything is finally intrinsic.) But the notion of the monad also has the advantage, unlike most doctrines of a world, of specifying this structure as a kind of totality, no matter how ultimately ungraspable or unknowable in its extent and finite detail: this third feature also suits the concept to aesthetic experience (based on a work) more obviously than to the inner-worldly data of phenomenology (which however tries to recuperate that data in something like a monadic fashion).

Some of these features would seem to have relevance to the symbolic structure of *The Magic Mountain* and in particular to the Alpine sanatorium which gives its narrative a frame. The notion of the symbol has fallen into some discredit today, owing to the primacy of allegory, both as a theory and as a mode; but it surely served as the backbone of the older Mann criticism, for which the sanatorium was a microcosm of European society before World War One, and an equivalent to all those older closed social structures—Settembrini himself compares it to a steamship—whose very closure encourages symbolic readings of this or that kind.

I have two observations about this approach, whose priorities tend to move Mann in the direction of Kafka, in their emphasis on the nature of the institution that surrounds the cast of characters. And it is certain, not merely that Settembrini identifies the institution as an outworn form of tyranny, as a superstitious survival of the powers of the ancient regime, but also that Mann sounds a Kafka-like note in other contexts: Hofrat Behrens, for example, describes himself as a "bureaucrat in the service of death." But I think that here as elsewhere (the episode in *Doktor Faustus* having to do with Leverkühn's venereal doctors, for example), the Kafka-like resonances constitute merely one optional mode or style among many others in Mann's composition (which, to be sure, like so much else in modern literature, is in reality closer to those vast compendia of different discourses that Northrop Frye evoked under the term "Menippean satire" than it is to the novel as a traditional form). It coexists, for example, with a more properly Russian or Dostoyevskian mode (as when Herr Ferge describes the wolves on the Russian steppe), and the juxtaposition also suggests that these "modes" are perhaps better to be considered as literary allusions.

The other observation to be made about the sanatorium as "symbol of pre-World War One society" is that this is an illusion specifically projected by the structure of the *Zauberberg* itself which is designed, in advance, to appear belated, and a message in a bottle or a recapitulation of a vanished past. But this is so, not particularly because the war intersected with Mann's first ideas for what was then to have been a novella "about the length of *Death in Venice*"; but rather because the very reading mode itself of which it is the monument is itself in eclipse, something then proleptically signaled in advance (in a kind of fictive premonition) in the form of the media and specifically of film and phonograph (the other machinery, that of the X-ray, for instance, is treated like the magic of a *Hexenküche* and exorcised *à la Doktor Faustus* as an archaic survival). So also with the larger generic structure which appeals to the *Bildungsroman*, and which is itself already extinct by the time the book is published, as Franco Moretti has pointed out. But this is not accident, but design: Thomas Mann wishes the book to be somehow historically posthumous, as the final form of a closure which secures the monadic features of the novel at the same time that it is reconfirmed by the omnipresence of the sanatorium as a vast unified overarching spatial and social institution. This symbolic institution then naturally enough begins to entertain both metaphoric and metonymic relations with a world posited as being outside of it, but which it of course first brings into being in the form of the "flatland", the "real world" down below and out there. Metonymically, the Berghof is different from that real world; metaphorically, it is identical with it; and the context can play off one or the other of these interpretive strategies at will. But the rhythm of the interpretive opposition itself is not something we derive from the setting, but have already made the apprenticeship of elsewhere as we shall see shortly.

This is then the context in which, returning to the monad as a paradigm of aesthetic theory, we must also mention Marcuse's conception of the "affirmative character of culture,"[10] where "affirmative" means anything but a positive feature—it designates indeed the complicity of culture with what is—but where the peculiar property of culture to float above reality as its phantom mirror-image (or as that "inverted world" as which Hegel characterized the ensemble of the invisible physical laws of a visible physical nature, in the *Phenomenology*) allows it to shift imperceptibly back and forth between an implicit Utopian critique of the status quo of Being and the latter's mere replication and perpetuation in thought and symbolic experience. This, which can also serve as yet another figure for the paradoxes of the work of art in its separation from outright being, also conveys something of the guilty ambivalence of art and culture in general, in a way that the author of *Tonio Kroeger* would have welcomed, and which it is surely the burden of *The Magic Mountain* to emphasize, at least as long as we remain under its spell—that is, continue to read.

Yet a fourth and final evocation of Leibniz is needed to return us more completely to the text and to the way in which it secured its peculiar aesthetic autonomy: for, although it has been mentioned in passing, it is now important to stress the way in which the monads, no matter how simple and how lacking in the more complex intellectual faculties, nonetheless continue to feel and to serve as the recording apparatus for a wealth of minute sensations or, as he calls them, perceptions: even in a swoon or "deep dreamless sleep," "it does not follow that the simple substance has no perception at all ... when there are a very great number of small perceptions with nothing to distinguish them, we are stupefied, just as it happens that if we go on turning round in the same direction several times running we become giddy ..."[11] But this dizzying aggregation of "small perceptions" is precisely what characterizes, if not writing in general, then at least the reading of this deliberately sensorial and symptomatological writing, as it minutely activates features of the reading body that serves it as a kind of ultimate template or monadic outer environment.

Yet it should not be thought that the flush, or blushing—to return to that symptom one final time—is a merely formal device for attaching the reader's body to the reading apparatus as such (as one might, alternatively, appeal to breathing as to something always present and ready to hand in whatever body). But blushing, and its social concomitant, shame, are at the very heart of the novel's content as well, since it is around them that Hans's relationship to sickness and death is primarily organized: it is not merely that the dying organism is embarrassed about its condition ("how strange is this shame of the living creature that slips away into a corner to die, convinced that he may not expect from outward nature any reference or regard for his suffering or death" [LP533, W522, D755]). Rather, in some deeper way, it is the meaning of sickness and death that is itself at stake: if sickness, indeed, has something to do with the body's autonomy (the "munter Betrieb"—to the point where one of the novel's comic climaxes comes when the Hofrat frightens Hans's uncle away with a joyous evocation of the scatological decomposition of the corpse [LP438–9, W431, D620]), then it needs to be remembered that the classical analysis of comedy and humor, above all Bergson's, also insists very much on this comic independence of the machine from the spirit. Is sickness here then somehow ridiculous, or an object likely to provoke titters or sniggers? Can one laugh at nature as such? Certainly some extreme and ultimate forms of satire (Swift, for example) have reached that point; something less absolute is at work here, where from the very outset a doubtful note is sounded:

> Then he began eating rice with cinnamon and sugar, his eyes roving over the table full of other inviting viands, and over the guests at the six remaining tables, Joachim's companions and fellow victims, who were all inwardly infected, and now sat there breakfasting. (LP43, W41, D58)

This sudden appearance of the shameful is in a minor and muted way comparable to the great moment in Proust when the bearer of a far greater shame, the Baron de Charlus, appears, his eyes "percés en tous sens par des regards d'une extrême activité comme en ont seuls devant une personne qu'ils ne connaissent pas des hommes à qui, pour un motif quelconque, elle inspire des pensées qui ne viendraient pas à tout autre":[12] but in Proust this shame is a hermeneutic engine that inspires a veritable archeology of the Other and everything that is unknowable and unforeseeable, whipping curiosity into the very frenzy of passion and morbid jealousy. In Mann, shame is a different kind of epistemological clue: it gives Hans Castorp his first real "thoughts" (which will gradually lead on to that "taking stock" ["regieren"—Woods translates "playing king"; LP390, W383, D552]—which is on a standard reading of the *Bildungsroman* the very fruit of his unplanned education)—namely the wonderment about Frau Stoehr, and how anyone so stupid could be touched by the glamour of illness: "One always has the idea of a stupid man as perfectly healthy and ordinary, and of illness as making one refined and clever and unusual" (LP97, W95, D135); it is a first idea which Settembrini is right to denounce as a threat to Enlightenment. Shame is also, to be sure, as in *Death in Venice*, a sign of the break-up of repression; complacency in it yet another of those disciplined indisciplines of which we have already spoken, that promise to lead on into unknown "educational" developments, a feeling that indeed may have some "advantages, even, that were well-nigh boundless in their scope. He tried to put himself in Herr Albin's place and see how it must feel to be finally relieved of the burden of a respectable life and made free of the infinite realms of shame; and the young man shuddered at the wild wave of sweetness which swept over him at the thought and drove on his labouring heart to an even quicker pace" (LP81, W79, D111–12).

But the motif of shame, and everything disgraceful and ignominious about illness, does not lead Hans to some new liberation and affirmation of freedom so much as it does to his most detestable persona, that of the prurient visitor to bedridden invalids, of the solemn wellwisher devoured by a kind of morbid voyeurism. Now it is the reader who is ashamed for Hans in the chapter significantly entitled "The Dance of Death", in which the dying, in all their pitiful variety (young girls, businessmen, children), all fail to live up to his high standards: for none of these people in the supreme role of the last illness is free from the pettiest human interests and foibles. Thus the Widow Hessenfeld, whose gamblings and flirtations "were not such as could be taken seriously by Hans Castorp, who even felt that her mere presence was prejudicial to the dignity of a serious cure. For he was inwardly concerned to protect that dignity and uphold it in his own eyes—though now, after nearly half a year among those up here, it cost him everything to do so. The insight he gradually won into their lives and activities, their practices and points of view, was not encouraging" (LP296–7, W291–2, D417). "None of this was really serious," he feels (299) confronted by different attitudes of the sick, while confronted by yet different destinies and characters:

> [Popov] was not a man to strengthen Hans Castorp's respect for suffering; his wife, too, after her fashion, only added to those impressions of frivolous irregularity against which Hans Castorp wrestled and which he sought to counteract by coming into closer touch, despite the prevailing attitude, with the suffering and dying in the establishment. (LP300, W295, D422)

But despite Hans's priggishness, perhaps indeed because of it, these are among the most moving pages in *The Magic Mountain* and the most terrible, those which, along with the story of Joachim's last days, inscribe death itself, not without a certain sentimentality, in something other than merely thematic or cerebral fashion. But all of this is already latent in the flush itself—fever and shame altogether—and the privileged mediation between our own mortal body reading and the work that seeks complicity with it as we do so.

3. Autonomy and Externality

At that point, then, the setting into place of relatively simple sensations—the various flushes and blushing that anticipate the state of full-blown fever, the horror of the heavy meals as those are lavishly enumerated for us, the science-fictional sterility of the air itself (which "had no perfume, no content, no humidity" (LP8, W9, D11): all gradually construct a state in which more complex operations can be undertaken, at the same time that they document the authenticity of the mere words by the memory of physical sensations, and also serve as the points of addiction for the appropriately modernist readers (of the inaugurators of the modern—Poe, Baudelaire, Wagner—Adorno has indeed aptly noted that they were all "addictive types"). Meanwhile, even the most windowless of monads needs some sense of an exterior or an outside reality from which it can be thus reassuringly sheltered: this is, for example, an intuition furnished us by Hans's cigar (a luxury shipped up from the flatland) which is gradually denatured by its new environment (both institutional and in the receptivity of Hans's already infected body) and which then only gradually redeploys its pleasures within that environment as something now completely inside it.

Yet this is only a minor figure for the process of interiorization and the way in which it needs to construct a complementary exteriority: the stronger image is more openly coded as reading itself: this is the *Liegekur,* in which Hans is initiated into the mysteries of "horizontal living" (LP73, W71, D101) and in particular into the practices of wrapping the resting body in the blankets that are to be its envelope:

> [Joachim] turned on the light, lay down with a thermometer in his mouth, and began, with astonishing dexterity, to wrap himself in the two camel's-hair rugs that were spread out over his chair. Hans Castorp looked on with honest admiration for his skill. He flung the covers over him, one after the other: first from the left side, all their length up to his shoulders, then from the feet up, then from the right side, so that he formed, when finished, a neat compact parcel, out of which stuck only his head, shoulders and arms. (LP88, W86, D121)

"You'll learn," adds Joachim to Hans, "tomorrow we must certainly get you a pair of rugs ..." In such a condition, Castorp will be able to approximate the situation of the reader, turned inward, and leaving a few organs, such as a cold nose, hostage to the outside world—the merest physical reminder of the existence of an exterior, to the degree to which that reminder is urgently required by the warmth and comfort of the interior as what comes to negate just that outside or external reality. This shred of external reality required by the process of monadization or autonomization—it can be as little as the object of the negation in the very concept of "windowless"—evidently stands as the last scrap of content in a henceforth purified work that is to approximate Mallarmé or Flaubert's conception of *Madame Bovary* as "a book about nothing." Its residual externality can also be grasped as the past, as what falls outside the work and stands as its historical or temporal preconditions: whence that second chapter on Hans's patrician merchant family, a kind of reprise of *Buddenbrooks,* whose essentials, however, lie in the transformation of the grandfather into a dead effigy and image of himself—a realer grandfather "clothed for ever in his true and proper guise" ... "not like grandfather at all, more like a life-size doll" (LP27, W27, D37) or better still approximating those portraits on the wall that are the end products of the family history: yet this substitution by the image, or a flesh-and-blood old man whom Hans considers little more than "an interim grandfather, as it were" (LP25, W25, D34), marks the interiorization process itself, the drawing of the referent within the reading spell of the work, its transformation into sheer representation. To the same degree, then, it can perhaps be suggested that—until the war in the last pages—the only genuine "foreign body" in this work, a true object that has come down through time, is the ancient "christening basin" from the distant past which the grandfather shows Hans on solemn occasions—something like a Wagnerian grail that proclaims its kinship with a very different generational time from the fictive reading time we enter at Davos.

For it should be clear that—following the example of that book Viktor Shklovsky called the most novelistic of all novels, *Tristram Shandy*—time in *The Magic Mountain* in all its various perplexing guises—rapid time, the time of boredom and waiting, cyclical time, the time of the great seasons; the units of time as well ("our smallest unit is the month," Settembrini explains [LP58, W56, D79]), along with the paradoxes of the memory of time (filled time flies by rapidly but is remembered as long; empty time goes by painfully slowly but is remembered in a brief flash [LP104–5, W102, D143])—all these representations of time, often as probing as anything in St Augustine, are themselves the after-effects of reading time itself; or rather the concrete experience of this last has, in a kind of sleight of hand, been imperceptibly substituted for that "real" or existential time of which it is so often a question in these pages. Proust is in that sense more referential, and depends on the assent and the confirmation of a personal or biographical memory in the reader to evaluate his accounts of time and memory: nothing can take the place of the madeleine experience, which must therefore simply be taken on faith. But in *The Magic Mountain*

> it is in accordance with [the laws of storytelling] that time seems to us just as long, or just as short, that it expands or contracts precisely in the way, and to the extent, that it did for young Hans Castorp, our hero ... [LP183, W180, D256]

And these laws are precisely those first enunciated in *Tristram Shandy*:

> I am this month one whole year older than I was this time twelve-month; and having got, as you perceive, almost into the middle of my fourth volume—and no farther than to my first day's life—'tis demonstrative that I have three hundred and sixty-four days more life to write just now, than when I first set out; so that instead of advancing, as a common writer, in my work with what I have been doing at it—on the contrary, I am just thrown so many volumes back—was every day of my life to be as busy a day as this—And why not?—and the transactions and opinions of it to take up as much description—And for what reason should they be cut short? as at this rate I should just live 364 times faster than I should write—It must follow, an' please your worships, that the more I write, the more I

> shall have to write—and consequently, the more your worships will have to read. Will this be good for your worships' eyes?
>
> It will do well for mine; and, was it not that my Opinions will be the death of me, I perceive I shall lead a fine life of it out of this self-same life of mine; or, in other words, shall lead a couple of fine lives together.
>
> As for the proposal of twelve volumes a year, or a volume a month, it no way alters my prospect—write as I will, and rush as I may into the middle of things, as Horace advises—I shall never overtake myself whipped and driven to the last pinch; at the worst I shall have one day the start of my pen—and one day is enough for two volumes—and two volumes will be enough for one year.
>
> Heaven prosper the manufacturers of paper under this propitious reign, which is now open to us—as I trust its providence will prosper every thing else in it that is taken in hand.[13]

This is, then, a first approach to the new kinds of content with which the monad of the work can be endowed; despite our abstraction from the world (sealed up in the warm rugs, in the cocoon, of the new artificial experience), a new kind of temporality is found to be generated there, one which can then be supposed to depend in no small measure on length as such, since otherwise the shifting of gears made possible by intricate self-reference and narrative variation, but also by the sheer primitive accumulation of reading capital in the form of memory, cannot take place.

It is not only length that it formally implied and gradually required in the modern, however: Schoenberg's *Pieces for Orchestra* and any number of other expressionist works—as well as certain kinds of not necessarily minimalist poetry—suggest that a violence of extreme concision can do as well (and indeed it would be possible to show that the inaugural modern gesture of *Madame Bovary* consists in excision and leaving out)—any violence to normal or habitual everyday time is enough to foreground the process of aesthetic perception, to make the work be noticed as such, at the same time that a continuum very different from the outside world is brought into being. But the postulate of great length is also a fundamental formal one—length in and for itself, one is tempted to say, even though as we shall see in a moment it can never be that exactly, and must search for content and a way of excusing and justifying its inexplicable persistence. Wagner's endless melody, the immense dilation of Mahler's symphonic movements, the aspiration of the naturalist novel to vast cycles, within which the individual work cannot exactly be said to end—all of these foreshadow the life-tasks of the great moderns, the well-nigh interminability of their projects which also promise a kind of magical immortality as long as the work lasts, everything contingent and empirical in the creator's life now somehow transfigured by its transformation into the potential content of the work itself. The ending of such works then tends to become something like the idea of an ending rather than the thing itself: precisely because it is the idea of an ending that has to be produced, so that the decision of Gertrude Stein about *The Making of Americans*, a book that was to describe "completely" every type of human being that ever existed or could exist, is the supremely exemplary one (she stopped writing it, she tells us, when she understood that she really would be able to finish it!). This is the sense as well in which, if *The Waste Land* is minimalist, the failure of *The Cantos* comes not from its unfinished character or Pound's inability to finish it, but rather from the absence of any idea of an ending, an absence we begin to feel and miss as the pages pile up (and something similar might be said for Musil's *The Man without Qualities*: the fact of the war, as a necessarily conclusion, is insufficient, whereas the war has been sewn cunningly into *The Magic Mountain*, like a sound that threatens sleep, which we weave back into our dream in order to postpone waking). In this case, however, the length is explicitly affirmed as the desire to keep on reading (like the wish to remain asleep), and wills itself, as has been said, as addiction fully as much as habit: everything problematic in Mann and in his book arises from this peculiar voluntarism, which constitutes a peculiar acknowledgement of and appeal to the reader rather different from the blank eye that most modern works purport to turn.

4. Form-Problem: Three Times

Nonetheless, reading time itself must have content: and we now approach something like the fundamental form-problem of the work itself, or rather its zero moment, the achievement of a kind of absolute monadic emptiness and separation which is too unstable to last. This is then the point at which we must posit something like a transcendental aesthetic deduction, very different from what Kant meant by these terms and more approximating the conceit of Fichte who wished at least to conceptualize in imagination a philosophical equivalent of the big bang, or of creation itself, a positing of how, given the empirical existence of subjects and objects, we might somehow work our way back to a primal *a priori* situation in which that existence could be somehow, not merely justified, but as it were replayed in all the logical necessity of its emergence. Despite some similarities, it seems to me that Fichte's great imaginative act is very different from the neo-Platonist emanations, which are not deduced, exactly, but rather narrated, as something that happened in the past, that can be recaptured mythically, in a vision. But Fichte's primal moment—because it is also his cogito—is always present, and can thus at least potentially always be reinspected (by the deducing mind) if not exactly reenacted: meanwhile it is so abstract (the emptiness of sheer identity, the A = A, out of which the not-A is to be generated, and the not-self or in other words the whole of the material world suddenly and convulsively brought into being by the sheer punctual positing of the abstract self as such) that, although containing all content within itself, it has no content either, and thus cannot exactly be narrated, let alone remembered. Finally, in Fichte, this logical moment is so performative that it cannot exactly be argued, but only designated, so that Fichte will spend the rest of his life writing prefaces that continue to summarize and reformulate the initial system. But like Leibniz's concept of the monad, this great deduction of Fichte is more obviously relevant to the aesthetic sphere, and may also be read as a kind of unconscious premonition of that, or a foreshadowing of it, if not a projection of the aesthetic back into the epistemological.

A similar act of deduction is to be performed here, on the occasion of *The Magic Mountain*: it must somehow recover the process whereby content is generated out of the empty situation of the reading monad. But that process can scarcely come as a surprise, inasmuch as "dualism, antithesis, is the moving, the passionate, the dialectic principle of all Spirit" (as Naphta puts it [LP374, W368, D529]): "To see the world as cleft into two opposing poles, that is Spirit." To put it this way is to suggest that this intellectualizing formulation is in place from the outset; yet, as the conversations of Naphta and Settembrini suggest, it is itself a late product in the book's dialectical evolution.

We must therefore retrace our steps, to the very beginning, where only a rudimentary and larval dualism can be witnessed, in the very presence of the two cousins themselves, who constitute what Beckett calls a pseudo-couple:[14] the complementary combination of two imperfect subjectivities: Bouvard et Pécuchet, Ham and Clov, Frédéric and Deslauriers, let alone Holmes and Watson or Dante and Vergil. As can be seen, various kinds of hierarchical order are possible in these combinations, but their crucial feature is the incapacity of the isolated subject to stand alone (as Aristotle thought a substance, or a substantive, should be able to do: the self-sufficiency of what is itself a prime mover). But actually I prefer to speak of the incapacity of the narrative of the isolated subject to constitute itself, since mere psychology menaces any discussion of the subjectivity or "the subject" in and of itself, while our formulation then would turn out to presuppose and to privilege some autonomy of the individual subject that belongs rather, as an ideology, to the heyday of competitive capitalism. We must not prejudge the outcome of this evolutionary and pedagogical development; nor must we count it in the subjective terms in which it is normally formulated, owing to the time-honored generic label—*Bildungsroman*, or novel of formation and education—which is here traditionally maintained. It is enough to note that "the cousins formed a miniature group by themselves in the society of the cure" (LP238, W235, D334); and also that when the pseudo-couple breaks up, and Joachim in a most undisciplined and unsoldierly, un-Germanic spirit of revolt tears himself away from the Berghof to return to the flatland, we find confirmed the impression that the whole work has dialectically acceded to a new level of organization (of which more below).

A second stage in this amoeba-like production of the object out of the subject, and unlike out of life—the Fichtean fiat whereby Nature surges into being alongside the Self—is reached with the awakening of the erotic proper: it is not to endorse or propose any specific psychoanalytic theory about what are recognized today to be not merely plural but also culturally and historically multiple homosexualities, to observe the fundamental structuring role of narcissism in that "bisexuality" so complacently indulged here, in the return of Hans's childhood memory of the student Hippe and the episode of the borrowed pencil (an episode which, like so much else in Mann, underscores its own "significance," rendering the usual sniggers about the discovery of phallic symbols unnecessary, yet endowing its later return in the "mature" love story with all the sleepwalking power of a dream's secret overdetermination). This kind of narcissism can generate an other from the self, and a like from like, on condition of the smallest proximate mark of difference (Lacan's "trait unaire"), namely the "Asiatic" "Kirghiz eyes above the prominent cheekbones" (LP123, W118, D167), and it is indeed this new supplement of signifier, however, libidinally charged, that ushers in the full-blown Other of the Polish woman, Clawdia Chauchat, whose meaning and function is fully as much the East as it is sexual differentiation.

But we must not omit that dimension of the symptom already mentioned above which here deploys its unexpected—its necessarily or expectantly unexpected—power with a shocking force, since it is none other than the teeth-rattling sound of Clawdia slamming the door

> which occurred while they were having the fish course. Hans Castorp gave an exasperated shrug and angrily resolved that this time he really must find out who did it. He said this not only within himself, his lips formed the words. "I must find out" he whispered with exaggerated earnestness. Miss Robinson and the schoolmistress both looked at him in surprise. He turned the whole upper half of his body to the left and opened wide his bloodshot blue eyes. (LP76, W74, D105)

Indeed, one may even say that if love there is, it is the falling in love with a painful auditory and tactile stimulus, an external discomfort that forces the organism into the internal expansion of development and *Bildung*.

In that case, if it is a continuous and evolutionary picture of development that is sought, and if the leitmotiv of narcissism is a plausible guiding thread, then it might be possible to go on and affirm that the larger notion and category of "love" developed in this novel (and deployed in its closing sentence) logically moves from the external other of another sex to the once again internalized object of artistic apprehension and consumption (in the climactic chapter on the phonograph records): music thus coming to be what is closest to me while remaining differentiated, what becomes mine by my appropriation and can thus be loved in some heightened or transcendental Hegelian narcissism as my other self—what also dispels death, since once I have known it, I have also known a Schopenhauerian annulment of the grasping worldly individual ego and am thus already at one with extinction and nirvana; or on the other hand I have known the essential experience in life and thus no longer have anything to miss or to regret.

Nor is this wrong exactly, but it smoothes over the discontinuities which are the bony structure of this text and also the source of its temporal varieties. For it is equally possible to argue that the primal dualism in question here emerges by way of discontinuous thrusts, of an almost geological character. It is thus wrong to reduce the first larval state of the pseudo-couple to latent homosexuality (in order to smooth over the emergence of the second or erotic stage); just as it would be a pity to reduce to that second stage of an ideal or romantic homosexuality the breakthrough, in some third moment, of a new and heightened form of dualism in the outbreak of those philosophical disputations which have become for many people the hallmark of this novel if not of the work of Thomas Mann generally. To be sure, psychological motivations can be adduced for this prodigious shifting of gears towards ideas and speculative speeches: not only is Settembrini by nature and temperament "anxious to exercise influence ... Hans Castorp, for his part, fairly yearned to be influenced" (LP149, W146, D208): a syndrome that here goes a little further than mere proto-fascist suggestibility (as in "Mario and the Magician"), even though family history would seem to provide the Oedipal preconditions for this pedagogical receptivity.

But there are other preconditions, and they must also be taken into account in a situation in which, all the while assuring us of Hans's average nature and thus the relative impersonality of his story, the author hastens to remind us (bidding Hans himself farewell) that "after all, it was your story, it befell you, you must have more in you than we thought" (LP715, W706, D1021). He has meanwhile himself carefully planted the seed of another, social and historical kind of story in the early flashback chapter in which Hans is shown to betray a certain fundamental indifference towards the bourgeois callings of a secular society, an inability "to believe in work as a positive value, a self-justifying principle" (LP34, W33, D46): something not yet in Mann's view a positive matter, but only a privation that under certain circumstances alone (those of this novel, for example) can be found to be promising, or to lead somewhere:

> In an age that offers no satisfying answer to the eternal question of "Why?" "To what end?" a man who is capable of achievement over and above the average and expected modicum must be equipped either with a moral remoteness and single-mindedness which is rare indeed and of heroic mould, or else with an exceptionally robust vitality. (LP32, W31, D44)

Hans is not driven by such demonic forces (which Lukács already theorized as a form-problem in the modern drama, where only pathology motivates real action[15]), so that this characterization stands as Mann's equivalent for Lukács's other formulation, concerning Scott's average heroes (in his analysis of what really amounts to his own version of the *Bildungsroman* in the form of the properly historical novel).[16] But he has not yet sunk, on Northrop Frye's cyclical ladder of forms, to the bereft condition of the anti-hero who has no motivation at all, but at best lives the heroism of the "great refusal." We have already hinted at several points in passing that in this particular *Bildungsroman*, at least from the standpoint of the hero's developing subjectivity, it will be a question not so much of developing a strongly centered subjectivity or personality but rather of getting rid of that, *à la* Schopenhauer: so that at his beginning Hans is in a certain way at his end already, this indifference or lack of ambition being itself what is wanted as a goal for development in the first place, although presumably "at some higher level."

5. The Two-volume Principle

But it is precisely that higher level—with its vague overtones of dialectical or evolutionary spirals, and the unexamined stereotypes of *Bildung*—that we first need to clarify, something that will happen here by way of the hypothesis that we have here to do, less with a view of the content (in some new conception of what "development" might mean either in the psychological, the spiritual or the subjective sense), than with an innovation in form, and more specifically with the articulation of some new formal category that Mann may be said to have pioneered, even though it has its analogies in the production of the other great moderns. The indispensable critical reference here is Proust's celebration of Flaubert as "un homme qui par l'usage entièrement nouveau et personnel qu'il a fait du passé défini, du passé indéfini, du participe présent, de certains pronoms et de certaines prepositions, a renouvelé presque autant notre vision des choses que Kant, avec ses Catégories, les théories de la Connaissance et de la Realité du monde extérieur".[17] The point is that Kant did not invent the categories themselves (whose codification we owe to Aristotle) any more than Flaubert invented the tense system of modern French; but there is a sense in which Kant "produced" the Categories as a concept by systematizing them in such a way that the term now seems to stand for the unity of a permutation scheme, rather than a generic word for a random collection of grammatical features. Following Proust's powerful comparison, then (in an essay that goes on to deny Flaubert any distinctive metaphorical power), we may suggest that Flaubert's systemic reorganization of the tense system as a set of relationships (such that the alternation of *passé simple* and *passé imparfait* always signals a shift in gears, without any specific temporal meaning being permanently attached to either term) marks as it were the emergence of a new *category* in the realm of narrative—a category, rather than a new form as such, which might rather suggest the idea of a new story type, or a new "technique" for organizing the retelling of events. Cross-cutting in the filmic sense (developed in the country fair scene of *Madame Bovary* and then readapted by Joyce in the Wandering Rocks chapter of *Ulysses*) might be said to be a new technique in this sense; while the Gothic novel in the England contemporary with the French Revolution has sometimes been taken to constitute a new kind of story altogether. Nor would the idea of a new category be synonymous with that of a new mode, such as what Hammett and Chandler impose on the detective story, let alone of a new style as such, something observable everywhere in the modern (after Flaubert, but not including him). Rather, as the example of a new formal category (with all due historical antecedents), it may be suggestive to point to Joyce's chapter divisions in *Ulysses*, whose novelty is only rationalized after the fact by the *Odyssey* parallel and the other thematic identifications (parts of the body, colors, rhetorical figures, etc.). To be sure, the immense dilations of Flaubert's chapters, in *L'Éducation sentimentale*, mark the break with the conventions of the various earlier or traditional novelistic practices, and endow the very conception of a chapter unity (and of the break between chapters) with a kind of autonomy or semi-autonomy they did not have before: now the length of the chapters and the nature of the break reconstitute themselves into a relatively independent art language which can be modulated or deployed above or in addition to the organization of the narrative itself and its sentences.

The term "level" imposes itself here, and is perhaps useful insofar as it suggests parallels in the emergence of new interests and attentions in painting or music, where, above and beyond the construction of the figure, a kind of supplementary interest in the disposition of the paint itself as such may be seen to be added to the older and more codified forms of viewing. But the term is also misleading to the degree to which it suggests that the new thing is something like an element or medium in its own right (as is of course the foregrounding of the sheer painterliness of oil paint, or the coloration of the musical instruments): here, in the chapter breaks, a mere empty relationality is at stake: so that when the autonomy of the chapter form leads

Joyce to endow each of his successive chapters with different styles, and to reorganize each one from within, this is not the result of changes in the content nor even a new conception of narrative, but rather, as with Kant or Flaubert's tenses, the consequences of a new system of abstract combinations through which the content is to be processed.

It is something analogous, but distinctive, that we find ourselves observing in the development of *The Magic Mountain*, where to be sure the later chapters transform the earlier more personal themes and experiences and recast those on the level of political and metaphysical reflection. But it is precisely the nature of this classification scheme that is at stake here, for the book itself seems to produce and impose it; and it may be suspected that some deeper formal principle is at work to endow even that conventional opposition between the personal and the collective—if that is what is going on here—with the sense of that progression we palpably feel. But who can think that the love affair with Clawdia is particularly personal, or more so than the great conversations with Naphta and Settembrini? We need to look elsewhere for an explanation of what has been modified here, and the climax of the courtship of Clawdia suggests one, insofar as that coincides with the completion of the first volume.

From another perspective, no doubt, the empirical fact of the two-volume format is utterly contingent: it has indeed been effaced from the English translation, although not from any of the one-volume German editions, where the first five chapters are still designated as "erster Band," the enormous sixth and seventh chapters corresponding to the whole of the second volume. A rather different "category" is to be sure at work in the chapter divisions themselves, where the magic number seven, evoked any number of times in passing, gives the deeper motive for that particular organization of the materials (and perhaps also for the sheer length of the novel, which must not stop until it has faithfully worked its way through its seventh and final stage). But it is striking to see this second, two-volume organizational system cut across the seven-fold chapter sequence in this way, and the uneven distribution already mentioned suggests that, however hallowed the sheer number of chapters to be composed, their internal consistency will surely be found to vary according to their lengths (these increasing in volume one at the general ration of 25 and 25, 75, 125, and 250 pages respectively; while the 300-page format of the two final chapters is more evenly distributed). I want to suggest that we have to do here with the superposition of several distinct kinds of classification schemes, as Lévi-Strauss might have called such organizational principles in his analogous unpacking of conventional historical narratives into heterogeneous systems.

That what we may begin to call the "two-volume principle" is not a mere accident (or that if it is an accident, imposed by book publishing as such, it is one that has been drawn back into the work and reinteriorized in the form of a henceforth purely artistic necessity, like those imperfections of the canvas in Hofrat Behren's Sunday paintings, whose occasional "roughness ... had been dextrously employed to suggest the natural unevennesses of the skin" [LP258, W254, D362]), the very content of the gap suggests (the physical consummation of Hans's love is omitted in the break between the volumes), but also the stylistic organization: for Chapter 5 concludes with the delirious love scene in French ("N'oubliez pas de me rendre mon crayon"), while Chapter 6 renews the tolling rhythm of the deeply philosophical reflections themselves ("Was is die Zeit?"). This is surely a moment which corresponds musically to the change of movements in sonata form; and it is no doubt primarily in terms of properly musical categories that Mann thought of such shifts, for he was proud of Mahler's interest in his works, and specifically went so far as to boast: "was ich machte, meine Kunstarbeiten, urteilt darüber, wie ihr wollt und müsst, aber *gute Partituren waren sie immer*."[18] Nor is it indifferent that Naphta only appears in Volume II, significantly announced by the words "noch jemand," while the later reappearance of Clawdia is like a musical motif which has been demoted, from primary to secondary and functional status.

At any rate, it would be preferable to look for the sources of this "two-volume principle" less in the intellectual or narrative content of the chapters themselves than in its precedent in literary history. That precedent can indeed perhaps itself account for (o: at least authorize) the subsequent temptation of the more "philosophical" interpretations (existential/political, individual/collective), for on my view it is none other than the two parts of Goethe's *Faust*, so preeminently underscored in their fateful symmetry by the gap of an entire long lifetime (the essentials of *Faust* I completed in Goethe's youth, the second part only appearing some sixty years later on the eve of his death in 1832). But Goethe himself motivated the twofold organization in advance, in the words with which Mephistopheles maps out the trajectory of the rejuvenated Faust's new life:

> "Erst die kleine Welt and dann die gross ..."

He means thereby to designate the leap from the provincial idyllic German village to the urbane court of the Holy Roman Emperor in Vienna; but also that from the personal love drama with Gretchen to the affairs of state of Part II (in which even the legendary "marriage of Faustus and Helena" is a matter of high politics and a kind of philosophical "raison d'état"). It is tempting to compare the juxtaposition of these two great and qualitatively different slabs of time with other period oppositions or dualisms, such as that so recently developed by Burke and Kant between the beautiful and the sublime. But it is more appropriate to follow Lukács here in positing a deeper ideological resonance between Goethe and Hegel, and indeed to confirm his sense of the "elective affinities" between *Faust* and Hegel's *Phenomenology* of 1807. The latter would be relevant for us in any case, not only because it has so often been described as a *Bildungsroman*, nor even specifically because its unspecified point of formal influence and of literary reference has been affirmed to be Marivaux's *Bildungsroman*, *La Vie de Marianne*—one of the few examples of the form before Goethe, and a text that obviously loops Hegel back into our own generic system of reference—but above all because so many people, despite Mann's avowed philosophical links with the anti-Hegelian Schopenhauer, and his relative coolness (like that of Benjamin) to Hegelianism as such, have persisted in finding various features of *The Magic Mountain* "dialectical." (We will ourselves continue to do so; see below.)

But in the spirit of the present analysis, it will be more appropriate to interrogate the form of the *Phenomenology* in this respect, than to compare moments of its content: we find that here too the scoring of a fundamental break plays a constructional role, Hegel being above all musical in his organization of separate moments over against each other, the blanks between them marking a shifting of gears of a well-nigh generic type and separating different temporalities and rhythms, different kinds of objects (cognitive versus experiential, mythic versus analytic) and even different moments of history. Despite the (stereotypical) value accorded the triad (or indeed the Trinity) in Hegel, we also find these chapters disposed against each other in fundamental (dualistic) oppositions: and the organization of these eight chapters, far from presenting the simplicity of Goethe's two parts, now approaches the complexity of Mann's multiple grids.[19] In the *Phenomenology* we are in particular forced to notice the syncopated or non-synchronous effects of two distinct sets of oppositions that cut across each other throughout: one is that between consciousness and self-consciousness, the other is that between phenomena of consciousness in general (including both of the previously mentioned moments) and phenomena of "spirit," or in other words between individual and collective or cultural phenomena: here, then, an opposition between life and reflexivity is played off against an opposition which looks a little like the traditional dualism between the individual and society, which in fact it implicitly displaces and reorganizes. Here indeed seemingly general non-individual matters such as science itself are ranged under the category of consciousness (which would seem to have governed individual or existential data), while certain kinds of ethical experience that we would today be tempted to deal with psychologically (moralizing, the so-called "beautiful soul") are rather assigned to *Geist* or to objective spirit as such. (Already this bears a striking resemblance to the "order of topics" in *The Magic Mountain*, where Hans's reading in the sciences and his ruminations about organic life precede the great debates on the social and metaphysical order of Volume II.)

But traditionally, the *Phenomenology* has been compared to the *Bildungsroman* because it seems to move from a situation of mere sentience (the first moment of pure physical sensation and the impoverished rendering of the "here" and "now") all the way to a disembodied consciousness that stands above all History and includes all the stages of the past within itself, reconciling all that struggle and blood, all those incompatible passions and ideologies, by its infinite comprehension, essentially enabled by the hard-won conviction that whatever happened had to happen in the way it did. What interests us here, however, is rather the matter of the ascension itself, the "effect" of a ladder of forms, which has been seen as the result of the superposition of various grids or classification schemes, that seem by their opposition to generate "higher" or at least antithetical "levels" or moments out of each other. It is a formal lesson that could never have been learned from Schopenhauer, but might well owe something to the "idea" of Hegel and his *Phenomenology of Spirit,* if not to the text itself; although I reserve the right to argue that there is also something Hegelian, in a more profound sense, about the ultimate experience of "love" as the interiorization of the other to which Hans finally comes. It is also worth noting, for future reference, about Hegel, that it is not merely the conception of distinct "moments" but also their increasing heterogeneity, as we approach the more historical and cultural dimensions, that alert us to greater episodic discontinuities in the subject matter from the vantage point both of the end of *Faust* II and of the end of *The Magic Mountain.*

6. The Metamorphosis of Opposition

In any case it now remains to see why the dualisms of a generally philosophical (and always rhetorical) disputation are required for this process, although in the final philosophical encounter of Naphta and Settembrini their debates seem to reach a kind of reflexivity in which the very nature of intellectuals is touched on (in the mirror images of conspiracy, Naphta as Jesuit and Settembrini as freemason), and the value of rhetoric and eloquence, and ultimately of Literature and letters itself, brought into question: Naphta's vilification of Vergil will in particular precipitate the final catastrophe. But it must be understood, not merely that a modernist work which questions Literature implicitly raises itself out of that condition into a more secure transliterary one, but also that for the Mann of that interminable precursor text the *Betrachtungen eines Unpolitischen* (*Reflexions of an Unpolitical Man*, written during the war and published in 1918), the "literary"—far from being the true object of the modern or modernist aesthete—is rather allied to the political in the form of the French-style "man of letters," "engagé" already in a civic sense (in the tradition that runs from

Voltaire to Romain Rolland); so that what would today be stigmatized as "literature"—namely high art in general—is here rescued in another sense even by way of Naphta's assault on it (mass culture is itself, typically but with great intelligence, associated with the visual and in particular with film and filmic time, in a luminous excursus [LP316ff, W310ff, D445ff]). Meanwhile, the association tends to cast some doubt on Settembrini's ringing assertion—"There is nothing that is not politics. Everything is politics" (LP515, W505, D729)—which can be thought to be virtually the inaugural moment of the modern as such, from Pound to Mayakovsky, and which comes indeed to be endorsed more whole-heartedly in its obvious or exoteric sense by Thomas Mann himself from the late 1920s onwards.

But the dualist habit—

> "Form," [Settembrini] said; and Naphta rejoined bombastically: "The Logos." But he who would have none of the Logos answered "Reason," and the man of the Logos retorted with "Passion" ... "The Object," cried one, the other: "The Ego!" "Art" and "critique" were bandied back and forth, then once more "nature" and "soul," and as to which was the nobler and concerning the "aristocratic problem." But there was no order nor clarity, not even of a dualistic and militant kind. Things went not only by contraries, but also all higgledy-piggledy. The disputants not only contradicted each other, they contradicted themselves ... (LP466, W457, D659)

—finds its concrete regrounding in the situation of the *Betrachtungen* in which it is the national spirit for which that erstwhile first person of Mann himself speaks: "the true opposition between music and politics, between Germany and Civilization" (24), this last taken in the then current (Spenglerian) acceptation of the institutions and technologies of modern society as opposed to culture. *Betrachtungen*—an odd and exasperating non-book, in which a flow of literary and linguistic energy was clearly released, in a cathartic way, and about which Mann himself was later to be apologetic, describing it as a kind of "poem" ("*beinahe zu einer Dichtung*") —neither work of art nor expository work proper—is a lengthy patriotic disputation with his brother Heinrich Mann, over what he considered an attack on his own essay on Frederich the Great, published early in the war and clearly a nationalistic text. *Betrachtungen* is most fascinating for the way in which its argument rebounds in all kinds of unexpected places and topics (very much in that like the later Settembrini–Naphta discussions), and also for the significant way in which all these dualisms are asymmetrically dialectical rather than Manichaean. Yet as the starting point suggests, this ostensible patriotism is rooted in subalternity; Mann speaks here out of the sense, not merely that Germany is the injured party (as he is himself), but also that it is France (and its associated values, the West, literature, politics, civilization, democracy, etc.) that is the hegemonic power, so that an apologia for

Germany must necessarily be reactive. Thus, a defense of Germany will be non- or anti-political; or rather, its politics must be anti-politics, aesthetics rather than politics, etc. Then in that case, the problem for the aesthete—which the author himself came to realize, when he finally decided to put an end to a dialogical or agonistic monologue that might well have been indefinitely prolonged—is that the irony and aestheticism defended here in the name of Germany is still insufficiently ironic and aesthetic, insofar as Thomas Mann here still takes a position and defends something, occupies one of the two fundamental oppositions when according to the logic of one of them he should be somehow serenely above that passionate commitment as well. He is still thus a character, rather than the Author himself; and it will be the removal of the traces of that commitment—and a consequent shift in perspective that now also opens the way for a more consequent sympathy with the "French" political and rhetorical position of the former "frère ennemi," now occupied by Settembrini's liberalism—that we observe in *The Magic Mountain*: first of all, by the virtual disappearance, from this "concert of nations" of any French character as such; then, by the virtual neutralization of the German position, which, while technically occupied by the protagonist and his cousin, has been carefully reduced to the German cultural habits of orderliness and quasi-military obedience (a form of repression which thus clears the way for the great libidinal "breakthroughs" of which Mann was something like the epic poet). Now the national oppositions are reorganized into shifting pairs of dualisms in which the anxiety about the opposition between France and Germany is somehow displaced by that between Europe and Asia, but also knows any number of other forms as well—the Enlightenment versus medieval Catholicism, the Roman tradition versus the Judaic, liberalism versus communism, etc.; while the classic solution of the mean—Germany itself as the median between France and the East, or between Western commercialism and Eastern authoritarianism—falls out (only to return in *Doktor Faustus*, as a problem rather than a solution).

This is to say that the very motivation of the dialectical oppositions generated in *Betrachtungen* changes here, while retaining the positions thus generated as a kind of raw material. For here I am tempted to say that the very principle of opposition or dualism itself is now made the definitive answer to the Fichtean problem already raised: how can the object be produced by the subject, or nature by the self, or content out of reading?

In this respect, it is crucial not to freeze any of these dualisms over, but to develop a keen awareness of the way they shift and regroup: first, the pseudo-couple of the two cousins against the other nationalities, and then against Settembrini seen as demonic if not "Satanic" (a far cry from his later role as the supreme humanist and the spokesman for reason and light as well as for a relatively tame bourgeois liberalism). Then, as the figure of Clawdia emerges from the indistinct mass of the various comic nationalities, and is invested with the erotic, a new dualism comes into being which opposes her to Settembrini (or more correctly, the reverse): she is thus explicitly glossed as a Circe figure who by way of *Walpurgisnacht* spells and revels keeps Hans chained to the bewitched mountain, to death and illusion, and distracts him from the life tasks in the real world to which Settembrini summons him. Later on, finally, after the definitive opposition between Settembrini and Naphta has emerged, we find both sent off "back to back" by the irruption of a new character, Mynheer Peeperkorn, who treats both indifferently as specimens of the intellectual and the academic and "opposes" them as physical consumption and life appetite.

Yet the Settembrini–Naphta debates have always rightly been considered the privileged locus of dualism in this novel, and justly admired for the elegance with which the stray thoughts and remarks of idle small talk are unexpectedly teased into the most lofty themes of philosophical speculation, and become the occasions for a veritably Platonic symposium in which one impoverished set speech provokes another, each one drawing Hans's enthusiasm and convictions (along with the reader's) in the opposite direction. Mann's own inner ambivalences—perhaps one should say, his disposition to revel in those ambivalences, and to indulge each contradiction at great length—play no little part in the oscillation of the reader back and forth across positions whose evaluation is also a matter of objective and historical ambiguity.

For these conversations—in which the very spirit of dualism is suddenly thematized as such and raised to reflexivity (we have already quoted its explicit evocation at the first appearance of Naphta, [LP374, W368, D529])—have as their content function the *Aufhebung* of the various preceding treatments of illness and physical decay onto a different and more intellectual level, which eventually proves to be that of politics and political theory in the largest sense—although the first skirmish begins, logically enough, with the current world situation, which allows the participants economically to invoke the church on the one hand, the world republic on the other, and to raise issues of nationalism, colonization, a "bourgeois acceptance of life," economics, and quietism versus praxis, in passing.

These topics must then be sharpened into ideological—or better still, "world-historical"—significance, they must enable the appearance of the great *Weltanschauungen* (in the second dialogue), before in a climactic third session the two counterpositions, now already largely associated with life and death, with the powers of light and the powers of darkness, are then brought to bear on matters of the body, corruption, torture, guilt, suffering and disease: as it were to authorize and certify their assumption into that "higher realm" of the *logos*, of political philosophy and metaphysics, of eloquence and the vocation of the intellectual. The latter will then be explored in the subsequent, and henceforth secondary development of these discussions, which thereby also now radically bifurcate from the matter of Hans Castorp's experience of art as such: just as in *Betrachtungen*, the rhetorical concerns of the Francophile and political "man of letters" were sharply distinguished from the German aesthete's unpolitical practice of music and irony.

But although these powerful dualisms of life and death are surely deployed and rehearsed in order to make us think so, nothing is less certain than that we here witness a perpetual "renversement du pour au contre" in which Manichaean opposites are evenly matched and any thinking person could be seduced into momentarily adopting either side and endorsing either the negative or the positive. The procedure was presumably devised in order to make possible some virtually psychoanalytic working through, acting out, and purgation of the political positions taken in *Betrachtungen* (indeed Mann says so explicitly in his lecture on the novel, reprinted in Lowe-Porter's translation, p. 721). In fact, however, no one in this novel takes the position of German nationalism, and of the metaphysical vocation of Germany to save Europe from the shallow materialism of the West, that Mann endorses in that interminably argued work: there are many nationalities here, but (save for the anti-Semitism that explodes as a symptom in the final pages) no nationalism as such, both Settembrini and Naphta being in their specific ways trans- and inter-nationalists. Thus, both their positions amount to a transcendence of that so tenaciously argued for in *Betrachtungen*, which may thus arguably be seen as the more dialectical work, in that its apolitical position finds itself forced by the very movement of the argument to acknowledge itself as political. This is to say that whereas Settembrini's and Naphta's positions are genuinely symmetrical (and thus Manichaean), the positions in *Betrachtungen*—France as a dominant or hegemonic political, literary and secular culture, Germany as the aestheticizing underdog—more dynamically represent the dissymmetries of the same–other opposition.

We must here, it seems to me, also distinguish between something like the structural and the dialectical uses of such dualisms, respectively. Classically, the structural opposition (as ultimately codified in Greimas's semiotic square, for example) is a means whereby from one seemingly isolated or free-standing term, an entire semantic universe can be generated, largely by way of various kinds of negation. This semiotic bootstrapping, or as it were a kind of Munchausen logical generation of the whole universe itself, then largely corresponds to the self-generative process of this particular novel, which, as we have suggested, begins within the zero of the isolated individual readerly body, within the cocoon of reading itself, and must thus slowly generate a whole world out of its starting point: body warmth generating both life and disease or death, just as little by little eros generates the intellectual or the political; this last, by way of a dramatic mitosis, separating out into a whole historical variety of world-views, only then to be rebuked and reduced to merely intellectual status by a "life affirmation" whose dramatic ephemerality is survived, in ever more troubled times, only by art itself, that is to say essentially by the work we have been reading. But each new moment must be an absolute beginning—*noch jemand!*—a discontinuous irruption of what could not have been foreseen in the previous avatar: a display of sheer irreducible contingency fully as much as a logical sequel whose deeper continuities can only be subsequently appreciated or measured.

Dualism is thus required as something like a principle of production in this constructional situation, all the while it is used to suggest a kind of ideological malleability and an indifferent flowing back and forth from one incompatible stance to another. The ideological suggestion is secretly reinforced by the other fundamental dualism at work here, the primal dualism, from which all these lesser ones spring, but which is here as it were dissociated from its worldly manifestations in such a way that it seems to reverse them and recombine with all of them freely. This is of course the dualism of good and evil, or of positive and negative: and its most dramatic exercise will be to suggest in various reversals that death is good, or that sickness is positive, and so forth.

7. Irony and Aestheticization

Such effects—which masquerade as a kind of dialectic—are however much closer to the ideological stance of irony, celebrated by Mann in *Betrachtungen* and adopted by him elsewhere as a kind of thematic badge; but his idiosyncratic use of the term needs to be appreciated before this particular view is endorsed either. For irony in both works essentially means aestheticization, the capacity to take an aesthetic view of both positions, that is to "appreciate" both from the standpoint of aesthetic contemplation: a capacity for which Mann celebrates Flaubert and Tolstoy in *Betrachtungen* (pp. 214–22), where for example at the end of *Madame Bovary* it is the power of Flaubert to convert both ideological sides, the priest and the freethinker, into the unity of a single image that is at issue.

If so, then what must be located is the process whereby these philosophical discussions and debates are transformed into aesthetic material as such and thereby enabled to become the substance of the work itself. But that is surely no mystery, for it is by way of Hans's essentially aesthetic apprehension of the discussions that their aestheticization and internalization (in the monad of the work) becomes possible. His affirmation or approval is not particularly necessary: that he should react to Settembrini as an "organ-grinder" (LP56, W54, D77) secures an aesthetic distance from the personage fully as much as his naïve admiration for the latter's fine language ("the words come jumping out of his mouth so round and appetizing" [LP101, W99, D139]), while later on it is aesthetic admiration rather than genuine rhetorical conviction and persuasion that marks the progress of the great debates. To Naphta, he throws the sop of experiential rumination—"Devotion, retirement,—there is something in it, it sounds reasonable. We practice a pretty high degree of retirement from the world, we up here. No doubt about it" (LP376, W370, D533)—while also equally seconding Settembrini in the appropriate moments: "No, here I must really corroborate Herr Settembrini ... my cousin and I have had the privilege of frequent conversations with him on this and kindred subjects ... so I can vouch for the fact ... that Herr Settembrini spoke more than once, with great enthusiasm, of the revolutionary principle" etc. (LP381, W375, D539).

That Hans listens to the sound of language fully as much as to its meanings is then corroborated by another feature of this novel—another manifestation of its complacencies—that has the function of a weaving together of its nomadic languages. This is Hans's "taking stock," which is to say the gradual construction in him of a kind of private language put together of expressions that have come to have some special meaning for him, or to have been the object of long quizzical perplexity. But this private language also secures the alienation of ordinary daily speech from its context and its readaptation into the milieu of the monad itself: by means of Hans's ruminations, an impersonal German vocabulary stock and collection of expressions is personalized and comes to be at one with the specific style of *The Magic Mountain* itself—a rather different procedure from the way in which personal style is imposed by fiat in the other great moderns. It is however again the consequence (or the achievement, if one likes) of a kind of aesthetic self-indulgence ratified into a virtually ethical imperative, to abandon one's self to such seemingly aberrant habits of mind, to a dwelling on inconsequential turns of phrase, until those become themselves the charged locus of a meaning that can be repeated.

Something may also be said in this connection about the development of Hans's subjectivity: the true story of his *Bildung* as a subject, which we have sought to downplay until now since it has seemed to mark a radical misunderstanding, either of what it is desirable for consciousness to evolve into, or of what is actually happening in this novel. But the relationship to language, and this aestheticization of events and experiences, can also be observed in Hans's "impertinence," noted by Frau Chauchat and others: that is, his sleepwalking freedom at externalizing all these inner perceptions and at describing his mental reactions to others (as when, later on, he actually tells Settembrini he first thought he looked like an organ-grinder). But this impertinence is quite different from arrogance, or from the indifference of powerful, "centered" personalities; rather it is itself a sign of Hans's subjective subalternity, and is authorized by his own secondary standing, by his submission to others and to the situation, or even, by his posture as a kind of apprentice (who entertains no hope of evolving into a master in his own right). Thus, what may be called a kind of aestheticizing impertinence is itself a stage towards the real "development" or *Bildung* foreseen in this *Bildungsroman*, which posits the Buddhist extinction of the personality, or at least its decentering, the indifference to one's own subjectivity as such, rather than the conquest of a Self traditionally celebrated in the era of ego psychology and of the ideology of modernism.

Such is surely the meaning of one of our final glimpses of Hans, who has now finally arrived at the "bad Russian table" and sits there, "wearing a recent little blond beard, vaguish in cut, which we are disposed to regard as a sign of philosophic indifference to his own outer man. Yes, we will go even further, and relate his carelessness of his person to the carelessness of the rest of the world regarding him" (LP706, W696, D1008). But this fate has already been long since prepared in the remarkable episode in which Hans receives a visit from his uncle—one of the only moments in the *Zauberberg* in which the narrative does not take Hans's point of view on events, but rather sees him from the outside—which is of course precisely the function of this particular episode. For now, once again, from the standpoint of the uncle, we reexperience everything Hans confronted when he first arrived; but from a more "advanced" standpoint. The uncle, properly horrified and alerted, is able to flee; but not without having been able to observe Hans's "serene, unfeigned, unmistakable sang-froid, which was like a suit of armor; like his indifference to the chill of that autumn evening, like his little phrase 'We don't feel the cold' " (LP431, W423, D609). This is a Hans to whom we are unaccustomed (seeing him generally from the inside, in terms of his own lively interests and curiosity); but it prepares us for the impersonal, aesthetic Hans of the final stage, the posthumous body to be sent into the holocaust of the Great War.

8. Is It Dialectical?

What seems dialectical about Mann's "irony," however, has another more historical source, consistent with the origins of dialectical thinking itself in the paradoxes of an essentially historical situation, namely, the transition from the *ancien régime* to bourgeois capitalism, and the resultant problems of judgement (most famously articulated in *The Communist Manifesto*). For the bourgeois order is at one and the same time freer and more open than the feudal forms that preceded it, and also the bearer of new kinds of alienations, of qualitatively different types, that had no equivalent in the still relatively human brutalities and personal violence of the old order. Whence the emergence of a third or Utopian term which would be the negation of both systems, and which would thus logically offer a solution to the otherwise insoluble movement back and forth between them, comparing their properties. It is this surreptitious substitution of a triad for a dualism or beneath the dualism which constitutes the dialectic and its new logical capacities; and it will be seen that it also represents cognitive possibilities that cannot be matched by structural oppositional combinations of whatever complexity. Nor is this putative power of the dialectic denied anywhere in modern or contemporary thought; rather, if I understand the critics and opponents, what is denied is its existence, its possibility as a concrete form of thinking.

At any rate, it will now be clear that the elasticity of the great arguments in *The Magic Mountain* derives essentially from this tripartite system, and accounts for the way in which the figure of Settembrini—at first Satanic, since in the eyes of the orderly German cousins he embodies the culturally unthinkable form of critique itself—slowly becomes a relatively more one-dimensional manifestation of Western liberalism. But this is because Naphta embodies both the other systemic possibilities: speaking first for the Church and for what looks like a kind of clerical reaction and obscurantism, he can be rightly thought—not only by Settembrini—to incarnate those more medieval elements of superstition and tyranny denounced by the Enlightenment at the heart of the *ancien régime*.

But, very consistent with the rethinking of the medieval going on elsewhere in this same period (e.g. Mumford on the medieval city), a rather different acceptation of the meaning of this period and its ethos can emerge, which is brilliantly formulated by Naphta as "the anonymous and the communal" (LP393, W386, D556): a formula perhaps now more attractive to us in the postmodern than to Mann's first Weimar readers, since it seems to promise a social resolution of those problems of "the centered subject" and of generalized or atomized individualism of which we have become so much more keenly aware. This is why the ultimate peripeteia comes with such logical force: it is no doubt related to that other duality in Naphta ("both natural aristocrat and Natural Revolutionary" [LP443, W436, D627]) which grounds this one, namely that he represents both Judaism and Catholicism all at once, as it were the two non-national principles that could not be well accommodated to the national guest-list of the Berghof (whereas Settembrini's nationality confirms the unity of rhetoric, Roman culture, classical politics, and Resorgimento liberalism). The later revelation that Naphta is a Jesuit (like the accompanying one about Settembrini's freemasonry) is more melodramatic, in the sense of the sham thunderclaps of the wellmade plot: the unveiling of stereotypical masks of villainy that, casting doubt on both political positions, prepare the vitalistic disabusement of the Peeperkorn episode.

But the leap from Naphta's medievalism to communism itself is more fundamental: it makes of his repudiation of the Western liberal and parliamentary ethos something more than merely regressive opinion, and endows it with the threatening overtones of a real future about which Mann was willing to be appropriately ambiguous (the physical and characterological attributes of Naphta are, as is well known, borrowed from Georg Lukács, just as those of Peeperkorn are borrowed from Gerhard Hauptmann).

This dialectic, once set in place, can then be activated on the occasion of the other dualisms in the work, most notably those having to do with sickness and with death: for even this last, under the guise of art, is able with the proper aesthetic bewitchment to give off Utopian overtones. We must, however, also record the last avatar of the more purely structural (not to say Manichaean) form of a pure and unresolvable dualism itself. For one final logical possibility remains to be worked out—one final challenge to the Fichtean scheme of things demands a response—and it is a matter of no little admiration to watch Mann rise to this ultimate occasion, in the chapter entitled "Snow." Here, uniquely in high modern literature, with the single exception of Conrad, the self is able to generate an absolute non- or anti-self over against it, in the form of a baleful Nature, an immeasurable force that seeks, as Conrad puts it in *Typhoon*, to do you personal harm. To be sure, Hans seeks the snowstorm out, by a kind of provocation; still, once caught in it he too must face this "unparalleled outrage directed at his feelings" and is in a position to measure the truth of Conrad's magnificent evocation: "A furious gale attacks him like a personal enemy, tries to grasp his limbs, fastens upon his mind, seeks to rout his very spirit out of him".

9. Dissolutions

But now, after this twofold climax of the principle of duality, in the Naphta–Settembrini debates on the one hand and the ultimate confrontation with nature on the other, the movement of the narrative towards what one remains tempted to call higher and higher moments or stages, ever more complex combinations, is broken: the work continues, but now by way of enormous and discontinuous, rather static episodes of a very different kind (but for which "Snow" was already a preparation, consisting as it does in a virtually self-complete anthology-piece structure). As has been said, the parallels here with Hegel and Goethe are only intensified, owing to the seemingly more exemplary and didactic quality of their closing episodes as well—the discontinuous historical moments of culture and religion in Hegel, the fable of Philemon and Baucis in *Faust* II. Those discontinuities, however—relatively aberrant in the context of neoclassicism, romanticism or realism—become prophetic as the logic of the modern comes into view, with its well-nigh organic commitment to autonomization as such (Joyce's "organ" motifs in fact signify autonomous functions, rather than the symbolic unification that passes under the aegis of the slogan of the organic in a romantically derived ideological tradition). The comparison of Mann with Joyce's multiple stylistic powers is no longer taken very seriously (although if it were limited to the Oxen of the Sun chapter, it would have more force, since Mann is very expert indeed at imitating written styles, as witness in particular the medievalisms of *Doktor Faustus*): but a deeper kinship can nonetheless be argued (in Proust, it would presumably hold with what Malraux called the latter's "art d'aveugle," his purely oral capacity to imitate other voices).

This well-nigh stylistic autonomization can best be observed in the extended Peeperkorn episode, which also rehearses, for one last time, but in its own dramatic and as it were most undisguised form, the peculiar operations of that generation of content from emptiness, of plot and event from the static abstraction and otherworldliness of the reading situation, that characterizes the specific form-problem of this unique work. For Peeperkorn himself—designed to be the very embodiment of the life force itself, at least in so far as life-affirming appetite is concerned, but also collectively, in the great festivals of eating and drinking and gambling over which he presides—is also the very epitome of a character without content, and suggests that the very notion of formalism implied by these terms is susceptible of a different kind of enlargement than the practices of sheer abstraction or of aestheticism normally convey. For being everything, Peeperkorn cannot really be anything: nor does he have anything to say—except everything! It is not merely that his sentences remain unfinished:

> Those adequate, compelling, cleanly attitudes of the hands—so varied, so full of subtle nuances—possessed a technique like that of an orchestra conductor. He would curve forefinger and thumb to a circle; extend the palm, that was so broad, with nails so pointed, to hush, to caution, to enjoin attention—and then having by such means led up to some stupendous utterance, produce an anticlimax by saying something his audience could not quite grasp. (LP550, W540–1, D781)

This is at it were the empty Idea of "a personality" (560): that it has some connection with demagogy, and can even be turned into an anachronistic anticipation of the *Führerprinzip*, Hauptman's own later evolution, as well as stray remarks and ironies of Mann here testify,[20] particularly insofar as it is a question of "that certain shrewd geniality native to him, which found everything fish to his net, and not only bound to him people of the most diverse tastes and characters, but exerted enough power to bind them to each other" (LP580, W571, D825). The destructive and self-destructive features of this empty power are also noted: but it is rather with the constructional principle that we are here concerned, and in particular the remarkable way in which a climactic moment is achieved: namely, the waterfall sequence, in which Peeperkorn's great speech, which, accompanied by the most vivid expressions and visible gestures, presumably transmits some of the most vital secrets of human experience, is utterly inaudible to everyone, being drowned out by the sound of the falling cataract.

Stylistically, however, the leitmotif of this enormous episode—which otherwise tantalizes us with its lack of content—finds its deeper motivation in the phenomenon of bodily appetite: as it were inflecting in the direction of taste what had hitherto been able to operate on the level of the epidermic flush. We have already seen a unique deployment of taste at its characteristic work in the sentence about champagne quoted early on: now however it is appropriate to marshal other forms of essentially liquid sampling:

> Peeperkorn indicated the medicine bottle on the table, a brown liquid, of which he took a spoonful from Frau Chauchat's hand. It was an antipyretic, chiefly quinine, he said. He made his guest try its characteristic bitter and pungent taste; and had much to say in praise of the wonder-working, germ-destroying properties of the drug, its tonic quality, its wholesome effect in regulating the temperature. It slowed down protein catabolism, promoted assimilation, etc., etc. (LP577, W568, D821)

These tastes are juxtaposed in the text like so many new kinds of raw materials, like oil colors on a medium: they reach into the reading body on the one hand and out across the imperial world system on the other, where the intimate relationship between Holland and Indonesian jungles are explicitly evoked, enlarging the purely European set of characters on a global scale, and setting in place new tones, which prove to be toxic as well as merely pungent and stimulating. It is this aestheticization of the Peeperkorn episode that makes its external appearance susceptible to assimilation into the sensory-contemplative dimension of the monad. Thus, not only will this particular stylistic dominant reach a climax when Peeperkorn poisons himself, but the whole episode is taken leave from in the characteristically aesthetic-static mode of a visual tableau, from which, as in a retreating zoom shot, we withdraw to a prodigious distance.

> The door to Peeperkorn's salon stood open, also that to his bedroom, where all the lights were burning. The two physicians, the Directress, Madame Chauchat, and the Malay were within, the last-named dressed not as usual, but in a sort of national costume, with a striped garment like a shirt, very long wide sleeves, a gaily coloured skirt, and a curious, cone-shaped hat made of yellow cloth on his head. He wore an ornament of amulets on his breast and stood with folded arms at the head of the bed, wherein Pieter Peeperkorn lay on his back, his arms

> stretched out before him. Hans Castorp, paling, took in the scene. Frau Chauchat sat with her back toward him in a low chair at the foot of the bed. Her elbows rested on the coverlet, her chin was in her hands, whose fingers were buried in her upper lip, and she gazed into the face of her protector. (LP622, W613, D887)

It is also worth noting that it is in this atmosphere of a new kind of physical expressivity that Hans arrives at a formulation for his own education which has its own peculiarly physical and bodily overtones: evoking this "alchemistic-hermetic pedagogy, transubstantiation, from lower to higher, ascending degrees" (LP596, W587, D849).

The formula is itself, however, under the spell of the stylistic dominant of Peeperkorn, for the very notion of development breaks off at this point, yielding the final punctual episodes under the sign of collective depression and collective mania, which now as in some final inverted Hegelian level, begin to convey the sense of a very madness of the times themselves breaking in on us. It is not normally appropriate to juxtapose Mann with Brecht, who loathed him for all kinds of reasons (but principally, surely, for the mandarin stance of aestheticism and of the demiurgic writerly and ironic pretensions he liked to affect); nonetheless even dialectically there is much in common between the ultimate dissolution of Mahagonny—

> giant demonstrations against inflation which heralded the end of the city

—and these last symptomatic crazes (the phonograph, table-turning and seances, the duels and fights) that sweep through *The Magic Mountain* itself (completed after all in that 1920s Weimar which is refracted back into the ostensible pre-World War One setting of the novel). This is then some ultimate supremely formal development of Mann's aesthetic of the symptom, which reaches out from a purely bodily sensorium into this virtually "public-sphere" diagnosis, this interpersonal sensorium of suggestivity and irritability, the hypersusceptibility to the most minute shifts and changes to the collective atmosphere: something of which the war may be said to be the definitive annulment in a physical indistinction and oppression in which the outside and inside are confounded indistinctly in exactly the opposite sense. The affirmation of art then, in the form of the Tannenbaum song, returns us to Schopenhauer's conception of art as a provisional nirvana, and the extinction of the worldly desiring consciousness: this was the sense in which Hans's operas all meant death. But now, after so many pages, "art" is also the memory of the extended reading experience that finally designates itself in conclusion, in the reflexivity both characteristic of modernist form production in general—in the way in which detached sign-systems need to reground themselves in their own minimal reference in the absence of more conventional contexts—and also of this unique monument to aestheticism, as ambiguous as the very ambiguities in which it so triumphantly revels.

(*1992*)

Notes

1 Walter Benjamin, *Gesammelte Schriften*, volume II-2, p. 446 (Frankfurt, 1977).
2 Maj Sjöwall and Per Wahlöö, *The Fire Engine that Disappeared* (New York, 1971), p. 34.
3 Jane Feuer, *The Hollywood Musical* (Bloomington, 1982).
4 Emile Zola, *La Débacle*, in *Les Rougon-Macquart* (Paris, 1967), volume V, p. 446.
5 Sigmund Freud, *The Standard Edition* (London, 1959) volume IX, p. 175.
6 The quotes in the text are mainly drawn from H.T. Lowe-Porter's translation (New York, 1967), designated LP in the text; accompanying those references are the page numbers in John E. Woods's 1995 translation (New York), designated W, and to the German original in the so-called *Stockholmer Gesamtausgabe* (Stockholm, 1950), marked D. Thus, the present reference should read LP273, W269, D384.
7 See Janice Radway, *A Feeling for Books* (Chapel Hill, 1997).
8 *Death in Venice and Other Stories*, trans. H.T. Lowe-Porter (New York, 1991) p. 6.
9 Kant, *Critique of Judgement*, 55, paragraph 10. Michael Fried's notion of absorption, in *Theatricality and Absorption* (Chicago, 1988), is also relevant here.
10 Herbert Marcuse, *Negations* (Boston, 1968).
11 Leibniz, "*Monadology*" trans. G.H. Parkinson, in *Philosophical Writings* (London, 1973), p. 182.
12 Marcel Proust, *À la recherche du temps perdu* (4 vols; Paris, 1987–89), II, pp. 110–11.
13 Laurence Stern, *Tristram Shandy*, Chapter XIII, Book IV.
14 In Samuel Beckett, *Mercier and Camier* (Paris, 1970); but see, for a fuller discussion, my *Fables of Aggression* (Berkeley, 1979), pp. 58–61.
15 Georg Lukács, *Entwicklungsgeschichte des modernen Dramas* (Darmstadt, 1981, [1911]).
16 Georg Lukács, *The Historical Novel* (Lincoln, Nebraska, 1983).
17 Marcel Proust, *Essais et articles* (Paris, 1994), p. 282.
18 Thomas Mann, *Betrachtungen eines Unpolitischen* (Frankfurt, 1988), p. 311.
19 But see Otto Pöggeler, *Hegels Idee einer Phänomenologie des Geistes* (Munich, 1973) for a more scholarly account of the overlapping organizational schemes.
20 My favorite sentence stages Hauptmann's collaboration: "Er blieb in Deutschland, hisste die Hakenkreuzflagge, schrieb 'Ich sage Ja!' und liess es sogar zu einer Entrevue mit Hitler kommen, der eine schmähliche Minute leng seinen stupiden Basiliskenblick in die kleinen und blassen, recht ungoethschen Augen bohrte und weiter 'schritt.' "

"... letting it go so far as a meeting with Hitler, who bored his stupid basilisk stare into the small, pale, truly ungoethean eyes for one long disgraceful minute and then 'strode' on." *Die Entstehung des Doktor Faustus* (Amsterdam, 1949), p. 174.

4

Kafka's Dialectic

Kafka's stories fatally lend themselves to interpretation, which is not only the question about what they mean, but also and even more fundamentally, what they are about. You do not have to posit some heavy-handed message (*Angst* or the "human condition") provided you have nailed down the deeper subject matter, which seems generally to fall into one of the following three options: the Oedipus complex or at least the guilt of subalternity; bureaucratic dictatorship or the dystopia of modernity; or, finally, God and our relationship to him or to his absence. With very little ingenuity these three levels can be superimposed and conflated: authority now staged as the father, the state, or God himself. But are these interesting subjects nowadays? Are messages about them really still worth pondering? (Even given a more perennial Jewish-identity spin?)

Perhaps it would be more productive to interrogate the reading experience itself, surely the most reliable source of testimony about Kafka's fascination, and the pleasure we still take in reading him (even after the familiar nightmares have all been catalogued and conventionally stereotyped). Any unprejudiced reader will then observe that reading Kafka plunges us into a well-nigh interminable weighing of alternatives, a tireless passage back and forth between the pro and the contra, each of which then unfolds into its own interminable consequences, and so on into that infinity which can be broken off at any point and which explains why the "unfinished" state of so many of Kafka's texts seems to make no difference at all to the general reader.

This is presumably to say that with signal exceptions these narratives are rarely stories in the sense in which the latter generally reach some kind of definitive conclusion (Gregor's death, Josef K.'s execution). It could even be argued that those seeming exceptions are themselves relatively unexceptional insofar as the perfunctory ending might have itself been indefinitely postponed or delayed, adding any number of additional pages (filled with more of the inexhaustible inventory of alternatives we have been characterizing) to the total.

That the procedure is not altogether incompatible with narrative as such may be judged by inspection of the one group of novels that proceeds very much in the same way: I mean certain key works of the English eighteenth century, in particular *Tom Jones* and *Clarissa*, in which each new turn of the plot seems to provoke a thorough acting out of all the possible consequences of the new situation, before the latter is decisively modified in turn (leading on to a new series). But in these novels, the various logical alternatives are all embodied in the diegetic reality itself, in the various and logically varied results of an act in the real world itself. Whereas in Kafka, they strike one as a subjective brooding on interminable logical possibility, even where (as in "The Metamorphosis") they do actually happen. But in this last, one is tempted to throw these events back into the conditional as such and to see them as a list of answers to the question, What if I were turned into a giant bug? And this is a conditional we do not find at work in the eighteenth century realist novels.

The answers to that initial question are of course well known, but we can glimpse the general process of logical permutation by way of a rough summary. The beetle-like starting point includes that part of the "definition" beetles share with turtles, namely, that once on their backs they cannot turn over. But how will Gregor's non-appearance be read? Laziness (he is always early), sickness ("during his five years' employment he had not been ill once"[1]). The other possibilities are enumerated (from beyond the locked door) by the chief clerk: he is by nature troublesome and provocative ("making a disgraceful exhibition of yourself"— 97/71); or else he has absconded with some of the funds.

Gregory answers his callers; but there is of course the other alternative: that they cannot understand what now passes for his voice. Reactions to his appearance are also suitably varied: the "loud 'Oh!' " of the chief clerk, the mother first approaching and then falling back, the father's clenched fist (the sister's behavior will be added in the second part, in which these reactions themselves enter into a variation scheme).

But first: the various possibilities of nourishment are clearly to be explored. Then there is space itself, the room furnished and unfurnished. Now finally the mother's pity is contrasted with the father's anger (while yet a third logical possibility is given in the sister's more active and protective stance). The attention to space is accompanied by the variation in Gregor's physical being: after the initial paralysis in part one, he can move (and the movement in and out of the room is a fundamental option); he can hide behind the sheet; or he can walk on the ceiling, or he can, in one of the most significant climaxes in the novella, be inspected splayed out clinging to the wall. The mother's fainting spell and the father's ominous transformation (also significant in other ways for Kafka) complete this development, which will now, in part three, require the addition of external spectators and their new and distinct reactions: the charwoman is neither afraid nor startled but threatens to strike this seemingly hostile occupant; while the lodgers take him as a pretext for demanding their rent back.

Yet now, in this third section as a whole, a new alternative is explored: from being a scandal and a perpetual source of horror, Gregor will have become familiar and even scarcely worthy of notice. In this alternative, there is very little that is new to explore in the range of objective possibilities; the variations are all in the observers. Thus, after a kind of competition with the mother, the sister from being self-sacrificing and protective becomes egotistical: she cannot stand it any longer and reverses her sibling identification ("if this were Gregor he would have realized long ago that human beings can't live with such a creature and he would have gone away on his own accord"—134/107).

Now, indeed, a larger alternative presents itself: we can see all this, not through Gregor's point of view, but from the outside, through the eyes of a genuine third person. At this point Gregor disappears (dies) and the very tonality of the novella is transformed. From the confinement situation, the world is reborn; from death we shift to life, the springtime, the walk in the country, the very rebirth of the daughter herself.

This ending (or coda) is indeed the most euphoric and paradisal moment in Kafka, a vision of a new heaven and earth into which the family tentatively steps forth in their Sunday best: for this is now, for the first time, a world without guilt, this last having been loaded onto the scapegoat Gregor and driven out into the wilderness. It is not, one would want to add, a personal matter, a decision by the writer that the family was in the right after all, and Gregor truly guilty of all the accumulated counts of the indictment that Georg Bendemann, for example, has to bear (in "The Judgement"): that judgement is in fact undecidable and forever swings back and forth between the warring parties. This new purification is, however, beyond individuals and the categories of their individual subjectivities; it is a transformation of the world itself (about which one would only want to pause to ask a question about shame as such, and whether it is a containment of guilt or on the contrary its distant origin).

Now what should have been a study in unrelieved dreariness becomes a joyous and redemptive celebration of life itself: "And it was like a confirmation of their new dreams and excellent intentions that at the end of their journey their daughter sprang to her feet first and stretched her body" (139/113). Indeed, one is tempted to think that the whole baleful Gregor narrative was itself required "merely" to motivate and enable this extraordinary and life-enhancing euphoria, this joyous ending (which is recapitulated even more emblematically at the end of "The Hunger Artist" when the panther, the very embodiment of the life force, takes the protagonist's place in his abandoned cage).

I have omitted several crucial features from this summary: most notably the family's economic situation, the transformation of the father, the framed picture on the wall, and music itself, the vocation of the daughter, or finally, the more ominous possibility that the final euphoric elevation is little more than a ruse for the family's exploitation of the daughter (the advantageous marriage!) in place of the no longer serviceable son. I have also omitted the dialectical shift in the narrative tone itself (which is scarcely limited to the final paradisiac vision): we will at least return to this shift later on. What it is now essential to observe is that what we may now speak of as Kafka's narrative procedure here still operates on the level of the diegetically real, that is, on the objective events of the story (which, far from fantastic, seem as realistic as in any nineteenth century novel).

But it is important to be clear about what such a "procedure" is: to call it a method is misleading to the degree to which it suggests a cut-and-dried or mechanical formula for processing the narrative raw material. Everyone knows, on the contrary, how various and varied the latter is in Kafka's hands and that it is the remarkable invention and inventiveness of this writer that allows us to continue to read and to reread him, not even for the narratives themselves (with which we are all long since familiar) but for each individual sentence and the following one.

So it is scarcely with the intent to slight Kafka's genius for writing narrative sentences that (imitating his own stylistic tics) we now pause to wonder whether the word "invention" is the right one here. It cannot, at least, be meant to characterize the developments of the plot itself, which after the initial situation are more or less predictable: or perhaps it would be better to say that they are predictable if one has already grasped a procedure in which we posit now one logical possibility and then its logical alternative, after the fashion we have begun to outline above. What is unpredictable on the level of these simple yet amazing sentences, these neutral yet arresting notations, is nonetheless predictable on the narrative and diegetic level where they clearly register one after another the only possibilities conceivable in the situation at hand.

There is here then something of a logical saturation at work, reminding us of an old structuralist aesthetic, which had never seemed altogether convincing in general but which suddenly springs into life when we think of Kafka. Indeed, it was something of a structuralist doxa (to be found in Greimas, Barthes, and possibly Genette and others as well if not in Lévi-Strauss himself for whom the possibilities were infinite) that the underlying conceptual or categorial scheme of every work was something like a machine for producing logical permutations or alternative possibilities, whether by inversion or negation, contradiction, neutralization, or what slowly turn out to be a variety of operations for producing variations as such. These operations do not only have to be seen in relationship to the acts as such; or rather, often they seem to lie within each act as its inner possibility, which is not only the possibility of being and nothingness, that the act may be performed or not performed, but inside, in its modes as well as in its microscopic unfolding.

The process is thus something like the inversion (and thus the structural equivalent) of that passage in Proust of which Barthes was so fond: the evocation of the incomprehensible silence of the elevator boy to the narrator's polite question:

> Mais il ne me répondit pas, soit étonnement de mes paroles, attention à son travail, souci de l'etiquette, dureté de son ouïe, respect du lieu, crainte du danger, paresse d'intelligence ou consigne du directeur.[2]

Here in Proust a single act or gesture (or non-act and non-gesture) is multiply transformed by a substitution in its possible motivations; where in Kafka it is the motivation which remains the same (self-preservation), whereas the gestural possibilities are logically varied and experimentally substituted for one another.

But was it not this same Barthes who also theorized the fan-like structure of possibilities and permutations that lay within a single gesture or act, or indeed within the ever more microscopic components of an act? Indeed, in *S/Z* the oddly named proairetic code (*proairesis* means *choice* in Aristotle[3]) designates this fan-like opening up of possibilities:

> Qu'est-ce qu'une suite d'actions? le dépli d'un nom. Entrer? Je peux déplier en: "s'annoncer" et "pénétrer". Partir? Je peux déplier en: "vouloir", "s'arrêter", "repartir".[4]

But for Kafka, we must transform the very structure of the fan itself to include all manner of structural variants, which include a negation (not to do it, then to do it anyway), secondary consequences and the need to address them by lateral acts, all kinds of more general cancellations and revisions, and so forth. The act itself becomes the center of a Greimas square that produces ever new possibilities out of itself and also seems uniquely to document that short-lived structuralist aesthetic whereby closure is reached when all the logical possibilities and permutations are reached, and the finished object, now a work of art, is thereby by definition endowed with value.

The problem with this view lay in its static or non-temporal dynamic, which it evidently owed to its assimilation to logical models as such: in other words, beginning with the basic machinery of something like the Klein group or the Greimas square, no particular direction was given for the inventory of these various logical possibilities, which could be enumerated in any order one liked and which then as the subtlety of the logical instruments became more and more refined, threatened to turn into an infinite series. Greimas's suggestion that the narrative merely generated in turn the solutions proposed by the various faces of the square did not seem to address this problem very adequately. Reidentified as the phenomenon of closure, however, a more abstract solution did seem to propose itself, namely that the work simply exhausted the various possibilities of a given scheme or starting point and then stopped, being at that point complete. This solution left the question of the number of logical possibilities open, but at least satisfied the ancient longing of all aesthetics to theorize the form of closure to be operated by a work or a genre.

But this is at least what we find in Kafka, who can be said to a far greater degree than any other writer to open up a given situation to the whole range of its possibilities—rather than, as in most narratives, to settle for one decisive realization after another—in such a way that of him, uniquely, we may say that he does indeed stop when the possibilities are exhausted and the list comes to an end (no matter whether this closure is designated by the narrator's death or disappearance). No matter, either, when the initial situation seems to offer no alternate possibilities: this is indeed the starting point of "A Report to an Academy": "for the first time in my life I could see no way out" (252/168). But this very absence of possibilities not only becomes the starting point of a new and unexpected permutation (in that case, why not cease to be an ape and turn into a human being?), but also seems to make a new metaphysical statement about human life (defined precisely as the opposite of the ape's "freedom"), and also to approach a kind of reflexive awareness of his own writing procedures themselves, which must pass through the initial "no way out" of the starting point in order to reach this characteristic movement of the careful enumeration of logical alternatives which is the key to Kafka's style.

But this is quite the opposite of inventiveness: it is as though, with the starting point, with the initial situation or given of the text—Gregor as a bug, the ape become human, fasting as a public art—invention ceases and something else takes its place. Inventiveness lies in the starting point alone, the initial inspiration, *Einfall*, datum, unconscious image or whatever; thereafter follows a patient, logical exploration and execution, concluded either by death or by the writer's own boredom as he lets the fragment fall.

This is not the whole story, but it does allow us to posit some initial dissociation within Kafka's work, a peculiar distribution of tasks or division of labor which may well serve to characterize his uniqueness for us at the same time that it raises other questions. We may thus redeploy Coleridge's old distinction between Fancy and Imagination in such a way that Imagination designates this first idea for the text which falls from the ceiling or from heaven—what if I were a bug?—while Fancy then comes to name that laborious and patient process of making an inventory of the consequences in a supremely logical fashion which also libidinally absorbs all the jouissance of the writer's elaboration of each successive sentence (along with the reader's reading of them). This may also go some distance towards solving the problem of the nightmarish or the dystopian in Kafka, which has not often seemed confirmed by the reader's experience even though it ought to be sufficiently documented by the texts themselves. But on the basis of the dissociation proposed here, it will be enough to posit the anxiety of the nightmare as the property of the initial act of Imagination (whether it springs from the unconscious or not), whereas the satisfactions of Fancy, utterly different from that first lightning bolt, are those of production and consumption and result from the rich content of what is now not at all a paralysis but rather a labor and a productivity.

But this duality also determines a duality of interpretations as well, or rather—since this wording seems simply to suggest polysemia or multiple meanings or whatever—an incommensurability of interpretive dynamics and methods. Thus, the psychoanalytic temptation—which could also include the biographical and the historical or political (the omnipresent Austro-Hungarian Empire, the bureaucratic empire and its nomads, the barbarians beyond the wall)—is essentially applicable only to the moment of Imagination, to the setting up of the situation. The execution of the text, the exercise of something like Fancy in the elaboration of the sentences, is not interpretable in this way; even though as we shall see later on it may lend itself to more purely philosophical analysis.

Thus, the crucial theme of the father is clearly enough inscribed in the starting point of "The Metamorphosis": Georg is supporting the family, or if you prefer, the family is exploiting him by way of a duty that has been imposed on him. The father is thus by definition weak, aged, infirm, incapable (both in the sense of the business he has mismanaged and in that of what can be demanded of him in the way of work); and the historically crucial story "The Judgement"—which is virtually the detonator of all of Kafka's mature work—sets up a similar situation, even though here it is the protagonist's complacency with his achievements, his good feeling about himself and his powers, his self-satisfaction and calm happiness, which is presupposed, rather than Gregor's sense of inferiority and subalternity, guilt, self-loathing, and all the other forms of affect that might be associated with being a bug of some kind.

Now clearly in Freudian terms the reversal, whereby Georg's father is unexpectedly transformed into the accuser, the relations are reversed, the father is strong and Georg is weak, corresponds to that "splitting" whereby a "bad" father is separated from a "good" one (Freud's example is another literary work, Hoffmann's "The Sandman"). The bad father figure then becomes the ogre and then even the devil himself, whereas the good one is impotent and unable to shelter or save the hero, whom the bad father positively wishes to harm, as in those primal myths where the father either kills the children (Ivan the Terrible, Philip II), or eats them (Saturn). Only in this temporal reversal, the good father turns into the bad father before our very eyes, and from an invalid becomes a giant: " 'No!' cried his father, cutting short his answer, threw the blankets off with a strength that sent them all flying in a moment and sprang erect in bed" ("The Judgement", 84/83). But in this initial story the transformation is mostly registered in the father's aggressive dialogue. In "The Metamorphosis" the visual and physical transformation is far more evident: "standing there in fine shape ... his black eyes darted fresh and penetrating glances, etc." (121/95); and above all, the following detail: "Gregor was dumbfounded at the enormous size of his shoe soles" (121/95), an observation which ostensibly redramatizes Gregor's new floor-level position and his size, but which does double-duty to suggest the presence of the ogre. Meanwhile, the father of "The Judgement" simply condemns the protagonist to death; while here a good deal more lethal detail is provided, not only the kicks, but above all the little apples with which he pelts his son, the last one breaking the carapace and leaving a festering wound.

Indeed, all of these developments do double-duty, for they are generated by the same alternating logical process which we have identified more generally: the father is either feeble or strong; he either protects or attacks, and so forth. But the dark and baleful content of the Oedipal situation spreads out through the subsequent text and is able to invest such details and such alternation with an electrifying charge, making such moments over into dramatic episodes in their own right.

Indeed, we may go even further than this, and suggest that such dramatic effects are not so much dependent on their psychoanalytic content as they are on the pure form of the reversal as such, the peripeteia. And even the peripeteia itself as pure form is here revealed to be the narrative structure generated by the logical alternations to which we have referred. For "The Judgement" can also be seen as a simple alternation, in which a first position, in which Georg is subject, seeing the world on the outside (in some contentment with it), is then submitted to the opposite logical possibility, in which he becomes object, and is then seen successively through the judging eyes of the father, the friend, the outside world, and so forth. Which is then the primordial form on which the other depends? Without prejudicing the issue with any indefensible generalization or universalizing metaphysical proposition, we may at least affirm that here, in Kafka, if not elsewhere, it seems clear that peripeteia is generated out of logical alternation and is at least in this unique work subordinated to it. Indeed we will see later on, when we come to "The Burrow," that even this apparent struggle between two protagonists, between self and Other, is not really to be grasped as an interpersonal drama but that in fact the seemingly human duel is itself only a projection of the logical system.

And this simplest reversal of all (which has the effect of a reversal from good to bad or vice versa, from center to margin, from inside to outside) can then be inspected in other texts, such as "Jackals and Arabs," where the demonic visions of persecution and revenge of the former are suddenly reversed by the latter's awakening and their bluff common sense and good humor. But it is above all in "The Village Schoolmaster" that this well-nigh permanent reversibility receives something like a definitive form: the modest yet somehow repulsively insidious protagonist ostensibly defends the village schoolmaster, but is at the same time according to the rhythms of alternation put in his place by the latter, in some much enlarged version of the son–father relationship in which the son seeks to help the father in an ambiguous way which also undermines the latter and whose deeper treachery the latter clearly grasps.

Yet it is not to be expected that these uneven and shifting duels between the function of Imagination (as it tends to express personal content of the psychoanalytic type) and the pure form of Fancy as it parses the situation like a sentence and works out one after another all its possible permutations—it is not to be expected that this crucial operation within Kafka's writing, this central mechanism in the production of the texts themselves, would pass unnoticed by whatever regulatory agency controls their interactions and their ratio to one another.

One way of showing this would be to observe that having banned interpretation from the whole of the process by way of limiting it to one instance only, namely that of the Imagination that establishes the initial situation or starting point of the text (its *Einfall*, in musical terms), we have merely opened the door to the return of interpretation on a higher level. Insofar as the content of Imagination is the only one of these instances that really opens on to the outside (or the extrinsic), it has seemed plausible to allow the latter to return in the form of external diagnoses. What this restriction on interpretation has unwittingly and as it were laterally achieved is to generate, however, what looks like a new dualism on the level of the instances themselves, that very opposition of Imagination and Fancy, or of content and execution, which then itself becomes susceptible to interpretation at that higher level in its own right.

But perhaps a different kind of hypothesis will dramatize this development more productively, and it is one that has the advantage of disposing of one of the central topics and enigmas of traditional Kafka criticism. This is the matter of the Law, as it is most notably exemplified in the agonizing uncertainties of the two major novels, and in such shorter texts as the canonical "Before the Law," or the various Chinese-imperial fantasies ("try with all your might to comprehend the decrees of the high command, but only up to a certain point"—"The Great Wall of China", 240/337; "this is a misunderstanding of some kind"—"An Old Manuscript", 417/48; or indeed the very secret of "An Imperial Message"). To the incomprehensibility of this Law may be added the refusal to abrogate it in the story entitled "The Refusal"; or, most movingly of all, the refusal of the mouse people to grant Josephine any exemptions in her obligations as a citizen: "Our people, so easily moved, sometimes cannot be moved at all"; "... the people show themselves here in their cold, judicial aspect ... like a grown-up person deep in thought turning a deaf ear to a child's babble, fundamentally well disposed but not accessible" ("Josephine the Singer, or the Mouse People", 372/204–5, 374/207, where even the shift from "cold" to "well disposed" is an alternation). Here indeed the definitive and nightmarish transformation of the "well-disposed" father into the "cold" and malevolent ogre has been downgraded to a mere moment in the perpetual back and forth of possibilities.

It is no doubt both plausible and inevitable that our own training in Freudianism should lead us to posit the inaccessible Father as the source of the Law and its incomprehensibility: for even the innermost judgements of the daily other are inaccessible to us, let alone those in some absolute Otherness. But I would like to propose a different reading, namely that the Law is simply the aftereffect of the decisionism of the Imagination or the starting point, which can no longer be challenged from within the text. It is thus and not otherwise: no point in wishing it were otherwise or in wondering why it is like that. It is within the fiat of the Imagination that Fancy must now do its humble work, without question, yet full of perpetual wonderment: the theme of the Law is thus ultimately auto-referential. It does not designate the external fact of the biographical father or Oedipus complex, but rather the very structure of this storytelling as such, which imposes the order of the Law on its execution. The latter, which to be sure sometimes even involves a literal execution ("The Judgement", "In the Penal Colony"), rehearses something like the dynamic of André Jolles's *casus*—a universal but empty statute to which the various concrete cases seek to adjust themselves uneasily, returning over and over again to the lack of fit and the new qualifications that the ultimate incommensurability of Universal and Particular always seems to demand.[5]

In a way the ultimate allegory of the Law is to be found in "The Hunter Gracchus," who alone in his immortality as a dead man sailing down through the ages of time and history, and docking intermittently in the latter's ports of call before moving on again, offers a different version of the immutable universal in which nothing changes (Gracchus is dead) and nothing ever happens (he is immortal). His journey, and the history of his anchorages, is then in its interminable formalism not dissimilar from Fancy's task of writing down its sentences (I have elsewhere suggested that Dürer's *Melencolia* is itself an allegory of Fancy and Imagination, the latter the great mourning angel in black, the former the cherub endlessly scribbling on its sheets of paper).

But to say that Imagination is the place of interpretation is not at all to say that Fancy has no relationship to the latter. Its interminable logical alternations cannot, to be sure, be interpreted in their own right: but it can be said that the reason this instance is not subject to interpretation lies in the paradoxical fact that it is itself a virtual frenzy of interpretation as such. We might have adduced "Report to an Academy" or "The Village Schoolmaster" as the very prototypes of such an interpretive process, each one indeed beginning with an incomprehensible given or starting point (the now inaccessible freedom of the initial ape nature, or the appearance of the giant mole itself, never adequately accounted for), if we did not already possess, in "Investigations of a Dog", an almost explicit demonstration of the interpretive drive along with a permanently thwarted attempt to explain this very vocation, one which significantly involves sexuality and music, silence and collectivity.

But it is rather to an equally unpublished or posthumous work, "The Burrow", that we turn in order to observe the moment in which the very theme of Fancy's productivity seems to rise to the surface in a well-nigh thematic way. For here it is not the unfolding events themselves which disclose their contradictory possibilities one after another, it is rather the possibility of those possibilities which is narrated. The nameless narrator (another unspecified Kafka animal of some sort) describes his burrow in an orderly way, from entrance to central storage room (*Burgplatz*, here translated "castle keep"); yet with each detail there rise the ghostly alternatives of what it might have been better to have done in its place; and satisfaction at the completion of the burrow, the comforts of its isolation and stillness, increasingly alternate with a sense of the vulnerability of the protagonist whose apprehensions rise to the point at which it is the very burrow itself which turns out to be the very source of the danger:

> Simply by virtue of being owner of this great vulnerable edifice I am obviously defenseless against any serious attack. The joy of possessing it has spoiled me, the vulnerability of the burrow has made me vulnerable; any wound to it hurts me as if I myself were hit (355/440).

Still, this seemingly climactic peripeteia is reached on the heels of any number of smaller ones, themselves organized according to the recto and verso of a narrative perspective in which we are first shown the burrow from the inside, until the narrator decides that it is more prudent to guard it by observing approaches to it on the outside, concealing himself in view of the entryway ("at such times it is as if I were not so much looking at my house as at myself sleeping, and had the joy of being in a profound slumber and simultaneously of keeping vigilant guard over myself"—334/420).

In keeping with some ancient pre-Hegelian rhythm of triplicity, the third part of the novella then witnesses the return of the protagonist to the inside, and catalogues not only his now unrealizable plans for strengthening the burrow's defenses and rebuilding it in all kinds of new ways, but also summons up the mirage of a ghostly yet hostile and ferocious other fatally burrowing its way towards the site with the murderous intent of a final encounter. But this other, whose threat becomes more and more imaginable as the novella prolongs itself, has already been sketched out by the movements of the narrator, whose positioning as an observer outside the burrow (in the second "movement" of the novella) offers a virtual acting out of the role of the alien predator itself. Here, then, as elsewhere in Kafka, the apparent other or interlocutor/enemy proves to offer something like a projection of the protagonist/narrator himself, whose weakness calls for the strength of the other, whose guilt and abjection call for the latter's judgement, even his moments of satisfaction deserving the emergence of an other who can rebuke and denounce him. Yet it is worth insisting that such projection is less a psychological than a logical matter: the other is in that case simply the negative of the self, the alternate possibility, the logical variation, the outside of an inside. For in Kafka, as we shall see shortly, the true Other of the self is not another self but rather the collectivity as such.

"The Burrow" is thus a significant document for our argument here insofar as it marks a level of reflexivity in which it is not the enumeration of the various logical possibilities itself, so much as the consciousness of that enumeration which constitutes the surface of the tale (or its *isotopie*, as Greimas calls it). We do not here, as in "The Metamorphosis" or indeed in most standard narration, follow the events as they succeed each other: emphasis is displaced from objectivity to what it would be better none too hastily to call subjectivity, so that it is the imagining of the various alternatives that the sentences narrate. The dualism of the Kafka narrative, which we have allegorized as the opposition between Imagination and Fancy, is now revealed to be that of self and consciousness. That "self" or identity—about which so much of modern philosophy teaches us that it is not the same as consciousness, that it is itself an object for that impersonal stream of consciousness which has no identity in its own right—that self becomes defined by the initial situation, the inspiration or *Einfall*, the *donnée* or datum of the point of departure: Fancy meanwhile, the enumeration of the logical alternatives, the slow piling up of one sentence after another, now takes the place of consciousness itself, that medium from which we can never (even in sleep) really free ourselves, but which for the most part we ignore by way of our *In-der-Welt-sein*, our practical distraction in the world's business, only in such moments of obsession as we find here coming to reassert its inescapable presence and the human requirement that we keep on thinking one thought after another.

For if the imagined situation is the place of *Angst* or anxiety, this execution of the tireless composition of successive sentences is that of *Sorge*, which the Heideggerians dutifully translate as Care, but which it is surely more appropriate to identify as Worry: constantly leaping ahead of ourselves and thinking of the next step, very much in the spirit of the *pro* and *contra*, the imagined consequences of first this and then that logical alternative. *Sorge* is for Heidegger the central and permanent experience of human reality (or *Dasein*), yet as he presents it, intensifying and dramatizing Worry in order for it to become visible in its own right, he thereby tends to lend its enlargement pathological features which we may also recognize as those of that "obsessional neurosis" dear to French psychiatry and in particular to Lacan (for whom it is the alternate typological category to the more familiar hysteria). Both these concepts, both these terms, are diagnoses and interpretations of the phenomenon we found in Kafka, and they have no particular force or validity except to underscore the role this phenomenon has played in any number of modern systems. Indeed, it would be tempting to search for other such equivalents, perhaps locating one in the very habits of bureaucracy (from *Bouvard et Pécuchet* to "Bartleby" and beyond), in which the imperatives of correctness and legality inspire a fear that determines a constant monitoring of the self. But this social equivalent is no more binding on us (despite its biographical relevance) than the other existential or psychoanalytic representations or models. All these diagnoses are interpretations of what in Kafka's text remains an unnamed and unique dynamic of production and a kind of perpetual present of the text in that very process of producing itself. The more interesting question is thereby avoided by such interpretations, namely of how it is that this obligation imposed on the reader—to live through every movement of consciousness in its worrying exploration of all the alternatives—an imprisonment in sentences which Kafka's former ape would certainly have characterized by the words "no way out!"—of how it is that such an experience can determine the jouissance and the passionate libidinal investment to which we have already referred.

All of which presupposes a text in which nothing happens (and which perhaps might bear more resemblance to a novel of Beckett than to the present stories); but we have omitted until now the unexpected peculiarity of what may be called the third and final movement of so many of these texts, very much including "The Burrow." For what begins to happen here is that the temporality which was only implicit in the execution of the text and the piling up of its sentences and alternatives, now becomes foregrounded in its own right, making itself felt less as a new theme than as a new kind of weariness, which is in many cases even a weariness with weariness itself. Slowly time begins to spread through these sentences like an immense stain; the protagonist suddenly begins to grow old; the alarming situation itself becomes familiar to the point of revulsion. So it is that poor Gregor sinks to the level of being a mere nuisance, a familiar but annoying daily burden along with so many others, an awkward fact of life it is permitted to grow impatient with, and to wish to get rid of. The narrator of "The Burrow" now realizes his mistakes and what he should have done or built in the first place, but no longer has any energy to do so. Josephine, meanwhile, in the most sublime of Kafka's stories, fades back into the crowd and disappears, "being forgotten like all her brothers" (376/209).

It is an instructive warning: the deepening and hastening of the passage of time, the realization that time passing inscribes itself in ageing, is here conjoined with forgetting, with consignment to oblivion: and yet in the usual unexpected changing of valences, being forgotten is no longer a negative or painful matter but rather a source of euphoria, a glorious destiny, a happy ending: redemptive or providential accents which in Kafka are somehow more precious than they would be in writers of more cheerful or optimistic dispositions. This is no doubt the euphoria that can only be properly experienced in melancholy and at the price of the latter.

Yet it is not the only tonality that the renewed temporality of these third movements (which are not yet codas, such as the panther in "A Hunger Artist") can convey. For whatever the redemptive possibilities, there is also the waning of a whole world to consider, as the classical sketches above all make us feel. Consider the slow degradation of the legends of Prometheus: according to the final version "everyone grew weary of the meaningless affair. The gods grew weary, the eagles grew weary, the wound closed wearily. There remained the inexplicable mass of rock" ("Prometheus," 432/351). Somewhat like Freud's peculiar notion of "the waning of the Oedipus complex," there is in these narratives equally a kind of waning of the original situation, in weariness and boredom, in the stagnation of a present that has grown too familiar to notice: and now the text and its sentences express this weary passage of time before breaking off altogether, or shifting keys in some final reversal.

Yet the world is also to be blamed for this gradual withdrawal of interest, as the fate of the horse of Alexander the Great makes clear: "people tell themselves that, modern society being what it is, Bucephalus is in a difficult position ... Nowadays—it cannot be denied—there is no Alexander the Great ... no one, no one at all, can blaze a trail to India ... Today the gates have receded to remoter and loftier places" ("The New Advocate," 415/139–40). Accordingly, Bucephalus takes to his law books and becomes an advocate. The god Poseidon, meanwhile, is in the *entzauberte Welt* of modern bureaucracy and modern bourgeois people, reduced to being the chief administrator of Earth's waters: "here he was sitting in the depths of the world's ocean endlessly going over the accounts, an occasional visit to Jupiter being the only interruption of the monotony" (435/354).

But it is in the fateful destiny of the hunger artist that we can most clearly observe the deleterious effects, not only of fashion but of the fickle tastes of the modern middle-class public. Yet it is in the changes in the latter that temporality and the passage of time can alone be registered, even though the beginnings of this "change in public interest" are difficult to pinpoint: "It seemed to happen almost overnight; there may have been profound causes for it, but who was going to bother about that; at any rate the pampered hunger artist suddenly found himself deserted one fine day by the amusement-seekers, who went streaming past him to other more-favored attractions" (273/189).

This anti-modernist Kafka, for whom change and neglect are identified with the coming of the banal and drab bourgeois world with its fashions and superficial crazes, would seem to imply nostalgia for a different one, situated in an all but forgotten past. But I think this is not the case with Kafka: the old imperial world of horsemen and barbarians, of the great wall and the forbidden city, is I think scarcely the object of regret, even though the collectivity it includes and produces within and against itself, the "we" of the harassed artisans and tradesmen in "An Old Manuscript," is very much more to the point. There is indeed here some kinship with Brecht's peasantry, this village collectivity of the shtetl and the obedient townspeople, who "play" at sleeping "in houses, in safe beds, under a safe roof" whereas "in reality they have flocked together as they had once upon a time and again later in a deserted region, a camp in the open, a countless number of men, an army, a people, under the cold sky on cold earth" (436/354, "At Night"). And this is no doubt very much Josephine's mouse people, short-lived, permanently threatened and vulnerable, and designating a first-person plural voice to the anonymous chronicler who prophecies forgetfulness and oblivion. But I think this is not nostalgia, and that it is the historical and political greatness of Kafka to have refused subjective *Angst* and the individualism of interpersonal relations and to have reinvented this truly epic structure in which the only viable partner of the lone named individual is the collective itself, the tribe, the people.

This mood-swing, this salvational euphoria, the unexpected reversal of the very dialectic of affect, is not personal or individual: its condition of possibility does not lie in the people who participate in it, and whose selfish intrication in their own interests—now we can marry our daughter, etc.—does not stain the final elevation with any *irony*. For very precisely this moment signals the disappearance of the categories of the individual and of the personality, which have died with Gregor, and the passing of the world into a state beyond human individuals, such as has also been characteristic of modern philosophy, with the return of Heidegger from an individualistic existentialism to the being of the pre-Socratics, or the displacement, in Deleuze, of psychology or existentialism by great supraindividualistic forces and rhythms. Here also, for better or for worse, we are granted the briefest of glimpses into such a world of forces and *Stimmungen*, the very moods and affect of being itself.

This final upswing is characteristic of much of Kafka's work, as with the panther at the end of "A Hunger Artist," who replaces the latter's feebleness, guilt and failure with the vibrancy of sheer life. But in the very last text, something even more peculiar happens to what stands as the equivalent of the final "happy ending" of this type. For Josephine vanishes, and is at the same time then raised into the pantheon of the heroes and legendary demigods of the mouse people: the usual happy ending by way of glory and posterity handed down to us from Homer and by now a little shopworn in the process. For that traditional apotheosis involved the construction and prolongation of some properly historical memory, one no doubt to be reinvented and recreated by generations of bards and praise-singers (of which, incidentally, Josephine was never one in the first place). But the mouse people have no history ("generally speaking we ignore historical research entirely"), and therefore there is no register or element in which Josephine's immortal name can be preserved and handed on down. In fact, therefore, she will gradually (or swiftly, given the rapidity of the generational changeover among the mice) be forgotten: and it is this which makes up the uniqueness of her final destiny, and of the final ending of this last story of all: for it is in being forgotten that Josephine will have become immortal, her glory lies precisely in this oblivion (which she shares with all the lives of the mouse people), her apotheosis lies very precisely in her utter disappearance from the world and from collective memory: "she will rise to the heights of redemption and be forgotten like all her brothers." And this also seems to be how Kafka, who asked that all his works and manuscripts be burned, turned his own imminent death into some sort of bizarre happy ending, "afin que," as the Marquis de Sade says in his Testament, "les traces de ma tombe disparaissent de dessus la surface de la terre comme je me flatte que ma mémoire s'effacera de l'esprit des hommes ..."[6]

But there remains a final turn of the screw: for, history or not, Josephine's name has survived, by being told by someone who is precisely not a a bard or a singer, but rather the prototypical representative of the Kafka collective enunciator, who says "we" and who folds back into the masses of the mouse people, representing them at the same time that he affirms their quintessential anonymity. Thus there is a praise song after all, and the people who have no historical memory and to whom others must give or lend a voice, here remember and exercise their collective voice—witnesses, like the builders of the great wall or the other spectatorial and passive generations who fill Kafka's works—distant and somehow unmoved, objective without any lack of sympathy: very much like that calm implacable unshakable refusal opposed to her demand for special exemptions—"a cold, judicial aspect ... a stony imperturbable front"—such is the patient enumeration of Josephine's excesses, her peculiarities, her inexplicable greatness, as well as of the perplexity at accounting for all these things. It is as though this ultimate emergence of the collective voice, of the people's impersonal narrator, was the final stroke in the eclipse of those individual characters or named personalities of which Josephine was the last. Her disappearance is thus a peculiar and yet self-defeating triumph of the collectivity, to which its dialectical union of opposites lends a single piping note indistinguishable from silence.

(*2005*)

Notes

1 All page references in text are to English edition followed by German edition. Franz Kafka, *Complete Stories* (New York, 1995); *Sämtliche Erzählungen* (Frankfurt, 1973).
2 See Marcel Proust, *A l'ombre*, vol. II (Paris, 1987–1989), p. 26.
3 Aristotle, *Nichomachean Ethics*, book III, chapter 2.
4 Roland Barthes, *S/Z* (Paris, 1970), p. 88.
5 André Jolles, "Kasus" in *Einfache Formen* (Tübingen, 1982).
6 D.A.F. de Sade, *Oeuvres*, vol. II (Paris, 1966). Gilbert Lély, *Vie de Sade* (Paris, 1965), p. 632.

5

Allegory and History: On Rereading *Doktor Faustus*

Is Thomas Mann outmoded? It is a question that engages both form and content (unless that distinction is equally outmoded). To be sure, *Buddenbrooks* is a classic (but that is just another way of becoming outmoded); while the great debates of *The Magic Mountain* between liberalism and communism (or fascism) are now, for many, equally dated. Who has ever read the *Joseph* tetralogy (the question can probably be translated into the obsolescence of the New Deal)? As for *Doktor Faustus*, a work for which even the most dismissive critics are sometimes willing to make an exception, is its equation of Nazism with diabolism really relevant any longer, in a world-historical situation in which neither Nazism nor diabolism any longer exist: which is to say that both the problem (Nazism) and the solution (the Devil, evil) have now vanished from History (or, what amounts to the same thing, have entered it). Unlike Proust, Joyce or Kafka, it is said, Mann never really challenged the mode of the realistic novel he inherited from the nineteenth century; in addition, he reveled in a mandarin role which is no longer socially available: the great and public Man of Letters, as opposed to the unlucky genius or bohemian outsider as which so many of the other "great moderns" can be identified (that he should endlessly have written about this very opposition—the children of light, Goethe and Tolstoy, versus the children of darkness, Nietzsche and Dostoyevsky—may only be thought to have rubbed it in further). In this respect, we may feel about Mann as we sometimes feel about Aristotle's recipe for happiness (healthy and male, rich, intellectually inclined, with large and prosperous family). These reactions cannot be refuted, since they are generational, which is to say, historical; they can only be radically displaced by readings no longer complicit with the older stereotype.

I

For one thing, *Doktor Faustus* is only a nineteenth-century realistic novel in appearance: it does not proceed by the accumulation of one scene after another, but rather offers a series of foreshortenings only occasionally enlivened by the flash glimpse of a gesture (as often verbal as corporeal). The scenes we are offered in a traditional spectatorial way (shot, countershot, full dialogue) tend in fact to be those from which the narrator was absent (the conversation in which Adrian requests Rudi's intermediation in the marriage proposal, for example). To be sure, the narrator always anticipates our "objections," which is to say our aesthetic attention to this punctum or peculiarity:

> ... what happened and how it happened—I know, let the objection be ten times raised that I could not know it because I was not there. No, I was not there. But today it is psychological fact that I was there, for whoever has lived a story like this, lived it through, as I have lived this one, that frightful intimacy makes him an eye- and ear-witness even to its hidden phases (XLI; LP 434; W 455; D 648).[1]

As a formal disclaimer this is exceedingly weak and unconvincing; but we have to understand it in a different way, namely that the structural feature (direct versus indirect narrative, presentation rather than relation) also includes another symbolic meaning, above and beyond its own fact of existence. Zeitblom's absence/presence is that of Thomas Mann himself, with respect to the Germany whose destiny he is narrating without sharing it: symbolically then, the formal feature has its own signifying role to play and exists in itself and not merely for its instrumental function in advancing the narrative. We must thus be very careful in observing and enumerating the formal peculiarities of this novel, about which I will suggest that they are also allegorical. In recent criticism, I believe that the notion of an "ideology of form," that of the possibility of an ideological message vehiculated by the form of a work rather than by its content, has come to be widely accepted. Here, we must come to terms with something like the reflexivity of that process: an artwork which, only too aware of the ideological and signifying properties of form as such, draws them into itself and internalizes and repotentiates them in the form of what I am calling allegory. (To be sure, it does not thereby escape ideology as such, a dimension which is properly inescapable in class society: but generates its own ideological functions and overtones at a higher level, an inevitability which can be identified as a kind of Gödel's law of the social.)

But the foreshortening I have been discussing—the predominance of telling over showing, the essentially indirect and mediated character of the narration (*récit* rather than *roman*, to use a terminology that Gide popularized from Ramon Fernandez)—is scarcely to be grasped in a privative or negative way, since its dialectical result is the production of an artistically rich opposite number, what I will call anecdotal gesturality. This is the way in which a long evocation, of discussions, speeches, situations, the characteristics of a situation, suddenly crystallizes in a single vivid narrative event, such as the French peasant woman shaking her fist at the German troops and crying, "*Je suis la dernière! [...] Méchants! Méchants! Méchants!*" (XXXI; LP310; W327; D464). The whole of World War One is here encapsulated, nothing further in the way of concretion needing to be added; and I have characterized such moments in terms of Brechtian gesturality (the *gestus*) rather than in the conventional terminology of the image, in order to underscore the productive energy of such moments, the way in which one feels the narrative palpably to contract and to bring a single quotable expressive dramatic feature into being, which is at one and the same time the climax of a certain temporal and narrative process. The narrative is comparable to an oratorio rather than to an opera: long choral and orchestral sections (long patches of indirect discourse) are then punctuated by the occasional formal aria or "number." Nothing like this in Proust or Joyce, or even, I believe, in *The Magic Mountain*; and it is what, in a famous letter to Adorno, Thomas Mann himself (perhaps inexactly, in the light of the Eisensteinian tradition) terms *montage*, namely the insertion of materials quoted from other often historic sources.[2] I call this anecdotal because it is precisely this kind of striking detail that we do tend to pass on to other people in the form of the anecdote: so that this one, from the German troop movements in France during World War One, might well have been something Mann heard from a witness, or found set down in a book of memoirs.

For the most part, however, these are essentially verbal gestures (and indeed the literature of the anecdote tends overwhelmingly, like that of jokes, to turn on the *pointe* or punchline): thus at the end of a long summary of his "speculations" on the elements, on arriving at those inorganic compounds which imitate organic life as though longing for transubstantiation into the higher form, Adrian's father murmurs, tears coming into his eyes, "Und dabei sind sie tot!" (III; LP20; W23; D35: "and for all that, they are dead!")—a reflexion which not unsurprisingly causes his son to shake with poorly repressed laughter. Such is also the termination of one of Kretschmar's great lectures, which marry the practice of pedagogy to modernist narration as such (see below), but also endow the former with the extraordinary materiality of the stuttering of Adrian's teacher. The account of the latter is already dramatic and gestural:

> Inevitably, from time to time, while constantly and only too justifiably awaited, came the moment of disaster; and there he stood with red, swollen face on the rack; whether stuck on a sibilant, which he weathered with wide-stretched mouth,

> making the noise of an engine giving off steam; or wrestling with a labial, his cheeks puffed out, his lips launched into a crackling quick-fire of short, soundless explosions; or finally, when with his breathing in helpless disorder, his mouth like a funnel, he would gasp for breath like a fish out of water; laughing with tears in his eyes, for it is a fact that he himself seemed to treat the thing as a joke. (VIII; LP50; W54; D77–8)

But this is not yet the anecdotal *pointe*: it is what happens all the time, and not the unique event, once and for all. Indeed, it is an exercise of that malicious and satiric art of portraiture which is also a specialty of this writer and an equally old-fashioned form, as we shall see in a moment. It is as though in this late work—and in pronouncing this expression the reference to Adorno's famous essay on "Beethoven's Late Style"[3] (itself "quoted" and inserted into the montage of one of Kretschmar's lectures) is obligatory—the various skills and strengths Thomas Mann drew on and combined to produce the narrative density of his earlier works here began to separate out from each other and to be exercised independently, in a kind of bravura isolation, in cadenzas designed specifically for their exhibition.

Here at any rate is the anecdotal climax of the tortured delivery, at the moment when the stutterer is evoking that "universal machine" that is the piano:

> But piano lessons should not be—or not essentially and not first and last—lessons in a special ability, but lessons in m–m–
>
> "Music!" cried a voice from the tiny audience, for the speaker could simply not get the word out, often as he had used it before, but kept on mumbling the *m*.
>
> "Yes, of course," said he, released and relieved. Took a swallow of water and went his way. (VIII; LP62; W69; D96)

The stutterer is released—and this is to be taken in an almost theological sense, in the very spirit in which Prospero "releases" Ariel at the end of *The Tempest*: "Then to the elements. Be free, and fare thou well!"—the words Adrian speaks at the death of little Nepomuk (XLV; LP479; W503; D714). Clearly, the disability plays a thematic role as well, and by placing a barrier to language (as well as foregrounding its sonorous, yet dissonant and rhythmic dimension) leaves only the non-verbal language of music open to us. Meanwhile Kretschmar's teaching is now susceptible to registration in its energy level, in the degree of force necessary to overcome the impediment, thereby preparing us for the formulation that will both identify it and give us an early clue about Adrian's vocation itself, and the peculiar nature of his fate: underscored by the all-important comment, heightened by the anecdotal format into well-nigh italic emphasis, which concludes this all-important chapter:

> "A gift of life like music," I responded, "not to say a gift of God, one ought not to explain by mocking antinomies, which only bear witness to the fullness of her nature. One must love her."
>
> "Do you consider love the strongest emotion?" he asked.
>
> "Do you know a stronger?"
>
> "Yes, interest." (VII; LP69; W76–7; D107)

Zeitblom's reply functions as the translation, the thematic transfer onto other allegorical levels, which will be developed in the later sections of the novel:

> "By which you presumably mean a love from which the animal warmth has been withdrawn."

And Adrian's reply then confirms the anecdote and seals the chapter with the gesture of opening:

> "Let's agree on the definition!" he laughed. "Good night!"
>
> We had got back to the Leverkühn house and he opened his door.

"Interest" thus points ahead to coldness and to a purely intellectual and "inhuman" obsession, but backwards towards Kretschmar's pedagogy:

> Wendell Kretschmar honoured the principle, which we repeatedly heard from his lips, first formed by the English tongue, that to arouse interest was not a question of the interest of others, but of our own; it could only be done, but then infallibly was, if one was fundamentally interested in a thing oneself, so that when one talked about it one could hardly help drawing others in, infecting them with it, and so creating an interest up to then not present or dreamed of. And that was worth a great deal more than catering to one already existent. (VIII; LP50–51; W55; D78–79)

Obscurely, this conception of pedagogy communicates in a subterranean way with what Mann himself described as "montage,"[4] but now a "montage" of his own interests (rather than the Eisensteinian montage of spectatorial "attractions")—and also at one and the same time with a modernist conception of the "Book of the World" which includes, as we shall see later on, the epistemological dimensions of the world itself. The novel thereby projects its own disposable canon, much like contemporary theory.

Still, the redefinition of the older and more familiar effects that have been called on to define the aesthetic—catharsis, beauty, emotion (the being moved to tears or laughter), empathy and the like—in terms of "interest" now conceived as an all-consuming fiery-cold passion and a hyper-intellectuality marks yet another way in which the novel interiorizes and thematizes its own mode of reading and attention, and makes our own relationship to the text into an allegory of its deeper and more sinister secrets.

Of course the pedagogical lecture—like the sermon itself, of which the Devil's account of hell to Adrian, comparable only to the great sermon in *Portrait of the Artist as a Young Man*, is an extraordinary sample, deeply rooted in the horrendous tirades of the Thirty Years' War on both confessional sides—may also be considered as an archaic form of genre, inserted into a text that comes more and more to resemble Frye's omnibus or encyclopedic form. Clearly, however, the satiric portrait (mentioned above) is just such an archaic form in its own right, which reaches its fullest development in the French classical period, from LaBruyère's *Caractères* and Saint-Simon's incidental portraits in the *Mémoires*, but which stretches back to antiquity and the literary practices of the Roman Empire. It is clearly no accident that such portraits and literary caricatures should be associated with social spaces so sophisticated (or decadent, depending on your point of view) as the era of Petronius or the *grand siècle*, with which it is fitting to associate pre-World War One Munich or the Weimar era (one understands that this extraordinary gallery of upper-class social types originated in a satirical project Mann abandoned at the time, but returned to quarry during World War Two in the *Faustus* project). But here the satire is sharpened by a historical prognosis more sharply focused than any moralizing denunciation of social degeneracy or decline: for the comedy (see Chapters XXVIII and XXXIV) lies in the contrast between the mentalities of these highly specialized and cultured intellectuals and the political regression they call for: the sacrifice of the bourgeois individual to the renewed "Gemeinschaft," and the denunciation of parliamentary democracy in favor of a new authoritarianism (of which Sorel and Mussolini are the heralds). This is thus the comedy of pre-fascism, and an exploration of the emergence of a Hitlerian climate, not among the poor, the unemployed and the veterans who made up the bulk of Nazi voters, but rather in the intelligentsia and the social elite.

This series of borrowed fixed forms and genres, to which we must add the chapter-long solo monologue of Saul Fitelberg (XXXVII), an ostentatiously bravura piece if there ever was one, are less to be considered as parodies (in Adrian's sense) than as pastiche, and as formal allusions (comparable to the more customary thematic or verbal ones). It is thus unsurprising that at the end of this enumeration we must register the appearance of "the novel" itself: the bourgeois melodrama, which finds its rich unfolding in the sad story of the Rodde family, with its tragic climax in the fate of Rudi (one does not exactly want to include the final episode of the miraculous child, which might perhaps stand as the sublimation of bourgeois melodrama if not even its sublime). It is clear why Mann needed to impose these otherwise interpolated narratives on top of his fundamental narrative line of an artistic life which, after its initial formation (and the diabolical events which supply its energy), is necessarily reduced to a series of imaginary works without much action. Yet this structural necessity is then overdetermined and redeemed by the variety of smaller fixed forms, perhaps less reminiscent of Joyce and *Ulysses*, than of Alban Berg's *Wozzeck*, also constructed out of a variety of traditional fixed forms which remain subcutaneous to the operatic narrative.[5]

Whatever the necessity of this purely formal montage of traditional organizational figures and patterns, however, it also corresponds to the deepest subject of the work itself: the impossibility of the new, the return of the archaic. On the political level, this combination of a new technological Novum with the most archaic revivals (hyperrationality with irrationality) corresponds to Nazism itself, of which Heidegger thought for a while that it had succeeded in finding a historically original use of technological modernization in the service of Being,[6] but whose innovative combinations of new industrial possibilities (the radio, the VW, the Autobahn, television, etc.) with the pseudo-archaic rituals of the Nuremburg rallies and the like are well-known. On the level of art, it is precisely the demands made by modernity/modernism that determine Adrian's desperate pact. Not only is the making of art increasingly difficult, after the immense musical developments of the nineteenth century, but all achievement has become inhuman in its demands in the twentieth century:

> I had I suppose a good toward wit and gifts graciously given me from above which I could have used in all honor and modesty, but felt all-too well: it is the time when uprightly and in pious sober wise, naught of work is to be wrought and art grown unpossible without the divel's help and fires of hell under the cauldron ... (XLVII; LP499; D744; W523)

Thus Adrian, in his final public confession (where the undertone of Luther's skepticism about the efficacy of "good works" is still alive); nor is this merely to be read in an aesthetic sense, but in that full desperation of the anti-modernist tradition, of which Heidegger's diagnosis of technology remains more alive than many other strands. And it is equally important to understand the outmoding of *Doktor Faustus* (if such a thing has taken place) in that same spirit, in a postmodernity which no longer fears technology, or in which, in other words, nature itself has been effaced (nature now itself having become genetic and ecological technology); and also because the very structure of the technology in question—no longer heavy-industrial but cybernetic—has altered beyond recognition. It is not so much the diabolical features which the postmodern eschews as unacceptable romanticism, but very precisely this sense of the human impotence conditioned by a technological age and the increasingly insuperable difficulties faced by the individual in praxis and poesis alike. The Frankfurt School dramatized this diminution in subjective autonomy by comparing it to the way in which the great trusts and monopolies, the great corporations, superseded that first age of entrepreneurship of which the robber barons were still the heroic emblems.

Yet the remarks of the Devil carefully enumerate the aesthetic forms in which this socio-economic or world-historical crisis inscribes itself:

> Every composer of the better sort carries within himself a canon of the forbidden, the self-forbidding, which by degrees includes all the possibilities of tonality, in other words all traditional music. (XXV; LP239; D358; W254–5)

This is very specifically Adorno's theory of the modern, or at least of modernism's telos, the ceaseless drive for ever-greater innovation, the restless search for the Novum, the "hunger and thirst" for which in art is as great as that for accumulation in capital, according to a famous observation of Marx. Yet Adorno's remarkable philosophical "solution" to the conundrum of this strange spectacle is to invert it into a negative or privative formulation. It is not because the new and novelty are attractive in their own right: it is rather because the old and traditional have become unacceptable and taboo, that modernism is driven forward into the unknown.[7] Forms wear out, tonal effects are no longer audible, the emotions themselves become stereotypical and caricatural, familiar words cease to have any bite or power, the color schemes are banal and the tastes of an older art insipid. And to be reckoned into this wholesale deterioration is the immense expansion of art and culture as such, in the light of which it is increasingly problematical to do anything at all that has not been repeated over and over again.

There are two solutions to this historical dilemma, both of which Adrian refuses. This first is the well-known resort to parody, to the manipulation of dead forms in a kind of second-degree construction:

> I: "A man could know that and recognize freedom above and beyond all critique. He could heighten the play, by playing with forms out of which, as he well knew, life has disappeared."
>
> He: "I know, I know. Parody. It might be fun, if it were not so melancholy in its aristocratic nihilism. Would you promise yourself much pleasure and profit from such tricks?"
>
> I (retort angrily): "No." (XXV; LP 241; W 257; D 362)

The second solution is the equally famous "end of art":

> The prohibitive difficulties of the work lie deep in the work itself. The historical movement of the musical material has turned against the self-contained work. It

> shrinks in time, it scorns extension in time, which is the dimensions of a musical work, and lets it stand empty. Not out of impotence, not out of incapacity to give form. Rather from a ruthless demand for compression, which taboos the superfluous, negates the phrase, shatters the ornament, stands opposed to any extension of time, which is the life-form of the work. Work, time, and pretence [*Schein*], they are one, and together they fall victim to critique. It no longer tolerates pretence and play, the fiction, the self-glorification of form, which censors the passions and human suffering, divides out the parts, translates into pictures. Only the non-fictional is still permissible, the unplayed, the undisguised and untransfigured expression of suffering in its actual moment. Its impotence and extremity are so ingrained that no seeming play with them is any longer allowed. (XXV; LP241; W256; D360–1)

This also Adrian repudiates ("Touching, touching: the devil waxes pathetic. The poor devil moralizes. Human suffering goes to his heart. How high-mindedly he shits on art!"). What remains is no doubt what Adrian himself is supposed, with the Devil's help, to have achieved during his most productive years, namely the great Oeuvre itself, "late style" as such the Book of the World, *opera mundi*,[8] indeed not one but two of them (shades of Joyce!), whose cosmic reach defines the objective (*Apocalypse*) and the subjective (*Lamentations*) alike; and may be thought to project Mann's ambitions for his own book, but in some sense (Ernst Bloch's) as a work-to-come, as the not-yet-existent, which is according to Bloch the ontological hole at the center of the artist's novel as such.[9] Indeed, if it is preferable to consider all works, especially the most ambitious, as failures, then it becomes clearer how "loser wins" (to use Sartre's phrase) and how a failure—incomplete, fragmentary, and even unrealizable, in the impossibility of all representation—can become a success by projecting its own concept in the absence of its realization. In that sense, *Doktor Faustus* projects the idea of an art that does not yet exist and perhaps never could.

II

Such are some of the formal considerations to which this novel gives rise; but we have not yet mentioned something that is neither form nor genre, namely allegory, which can at best be grasped at what Hjelmslev might call the "form of the content." It is crucial, for the understanding of allegory, that it not be confused with symbols or with metaphorical processes in general, with which, to be sure, this novel is well-provided. Our initial training in this kind of reading takes place early, in Chapter III, in the portrait of Adrian's father and his hobby of "speculating the elements," a detail of which has already been touched on above. In the organic sections of this rather alchemical lesson, however, we are treated to an exhaustive and unforgettable survey of camouflage in the animal kingdom, and in particular to the ways in which a certain butterfly (*Hetaera esmeralda*) insinuates itself into the landscape, its wings transparent save for breathtaking spots of color (similar creatures are avoided by predators despite their beauty and owing to thei: loathsome taste and poisonous attributes). That this particular lepidopteron becomes a personal symbol for Adrian (the letters of its name later on forming a recurrent musical theme or row) is, to be sure, part of the book's official business. The theme of mimesis, however, which the chapter also insistently vehiculates and foregrounds, is another matter. No doubt, Thomas Mann found it, complete with a rich apparatus of materials and illustrations, in a famous work of Roger Caillois[10] which also (independently) startled and impressed Walter Benjamin and Mann's later "musical-advisor"-to-be, T.W. Adorno. Mimesis is here, however, grasped as a dimension of the material universe, and indeed a kind of universal law, whose operations, as we have seen, Adrian's father detects in the inorganic as well as the organic world. Here, then, the novel seems to be pushing at its own limits, and straining to take in, far beyond the little provincial town of Kaisersaschern and indeed far beyond the special case of Germany itself, the whole warp and woof of the physical universe. It is an impression only reinforced later on, when in the immediate pre-World War One Munich period (in Chapter XXVII) Adrian playfully sets to music a kind of Jules Verne tale of a descent into the deep in a diving bell, and the wondrous luminescent creatures to be found there. Here too a whole realm of what may indifferently be called scientific content or cosmological perspectives is inserted into the text in order to enlarge its framework or indeed its frame of reference.

Indeed, the Book of the World wishes to be cosmological as well as historical and psychological; it wishes to devise an instrumentarium such that physics and chemistry, the subatomic and the dust of the galaxies, can be registered and "set to music." From Dante to Joyce, such works scarcely rise to the occasion unless they make an effort to envelop and include the science of their period. From our current perspective, these efforts can be identified as the features of a first, pre-Christian and Alexandrian allegorical tradition, whose fundamental characteristic consists in its tripartite organization. This particular kind of allegory was developed in order to endow the Homeric poems—the basic texts of classical pedagogy—with overtones and meanings, intellectual and disciplinary content, which would today be considered arbitrary and awkward. Thus a literal level of this or that Homeric battlefield, strewn with a still-unparalleled butchery and carnage, is read on another level as the battle between the virtues and the vices: this is the not unfamiliar moral level that continues on through Prudentius and the *Roman de la rose*, and has done so much, in its clumsy literality, to discredit allegory in general. But the scientific materials we have been discussing point to a less familiar third level which seals the form and lends Alexandrian or tripartite allegory its structural originality: this is the level of the cosmological, in which the Homeric characters, not content with hacking away and maiming one another in some crude, rough-and-ready mimesis of the struggle of the various virtues and vices, also represent the elements themselves, the planets or the atoms, for example, as they intersect and collide, interact, and figure forth an immense pattern and panorama of the very building blocks of the universe. I hazard the guess that any introduction of scientific materials as such (as in Pynchon, for example) always threatens to draw the work into the logic of the tripartite scheme and to reorganize it into one version or another of the Alexandrian allegory: thus here the ethical dimension is given in the contrast between Zeitblom and Adrian himself, Catholic-humanist and protestant-demonic, and ultimately seeks to reestablish an ideology of the natural and the un- or preter-natural along tripartite lines.

The Church fathers, however, invented an allegorical pattern utterly distinct from this one, a dynamic structure organized around four levels rather than three, and were able, by incorporating the life of Christ as its first allegorical dimension, to introduce narrative into the static Alexandrian scheme and to make the new scheme susceptible of registering that properly historical movement with which Christianity revolutionized the thought patterns of the classical world. I will not recapitulate the enormous literature on the fourfold allegorical scheme,[11] save to reidentify its levels as follows:

ANAGOGICAL (history, the fate of human kind)
MORAL (the fate of the individual subject)
ALLEGORICAL (the life of Christ)
LITERAL (the text itself, in its first application the Old Testament)

I now want to show that Thomas Mann has offered us a peculiarly ambivalent structure, which can be taken indifferently as a tripartite or fourfold allegory: as a cosmological Book of the World, or alternately, and in keeping with the great thunderclap of Viconian modernity, the *verum factum*, which posits our possibility of understanding history but not nature, as a narrative which seeks, in its own (Germanic) idiosyncratic way, to tell "the tale of the tribe."

But in order to apply our scheme properly, we need to reach some agreement on the nature of the literal level itself. I have already tried to show that *Doktor Faustus* significantly distances itself from the full-frontal representation of the realistic tradition; this means, I think, that we cannot simply assume that the literal level is embodied in the life of Adrian (which I propose to shift, indeed, to the second, or allegorical, level: the

Christological allusions need not be heavy-handedly underscored, and in any case probably come more from Nietzsche than from the New Testament). No, what is literal in this novel is the writing of it,[12] in which finally (and more successfully than in Gide's personal diary of the *Faux-monnayeurs*) Thomas Mann's composition of the book (as related in *Die Entstehung des Doktor Faustus*) folds back into Zeitblom's own: they start writing the novel on the same day, hear the same news reports on the "progress" of the war (the Nazi retreat from Stalingrad), and slowly work their way forward through the war (although Thomas Mann lags a year or so behind Zeitblom in the completion of the text). The temporality of the text is a kind of somber replay of the intertwinings of *Tristram Shandy* ("it is now one month since I began writing this and my hero is still only one week old; at this rate ..."), in which, as the Devil wisely observes, fiction begins to take a back seat to historical fact ("only the non-fictional is still permissible"), and the real-life destiny of Nazi Germany (along with that of Thomas Mann himself—will he die at seventy, will this be his last book, is it not too difficult to write?) endows the imaginary characters with something of the tragic density of the real.

We may pause for a moment to interrogate the Zeitblom style, less mandarin (the word is used frequently about Thomas Mann) than philological in the sense of that German philology (from Wolf down to Spitzer and Auerbach) which identified itself as a successor to Renaissance humanism. Certainly the possibilities of German syntax are here ostentatiously articulated in a way I would hesitate to identify as narcissistic complacency (even though in context these stylistic mannerisms can take on a variety of different connotations, as in the fussiness and self-consciousness with which Felix Krull "sets pen to paper"). The relative impersonality of Wordsworth's "egotistical sublime" seems to me more suitable, and indeed characterizes Thomas Mann's relationship to his writing in general, the reading of which does not often arouse that irritation and annoyance Freud ascribed to the expression or betrayal of other people's desire, even though it invokes the first person unashamedly as the fixed point around which these sentences turn.[13] Kleist is invoked in the *Gesta romanorum* chapter (XXX), with reference to the famous essay on marionettes (whose pure materiality alone is comparable to the pure spirituality of grace); but the latter calls to mind not only Kleist's own internally self-complicating sentences, but also the companion piece, "On the gradual completion of thinking by speaking," in which meaning comes as the result of finishing your sentence. (It is worth noting the contrast between the two kinds of examples given in this essay by Kleist: the first, the fiery orations of the French Revolution; the second, the dry and reified schoolboy lessons on the state and private property: the implication is clear—the revolutionary now is the "constituent power" of emergent language, which becomes static and ossified when consigned to paper and to the institutions.) In any case, of Zeitblom's writing one must observe, first, that modern syntax is itself a symbolic act, that of the conquest by humanism and civilization over the unruly archaism of the medieval, in some straight line running from the imitation of the classical languages to the standardization of the modern. Whence, among many other motivations (self-concealment for example), the ultimate submersion of Adrian in the older (and thus more "theological") jargon in which he delivers his final public confession:

> I need not have been so agonized over his various irregularities of pronunciation, for he used in part, as he had always enjoyed doing in writing, a sort of elder German, with its defects and open sentence-structure, always with something doubtful and unregulated about it: how long ago is it, indeed, that our tongue outgrew the barbaric and got tolerably regulated as to grammar and spelling! (XLVII; LP495–6; W520, D738)

We should also note in passing an effort to encompass the wealth of dialects that make up the Germanness which is the central problem of this novel; and also the unique position of Switzerland where Mann elected to spend the end of his life—Swiss German being the language of the divine child who is Adrian's final love object, and indeed constituting for Mann the only truly Western European form of German, freed from the demonic curse of Central Europe.

But the self-interruptions and throat-clearing of this narrative style, ostentatiously underscored by the narrator himself through elaborate apologies for it which only hold up the narrative further, is also to be grasped in all its charged temporal ambivalence. It can first be identified as fear: an anxiety before what is to come, the collapse of the Reich, the sinking of Adrian himself into syphilitic paresis, the imminence of the unthinkable and the inevitable. But as with all ambivalence, this hesitation and drawing back, this "resistance" (in the strict sense of the psychoanalytic session), must also be grasped in everything it has of a libidinal positivity and satisfaction. One does not, in other words, want it to come to an end in a different sense as well: let the writing process, the process of deferral, last, let's not come to the end of the book, the biography, too quickly! Nor should we neglect the profound guilt inherent in this ambivalence: Zeitblom must wish for the defeat of his own country, for the thorough destruction, not merely of the Hitlerian Reich but of everything in the German past that found its culmination in the latter, that is, of Tradition itself, of which Zeitblom is in some professional sense the guardian (V; LP30; W33–4; D49–50). This is, I think, the other side of the trembling hand with which Zeitblom sets his *récit* down; it is the other face of that "agitated state in which I have found myself ever since beginning this biographical enterprise" (IV; W30; but see LP27; D45). But what Woods translates negatively here is the word *Aufregung*, which can also simply mean "excitement"; or, to speak more precisely, which carries within itself a notion of internal commotion which can connote both stimulation and agitation in much the same way that it is sometimes difficult to distinguish between anxiety and anticipation. The reader response here operates in obedience to what we may call the Kretschmar principle: it is because Zeitblom himself lives the internal and syntactical excitement of his sentences that the reader is able to dwell on them with much the same delectation. Syntax here becomes transformed into the symbolic perception of temporality itself: thus enlarged and foregrounded, it becomes the very incarnation of time itself; and can thereby serve as a literal foundation upon which the other allegorical levels are constructed, insofar as its symbolic or connotational opening points beyond the literal meaning of the sentences in question.

It is then their movement back and forth between the various historical dimensions in question here—the artist's life in Wilhelminian and Weimar Germany, the onslaught of allied forces on Fortress Europe, the pages slowly piling up in Zeitblom's isolation (and in Thomas Mann's study in Pacific Palisades), the peculiar destiny of Central Europe itself, birthplace of the Reformation and site of the Thirty Years' War (and of so much else that was later to "astound" the world)—which by figuring these distinct temporalities as the entanglement of separate threads eventually brings us to unite them in a process of allegorical differentiation.

Discontinuity—the interruption of one of these temporalities by another one—is thus here the very operator of allegorical signification (a word meant to emphasize a generative process absent from the term "structure"). It makes for the possibility of isolating the second level—Adrian's life as a composer, the properly musical content—in some more autonomous and specialized fashion than was possible in the tripartite allegory, in which the details of musical technique simply folded back into a more global moral lesson—and thus it makes also for a kind of non-fictional semi-autonomy of these dimensions in comparison with the homogeneous representational *isotopies* of classical realism. Now for example we can focus on the whole question of relationality as it emerges technically from the crisis of the tonal system: "Beziehung ist alles" (D74; W51; LP47: "relationship is everything"). The isolated note is meaningless in and of itself; it takes on musical value only by a specific tonal context. Yet in the tonal system that context is inherently "zweideutig" (W "ambiguous"; LP "equivocal"); it can be displaced in different directions:

> And he played a chord: all black keys, F sharp, A sharp, C sharp, added an E, and so unmasked the chord, which had looked like F-sharp major, as belonging to B major, as its dominant. "Such a chord," he said, "has of itself no tonality.

> Everything is relation, and the relation forms the circle." The A, which, forcing the resolution into G sharp, leads over from B major to E major, led him on, and so via the keys of A, D, and G he came to C major and to the flat keys, as he demonstrated to me that on each one of the twelve notes of the chromatic scale one could build a fresh major or minor scale. (VII; LP46; W51; D73)

This is the unstable classical system which is coming apart in the twentieth century; and the twelve-tone system, which replaces a given tonality by the specific row of all twelve notes in a determinate series, is in some unspecified sense meant to change our whole mode of auditory perception and to replace tonal attention with a radically different kind.[14]

In fact, the novel skirts this difficult problem, which raises the specter of Ernst Bloch's great account of the artist novel as the inversion of the detective story and the "representation" of a hole or a blank at the center of its own narrative: the work of art of the future, the work of art to come; and along with that the very mode of perception to come, the Superman, the communist New Man of the future, what is properly Utopian and unimaginable. But a novel cannot teach us, even prophetically, those new habits and perceptions; and the work of art of the future—no matter how fully projected it might be, as were, with Adorno's help, the great final masterpieces of the *Apocalypse* and the *Lamentations of Doktor Faustus*; and some more humble thematics must be found for what we cannot yet know or see. This theme (not at all external to the Schoenberg problematic but already inherent in it) will be that of polyphony, of the horizontal as opposed to the vertical combination of orchestral harmonies in the now-classical tonal works of the "realistic" nineteenth century. The tonal system begins to sink under the weight of its own richness and of the ever more massive weight of ever more numerous combined orchestral sonorities: its epitaph might indeed be that "black square" which is the ultimate static dissonance, the twelve combined tones of the scale that concludes Berg's *Lulu*.

The twelve-tone system on the contrary permits a return to those blessed polyphonic times in which "the same" echoed and responded to itself on all the levels of a sound mass in constant movement. But in what sense does this offer a new possibility of representation and allow us however imperfectly to fill in that empty or blind spot of the future that Bloch identified as being central to the artist novel? It does so by way of its allegorical possibilities, or perhaps I should say by leapfrogging onto the next levels of allegorical significance.

For the horizontal, or polyphony, which stands as the archaic moment which Leverkühn's modernity will mine in order to escape from tonality's contradictions, can also be isolated and dramatized as a social form. We need only return to Adrian's childhood (IV) and the musical round in which "barnyard Hanne" leads the singing children:

> In this way we were always separate from each other in time, but the melodic presence of each kept together pleasantly with that of the others and what we produced made a graceful web, a body of sound such as unison singing did not; a texture in whose polyphony we delighted without inquiring after its nature and cause ... None of us was aware that here, led by a stable-girl, we were moving on a plane of musical culture already relatively high, in a realm of imitative polyphony, which the fifteenth century had had to discover in order to give us pleasure. (IV; LP 28–8; W32; D48)

In the harmonic system, the notes are either masters or servants (shades of Johann Conrad Beissel!) and must slavishly surrender themselves to their unequal roles in (borrowing from Mumford) what might be called a small and artistic mega-machine. Here a kind of equality unites voices none of which can be said to be truly individualistic yet, like those handicraft artisans whose individual craft is distinct and meaningful in and of itself and yet contributes to the prosperity of the whole village. I have allowed a social metaphorics to seep into this description in order to defend the proposition that on another level altogether the opposition between the horizontal and the vertical, between polyphony and harmony, is somehow "the same" as that between *Gesellschaft* and *Gemeinschaft*, between the older organic communities and the new industrial agglomerations of the late-nineteenth-century city. We do not often remember today (but Mann's Munich chapter—XXVIII—underscores it) that *Gemeinschaft* was once a popular Nazi word, redolent of the "völkisch" and of German nationalism, when not the return to the German archaic and mythic. On this level, Adrian's attempt to "overcome modernity"[15]—to harness the powers of the archaic past in order to resolve the crisis of the musically modern—is identified with the Nazi combination of mythic demagogy and spectacle with the technologically most advanced industrial equipment in all domains. But here we have (as Zeitblom might have said) gotten ahead of ourselves and anticipated the climax of our not yet completed story.

For, as I will want to claim this social thematic for the fourth and final "anagogical" level of the fourfold scheme, we must first to come to terms with the third or moral one, the fate of the individual soul. I want to gather on this particular level the war itself as a time line: and this is already paradoxical in the light of the psychological or existential restriction of the traditional third (or moral) allegorical sense. Yet, equally paradoxically, it does not seem to me that the entire historical phenomenon of Hitlerism belongs here either (and indeed, we will find ourselves positioning it on some fourth or collective level): there is an excellent reason for this, and it lies in the deeper ambiguity (*Zweideutigkeit*) of the work as such (and of Thomas Mann's relationship to Nazism, whose "romantic" roots he also shared[16]). This constitutive ambiguity has as its consequence that Nazism itself as a historical moment and a social movement will be unrealizable as the operator of the kind of ethical oppositions required on this particular level: whatever ethical binary Nazism generates will at once be drawn into dialectical reversals and Nietzschean transcendences. Unfortunately, in order for ambiguity itself to become a fundamental theme and to find concrete representation, the stark contrast of good and evil must somehow already be in place, something more evident for the theologians of the late Middle Ages (*et encore!*) than for ourselves.

But such ambivalences completely disappear when we have to do with World War Two, the last "just war" as it has been called, and a Manichaean operation in which no doubt any longer subsists as to the identification of good and evil. The war thus presents the ultimate moment of existential choice when the individual must take sides and "irony" is no longer possible. But the war also has another aesthetic bonus, namely, that it is a temporal process, one with an intensifying tempo as well as, at least after Stalingrad (and after the chronological beginning of the composition of this book) an inevitable and fatal, predetermined outcome. This temporality can then be borrowed and transferred to the other levels, of Adrian's doom as well as of Zeitblom's writing. At the same time it opens up that exterior or outside of the monadic work (which Adorno felt to be both unrepresentable and indispensable for any work of art) and at the same time draws it inside the form, in that dialectic of identity and difference we have already noted (the tempo of current events and world history is radically distinct from existential experience, let alone the reading process, but yet is part of the latter by way of that very difference and incommensurability).

As far as the experience of the individual soul, however, the war provides an original thematic we would not have been likely to find articulated in this transferrable way in any other area of the raw material: I mean the "psychology of the breakthrough" (XXX; D459; W323; LP306): a leitmotif which runs through the book on all levels with all its possible variations (thus *durchbrechen* is also to interrupt: but not all interruptions are real breakthroughs). At its starkest, this is very much a geopolitical theme, which is derived from Germany's lateness and isolation as a world power, without respect, without allies, without colonies, without an army (after Versailles), without *Lebensraum*, etc. Both wars can then be seen as a final, desperate, convulsive attempt to break out of that isolation, and to establish or invent some new relationship to the outside world (Mann's infamous *Betrachtungen eines Unpolitischen—Reflexions of an Unpolitical Man*—are the obvious reference to document this internal German national feeling).

It is irrelevant to decide whether this national feeling was ill- or well-founded: and indeed it is hard to see how any imputed collective representation of this kind can be either true or false. What is more important for our purposes is that "breakthrough" then takes on a far more restricted and concrete sense in terms of precisely those military movements that attention to the temporality of the war focuses on. The Western front, in both world wars, is the locus of repeated attempts to "break through" (most notably in the famous Schlieffen Plan, which failed in World War One and succeeded in Hitler's *Blitzkrieg*); we do not particularly associate the "breakthrough" with eastern momentum on the Eastern front, but it certainly comes into play in the grimmest form when the Red Army begins to move west.

At any rate this figure becomes a most tangible one indeed on the battlefield, after which its transfer to the psychological—to Adrian's desperate search for *Hetaera esmeralda*, for example—seems as appropriate as it is unproblematic. At that point, the figure becomes available for a wide variety of applications and articulations: this is, for example, what Zeitblom has to say about the Wilhelminian era:

> Culture had been free, had stood at an admirable pinnacle, and if it had long since grown accustomed to being totally irrelevant to the state, its younger representatives wished to regard the great national war that had now broken out as the means for breaking through to a new form of life in which state and culture would be one. (XXX, W317; LP300; D450)

This particular articulation, however, now shifts us back to the fourth or final, collective, level of this tiered allegory, and prompts us in conclusion to venture a few speculations on what could be taken as the book's "ultimate" meaning, even though it is only one allegorical meaning among others. Wrapped in this question, however, is another one about the novel's universality, in a perspective for which that ultimate level of the collective can only turn on an interrogation of Germany itself, of the German destiny and German exceptionalism: a theme that threatens immediately to deteriorate into the commonplace astonishment at the combination of civilization and barbarism that runs throughout German history, uniting Beethoven and Hitler, and inscribing itself into figures like Luther and Nietzsche. It would be facile and unsatisfying to remind ourselves that all national traditions are unspeakably bloody (whatever their own national history books may attempt to tell them); more discouraging to remember that not all national cultures are as illustrious as this one. The framework of modernity and modernization may provide a more workable context in which to argue (as Hegel always did) that the exception *is* the rule, and that there are in that sense no averages. Still, the diagnosis of modernity here as a pact with the archaic may no longer be very compelling in a postmodernity which has eliminated the last traces of the archaic so thoroughly that only the latter's images remain. (Yes, it is still a question of the attractiveness of this quintessentially modernist work for a postmodern readership that has been only too successful in reappropriating the other modernist "classics" such as Joyce, Proust or Kafka.)

I think that the passage quoted immediately above sets us on a more productive line of inquiry: it posits, indeed, the ideal of Wilhelminian youth, those who are about to become the citizens of the Weimar Republic, if not of the kingdoms of the dead, as a new synthesis of dimensions hitherto separated, in this particular case the state and culture as such. To put it this way is however to remember that this particular micrological figure (as Adorno might have called it) knows stronger and more insistent formulations throughout the novel, and in particular an opposition between the "cultic" or religious function of art in traditional society and its secular status as mere "culture" in this one. Indeed, if Adrian has any social or political thoughts at all, they turn on this question, whose significance he learned from Kretschmar (VIII; W64; LP59; D91–2). Not only does the youthful composer betray nostalgia for an older situation, in which church and state are not yet separate:

> "I cannot go with you in your radicalism—which certainly will not long persist, as it is a student license—I cannot go with you in your separation, after Kierkegaard, of Church and Christianity. I see in the Church, even as she is today, secularized and reduced to the bourgeois, a citadel of order, an institution for objective disciplining, canalizing, banking-up of the religious life, which without her would fall victim to subjectivist demoralization, to a chaos of divine and demonic powers, to a world of fantastic uncanniness, an ocean of Daemony. To separate Church and religion means to give up separating the religious from madness." (XIV; LP119; W128; D180–1)

Adrian's "explosive antiquarianism" (XXXIV, W 396) thus also very specifically posits a reunification of church and state in the name of music, an ideological temptation he very much shares with the pre-fascist Weimar intellectuals we have already mentioned, and which is as always best articulated by the Devil himself:

> "Do you understand? Not only will you break through the paralysing difficulties of the time—you will break through time itself, by which I mean the cultural epoch and its cult, and dare to be barbaric, twice barbaric indeed, because of coming after the humane, after all possible root-treatment and bourgeois raffinement. Believe me, barbarism even has more grasp of theology than has a culture fallen away from cult, which even in the religious has seen only culture, only the humane, never excess, paradox, the mystic passion, the utterly unbourgeois ordeal." (XXV; LP 243; W259; D365)

It seems to me less interesting to speculate about the religious, medieval, cultic remnants at work in modernist conceptions of the great work (as in that mesmerization by Dante's *Commedia* we also find at work in Joyce)—or even about the religious frameworks of Adrian's two great final compositions—than to re-pose the problem in terms of differentiation.

Luhmann indeed identified the latter as the very process of the coming into being of modernity itself:[17] whether this account serves as a definition or merely as a formal description is another matter we do not have to deal with here. But as secularization is the crudest characterization of this process, it is well to remind ourselves of an earlier figure in Thomas Mann's work, a figure who serves as a locus for these dilemmas in a historically different way than that in which *Doktor Faustus* confronts them, but whose example is nonetheless instructive: I refer to the figure of Naphta in *The Magic Mountain*, and to the obsession of this communist Jesuit with the reunification of church and state along medieval lines. Indeed, we know that at the time Thomas Mann elaborated the figure of Naphta he was much taken with a book that for him underscored the analogies between Bolshevism and the medieval *Weltanschauung*.[18] Following Luhmann, then, one is tempted to suggest that the great temptation of modernity, its diabolical one, is indeed very precisely this regression on the process of differentiation, its attempt to recombine levels such as those of church and state which have already been fatally separated by history, the desperation with which it tries to reunite its oppositions by an act of violence. To read Mann's vision of the German destiny in this way is not only to rearticulate it in postmodern rather than in modern terms: it is also to measure the distance between the overcoming of differentiation he thus fearfully contemplates (and it is a vision that has given rise to a good deal of anti-Utopian rhetoric and philosophizing in recent, post-Cold War years) and the rather different kind of dedifferentiation, the folding back in upon each other of hitherto specialized and separate levels, that defines the postmodern as such.

As far as *Doktor Faustus* is concerned, however, it should also be remembered that the allegorical operation is itself a unique and historically idiosyncratic mode of differentiation: the novel thus contemplates, as a baleful temptation, the very nostalgia for reunification and re-identification which would abolish it as an allegory in the first place.

(1997)

Notes

1 All quotations are from H.T. Lowe-Porter's translation (New York, 1948), which, despite all very pertinent objections, I prefer to the new one by John E. Woods (New York, 1999); henceforth after the chapter number, page numbers are given within the text to Lowe-Porter (LP), Woods (W), and to the German original (D) published by Fischer Verlag (Frankfurt, 1951).

2 See Adorno/Mann, *Briefwechsel 1943–1955* (Frankfurt, 2003), pp. 18–20.
3 See Adorno, *Essays on Music*, ed. Richard Leppert (Calif., 2002), pp. 564–7.
4 See Mann's letter to Adorno of December 30, 1945, in Adorno/Mann, *Briefwechsel 1943–1955* (Frankfurt, 2003), pp. 18–22.
5 See Pierre Boulez, "*Wozzeck* and Its Interpretation," in his *Orientations* (Harvard, 1986), pp. 374–9.
6 See my "Heidegger and Fascism" (forthcoming). Heidegger's diagnosis of technology is to be found in "Die Frage nach der Technik," in *Vorträge und Aufsätze* (Pfullingen, 1954), pp. 9–40.
7 See Adorno, *Aesthetische Theorie* (Frankfurt, 1997), p. 57 (trans. Hullot-Kentor, Minnesota, 1997), p. 34.
8 See Franco Moretti, *The Modern Epic* (London, 1996).
9 Ernst-Bloch, "Philosophische Ansicht des Künstlerromans," in *Verfremdungen* I (Frankfurt, 1963), pp. 64–80.
10 Roger Caillois, *Méduse et cie* (Paris, 1960).
11 But see Henri de Lubac, *Exégèse mediévale* (Paris, 1959–64, 4 vols.), in particular vol. I, pp. 139–69 and pp. 200–7.
12 The literal level of *The Magic Mountain*, on the other hand, seems to me to be constituted by phenomenological time, that is to say, by the time of reading rather than that of writing.
13 See "Creative Writers and Daydreaming," in Sigmund Freud, *The Standard Edition* (London, 1959), volume IX, pp. 152–3. None of this holds true, however, the moment the reader emerges from the spell of these sentences: the denunciation of Thomas Mann's character in the biographical literature has become almost universal in recent years.
14 The classical discussion (which Mann read in manuscript as he was composing *Doktor Faustus*) is Adorno's *Philosophie der neuen Musik* (Frankfurt, 1958).
15 The allusion is to the historically significant Japanese philosophical symposium of 1942, described by Harry Harootunian, *Overcome by Modernity* (Princeton, 2000), chapter 2.
16 This is the (rather single-minded) argument of Hans Wisskirchen, *Zeitgeschichte in Thomas Mann* (Thomas Mann Studien VI: Bern, 1986). To be sure, this objection still very much relies on the very opposition it criticizes Mann himself for: the positing of an "irrational" tradition to German culture (from the Schlegels, or even Luther, to Nietzsche and beyond), to which a rational or Enlightenment minority tradition is opposed (Lessing, Goethe, Heine, Marx, and Heinrich, if not Thomas Mann). This opposition between the rational and the irrational is still central both for Lukács and for Habermas: one may wonder if it is still operative in the postmodern.
17 Niklas Luhmann, *The Differentiation of Society* (Columbia, 1982). But see on this also *A Singular Modernity* (London, 2002).
18 Wisskirchen, op. cit., pp. 61ff.

THREE

6

Ulysses in History

I had it in mind, in what follows, to say something about the two most boring chapters of *Ulysses*: most people would agree that these are surely the Eumaeus and the Ithaca chapters, the scene in the cabmen's shelter and the catechism. I have found, however, that in order to do that properly one must necessarily speak about the rest in some detail so that finally those parts are greatly reduced. One of the things such a subject leads you to consider, however, is boredom itself and its proper use when we are dealing with literary texts of this kind, and in particular the classical texts of high modernism or even postmodernism. I will still say something about that—I think there is a productive use of such boredom, which tells us something interesting about ourselves as well as about the world in which we live today—but I also mean to use this word in a far less positive sense, so I will do that first and say that if there are boring chapters of *Ulysses*, with which we must somehow learn to live, there are also boring interpretations of *Ulysses*, and those we can really make an effort to do without, sixty years after its publication, and in a social and global situation so radically different from that in which the canonical readings of this text were invented.

It would be surprising indeed if we were unable to invent newer and fresher ways of reading Joyce; on the other hand, the traditional interpretations I am about to mention have become so sedimented into our text—*Ulysses* being one of those books which is "always-already-read," always seen and interpreted by other people before you begin—that it is hard to see it afresh and impossible to read it as though those interpretations had never existed.

They are, I would say, threefold, and I will call them the mythical, the psychoanalytical, and the ethical readings respectively. These are, in other words, the readings of *Ulysses*, first in terms of the *Odyssey* parallel; second, in terms of the father–son relationship; and third, in terms of some possible happy end according to which this day, Bloomsday, will have changed everything, and will in particular have modified Mr Bloom's position in the home and his relationship with his wife.

Let me take this last reading first. I will have little to say here about Molly's monologue, and only want now to ask not merely why we are so attached to the project of making something decisive happen during this representative day, but above all to ask why we should be committed to this particular kind of event, in which Mr Bloom is seen as reasserting his authority in what can therefore presumably once again become a vital family unit. (You will recall that he has asked Molly to bring him breakfast in bed the next day—the triumph over his suitors!) In this day and age, in which the whole thrust of a militant feminism has been against the nuclear and the patriarchal family, is it really appropriate to recast *Ulysses* along the lines of marriage counseling and anxiously to interrogate its characters and their destinies with a view towards saving this marriage and restoring this family? Has our whole experience of Mr Bloom's Dublin reduced itself to this, the quest for a "happy ending" in which the hapless protagonist is to virilize himself and become a more successful realization of the dominant, patriarchal, authoritarian male?

Still, it will be said that this particular reading is part of the more general attempt to fit *Ulysses* back into the *Odyssey* parallel. As for the mythical interpretation—the *Odyssey* parallel undoubtedly underscored for us by the text itself as well as by generations of slavish interpreters—here too it would be desirable to think of something else. We are today, one would hope, well beyond that moment of classical modernism and its ideologies in which, as Sartre said somewhere, there was a "myth of myth," in which the very notion of some mythic unity and reconciliation was used in a mythical or, as I would prefer to say, a fetishized way. The bankruptcy of the ideology of the mythic is only one feature of the bankruptcy of the ideology of modernism in general; yet it is a most interesting one, on which it might have been instructive to dwell. Why is it that, in the depthlessness of consumer society, the essential surface logic of our world of simulacra—why is it that the mythic ideal of some kind of depth integration is no longer attractive and no longer presents itself as a possible or workable solution? There is kinship here, surely, between this waning of the mythic ideal or mirage and the disappearance of another cherished theme and experience of classical or high modernism, namely that of temporality, "durée," lived time, the passage of time. But perhaps the easiest way to dramatize the breakdown of myth and myth criticism is simply to suggest that we suddenly, with anthropologists like Lévi-Strauss, discovered that myths were not what we thought they were in the first place: not the place of some deep Jungian integration of the psyche, but quite the opposite, a space preceding the very construction of the psyche or the subject itself, the ego, personality, identity and the like: a space of the pre-individualistic, of the collective, which could scarcely be appealed to offer the consolations that myth criticism had promised us.

On the other hand, we can scarcely hope to read *Ulysses* as though it were called something else. I would suggest, then, that we displace the act or the operation of interpretation itself. The *Odyssey* parallel can then be seen as one of the organizational frameworks of the narrative text: but it is not itself the interpretation of that narrative, as the ideologues of myth have thought. Rather it is itself—qua organizational framework—what remains to be interpreted. In itself, the *Odyssey* parallel—like so much of that whole tradition of the classical pastiche from Cocteau or even from *La Belle Hélène* all the way to Giraudoux or Kafka or even John Barth or Pelevin—functions as wit: a matching operation is demanded of us as readers, in which the fit of the modern detail to its classical overtext is admired for its elegance and economy, as when, in *Ulysses*, Odysseus's long separation from Penelope is evoked in terms of a ten-year period of coitus interruptus or anal intercourse between the partners of the Bloom household. You will agree, however, that the establishment of the parallel is scarcely a matter of interpretation—that is, no fresh meaning is conferred either on the classical Homeric text, or on the practices of contemporary birth control, by the ironic matching of these two things.

Genuine interpretation is something other than this, and involves the radical historization of the form itself; what is to be interpreted is then the historical necessity for this very peculiar and complex textual structure or reading operation in the first place. We can make a beginning on this, I think, by evoking the philosophical concept, but also the existential experience, called "contingency." Something seems to have happened at a certain point in modern times to the old unproblematic meaning of things, or to what we could call the content of experience; and this particular event is as so often first most tangibly detectable and visible on the aesthetic level. There is something like a crisis of detail, in which we may, in the course of our narrative, need a house for our characters to sleep in, a room in which they may converse, but nothing is there any longer to justify our choice of this particular house rather than that other, or this particular room, furniture, view, and the like. It is a very peculiar dilemma, which Barthes described as well as anyone else, when he accounted for the fundamental experience of the modern or of modernity in terms of something like a dissociation between meaning and existence:

> The pure and simple "representation" of the "real", the naked account of "what is" (or what has been), thus proves to resist meaning; such resistance reconfirms the great mythic opposition between the *vécu* [that is, the experiential or what the existentialists called "lived experience"] and the intelligible; we have only to recall how, in the ideology of our time, the obsessional evocation of the "concrete" (in what is demanded of the sciences, of literature, of social practices) is always staged as an aggressive arm against meaning, as though, by some *de jure* exclusion, what lives is structurally incapable of carrying a meaning—and vice versa.[1]

One would only want to correct this account by adding that the living, life, vitalism, is also an ideology, as it is appropriate to observe for Joyce himself more generally; but on the whole Barthes's opposition between what exists and what means allows us to make sense of a whole range of formal strategies within what we call the high modernisms. These range clearly all the way from the dematerialization of the work of art (Virginia Woolf's attack on naturalism, Gide's omission of the description of people and things, the emergence of an ideal of the "pure" novel on the order of "pure poetry") to the practice of symbolism itself, which involves the illicit transformation of existing things into so many visible or tangible meanings. I believe that today, whatever our own aesthetic faults or blinkers, we have learned this particular lesson fairly well: and that for us, any art which practices symbolism is already discredited and worthless before the fact. A long experience of the classical modernisms has finally taught us the bankruptcy of the symbolic in literature; we demand something more from artists than this facile affirmation that the existent also means, that things are also symbols. But this is very precisely why I am anxious to rescue Joyce from the exceedingly doubtful merit of being called a symbolic writer.

Yet before I try to describe what is really going on in the text of *Ulysses*, let me do something Barthes did not care to do, in the passage I quoted, and designate the historical reasons for that modernist crisis, that dissociation of the existent and the meaningful, that intense experience of contingency in question here. We must explain this experience historically because it is not at all evident, and particularly not in the ideological perspective—existential or Nietzschean—which is that of Roland Barthes, among many others, and for which the discovery of the absurd and of the radical contingency and meaninglessness of our object world is simply the result of the increasing lucidity and self-consciousness of human beings in a post-religious, secular, scientific age.

But in previous societies (or modes of production) it was Nature that was meaningless or anti-human. What is paradoxical about the historical experience of modernism is that it designates very precisely that period in which Nature—or the non- or anti-human—is everywhere in the process of being displaced or destroyed, expunged, eliminated, by the achievements of human praxis and human production. The great modernist literature—from Baudelaire and Flaubert to *Ulysses* and beyond—is a city literature: its object is therefore the anti-natural, the humanized, *par excellence*, a landscape which is everywhere the result of human labor, in which everything—including the formerly natural, grass, trees, our own bodies—is finally produced by human beings. This is then the historical paradox with which the experience of contingency confronts us (along with its ideologies—existentialism and nihilism—and its aesthetics—modernism): how can the city be meaningless? How can human production be felt to be absurd or contingent, when in another sense one would think it was only human labor which created genuine meaning in the first place?

Yet it is equally obvious that the experience of contingency is a real or "objective" one, and not merely a matter of illusion or false consciousness (although it is that too). The missing step here—the gap between the fact of the human production of reality in modern times and the experience of the results or products of that production as meaningless—this essential mediation is surely to be located in the work process itself, whose organization does not allow the producers to grasp their relationship to the final product; as well as in the market system, which does not allow the consumer to grasp the product's origins in collective production.

This may or may not be the moment to insert a general lecture on alienation and reification, on the dynamics of capital and the nature of exchange value, at this point: I do want to dwell at somewhat greater length on one of the basic forms taken by reification as a process, and that is what can be called the analytical fragmentation of older organic or at least "naturwüchsige" or traditional processes.[2] Such fragmentation can be seen on any number of levels: on that of the labor process first of all, where the older unities of handicraft production are broken up and "taylorized" into the meaningless yet efficient segments of mass industrial production; on that of the psyche or psychological subject, now broken up into a host of radically different mental functions, some of which—those of measurement and rational calculation—are privileged while others—the perceptual senses and aesthetic generally—are marginalized; on that of time, experience, and storytelling, all of which are inexorably atomized and broken down into their most minimal unities, into that well-known "heap of fragments where the sun beats"; the fragmentation, finally, of the older hierarchical communities, neighborhoods, and organic groups themselves, which, with the penetration of the money and market system, are systematically dissolved into relations of equivalent individuals, "free but equal" monads, isolated subjects equally free to sell their labor power, yet living side by side in a merely additive way within those great agglomerations which are the modern cities.

It is incidentally this final form of reification which accounts for the inadequacy of that third conventional interpretation of *Ulysses* mentioned above, namely the fetishization of the text in terms of "archetypal" patterns of father–son relationships, the quest for the ideal father or for the lost son, and so forth. But surely today, after so much prolonged scrutiny of the nuclear family, it has become apparent that the obsession with these relationships and the privileging of such impoverished interpersonal schemas drawn from the nuclear family itself are to be read as breakdown products and as defense mechanisms against the loss of the knowable community. The efforts of Edward Saïd and others to demonstrate the omnipresence of such familial schemes in modern narrative should surely not be taken as an affirmation of the ultimate primacy of such relationships, but rather exactly the reverse, as sociopathology and as diagnosis of the impoverishment of human relations which results from the destruction of the older forms of the collective.[3] The father–son relationships in *Ulysses* are all miserable failures, above all others the mythical ultimate "meeting" between Bloom and Stephen; and if more is wanted on this particular theme, one might read into the record here the diatribes against the very notion of an Oedipus complex developed in Deleuze and Guattari's *Anti-Oedipus*, which I do not necessarily endorse but which should surely be enough to put an end to this particular interpretive temptation.

But the psychoanalytic or Oedipal interpretation was itself only a subset of the *Odyssey* parallel or mythological temptation, to which, after this digression, I promised to return. What I wanted to suggest about the kind of reading determined by the *Odyssey* parallel in *Ulysses* is that this parallelism, and the kind of matching it encourages between the two levels of written and over-text, functions as something like an empty form. Like the classical unities, it offers a useful but wholly extrinsic set of limits against which the writer works, and which serve as a purely mechanical check on what risks otherwise becoming an infinite proliferation of detail.[4] The point is that, as we suggested a moment ago, the older traditional narrative unities have disappeared, destroyed in the process of universal fragmentation: the organic unity of the narrative can thus no longer serve as a symbol for the unity of experience, nor as a formal limit on the production of narrative sentences: the single day—that overarching formal unity of *Ulysses*—is a meaningful unit neither in human experience nor in narrative itself. But at that point, if what used to be experience—human destiny and the like—is shattered into such components as taking a walk at lunchtime from your place of business to a restaurant, buying a cake of soap, or having a drink, or visiting a patient in a hospital—each of these components being then in itself infinitely subdivisible—then there is absolutely no guarantee that the transformation of these segments into narrative sentences might not be infinitely extended and indeed last forever. The *Odyssey* parallel helps avoid this unwelcome development and sets just such external limits, which ultimately become those of Joyce's minimal units of composition—the individual chapters themselves.

But alongside the type of reading encouraged by the mythic parallels—which I have called a matching up—there is a rather different form of reading which resists that one in all kinds of ways, and ends up subverting it. This is a type of reading that interrupts the other, consecutive kind, and moves forward and backwards across the text in a cumulative search for the previous mention or the reference to come: as Kenner and others have pointed out, it is a type of reading, a mental operation, peculiarly inconceivable before printing, before numbered pages, and more particularly before the institutionalization of those unusual objects called dictionaries or encyclopedias.[5] Now one is tempted to assimilate this kind of reading to the more customary thematic or thematizing kind, where we compile lists of recurrent motifs, such as types of imagery, obsessive words or terms, peculiar gestures or emotional reactions; but this is not at all what happens in *Ulysses*, where the object of the cross-referencing activity is always an event: taking old Mrs Riordan for a walk, the borrowed pair of tight trousers worn by Ben Dollard at a memorable concert, or the assassination in Phoenix Park twenty-two years before. This is to say that these seemingly thematic motifs are here always referential: for they designate content beyond the text, beyond indeed the capacity of any of the given textual variants to express or exhaust them. In such cross-referencing, indeed, one can say that the referent itself is produced, as something which transcends every conceivable textualization of it. The appropriate analogy might be with the return of characters in Balzac's *Comédie humaine*, where the varying status of a given character—the hero in one novel, a character actor in a second, a mere extra in a third and part of an enumeration of names in a fourth—tends effectively to destabilize each of the narrative forms in question, and to endow them all with a transcendental dimension on which they open so many relative perspectives.

The analogous recurrence of events and characters throughout *Ulysses* can equally be understood as a process whereby the text itself is unsettled and undermined, a process whereby the universal tendency of its terms, narrative tokens, representations, to solidify into an achieved and codified symbolic order as well as a massive narrative surface, is perpetually suspended. I will call this process "dereification," and I first want to describe its operation in terms of the city itself. The classical city is not a collection of buildings, nor even a collection of people living on top of one another; nor is it even mainly or primarily a collection of pathways, of the trajectories of people through those buildings or that urban space, although that gets us a little closer to it. No, the classical city, one would think—it always being understood that we are now talking about something virtually extinct in the age of the suburb or megalopolis or the private car—the classical city is defined essentially by the nodal points at which all those pathways and trajectories meet, or which they traverse: points of totalization, we may call them, which make shared experience possible, and also the storage of experience and information, which are in short something like a synthesis of the object (place) and the subject (population), focal points not unlike those possibilities of unifying perspectives and images which Kevin Lynch has identified as the signs and emblems of the successful, the non-alienating city.[6]

But to talk about the city in this way, spatially, by identifying the collective transit points and roundabouts of temple and agora, pub and post office, park and cemetery, is not yet to identify the mediation whereby these spatial forms are at one with collective experience. Unsurprisingly that mediation will have to be linguistic, yet it will have to define a kind of speech that is neither uniquely private nor forbiddingly standardized in an impersonal public form, a type of discourse in which the same, in which repetition, is transmitted again and again through a host of eventful variations, each of which has its own value. That discourse is called gossip: and from the upper limits of city life—the world of patronage, machine politics, and the rise and fall of ward leaders—all the way down to the most minute aberrations of private life, it is by means of gossip and through the form of the anecdote that the dimensions of the city are maintained within humane limits and that the unity of city life is affirmed and celebrated. This is already the case with that ur-form of the city which is the village itself, as John Berger tell us in *Pig Earth*:

> The function of this gossip which, in fact, is close, oral, daily history, is to allow the whole village to define itself ... The village ... is a living portrait of itself: a communal portrait, in that everybody is portrayed and everybody portrays. As with the carvings on the capitals in a Romanesque church, there is an identity of spirit between what is shown and how it is shown—as if the portrayed were also the carvers. Every village's portrait of itself is constructed, however, not out of stone, but out of words, spoken and remembered: out of opinions, stories, eye-witness reports, legends, comments and hearsay. And it is a continuous portrait: work on it never stops. Until very recently the only material available to a village and its peasants for defining themselves was their own spoken words ... Without such a portrait—and the gossip which is its raw material—the village would have been forced to doubt its own existence.[7]

So in that great village that is Joyce's Dublin, Parnell is still an anecdote about a hat knocked off, picked up and returned, not yet a television image nor even a name in a newspaper; and by the same token, as in the peasant village itself, the ostensibly private or personal—Molly's infidelities, or Mr Bloom's urge to discover how far the Greek sculptors went in portraying the female anatomy—all these things are public too, and the material for endless gossip and anecdotal transmission.

Now for a certain conservative thought, and for that heroic fascism of the 1920s for which the so-called 'masses' and their standardized city life had become the very symbol of everything degraded about modern life, gossip—Heidegger will call it "das Gerede"—is stigmatized as the very language of inauthenticity, of that empty and stereotypical talking *pour rien dire* to which these ideologues oppose the supremely private and individual speech of the death anxiety or the heroic choice. But Joyce—a radical neither in the left-wing nor the reactionary sense—was at least a populist and a plebeian. "I don't know why the communists don't like me," he complained once, "I've never written about anything but common people." Indeed, from the class perspective, Joyce had no more talent for or interest in the representation of aristocrats than Dickens; and no more experience with working-class people or with peasants than Balzac. (Beckett is indeed a far sounder guide to the Irish countryside or rural slum than the essentially urban Joyce.)

In class terms, then, Joyce's characters are all resolutely petit-bourgeois: what gives this apparent limitation its representative value and its strength is the colonial situation itself. Whatever his hostility to Irish cultural nationalism, Joyce's is the epic of the metropolis under imperialism, in which the development of bourgeoisie and proletariat alike is stunted to the benefit of a national petit-bourgeoisie. Indeed, precisely these rigid constraints imposed by imperialism on the development of human energies account for the symbolic displacement and flowering of the latter in eloquence, rhetoric and oratorical language of all kinds: symbolic practices not particularly essential either to businessmen or to working classes, but highly prized in precapitalist societies and preserved, as in a time capsule, in *Ulysses* itself. And this is the moment to rectify our previous account of the city and to observe that if *Ulysses* is also for us the classical, the supreme representation of something like the Platonic idea of city life, this is also partly due to the fact that Dublin is not exactly the full-blown capitalist metropolis, but like the Paris of Flaubert, still regressive, still distantly akin to the village, still un- or under-developed enough to be representable, thanks to the domination of its foreign masters.

Now it is time to say what part gossip plays in the process of what I have called dereification, or indeed in that peculiar network of cross-references which causes us to read *Ulysses* backwards and forwards like a handbook. Gossip is indeed the very element in which reference—or, if you prefer, the "referent" itself—expands and contracts, ceaselessly transformed from a mere token, a notation, a short-hand object, back into a full-dress narrative. People as well as things are the reified markers of such potential storytelling: and what for a high realism was the substantiality of character, of the individual ego, is here equally swept away into a flux of anecdotes—proper names on the one hand, an intermittent store of gossip on the other. But the process is to be sure more tangible and more dramatic when we see it at work on physical things: the statues, the commodities in the shop windows, the clanking trolleylines that link Dublin to its suburbs (which dissolve, by way of Mr Deasy's anxieties about foot-and-mouth disease, into Mr Bloom's fantasy projects for tramlines to move cattle to the docks); or the three-master whose silent grace and respectability as an image is at length dissolved into the disreputable reality of its garrulous and yarn-spinning crewman; or, to take a final example, that file of sandwich men whose letters troop unevenly through the text, seeming to move towards that ultimate visual reification fantasized by Mr Bloom virtually in analogue to Mallarmé's "livre":

> Of some one sole unique advertisement to cause passers to stop in wonder, a poster novelty, with all extraneous accretions excluded, reduced to its simplest and most efficient terms not exceeding the span of casual vision and congruous with the velocity of modern life. (592)[8]

The visual, the spatially visible, the image, is, as Guy Debord has observed, the final form of the commodity itself, the ultimate terminus of reification. Yet even so strikingly reified a datum as the sandwichboard ad is once again effortlessly dereified and dissolved when, on his way to the cabman's shelter, Stephen hears a down-and-out friend observe: "I'd carry a sandwichboard only the girl in the office told me they're full up for the next three weeks, man. God, you've to book ahead!" (505). Suddenly the exotic picture-postcard vision of a tourist Dublin is transformed back into the dreary familiar reality of jobs and contracts and the next meal. Yet this is not necessarily a dreary prospect; rather it opens up a perspective in which, at some ideal outside limit, everything seemingly material and solid in Dublin itself can presumably be dissolved back into the underlying reality of human relations and human praxis.

Yet the ambulatory letters of the sandwich men are also the very emblem of textuality itself, and this is the moment to say the price *Ulysses* must pay for the seemingly limitless power of its play of reification and dereification; the moment, in other words, to come to terms with Joyce's modernism. Stated baldly, that price is radical depersonalization, or in other words, Joyce's completion of Flaubert's programme of removing the author from the text—a programme which also removes the reader, and finally that unifying and organizing mirage or aftermirage of both author and reader which is the "character," or better still, "point of view." What happens at that point can perhaps oversimply be described this way: such essentially idealistic (or ideal, or imaginary) categories formerly served as the supports for the unity of the work or the unity of the process. Now that they have been withdrawn, only a form of material unity is left, namely the printed book itself, and its material unity as a bound set of pages within which the cross-references mentioned above are contained. One of the classic definitions of modernism—that of Clement Greenberg—isolates the increasing sense of the materiality of the medium itself (whether in instrumental timbre or oil painting), the emergent foregrounding of the medium in its materiality. It is paradoxical, of course, to evoke the materiality of language; and as for the materiality of print or script, that particular material medium is surely a good deal less satisfying or gratifying in a sensory, perceptual way than the materials of oil paint or of orchestral coloration; nonetheless, the role of the book itself is functionally analogous, in Joyce, to the materialist dynamics of the other arts.

Now in one sense textualization may be seen as a form or subset of reification itself: but if so, it is a unique type of reification, which unbinds fully as much as it fixes or crystallizes. It may, indeed, offer the most appropriate contemporary way of dealing with the phenomena Joseph Frank described in his now classic essay as "spatial form". I am thinking, for instance, of the moment in which a remarkable and ingenious method for cabling news of the Phoenix Park murders across the Atlantic is described: the reporter takes an ad (Mr Bloom's "one sole unique advertisement") and uses its spatial features to convey the trajectory of the killers and the map of the assassination (112). This is to institute a peculiarly fluid relationship between the visually reified and the historically eventful, since here these categories pass ceaselessly back and forth into one another.

The climax of this development is in many ways reached in the Nighttown section, itself a prolongation of that comparable movement and outer limit reached by Flaubert in *La Tentation de Saint Antoine*. Indeed, it would have been pleasant to discuss the peculiar representational space generated by these two "reading plays," these two seeming eruptions and intrusions of a properly theatrical space in that very different space—no matter how experimental—of narrative or novelistic representation. The comparison would show that this new space, with its ostensibly theatrical form (scenic indications, character attributions, printed speeches, notations of expression), has nothing to do with the closure of traditional theatrical representation; far more to do, indeed, with that space of hallucination in terms of which Flaubert often described his own creative processes, and which, in *Saint Antoine*, he represents as follows:

> And suddenly there move across the empty air first a puddle of water, then a prostitute, the edge of a temple, a soldier's face, a chariot drawn by two white horses rearing. These images arrive abruptly, jerkily, detached against the night like scarlet paintings on ebony. Their movement grows more rapid. They follow each other at a dizzying rate. At other times, they come to a halt and gradually waning, melt away; or else they fly off, and others take their place at once.[9]

Hallucinatory experience of this kind can be described, in the language of Gestalt psychology, as the perception of forms without background, forms or figures sundered from their ground or context, and passing discontinuously across the field of vision in a lateral movement, as though somehow on this side and nearer than the objects of the visible world. The instability of space or experience of this kind lies in the failure of the discrete or isolated image to generate any background or depth, any worldness in which it can take root. On the printed page, this essentially means that the ground, the anticipatory–retrospective texture, of narrative—what Greimas calls its *isotopies*, its ana- and cata-phoric relationships—is ruptured: it therefore falls to the typographic and material mechanisms of theatrical and scenic directions to bind (or rebind) these discontinuous images together. Typography thus becomes an event within the text among others. Or, if you prefer, since it is the reified sense of the visual which has here been solicited and stimulated, this sense will now begin to function as it were in the void, taking as its object the material signifiers, the printed words themselves, and no longer the latter's signifieds or representations or meanings.

At any rate, this peculiar climax of *Ulysses* in the seeming immediacy of a theatrical representation which is in reality the unmediated experience of the printed book will now help us to understand two kinds of things: the peculiarly anticlimactic nature of the chapters that follow it (I'm getting to them, at last!), and the ground on which the depersonalized textualization of the narrative of *Ulysses* takes place, what one is tempted to call a kind of "autistic textualization," the production of sentences in a void, moments in which the book begins to elaborate its own text, under its own momentum, with no further need of characters, point of view, author or perhaps even reader:

> Mr Bloom reached Essex bridge. Yes, Mr Bloom crossed bridge of Yessex. (215)

> Love loves to love love. Nurse loves the new chemist. Constable 14A loves Mary Kelly. Gerty MacDowell loves the boy that has the bicycle. M.B. loves a fair gentleman. Li Chi Han lovey up kissy Cha Pu Chow. Jumbo, the elephant, loves Alice, the elephant. Old Mr Verschoyle with the ear trumpet loves old Mrs Verschoyle with the turnedin eye. [...] You love a certain person. And this person loves that other person because everybody loves somebody but God loves everybody. (273)

The point I want to make about passages like these, and they are everywhere in *Ulysses*, is that "point of view" theory does not *take* on them, nor any conceivable notion of the Implied Author, unless the IA is an imbecile or a schizophrenic. No one is speaking these words or thinking them: they are simply, one would want to say, printed sentences.

And this will be my transition to the two most boring chapters of *Ulysses*, and thence to a close. Because what happens in the Eumaeus chapter is that, so to speak, Joyce lapses back into more traditional narrative "point of view": that is, for the first time in *Ulysses*, we once again get the "he thought/she thought" form of indirect discourse, what I will call the third person indistinct, and a henceforth conventional belief in that central reflective consciousness which is both appropriate and ironic in the chapter in which Bloom and Stephen are finally able to sit down together, two closed or solipsistic monads projecting that most boring theme of our own time, namely "lack of communication." Indeed, I am tempted to say, judging from the sentence structure, the elaborate periphrases, the use of occasional foreign expressions as well as cautiously isolated "colloquial" ones, that this chapter really constitutes Joyce's attempt at a parody or pastiche of a writer he had no particular sympathy or respect for, namely Henry James. (If so, it is not a very good pastiche, and only our supreme belief in Joyce's power of mimicry, in his ability to do anything stylistically, has prevented us from noticing it.) Or better still, this chapter deploys the stylistic mannerisms of Henry James in order to record a social and psychological content characteristic, rather, of James's enemy brother and archetypal rival, H.G. Wells—that is, an essentially petit-bourgeois content whose comfortable fit with the Jamesian narrative apparatus is somehow humiliating for both of them and sends both off back to back, as though their well-known differences on the form and function of the novel were less the taking of incompatible positions than—to use a more contemporary expression—mere variants within a single problematic, the problematic of the centered subject, of the closed monad, of the isolated or privatized subjectivity. The theory and practice of narrative "point of view," as we associate it with Henry James, is not simply the result of a metaphysical option, a personal obsession, nor even a technical development in the history of form (although it is obviously also all those things): point of view is rather the quasi-material expression of a fundamental social development itself, namely the increasing social fragmentation and monadization of late capitalist society, the intensifying privatization and isolation of its subjects.

We have already touched on one aspect of this development—reification—which can now be characterized in another way, as the increasing separation, under capitalism, between the private and the public, between the personal and the political, between leisure and work, psychology and science, poetry and prose, or, to put it all in a nutshell, between the subject and the object. The centered but psychologized subject and the reified object are indeed the respective orientations of these two concluding chapters, Eumaeus and Ithaca: and it is as though Joyce meant here to force us to work through in detail everything that is intolerable about this opposition. What we have been calling boredom is not Joyce's failure, then, but rather his success, and is the signal whereby we ourselves as organisms register a situation but also forms that are finally stifling for us.

This is perhaps a little easier to show in the Ithaca or catechism sequence: the format—question and answer—is not really, I think, a return to the experimentation—better still, the textualization—of the earlier chapters. It is rather that quite different thing—the construction of a form of discourse from which the subject—sender or receiver—is radically excluded: a form of discourse, in other words, that would be somehow radically objective, if that were really possible. And if it is observed that even this seemingly sterilized alternation of question and answer turns increasingly, towards the end of the chapter, around Mr Bloom's private thoughts and fantasies, in other words, around the subjective rather than the objective, then I will reply by noting the degree to which those fantasies (Mr Bloom's "bovarysme," tactfully called "ambition" by Joyce) are henceforth inextricably bound up with objects, in the best consumer society tradition. These are falsely subjective fantasies: here, in reality, commodities are dreaming about themselves through us.

These two final Bloom chapters, then, pose uncomfortable questions, and not least about narrative itself: the subjective or point-of-view chapter, Eumaeus, asks us why we should be interested in stories about private individuals any longer, given the extraordinary relativization of all individual experience, and the transformation of its contents into so many purely psychological reactions. Meanwhile, the objective chapter, Ithaca, completes an infinite subdivision of the objective contents of narrative, breaking "events" into their smallest material components and asking whether, in that form, they still have any interest whatsoever. Two men have a discussion over cocoa, and that may be interesting at a pinch; but what about the act of putting the kettle on to boil—that is a part of the same event, but is it still interesting? The elaborate anatomy of the process of boiling water (548–50) is boring in three senses of the words (1) it is essentially non-narrative; (2) it is inauthentic, in the sense in which these mass-produced material instruments (unlike Homer's spears and shields) cannot be said "to be organic parts of their users' destinies"; finally, (3) these objects are contingent and meaningless in their instrumental form, they are recuperable for literature only at the price of being transformed into symbols. Such passages thus ask three questions:

1 Why do we need narrative anyway? What are stories and what is our existential relation to them? Is a non-narrative relationship to the world and to Being possible?
2 What kind of lives are we leading and what kind of world are we living them in, if the objects that surround us are all somehow external, extrinsic, alienated from us? (It is a question about the simulacra of industrial society, essentially a question about the city, but in this form at least as old as the interrogation of the 'wholeness' of Greek culture by German romanticism.)
3 (A question I have already raised but which remains seemingly unanswered, namely) How can the products of human labor have come to be felt as meaningless or contingent?

Yet to this last question at least, Joyce's form has a kind of answer, and it is to be found in that great movement of dereification I have already invoked, in which the whole dead grid of the object world of greater Dublin is, in the catechism chapter, finally, disalienated and by the most subterranean detours traced back ... less to its origins in Nature, than to the transformation of Nature by human and collective praxis deconcealed. So to the vitalist ideology of Molly's better-known final affirmation, I tend rather to prefer this one:

> What did Bloom do at the range?
>
> He removed the saucepan to the left hob, rose and carried the iron kettle to the sink in order to tap the current by turning the faucet to let it flow.
>
> Did it flow?
>
> Yes. From Roundwood reservoir in county Wicklow of a cubic capacity of 2,400 million gallons, percolating through a subterranean aqueduct of filter mains of single and double pipeage constructed at an initial plant cost of £5 per linear yard ... (548)

(*1980*)

Notes

1 Roland Barthes, "L'Effet de réel," *Communications*, no. 11 (1968), p. 87.
2 See for a more detailed account of reification my *The Political Unconscious; Narrative as a Socially Symbolic Act* (London and Ithaca, 1981), esp. pp. 62–4, 225–37, and 249–52.
3 Edward Said, *Beginnings* (New York, 1975), pp. 137–52.
4 For further remarks on the proliferation of sentences see my *Fables of Aggression: Wyndham Lewis, the Modernist as Fascist* (Berkeley, 1979).
5 See Hugh Kenner, *Flaubert, Joyce, Beckett; the Stoic Comedians* (Boston, 1962). Also the work of Marshall MacLuhan and Walter Ong.
6 Kevin Lynch, *The Image of the City* (Cambridge, MA, 1960).
7 John Berger, *Pig Earth* (New York, 1981), p. 9.
8 *Ulysses* (New York, 1986), p. 720; all references in the text are to this, the one-volume Gabler edition.
9 Gustave Flaubert, *La Tentation de Saint Antoine* (Paris, 1951), vol. 1, p. 69.

7

Modernism and Imperialism

This is a time in which, at least in part owing to what is called post-modernism, there seems to be renewed interest in finding out what modernism really was, and in rethinking that now historical phenomenon in new ways, which are not those we have inherited from the participants and the players, the advocates and the practitioners themselves. But this has also been a time, over perhaps an even longer span of years, in which the matter of what imperialism still is and how it functions has been a subject of intense debate and discussion among the theorists, and not only the economists, the historians and the political scientists. A range of very complex theories and models indeed—probably more incomprehensible than most forms of contemporary literary theory—have come into being which any serious discussion of this issue has to acknowledge.

Any discussion of the relationship of modernism and imperialism will therefore generally require, not one, but two lengthy preambles, before it reaches its topic. It is, however, important to be clear in advance of what that topic is: it will not, in the present case, involve what can be called the literature of imperialism, since that literature (Kipling, Rider Haggard, Verne, Wells) is by and large not modernist in any formal sense, and, emerging from sub-canonical genres like the adventure tale, remained "minor" or "marginal" during the hegemony of the modern and its ideology and values (even Conrad explicitly draws on more archaic storytelling forms).[1]

The hypothesis to be explored here is both more formalistic and more sweeping than the affirmation that imperialism as such produced its specific literature and left palpable traces on the *content* of other metropolitan literary works of the period.[2] I want in fact to suggest that the structure of imperialism also makes its mark on the inner forms and structures of that new mutation in literary and artistic language to which the term "modernism" is loosely applied. This last has of course multiple social determinants: any general theory of the modern—assuming one to be possible in the first place—would also wish to register the informing presence of a range of other, historically novel phenomena: modernization and technology; commodity reification; monetary abstraction and its effects on the sign system; the social dialectic of reading publics; the emergence of mass culture; the embodiment of new forms of the psychic subject on the physical sensorium. Nor is the relative weight and importance of the emergence of a whole new global and imperial system in this constellation of "factors" at all clear even in a speculative way. The present essay is limited to the isolation of this determinant alone, to the registration of the presence of a new space, which cannot be reduced to any of those aforementioned factors.

However extrinsic and extra-literary the fact of imperialism may at first seem, there is at least a chronological justification for exploring its influence. If we take, as the codification of the new imperialist world system, the emblematic date of 1884—the year of the Berlin Conference, which parcelled Africa out among the "advanced" powers—a whole range of literary and artistic events spring to mind which at the very least suggest analogous breaks and emergencies: the death of Victor Hugo in the following year, for example, has often been seen as the inaugural moment of that whole new symbolist and Mallarméan aesthetic which his disappearance suddenly revealed to have already existed in full development behind his massive presence. The choice of such emblematic breaks is not ~~an~~ empirically verifiable matter but a historiographic decision; nor are chronological parallels of this kind much more at the outset than incentives to construct new and more complex and interesting historical narratives, whose usefulness cannot be predicted before the fact. But when, as we shall see, the parallel also seems to hold at the other end of such chronological series and the end of modernism to coincide with the restructuration of the classical imperialist world system, our curiosity as to possible interrelationships can surely only be sharpened.

For the emphasis on form and formal innovation and modification implies that our privileged texts and objects of study here will be those that scarcely evoke imperialism as such at all; that seem to have no specifically political content in the first place; that offer purely stylistic or linguistic peculiarities for analysis. One of the more commonly held stereotypes about the modern has of course in general been that of its apolitical character, its turn inward and away from the social materials associated with realism, its increased subjectification and introspective psychologization, and, not least, its aestheticism and its ideological commitment to the supreme value of a now autonomous Art as such. None of these characterizations strikes me as adequate or persuasive any longer; they are part of the baggage of an older modernist ideology which any contemporary theory of the modern will wish to scrutinize and to dismantle. But there is something to be said, in the present context, for beginning with the formalist stereotype of the modern, if only to demonstrate with greater force the informing presence of the extraliterary, of the political and the economic, within it.[3]

But such is not the only restriction on the present topic: it also involves some restrictions that concern its other term—imperialism—which must also now be delimited. I take it, for instance, that only those theories of imperialism which acknowledge the Marxist problematic (in however heretical or revisionist a fashion) are of concern here, since it is only within that problematic that a coordination between political phenomena (violence, domination, control, state power) and economic phenomena (the market, investment, exploitation, underconsumption, crisis) is systematically pursued. Exclusively political theories of imperialism (such as Schumpeter's) slip not merely towards moralizing, but also towards metaphysical notions of human nature (the lust for power or domination), which end up dissolving the historical specificity of the thing itself and disperse the phenomenon of imperialism throughout human history, wherever bloody conquests are to be found (which is to say: everywhere!). At any rate, if it is the link between imperialism and modernism that is in question here (and between imperialism and Western modernism at that), then clearly imperialism must here mean the imperialist dynamic of capitalism proper, and not the wars of conquest of the various ancient empires.

But even in the case of Marxist theories of imperialism, a further historical qualification now needs to be set in place: namely that the Marxist approach to imperialism was crucially modified and restructured in the mid-twentieth century.[4] People generally remember that Lenin wrote a very influential pamphlet on imperialism during World War One; they probably suspect anyone who uses this word "imperialism" too frequently of being a Marxist; and if they have had any greater exposure to these discussions, they know that the term has something to do with the problems of Third World societies and with under-development, with the debt as well, with the International Monetary Fund and American investments and bases abroad, with support for dictators and anxieties about Soviet influence, and perhaps only ultimately—in the last instance!—with marines and gunboat intervention or with a formal colonial structure. What must now be observed is that the term "imperialism" when used in the so-called Marxian classics—in Marx himself, in Lenin, in Hilferding and in Bukharin, with a certain exceptionality for the work of Rosa Luxemburg—has none of these connotations. For the most part, the older Marxist theorists of imperialism followed Marx himself (in the famous letters on India) in assuming that capitalist penetration would lead directly to positive economic development in what are now known as Third World countries. The very widely held contemporary belief—that, following the title of Walter Rodney's influential book, capitalism leads on the contrary to "the development of underdevelopment," and that imperialism systematically cripples the growth of its colonies and its dependent areas—this belief is utterly absent from what may be called the first moment of Marxist theories of imperialism and is indeed everywhere explicitly contradicted by them, where they raise the matter at all.[5] The point is, however, that they do not often raise the matter in that form for the good reason that during this period the word "imperialism" designates, not the relationship of metropolis to colony, but rather the rivalry of the various imperial and metropolitan nation states among themselves. It becomes immediately clear, then, that we risk all kinds of historical confusions and anachronisms if we ignore this usage and transfer our own contemporary sense of the word to contexts in the modernist period.

For it is in our time, since World War Two, that the problem of imperialism is as it were restructured: in the age of neo-colonialism, of decolonization accompanied by the emergence of multinational capitalism and the great transnational corporations, it is less the rivalry of the metropolitan powers among each other that strikes the eye (our occasional problems with Japan, for example, do not project that impending world-war-type conflict that nagged at the awareness of the *belle époque*); rather, contemporary theorists, from Paul Baran on to the present day, have been concerned with the internal dynamics of the relationship between First and Third World countries, and in particular the way in which this relationship—which is now very precisely what the word "imperialism" means for us—is one of necessary subordination or dependency, and that of an economic type, rather than a primarily military one. This means that in the period from World War One to World War Two the axis of otherness has as it were been displaced: it first governed the relationship of the various imperial subjects among each other; it now designates the relationship between a generalized imperial subject (most often the US, but frequently enough also Britain or France and Japan, not to speak of those new kinds of metropolitan centers which are South Africa or Israel) with its various others or colonies. That would be the historical way of putting it; but since (naturally enough) we think we have discovered some more basic truths about the dynamics of imperialism than our forefathers in Lenin's time, one could also describe the displacement this way: in that older period, from 1884 to World War One, the relationship of domination between First and Third World was masked and displaced by an overriding (and perhaps ideological) consciousness of imperialism as being essentially a relationship between First World powers or the holders of Empire, and this consciousness tended to repress the more basic axis of otherness, and to raise issues of colonial reality only incidentally.

Culturally, the causes as well as the effects of this shift can be rapidly evoked. We think about the Third World in a different way today, not merely because of decolonization and political independence, but above all because these enormously varied cultures all now speak in their own distinctive voices. Nor are those voices any longer marginal ones, that we are free to overlook; at least one of them—Latin American literature, since the *boom*—

has today become perhaps the principal player on the scene of world culture, and has had an unavoidable and inescapable influence, not merely on other Third World cultures as such, but on First World literature and culture as well. It would be easy to demonstrate a presence of other such voices in First World cultural situations outside the US as well, as for example in Britain today. Meanwhile, it is significant that in the US itself, we have come to think and to speak of the emergence of an internal Third World and of *internal* Third World voices, as in Black women's literature or Chicano literature for example. When the other speaks, he or she becomes another subject: which must be consciously registered as a problem by the imperial or metropolitan subject—whence the turn of what are still largely Western theories of imperialism in a new direction, towards that new other, and towards the structures of underdevelopment and dependency for which we are responsible.

But in the modernist period this is by no means the case. The prototypical paradigm of the Other in the late nineteenth century—in Zola's *La Débâcle* (1892), for example—is the other imperial nation state: in this case, the Germans, who are the quintessential ogres and bogeymen of childhood nightmare, physically alien and terrifying, barbarous, uncivilized, and still not terribly remote, as stereotypes, from the archaic "wild man of the middle ages," who incarnates everything fascinating and frightening about the unbridled id for an agricultural or village society.[6] Such "others" will then circulate in paler and more respectable forms in high literature during this period—as in the various foreigners who add an exotic note to high society in the English novel (E.M. Forster's Germans, in *Howards End*, function to reverse this xenophobia in a kind of therapeutic liberal tolerance and self-critique); while the more radical otherness of colonized, non-Western peoples tends to find its representational place in that non-canonical adventure literature of imperialism to which we have already referred.[7]

But this masking of one axis of otherness by a very different one, this substitution of rivalry for exploitation, and of a First World set of characters for a Third World presence, may be thought of as a strategy of representational containment, which scarcely alters the fundamental imperialist structure of colonial appropriation, or of what Jacques Berque has memorably called the "dépossession du monde" of the colonized peoples. Its effects are representational effects, which is to say a systematic block on any adequate consciousness of the structure of the imperial system: but these are just as clearly objective effects and will have their most obvious consequences in the aesthetic realm, where the mapping of the new imperial world system becomes impossible, since the colonized other who is its essential other component or opposite number has become invisible.

It is in this situation that modernist representation emerges: and this is indeed in general the relationship of formal and cultural change to what we have called its social "determinants," which present a radically altered situation (new raw materials of a social, psychological or physical type) to which a fresh and unprecedented aesthetic response is demanded, generally by way of formal, structural and linguistic invention. But what the new situation of imperialism looks like from the standpoint of cultural or aesthetic production now needs to be characterized, and it seems best to do so by distinguishing its problems from those of an internal industrialization and commodification in the modernizing metropolis. This last seems most often (paradoxically) to have been lived in terms of a generalized loss of meaning, as though its subject measured the increase in human power negatively, by way of the waning of tradition and of religious absolutes, at the same time that the fact of praxis and production was only too susceptible to distortion by and concealment beneath the reifying logic of the commodity form.

What is determined by the colonial system is now a rather different kind of meaning-loss than this one: for colonialism means that a significant structural segment of the economic system as a whole is now located elsewhere, beyond the metropolis, outside of the daily life and existential experience of the home country, in colonies over the water whose own life experience and life world—very different from that of the imperial power—remains unknown and unimaginable for the subjects of the imperial power, whatever social class they may belong to. Such spatial disjunction has as its immediate consequence the inability to grasp the way the system functions as a whole. Unlike the classical stage of national or market capitalism, then, pieces of the puzzle are missing; it can never be fully reconstructed; no enlargement of personal experience (in the knowledge of other social classes, for example), no intensity of self-examination (in the form of whatever social guilt), no scientific deductions on the basis of the internal evidence of First World data, can ever be enough to include this radical otherness of colonial life, colonial suffering and exploitation, let alone the structural connections between that and this, between daily life in the metropolis and the absent space of the colony. To put it in other words, the former—daily life and existential experience in the metropolis—which is necessarily the very content of the national literature itself, can now no longer be grasped immanently; it no longer has its meaning, its deeper reason for being, within itself. As artistic content it will now henceforth always have something missing about it, but in the sense of a privation that can never be restored or made whole simply by adding back in the missing component: its lack is rather comparable to another dimension, an outside like the other face of a mirror, which it constitutively lacks, and which can never be made up or made good. This new and historically original problem in what is itself a new kind of content now constitutes the situation, and the problem, and the dilemma, the formal contradiction, that modernism seeks to solve; or better still, it is only that new kind of art which reflexively perceives this problem and lives this formal dilemma that can be called modernism in the first place.

Now of course one's simplest first thought, faced with this problem of a global space that like the fourth dimension somehow constitutively escapes you, is no doubt to make a map: nor is *Ulysses* by any means the first, let alone the only literary work of the imperialist period that stakes its bet on the properties of maps. The very title of Conrad's *Heart of Darkness*, whatever other resonances it comes to have, is literally determined by the reference to cartography. But cartography is not the solution, but rather the problem, at least in its ideal epistemological form as social cognitive mapping on the global scale. The map, if there is to be one, must somehow emerge from the demands and constraints of the spatial perceptions of the individual; and since Britain is generally thought of as the quintessential imperialist power, it may be useful to begin with a sample of what looks like a relatively pre-modernist English spatial experience:

> The train sped northward, under innumerable tunnels. It was only an hour's journey, but Mrs Munt had to raise and lower the window again and again. She passed through the South Welwyn Tunnel, of tragic fame. She traversed the immense viaduct, whose arches span untroubled meadows and the dreamy flow of Tewin Water. She skirted the parks of politicians. At times the Great North Road acompanied her, more suggestive of infinity than any railway, awakening, after a nap of a hundred years, to such life as is conferred by the stench of motor-cars, and to such culture as is implied by the advertisements of antibilious pills. To history, to tragedy, to the past, to the future. Mrs Munt remained equally indifferent; hers but to concentrate on the end of her journey, and to rescue poor Helen from this dreadful mess.[8]

This episode, from the opening pages of *Howards End*, is characteristic of Forster's duplicities, and offers an amiable simplicity filled with traps and false leads. Pockets of philosophical complexity are hidden away beneath its surface, and they include reflections on nature and industrialization, on authentic and inauthentic existential time (Mrs Munt's version of Heideggerian *Sorge*), and a firm but tactful consciousness of English class realities. The novel will then undertake to spell these out and to make sure that what the reader has been encouraged to overlook here becomes at length an unavoidable message, in terms of which we may then leaf back and gloss the present text in some detail. But it will remain a gloss on what is essentially a spatial representation and a spatial perception: the philosophical thoughts (which in any case involve space, as we shall see) will finally have been dependent on space, and inexpressible without it. This is of course a cinematographic kind of space, with its Einsteinian observer on a train moving through a landscape whose observation it alters at the very moment that it makes it possible. But what is most significant is not some possible influence of nascent cinema on Forster or on the modernist novel in general, but rather the confluence of the two distinct formal developments, of movie technology on the one hand, and of a certain type of modernist or proto-modernist language on the other, both of which seem to offer some space, some third term, between the subject and the object alike. Cinematographic perception is in that sense neither subjective nor psychological: there is nothing private or personal about it (and it was for that reason that I suggested, above, that characterizations of the modern as some inward turn were misleading). But it is not objective either in any conventional sense of realism or empiricism: nothing is indeed quite so perverse or aberrant for the truly postmodern person as the polemic expression "photographic realism"—as though photography, today so mysterious and contradictory an experience, had anything reassuringly trustworthy or reliable about it, for us a most unlikely guarantor of verisimilitude! This is why, although the category of *style* remains a fundamental one of the various modernisms, emerging with them and disappearing again when the psychic subject is notoriously eclipsed in the postmodern moment, it seems urgent to disjoin it from conventional notions of psychology and subjectivity: whence the therapeutic usefulness of the cinematographic parallel, where an apparatus takes the place of human psychology and perception. But this can most effectively be achieved by recoordinating the concept of style with some new account of the experience of space, both together now marking the emergence of the modern as such, and the place from which a whole bewilderingly varied set of modernisms begins to flourish.

Forster, at best a closet modernist, may seem an unlikely enough illustration of this process; but it was its tendential emergence that interested us, and not the full-blown thing itself. Meanwhile, if it is argued that England, the very heartland of imperialism, is also that national terrain which seems to have been the least propitious for the development of any indigenous modernism,[9] then that is surely also relevant for our present topic.

Yet at least one moment in the present passage seems to hold all the possibilities of some properly modernist language, past and future, instinct within itself, from Baudelaire to Eliot: a figure which speeds by like Mrs Munt's surroundings, only its false modesty drawing attention to itself (as always in Forster). It is "the great North Road ... suggestive of infinity", where the word "infinity" oddly disrupts the conventional description of the journey, seeming to open up some strange space outside the empirical world alongside it. Technology is of course the operator here, and in the light of Forster's anti-technological bias (as in the SF story "The Machines Roll") it is well to remember that modernism is not so much characterized by a position against or for technological modernity (think of the enthusiasm of the Futurists!) so much as by its inevitable inclusion. Here, indeed, it is perhaps less the train than rather speed itself which is included; and at first the Great North Road comes before us as the device by which that phenomenon is represented and indeed registered: the Eisensteinian parallel whereby a trajectory that cannot be visualized in itself is conveyed first through the indirection of its passing scenery, and then at length by the isolation of but one item in that changing scenery (an item that is therefore both still and in movement all at once), the cinematographic evocation of the great sweep and curve of the road as it both follows and diverges from the train tracks. Yet as Forster repeatedly uses his peculiar word "infinity," we come to realize that this metonymic continguity of the ancient highway with the modern railroad is not only a way of representing the latter, but rather a way in which the latter's modernity can be pressed into the service of disclosing some third reality, which is neither traditional nor modern empirical space, but rather the pressure of something more transcendent, a kind of Kantian sublimity, against the here and now. That other, vaster, unrepresentable space stands to the nameable and perceivable physical objects as the abstract word "infinity" does to the conventional language in which it is embedded, as with the gesture of an afterthought or an insignificant aside (recalling, however, some of the other strange abstractions that punctuate the narrative language of this period, like the expression "material interests" in *Nostromo*).

Yet now the same duality reappears within the structure of this figure itself and it is undecidable whether the Great North Road is the tenor or the vehicle; whether the roadway is intended, as in analogous moments in Baudelaire, to concretize the nebulous metaphysical concept "infinity," and by a momentary transfer of its visual properties to make that vague but lofty word a more vivid linguistic player in the textual game; or whether, on the other hand, it is rather the metaphysical prestige of the more noble idea that is supposed to resonate back on the banal highway, lending it *numen* and thereby transforming it into the merest promise of expressivity without having to affirm it as some official "symbol" of the conventionally mendacious kind. Modernism is itself this very hesitation; it emerges in this spatial gap within Forster's figure; it is at one with the contradiction between the contingency of physical objects and the demand for an impossible meaning, here marked by dead philosophical abstraction. The solution to this contradiction, which we call "style," is then the substitution of a spatial or perceptual "meaning" (whatever that now is) for the other kind (whatever that was, or might be in the future).

An even more articulated allegory of this process, whereby commonsense space perception is disrupted by the emergence here and there of a dawning sense of the non-perceptual spatial totality (Forster's "infinite"), is to be found in Virginia Woolf's far more overtly "modernist" text *To the*

Lighthouse, where the interruption of a network of physical trajectories to and from the island takes the form of Lilly Bristow's painting;

> and so, lightly and swiftly pausing, striking, she scored her canvas with brown running nervous lines which had no sooner settled there than they enclosed (she felt it looming out at her) a space. Down in the hollow of one wave she saw the next wave towering higher and higher above her. For what could be more formidable than that space? Here she was again, she thought, stepping back to look at it, drawn out of gossip, out of living, out of community with people into the presence of this formidable ancient enemy of hers—this other thing, this truth, this reality, which suddenly laid hands on her, emerged stark at the back of appearances and commanded her attention.[10]

Woolf's confrontation with this non-empirical space beyond space, this unrepresentable totality, is far more dramatic in its personification and its evocation as an event, than Foster's modest allusion, yet the aesthetic framework, which alone motivates the figural appearance of this new space, is at once what also threatens to undermine it, and to tempt the reader back into the conventional meanings of art or mysticism.

Yet Forster's figure also turns out to have a more conventional "meaning," as the rest of his novel instructs us: it will be perfectly proper to unravel it, provided we do not lose sight of its initial spatial and perceptual ground, and of the work of some new modernist language on our bodies and our sensorium that is its precondition. He goes on, indeed, to develop his ethos of place, as "the basis of all earthly beauty" (204), which he elaborates into something like a twofold salvational system, the twin paths of intimate human relations and of an immediate landscape. "We want to show him," says Margaret about the wretched Leonard Bast, "how he may get upsides with life. As I said, either friends, or the country, some ... either some very dear person or some very dear place seems necessary to relieve life's daily grey, and to show that it is grey. If possible, one should have both" (145). The place is of course the country house itself, the Howards End of the title; and the "dear person" the late Mrs Wilcox, who begins to merge with her dwelling to the point of becoming almost literally a "genius loci." Yet the representational dilemma remains, as in our earlier figure: Mrs Wilcox as a character draws her possibilities from that concrete place which is Howards End, while this last draws its evocative power from the spirit of Mrs Wilcox. The transformation of chance encounters ("only connect") into a Utopian social community presided over by a woman who is its providential spirit in a virtually literal sense; and the recovery of a Utopian landscape orchestrated by the well-nigh Shakespearean glorification of an ideal (and an anti-patriotic) England in Chapter XIX—the combination, indeed, the identification of these two visionary constructions is Forster's political as well as his aesthetic agenda in this novel.

Yet as he himself makes clear, it is not evident that the operation can be historically realized and completed (even though the novel itself gets written). For he will go on to suggest that the tendential conditions of modern civilization—"modernization" now, rather than aesthetic "modernism"!—are in the process of closing off one of these two avenues of personal and spiritual "salvation" (if that is not too lofty a word for it). Landscape is in the process of being obliterated, leaving only the more fragile and ephemeral safety net of the interpersonal behind it:

> London was but a foretaste of this nomadic civilization, which is altering human nature so profoundly, and throws upon personal relations a stress greater than they have ever borne before. Under cosmopolitanism, if it comes, we shall receive no help from the earth. Trees and meadows and mountains will only be a spectacle, and the binding force that they once exercised on character must be entrusted to Love alone. (261)

But what we must now add, and what now returns us to our starting point, is that London is very precisely that "infinity" of which we caught a glimpse on the Great North Road, or at least a "caricature" of it (Forster's word, p. 280). But now suddenly a whole set of terms falls into place and begins to coincide: cosmopolitanism, London, the nomadic, the stench of motorcars, antibilious pills, all begin to coalesce as a single historical tendency, and they are unexpectedly at one with "infinity" itself, which equally unexpectedly becomes the bad opposite of place, of Howards End, of the salvation through the here and the now (and incidentally of the regeneration of some older England that never existed, the Utopian England of Chapter XIX). But this is not simple romantic anti-urban or anti-modern nostalgia; it is not at all the conservative revulsion before the faceless industrial masses of *The Waste Land*, the modern urban world. And that for a final decisive reason, a final identification in this linked chain of phenomena: for infinity in this sense, this new grey placelessness, as well as what prepares it, also bears another familiar name. It is in Forster *imperialism*, or Empire, to give it its period designation. It is Empire which stretches the roads out to infinity, beyond the bounds and borders of the national state, Empire which leaves London behind it as a new kind of spatial agglomeration or disease, and whose commercialism now throws up those practical and public beings, like Mr Wilcox, around whose repression of the personal Forster's message will also play, taking on new forms we have no time to examine here:

> In the motorcar was another type whom Nature favors—the Imperial. Healthy, ever in motion, it hopes to inherit the earth. It breeds as quickly as the yeoman, and as soundly; strong is the temptation to acclaim it as a super-yeoman, who carries his country's virtue overseas. But the Imperialist is not what he thinks or

> seems. He is a destroyer. He prepares the way for cosmopolitanism, and though his ambitions may be fulfilled, the earth that he inherits will be grey. (323)

With this identification—the coincidence of "infinity" with "imperialism"—we come full circle, and a component of the imperialist situation appears in human form, or in the representational language of a narrative character. Yet the representation is incomplete, and thereby epistemologically distorted and misleading: for we are only able to see that face the "Imperial type" turns inward, towards the internal metropolitan reality. The other pole of the relationship, what defines him fundamentally and essentially in his "imperial" function—the persons of the colonized—remains structurally occluded, and cannot but so remain, necessarily, as a result of the limits of the system, and the way in which internal national or metropolitan daily life is absolutely sundered from this other world henceforth in thrall to it.[11] But since representation, and cognitive mapping as such, is governed by an "intention towards totality,"[12] those limits must also be drawn back into the system, which marks them by an image, the image of the Great North Road as infinity: a new spatial language, therefore—modernist "style"—now becomes the marker and the substitute (the "tenant-lieu," or place-holding, in Lacanian language) of the unrepresentable totality. With this a new kind of value emerges (and it is this which is generally loosely and misleadingly referred to as modernist aestheticism): for if "infinity" (and "imperialism") are bad or negative in Forster, its perception, as a bodily and poetic process, is no longer that, but rather a positive achievement and an enlargement of our sensorium: so that the beauty of the new figure seems oddly unrelated to the social and historical judgement which is its content.

What I have tried to suggest about this "event" on the border or limit of representation might also have been shown for the representation of inner or metropolitan space itself, for the national daily life which must remain its primary raw material.[13] Because in the imperial world system this last is now radically incomplete, it must by compensation be formed into a self-subsisting totality: something Forster uniquely attempts to achieve by way of his providential ideology, which transforms chance contacts, coincidence, the contingent and random encounters between isolated subjects, into a Utopian glimpse of achieved community. This glimpse is both moral and aesthetic all at once, for it is the achievement of something like an aesthetic pattern of relationships that confirms it as a social reality, however ephemeral: and the coincidence of the social (grasped in moral terms) and the aesthetic is then what allows other related works (such as those of Virginia Woolf) to refocus it by way of operations which look more aestheticizing than Forster's. Here also the internal social totality will remain incomplete; but the internal social classes are nonetheless explicitly designated by their absence (thus, Leonard is carefully characterized as non-proletarian, as standing "at the extreme edge of gentility. He was not in the abyss but he could see it, and at times people whom he knew had dropped in, and counted no more") (45). This internal subsumption is sharply to be distinguished from the exclusion of an external or colonized people (whose absence is not even designated): the distinction would correspond roughly to that which obtains in Freud between repression (neurosis) and foreclusion (psychosis).

The hypothesis suggested here—between the emergence of a properly modernist "style" and the representational dilemmas of the new imperial world system—will be validated only by the kind of new work it enables: by some fresh (formal and structural) approach to the moderns able to formulate their historical specificity more adequately for us today than the descriptions we have inherited from their contemporaries. Yet there is also another way in which such a hypothesis might be "verified," at least by way of an Einsteinian "thought-experiment": this would be something like a principle of experimental variation or aesthetic falsifiability, in which this particular metropolitan or First World modernist laboratory experiment is tested against radically different environmental conditions. These are not, in this period, to be found in what will come to be called the Third World, or in the colonies: there the face of imperialism is brute force, naked power, open exploitation; but there also the mapping of the imperialist world system remains structurally incomplete, for the colonial subject will be unable to register the peculiar transformations of First World or metropolitan life which accompany the imperial relationship. Nor will it, from the point of view of the colonized, be of any interest to register those new realities, which are the private concern of the masters, and which a colonized culture must simply refuse and repudiate. What we seek, therefore, is a kind of exceptional situation, one of overlap and coexistence between these two incommensurable realities which are those of the lord and of the bondsman altogether, those of the metropolis and of the colony simultaneously. Our experimental variation, then, would presuppose, were it possible in the first place, a national situation which reproduces the appearance of First World social reality and social relationships—perhaps through the coincidence of its language with the imperial language—but whose underlying structure is in fact much closer to that of the Third World or of colonized daily life. A modernism arising in these circumstances could then be inspected and interrogated for its formal and structural differences from the works produced within the metropolis and examined above. But at least one such peculiar space exists, in the historical contingency of our global system: it is Ireland, and the uniqueness of the Irish situation will now allow us, as it were experimentally, to verify our argument up to this point. For it allows us to make a deduction, as it were, *a priori* from our hypotheses, and then to compare that deduction with the historical realities of Irish culture. If the thesis is correct, then, we may expect to find, in some abstractly possible Irish modernism, a form which on the one hand unites Forster's sense of the providential yet seemingly accidental encounters of characters with Woolf's aesthetic closure, but which on the other hand projects those onto a radically different kind of space, a space no longer central, as in English life, but marked as marginal and ec-centric after the fashion of the colonized areas of the imperial system. That colonized space may then be expected to transform the modernist formal project radically, while still retaining a distant family likeness to its imperial variants. But this "deduction" finds immediate historical confirmation, for I have in fact been describing *Ulysses*.

For in *Ulysses* space does not have to be made symbolic in order to achieve closure and meaning: its closure is objective, endowed by the colonial situation itself—whence the non-poetic, non-stylistic nature of Joyce's language. In Forster, the deeper reality of the encounter, the coincidence, the determinate meetings or the five-minute lag that prevents them from coming about, are played off against the metropolis, which "one visualizes as a tract of quivering grey, intelligent without purpose, and excitable without love; as a spirit that has altered before it can be chronicled; as a heart that certainly beats, but with no pulsation of humanity" (108). In Joyce, the encounter is at one with Dublin itself, whose compact size anachronistically permits the now archaic life of the older city-state. It is therefore unnecessary to generate an aesthetic form of closure distinct from the city, which in First World modernism must be imposed by the violence of form upon this last as compensation.

One wants, indeed, to go even further than this and to assert that what has been seen as the linguistic dimension of modernism proper—namely, "style" as such, as something like an absolute category of the modern canon—is also absent in Joyce. The spatial poetry that has been detected in Forster has, for one thing, no equivalent in *Ulysses*. "Am I walking into eternity along Sandymount strand?" is thrust back into Stephen's consciousness and marked as subjective. At the other end of the continuum, the great anamorphic spaces of the Nighttown chapter take place much too close to the eye, as it were, to be characterized in terms of images. A personal style, evolving towards the conventionally modern, can be detected in early Joyce, and may be identified by way of traces of Walter Pater's mannerisms: all that survives of that in *Ulysses* is the self-conscious placement of crucial adverbs. Otherwise, style, as a category of some absolute subject, here disappears, and Joyce's palpable linguistic games and experiments are rather to be seen as impersonal sentence combinations and variations, beyond all point of view ("Love loves to love love. Nurse loves the new chemist. Constable 14A loves Mary Kelly. Gerty MacDowell loves the boy that has the bicycle

... "etc.): whence one's occasional sense that (as with revolutionary modes of production) Joyce leaps over the stage of the modern into full post-modernism. The pastiche of styles in the Oxen of the Sun not merely discredits the category of style as such, but presents an enumeration of English styles, of the styles of the imperial occupying armies.

Even the matter of coincidence indeed—so crucial in Forster and Woolf—takes on a different meaning in Joyce, where such intersections are everywhere, but have little of the dubious providentiality they project in our other works (a partial exception needs to be made here for the father–son thematics). Leonard catches sight of Margaret and Mr Wilcox in Saint Paul's at a climactic moment; Stephen catches sight of Mr Bloom in a more doubtful, but also more aesthetic moment; yet this last does not raise the same questions as the former. London (or the Manhattan of *Manhattan Transfer*) are agglomerations (and metropolises) in which such encounters are sheer coincidence; Dublin is a classical city in which they are not merely normal but expected. This is to say that a concept of the urban is present in *Ulysses* which contains and motivates those very encounters and intersections crucial to the modern, but lends them a different resonance. But Dublin, as we have said, remains classical because it is also a colonial city: and this "peculiarity" of Joyce's narrative content now determines a certain number of other formal results. For one thing, encounters in Joyce are already (or perhaps I should say, still) linguistic: they are stories, gossip, they have already been assimilated into speech and storytelling while taking place, so that the demiurgic transformation of the modernist poet or writer—the need to invent a new speech in order to render the freshly revealed, non-linguistic contingencies of modern life—is in Joyce short-circuited. Meanwhile, this essential linguisticality of *Ulysses*—a book, as he said himself, about "the last great talkers"—is itself a result of imperialism, which condemns Ireland to an older rhetorical past and to the survivals of oratory (in the absence of action), and which freezes Dublin into an underdeveloped village in which gossip and rumor still reign supreme.

Meanwhile, history itself, which must elsewhere be imported and introduced by fiat, is here already part of the urban fabric: the occupying army is present, it is perfectly natural for us to encounter its soldiers, as it is to witness the viceregal procession; the spasmodic efforts at militancy—such as the assassination of the Invincibles—are still vivid in the collective memory, and the appearance of one of the survivors is a Proustian shock, no doubt, but perfectly plausible. It is normal for the British intelligentsia to visit this interesting cultural backwater; normal for the nationalist debates (very specifically including the one around the national language) to sputter on in pubs, bars and meeting places; while the very fact of the pub itself, of public space in which you meet and talk, is itself a happy survival of an older urban life, which will have no equivalent in metropolitan literature, where meetings between disparate characters must be more artificially arranged, by means of receptions and summer houses.

Even the one section of *Ulysses* which resembles a rather different modernist approach towards space—the Wandering Rocks, which is the direct inspiration of Dos Passos and his discontinuous literary cross-cutting—is the exception that proves the rule, since these palpable discontinuities are already mere appearance: we know already in fact that these disjoined characters are already connected, by acquaintance and history, and that a shift in perspective would at once cause the illusion of external chance and coincidence to vanish utterly away. The *Odyssey* parallel itself—which may superficially as an aesthetic design and allusion resemble the painting in Virginia Woolf's *To the Lighthouse*—must also be rethought in the context of imperialism. It is of course the great formal pretext, whose setting in place then allows Joyce to elaborate the contingencies of his individual chapters without any deeper motivation (the other levels of the parallels, the colors, the tropes, the organs of the body, rather resemble Freudian "secondary elaboration" than genuine symbolism): but what must be stressed is that it is not the meaning of the *Odyssey* which is exploited here, but rather its spatial properties. The *Odyssey* serves as a *map*: it is indeed, on Joyce's reading of it, the one classical narrative whose closure is that of the map of a whole complete and equally closed region of the globe, as though somehow the very episodes themselves merged back into space, and the reading of them came to be indistinguishable from map-reading. None of the other classical parallels in modern literature has this peculiar spatial dimension (think for example of the various subjects of Greek tragedy); indeed, it is as though this Third World modernism slyly turned the imperial relationship inside out, appropriating the great imperial space of the Mediterranean in order to organize the space of the colonial city, and to turn its walks and paths into the closure of a form and of a grand cultural monument.

(*1990*)

Notes

1 See Martin Green, *Deeds of Empire* (New York, 1979); Philip D. Curtin, *The Image of Africa: British Ideas and Action 1780–1850* (Madison, 1964); Brian Z. Street, *The Savage in Literature: Representations of "Primitive" Society in English Fiction 1858–1920* (London, 1972); and especially Edward Said, "*Kim*: The Pleasures of Imperialism," in *Raritan* VII: 2 (Fall, 1987), 27–64, reprinted in his *Culture and Imperialism* (New York, 1993).

2 In what follows, the word "metropolis" will designate the imperial nation state as such, "metropolitan," then applying to its internal national realities and daily life (which are of course not exclusively urban, although organized around some central urban "metropolis" in the narrower sense).

3 Two other essays of mine explore the links between a modernist poetics and what we might today call Third World space: see essays 9 and 11, below on Stevens and Rimbaud.

4 I draw here essentially on Anthony Brewer's excellent *Marxist Theories of Imperialism: A Critical Survey* (London, 1980).

5 Bill Warren's *Imperialism: Pioneer of Capitalism* (London, 1980) may be seen as a contemporary reformulation of these classical positions.

6 The reference is to Edward J. Dudley and Maximilian Novak, eds., *The Wild Man Within: An Image in Western Thought from the Renaissance to Romanticism* (Pittsburgh, 1973).

7 The signal exception being, of course *A Passage to India* by this same author, about which see below.

8 E.M. Forster, *Howards End* (London, 1910; New York, 1921), pp. 14–15; henceforth all references will be given in the text to this edition.

9 It is, I take it, the position of Terry Eagleton's stimulating *Exiles and Emigrés* (New York, 1970), that all the most important modern writers of what we think of as the *English* canon are in fact social marginals of various kinds, when not outright foreigners. The analogy to be explored with Britain is of course the Austro-Hungarian empire, which was an extraordinarily rich terrain for a variety of the most important modernisms in all the arts (and in philosophy as well). Hugo von Hofmannsthal may here be taken as the non-ethnic Austrian norm, from which these modernisms are the deviation: his "Letter from Lord Chandos" is a paradigmatic text about the discovery and subsequent repudiation of the "modern."

10 Virginia Woolf, *To the Lighthouse* (London, 1927), p. 236.

11 Africa is set in place by the mediation of Charles Wilcox, who works in Uganda for his father's Imperial and West African Rubber Company (see pp. 195–6). About *A Passage to India*, what needs to be said here is (a) that Forster's luck lay in the fact that one of the many Indian languages is the one called Indian English, which he was able to learn like a foreign language; and (b) that the novel is restricted to British and Muslim characters—(Islam being, as Lévi-Strauss instructs us in *Tristes Tropiques*, the last and most advanced of the great Western monotheisms)—the Hindus being specifically designated as the Other, which is inaccessible to Western representation.

12 George Lukács, *History and Class Consciousness* (Cambridge, MA, 1971), p. 174 (where the German "*Intention*" is translated "aspiration").

13 My oldest thoughts on all this were stimulated into being by Gertrude Stein's remarkable "What is English Literature?" in *Lectures in America* (Boston, 1985). "If you live a daily life and it is all yours, and you come to own everything outside your daily life besides and it is all yours, you naturally begin to explain. You naturally continue describing your daily life which is all yours, and you naturally begin to explain how you own everything besides. You naturally begin to explain that to

yourself and you naturally begin to explain it to those living your daily life who own it with you, everything outside, and you naturally explain it in a kind of way to some of those whom you own." (41) For more on this work of Stein see below, essay 17.

8

Joyce or Proust?

Canonical questions are as contradictory for modernism as they are unavoidable. Only by putting heterogeneous (or singular) works together can some larger notion of "modernism" be constructed; and yet the works in question for the most part came into being by way of fierce resistance to the art objects all around them, whether of mass cultural or of high aesthetic origin. Still, the construction of the modern proceeded by way of intimidating juxtapositions, poets from a few selected languages, or Joyce alongside Proust, with Thomas Mann in some proximate distance, until he was replaced by the less assimilable Musil (Kafka always occupying an uncomfortably unclassifiable position with respect to these architectonic designers). Now, in the catastrophe of the postmodern, most of these canonical groupings—like the old-fashioned tableaux of nineteenth-century or seventeenth-century paintings—have disintegrated, leaving the surviving figures—Joyce, Proust, Kafka—visible like the occasional lone high-rise in a landscape of rubble. But the very manner of their survival provides some interesting and unexpected answers, which scarcely confirm any of the standard canonical verbiage about greatness, genius or eternal art.

Where these works survive and are still eagerly read, one can observe, I think, the complete falling away of the traditional interpretations and meanings that used to accompany them like an indispensable entourage of bodyguards, drivers and public relations experts. No one is now interested in the madeleine or "involuntary memory"; no one cares about the father-son relationships in *Ulysses* or the *Odyssey* parallels; above all, no one needs the humanist generalizations that purport to attach these texts to vague but universalizing and normative conceptions of life and experience. It is certainly refreshing to be done with these stereotypes of the general education course, the "history of ideas," and the more "literary" segments of the book-reviewing industry; bracing to find oneself in the post-atomic atmosphere of a cultural multiplicity and fragmentation which cannot be legitimated and codified or authorized in any of the boring old ways. One's pleasure in this new freedom is only stimulated by an obvious dilemma, since not only the modernist cultural authorities, but also clearly enough the authors themselves, believed in their interpretive scaffolding and took the system of the physical organs, or the identity of the Swann and Guermantes "ways" seriously, and not only as constructional devices and organizational pretexts. What to do now, in postmodernity and its readings, when such devices have become unacceptable? Do not these vast "texts" then break down into so many discontinuous moments of sheer textuality and, thus textualized, lose any further claim to be interpreted as aesthetic totalities? Or does the question of what counts as a textual singularity not fatally revive, by way of Viconian or other circularities, all the old aesthetic speculations as to some narrative essence of poetic language in the first place?

Yet another comparison of Proust and Joyce and their singularities is not likely to provide answers to these questions, but perhaps it will be able to touch on the constructional problems in passing, always mindful of the way in which construction and interpretation intersect. Certainly the reflexions that follow start from the premise that Proust and Joyce had nothing whatsoever in common, save perhaps for pathological jealousy:[1] both books are deeply marked by it, even though Joyce motivates this "device" (as the Russian Formalists might have called it) far more successfully than Proust, in whom its extensive indulgence scars the uncorrected text of *La Prisonnière* with repetitions that have no equivalent elsewhere in these pages. Yet even to name this obsession (whether we want to call it jealousy or something else) is already to take a position outside the work. It is not because such a position is clinical or diagnostic that it must alert suspicion: rather, it is because the diagnosis is in reality yet another interpretation which seeks to unify these texts in an operation not different in kind from those we have enumerated above. Thus, the "deeper meaning" of the work is jealousy, now perhaps taken in Heideggerian fashion as a fundamental expression of our being-in-the-world and our relationship to the Other. Why not? The conceit is fresher than the traditional versions, and might well lead us into new and unrehearsed textual discoveries.

Yet the objection remains, which has to do with the position from which the interpretation is staged, rather than with its accuracy or productivity. Such attempts to unify two long and heterogeneous texts express indeed what Lukács might have called an "aspiration to totality," but which Coleridge named the Imagination, the unifying force of textual production fully as much as of textual reception. It is the Imagination that seeks to draw all the elements of our reading into the form of a "concrete universal," and to translate the many local acts of sentence perception into a meaningful and somehow unified process which we can characterize with a theoretical formula or matheme. And to the degree to which these books stage themselves as *le Livre*, or the Book of the World, this impulse is surely not illegitimate but shared by the authors themselves, as has already been pointed out.

The usefulness of Coleridge's idea lies, however, not in its criteria for judgement, but rather very specifically in its structure as an asymmetrical binary opposition: for the impulse that stands opposed to that of the Imagination is identified as the decorative activity and embroidery of Fancy as such, for Coleridge the very sign and symptom of eighteenth-century rhetoric, which can for us, however, be reinterpreted in terms of sensory immediacy and the minutiae of the here-and-now. At this point, then, Coleridge's great distinction takes on the metaphysical proportions of a vision of the world's gap, between an absent totality and a meaningless contingency, or between form and content, or spirit and matter, what Heidegger calls World and Earth, collective history and existential individuality. It thereby becomes the very situation of the great modernists themselves, whose inventions are all original, and impossible, solutions for overcoming this gap between the overall organizational Idea and the local activity of the individual sentence. It is a gap which remains concealed in traditional storytelling and in that realism which in the nineteenth-century comes to be taken as a natural or common-sense representation of reality: traditional storytelling opts for the Imagination, while the nineteenth-century novel attempts a precarious balance between *récit* and *roman*, between summary and scene, between telling and showing. But the mark of the emergence of modernism is to be detected in the weakening of any naturalized belief in the tale type or the shape of destiny, in the reliability of Imagination itself, which it must seek to strengthen and to reinstate artificially by way of ingenious architectonic schemes.

Still, could one not argue for a view of Proust or Joyce which saw each as a unified linguistic process, a mode of the production of language as it were, which seeks tirelessly to assimilate all the materials of the outside world into a specific style or linguistic medium? This would seem to be a more apt characterization of Proust than Joyce, who transcends style itself in so many ways and leaves his own personal style—a set of *fin-de-siècle* mannerisms *à la* Walter Pater—behind him dissolving like a mirage around the character of Stephen. It might be better to insist on the orality of both texts: Joyce's as the epic of the last great talkers, as he himself put it; Proust's as the infinite monologue of a witty and erudite salon commentator whispered in your ear. We will see, however, that language plays a rather different role in the construction of these totalities than the positive one implied here.

1. Missing Portions I: Falling through the Cracks

Indeed, the constructional problem posed by any totality is not that of inclusion but that of the inevitable and necessary leaving out of content, and thereby that of the masking of those omissions, in order to legitimate the totality effect as such. Since the totality—whether it is conceived as History or Being, as capitalism or Utopia—is clearly unavailable for sense perception or for any immediate appropriation, the effort might better be described, in the Heideggerian formula, as an attempt to make the absent totality appear, to cause it to rise into visibility, in what must inevitably be an ephemeral apparition or glimpse, the event of an appearing which has however its own specific conditions of possibility.

Proust knew something about the process of leaving out, and the way in which successful omission must bear, not on a mere detail, but on a whole strategic dimension of the representation in question. It is something he explicitly discusses in connection with what one may consider (along with the pastiche of the Goncourt brothers' florid account of the Verdurin circle in the last volume) a text in competition with his own, namely, the memoirs of high society left behind by one of his own characters. For it turns out—in a paradigmatic Proustian reversal—that the nondescript old friend of his grandmother's whom the narrator meets at the seaside is not only herself a Guermantes in her own right, but also one of the most celebrated diplomatic hostesses of the age, whose salon has welcomed virtually all the major political figures of pre-war Europe. But the narrator's mistake in underestimating Mme de Villeparisis is not one any reader of her *Memoirs* would be likely to make, inasmuch as there

> certaines relations médiocres qu'avait l'auteur disparaissent, parce qu'elles n'ont pas l'occasion d'y être citées; et des visiteuses qu'il n'avait pas n'y font pas faute, parce que dans l'espace forcément restraint qu'offrent ces Mémoires, peu de personnes peuvent figurer et que, si ces personnes sont des personages princiers, des personnalités historiques, l'impression maximum d'élégance que des Mémoires puissant donner au public se trouve atteinte.[2] (P II 491–2)

> certain unimportant friendships of the author have disappeared because there is never any occasion to refer to them; while the absence of those who did not come to see her leaves no gap because, in the necessarily restricted space at the author's disposal, only a few persons can appear, and if these persons are royal personages, historic personalities, then the utmost impression of distinction which any volume of memoirs can convey to the public is achieved. (SM I 854)

This is, as it were, a principle of the positivity of the form itself, which can only register presence, and from which absences are themselves as it were omitted: thus what in fact marks Mme de Villeparisis's salon as a second-rate one, the deliberate abstention from it of any number of fashionable figures, will not be registered for any future reader, who will only note the frequentation by the great names in the history books.

Another principle at work in this strikingly dialectical process of omission (in which it is the omission which is itself omitted) needs to be mentioned at this point; and it has to do with what we may call the synchronic dimension of the Proustian present and the role it plays in the misunderstandings of later generations of readers, which is to say in Proust's very conception of the historical past as such. Like the American in the last volume, readers of later generations have no conception of the systematicity of the *haut monde* of this period and cannot situate the often unfamiliar names in the lofty circles they then inhabited:

> Au judgement de Mme Leroi, le salon de Mme de Villeparisis était un salon de troisième ordre; et Mme de Villeparisis souffrait du jugement de Mme Leroi. Mais personne ne sait plus guère aujourd'hui qui était Mme Leroi, son jugement s'est évanoui, et c'est le salon de Mme. de Villeparisis, où fréquentait la reine de Suède, où avaient fréquenté le duc d'Aumale, le duc de Broglie, Thiers, Montalembert, Mgr Dupanloup, qui sera considéré comme un des plus brillants du XIXe siècle ... (P II 492)

> In the opinion of Mme Leroi, Mme de Villeparisis's parties were third-rate; and Mme de Villeparisis felt the sting of Mme Leroi's opinion. But hardly anyone today remembers who Mme Leroi was, her opinions have vanished into thin air, and it is the drawing-room of Mme de Villeparisis, frequented as it was by the Queen of Sweden, and as it had been by the Duc d'Aumale, the Duc de Broglie, Thiers, Montalembert, Mgr Dupanloup, which will be looked up as one of the most brilliant of the nineteenth century ... (SM I 854)

What only needs to be added is that Proust himself does not merely assign the correct values to the various aristocratic characters he mentions: he also inserts and includes an account of the mechanisms by which those values and that system are later on misperceived and misinterpreted.

That omission can take on more empirical forms, the four-volume Tadié edition of 1987–9 richly instructs us, for its notes contain an impressive number of significant yet suppressed episodes, such as Odette's clandestine affair with Dr Cottard (an episode which Raoul Ruiz's splendid film of *Le Temps retrouvé* reinstates). These episodes and anecdotes, however, whatever their intrinsic interest, are testimony to an even more significant structural peculiarity of Proust's text to which we will return later, namely its capacity for infinite expansion and very precisely for the insertion (or reinsertion) of any number of interpolated episodes of precisely this kind.

For suppressions are also additions, to the degree to which they can be restored; and the suppression of such new material is not unlike the way in which, in this text, memory restores the forgotten past, itself so often in Proust compared to spatial dimensions, like parts of a house—staircases, upper storeys—which are suddenly added and become illuminated and open for representation.[3] The point, however, is that other parts of these spaces vanish without a trace: thus any visitor to the museum in Illiers (the original Combray of Proust himself) will be stunned to find a profusion of Algerian artifacts and souvenirs, rugs, memorabilia of all kinds. We have long since accustomed ourselves to thinking of Joyce as a postcolonial writer; but we are certainly ill prepared to try out such a focus on Proust. It turns out, however, that the husband of the famous Tante Léonie (the despotic Louis XIV of the household and village) was a functionary in Algeria, the future site of one of the major wars of national liberation of the twentieth century (and of the nineteenth century as well). Surely the Freudian concept of repression is exceedingly appropriate, indeed well-nigh unavoidable, when contemplating the removal without a trace of this character and the social and historical raw material associated with him; it is very much a dog which did not bark in the night.

Finally, the most important dimension strategically omitted from these volumes, and the one which he himself designates at crucial points in the narrative, is paradoxically the omission of daily life itself. This will be a perverse judgement for those for whom the "iterativity"[4] of *Combray* constitutes the very essence of the representation of the everyday and its conquest and appropriation by narrative language. But this is to ignore the process whereby everyday life and existential experience are everywhere in Proust translated and transmuted into anecdote, into gossip and the traffic in witty and often cruel and pointed stories framed in order to be told to other people (in the event, to ourselves as readers). We will return to this fundamental omission later on, but it suffices for the moment to sample what the narrator considers to have been the low points of his existence:

> Je suis pourtant ici en pleine nature, eh bien, c'est avec froideur, avec ennui que mes yeux constatent la ligne qui sépare votre front lumineux de votre tronc d'ombre. (P IV 433)

> Behold me in the midst of nature's beauty and yet it is with indifference and ennui that my eyes take note of the line that separates the sun-bathed foliage from the shadowed trunk...(SM II 983)

Such complaints bear centrally on the very texture of time itself, the reality of everyday temporality in Proust, a self-perpetuating existential dissatisfaction which for once, significantly, fails to be translated into anecdotes and storytelling, into witty self-deprecation or satiric projection. Certainly, nothing in Proust is immediate in the philosophical sense, indeed the very burden of Proustian representation lies in thoroughgoing attack on immediacy as we shall see. Yet the dimension of gossip and storytelling masks this immediacy with a consumable narrative which is here stripped away, allowing us to glimpse the empty time of boredom that lies beneath and that is, with one signal exception, properly unrepresentable. From this perspective it may be seen that even the sufferings of jealousy, as they come to dominate the later pages of the novel, are in effect a cover and a concealment of this deeper futility: jealousy foregrounds the event of loss and exemplifies that suffering which Proust was to theorize as essential to the very content of art as well as to its production.[5] Here, however, what is deplored is that very absence of the "talent" which might have succeeded in producing narrative in the first place (and yet, by another "narrative" reversal, this plaintive litany of weaknesses is required in order to transform the imminent burst of joy and creativity into an event about which one can precisely tell a story, the story Proust tells us in his last volume).

Omission in Joyce is evidently a more straightforward affair: I remember being startled by Hugh Kenner's observation[6] that, between the discomfiture with the Citizen and the onset of that summer evening which "had begun to fold the world in its mysterious embrace"[7] (284), another event took place which was apparently not of sufficient significance to merit chapter status (unless the "significance" is limited to finding an *Odyssey* parallel, in which case the birth that follows is scarcely fully motivated either). This was a visit to the widow Dignam with the intent of offering the bereaved family a modest collection of funds, an event succinctly noted in the Gerty MacDowell chapter as follows:

> Houses of mourning so depressing because you never know. Anyhow she wants the money. Must call to those Scottish Widows as I promised. (311)

What is it that we "never know"? Whether they are really grieving or not? What to say to the bereaved (whether sincere or not)? The sincerity of one's own expressions of regret (or even of sympathy)? Dignam is not someone with whom the abstemious Bloom could have been expected to have much in common. Memories of the little boy underscore the differences (even though they tend to recall Mr Bloom's grief at the loss of his own father):

> The last night pa was boosed he was standing on the landing there bawling out for his boots to go out to Tunney's for to boose more and he looked butty and short in his shirt. Never see him again. (207)

But Mr Bloom does see him again, in the Nighttown phantasmagoria:

> The beagle lifts his snout, showing the grey scorbutic face of Paddy Dignam. He has gnawed all. He exhales a putrid carcassfed breath. He grows to human size and shape. His dachshund coat becomes a brown mortuary habit. His green eye flashes bloodshot. Half of one ear, all the nose and both thumbs are ghoul-eaten ... He lifts his mutilated ashen face moonwards and bays lugubriously. (385)

Still, it could be argued that even this nightmarish vision does not approach the interstices of the content, the real void between the events *Ulysses* does represent, insofar as it refers back specifically to Mr Bloom's reveries and associations during the cemetery chapter, or, in other words, to positive elements already present in the text itself, to a fantasy about the world under the earth and the fate of the dead which is not itself an absence or a gap but rather itself something existing in the world, precisely *qua* fantasy or daydream:

> Wait. There he goes.
> An obese grey rat toddled along the side of the
> crypt, moving the pebbles....
> Wonder does the news go about whenever a fresh one
> is let down. Underground communication. We learned
> that from them ... (94)

To be sure, these are not the positivities of empiricism, but rather linguistic positivities: Joyce presupposes that the ontic has already been transmitted into the various inner languages of his characters, which range from those of the literary intellectual or the newspaperman, all the way to the genuine Dubliners, the denizens of the pubs. Only Bloom's "style" is somehow arbitrary; Joyce asks us to accept as "natural" these famous "telegraphic" reveries, which are unmotivated, save for the interest in technological inventions or get-rich-quick schemes ("we learned that from them"), in other words the *Popular Mechanics* or *Reader's Digest* version of modernity. But this linguistic persona is not as plausible as that of Proust (the salon raconteur), not because it is not fully worked out verbally, but because the social type is not really validated by social convention: in that sense Mr Bloom is more American than he is Jewish or Irish, if those stereotypes mean anything.

At any rate, Mr Bloom's associations fill up the empty spaces of that to which we are positively present—in a decoration very consistent with what Coleridge called Fancy; but, save for the visit to the Dignams, they do little to hint at the gaps and empty spaces between those positivities, which also include past and future, insofar as those memories and anticipations are part of the ontic present. But the presumptive breaks in that present, the dim suspicion that Odysseus had himself made other stops on his home journey which Homer failed to note down—no such nagging suspicions distract us from the here-and-now of the text, and it is worth asking how that can possibly be so.

2. The Totality-effect

Form is in other words what has the function of preventing such questions from arising: for it is clear that the text cannot include everything, but also that it can take its precautions to ensure that the omissions we have hypothesized are never noticed. This is then where the *Odyssey* parallel comes in, as well as all the humanist interpretations we have vilified in passing. For a comprehensive interpretation (father–son relationship as historical tradition, or unity of the nation, or the fatal ruptures in both of these) has at least the merit of signaling completion (as do Joyce's own suggestions: the complete collection of the organs of the body, the complete dictionary of rhetorical figure, etc.). The *Odyssey* signals completion in another way: by way of the sixteen episodes, nothing to be added or subtracted, Homer constituting in effect a second nature in terms of which this modern selection is naturalized and its motivation secured.

To be sure, the unity of the chapter itself has another genealogy, closer to home: it lies in the pioneering organization of the individual chapter by Flaubert, in *L'éducation sentimentale*, which foregrounds an immense affective logic, sweeping more immediate chronological and even thematic units together into one larger unification of a different type altogether. Zola then institutionalizes the form in the *Rougon-Macquart* series, where each chapter, now standardized in length and narrative function, serves an equivalent function in that prodigious codification which is the production of form in naturalism. Joyce certainly explodes that uniformity and the equivalence on which it is based, without returning to any of the longer temporal rhythms which Flaubert's chapters subsumed: in Joyce what is retained of this earlier development is simply the ratification of the pure form itself. The chapter is here in *Ulysses* always a complete unit, the very sign of completeness as such, which on the one hand approaches the luminous abstraction of the Platonic idea, while on the other it begins to portend the dialectical category of totality. Yet each "Idea" is different from every other in this constellation which is *Ulysses*: each quasi-totality is a monad both unlike every other and yet so proximate as to differ only slightly and imperceptibly and to escape categories of analogy altogether. Why should there not have been more such chapters? Could there not have been more than the twelve, without disturbing our feeling, about the book as a whole, that it is enough? We are here flying beneath the radar ceiling of quantity, the vanishing point is so cunningly placed as to foreclose any glimpse of a further horizon.

Yet I am tempted to dramatize this unique formal innovation in yet another way, which finds encouragement in Proust's great comment on Flaubert's use of the *passé simple* (or rather of his deployment of the alternation between *passé simple*, or preterite, and imperfect), namely that it was as revolutionary a historical event as Kant's invention of the categories.[8] Yes, it is precisely the notion of the category (the category of the category, as Derrida liked contemptuously to put it) that is called for here to convey the portentousness of Joyce's innovation. For it is precisely as a new mode of organizing human experience that Joyce's form production must here be appreciated, and what better way to do justice to it than to claim that in *Ulysses* Joyce invented the single day as a new category of lived experience.

The implication is that something like a revolution in daily life, in the everyday or the quotidian, is to be grasped here: unless we want to go so far as to associate this new form with the very invention of daily life as such in modernity, along with the claim that however people lived temporality in older modes of production, it was not by way of what we now call everydayness, a phenomenological essence in which the industrial-urban, wage-labor, centered subjectivity, and the nuclear family all "participate" as well (to use Plato's conceptuality). Compare this emergence with a contemporaneous but unrelated development in Freud: the discovery that the dream material must always take its pretext and its starting point in the events of the previous day; and we will begin to appreciate the privilege and the burden of this new kind of temporality.

We can also celebrate it in Lacanian terms as the emergence of a new signifier, for it is that as well, nor is it sufficiently appreciated that the Lacanian doctrine of the signifier is not one of immutability and of eternal structures but rather a matter of historical innovation, at whatever geological pace:

> The day is a being distinct from all the objects it contains and manifests, it's probably even more weighty and present than any of them, and it's impossible to think of it, even in the most primitive human experience, as the simple return of an experience.
>
> It suffices to mention the prevalence of a rhythm of sleep in the first few months of human life for us to have all sorts of reasons to believe that it isn't due to any empirical apprehension that at a given moment—this is how I illustrate the initial symbolic nihilations—the human being detaches itself from the day. The human being is not, as everything leads us to think is the case for the animal, simply immersed in a phenomenon such as that of the alternations of day and night. The human being poses the day as such, and the day thereby becomes presence of the day—against a background that is not a background of concrete nighttime, but of possible absence of daytime, where the night dwells, and vice versa moreover. Very early on, day and night are signifying codes, not experiences. They are connotations, and the empirical and concrete day only comes forth as an imaginary correlative, originally, very early on.[9]

It is then this category of the single day as a supreme unity of human temporality that serves to ratify Joyce's totality-effect by excluding the unwanted questions about further inclusions and new material not contained already within the text.

We might also have dwelt for a moment on the formal innovation of Joyce's ending as well: for on the face of it a totality cannot be concluded as it is somehow outside of time, while night apparently naturalizes the end of the day sufficiently to bracket the question permanently. Yet a text's sentences are not out of time, and Joyce has here also projected a momentous formal innovation, in which *Ulysses* is completed not by one but rather by two endings. On the one hand, the Nighttown chapter recombines all the elements of the preceding chapters, producing all kinds of new relationships between them in a delirium of what Freud called, in the dream work, "secondary elaboration."[10] Joyce thereby opens a place for that other form of modernist temporality which is the musical *coda*, in which, as in a decompression chamber, all the momentous textual developments of the preceding book are slowly discharged and diffused, disseminated into the *informe* beyond the book. At the very same time, however, even this leisurely coda is brought to an abrupt and scandalous ending, a pistol-shot of an altogether different temporality, with the unexpected change in gender and the very different performative voice of Molly's invincible monologue which cancels all the earlier masculine languages of *Ulysses*, and concludes—the famous final Yes—with a negation of the negation, as we shall see.

Several "categories"—or Platonic Ideas—of ending and concluding are at stake here; and it is enough to claim that the Nighttown chapter realizes as it were in pure spirit what the mechanical practice of dénouement, the final tying together of the loose ends, the fulfillment of all the carefully planted clues and secondary characters, the great recognition scenes as well (Mamma! Papa! Our son!), had aimed at in the well-made plot—just as the category of the single day as it were sublimates the whole multifarious historical tradition of the "unities" and projects it into the heaven of pure form. In this Joyce's macro-text echoes the bravura flourishes that conclude the individual chapters—"laud we the gods," "like a shot off a shovel," where it is the radical shift in tone that announces conclusion—*dixi*, I have spoken.

Indeed, with Proust it is far more decisively on that micro level that we find any comparable form production, and the elaboration of mechanisms designed to exclude questions about the text's inclusions and its completeness. To be sure, Proust has his own equivalent of the production of external framing devices (on the order of Joyce's chapter systems): these are what Joseph Frank called spatial forms and they organize the immense work into a few great set-pieces, such as the ultimate convergence of the Swann and Guermantes "ways" (the English expression is far more useful in making the point), or the well-nigh interminable matinées and receptions, teas, dinners, soirées, in which the narrative work of the book gets done, its anecdotes interpolated thematically within these units: if the one-time Saturday/Sunday walks of Combray recapitulated not only the summer routine but the whole childhood of the narrator, so too these unique events in time (as when Swann tells the Duchesse de Guermantes that he is dying) serve at one and the same time as containers for the whole biographical material of lives that stretch from the Dreyfus case to World War One and beyond.

At the same time, it must be noted that Proust's most striking innovation lies in the elaboration and development of the form of the paragraph itself, from a typographic convenience to a habit of thought and the very vehicle for meditation and commentary itself. It is enough to review in one's mind the characteristic falling cadences of these paragraphs—"ma mère ne vint pas," "the whole world in a cup of tea"—to realize that such prestidigitation imposes a requirement of rhetorical conclusion on the mind itself and the imperative for thought to fall back unexpectedly on its feet, in an iteration of the unpredictable formally analogous to what is demanded of his characters who always turn out to be radically other than they first seem. Yet the closure of this succession of formed paragraphs allows for an unregulated insertion of all kinds of new material, as the inspection of any one of Proust's notebooks testifies. Here too then, as in the macro-form, the question arises as a reversal of that suggested by Joyce's practice, namely how, faced with a text in which insertions and accretions are not only possible, but like the great coral reefs have actually produced the text we currently have—how, under such conditions, any sense of completeness or totality is possible; or rather, following the formula we have found useful and alone productive here, how such questions can possibly be formally excluded, in advance, by these procedures.

3. Autonomization and Language

The preconditions for the autonomy of the aesthetic totality can also be formulated in a different way, in terms of the problem of reference. It should be clear that autonomization, in modernism, far transcends the limited philosophico-aesthetic problem the tradition theorized as the autonomy of the aesthetic as such: for now the work itself has become a totality, assuming all those claims to the Absolute which Hegel made in the name of philosophy (the latter only coming due after the "end of art"). Is not then reference one of the ultimate forms of the denial of precisely that autonomy? and a reminder that the object of the work's language is always to be found somewhere outside itself, and always secures some fundamental dependence of the work on something other than itself?

Yet paradoxically, this impurity of the aesthetic totality, its contamination by what is, by its inevitable wordliness, is felt most strongly not in its relationship to the objects that language names and designates, so much as in the way it eats away at the very heart of language itself in the form of the external listener always posited by the speaker, of the receiver always posited by the linguistic act. Communication as such (like a coin one speaker presses into the hand of his listener, says Mallarmé) can always be somehow interrupted or suspended by the containment of a garden-variety aesthetic autonomy of the type initially theorized by Kant. But that kind of deformation of the linguistic act, its appropriation and deviation by the very aesthetic institution itself, is likely to find itself heightened and intensified beyond all recognition in modernism's more desperate search for autonomy in a mass cultural situation in which everything is now threatened by the communicational.

The modernist "solutions" to this problem have often (particularly by Adorno) been characterized as a new form of reification in which the work resists the commodity reification of the world around it, in which the work makes itself into a commodity in order homeopathically to undermine commodity reification itself, thereby assuming a Utopian function. Yet this is a perverse formulation, insofar as the work must then also avoid a degradation into outright nonsense and babble, into the objectivity of pure sound: and this even though artists like Khlebnikov and Malevich seem to have posited just that, and theorists to have endorsed them (Deleuze in his critique of conversation and his celebration of nonsense,[11] and Lacan in his notion of the *lalangue*[12]). It is true that such outcomes foreclose the consumption which necessarily fulfills every successful artwork, and which (along with markets and other institutions) confirms the inevitable status of art as a commodity in the last instance. And is not Mr Bloom an advertising agent, purveying images that incite to commodity consumption to the degree to which they are themselves commodities? "Proust" is also a kind of commodity producer, insofar as his social success in the *haut monde* will be judged on the consumption of a steady stream of anecdotes, *traits d'esprit*, "astute" perceptions, and the witty repartee indispensable to the life of any salon.

I will, however, suggest that Joyce and Proust alike offer the spectacle of techniques for the autonomization of language which can be theorized in a different way, one that might currently be more productive than the rather exhausted dead ends of reification theory or of the theory of the image as commodity. This perspective will return to the linguistic act as such, and will propose to grasp these so palpably spoken and oral voices in terms of the detachment from the speech act itself of either the pole of reception or that of enunciation. The bracketing of either of these poles, indeed, will be enough to secure the existence of the text as a kind of free-floating and autonomous totality, even though, in the case of these two writers, the results are structurally as well as aesthetically virtually antithetical. Yet we may think of a distant analogy in the psychoanalytic session as such, in which the patient speaks interminably to an Other who fails to respond, that is to say, to receive in any conventional communicational fashion. We also, if we think about it intently enough, are always surrounded by messages which seem to have no sender, a whole universe of preexisting and ongoing textual processes which imperatively solicit our attention.

In any case, and whatever the situation with Joyce, the characterization of Proust's verbal generosity as a discourse without a receiver seems willful enough and demands justification. His genius for mimicry has often been noticed ("son art d'aveugle," says Malraux), yet less often his capacity for imitating himself and for reproducing, as it were in the void, that conversational gift which was his stock in trade and which finds itself amply documented in his letters (where the pole of the receiver is so strong that they are conventionally taxed with flattery and obsequiousness). In order to witness this process with the naked eye, we need to find an instance in which he makes conversation out of his lack of interest in making conversation in the first place: unsurprisingly, such language will emerge from those very moments in which, as we have shown, the narrator touches on the low points of everyday life itself, and of a temporality about which there is nothing to say, and from which no anecdotes can be fashioned, no interesting "pointe" can be drawn:

> "Trees," thought I to myself, "you have nothing more to say to me; my deadened heart no longer hears you. Behold me in the midst of nature's beauty and yet it is with indifference and ennui that my eyes take note of the line that separates the sun-bathed foliage from the shadowed trunk. If there was once a time when I was able to believe myself a poet, I now know that I am not. In the new chapter of now arid life which is opening before me, perhaps men might be able to give me the inspiration I no longer find in nature. But the days when I might possibly have been able to sing her praises will return no more." And yet, even as I offered myself the consolation of this possible study of human beings taking the place of the departed inspiration of nature, I knew that I was merely offering myself a consolation which I knew had no value. If I really had the soul of an artist, what pleasure would I not derive from the sight of that curtain of trees lighted by the declining sun, and in those little flowers growing along the roadbed and raising their heads almost to the step of the railway carriage, so near that I could count their petals, but I shall take good heed not to describe their colour, for who can hope to convey to another a pleasure he has not himself felt? A little later it was with the same indifference that I noted the gold and orange disks with which the same setting sun riddled the windows of a house; and finally, as the hour advanced, I saw another house which seemed constructed of some material of a strange rosy pink. But I made these various observations with the same complete indifference with which, as I strolled with some lady in a garden, I might have noticed a leaf of grass and, a few steps further on, some object made of a substance similar to alabaster, the unaccustomed colour of which would not have roused me from the most languorous ennui; at most, out of politeness toward the lady and in order to say something and to shew that I had remarked the colour, I might have called attention, as we passed by, to the coloured glass and the bit of stucco. In the same way

> and only to clear my conscience, I pointed out to myself—as though to someone who was accompanying me and who could get more pleasure from it than I—the reflexions of fire on the windowpanes and the rosy transparence of the house. But the companion whose attention I had drawn to these curious effects must have been of a less enthusiastic disposition than many responsive folk who are enraptured by such sights for he had taken note of those colours without the slightest joy. (SM II 983–4)

> Arbres, pensai-je, vous n'avez plus rien à me dire, mon coeur refroidi ne vous entend plus. Je suis pourtant ici en pleine nature, eh bien, c'est avec froideur, avec ennui que mes yeux constatent la ligne qui sépare votre front lumineux de votre tronc d'ombre. Si j'ai jamais pu me croire poète, je sais maintenant que je ne le suis pas. Peut-être dans la nouvelle partie de ma vie, si desséchée, qui s'ouvre, les hommes pourraient-ils m'inspirer ce que ne me dit plus la nature. Mais les années où j'aurais peut-être été capable de la chanter ne reviendront jamais. Mais en me donnant cette consolation d'une observation humaine possible venant prendre la place d'une inspiration impossible, je savais que je cherchais seulement à me donner une consolation, et que je savais moi-même sans valeur. Si j'avais vraiment une âme d'artiste, quel plaisir n'éprouverais-je pas devant ce rideau d'arbres éclairé par le soleil couchant, devant ces petites fleurs du talus qui se haussent presque jusqu'au marchepied du wagon, dont je pourrais compter les pétales, et dont je me garderais bien de decrire la couleur comme feraient tant de bons lettrés, car peut-on espérer transmettre au lecteur un plaisir qu'on n'a pas ressenti?
>
> Un peu plus tard j'avais vu avec la même indifférence les lentilles d'or et d'orange dont il criblait les fenêtres d'une maison; et enfin, comme l'heure avait avancé, j'avais vu une autre maison qui semblait construite en une substance d'un rose assez étrange. Mais j'avais fait ces diverses constations avec la même absolue indifférence que si, me promenant dans un jardin avec une dame, j'avais vu une feuille de verre et un peu plus loin un objet d'une matière analogue à l'albâtre dont la couleur inaccountumée ne m'aurait pas tiré du plus languissant ennui, mais si, par politesse pour la dame, pour dire quelque chose et aussi pour montrer que j'avais remarqué cette couleur, j'avais désigné en passant le verre coloré et le morceau de stuc. De la même manière, par acquit de conscience, je me signalais à moi-même comme à quelqu'un qui m'eût accompagné et qui eût été capable d'en tirer plus de plaisir que moi, les reflets de feu dans les vitres et la transparence rose de la maison. Mais le compagnon à qui j'avais fait constater ces effets curieux était d'une nature moins enthousiaste sans doute que beaucoup de gens bien disposés qu'une telle vue ravit, car il avait pris connaissance de ces couleurs sans aucune espèce d'allégresse. (P IV 433–4)

So we here have a phenomenon analogous to what the philosophers ruminate when they theorize reflexivity or self-consciousness: there is some primary perception of the outside world ("to shew that I had remarked the colour"), and then there is the phantom "companion" to whom I address the observation, "out of politeness toward the lady and in order to say something." Yet this second self to whom he makes the observation—"to myself as though to someone who was accompanying me"—is "less enthusiastic" and indeed "takes note of those colours without the slightest joy." The first self is charged with the dual responsibility of making the perception and then of formulating it, the second self is the listener, who is in principle meant to receive the observation "with joy." But that joy, imputed to the receiver, is in reality the redoubled joyousness of the sender, who isolates a new object, a new color, a new tactility or material surface, and simultaneously expresses it by way of designating it ("zut! zut!" were the inarticulate cries of the young Proust in the face of a perception for which he claimed to have as yet no language, but for which, in reality, he had no listener and no public). We thereby deduce that Proust's own sentence production demands the replacement of the external receiver with the simulation of an internal one, or in other words a speech situation in which the pole of reception has been suspended altogether, leaving that face language turns to its other in a kind of miraculous suspension.

We may also deduce that Proustian time, the Proustian present, can only be this moment of sentence production, in which a voice tirelessly whispers the sentences of an infinite murmur into the absent ear of a non-existent other. This peculiar situation also explains the ultimate failure of the otherwise powerful Proustian aesthetic (impressionism, defamiliarization), which ought to culminate with an injunction to the reader to write his own book and take possession of his own experience, but which can instead only theorize a vacuous call for a kind of projection ("in reality each reader reads only what is within himself" etc. [P IV 610/SM II 1024]).

But if such moments have little consolation to offer theoreticians of self-consciousness or reflexivity, conversely they offer us a magnificent metaphysics of time, one in which that "enormous privilege of the present" of which Hegel so strangely spoke is affirmed with incomparable philosophical ingenuity and force. And this is why the traditional reception of Proust, in terms of the past and of memory, as well as of the latter's triumphant recovery by way of the aesthetic vocation, is so singularly misplaced and inconsequential: it is in Bergson rather than in Proust that the past exists somehow outside of time, serenely surviving all the latter's vicissitudes. In Proust, however, the moments of involuntary memory are mere transitional devices and organizational hinges: far from opening up the past all over again, they make it present "for the first time," like an alternate space opening up within the space of the current present. However much Proust himself participated in the mystification, we must therefore insist on the presence in his work of a different conception of time that coexists uneasily with this memory-obsessed past-oriented one, and that is to be found in the notion of experience that runs throughout the length of the novel, namely that there is no immediacy, that we never experience anything for the first time, but that it is in the present of writing and only then that we come really to experience it. The present is this second time of the writing of the sentence, and the past experience, whether it happened just now, or in some much earlier decade, does not happen until that present (which may to be sure in its turn never come into being).

We must now develop further the way in which Proust's sense of an absolute present performs this particular function. The doctrine whereby a present is only experienced "for the first time" in its aesthetic repetition is designed to exchange the passivity of some first reception for the sheer activity of the process of producing its "original," as it were: the philosophical equivalent might well be that astonishing notion of Fichte that the *I* needs to produce a *not-I* out of itself in order, by way of its receptive contemplation of the object, to affirm its own existence. Yet it is an emphasis that must also be corrected and modified in order to avoid any suggestion of idealism, of the omnipotence of subjectivity and the absolute malleability of external reality to its whims. This will be achieved, in Proust by a systematic dissolution of the idea of will-power (just as the construction of the very system of reexperience involved the discrediting of notions of immediacy). In this sense will-power corresponds to some principle of practical activity which seeks to intervene in the present and to modify it according to a project: indeed, were we to limit ourselves to this feature alone, the construction would truly look very much like Bergson's idealism, in which practical activity blurs the traces and always distracts from the stillness of pure perception—a view which then would go far towards restoring the stereotype of Proust's irrationalism, his substitution of sheer feeling and intuition for rational deliberation and choice.

Everything changes, however, when the moment is completed with its corollary, namely the reappropriation of the present in some second act which restores it as an experience "for the first time." But even this will be so only if we resist the trivialization of aestheticism and of the wonderment of art or writing, the transformation of life into work, the world ending up in a book, the triumphant reassertion of the artist's vocation, and so forth. This is not to deny the existence of the omnipresent motif of writing and artistic production in Proust (which can itself mean little enough to readers who are not themselves artists), but rather to insist on a further allegorical dimension in which writing is itself grasped as a figure for sheer activity and for production as such. What is energizing in Proust is indeed not some mystical inward spiral into the fascination of one's own past, nor is it the identification with the *fin-de-siècle* aesthetics of a few isolated modernist painters and composers: it is the liberation of Goethean forces of praxis and sheer activity, which, hobbled by a will-power busy struggling against its own inclinations, is able by shaking that inner tension off to find ("for the first time") a full identification with its own project.

And this is also the sense in which will-power—the attempt to appropriate experience simply by the taking of a thought, by conscious or rational decision, by a forcing of the situation—also adds to the moment of the past in question an element which is extraneous to it, which introduces an external motivation and as it were the gaze of another self on a place in which it does not yet exist: indeed will-power attempts to force the priorities and the projects of that external self onto a world utterly innocent of it, not understanding that

> at every moment, there was one more of those innumerable and humble "selves" that compose our personality which was still unaware of Albertine's departure and must be informed of it; I was obliged—and this was more cruel than if they had been strangers and did not share my susceptibility to suffering—to announce to all these beings, to all these "selves" who did not yet know of it, the calamity that had just occurred; each of them in turn must hear for the first time the words: "Albertine has asked for her boxes"—those coffin-shaped boxes which I had seen loaded on to the train at Balbec with my mother's—"Albertine has gone." Each of them had to be told of my grief, the grief which is in no way a pessimistic conclusion freely drawn from an accumulation of baneful circumstances, but is the intermittent and involuntary reviviscence of a specific impression that has come to us from without and was not chosen by us. There were some of these "selves" which I had not encountered for a long time past. For instance (I had not remembered that it was the day on which the barber called) the "self" that I was when I was having my hair cut. I had forgotten this "self," and his arrival made me burst into tears, as, at a funeral, does the appearance of an old retired servant who has not forgotten the deceased. (SM II 683–4)

> à chaque instant, il y avait quelqu'un des innombrables et humbles moi qui nous composent qui était ignorant encore du départ d'Albertine et à qui il fallait le notifier; il fallait—ce qui était plus cruel que s'ils avaient été des étrangers et n'avaient pas emprunté ma sensibilité pour souffrir—annoncer le malheur qui venait d'arriver à tous ces êtres, à tous ces moi qui ne le savaient pas encore; il fallait que chacun d'eux à son tour entendit pour la première fois ces mots: Albertine a demandé ses malles—ces malles en forme de cercueil que j'avais vu charger à Balbec à côte de celles de ma mere—Albertine est partie. A chacun j'avais à apprendre mon chagrin, le chagrin qui n'est nullement une conclusion pessimiste librement tirée d'un ensemble de circonstances funestes, mais la reviviscence intermittente et involontaire d'une impression spécifique, venue du dehors, et que nous n'avons pas choisie. Il y avait quelques-uns de ces moi que je n'avais pas revus depuis assez longtemps. Par exemple (je n'avais pas songé que c'était le jour du coiffeur) le moi que j'étais quand je me faisais couper les cheveux. J'avais oublié ce moi-là, son arrivée fit éclater mes sanglots, comme, à un enterrement, celle d'un vieux serviteur retraité qui a connu celle qui vient de mourir. (P IV 14)

Some day, no doubt, this failure of will-power to reappropriate the older moment will itself be remembered with bitter chagrin, as yet another defeat, yet another proof that Marcel is not up to the task (indeed, we have already quoted just such a passage).

But what is crucial is that this external element has no place in a moment which is, like Leibniz's monad, a kind of synchronic system in its own right, in which all the elements obey a specific logic which (as with Mme de Villeparisis's Memoirs) is violated if any of them are forgotten or left out. (Thus the Dreyfusard past—against the army, against the nation—is gradually effaced when its adherents have become anti-German militarists and xenophobic and patriotic proponents of precisely that nation itself.[13]) This monadic logic of the present of time (even when—particularly when—it has gone into the past) has several significant consequences which must be noted here.

First of all, it is the specific logic of an older moment which will resonate with a moment of the current present in an elective affinity which accounts for its possibility of reinvention or resurrection. Proust's myth of a so-called involuntary memory—authorized by Baudelaire[14]—serves as the operator for this transfer across time, this "blasting open of the continuum of chronological history," as Benjamin called it, who was influenced in his political theorization of Marx's *Eighteenth Brumaire*[15] by just this structure in Proust (just as he derived the whole motivation of his Arcades project—"waking up from the nineteenth century"—from Proust's opening pages). It is the laterality of our ordinary experience that accounts for these unexpected contacts across time: the present is ordinarily only glimpsed out of the corner of our eye, as we go about other business: its head-on perspective, with genuine depth and a well-nigh photographic fullness of detail, is lacking, unless and until, in the mystery of some well-nigh astronomical rotation of positions and their perspectives, time or history suddenly allows us the blinding revelation of the original foregrounded.

That "involuntary memory" (not Proust's phrase) is little more than a motivation for this process can be deduced from the presence, alongside this seemingly irrational proposition, of a second, wholly dialectical, critique of error and miscomprehension as such: a veritable pedagogy of perception in time, which seeks to restore (but for some "first time") the right way of thinking about the synchronic system constituted by every present of time (that is to say, by reality itself). Nor is this simply the affirmation of a specific view of temporality and experience: it is at one and the same time a thoroughgoing diagnosis and denunciation of empiricist and commonsense conceptual stereotypes. What is dialectical in Proust is then not only this indictment of a reified first-order thinking (like Hegel's *Verstand*), but his simultaneous insistence on the necessity of such errors and on the need to pass through such an inevitable diachrony of individual items, facts or static elements on our way towards a truth that can only come as their prodigious restructuration: a new monad of time that substitutes synchronicity and rationality in the place of the necessary error of commonsense everyday experience. Dialectical perception is the violent modification and rectification of those inevitable blind spots and structural misunderstandings which must necessarily serve as the first moment in the process: Proustian effects are at one with such always-startling restructurations and their reexplanations.

Nowhere are such "corrections" so strikingly visible to the naked eye as when it is a question, in the moment, of its quotient of futurity (rather than its shards of past temporalities). Here I believe that we must come to terms with an operation that may well seem reductive and ideological under present-day theoretical conditions: namely the containment of desire as such and its strategic domestication and limitation within the category of the wish, a far more modest and humble entity than its lofty metaphysical opposite number. For whatever the philosophical or theoretical context today, is not Desire always theorized, along the lines of Foucault's influential retheorization of power, as a capillary process which reaches into all the nooks and crannies of reality and leaves its subtle fingerprints on all our thoughts and deeds? Desire is multiply allegorical and insinuates itself into a variety of levels, redoubling conscious velleities with its own overdeterminations and parasitizing decision and the irrational alike. But the wish—to which Freud also had recourse in *The Interpretation of Dreams*, causing the greatest problems for his postmodern readership—the wish is stubborn and one-dimensional, it has an aim and an object and brooks no mere "symbolic" satisfaction.

The wish is therefore preeminently a category appropriate to the synchronic present of time and unlikely to overspill its boundaries or to contaminate the other temporal ek-stases. The wish, in Proust, is a constitutive feature of the present, whose structure indeed it defines; and a new present is silently designated by the volatilization of the old wish that vanishes without a trace, its place occupied by a new one that betrays not the slightest suspicion that something else once was there, and that it is itself something new and a mere replacement.

The wish is moreover what is called a zero-sum or off-on process: it is either granted or refused, it knows the most straightforward positive or negative outcomes; which are, nonetheless, subject to the most wondrous and contingent, unexpected, permutations. The wish is desire crystallized into an obsession, no longer some omnipresent fluid or element but rather the childish fetishization of some impossible whim, on which the whole of existence henceforth depends.

Nowhere are the effects of this new and artificial category more apparent than in the famous opening pages in which the child desperately waits in vain for its mother's goodnight visit and kiss. Here, as readers will recall, the ambiguities of the iterative are supremely mustered: it was always like this, but that particular night it was otherwise. My mother always gave me a goodnight kiss, except for those evenings when we had visitors. We thus posit a law together with its exception, which turns out, as Hegel, Marx and Lacan had long ago foreseen (and as Žižek more recently insists), to be the Law itself in the first place. What is representationally significant here is not, however, the psychological dynamic, but rather the way in which the category of the wish allows all the logically possible outcomes to be included in a narrative enumeration whose completion then signals the fulfillment and closure of the temporal monad itself. My mother always came; but not that evening. I asked her to make an exception—hope against hope: but the refusal is categorical—"ma mère ne vint pas." Yet to this negative is added an unexpected positive: however, she came anyway. Now it is a question of reaffirming the first negative, that of the law, by the invocation of the father figure, with his authority and taboos: the father arrives with all the inevitability of that negative, which all the parties expect as a destiny. But this time, exceptionally, he negates his own negation, and orders the mother to remain and to continue the visit: "Reste avec l'enfant." The truly sublime orchestral delirium with which Proust's narrative greets this unexpected transcendence of the Law—externalization of the father's visual gesture, evocation of the staircase itself from which the temporal camera draws away in a thrilling moment, only to prepare the utter resurrection of the entire house and village in that spatial reappearance of the full monad of the past that follows[16]—this dramatic freeze-frame of the instant, which summons all the techniques in the Proustian repertoire for its implementation, is not due I think to any merely affective or psychoanalytic content: it is rather the sign of the completion of the monad, in which—thanks to the narrative category of desire—all possible variants have been played out and all the logical possibilities exhausted.

What has been called the temporal monad—the absolute present in which in Proust reality alone exists, yet a present of the text as well into which its inevitable past and future have been drawn and transmuted—is itself a formal consequence, I have argued, of that suspension of the pole of the receiver or listener which endows Proustian language with an absolute presence of its own and lends the otherwise seemingly ephemeral passage of whispered sentences to take on the modernist effect of an aesthetic totality in its own right ("just as the earth, with no support, holds up in the air").[17] The bracketing of the receiver in Proust generates a mirage of the sender as a kind of transcendental subjectivity beyond all individuality, a kind of first-person aesthetic "subject supposed to know," always present, always speaking, inexhaustible and beyond all mortal vicissitudes, something Proust was careful to perpetuate by drafting his own ending first before writing the rest of the novel.

*

In the case of Joyce the blockage of communication is the inverse of this one, and involves the bracketing of the pole of subjectivity itself and the suppression of the place of the sender as such, producing the illusion of a language that speaks all by itself, without the intervention of human agency. Here an autonomy of language is secured by the systematic refusal of expression as such, as well as the strategic exploitation of all those features and dimensions of language susceptible of being abstracted from the normal operations of human expression and communication, human meaning, and of being potentiated as though each could somehow prolong its existence under its own power alone.

The Wandering Rocks episode offers a virtually definitional allegory of this process, where it is the things themselves—neither symbols nor signs in some sender's discourse—which incline their face towards a receiver. Thus the opening episodes program us to this interesting linguistic deformation:

> The lychgate of a field showed Father Conmee breadths of cabbages, curtseying to him with ample underleaves. (184)

Meanwhile the most unexpected features of the physical Dublin are ultimately drawn into the process, disposing themselves around the governor general's trajectory through the city:

> From its sluice in Wood quay wall under Tom Devan's office Poddle river hung out in fealty a tongue of liquid sewage. (207)

Finally the experiment is brought to a paradoxical end, in which even a repulse of the observer is converted, in a final flourish, into an acknowledgement of the latter's presence:

> ... and the salute of Almidano Artifoni's sturdy trousers swallowed by a closing door. (209)

The famous Sirens section—first of the more outrageously experimental chapters, which elicited from Ezra Pound the impatient observation, "A new style per chapter not required!"—now performs its abstraction in a new way, by retaining samples of the purely material language of the following narrative (both sound and script) which it purports to organize into a kind of musical score: keys and tempo at least being detectable here, in an alternation between the throbbing and the darkly booming and crashing (the bar girls versus Bloom), enlivened by piquant or comical trills (rocky thumbnail, hee hee, little wind piped wee, etc.). The concentration on the production of a pure soundtrack without evaluative meaning is then itself reinforced by the equal weight given to the most sublime note of the tenor

("It soared, a bird, it held its flight, a swift pure cry"—226) and the fart that concludes this exercise, whose deeper logic has to do, not so much with temporality in general, as with the time of waiting ("Pat is a waiter who waits while you wait"—230). Is then the fulfillment of time ("Time's livid final flame") the same as the fulfillment of the time of waiting? And is the latter to be found in the taste of food, in the climax of song, in seduction, or in physical relief? The scandal of this chapter lies in the way in which, within the chapters bound together in the book as a whole, this one asserts a kind of absolute autonomy and closure by way of its abstraction as temporally organized sound. Even the misguided attempts to make the narrative mean in the ordinary way, and incorrectly to reimport the communicational situation, have been drawn into the text and neutralized by the handicaps of the deaf waiter and the blind piano-tuner: allegorized in another way, perhaps, by the practical life failures of the two supremely successful vehicles of musical sound, the two singers Simon Dedalus and Ben Dollard.

I have observed elsewhere that something like a zero degree of the script of *Ulysses* is reached in those well-nigh schizophrenic passages in which the book begins to talk for itself and meaninglessly to repeat its own contents and to vary their succession in a purely mechanical way, as here: "He waits while you wait. While you wait if you wait he will wait while you wait" (230). Or better still, as the chapter itself "waits" for Mr Bloom to make his appearance: "Mr Bloom reached Essex bridge. Yes, Mr Bloom crossed bridge of Yessex" (215). This is certainly not something Mr Bloom himself is thinking ("To Martha I must write," etc.). Then who can be thinking it? Only the book itself, as in its imbecilic and mindless reaction to Bloom's profession of the doctrine of universal love in the next (Cyclops) chapter:

> Love loves to love love. Nurse loves the new chemist.
> Constable 14A loves Mary Kelly. Gerty MacDowell loves the boy that has the bicycle. M.B. loves a fair gentleman. Li Chi Han lovey up kissy Cha Pu Chow. Jumbo, the elephant, loves Alice, the elephant. Etc. (273)

The passage also usefully illustrates the difference between parody and pastiche, or between irony and a kind of blank or blind imitation of it: for no one is meant to be the target of this otherwise seemingly mocking and trivializing voice. Yet what is now, in the absence of irony, achieved and anticipated, is that rehearsal and permutation of all the individual contents of the preceding text which we will confront in the Nighttown section, in which the multitudinous elements, tokens, and counters of *Ulysses* are reunified, but in the non-signifying and one-dimensional meaninglessness of the oneiric as such, where hallucinations pass across the eye without the background of depth or context, as though under their own power (the great predecessor here being Flaubert's *Temptation of Saint Anthony*[18]).

The passage from one pub to another, in the next chapter, is then not only the leap from one organizational system to another, it is the transmutation of the aesthetic into the political, of music—which can, to be sure, as the glorification of the voice, have its political significance—to nationalism and to argument, debate, political passion. It is also a shift from an individual perception of sound, as a unique physical experience and event, to something like a political unconscious, a kind of cauldron of stereotypes in which a host of ideological languages float and ferment—medieval ones, bardic or clerical, visionary-Utopian figments, public-mediatic smears, even infantile babblings—released from all the layers of Ireland's past. It is therefore not quite right to continue to see the Cyclops chapter in a dualistic way, as an ironic montage of Ireland's present, degraded into petty squabbles, booze and gossip, and petit-bourgeois characters and concerns, with the echoes of some pseudo-noble Irish courtly and knightly romance era. For these last are themselves eaten away from within by modern trivialization:

> And there rises a shining palace whose crystal glittering roof is seen by mariners who traverse the extensive sea in barks built expressly for that purpose. (242)

The final phrase is of course a staple of modern commercial speech which has no semantic function in this account of the narrator's progress towards Barney Kiernan's (the palace in question): for if even the vision of the past is degraded by modernity, then the entire chapter sinks into a kind of monological expression of naturalist reality from which the shock effects of these crossings of multiple synapses—

> and they beheld Him, even Him, ben Bloom Elijah, amid clouds of angels ascend to the glory of the brightness at an angle of fortyfive degrees over Donohoe's in Little Green Street like a shot off a shovel. (283)

—lose their force. In any case, this particular effect reminds us that with the discussion of Jesus and the Jews new languages have been added to the older nationalist ones and stirred into the older mixture. Autonomy here is precisely this autonomization of all the ideological and stereotypical collective languages within some new collective element for which the anonymous narrator is but a place-holder and a frame.

Gerty MacDowell's chapter then restates the claims of meaning with an extravagance that unmasks sentiment and expression as the *bovarysme* of reading and romance, of the degradation of the popular media. The tension between these two chapters then produces the concept of "style" as a kind of free-floating linguistic object in its own right, an object whose varied historical manifestations are contradictory enough to generate the autopoiesis of the maternity chapter, a veritable evolutionary slide-show comparable to

Hegel's *Logic*. Yet to the autonomization of style is now replied a very different autonomization of the image, in the Nighttown phantasmagoria, while to the sentimental language of Gerty's daydreams is opposed the meaning-drained or exhausted bureaucratic-conventional journalese of the cabman's shelter. Here it is as though conventional language were restored, but without any vitality save the fulminating historical memory of the most significant political explosion in Dublin before the Easter Uprising (an event never foreshadowed or even conceivable in the framework of these pages, as we shall see). In the final occasion for these experimental deployments of the various isolated properties of language, then, the catechism chapter ingeniously restores pure sentence structure, by means of a kind of rote-like exercise of statements and their cataphoric echoes in the void. It should be noted that the catechism chapter is the only one in all of *Ulysses* in which the scene is a return to or repeat of the setting of a previous chapter: here the Bloom residence which has already figured in chapter 4. The very motivation, then, for some utterly unnarrative presentation also lies in this will to avoid the familiarity of place and its repetitions, or, if you prefer, to incorporate the Bloom biographical past in some new non-personal way.

At any rate, the catechism's questions and answers—through which this approach to the Real is conveyed—must also be grasped in the same way as the radical depersonalization of language. Unspeakable sentences: Ann Banfield's wonderful title reverberates throughout the modernist aesthetic, but it is time to think of it in a different way from writing or text. In the case of the catechism, the echoing back and forth of questions and answers marks a very specific pattern of aphasia, which is here the mode of the neutralization of language as a human, interpersonal, expressive element. Such depersonalization in general, whatever the specific strategy and form it may take, is one of the fundamental characteristics of all modernism, all modern art. I believe it emerges from the gradual and historical realization that consciousness as such cannot be represented, and that it must be conveyed indirectly, by way of the detour of things.

The play of oppositions that lends these various projections their tension may now be mapped out as follows:

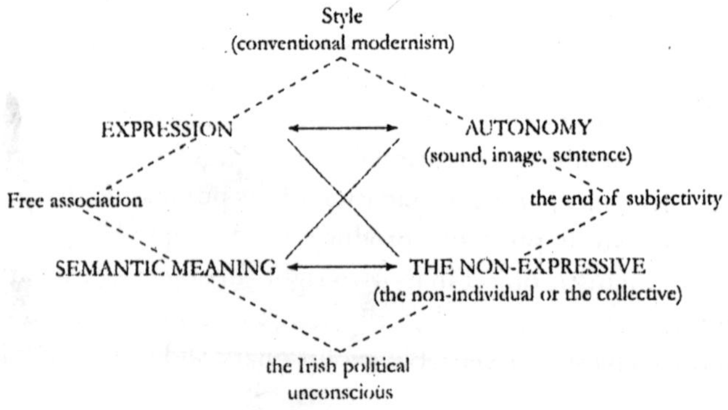

It is worth remembering that shifts of register and chapter divisions produced by this dialectic are criss-crossed and relativized by other kinds of divisions and organizational schemes in the novel, most notably the division into three parts; and also the one-day framework commented on above. (This multiplicity of schemata is comparable to what has been ascribed to *The Magic Mountain* in an earlier essay in this volume.)

At any rate, the greater complexity of the system described here is clearly due to the problem of projecting a language without a speaker, a problem more onerous than that construction of a language without a receiver or a listener we have attributed to Proust.

4. Missing Portions II: The Real

Can a future then fall through the cracks? This is the problem posed by two texts whose uniquely different modes of autonomization both conspire to eternalize the present. In a sense, Proust has it easier, since his very digressive/interpolative form allows for the folding in of new material virtually without limit. The initial situation is well-known: Proust's first volume—*Du côté de chez Swann*—is published in 1913 and a modest two-volume sequel (*Le Côté de Guermantes* and *Le Temps retrouvé*) stands ready and waiting as its completion. The immediate war crisis then brings an acute shortage of paper, which will last for the duration. Publication is accordingly postponed indefinitely: yet Proust does not use this time to start new projects, but rather to add new details and even new episodes to the proof of the existing volumes, at the same time that he fills in the temporal gap between them with wholly new and unexpected material—above all the entire affair with Albertine and the ramifications of the Charlus drama (to be sure, *Le Temps retrouvé*, which Ruiz reveals to have been a war novel, is enhanced by the experience of the bombing and blackout of wartime Paris under siege). Thus, when paper again becomes available an immense new novel has taken the place of the two-volume original and what we know as Proust will gradually heave into sight as the later sections are published (the last ones being, of course, posthumous). It is strange to think, not only that Proust died so young (at fifty-one) but also that this disappearance took place even before the 1920s became a distinctive entity; and the temptation is strong (and has frequently been succumbed to) to suppose that feeling his death approaching, he sought to provide an ending for the work as a whole and also to describe it (in the form of the death of Bergotte, "le petit pan de mur jaune"). But the ending had been planned out and written years in advance, and his final illness had nothing particularly fatal about it—the doctors (his brother Robert included) concluding that he simply let himself die—to which one is tempted to add the usual Proustian enumerative cadence: whether out of boredom, or the feeling that he had accomplished his life's work, or out of momentary despair, or by inattention and miscalculation, or simple fatigue ... etc., etc.

We are thus entitled to wonder what would have happened had Proust lived to the ripe old age of sixty, let alone something properly biblical. In a stunning essay,[19] Michel Butor speculates, not merely that Proust would have gone on writing and adding to the already voluminous *Recherche*—which seems plausible enough—but that he would have devised a new ending for his work, an ending already hinted at in some of the pages we already have. Indeed, the reader will remember the narrator's interest, during the final reception, in that belated "jeune fille en fleur" who turns out to be the daughter of his first love Gilberte and his best friend Robert de Saint-Loup.[20] Butor then boldly surmises that the work might have been concluded with an unexpected happy ending: the triumphal wedding between the narrator and Mlle de Saint Loup: it is the kind of unpredictable flourish in which Proust reveled, and makes for the most interesting dynastic and generational complications as well. Whether plausible or not, it is enough: Butor has succeeded in powerfully opening up this novel's virtualities and by liberating the productivity of new futures of the Proustian present has usefully broken the hold of the old boring cyclical theories of the novel and its putative closure. On the other hand, such is the peculiar nature of this agglutinative form that nothing stops us from speculating on even further additions after this one, which then, even as a future, loses its claim to be the final form of some Proustian "Real."

We shall not expect stray variants of *Ulysses* to offer any such possibilities: not only is *Ulysses* as "completed" as it ever will be, but the very perspective of the individual sentences, as we have insisted through these pages, enforces a kind of positivity quite inconsistent with reveries about "what might have happened next," "what becomes of all these characters," and even, "will Stephen actually leave Ireland?", "will he actually turn into Joyce himself, or at least a writer of Joyce's stature and accomplishments?" This is why Terry Eagleton's novelistic speculation, in *Saints and Scholars*, about Bloom's future in the Civil War is paradigmatically unsatisfying, since as a character Bloom cannot exist in that kind of narrative but only in the intense linguistic present of this one (whereas it seems perfectly legitimate to wonder what became of Mr Sherlock Holmes, and Balzac himself authorizes, nay encourages, us to reflect on Vautrin in his old age, etc.). Still, there is a certain truth in Eagleton's fanciful later glimpse: and that is the one grim future that lies in wait for this novel without any of the characters realizing it, namely the Easter Uprising and the end of this ineffectual Dublin of the colonial period. We have here a Real, if there ever was one, and it stands forever outside the text, not even the political memories of the old Invincibles are enough to "blast open" this particular historical continuum.

Yet this also is not the Real the text does manage to resonate, in what must surely stand as the affective nadir of this text. This very formulation stages our initial theoretical and formal problem: to touch on the Real is to glimpse the conscious subject in the moment of its dissolution, the moment in which it passes beyond itself; to read the significance of affect is already to approach impersonal states quite different from the subjective emotions an individual self or character may be described as having. In fact, we have shown that as Joyce's text, his language, become more and more autonomous, they can no longer be thought to be representational or to include "characters" who "have" various emotions and feelings. But if affect is no longer something subjective that subjects have or experience, then where is it? The traditional solution (that of Heideggerian or Sartrean existentialism) is that it is in the world; that it is the world that thus displays affect as a modality of being itself: "cette déchirure jaune du ciel au-dessus de Golgotha, le Tintoret ne l'a pas choisie pour signifier l'angoisse ... elle est angoisse, et ciel jaune en même temps ..."[21] But this is also a figure whose expressive ideology may no longer work for us today.

The dilemma is intensified when we have to do with that peculiar thing called anxiety (*Angst, angoisse*), which is surely not an emotion any longer, however little it can be called an affect either. Lacan follows Sartre in grasping anxiety not only as an instant, like a flash of sheet lightning, but also as the very mode of our fitful contact with the Real. We thereby seek to avoid it at all costs, and along with it, the Real whose approach and glimpse it betokens. Yet Sartre's characters still "have" anxiety, on the mode of an existential experience, of an event of subjectivity. It is not clear that Joyce's characters "have" named emotions of that kind, even when they suffer most acutely (Stephen's memory of his dying mother and his neglected sister, Mr Bloom's pang of jealousy).

Lacan has indeed explained, from a wholly different perspective why this must be so. Abandoning the whole issue of subjects and subjectivities, he turns instead to language itself, that is to say, to the very element—the Imaginary and the Symbolic—through which the Real would have by definition to be expressed or at least designated. The famous formula runs as follows (it is not exactly a definition): "The Real is what resists symbolization absolutely."[22] The Real can never be theorized in this sense, inasmuch as it is what falls outside the Symbolic Order, beyond the system of categories that organizes our meanings (and our Being-in-the-World as well). Indeed, insofar as the Imaginary is the very element of affect, it seems possible that an affective symptom would be more likely to find its conditions of possibility here than in the conventional categories of language. (We must add, without resolving the issue, that narrative as such makes a kind of third with respect to the Imaginary and the Symbolic, and does not quite fit into either order: narrative is, to be sure, the very inner essence of fantasy, which plays as fundamental a role in the Lacanian view of the subject as it does in Althusser's related definition of ideology, implicit in the latter's phrase "the 'representation' of the imaginary relationship of individuals to their Real conditions of existence."[23])

But fantasy and its multiple narratives are precisely the name for what is liberated by the impersonality of Joyce's autonomous language, as, in the Nighttown section, those non-signifying, non-communicating dimensions allow for a whole explosion and multiplication of selves: the Bloom Lord Mayor of Dublin certainly offering a defense against anxiety fully as much as do the images of the masochist Bloom submitting abjectly to the domination of Bella/Bello. We are here, to be sure, no longer in the realm of the personal subject or self: the exclusion of world and context which is the very mechanism of hallucination secures the possibility of many images of possible selves, all of which are then domesticated and reined back in by the sheerly enumerative and post-narrative frame of the catechism chapter, where the "Bloom of 7 Eccles Street foresees the Bloom of Flowerville," his retirement fantasy, and is able to list "in ascending powers of hierarchical order," his various "civic functions and social status":

> that of gardener, groundsman, cultivator, breeder, and at the zenith of his career, resident magistrate or justice of the peace, with a family crest and coat of arms and appropriate classical motto (Semper paratus), duly recorded in the court directory .... (588)

Alas, Mr Bloom has already reached the "zenith of his career," and even his current situation (as canvasser of advertisements for the newspaper *The Freeman*) does not seem likely to last long, nor is it much more substantial than the job Stephen has quit that very same day: "he ought to chuck that Freeman," Molly thinks, "with the paltry few shillings he knocks out of it and go into an office or something where he'd get regular pay or a bank where they could put him up on a throne to count the money all the day of course he prefers plottering around the house so you can't stir with him any side" (619). (The throne is of course a nice touch for the former future Lord Mayor of Dublin.)

Yet even these future fantasies within the present can be further stripped away and some ultimate reality asymptomatically approached without quite leaving "symbolization" altogether. This is then what the depersonalized language of the catechism chapter leaves us with:

> Reduce Bloom by cross multiplication of reverses of fortune, from which these supports protected him, and by elimination of all positive values to a negligible negative irrational unreal quantity.
>
> Successively, in descending helotic order: Poverty: that of the outdoor hawker of imitation jewellery, the dun for the recovery of bad and doubtful debts, the

poor rate and deputy cess collector. Mendicancy: that of the fraudulent bankrupt with negligible assets paying 1s 4d in the £, sandwichman, distributor of throwaways, nocturnal vagrant, insinuating sycophant, maimed sailor, blind stripling, superannuated bailiff's man, marfeast, lickplate, spoilsport, pickthank, eccentric public laughingstock seated on bench of public park under discarded perforated umbrella. Destitution: the inmate of Old Man's House (Royal Hospital), Kilmainham, the inmate of Simpson's Hospital for reduced but respectable men permanently disabled by gout or want of sight. Nadir of misery: the aged impotent disfranchised ratesupported moribund lunatic pauper. (596)

It is this "nadir of misery" that Molly's final Yes negates, affirming not Life itself but rather the pure present that excludes this future.

It remains to ask ourselves whether any reduction of this radicality is possible in Proust, where the persistent first person (despite the *tour de force* of the third-person Swann episode) would seem to guarantee a certain security against absolute depersonalization of the Joycean kind. It is a security of the speaking voice, which not even Death can challenge (witness the supreme death scenes, of the Grandmother and of Bergotte, challenges to which this voice supremely rises). Yet another fantasy narrative is present here from the very first pages, and that is the fantasy of the mother's comforting presence, alone broken and dispelled in one of those undeveloped later episodes, which might have become a whole book in its own right had Proust lived, and that is the long-anticipated visit to Venice. Here, indeed, we find the culmination of all those complaints about boredom and lack of feeling we have already touched on; but here also we find as it were the quasi-cause, the quarrel and break with the mother, that brutally leaves the narrator on his own as he has never been before:

Ma solitude irrévocable était si prochaine qu'elle me semblait déjà commencée et totale. Car je me sentais seul. Les choses m'étaient devenues étrangères, je n'avais plus assez de calme pour sortir de mon coeur palpitant et introduire en elles quelque stabilité. La ville que j'avais devant moi avait cessé d'être Venise. Sa personnalité, son nom, me semblaient comme des fictions menteuses que je n'avais plus le courage d'inculquer aux pierres. Les palais m'apparaissaient réduits à leurs simples parties et quantités de marbre pareil à tout autre, et l'eau comme une combinaison d'hydrogène et d'azote, éternelle, aveugle, antérieure et extérieure à Venise, ignorante des doges et de Turner. Et cependant ce lieu quelconque était étrange comme un lieu où on vient d'arriver, qui ne vous connaît pas encore, comme un lieu d'où l'on est parti et qui vous a déjà oublié. Je ne pouvais plus rien lui dire de moi, je ne pouvais rien laisser de moi se poser sur lui, il me laissait contracté, je n'étais plus qu'un coeur qui battait et qu'une attention suivant anxieusement le développement de *Sole mio*. J'avais beau raccrocher désespérément ma pensée à la belle coudée caracteristique du Rialto, il m'apparaissait avec la médiocrité de l'évidence comme un pont non seulement inférieur, mais aussi étranger à l'idée que j'avais de lui qu'un acteur, dont, malgré sa perruque blonde et son vêtement noir, j'aurais su qu'en son essence il n'est pas Hamlet. (P IV 232)

My irrevocable solitude was so near at hand that it seemed to me to have begun already and to be complete. For I felt myself to be alone. Things had become alien to me. I was no longer calm enough to draw from my throbbing heart and introduce into them a measure of stability. The town that I saw before me had ceased to be Venice. Its personality, its name, seemed to me to be lying fictions which I no longer had the courage to impress upon its stones. I saw the palaces reduced to their constituent parts, lifeless heaps of marble with nothing to choose between them, and the water as a combination of hydrogen and oxygen, eternal, blind, anterior and exterior to Venice, unconscious of the Doges or of Turner. And yet this unremarkable place was as strange as a place at which we have just arrived, which does not yet know us—as a place which we have left and which has forgotten us already. I could not tell it anything more about myself, I could leave nothing of myself imprinted upon it, it left me diminished, I was nothing more than a heart that throbbed, and an attention strained to follow the development of 'sole mio.' In vain might I fix my mind despairingly upon the beautiful and characteristic arch of the Rialto, it seemed to me, with the mediocrity of the obvious, a bridge not merely inferior to but as different from the idea that I possessed of it as an actor with regard to whom, notwithstanding his fair wig and black garments, we know quite well that in his essential quality he is not Hamlet. (SM II 837–8)

Here indeed one may truly speak of that misery evoked by Joyce, some ultimate point, not of suffering—which was for Proust a positive and indeed a productive experience and which is concentrated in the account of jealousy for Albertine—but rather of a stripping away of the surface of appearance to reveal a kind of dead extension beneath, a kind of zero degree of being of the world and of reality itself, a fabulous place-name from which the name and the image, the very "place" itself, have vanished away leaving nothing behind them but pure matter—"parties et quantités de marbre pareil à tout autre, et l'eau comme une combinaison d'hydrogène et d'azote." It is a matter without properties strangely akin, indeed, to the scientific dryness of the questions and answers of Joyce's catechism chapter; and leaves the question open whether this negative sublime, this stripping away of the very connotations of language, is not the closest literature can ever come to the Real itself.

(*2006*)

Notes

1 See Brenda Maddox, *Nora: The Real Life of Molly Bloom* (NY, 1998); and Jean-Yves Tadié, *Marcel Proust*, (2 vols, Paris, 1966).

2 All references to Proust's novel are given in the text as follows: first the volume and page number of the four-volume Jean-Yves Tadié edition of *A la recherche du temps perdu* (Paris, 1987–1989) designated as P; then to the two-volume Scott Moncrieff translation (final volume translated by F.A. Blossom), of *Remembrance of Things Past* (New York, 1932), designated as SM.

3 "The wall of the staircase, up which I had watched the light of his candle gradually climb, was long ago demolished ... immediately the old grey house upon the street, where her room was, rose up like the scenery of a theatre to attach itself to the little pavilion, opening onto the garden, which had been built out behind it for my parents ..." (SM I 28, 36).

"On ne pouvait pas remercier mon père; on l'eût agacé par ce qu'il appelait des sensibleries. Je restai sans oser faire un movement; il était encore devant nous, grand, dans sa robe de nuit blanche sous le cachemire de l'Inde violet et rose qu'il nouait autour de sa tête depuis qu'il avait des névralgies, avec le geste d'Abraham dans la gravure d'appr̀es Benozzo Gozzoli que m'avait donnée M. Swann, disant à Sara qu'elle a à se départir du côté d'Isaac. Il y a bien des années de cela. La muraille de l'escalier, où je vis monter le reflet de sa bougie n'existe plus depuis longtemps. En moi aussi bien des choses ont été détruites que je croyais devoir durer toujours et de nouvelles se sont edifiées donnant naissant à des peines et à des joies nouvelles que je n'aurais pu prévoir alors, de même que les anciennes me sont devenues difficiles à comprendre. Il y a bien longtemps aussi que mon père a cessé de pouvoir dire à maman: Va avec le petit ... Aussitot la vieille maison grise sur la rue, où etait sa chamber, vint comme un décor de theatre s'appliquer au petit pavillon, donnant sur le jardin, qu'on avait construit pour mes parents ..." (P I 36, 47)

4 Gerard Genette, *Narrative Discourse* (Ithaca, 1980).

5 See P IV 484/SM II 1020, ff: "Sometimes, when a painful study has been left merely sketched in, a new affection or fresh suffering to help us fill it in ..."

6 See Hugh Kenner, *Joyce's Voices* (Berkeley, 1978), pp. 91, 117–18. Kenner's explanation for this omission is too ingenious for its own good; his explanation for the "multiplicity of styles" falls into the point-of-view ("centered subject") trap by inventing, not one, but two, ominiscient narrators.

7 Pages references to *Ulysses* in the text designate Gabler's one-volume (New York) edition.

8 See Marcel Proust, "A propos du 'style' de Flaubert," in *Essais et articles* (Paris, 1994), p. 282.

9 Jacques Lacan, *Le Séminaire II* (Paris, 1981), pp. 148–9. And see also Martin Heidegger, *Sein und Zeit*, paragraph 80: "Dasein awaits with circumspective concern the possibility of sight, and it understands itself in terms of its daily work. The sun dates the time which is interpreted in concern. In terms of this dating arises the 'most natural' measure of time—the day, and because the temporality of that

Dasein which must take its time is finite, its days are already numbered ..." (*Being and Time*, trans. John Macquarrie and Edward Robinson [San Francisco, 1962], pp. 465–6).

10 Brill's original translation of "Überdeterminierung" was later replaced by the neologism "overdetermination", whose fortunes in Althusser's work and that of his followers are only too well-known. Freud originally meant that the elements of the dream material are elaborately cross-referenced during the dream work, with a complexity that can never be fully explored; the Althusserian use of the word simply means the multiple causalities of a historical event.

11 Gilles Deleuze, see *Cinéma II* (Paris, 1983), p. 299; and *Logique du sens* (Paris, 1969).

12 Elaborated in his seminar on Joyce, *Le Sinthome* (1975–1976).

13 "Who would have held it against Mme Bontemps that her husband had played in the Dreyfus case a part that had been sharply criticised by *L'Echo de Paris*? The entire Chamber of Deputies having at a certain moment turned revisionist, it was necessarily among former revisionists, as among former socialists, that one had had to look for recruits for the party of Law and Order, Religious Tolerance and Military Preparedness. Formerly M. Bontemps would have been cordially hated, because at that time the anti-patriots were dubbed Dreyfusards. But soon this name was forgotten and replaced by that of 'opponent of the three-year military service law.' M. Bontemps was, on the contrary, one of the authors of that law, therefore he was a patriot. In society (and this social phenomenon, it should be remembered, is merely one application of a much more general psychological law) new ideas, whether reprehensible or not, cause alarm only until they have been assimilated and surrounded by reassuring elements. It was the same with Dreyfusism as with Saint-Loup's marriage to Odette's daughter, a marriage which had provoked an outcry at first. Now that everybody who was 'anybody' was to be seen at the Saint Loups', Gilberte might have had the morals of Odette herself and people would have gone there just the same and would have commended her if she had censured like a dowager new moral ideas not yet assimilated. Dreyfusism had now been given its place in a whole category of respectable and accustomed things." (SM II 895)

"Qui eût pu tenir rigueur à Mme Bontemps que son mari eût joué un rôle, âprement critiqué par *L'Echo de Paris*, dans l'affaire Dreyfus? Toute la Chambre étant à un certain moment devenue révisioniste, c'était forcément parmi d'anciens révisionnistes, comme parmi d'anciens socialistes, qu'on avait été obligé de recruiter le parti de l'ordre social, de la tolérance religieuse, de la préparation militaire. On aurait détesté autrefois M. Bontemps parce que les antipatriotes avaient alors le nom de dreyfusards. Mais bientôt ce nom avait été oublié et remplacé par celui d'adversaire de la loi de trois ans. M. Bontemps était au contraire un des auteurs de cette loi, c'était donc un patriote. Dans le monde (et ce phénomène social n'est d'ailleurs qu'une application d'une loi psychologique bien générale) les nouveautés, coupables ou non, n'excitent l'horreur que tant qu'elles ne sont pas assimilées et entourées d'éléments rassurants. Il en était du dreyfusisme comme du mariage de Saint-Loup avec la fille d'Odette, mariage qui avait d'abord fait crier. Maintenant qu'on voyait chez les Saint-Loup tous les gens qu'on connaissait, Gilberte aurait pu avoir les moeurs d'Odette elle-même, que malgré cela on y serait 'allé' et qu'on eût approuvé Gilberte de blamer comme une douairière des nouveautés morales non assimilées. Le dreyfusisme était maintenant integré dans une série de choses respectables et habituelles." (P IV 305)

14 As in "La Chevelure" (No. XXIII of *Les Fleurs du mal* [1857; Paris, 1958]):

l'alcôve obscure
Des souvenirs dormant dans cette chevelure ...

15 Walter Benjamin, "Theses on the Philosophy of History," in *Illuminations* (NY, 1969), p. 261.

16 See above, note 3.

17 See Introduction, note 7, above.

18 Flaubert, *La Tentation de Saint Antoine*, in *Oeuvres I* (Paris, 1951), p. 69. "Et, tout à coup, passent au milieu de l'air, d'abord une flaque d'eau, ensuite une prostituée, le coin d'un temple, une figure de soldat, un char avec deux chevaux blancs qui se cabrent. Ces images arrivent brusquement, par secousses, se détachant sur la nuit comme des peintures d'écarlate sur de l'ébène."

19 Michel Butor, "Les Oeuvres d'art imaginaires chez Proust" in *Répertoire II* (Paris, 1964), p. 289.

20 See the extraordinary page in which Proust maps out the central position of Mlle de St. Loup: "Many were the paths of my life which met Mlle de Saint-Loup and radiated outward from her." (P IV 606/SM II 1110).

21 Jean Paul Sartre, "Qu'est-ce que la litterature?", *Situations II* (Paris, 1948), p. 6.

22 Jacques Lacan, *Le Séminaire I* (Paris, 1975), p. 80.

23 Louis Althusser, "Ideological State Apparatuses", in *Lenin and Philosophy* (NY, 2005), p. 162.

FOUR

9

Exoticism and Structuralism in Wallace Stevens

On the conventional periodizing account, Wallace Stevens's work, a monumental summa of the modernist languages in formation in the 1920s and 1930s and even the immediate post-World War Two era, constitutes the privileged object which a postwar "ideology of modernism"[1] seeks to theorize, as well as the prototype of everything in literature with which the 1960s wished to break. Yet perhaps there were other developments in the 1960s which Stevens can be said to have anticipated:

> This endlessly elaborating poem
> Displays the theory of poetry,
> As the life of poetry. A more severe,
>
> More harassing master would extemporize
> Subtler, more urgent proof that the theory
> Of poetry is the theory of life ....
>
> "An Ordinary Evening
> in New Haven" (486)[2]

It would be anachronistic to claim for Stevens's use of the term "theory" that later, charged meaning with which the development of the 1960s will invest it, becoming the designation of a new form of discourse that transcends the older separations of disciplinary categories of philosophy, criticism, belles-lettres, creative writing, and the like; still, Stevens's anticipation of this term may be taken as a warning that the Stevens phenomenon may well involve some initial lifting of the old barriers between "poetry" and "theory" and may involve the emergence of some new and as yet unclassifiable form of discourse.

Indeed, Frank Lentricchia has pointed out that the canonization of Wallace Stevens is not merely a kind of ultimate conclusion and ending for the modernist aesthetic generally: although it is that too, and Stevens's belated triumph over all his modernist rivals (Pound, Eliot, etc.) is consecrated by his institutionalization in the University as the supreme manifestation of New Critical poetic and aesthetic values, not unlike the analogous revival and canonization of Henry James during the same period as the supreme examplar of modernizing ironic narrative. But if that were all that was involved, the aforecited objections would have much merit, that Stevens's monumental work is at best to be taken as the canonical and hegemonic values of the ending 1950s, as that with which the poetry and the cultural thought of the 1960s must desperately break if it is to breathe and to "make it new." Yet this is to reckon without the theoretical component of Stevens's verse: Lentricchia goes on to underscore the hegemony of Stevens as a theoretician during this period, his immense influence as a strange new type of literary "critic" which is in many ways greater than that of his own prose commentators or of the founders of the New Criticism. *This* Stevens—the theoretician of poetry, rather than the poet, insofar as that distinction can be retained—will come to dominate the whole first moment of the emergent 1960s as well; and if in that case one wishes to say that what concerns us here is less the "historical" Wallace Stevens of the poetry than the "idea" of Wallace Stevens who came to be a critical fetish in this period, then the formulation may be pragmatically acceptable, even though it neglects the diachronic transformations of Stevens's own poetry (the emergence of a seemingly distinct and more philosophical-existential "late" Stevens) as well as the whole nature of the dialectic itself, for which there must necessarily be a constant interaction between subject and object, between the "idea" of a thing and the historical "thing itself."

Any evaluation of Stevens's work must start from an initial axiological paradox, which is surely more intense with Stevens than with any other major modernist figure. It must somehow be able to accommodate the seeming irreconcilable impressions of an astonishing linguistic richness on the one hand and an impoverishment or hollowness of content on the other, each of these in constant tension with one another and on various readings each seeming to draw the other into its force field and transfigure it. On the one hand, a familiar modernist practice of the unique personal or private style in these poems opens up into a wealth of vocabulary and syntactical fluidity that seems both absolute (no stammering, the voice never ends, is never reduced to silence or to awkwardness) and somehow impersonal again, as though this style were in reality something like an older rhetoric, with its collective, prepersonal capacities, its preexisting of the individual speaker who only needs to move in it as in an element. Therewith, however, one of the key features of the modernist will to style is lost: the necessity for its violent birth, for a painful conquest of the private voice over against the universal alienation of public speech: that "initial ugliness," as Gertrude Stein liked to say, "which it is our business as critics to recapture [even when standing in front of the insipid canonical loveliness of the Sistine Madonna] and which is that new style's struggle to be born." Nothing of a kind in Stevens: which is to say that in him, or for his discourse, it is for whatever reason no longer necessary to posit a whole universe of degraded speech, a whole world of prose, of the world of alienation and work, of universal instrumentalization and commodification, out of which and against which a specifically disalienating poetic language will emerge.

This extraordinarily supple and resourceful speech will then often seem to express its objects in some remarkably apt and unmediated way: more often, however, what I have called the inner hollowness of this verse will tend to return upon its language to cast some doubt upon the latter's density and authenticity. This steals upon one in those moments in which it becomes (momentarily) clear that Stevens's *only* content, from the earliest masterpieces of *Harmonium* all the way to the posthumous *Rock*, is landscape: and that not even in the visionary sense of many of the great nature poets, for whom the momentary epiphanies of place and object world are rare events, to be preserved over against the encroaching destruction of Nature as well as the alienating features of city or man-made environment. In Stevens, nature is, however, nothing but a given, a ready-made occasion for speech—birds, wind, mountains, the sun, always ready to hand whenever poetic speech needs some kind of objective content for its own production.

This is not to say that such content in Stevens is not also historically specific, as it necessarily always must be: there must be a historical precondition even for this seemingly ahistorical availability of abstract landscape for whatever poetic ends. In fact, landscape in Stevens has a twofold historical specificity, as a certain type of culturally marked geography, as well as a certain "vocabulary field" of specific and culturally marked place-names. But I will argue in this first moment that Stevens must repress this specificity, whose recognition would at once deflect his work into directions like those of Williams and Olson and raise social and historical issues that would at once undermine his remarkably self-contained or autonomous aesthetic vision.

The repression of the social origins of this neutralized landscape, henceforth given as a kind of abstract "vocabulary," a set of neutral counters for the exercise of poetic speech (not unlike those formal, geometrical vocabulary units of the great architectural modernists such as Le Corbusier), is determined by the subject–object framework of Stevens's poetic practice which we will characterize as rigorously epistemological in all the worst senses of this word. In Stevens we never have anything but an abstract subject contemplating an object world which is thereby construed as being equally abstract. As with the great "illustrations" of classical epistemology (in professional philosophy), where impoverished tokens from the external world (a desk, say) are drawn in as sheer indifferent "examples," the items of the external world must in Stevens equally be laundered of their cultural and social semantics, just as the social world and the existence of other people must equally be bracketed. But this observation is not a solution but a problem in its own right: it should logically lead to the attempt to establish the historical preconditions of even this peculiarly abstract possibility.

Indeed, the preliminary remarks on Stevens should not overhastily, in our present *historicist* and historicizing context, be taken as criticisms, not even yet as an ideological critique, of Stevens's work (we do not even yet, for one thing, know exactly what it is or does within that framework). At best, these must be seen as contradictions that will set ultimate limits for Stevens's "achievement," and these will be indicated in time: what is historically significant, however, is the work that is done within those limits. That it is avant-garde or elitist poetry goes without saying: but such extreme language experiments have themselves much to tell us about historical possibilities that one would not have been able to read off other kinds of texts (the latter may well be revealing in quite different ways, for which Stevens or vanguard modernism would be quite useless). In particular, however, as damaging as the restriction to an epistemological framework may be, we must here too immediately add the qualification that somehow, again in ways that remain to be determined, Stevens's poetry manages to transcend the limits of traditional epistemology: here, as in the gradual foregrounding of the theme of language in his work, he may best be read as registering a process analogous to that we will observe in French "structuralism," namely a dissolution of the older epistemological subject–object framework, which is bought at the cost of a certain reification of "Language."

The well-known problem of beginnings or of the starting point now imposes itself: we will begin with the phenomenon of the ease of speech that has already been mentioned. It is not a particularly unusual starting point: Wordsworth critics, for example, find their privileged points of departure in the distinction of moments in which poetic speech can flow from others which somehow block the latter and cause poetic language to return upon itself and interrogate its own conditions of productivity. Meanwhile, in other kinds of poets, the arbitrariness of certain poetic stances (the personal voice, say, or the prophetic mode, or the dramatic monologue) at once by their very artificiality designate the central problem of a more general blockage of other forms of poetic language. What we have to do with Stevens is artificially to reconstruct a certain stance or mental element that, once determined, accounts for this seemingly effortless coming into being of sentences, and of their content.

This may perhaps best be evoked by a contrast with the (contemporaneous) speech source of surrealist poetry, which laid claim to an equally effortless flow, although one of a clearly very different type. The problem is essentially one of distracting oneself from everything which intimidates or blocks speech: the surrealists found such an ideal locus of spontaneity through the systematic blocking off of conscious, rational, calculating mental and institutionalized thinking—in other words, by systematically suspending the "reality and performance principle" on the order of free association in Freudian analysis. But this very complex mental operation required them in effect, by their very effort and attention to that reality principle that has to be repressed, to preserve what they cancelled: so that the latter (or better still the inaugural opposition between common-sense prose reality and poetic language) returns on the poetic language, which, effortless in principle at least for the poetic producer, is then wildly dissonant for the reader and bears all the marks of the bracketing of reality that instituted it.

Nothing of the sort, as we have said, for Stevens's form of what may still in some way be characterized as free association. If so, then we would have to speak of something like a free association of *preconscious* material in Stevens, to distinguish him sharply and radically from the surrealists. The more appropriate point of reference, as we shall see, and one that anchors Stevens more firmly in our period than has hitherto been done, is with Lévi-Strauss's "discovery" of *pensée sauvage*, of the operation of great preconscious grids and associative systems, which, like a language or like several linguistic systems, subtend the thoughts of "primitive" peoples, that is, of tribal people who have not yet known abstraction in the modern or "scientific" sense (who precede the emergence of "philosophy" in ancient Greece). The indeterminacy in Lévi-Strauss, marked by our designation of such systems as being "like" languages, is not merely present in Stevens also: it marks out an ambiguous space that is the precondition of the "ease" of his discourse, namely a kind of no-man's-land in which words and images are not yet radically distinguished from one another. In any case, as has been widely observed, this ambiguity is at the very heart of the pseudo-concept of the "image" as well, about which it is never clear whether this word designates the thing of which the image is a representation, or the representation itself. The moment of "structuralist" reflexivity, in which language itself as a separate system is disengaged from *all* of its contents—whether images or things, signifieds or referents—is a later moment, which will in fact cancel this initial moment of possibility.

The latter is thus available only on condition that the systemic levels and their dynamics are not yet differentiated: a sense of the systemic relationship of words, which is not yet distinguished from a system of images, itself still naïvely able to be assumed to be a system of the objects themselves, the subsystems of the natural world, or what we have called Stevens's landscapes:

> Morning and afternoon are clasped together
>
> And North and South are an intrinsic couple
> And sun and rain a plural, like two lovers
> That walk away as one in the greenest body.
>
> "Notes Toward
> a Supreme Fiction" (392)

These differential relationships have not yet been dogmatically codified in terms of the binary opposition of structural linguistics: if "North" and "South" offer such a binary opposition in its pure state, the same cannot be said for "morning" and "afternoon"—elements of a larger system ultimately organized around "morning" and "evening" but eccentric to that opposition—and even more so for "sun" and "rain," in which these secondary or marginal or asymmetrical oppositions have been widened to include quite different semes, before being returned to the more conventional sexual opposition ("the lovers") and revealed to be the unity of growth by means of the adjective "greenest." No yoking of widely disparate contents in a jarring surrealist image here: there seems to be little enough resistance to the play of the mind across these signifying fields, and their reunification is a victory that is not bought at any particularly exorbitant or even visible cost.

The "still point" from which this kind of systemic exploration, this free association of the preconscious, is possible will then be initially one of cultural systems and collective associations (socially institutionalized in the collective *pensée sauvage*) as in Lévi-Strauss. It may be useful to mark the cross-reference to another significant "modernist" literary discovery, namely Flaubert's sudden awareness of the operation of bits of material language in consciousness, the not yet completely determinant yet ominous organization of the "mind" by clichés, commonplaces, forms of *bêtise* which are active in crystallized or reified phrases and bits of material speech. Only where in Flaubert these foreign bodies are immediately felt to be degraded speech (and through *bovarysme* already prophetically linked to the nascent media, the vehicles of propagation of these "pseudo-thoughts"), in Stevens there is no particular sense that these associative paths are in any way inauthentic (the same is true for Lévi-Strauss, but for a different reason, namely the restriction of his work to tribal peoples "before the fall," objects, in his Rousseau revival, of the celebration of something like "natural man"). Yet this is what accounts for the peculiar impersonality of Stevens's poetry and imagination: no sense of the urgent need to forge a private and uniquely personal style, to wrest one's individual *pensée sauvage* as an act of revolt from the standardized culture surrounding those last places of the authentic. Stevens's imagination situates itself at once in the universal, thereby forfeiting the peculiar glamor of the modernist poet as *poète maudit*, genius and unique stylist: *style* being above all the ambiguous and historical category in which, in high modernism, the specificity of the individual subject is expressed, manifested and preserved. This peculiarly unmodern commitment to collective association, to an already systemic cultural storehouse—a commitment that does not in Stevens involve the renunciation of the personal and the private, either, since in a sense it precedes the very emergence of the individual subject and of the latter's oppositions—accounts in another way for what we have called the hollowness or impoverishment of his content. Utopian in that it implicitly insists on the undegradedness of the cultural stereotypes, on their freshness and perhaps indeed their immediate or unmediated relationship to Nature itself, the reliance on collective automatisms, in a fallen society, cannot but constitute somehow, at some ultimate level, the zero degree or average common denominator of a fragmented and atomized *Gesellschaft*; hence the strategic limitation of this material to landscape, where those features may be expected to be least obvious and intrusive.

Still, there is much properly cultural material in Stevens, material that dates him oddly far more than the other great modernists of his generation, and read in a certain fashion obsessively evokes the glossy ads, the art deco, the fashions and interior design of the 1920s or the more elegant productions of the silent movie era:

> When the elephant's-ear in the park
> Shrivelled in frost,
> And the leaves on the paths
> Ran like rats,
> Your lamp-light fell
> On shining pillows,
> Of sea-shades and sky-shades
> Like umbrellas in Java.
>
> "Tea" (112)

Yet the high luxury of these characteristic interiors is a significant mechanism in the dynamics of Stevens's associative systems: these materials are allowed entrance to the verse, not because Stevens is particularly aware of their social and class character, as rather because—for obvious class reasons—they are felt in their elegance to be something like a subset of the natural. As in contemporary photorealism, people (debutantes, Jazz Age rakes, Newport aristocracy, and the like) are excluded, and only the Utopian *locus* of a peculiarly refined space for life remains behind (as also in some advertising). In fact, of course, such images are not natural, but form a specific "signifying field" among others in Stevens's imagination (others, related in different ways, would include the "popular American" field of associations, Whitman, "the emperor of ice cream," American birds, Indian imagery, a whole marked "American" vocabulary that intersects with various other specific vocabulary fields such as the "French," and so forth).

But what is important to us at present is the return of this seemingly alien content to the baseline natural system: this is achieved by means of a slippage from image to language. The glossy ad for an elegant boudoir, the luxurious empty place of reclining bodies, negligees, intimate receptions, now without any apparent discontinuity or shifting of gears finds fulfillment in an unexpected way, by the emergence of a place-name: Java. Indeed, place-names in Stevens (he who travelled so little in his life, and was proud of the fact) play a key role in the transformation of systems of natural or landscape *images* into more properly linguistic systems: the mystery of place-names, like those of proper names generally, lies in their coordination of a general cultural system (see Lévi-Strauss on the naming system for dogs, cats, birds and horses in our culture) with the unique deictic of the here-and-now, the named individual who is incomparable and presumably not systematizable. In Stevens, the place-name will be at one and the same time the very locus and occasion for a production of images: quasi-Flaubertian *bovarysme*, the daydream about the exotic place, the free association on Java, Tehentepec, Key West, Oklahoma, Tennessee, Yucatan, Carolina, and so forth—and the emergence of another level of systematicity in language itself (the generation of place-names out of each other, their association now as a proper vocabulary field), behind which yet a deeper system is concealed and active.

That deeper system, as the majority of place-names in Stevens can testify, centers on the exoticism of the South and most notably of the whole Caribbean area (Stevens was also proud, in particular, of never having been to Europe, a set of place-names that would have been peculiarly intrusive here as we shall see in a moment). We may thus generally characterize this new and very instinctive "signifying field" as corresponding generally to what would today be called the material of the Third World (yet another reason why there is some deeper logic in including Stevens in the movement of the early 1960's: only Crane of the great American modernists was also sensitive to the specificity of this material—Royal Palm or the seascapes—but Crane's aesthetics are very different from this and the resonance of his Caribbean has nothing in common with Stevens's assimilation of Third World realities to a place-name system and an occasion for infinite imagining reverie).

Yet it is clearly a peculiar view of the Third World, which one might seek to concretize by the experience of the world tour, the liner cruise through the islands, a peculiarly disengaged luxury tourist's contemplative contact with ports and maps (a specific moment, one would think, of aristocratic or moneyed tourism in the 1920s, which has little socially in common with the more universal tourism of the present day). This impoverished experience reconfirms our notion of the underlying purely epistemological stance of Stevens's work—a detached subject contemplating a static object in a suspension of praxis or even rootedness—and is documented in Stevens's one autobiographical "novel" or narrative, "The Comedian as the Letter C." Yet if this is the phenomenological experience, the "social equivalent" of Stevens's fascination with place-names, it also betrays a far deeper social and economic source which is that of the consumption of luxury products and objects at a particular moment in the development of modern capitalism, and reflects, one might say, a kind of luxury-mercantilist *Weltanschauung*, a view of the "world system" as so many sources for expensive imported goods. There is, in other words, a subterranean relationship between the "umbrella in Java"—the fantasy of the exotic holiday—and the "umbrella *from* Java," the luxury item whose own capacity to generate images, day-dreams and semic associations lies in its origins in a distant place and culture, and in the momentary function of a Third World handicraft industry to produce just such objects of consumption for the First World.

What we have called the Third World material in Stevens is thus not some mere private aberration in his work, not some mere adjunct due to the accidents of his personal history, his means, travel, and the culture of the age; but is rather a fundamental piece in the overall system, the way by which the latter comes to know a global closure and thus a universality (both Hartford and Yucatan, both First and Third Worlds) on which its other procedures depend. At the same time, by means of this crucial mediation of Third World material, a bridge is made between image and word (by means of place-names), and a transformation of purely social and cultural objects (the interiors, the furnishings, the Jazz Age luxury items) back into Nature and virtual landscape, since they all come to be associated with exotic *places*.

With the completion of his "world" by such Third World material, then, it would seem that an autonomous or semi-autonomous space has been achieved that can now be felt to "represent" the real world in its fundamental oppositions (nature versus culture, or in other words, landscape versus luxury consumption objects; and First World versus Third World). The next step in our inquiry is to investigate the process of autonomization by which this new "ideal" world of "representation" is felt to separate itself from the empirical one.

But we must first dispel the impression that this ideal sphere of images and words is some Parmenidean place of changelessness or of static being: our characterization of the content of Stevens's world as hollow or impoverished designated the nature of the link between the "ideal" and the "empirical" in Stevens. On the other hand, once we enter completely the realm of the "poem," it is clear that there is a great fluidity, a wealth of movement and micro-event that must now be accounted for in some more adequate fashion. We have suggested that the space of possibility onto which Stevens's imagination for whatever accidents of personal history or inclination happened—that space which unexpectedly opens up a seemingly limitless movement of poetic discourse, without barriers, in all directions—this space is essentially that designated by "structuralism" or by Theory as the Symbolic Order, or in a different way by Hegel as "objective spirit," or by Durkheim as "collective consciousness": that is, the ensemble of representations, representational systems, and their various levels (concepts, images, words) in which the individual consciousness or subject must dwell, and about which the thinkers of this period increasingly suspect that, more than a mere element for thought, or even constellations floating in the mind, this whole system may in fact determine and program individual consciousness to a far greater degree than had hitherto been imagined. This "discovery," if it can really be called that, is significantly contemporaneous with the emergence of media society (or of the *société de consommation*), and may thus be expected at least in part to register this tremendous quantitative increase in material images and representations of all kinds in the new cultural space in question. Always accepting the conception of a Symbolic Order as a kind of space and dynamic beyond the individual subject, we do not, however, necessarily need to endorse the various models and hypotheses devised by high structuralism to describe this new space, and essentially extrapolated from linguistic systems (binary oppositions, the Greimas semantic rectangle, even the more multidimensional projections of a Lévi-Strauss or a Foucault of immense systemic relations in constant transformation).

Stevens's freedom to move within the Symbolic Order is at least in part ensured by the absence of such codified models, which often restrict inquiry or exploration in advance. Now that Stevens's work is over and "complete," it would certainly seem possible to imagine an enlarged and complex structural analysis capable of mapping it out after the fact: here we will essentially be content to stress the multiplicity of subsystems in this ideal space, which is closed, if at all, only in the sense that the Einsteinian universe is closed, by folding back on itself, such that one never meets anything but contents of the same order, rather than, as in traditional closure, by the arrival at limits beyond which some radical otherness or difference from the system is felt to exist.

These "sub-systems," or "fields" as I prefer to call them, are thus in themselves capable of infinite expansion and combination: the dominant one, what in another kind of writer one would have been tempted to call that of the pastiche of Elizabethan language (what I have earlier characterized as the rediscovery, in a modernizing world of *styles*, of an essentially rhetorical practice in Stevens)—this field is capable of as much formal variety, of as unlimited a mutability, as clouds themselves (to use a characteristic Stevens image), and one could, in a pinch, dwell in it forever, were it not for the perpetually nagging sense that it is not itself really a world but merely a specific language. Each of these fields is thus essentially complete, with its own oppositions and its own rich possibilities of dissonance and contradiction: in such a field, for example, "grammarians" can be "gloomy" and still wear "golden gowns" (55). Such eventful tensions are felt to be an interesting heterogeneity only *within* the limits of the field itself: when, as we are admonished to do by the letter "G," we step outside that particular stylistic field, such variety once again falls back into a kind of homogeneity.

What has to be added, however, is the observation that there is also a play of eventfulness, of dissonance, of contradiction and variety or heterogeneity at the *intersections* between the various fields: as when a pseudo-Elizabethan vocabulary, for instance, like two galaxies colliding and interpenetrating on their distinct paths through space, momentarily knows interference with a pseudo-American, Whitmanesque, folkloric vocabulary field, all shot through with hoots and "barbaric" sounds and yawps. ... These intersystemic combinations ought clearly to produce an even richer sense of eventfulness than those that take place within any given system (all the more so since, as I have suggested, the systems involved are themselves disparate—some being systems of images, some of concepts, and some, simply, of vocabularies and "style").

Yet this is not necessarily the case either: in fact, what tends to happen when a single subsystem or field intersects with another is rather a bracketing or a distantiation in which each is precisely grasped as a "field," seen now for what is an ideal system of representations rather than a "world." Here, too, a certain current of structuralism, or rather of its immediate prehistory, coming upon an analogous phenomenon, has proposed a concept for this process which is relevant: this is Barthes's early notion of "connotation," derived from Hjelmslev and later repudiated in Barthes's middle or "mature" structuralist period. Connotation designated a set of messages given off, not by the "things themselves" but by the modes of representation of those things; a moment, in other words, in which (to use another characteristic formulation of the period) the medium turns into its own message, or rather begins to emit its own messages; in which the former "message" or denotation is henceforth only the occasion or pretext for new second-degree messages couched in the language of signs or styles or representational systems themselves. But Barthes's account, at least in relation to Stevens's poetry, needs to be elaborated and refined: for here it is clear that we have to do, not merely with isolated connotations, but with a play between whole "systems" of connotation among each other, systems in which reference withdraws in order the more surely to foreground style or representation as its new object (in that sense, the concept of connotation would offer yet an alternate model for theorizing the gradual autonomization of Stevens's systems, their reorganization into some ideal sphere beyond the empirical world itself). Thus, even this form of intersystemic play (as open-ended, clearly, as is each of the systems itself) ultimately undergoes an auto-referential momentum in which its very content, at the latter's strongest, ends up rather designating a play of forms.

With this, we may begin to observe the dynamics of autonomization proper as they can be viewed within the small-scale model or experimental laboratory situation of this poetic language:

Just as my fingers on these keys
Make music, so the selfsame sounds
On my spirit make a music, too.
"Peter Quince at the Clavier" (89)

It is the quintessential Kantian moment in which, as contemporary middle-class subjectivity is forced back inside its own head, the idea of the thing peels off the "thing itself," now forever out of reach—less, to be sure, as a Kantian noumenon than as an infinitely receding "referent," image separating from the thing, idea from image, word from idea, so that as the poem systematically drives itself deeper and deeper into the Symbolic Order, the "absent cause" of its content appears at ever greater distance in the imagined cosmos, its final symbolic form that "absolute referent," as Derrida has called it, the sun, in which, in some ultimate quintessence, all reference becomes itself concentrated and reduced to a point, a pure locus without dimension:

The sun no longer shares our works …
Not to be part of the sun? To stand

Remote and call it merciful?
The strings are cold on the blue guitar.
"The Man with the Blue Guitar" (168)

But this absolute referent was already present in various guises in the earlier poems, most strikingly perhaps in that remarkable exercise "Thirteen Ways of Looking at a Blackbird," in a form Stevens virtually invented for modern poetry, the theme and variations, where the referent is first the intense black point of the "eye of the blackbird," only to return in various forms of punctuation and interference within consciousness as the shadow cast by the real.

This is the most crucial moment in Stevens's poetic operation, the unresolvable contradiction on which the whole system turns and depends absolutely: reference must be preserved at the same time that it is bracketed, and that it is affirmed of it that it can never be known, that it stands outside the system. The system autonomizes itself as a microcosm, a self-contained faithful Utopian reflexion and representation of "things as they are": but in order to assure its continuing autonomy it must retain the link with the real of which it is the Hegelian "inverted World" or the complete mirror reflexion. This link with the real—what we will shortly characterize as the link between the autonomized *sign* (signifier/signified) and the referent—cannot within this system be theorized. We are therefore given two absolute and incommensurable, self-contradictory formulations: on the one hand, "nothing changed by the blue guitar" (167). Since the space of the Symbolic Order is the space of the images, ideas and names of "things as they are," the latter persevere serenely in their being, unmodified by their symbolic representation,

> nothing changed, except the place
>
> Of things as they are and only the place
> As you play them, on the blue guitar,
>
> Placed so, beyond the compass of change;
> Perceived in a final atmosphere...

Yet the opposite is also true, and its affirmation is equally necessary to the poetic system—namely, that in some Utopian sense, everything is changed by the "supreme fiction" of the Symbolic Order. Here is then once again the great paradox of the Symbolic Order thus conceived: it is both ideological and Utopian, both a simple reflexion or projection of the real with all its contradictions, and a small-scale model or Utopian microcosm of the real in which the latter can be changed or modified. One is reminded of Kenneth Burke's characterization of the ambiguity of the "symbolic act" and the cultural generally—on the one hand, a merely *symbolic* act which is not praxis and which changes nothing, yet on the other a genuine symbolic *act* which has at least the symbolic value of genuine praxis.

My point is that both of these contradictory formulations serve a non-theoretical function, namely to preserve the parallelism between a semi-autonomous symbolic space and the space of reality: this is a functional necessity for Stevens's system, since, as we shall see shortly, when in postmodernism the referent vanishes altogether, with it go the properly symbolic possibilities of Stevens's own specific subject–object relationship. Yet from this necessity (which Stevens must hold in being, which he must not allow to proceed further along the momentum of a properly post-modernist disintegration) a certain number of consequences flow—some of them ideologies, or strategies of ideological containment (in order to keep this contradictory system under control) and some of them inevitable structural results and limits of the system itself, among these that very quality of

Stevens's poetry which we posed as an initial problem, namely the ambiguous sense of richness and impoverishment.

We will formulate these structural consequences under three headings, with the preliminary reminder that the dialectic outlined up to this point is not ideological and does not yet imply the ideological critique of Stevens's work about to be summarized. Up till now, what we have described is an objective experience of a certain capacity of language or the Symbolic, which for whatever personal accidents Stevens felt himself impelled to explore, of which he made himself the objective vehicle or recording apparatus. The symbolic space opened up by Stevens's work, the autonomization of image from thing, idea from image, name from idea, is in itself neither true nor false, neither scientific nor ideological: it is an experience, and a historical experience at that, and not a theory about language or a choice susceptible of ethical or political judgement. But given the instability of this experience, which needs to be safeguarded and perpetuated by various strategies, the ideological now makes its appearance as what the Formalists would have called "the motivation of the device."

The strong form of ideology taken in Stevens's work is what we have since come to identify in the most general sense as existentialism (including within it that "fiction-making" thematics of Nietzsche's work which is its initial moment). Here the familiar and banal motifs of *Geworfenheit* and absurdity make their predictable appearance: the death of God, the disappearance of religion, now determine a radically meaningless world in which alone poetry or fiction can restore at least an appearance of meaning, assuming for the moderns the function that religion used to secure in more traditional social systems:

> The earth, for us, is flat and bare.
> There are no shadows. Poetry
>
> Exceeding music must take the place
> Of empty heaven and its hymns,
>
> Ourselves in poetry must take their place,
> Even in the chattering of your guitar.
>
> (167)

This ideology is then systematically elaborated and produced in the poems on death and the religion of art, from the early "Sunday Morning" on, in what are surely for us today the least interesting parts of the Stevens canon.

Yet what must be insisted on is the innate instability of existentialism (understood here as an ideology rather than as a technical and rigorous form of philosophical discourse). For as soon as we come to be convinced of the fictionality of meaning, the whole operation loses its interest; philosophies of "as if" are notoriously unsatisfying and self-unravelling. Yet when such an ideology unravels, then the very conception of fiction disappears along with it. In order to prevent this dissolution of the poetic system, something like an Absolute Fiction must be desperately maintained:

> But to impose is not
> To discover. To discover an order as of
> A season, to discover summer and know it,
>
> To discover winter and know it well, to find,
> Not to impose, not to have reasoned at all,
> Out of nothing to have come on major weather,
>
> It is possible, possible, possible. It must
> Be possible. It must be that in time
> The real will from its crude compoundings come,
>
> Seeming at first a beast disgorged, unlike,
> Warmed by a desperate milk. To find the real,
> To be stripped of every fiction except one,
>
> The fiction of an absolute—Angel,
> Be silent in your luminous cloud and hear
> The luminous melody of proper sound.
> "Notes Toward a Supreme Fiction" (403–4)

Here then the ultimate "referent" is affirmed by the very movement that denies it, and what is less an ideology than a desperate conceptual prestidigitation reaffirms the impossible, the silent Angel, the absent cause, the Absolute or necessary fiction.

Yet in a final moment this desperate systemic readjustment has practical consequences which are like the price to be paid for its continuing existence. This is the great lateral movement of autoreferentiality referred to in the beginning, in which the act of designating the absent referent (blackbird's eye or the sun itself, the impossible Angel) turns out at one and the same time to be a process of designating the Symbolic or poetic space in question as symbolic or poetic, as fictional, such that the poetry will now come to turn on itself and in all of its rotations continue to designate nothing but itself. Hence the richness and impoverishment we spoke of: infinitely rich as the projection of a whole world, a whole geography, this language at once empties itself by calling attention to its own hollowness as that which is merely the image of the thing, and not the thing itself. Yet at this point, at which Stevens would be indistinguishable from the autoreferentiality of high modernism generally, an unusual permutation takes place, and a new thing—theory itself—emerges. What before was merely "poetic" discourse, with its traditional and banal problems of the nature of specifically poetic discourse and of the aesthetic as non-practical and non-cognitive, suddenly opens up into a new form of discourse which is theoretical and poetic all at once, in which "the theory of poetry" becomes at one with "the life of poetry." Yet this emergence marks the originality of Stevens, now considered as a moment of the 1960s, a moment in which "poetry" also, in its traditional sense, dies and is transformed into something historically new, something that will gradually (in opposition to philosophy or literature alike) come simply to be designated as theory. It is the end of art, perhaps, in the Hegelian sense, but also its realization, and its transformation into the sphere of culture generally or of the Symbolic Order.

(1975)

Notes

1 See my *A Singular Modernity* (London, 2002), particularly pp. 197–200.

2 Parenthetical page numbers refer to *The Collected Poems of Wallace Stevens* (New York, 1969).

10

Baudelaire as Modernist and Postmodernist: The Dissolution of the Referent and the Artificial "Sublime"

The inaugural, the classical, status of Baudelaire in Western poetry can be argued in a number of different ways: a privileged theory of poetic value as it has been developed and transmitted by the modernist tradition is, however, a historicizing one, in which, for each successive period or moment—each successive new *present*—some new ghostly emanation or afterimage of the poet peels off from the inexhaustible text. There are therefore many Baudelaires, of most unequal value indeed. There is, for instance, a second-rate post-romantic Baudelaire, the Baudelaire of diabolism and of cheap *frisson*, the poet of blasphemy and of a creaking and musty religious machinery which was no more interesting in the mid-nineteenth century than it is today. This is the Baudelaire of Pound and of Henry James, who observed, "Les Fleurs du *mal*? Non, vous vous faites trop d'honneur. What you call *evil* is nothing more than a bit of rotting cabbage lying on a satin sofa." *This* Baudelaire will no doubt linger on residually into the *fin de siècle*.

Then there is the hardest of all Baudelaires to grasp: the Baudelaire contemporary of himself (and of Flaubert), the Baudelaire of the "break," of 1857, the Baudelaire the eternal freshness of whose language is bought by reification, by its strange transformation into alien speech. Of this Baudelaire we will speak no further here.

Instead, I propose two more Baudelaire-simulacra—each identical with the last, and yet each slightly, oddly, distinct: these are the Baudelaire inaugural poet of high modernism (of a today extinct high modernism, I would want to add), and the Baudelaire of postmodernism, of our own immediate age, of consumer society, the Baudelaire of the society of the spectacle or the image. As my title suggests, I will attempt a reading of this society in our present (and of the Baudelaire it deserves) in terms of the machine and the simulacrum, of the return of something like the "sublime." This will then be a speculative and prophetic exercise. I feel on more solid ground with that older period about which we are gradually reaching some general consensus, namely the long life and destiny of high modernism, about which it is safe to assert that one of its fundamental events concerned what we now call the "referent." It is therefore in terms of the disappearance of this last, its eclipse or abolition—better still, its gradual waning and extinction—that we will make our first approach to the poetic text.

Chant d'automne, part 1

Bientôt nous plongerons dans les froides ténèbres;
Adieu, vive clarté de nos étés trop courts!
J'entends déjà tomber avec des chocs funèbres
Le bois retentissant sur le pavé des cours.

Tout l'hiver va rentrer dans mon être: colère,
Haine, frissons, horreur, labeur dur et forcé,
Et, comme le soleil dans son enfer polaire,
Mon coeur ne sera plus qu'un bloc rouge et glacé.

J'écoute en frémissant chaque bûche qui tombe;
L'échafaud qu'on bâtit n'a pas d'écho plus sourd.
Mon esprit est pareil à la tour qui succombe
Sous les coups du bélier infatigable et lourd.

Il me semble, bercé par ce choc monotone,
Qu'on cloue en grande hâte un cercueil quelque part
Pour qui?—C'était hier l'été; voici l'automne!
Ce bruit mystérieux sonne comme un départ.

Autumnal 1

Soon cold shadows will close over us
and summer's transitory gold be gone;
hear them chopping firewood in our court—
the dreary thud of logs on cobblestone.

Winter will come to repossess my soul
with rage and outrage, horror, drudgery,
and like the sun in its polar holocaust
my heart will be a block of blood-red ice.

I listen trembling to that grim tattoo—
build a gallows, it would sound the same.
My mind becomes a tower giving way
under the impact of a battering-ram.

Stunned by the strokes, I seem to hear, somewhere,
a coffin hurriedly hammered shut—for whom?
Summer was yesterday; autumn is here!
Strange how that sound rings out like a farewell.[1]

Three experiences (to begin modestly, with the commonsense language of everyday life)—three experiences come together in this text: one is a feeling of some kind, strong and articulated, yet necessarily nameless (is it to be described as "anxiety" or that very different thing, "sadness," and in that case what do we do with that other curious component of eagerness, anticipation, curiosity, which begins to interfere with those two other affective tones as we reach the so characteristic final motif of the "départ"—voyage and adventure, as well as death?). I will have little to say about this affective content of the poem, since, virtually by definition, the Baudelaire that interests us here is no longer the Baudelaire of an aesthetic of *expression*: an aesthetic in which some pre-given and identifiable psychological event is then, in a second moment, laid out and expressed in poetic language. The poetic producer may well have thought of his work here in terms of some residual category of expression and expressiveness. If so, he has triumphantly (if even against his own will) undermined and subverted that now archaic category: I will only observe that as the putative "feeling" or "emotion" becomes slowly laid out in words and phrases, in verses and stanzas, it is transformed beyond all recognition, becomes lost to the older psychological lexicon (full of names for states of mind we *recognize* in advance); or, to put it in our own contemporary jargon, as it becomes transmuted into a verbal text, it ceases to be psychological or affective in any sense of the word, and now exists as *something else.*

So with this mention we will now leave psychology behind us. But I have suggested that two more "experiences" lend their raw material to this text, and we must now register their banal, informing presence: these are, evidently, a season—fall, the approach of a dreary winter which is also and even more strongly the death of summer itself; and alongside that, a physical perception, an auditory event or experience, the hollow sound of logs and firewood being delivered in the inner courtyard of the Parisian dwelling. Nature on the one hand, the city, the urban, on the other, and a moment in the interrelationship of these two great contraries in which the first, the archaic cyclical time of an older agriculture and an older countryside, is still capable of being transmitted through what negates it, namely the social institutions of the city itself, the triumphantly un- or anti-natural.

One is tempted, faced with this supreme antithesis between country and city, with this inner contradiction in the raw material of Baudelaire's text between precapitalist society and the new industrial metropolis of nascent capital, to evoke one of the great aesthetic models of modern times, that of Heidegger, in the "Origins of the Work of Art." Heidegger there describes the effect and function of the "authentic" work of art as the inauguration of a "rift" between what he calls World and Earth: what I will rewrite in terms of the dimensions of History and the social project on the one hand, and of Nature or matter on the other—ranging from geographical or ecological constraint all the way to the individual body. The force of Heidegger's description lies in the way in which the gap between these two incommensurable dimensions is maintained and held open: the implication is that we all live in both dimensions at once, in some irreconcilable simultaneity which subsumes older ideological oppositions like those of body and spirit, or that of private and public. We are at all moments in History and in matter; at one and the same time historical beings and "natural" ones, living in the meaning-endowment of the historical project as well as in the meaninglessness of organic life. No synthesis—either conceptual or experiential, let alone symbolic—is conceivable between these two disjoined realms; or rather, the production of such conceptual synthesis (in which, say, History would be passed off as "natural," or Nature obliterated in the face of History) is very properly the production of ideology, or of "metaphysics" as it is often called. The work of art can therefore never "heal" this rift: nothing can do that. What is misconceived is, however, the idea that it ought to be healed: we have here indeed three positions and not two. It is not a question of tension versus resolution, but rather of repression and forgetfulness, of the sham resolution of metaphysics, and then of that third possibility, a divided consciousness that strongly holds together what it separates, a moment of awareness in which difference relates. This is then, for Heidegger, the vocation of the work of art: to stage this irreconcilable tension between History and Nature in such a way that we live *within* it and affirm its reality *as* tension, gap, rift, distance. Heidegger goes on to assimilate this inaugural "poetic" act with the comparable acts of philosophy (the deconcealment of being) and of political revolution (the inauguration of a new society, the invention of new social relations).

It is an attractive and powerful account, and one can read "Chant d'automne" in this way, as staging the fateful gap between organic death, the natural cycle, and the urban, which here greatly expands beyond the city to include the repressive institutions of society generally—capital execution, war, ceremonial burial, and finally, most mysterious, the faint suggestion of the nomadic, of the "voyage" which seems to mark the interface between nature and human society. One can read the poem in that way, but at what price?

This is the moment to say that the limits of Heidegger's grand conception are less to be found in its account of the poetic act than in its voluntaristic implications for that other act, the act of reception or of reading. Let us assume that the poet—or the artist generally—is always in a position to open World and Earth in this fashion (it is not a difficult assumption to make, since "real" poetry does this by definition, for Heidegger, and art which does not do so is therefore not "really" art in the first place). The problem arises when the reader's turn comes, and in a fallen, secular or reified society is called upon (not least by Heidegger himself) to reinvent this inaugural and well-nigh ritualistic act. Is this always possible? Or must we take into account specific historical conditions of possibility which open or close such a reading? I pass over Heidegger's own sense of historical possibility in the fateful and unnameable moment in which he elaborated this meditation (1935). What is clear is that even this meditation must now return us to the historical in the drearier humdrum sense of the constraints, the situation, which limits possibility and traces the outer boundary even of that more transcendent vision of History as World.

So we now return to the narrower historical situation of this particular Baudelaire, which is the situation of nascent high modernism. Conventional wisdom already defines this for us in a certain number of ways: it is the moment, the Barthes of *Writing Degree Zero* tells us, of the passage from rhetoric to style, from a shared collective speech to the uniqueness and privacy of the isolated monad and the isolated body. It is also the moment, as we know, of the break-up of the older social groups, and not least those relatively homogeneous reading publics to whom, in the writer's contract, certain relatively stable signals can be sent. Both of these descriptions then underscore a process of social fragmentation, the atomization of groups and neighborhoods, the slow and stealthy dissolution of a host of different and coexisting collective formations by a process unique to the logic of capital which my tradition calls reification: the market equivalency in which little by little units are produced, and in the very act by which they are made equivalent to one another are thereby irrevocably separated as well, like so many identical squares on a spatial grid.

I would like to describe this situation, the situation of the poet—the situation this particular Baudelaire must resolve, in obedience to its constraints and contradictions—in a somewhat different, yet related way, as the simultaneous production and effacement of the referent itself. The latter can only be grasped as what is outside language, what language or a certain configuration of language seems to designate, and yet, in the very moment of indication, to project beyond its own reach, as something transcendental to it.

The referent in "Chant d'automne" is not particularly mysterious or difficult of access: it is simply the body itself, or better still, the bodily sensorium. Better yet, it is the bodily perception—better still, even more neutral a term, the *sensation*—which mobilizes the body as its instrument of perception and brings the latter into being over against it. The referent here is then simply a familiar sound, the hollow reverberation of logs striking the courtyard paving. Yet familiar for whom? Everything, and the very mysteries of modernism itself, turn on this word, about which we must admit, in a first moment, that it no longer applies to any contemporary readership. But in a second moment, I will be less concerned to suggest ways in which, even for Baudelaire's contemporaries, such a reference might have been in the process of becoming exotic or obscure, than rather to pose as a principle of social fragmentation the withdrawal of the private or the individual body from social discourse.

We might sharpen the problem of reference by prolonging positivist psychology itself—rigorously coeval with high modernism—and imagining the visual and graphic registration of this unique sound, whose "real nature"—that is to say, whose *name*—we could never guess from looking at its complex spatial pattern. Such registrations perpetuate the old positivist myth of something like a pure atomic sensation in the then nascent pseudoscience of psychology—a myth which in the present context I prefer to read as a symptom of what is happening to the body itself.

For this once "familiar" sound is now driven back inside the body of Baudelaire: a unique event taking place there and utterly alien to anything whose "experience" we might ourselves remember, something which has lost its name, and which has no equivalents: as anonymous and indescribable as a vague pain, as a peculiar residual taste in the mouth, as a limb falling asleep. The semioticians know well this strange seam between the body and language, as when they study the most proximate naming systems—the terms for wine-tasting, say—or examine the ways in which a physician *translates* his patients' fumbling expressions into the technical code of nosology.

But it is *this* that must now be historicized. I would like to make an outrageous (or at least, as they say, unverifiable) generalization, namely that before Baudelaire and Flaubert there are no physical sensations in literature. This does not quite mean advancing a proposition so sweeping as the proposition that (parodying Virginia Woolf) on or around 1857 we can observe a fundamental mutation in human nature. It does mean, more modestly, and on the side of the object (or the literary raw material), that free-floating bodily perception was not, until now, felt to be a proper content for literary language (you will get a larger historical sense of this by expanding such data to include experiences like that of anxiety—Kierkegaard is after all the contemporary of these writers). And it means, on the side of the subject, or of literary language itself, that the older rhetoric was somehow fundamentally nonperceptual, and had not yet "produced" the referent in our current sense: this is to say that even where we are confronted with what look like masses of sense data—the most convenient example will be, perhaps, Balzac, with his elaborate descriptions, that include the very smell of his rooms—those apparently perceptual notations, on closer examination, prove to be so many *signs*. In the older rhetorical apparatus, in other words, "physical sensation" does not meet the opacity of the body, but is secretly transparent, and always *means* something else—moral qualities, financial or social status, and so forth. Perceptual language only emerges in the ruins of that older system of signs, that older assimilation of contingent bodily experience to the transparency of meaning. The problem, however, and what complicates the description enormously, is that language never ceases to attempt to reabsorb and recontain contingency; that in spite of itself, it always seeks to transform that scandalous and irreducible content back into some thing like meaning. Modernism will then be a renewed effort to do just that, but one which, faced with the collapse of the older system of rhetorical language and traditional literary meaning, will set itself a new type of literary meaning, which I will term symbolic reunification.

But now we must observe this process at work in our poetic exhibit. The irreducible, the sonorous vibration, with its peculiar hollowness and muffled impact, is here a pure positivity which must be handled or managed in some fashion. This will first be attempted metonymically, by tracing the association of this positive yet somehow ominous sound with something else, which is defined as absence, loss, death—namely the ending of summer. For reasons I will develop later on, it seems useful to formulate this particular axis—positivity/negativity—as one of the two principal operative grids of the poem, the other being the obvious and well-known movement between metonymy and metaphor. The latter will then be the second option of the poetic process: the pure sensation will now be classed metaphorically, by way of analogies and similarities: it is (like) the building of a scaffold, the sound of a battering ram, the nailing up of a coffin. What must be noted here is that this alternate route, whereby the sensation is processed metaphorically rather than metonymically, also ends up in negativity, as though the poetic imagination met some barrier or loop which fatally prevents it from reaching relief or salvation.

This is of course not altogether true: and a complete reading of the poem (not my purpose here) would want to underscore the wondrous reappearance of the place of the subject in the next line—the naïve and miraculous, "Pour qui?" and the utter restructuration of the temporal system, in which the past is now abandoned, the new present— now defined, not negatively as the end of summer, but positively, as autumn—reaffirmed to the point at which the very sense datum of the sound itself becomes a promise rather than a fatality.

Let me now rapidly try to theorize the two principal strands of the argument, the one having to do with the production of the "referent," the other with the emergence of modernism. In "Chant d'automne" at least—and I don't want to generalize the model in any unduly dogmatic way—the high modernist strategy can be detected in the move from the metonymic reading of the sense datum to the attempt to reabsorb it in some new symbolic or metaphorical meaning—a symbolic meaning of a type very different from the older transparencies of the rhetorical sign to which I have already referred. What I have not yet sufficiently stressed is the way in which this high modernist or symbolic move is determined by the crisis of the reading public and by the social fragmentation from which the latter springs. Given that crisis, and the already tendential privatization and monadization of the isolated individuals who used to make up the traditional publics, there can no longer be any confidence in some shared common *recognition* of the mysterious sense datum, the hollow sound, which is the "referent" of the poetic text: the multiplication of metaphorical analogies is therefore a response to such fragmentation, and seeks to throw out a range of scattered frameworks in which the various isolated readers can be expected to find their bearings. Two processes are therefore here at work simultaneously: the sound is being endowed with a multiplicity of possible receptions, but as that new multifaceted attack on a fragmented readership is being projected (something whose ultimate stage will be described in Umberto Eco's *Open Work*[2]), something else is taking place as well, namely the emergence of a new type of symbolic meaning, symbolic recuperation, which will at length substitute itself for an older common language and shared rhetoric of what it might be too complicated to describe as a "realistic" kind.

This crisis in readership then returns us to our other theme, namely the production of the referent: a paradoxical way of putting it, you will say, since my ostensible topic was rather the "eclipse" or the "waning," the "disappearance" of the referent. I don't want to be overly subtle about all this, but it seems to me very important to understand that these two things are the same. The "production" of the referent—that is, the sense of some new unnameable ungeneralizable private bodily sensation, some new "thing-in-itself" that must necessarily resist all language but which language lives by positing—is the same as the "bracketing" of that referent, its positioning as the "outside" of the text or the "other" of language. The whole drama of modernism will lie here indeed, in the way in which its own peculiar life and logic depend on the reduction of reference to an absolute minimum and on the elaboration, in the former place of reference, of complex symbolic and often mythical frameworks and scaffolding: yet the latter depend on preserving a final tension between language and referent, on keeping alive one last shrunken point of reference, like a dwarf sun still glowing feebly on the horizon of the modernist text.

When that ultimate final point of reference vanishes altogether, along with the final desperate ideology—existentialism—which will attempt to theorize "reference" and "contingency"—then we are in postmodernism, in a now wholly textual world from which all the pathos of the high modernist experience has vanished away—the world of the image, of textual free-play, the world of consumer society and its simulacra.

To this new aesthetic we must now turn, for as I suggested it also knows remarkable anticipations in the work of Baudelaire. There would of course be many ways of approaching postmodernism, of which we have not even time enough to make a provisional inventory. In the case of Baudelaire, one is rather tempted to proceed as follows, by recalling the great dictum of the philosopher already mentioned, "Language is the house of being." The problem then posed by postmodernism, or more narrowly by the postmodernist elements in Baudelaire, could then be conveyed by the question of what happens when Language is only the *apartment* of Being; when the great urban fact and anti-nature spreads and abolishes the "path through the field," and the very space and coordinates of some Heideggerian ontological poetry are radically called into question.

Consider the following lines, for example, from "Alchimie de la douleur":

> Et sur les célestes ravages
> Je bâtis de grands sarcophages.

> and on celestial shores I build
> enormous sepulchres.[3]

The entire poem amounts to a staging of or meditation on the curious dialectic of Baudelaire's poetic process, and the way in which its inner logic subverts itself and inverts its own priorities, something these concluding lines suggest rather well. It is as though the imagination, on its way toward opening, or toward the gratifications of some positive and well-nigh infinite wish-fulfillment, encountered something like a reality principle of the imagination or of fantasy itself. Not the transfigured nature of the wish-fulfillments of paradise, but rather the ornate, stubborn, material reality of the coffin: the poetic imagination here explicitly criticizes itself, and systematically, rigorously, undermines its first impulse, then in a second moment substituting a different kind of gratification, that of artisanal or handicraft skill, the pleasures of the construction of material artifacts. The role of the essentially nostalgic ideal of handicraft labor in Flaubert and Baudelaire has often been rehearsed; as has Baudelaire's fascination for un- or anti-natural materials, most notably glass, which Sartre has plausibly read as part of a whole nineteenth-century middle-class ideology of "distinction," of the repression of the organic and the constriction of the natural body. But this essentially subjective symbolic act, in which human craft manufacture is mobilized in a repression of the body, the natural, the organic itself, ought not to exclude a more "objective" analysis of the social history of those materials, particularly in nineteenth-century building and furnishings, a perspective which will be appropriate for our second exhibit, "La Mort des amants."

Nous aurons des lits pleins d'odeurs légères,
Des divans profonds comme des tombeaux,
Et d'étranges fleurs sur des étagères,
Écloses pour nous sous des cieux plus beaux.

Usant à l'envi leurs chaleurs dernières,
Nos deux coeurs seront deux vastes flambeaux,
Qui réfléchiront leurs doubles lumières
Dans nos deux esprits, ces miroirs jumeaux.

Un soir fait de rose et de bleu mystique,
Nous échangerons un éclair unique,
Comme un long sanglot, tout chargé d'adieux;

Et plus tard un Ange, entr'ouvrant les portes,
Viendra ranimer, fidèle et joyeux,
Les miroirs ternis et les flammes mortes.

The Death of Lovers

We shall have richly scented beds—
couches deep as graves, and rare
flowers on the shelves will bloom
for us beneath a lovelier sky.

Emulously spending their last
warmth, our hearts will be as two
torches reflecting their double fires
in the twin mirrors of our minds.

One evening, rose and mystic blue,
we shall exchange a single glance,
a long sigh heavy with farewells;

and then an Angel, unlocking doors,
will come, loyal and gay, to bring
the tarnished mirrors back to life.[4]

I am tempted to be brutally anachronistic, and to underscore the affinities between this curious interior scene and the procedures of contemporary photorealism, one of whose privileged subjects is not merely the artificial—in the form of gleaming luxury streets of automobiles (battered or mint)

—but above all, interior scenes, furnishings without people, and most notably bathrooms, notoriously of all the rooms in the house the least supplied with anthropomorphic objects.

Baudelaire's sonnet is also void of human beings: the first person plural is explicitly displaced from the entombed chamber by the future tense of the verbs; and even where that displacement weakens, and as the future comes residually to fill up the scene in spite of itself, the twin protagonists are swiftly transformed into furnishings in their own right—candelabra and mirrors, whose complex four-way interplay is worthy of the most complicated visual illustrations of Jacques Lacan.

But I am tempted to go even further than this and to underscore the evident paradox—even more, the formal scandal—of the conclusion of this poem, whose affective euphoria (and its literal meaning) conveys the resurrection of the lovers, while its textual elements in effect produce exactly the opposite, the reawakening of an empty room from which the lovers are henceforth rigorously absent. It is as though the text had profited from the surface or manifest movement of its narrative toward the wish fulfillment of resurrection, to secure a very different unconscious solution, namely extinction, by means of assimilation to the dead (albeit refurbished) boudoir. Here "interior" knows its apotheosis, in very much the spirit of Adorno's pages on Kierkegaard where the passion for Biedermeier furnishings and enclosed space becomes the symbolic enactment of that new realm of the private, the personal, of subjective or inner life.[5]

Yet Baudelaire goes a good deal further than Kierkegaard in this historical respect, and we will not do proper justice to this glorious poem without registering the properly dreadful nature of its contents: what is tactfully conveyed here is indeed to be identified as the worst Victorian kitsch already on its way to the modulation of fin de siècle decadence, as most notably in the proto-Mallarméan flowers, of which we can at least minimally be sure that "in real life" they are as garish as anything Des Esseintes might have surrounded himself with. Even the "soir fait de rose et de bleu mystique" is mediated by the most doubtful pre-Raphaelite taste, if I may use so moralizing a word.

Now this presents us with an interesting axiological problem: in our engrained Cartesianism, it is always difficult to imagine how a whole might possess value whose individual parts are all worthless; meanwhile, our critical and aesthetic traditions systematically encourage us in a kind of slavish habit of apologia in which, faced with a text of great value, we find ourselves rationalizing all of its more questionable elements and inventing ingenious reasons why these too are of value. But culture is often more complicated and interesting than this; and I must here briefly invoke one of the most brilliant pages in what remains I think Jean-Paul Sartre's greatest single book, *Saint Genet*, whose riches, remarkably, have still been little explored:

most notably the section in which he reveals the inner hollowness of Genet's sumptuous style. The principal category of Sartre's analysis is the concept of "le toc"—the phony, the garish, that which is in and of itself and in its very essence in bad taste, all the way from religious emblems and the Opéra of Paris, to the cheapest excesses of horrific popular thrillers, porn ads, and the junk adornments and heavy makeup of drag queens. In Genet, as Sartre shows us, the acquired mental habits of Bossuet's style and classical rhetorical periods reorder and stamp these tawdry materials with the tarnished aura of the sublime, in an operation whose deepest inner logic is that of *ressentiment* and of the imperceptible subversion of the bourgeois reader's most cherished values.

Baudelaire, of course, represents a very different order of elegance; his mastery of the raw material of bad taste will be more tactful and allusive, more refined; nor do I wish to follow Sartre along the lines of an analysis of individual or biographical impulses in this writer. Nonetheless, there are curious analogies between the Sartrean analysis and this extraordinary apotheosis of what should otherwise be an oppressively sumptuous interior, whose very blossoms are as asphyxiating as a funeral parlor, and whose space is as properly funereal as the worst Victorian art photographs. These characterizations are not, clearly, chosen at random: the logic of the image here conveys death and the funereal through its very tawdriness, at the same moment in which the words of the narrative affirm euphoria and the elation of hope.

We have a contemporary equivalent for this kind of stylistic operation, which must be set in place here: and this is the whole properly poststructural language which Susan Sontag was the first to identify as "camp,"[6] the "hysterical sublime," from Cocteau and Hart Crane to Jack Spicer and David Bowie, a kind of peculiar exhilaration of the individual subject unaccountably generated by the trash and junk materials of a fallen and unredeemable commodity culture. Camp is indeed our way of living within the junkyard of consumer society and positively flourishing there: it is to be seen in the very gleam and glitter of the automobile wrecks of photorealist paintings, in the extraordinary capacity of our own cultural language to redeem an object world and a cultural space by holding firmly to their surfaces (in mechanisms which Christopher Lasch and others would no doubt identify as "narcissistic"). Camp, better than anything else, underscores one of the most fateful differences between high modernism and postmodernism, and one which is also, I believe, operative in this strange poem of Baudelaire: namely what I will call the disappearance of *affect*, the utter extinction of that pathos or even tragic spirit with which the high moderns lived their torn and divided condition, the repression even of anxiety itself—supreme psychic experience of high modernism—and its unaccountable reversal and replacement by a new dominant feeling tone: the high, the intensity, exhilaration, euphoria, a final form of the Nietzschean Dionysiac intoxication which has become as banal and institutionalized as your local disco or the thrill with which you buy a new-model car.[7]

This strange new—historically new—feeling or affective tone of late capitalism may now be seen as something like a return of the "sublime" in the sense in which Edmund Burke first perceived and theorized it at the dawn of capital. Like the "sublime" (and "anxiety"), the exhilaration of which we are speaking is not exactly an emotion or a feeling, not a way of living an object, but rather somehow detached from its contents—something like a disposition of the subject which takes a particular object as a mere occasion: this is the sense in which the Deleuze-Guattari account of the emergence, the momentary and fitful sunburst of the individual psychological subject has always seemed exceedingly relevant:

> Something on the order of a subject can be discerned on the recording surface: a strange subject, with no fixed identity, wandering about over the body without organs, yet always remaining peripheral to the desiring-machines, being defined by the share of the product it takes for itself, garnering here, there, and everywhere a reward, in the form of a becoming or an avatar, being born of the states that it consumes and being reborn with each new state: "c'est donc moi, c'est donc à moi! ..." The subject is produced as a mere residue alongside the desiring machines: a conjunctive synthesis of consumption in the form of a wonderstruck: "c'était donc ça!"[8]

Such an account has the additional merit of linking up with the great Lacanian theme of "second death,"[9] and of suggesting why death and resurrection should have been so stimulating a fantasy-material for a poet intent on capturing the highs and the "elevations" of an intermittent experience of subjectivity. If the subject exists always and only in the moment of rebirth, then the poetic fantasy or narrative process must necessarily first work its way along the path of death, in order to merit this unique "bonus of pleasure" whose place is carefully prepared in advance for it in the empty, dusted, polished, flower-laden chamber. And the latter is of course, for us, as readers, the poem itself: the chamber of the sonnet, Donne's "pretty room" (and Mallarmé's), waiting to be the faithful (and joyous) occasion of our own brief, fitful, punctual exhilaration as subjects: "c'est donc moi, c'est donc à moi!"

Burke's problem, as he confronted an analogous and historically equally new form of affect—the sublime—was to find some explanation—not for our aesthetic pleasure in the pleasurable, in "beauty," in what could plausibly gratify the human organism on its own scale, but rather for our aesthetic delight in spectacles which would seem symbolically to crush human life and to dramatize everything which reduces the individual human being and the individual subject to powerlessness and nothingness.

Burke's solution was to detect, within this peculiar aesthetic experience, a relationship to being that might as well have been described as epistemological or even ontological (and incidentally a logic which is rigorously un- or a-symmetrical to that of his other term, "beauty"): astonishment, stupor, terror—these are some of the ways in which the individual glimpses a force which largely transcends human life and which Burke can only identify with the Godhead or the divine. The aesthetic reception of the sublime is then something like a pleasure in pain, in the tightening of the muscles and the adrenaline rush of the instinct of self-preservation, with which we greet such frightening and indeed devastating spectacles.

What can be retained from this description is the notion of the sublime as a relationship of the individual subject to some fitfully or only intermittently visible force which, enormous and systematized, reduces the individual to helplessness or to that ontological marginalization which structuralism and poststructuralism have described as a "decentering" where the ego becomes little more than an "effect of structure." But it is no longer necessary to evoke the deity to grasp what such a transindividual system might be.

What has happened to the sublime since the time of Burke—although he judiciously makes a place for a concept which can be most useful to us in the present context, namely the "artificial infinite"—is that it has been transferred from nature to culture, or the urban. The visible expression of the suprapersonal mode of production in which we live is the mechanical, the artificial, the machine; and we have only to remember the "sublime" of yesterday, the exhilaration of the Futurists before the machine proper—the motorcar, the steamship liner, the machine gun, the airplane—to find some initial contemporary equivalent of the phenomenon Burke first described. One may take his point about self-preservation, and nonetheless wish to formulate this affective mechanism a little more sharply: I would have said myself that in the face of the horror of what systemically diminishes human life it becomes possible simply to change the valence on one's emotion, to replace the minus sign with a plus sign, by a Nietzschean effort of the will to convert anxiety into that experience physiologically virtually identical with it which is eagerness, anticipation, anxious affirmation. And indeed, in a situation of radical impotence, there is really little else to do than that, to affirm what crushes you and to develop one's capacity for gratification in an environment which increasingly makes gratification impossible.

But Futurism was an experiment in what Reyner Banham has called the "first machine age": we now live in another, whose machines are not the glorious and streamlined visible vehicles and silhouettes which so exhilarated Le Corbusier, but rather computers, whose outer shell has no emblematic or visual power. Our own machines are those of reproduction; and an exhilaration which would attach itself to them can no longer be the relatively representational idolatry of the older engines and turbines, but must open some access, beyond representation, to processes themselves, and above all the processes of reproduction—movie cameras, videos, tape recorders, the whole world of the production and reproduction of the image and of the simulacrum, and of which the smeared light and multireflective glass of the most elegant post-contemporary films or buildings is an adequate *analogon*. I cannot, of course, pursue this theory of postmodernism in any more detail here; but returning one last time to "La Mort des amants" it is appropriate to see in the play of mirrors and lights of the funereal chamber some striking and mysterious anticipation of a logic of the future, a logic far more consonant with our own social moment than with that of Baudelaire. In that then, as in so much else, he is, perhaps unfortunately for him, our contemporary.

(*1985*)

Notes

1 Charles Baudelaire, "Chant d'automne" I, in *Les Fleurs du mal* (1857; Paris, 1958), p. 61. All subsequent references will be to this edition. Translation by Richard Howard, "Autumnal I," in *Les Fleurs du Mal: The Complete Text of The Flowers of Evil in a New Translation* (Boston, 1982), pp. 61–2. All subsequent translations will be from this edition. It will be clear that my interpretation would exclude the woodchopping sound Howard has added here; but also that I have omitted the subliminal comparison of the thud to a Poe-like beating heart.

2 And see also Victor Turner, *The Forest of Symbols*, for an account of the multiple interpretations of myth and ritual generated by multiple publics within Ndembu society.

3 Baudelaire, *Les Fleurs du mal*, p. 82. Translation, p. 78.

4 Baudelaire, *Les Fleurs de mal*, p. 149. Translation, p. 149.

5 Theodor W. Adorno, *Kierkegaard* (Frankfurt, 1974).

6 Susan Sontag, "Notes on Camp," in *Against Interpretation and Other Essays* (New York, 1966), pp. 275–92.

7 As my use of the word "affect" (in *Postmodernism, or, The Cultural Logic of Late Capitalism*) has been questioned by recent theorists such as Brian Massumi (*Parables for the Virtual*) and Sianne Ngai (*Ugly Feelings*), and in order to engage in a productive discussion of the postmodern rather than a sterile and purely terminological exchange, I will specify that the "waning of affect" on my usage designated a system of more traditional named emotions, and that it might well be preferable to reserve the less familiar word, with all the Heideggerian overtones of its *Stimmungen*, for the various highs and bad trips I saw as replacing the older named "feelings."

8 Gilles Deleuze and Felix Guattari, *The Anti-Oedipus: Criticism and Schizophrenia*, trans. Robert Hurley, Mark Seem, and Helen R. Lane (New York, 1977), p. 16; "c'était donc ça!" is best translated "wow!"

9 Jacques Lacan, "Kant avec Sade," in *Ecrits* (Paris, 1971), 2:119–48.

11

Rimbaud and the Spatial Text

I want to see if I can make a very schematic contribution to the problem of the preconditions, the conditions of possibility, of a particular realization of what we generally call modernism, namely the poetry of Arthur Rimbaud. The problem I want to focus on has to be initially distinguished from both the analysis of that poetry and its interpretation. But the question of the "objective" conditions of possibility of these texts must also be differentiated from the biographical approach, even from those sophisticated contemporary psycho-biographies which offer an expanded sense of the very complex determinations in the construction of what we used to think of as an individual psyche or subjectivity. Rimbaud's psyche will be taken here as an objective given, as one crucial factor, among others, of the conditions of possibility in question. And since we necessarily find ourselves in a pluralistic climate in which a host of labelled and personalized "methods" compete, honesty requires me to avow a kinship with the aims of Jean-Paul Sartre in his last work, most notably the long and unfinished Flaubert project: even though it seems possible that my own judgements of detail and of historical interpretation alike will be very different in spirit from those of Sartre in that work and elsewhere.

As I read those three thousand pages, Sartre's project presupposes something like a fundamental gap between subject and object in the modern world, a gap which it proposes to maintain methodologically in order to surmount it epistemologically. What I mean by that is that *The Family Idiot* presupposes two distinct kinds of explanations for "Flaubert": on the one hand, a subjective, familial, psychoanalytic one, which will turn on Flaubert's trauma, his famous seizure at Pont-L'Evêque in 1842; on the other, a set of social determinants which range from the strategic configurations of bourgeois ideology at Flaubert's moment to the socially symbolic value of the conception of art his generation inherited and modified. The three completed volumes of the work will then stage these two enormous loops as something like a preestablished harmony between the subjective and the objective: the extraordinary historical accident which makes of the

Flaubert, bearer of a kind of private neurosis on the one hand, and the privileged spokesperson and form-creator for that collective and "objective neurosis" which was the ideology and daily life practices of the mid-nineteenth-century bourgeoisie on the other. The unwritten final volume was then to have set all this in motion around *Madame Bovary*, considered as a symbolic act overdetermined by these two distinct impulses, which are however in the work of art uniquely fused and ultimately indistinguishable.

Something like this, on a far reduced scale, is what I propose to sketch out for Rimbaud. On the side of the subject, "Rimbaud" is to be understood as a distinct physical and experiential, phenomenological configuration, something I will call "the production of the adolescent body"; and this is, I believe, a historically new and specific *sensorium* for which a host of unique determinants made this particular figure a privileged recording apparatus. On the side of the objective dimension, or that of social history, "Rimbaud" marks the moment—and this prematurely and in a uniquely anticipatory and prophetic fashion—of the passage from market capitalism to the monopoly stage of capital (or to what Lenin called the "stage of imperialism"), the moment therefore, of a whole mutation in the world system, something which demands a little fuller explanation. We are, in other words, fairly familiar with the relationship between culture and the historical body; yet the way in which an individual consciousness can also in some sense be informed and determined, structurally constructed and influenced, by something so seemingly abstract as a far-flung geographical and international system—this is perhaps still a paradoxical or enigmatic notion.

I might begin its elaboration by suggesting that my own approach is more unified than Sartre's, in that both of the impulses I have mentioned—the subjective and the objective, the body and the world system—are essentially *spatial* and are thus distinct poles in the historical configuration and transformation of social space itself.

Insofar as global or planetary space is concerned, however, a more effective approach to that might well involve attention to the intelligibility of social units, such as the village, the city, and the like. This is the moment to complicate our presentation—but the complication is really essentially yet another point of differentiation from the Sartrean model—with an aesthetic and a formal accompaniment, namely a theory of the stages of form production and cultural languages which sees middle-class art as passing through the three moments of realism, modernism, and postmodernism. These moments roughly correspond to the three stages of capitalism itself—the market stage, the monopoly stage or stage of imperialism, and finally our own moment, the multinational stage or so-called late capitalism and globalization, whose peculiar adventure we cannot even touch on here.

The larger theoretical interest of the moment of Rimbaud, however, will now be hopefully clarified: its analysis can be expected to tell us something significant about the key transitional moment in which modernism proper emerges, and some of the features of my explanation are indebted to Lukács's pioneering views on that emergence, from which, however, I hope a certain dogmatic moralizing has been removed.

My own particular Lukács, however, is, as I have said elsewhere, the Lukács of *History and Class Consciousness*, that is, the theorist of "totality"; I believe indeed that it is possible to read the familiar aesthetic works, the essays on realism, in terms of the earlier theory, and it is in this way that I want to approach our immediate spatial and geographical problem here. The idea is that the unification of form, in art, is closely interdependent on the immanent intelligibility of social life, that is, on the persistence of certain local social totalities. The possibility of realism will thus be closely related to the persistence of a certain kind of community existence, in which the experience of the individual is not yet completely sundered from the mechanisms of the socio-economic: a kind of society then that one might still overhastily describe in terms of the rhetoric of transparency. Intelligibility here means that the experience of a given individual is still able to convey the structure of social life proper: so that the "realistic" narrative of the destiny of individual characters retains an epistemological value and is still able, according to narrative laws and logic, to convey something of the inner truth of social life itself.

It is this possibility which becomes problematical when the newly unified and post-revolutionary nation states of Europe enter their monopoly and imperialist stage, in other words, when the life of the metropolis comes to be increasingly and structurally dependent on a network of domination and a colonial base (raw materials, markets, intensified and brutal surplus extraction) outside its own national borders and in the field of the cultural Other, which we have come to term the Third World: a process which sets in with an irreversible intensity from the period of Rimbaud's production onwards, and essentially extends all the way up to World War Two and to the great moment of decolonization and neocolonialism which marks the passage to the third or multinational stage.

The crisis in realism can therefore be theorized or modelled in the following way: as a gap between individual and phenomenological experience and structural intelligibility. Or to put it more simply, if, in the newly decentered situation of the imperialist network, you live something strongly and concretely, it is unintelligible, since its ultimate determinants lie outside your own field of experience. If on the other hand you are able to understand a phenomenon abstractly or scientifically, if your abstract mind is able to assemble all the appropriate determinants, present and absent as well, then this knowledge fails to add up to a concrete experience, remains abstract and sealed away in the compartment of the mind reserved for pure knowledge and intellection.

Two immediate comments about this description: first, the notion of the compartmentalization of the mind into experience and knowledge is only part of an immense psychic fragmentation, of a specialization or division of labor of various mental functions according to the separate senses, sexuality, rationality, numeration, and so forth—and that very fragmentation (sometimes, following Lukács, I call it reification) is itself a historically original part of the process I am trying to describe here, and is evidently the mental analogue to the taylorization of the labor process during this same period.

The second observation is this: that the various aesthetic and philosophical movements which aim at a return to wholeness, or, as with Bergson or the phenomenologists, posit some original wholeness which the fallen human beings of daily life misrecognize—all of these are surely also to be understood as so many desperate, second-degree attempts to deal with the crisis of fragmentation itself. Among them, one would surely want to accord some supremely privileged place to modernism itself, an artistic language which both registers and replicates the reification. Elsewhere I've discussed such strategies in terms of the body and the senses or the sensorium, with a view towards showing how the fragmentation of the various physical senses from one another also provided the modernist artist with so many sealed compartments (the pure eye, the pure ear, even some "pure" linguistic apparatus) in which to restore unity in a purely symbolic fashion. But I must not omit to remind us here that the most influential of these strategies is a far more pernicious and ideological gesture, in which it is subjectivity as a whole which is sealed off from a now dead and inert objectivity: generating a whole new field in which a whole new literature of inwardness and introspection can flourish.

The peculiar greatness and originality of Rimbaud—due at least in part to his prophetic or annunciatory situation—is that in his work none of these "strategies" has had time to freeze over into what Gadamer would have called a "method" or Barthes "an established, canonical, institutional system of signs." Returning to the matter of the geographical, of the abstract idea of the map as opposed to the bodily experience of a marginalized and in itself unintelligible here-and-now, I have in mind shortly to try to show the role played in Rimbaud's poetic production by the evocation of exotic parts of the world—Africa, the Far East, a delirious tropics, a phantasmagorical Germany—not to speak of the very real personal shock of contact with London itself, supreme metropolis of capitalism and also the very center of the shipping networks which will increasingly unite a world drawn together by colonization.

Central among these references is of course the great section "Mauvais sang" (Tainted Blood), in *A Season in Hell*: this extraordinary chapter—

which describes the attempt to daydream the self back through history, the imagination fighting desperately against the dead weight of Christianity that it finds there everywhere—attempts a series of identifications with the underclasses, from mercenaries, lepers, convicts, all the way to the lengthy acting out of the tribal African on whose shores slavers, Christian colonizers and the colonial soldiers of Europe disembark—a scene that it might have been interesting to compare with Whitman's slave market sequence. Unfortunately we have no further time to consider *A Season in Hell* here. But I'm anxious that this geographical Unconscious of colonialism be understood in a more generalized sense: I will refer to my discussion of the role of abstract geographical and exotic fantasy in the form production of Wallace Stevens (see essay 9 above). A rather different light is then cast on this by Terry Eagleton's insight, in *Exiles and Emigrés*, that virtually all the great modern 'British' writers have either been foreigners, women or internal emigrés—as though the establishment culture of English imperialism was unable to achieve a vision of its own Other or Outside sufficient to confer form on its own subjective experiences. Nor should it be supposed that those Others, and Third World culture generally, do not suffer an analogous yet inverted version of this same situation: as Susan Willis has shown in her discussion of the role of maps and floating airplane's-eye-view totalization in some of the greatest Caribbean poets. Finally, of course, another dimension of all this has been spelled out by Edward Said in his now classic *Orientalism*.

But we're beginning to run ahead of ourselves, and must now return to the other pole of Rimbaud's spatial text, namely the body, whose unique historical disposition and sensorium serves as something like a registering machine or libidinal apparatus for capturing the peculiar resonances of the colonial world system. For purposes of exposition, I'm going to begin a schematic discussion of the body in Rimbaud with a fairly traditional "influence" approach, namely a rather preposterous suggestion by Enid Starkie in her classic biography that when Rimbaud said "alchemy" he meant exactly that, and that his images and figures are explicitly informed by a conscious conception of the traditional vision of the "grand oeuvre" or the transmutation of baser metals into gold:

> There are seven stages, or processes, in the production of the gold: calcination, putrefaction, solution, distillation, sublimation, conjunction and finally fixation. They produce, during the processes, and in their correct progression, the various colours which are proof that the experiment is proceeding satisfactorily: There are three main colours. First the black—the indication of dissolution and putrefaction—and when it appears it is a sign that the experiment is going well, that the calcination has had its proper effect of breaking down the various substances. Next comes the white, the colour of purification; and the third is the red, the colour of complete success. There are intermediary colours as well, passing

> through all the shades of the rainbow. Grey is the passage from black to white; yellow from white to red. Sometimes the gold is not produced even when the red appears, then, says Philalèthe, it moves on to green, remains there for a time and turns blue. Care must be taken at this point that it does not return to black, for then the process would have to be begun all over again. If success comes then the gold should appear after the blue, grains of philosopher's gold. Sometimes the gold is in grains, but sometimes in liquid form, *aurum potabile* it is called, the elixir of long life. The whole process is sometimes described as the four ages, or the four seasons.[1]

I've found this description useful, not because I believe it to be the key to Rimbaud which Starkie thinks it is, but rather because the alchemical process offers a convenient shorthand impressionistic and figurative account of a physiological experience I take to be more basic in Rimbaud: namely a certain sense of the perseverance of identity through metamorphosis, a certain feeling for the way a single object or element, like Monet's haystacks, is transfigured by alterations in its lighting, exterior weather, metereological context, and so forth.

To put it that way, however, is still to give a rather static and external, contemplative picture of this process, which is on the contrary *lived*, I will argue, as an experience of *fermentation*. Nothing is indeed quite so striking in Rimbaud as a certain dominant rising and falling movement, whose element is liquid and which may even be primarily conveyed as a surging and ebbing movement of liquid *within* liquid. My examples must necessarily be abbreviated and few; I will take my master text, here from "Les Chercheuses de poux," translated by Paul Schmidt as "The Ladies who look for lice," which reads as follows:

Les Chercheuses de Poux

Quand le front de l'enfant, plein de rouges tourmentes,
Implore l'essaim blanc des rêves indistincts,
Il vient près de son lit deux grandes soeurs charmantes
Avec de frêles doigts aux ongles argentins.

Elles assoient l'enfant devant une croisée
Grande ouverte où l'air bleu baigne un fouillis de fleurs,
Et dans ses lourds cheveux où tombe la rosée
Promènent leurs doigts fins, terribles et charmeurs.

Il écoute chanter leurs haleines craintives
Qui fleurent de longs miels végétaux et rosés,
Et qu'interrompt parfois un sifflement, salives
Reprises sur la lèvre ou désirs de baisers.

Il entend leurs cils noirs battant sous les silences
Parfumés; et leurs doigts électriques et doux
Font crépiter parmi ses grises indolences
Sous leurs ongles royaux la mort des petits poux.

Voilà que monte en lui le vin de la paresse,
Soupir d'harmonica qui pourrait délirer;
L'enfant se sent, selon la lenteur des caresses,
Sourdre et mourir sans cesse un désir de pleurer.[2]

The Ladies Who Look for Lice

When the child's forehead, red and full of pain,
Dreams of ease in the streaming of white veils,
To the side of his bed two lovely sisters come
With delicate fingers and long silvery nails.

They take the child with them to an immense
Window, where blue air bathes a flowery grove,
And through his heavy hair, as the dew descends,
Their terrible, enchanting fingers probe.

He listens to their fearful slow breath vibrate,
Flowering with honey and the hue of roses,
Broken now and then with whispers, saliva
Licked back on their lips, a longing for kisses.

He hears their lashes beat the still, sweet air;
Their soft electric fingers never tire—
Through his gray swoon, a crackling in his hair—
Beneath their royal nails the little lice expire.

Within him then surges the wine of Idleness,
Like the sweet deluding harmonica's sigh;
And the child can feel, beneath their slow caresses,
Rising, falling, an endless desire to cry.[3]

I want to linger on a somewhat more detailed reading of this poem, which is a rather central piece in my argument. It has as I see it three basic moments: the first one in which the body is still fantasized as a closed unity, a kind of self-sufficient element or vessel, whose outer limit, edge, rind, promontory, gives onto nothing but is sensitized or problematized by torment of bug bites. Sleep—or better still "indolences," to use Rimbaud's own word—will, the child thinks, still restore that unity: "l'essaim blanc des rêves" will fold into the raging itchy spots and annul them. Yet now something approaches from the real outside, the unsuspected real exterior world beyond that closed body. I don't want to get into vulgar psychoanalysis, but the two sisters are clearly figures of the Horrible Mother, the Ogress who haunted and maimed Rimbaud's biographical life, and whose nails have something predatory and decoratively terrifying about them.

Now the second moment begins, in which we attend, through as yet unexercised senses, to that whole outer world. The primary unity is still given for another moment in the unity of the blue air and the tangle of "fleurs" (this replicates dreams/itchy bites) and then in the dew falling in the child's hair. But now something new: touch—a strange metallic contact, not the caress of skin or fingertips, but the exploration of fingernails, as of some delicate machine. And at that point then also, sound: the liquid noises of lips and breathing, the electrical clicking of eyelids and then of the cracking of lice between long sharp nails. All this, and the emanation of perfume or fragrance, takes place on the outside, wanders over the surface, yet includes the menace of a kind of penetration, even more frightening for its delicacy, an approach to the violation of the sealed adolescent body.

I want to note two features of this section: first, the buccal sounds, "salives reprises," the drawing back in of saliva and breath—this is the first sketch of that rising and falling movement we will underscore in a moment. Then the inorganic clicking sound itself: minute, electrical, deadly, blood-spilling in its very delicacy—I feel myself that it may not be too exaggerated to read here an anticipation and a foreshadowing of that new thing, the modern firearm, the machine gun, first deployed in the Franco-Prussian war and then the object of Rimbaud's later colonial commerce in an Africa under full colonization. It is the bodily modification of this new military technology, the production, by industrial capital, of a whole new and threatening sensorium of the body menaced over distance to the accompaniment of strange and inoffensive whistling, as of bees around your head (Zola's image in *La Débâcle*), which is here in emergence.

So now finally to the last moment, the great shift in level, the great release of a new *Stimmung* which we should not be tempted to trivialize and banalize too rapidly under the known quantity of a concept of adolescent sexual desire. Here we have then finally the full of what I have called fermentation—the ebbing and falling as of a tide of the "desire to weep," surging and dying away and yet never overflowing its boundaries, reconfirming the sealed body, a perpetual inner displacement of liquid volumes, which is identified as wine, as the delirium of music, and at length, the final word for this corporeal monad in full transformation and yet at full rest—*paresse*, indolence, idleness as some ultimate full, troubled yet self-sufficient state of being.

Let me now reinforce this peculiar inner movement with two stanzas which I must hack awkwardly from "Le bateau ivre":

Et dès lors, je me suis baigné dans le Poème
De la Mer, infusé d'astres, et lactescent.
Dévorant les azurs verts; où, flottaison blême
Et ravie, un noyé pensif parfois descend,

Ou, teignant tout à coup les bleuités, délires
Et rhythmes lents sous les rutilements du jour,
Plus fortes que l'alcool, plus vastes que nos lyres,
Fermentent les rousseurs amères de l'amour!

Now I drift through the Poem of the Sea;
This gruel of stars mirrors the milky sky,
Devours green azures; ecstatic flotsam,
Drowned men, pale and thoughtful, sometimes drift by.

Staining the sudden blueness, the slow sounds,
Deliriums that streak the glowing sky,
Stronger than drink and the songs we sing,
It is boiling, bitter, red; it is love![4]

These various versions, of which there are many more for which we have no time, would have served, for an older phenomenological criticism, to designate, at the heart of this poetry, a nameless yet precise physiological experience—what I've termed fermentation, following Rimbaud himself (the word is omitted by Schmidt)—and which it is the task of the poet, as he tells us in *A Season in Hell*, to register: "Ce fut d'abord une étude. J'écrivais des silences, des nuits, Je notais l'inexprimable. Je fixais des vertiges."[5] A whole new grammar corresponds to this vocation, a whole new practice of plural substantives and of multiplied apostrophes, as well as a curious and innovative production of self-modifying verbs ("les fleurs de rêve tintent, éclatent, éclairent"[6]), which seems to me to be linked to a whole new conception of rhyme itself, as in "Veillées I":[7]

Veillées I

C'est le repos éclairé, ni fièvre ni langueur, sur le lit ou sur le pré.
C'est l'ami ni ardent ni faible. L'ami.
C'est l'aimée ni tourmentante ni tourmentée. L'aimée.
L'air et le monde point cherchés. La vie.
—Etait-ce donc ceci?
—Et le rêve fraîchit.

Vigils I

This is a place of rest and light,
No fever, no longing,
In a bed or a field.
This is a friend, neither ardent nor weak. A friend.
This is my beloved, untormenting, untormented. My beloved.
Air, and a world all unlooked for. Life.
... Was it really this?
For the dream grows cold.[8]

I think we must resist the temptation to confer an immutable and metaphysical signification to rhyme in general; on the other hand, that a peculiar rhyming structure (coming out of the refrain structure of the earliest verse) has a fairly precise private meaning in Rimbaud's practice seems to me incontrovertible; and it is a meaning I would want to describe in terms of the persistence of a certain identity through metamorphosis, the way in which a substance (as in the alchemical process) retains a troubled and bewildered continuity of being across a range of organic transformations in its flesh, its colors and its very texture ("nudité qu'ombrent, traversent et habillent les arcs-en-ciel, la flore, la mer"[9]): now we can better grasp the phenomenology of Monet's haystacks and cathedrals.

I will want shortly to suggest that such fermentation is to be understood as the effects of the mutability of a range of contextual frameworks around a single substance; and you will have understood that those absent, fantasized, yet perpetually shifting "frameworks" are at one with the whole new global geographical system I mentioned earlier. For the moment, however, and on the level of the individual body, this fermentation can be identified as that of adolescence, and its aesthetic registration can thus be taken as the virtual "production" of the adolescent body itself.

Fermentation, however, is only one privileged or symbolic bodily phenomenon in a constellation of others which form something like the semiotic *system* of Rimbaud's body or sensorium. Here I must however proceed even more schematically, with the briefest of examples. The other three terms of such a system seem to me to be those of rage, of the insipid, and of what in Rimbaud's private language is called "le bonheur" (happiness). Rage, storm, the moment in which the body seems on the point of exploding:

Qu'est-ce pour nous, mon coeur, que les nappes de sang
Et de braise, et mille meurtres, et les longs cris
De rage, sanglots de tout enfer renversant
Tout ordre; et l'Aquilon encor sur les débris;

What do we care, my heart, for streams of blood
And fire, a thousand murders, endless screams
Of anger, sobs of hell, order destroyed in a flood
Of fire, as over all the North Wind streams[10]

This is, I believe, the political or revolutionary pole in Rimbaud, the moment of revolt—both social and physical—which for all intents and purposes disappears from his world with the bloody repression of the Paris Commune.

The insipid (the more expressive French word is "fade") is, one would think, something like the opposite term to this one: a kind of inner stagnation or stasis, in which an inner tonality or perceptual flavor is given, without its being perceptually identifiable, since the movement of fermentation has been momentarily arrested, and in the absence of metamorphoses into something else there is no way to fix or to demarcate, to identify or to name, the perception or the taste in question:

Que pouvais-je boire dans cette jeune Oise,
Ormeaux sans voix, gazon sans fleurs, ciel couvert.
Que tirais-je à la gourde de colocase?
Quelque liqueur d'or, fade et qui fait suer.

What could I drink from this young Oise,
Tongueless trees, flowerless grass, dark skies ...
What could I draw from the round gourd that grew there?
Some tasteless golden draught to make me sweat.[11]

The mystery of "le fade," the insipid, along with the accompanying sealing of the body over upon itself, is in Rimbaud generally accompanied by sweat on the outer surface. I will very rapidly suggest, without being able to defend this peculiar hypothesis any further, the intimate signifying relationship between this datum and the privileged theme of work and workers in Rimbaud,[12] as well as the relationship of dawn to noon, the emergence into the social world of the city at work and of the sun at its zenith.

Finally, most enigmatic, "le bonheur," which seems to me to mark the relief of a windless absence of inner bodily feeling, a kind of extraordinary calm more negative than positive, in which the various other perceptual tides have momentarily been stilled or suspended. "Veillées I" can again exemplify this moment, which is sometimes, as in "Being Beauteous" or "Génie," projected outwards into a mirage of the ideal double, supreme, new, and perfect, to use some of the most characteristic markers for what we must however take to be an illusion: this state is not the prophetic annunciation of the radically new, but rather merely a moment of radical exhaustion and privation, an emptiness rather than a plenitude on the point of emergence.

This system can then be formalized, if we articulate its various terms and elements into the twin oppositions of stasis versus change on the one hand, and closure/plenitude versus emptiness on the other (see figure):

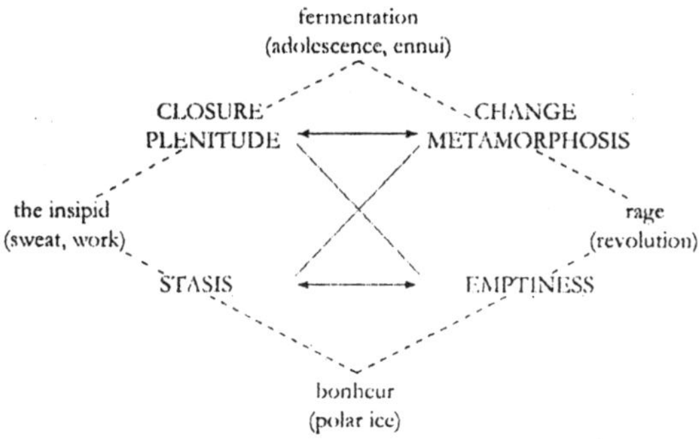

You will note that in the neutral term, "bonheur," I have introduced an exemplification not mentioned until now, namely the ice and snow of the arctic pole—images from Poe's "Gordon Pym" or from Verne which begin obsessively to invade *Illuminations* and which may thus serve as a way of modulating towards our other theme here, namely the global, geographical colonial world-system as it inscribes itself in these poems and develops a resonant interaction with the sensory or bodily system of the individual subject outlined above.

The movement from the verse to the prose poems can largely, but not exclusively, be understood as the displacement of a movement of bodily fermentation or metamorphosis towards that of a metamorphosis of cultural and geographical systems. As with the more purely physical experience, this movement, this rotation of a semiotic system, desperately seeks to transcend itself, to issue into the radically new, into genuine transformation and the Novum, and to constitute something more than a mere permutation in a closed combinational field. It is therefore as though the question posed by such prose poems could be formulated as follows: not, How to find or invent a radically new body? but rather, How will the world end? (it being understood that with the defeat of the Commune in May, 1871, no further visions of social and revolutionary transformation are concretely available to the political unconscious): only destruction and Apocalypse, then, the end of the world, remains as an imaginative possibility and as a formal principle for the closure of these poems:

> Non! Le moment de l'étuve, des mers enlevées, des embrasements souterrains, de la planète emportée, et des exterminations conséquentes, certitudes si peu malignement indiquées dans la Bible et par les Nornes et qu'il sera donné à l'être sérieux de surveiller.—Cependant ce ne sera point un effet de légende!

No! This is the time of the sweat bath, of oceans boiling over,
Of underground explosions, of the planet whirled away,
Of exterminations sure to follow;
Certainties only vaguely indicated in the Bible,
—Or by the Norns—
Which the serious man will be asked to observe.
Though the entire effect will be scarcely one of legend![13]

I want to argue, however, that this new vision of the end of the world (curiously inverted in the greatest of all the prose poems, "Après le déluge," which begins with the end of the world and works drearily backwards into civilization and the misery of the adolescent) involves a displacement of terms from the position of what we have called "rage" to that other, far less dynamic term which marks the moment of stillness or suspension. This is, however, something best demonstrated in the analysis of a single fundamental text, "Métropolitain":

Métropolitain

Du détroit d'indigo aux mers d'Ossian, sur le sable rose et orange qu'a lavé le ciel vineux viennent de monter et de se croiser des boulevards de cristal habités incontinent par de jeunes familles pauvres qui s'alimentent chez les fruitiers. Rien de riche.—La ville!

Du désert de bitume fuient droit en déroute avec les nappes de brumes échelonnées en bandes affreuses au ciel qui se recourbe, se recule et descend formé de la plus sinistre fumée noire que puisse faire l'Océan en deuil, les casques, les roues, les barques, les croupes.—La bataille!

Lève la tête: ce pont de bois, arqué; les derniers potagers de Samarie; ces masques enluminés sous la lanterne fouettée par la nuit froide; l'ondine niaise à la robe bruyante, au bas de la rivière; ces crânes lumineux dans les plants de pois,—et les autres fantasmagories,—la campagne.

Des routes bordées de grilles et de murs, contenant à peine leurs bosquets, et les atroces fleurs qu'on appellerait coeurs et soeurs, Damas damnant de langueur,—possessions de féeriques aristocraties ultra-Rhénanes, Japonaises, Guaranies, propres encore à recevoir la musique des anciens—et il y a des auberges qui pour toujours n'ouvrent déjà plus—il y a des princesses, et si tu n'es pas trop accablé, l'étude des astres—le ciel.

Le matin où avec Elle, vous vous débattîtes parmi les éclats de neige, les lèvres vertes, les glaces, les drapeaux noirs et les rayons bleus, et les parfums pourpres du soleil des pôles,—ta force.

Metropolitan

From the indigo straits to the oceans of Ossian,
Across orange and rosy sands washed in the wine-dark sky
Boulevards of crystal rise, crisscross—

They swarm instantly with the young families of the poor,
Fed from the fruit-sellers' stands—Nothing too rich.
This is the city!

Fleeing out of the bituminous waste
In rout through sheets of mist rising in terrible bands
To the hovering sky, high, then low, full of the blackest,
Most sinister smoke of a mourning Ocean,
Roll helmets, wheels, wagons, and horses' flanks—
This is battle!

Lift up your head: this high-arched wooden bridge,
The straggling kitchen gardens of Samaria;
Painted masks beneath a lantern beaten by cold nights,
A stupid water nymph in shrieking garments
Deep in the riverbed.
Gleaming skulls in the garden vines,
And other phantasmagorias—
This is the country.

Highways edged with iron grilles and walls,
Barely holding back their groves,
The terrible flowers called sisters, called hearts—
Damascus damned and endless—
The holdings of enchanted aristocracies
(High Rhenish, Japanese, Guaranian)
Still fit to resound with the music of the ancients.
—There are inns that will never ever open again;
There are princesses, and (if you are not yet overwhelmed)
The stars to gaze at—
This is the sky.

The morning when, with Her, you struggled
In the glaring snow; green lips, ice, black banners,
Blue rays of light,
And the dark red perfumes of the polar sun—
This is your strength.[14]

As is clear, the final strophe of this poem stages that whole landscape of ice to which we referred; and it equally clearly does so in order to bring resolution to the sequence of geographical and cultural motifs. Our initial question must therefore be: resolution of what? How are the constitutive tensions or contradictions in this sequence to be articulated?

City, battle, countryside, heavens: such are the formal rubrics of the four-strophe movement which precedes the ultimate neutralizing world of ice and snow. This movement is subtended, I will argue, by a whole phantasmal history of the world, by an unconscious yet well-nigh collective meditation on history and its contradictions, which now decisively absorbs the more seemingly individual thematics of the earlier poems. Let me, however, qualify this: I'm certainly not trying to say that some earlier subjective or personal thematics has here been somehow replaced by an objective one. Rather, along with Deleuze and others, I must feel that the separation between the subjective and the objective, the psychoanalytic and the social, between desire and politics, is an artificial one, and that desire and its fantasies are always social and political, while the political vision, wherever it exists intensely, must always be seen as a form, perhaps the strong form, of desire. The explicitation, therefore, in this poem, of its historical and political elements is not a turn to something else, but rather simply an enlargement of Rimbaud's earlier poetic obsessions.

Here, I think, at a moment in which France is passing belatedly into the industrial world, in which for the first time in French history a genuinely bourgeois regime is in the process of installing itself definitively, we can detect in Rimbaud's prose poem a meditation on the gap between the two great modes of production which, overlapping for a time, are in the process of displacing one another. The first strophe designates the City, the industrial and commercial metropolis which in Rimbaud's historical experience is embodied, not by Paris—a space of politics and revolution—but rather by London itself, the very center of the colonial world network, and an unimaginable and futuristic urban phenomenon which leaves its mark all over the later prose poems.

The second strophe then conjures up the phantasmagorical Other of the city, of urban civilization—namely the barbarian horde, what Deleuze calls the nomadic, the faceless swarm of the enemies of the city who mass beyond its outer walls and fortifications, but are set in flight by nascent civilization.

With the third and fourth strophes, however, we are clearly in a very different historical and social world, namely that of the great feudalisms, of peasant culture and samurai aristocracies, of fields and feudal warlords. The two strophes are differentiated in terms one would be tempted to characterize as those of social class, but also as those of base and superstructure. The third strophe, indeed, develops a vision of precapitalist agriculture and peasant holdings, along with the cultural dominants of that kind of society, magical and fairytale elements which in our society have been reduced to the materials of children's books.

The fourth then discovers the whole space of a feudal ruling class, a space which is however detectable only in its sealed absence, by the walls and fences which shut off the ruling-class enclave from the outside world. Even more striking, however, is the sense of the passage of time, of historical disappearance in this passage, in which one of Rimbaud's great motifs suddenly reappears, like a fateful and telltale symptom: "there are inns that will never ever open again." As against this world on the wane, then, we return to the opening strophes as the signs of a new world struggling to be born (and struggling to be conceptualized).

The landscape of ice and snow of the final strophe then blots all this out in peremptory fashion: overtones of a return to childhood games and loves—Citizen Kane's "Rosebud!"—organize a new and powerful neutral element—the arctic pole—capable of obliterating the new space of capital along with the archaic space of feudalism in a single all-engulfing movement.

In the larger context of the *Illuminations* generally, the two initial sets of paired strophes seem to me to correspond to one of the more haunting obsessions in Rimbaud's late poetry, most strongly expressed in the regressive movement of "Après le déluge": "Oh! les pierres précieuses qui se cachaient,—les fleurs qui regardaient déjà" (Oh, the precious stones returning into the earth,—the flowers again beginning to look at us).[15] Mineral versus vegetal, industrial capital versus the agricultural world of a precapitalist era: these are the terms in which Rimbaud's vision of the city—crystal, futuristic, with its great causeways *à la* Wells or Jules Verne, its Piranesi-like skylines, dizzying in their geometrical entanglement—are linked to the masses of the poor—decent, working poor—who are its human subjects.

It is useful to insist a little—not by way of critique but for purposes of historical specification—on everything which is partial, distorted, ideological, phantasmagoric, in this vision of imperial capitalism. Rimbaud as a marginal and a foreigner is excluded from any possibility of grasping that new social formation in any realistic or "scientific" way: he must therefore fantasize it from the outside in terms of the visions offered him by Jules Verne. Yet it is very precisely this failure of the imagination, this dissociation of sensibility, which then finds dialectical compensation in the even wilder visions of a barbarian horde, which appear as though in answer to the question: How will *this*, how will the city of the future, end?

But it is as if the poem undertook an implicit critique of precisely this vision of history—following the theme of barbarism and the barbarian back into the other related vision of a precapitalist feudalism—something which really did exist, but which can surely no longer be the agency of the end of capital, since it was this last that brought an historical end to the older society, leaving the "inns" empty.

The final apocalypse of snow oddly reintegrates one of the motifs of the first stanza, namely the whole vision of a crystal world proper: the very unnaturality, minerality, inhumanity of the metropolis—its affinity with the materials of glass, metal and crystal—now generates their ultimate strong form in the emergence of an ice age.

But to leave Rimbaud at that point would be to lose everything which is the most deeply energetic and poetic in this visionary writer: for—ultimate paradox—this glacial annulment of the world is in the climax of the poem suddenly transformed into the most stubborn of all Rimbaud's obsessions—the transformation of the body, the emergence of the New, the Utopian impulse itself, saluted here in a final moment with the symbolically charged words, "ta force." To understand how a vision of the blockage of history could be thus invested, against all hope, with a relentless drive towards the transfiguration of the world would be to stand at the very center of the unique complex which bears the name Arthur Rimbaud.

(*1981*)

Notes

1 Enid Starkie, *Rimbaud* (New York, 1961), pp. 162–3.
2 All quotations from Rimbaud's French are from the Pléiade edition of Rimbaud: *Oeuvres complètes*, ed. Antoine Adam (Paris, 1972). For the present quotation, see pp. 65–6.
3 See Paul Schmidt, *Arthur Rimbaud: Complete Works* (New York, 1976), pp. 76–7.
4 Rimbaud, p. 67; Schmidt, p. 120.
5 Rimbaud, p. 106.
6 Rimbaud, p. 122.
7 But see also 'Départ' and 'A une raison'.
8 Rimbaud, p. 138–9; Schmidt, p. 161. English can scarcely render the effect of Rimbaud's off-rhymes here.
9 Rimbaud, p. 122.
10 Rimbaud, p. 71; Schmidt, p. 85.
11 Rimbaud, p. 72; Schmidt, p. 139.
12 See, in particular, "Bonne pensée du matin."
13 Rimbaud, p. 150; Schmidt p. 169.
14 Rimbaud, pp. 143–4; Schmidt, p. 233–4.
15 Rimbaud, p. 121; Schmidt p. 219.

12

Towards a Libidinal Economy of Three Modern Painters

I

Questioned on her "attitude towards modern art," Gertrude Stein once remarked, "I like to look at it. That is, I like to look at the picture part of it; the other parts interest me much less." What I like to look at in De Kooning's paintings is the yellow. I like to look at the yellow parts of even those paintings I don't think much of. Next to the yellow, I like to look at the pink. Finally the grey. For me the name De Kooning means the chance to stare at these painted colors, not works of art or experiences of form, and certainly not the various figurative pretexts, although the remnants of the faces of women are certainly unavoidable.

So I take an irresponsible view of these "paintings," taking only what I like and ignoring the rest. The canvasses give me proof of the fragmentation of the modern senses and of the modern body. In the thinking part of my mind, I know where this fragmentation comes from; Schiller, Marx, Lukács, Weber, tell me how the development of capital enforces a kind of psychic "division of labor," the advanced form of which can be observed in just this reification and autonomization of the various senses from one another. In front of the paintings, however, all I know is that the eye finds a space of sheer colored paint before it, in which it can lead a life of its own, beyond hearing and taste, and beyond the clock time of everyday life.

The paintings let me glimpse this space, while doing other things that seem more suspect to me. If you look at them from a distance, across the circular stairwell of the Guggenheim, you register a rather different message: each canvas projects a garish and self-indulgent riot of solid colors, a whole ideology of pastel and "joyous" sensualism as inadmissible as any Renoir. Up close, however, you can forget this overall organizational "message" of the form, and concentrate on its bits and pieces, on these accidents that have something different in store for you.

How were they possible? Only a myth or genealogical fable can answer this question. In the beginning, you tell yourself, was Line. It was without color or density, as the charcoal sketches show us. But it was not the sculptural outline that the tradition associates with this term. Neither trace nor profile, draftsmanship or boundary, not the ideology of the straight line made loose and supple enough to circumscribe a silhouette; but rather compulsive involution, like tangled string. Left to itself, this linear impulse generates the disappointment of De Kooning's bronzes, Rodin in squiggles, as though dissolved into a blur of fibres by a Giacometti force field.

The impulse to Line, you have to understand, is not sufficient, only necessary. If you let it guide your reading of the paintings, you quickly find them reduced to expensive doodles: not action painting, or if Jackson Pollocks, then a Pollock whose brush is too heavy and dripping with color to move very fast. Let's say it openly: what is interesting here is never Line itself, but what is allowed to emerge between the lines, what you find yourself calling the "Flat." This is the secret tension in De Kooning's paintings, their storyline: not the melodramatic rivalry between figure and background, or even Line and Color, but the fascinating and inexplicable emergence of the flat, with stretches of painted color across which the eye skids without so much as raising a ripple.

Where does it come from? You have to imagine, I think, a process of effraction that seizes on the line itself, tangling it, as in the charcoal sketches, making it shiver and vibrate, shattering it rhythmically into pencil shadings, like so many overtones. Here some inner compulsion of line, some originary nervousness, makes it want to burst its two-dimensional limits and produce, out of its own inner substance, smears that coopt and preempt its primal adversary, the brush-stroke itself.

Digression on the brush-stroke, the very fingerprint of private style, of the unique and incomparable individuality of the modem "genius." No wonder a post-individualistic art like Warhol's paints it out, not merely for the purpose of mass reproduction (although this art marks the entrance of painting into the category of Walter Benjamin's "reproduceable work"), but above all as a sign that the individual subjectivity is irrelevant, that we are now beyond all that, somewhere else.

So you could see De Kooning as the meta-brushstroke, the mega-brushstroke, the enlargement of the real-life microscopic fingerprint of the normal brush into that immensely magnified space you find on the photographic blow-ups that hang near museum offices during fund-raising campaigns: enlargements of tiny sections of the old masters, to illustrate the authentication process or to show the use of X-rays in detecting earlier sketches beneath the familiar final surface. So here too, if you want, you could see these canvasses as the last gasp of some individualizing romanticism, as the celebration of some ultimate genius- or personality-cult, of

De Kooning's incomparable physical gesturality, in the form of just such gigantic, yet personal and unfalsifiable painted traces.

Clearly, I would rather not see them that way: De Kooning's style is unmistakable all right, but I would rather see its enlargement as a process that drives the personal beyond itself, in much the same way that the X-ray process of psychoanalysis blows your private thoughts and fantasies up to the point at which they become impersonal again, the algebra or syntax of the unconscious. Let me justify this preference: the older identification of brush-stroke with stylistic individuality took place within the opposition of color to line, romanticism to classicism. Line was here objectivity, the resistance of matter, the visible trace of Cartesian extension; color marking the place of the "secondary qualities," of the subjective projection of individual sense perception.

But now, in De Kooning, Line transforms itself into the brush-stroke itself, it splays out, fanning into distinct yet parallel ridges and streams of paint, refracting the original substance into strands that have different destinies, some mountainous and bristling, others trickling down the canvas in tears that no longer seem the marks and traces of *maladresse*. Line is now brush-stroke and color; its new structural opposite, the flat, is something that happens to the latter, rather than a place of freedom and of private, personal expression in its own right.

With these developments, we can construct the first great paintings of De Kooning's maturity, gigantic ideograms, Klines projected into a Utopia of a few solid colors. A standing tripod, great smears of brown and green, with an immense brush-stroke of bluish white, beside a deeper blue, with the hallucinatory De Kooning yellow already extended overhead: in *Painting 1959* the flat has already emerged as the space on which these messy brushstrokes overlap, to the point at which we can grasp its new specificity.

Imagine, alongside the movement of the brush, and the strands of paint it leaves to mark its path, a quite different operation, a lateral treatment of the wet oil to which, no longer coaxed out by the bristles that transmit it, a new and unaccustomed violence is now done, forcing the paint across its own grain, smoothing and levelling it crosswise, flattening the natural ridges of the brushstrokes and contaminating the primary colors by smearing and compressing them together in an implacable sideswipe.

We can dramatize this new way of laying paint, and its hostility to the linear multiplicity of the original brushstroke, by naming the two great tools or instruments which are the demiurges of these painted surfaces. Now the flat betrays the intervention, in the splayed and variegated ridges of the primal Brush, of a new and unexpected agency, the Palette-knife; and these non-figurative canvasses can be read as allegories of some primal dualism, like space and time, earth and sky, male and female, industry and agriculture, in which for all eternity Brush and Palette-knife pursue their eternal and irreducible combat. But does this local mythology of the eye, this archetypal cosmology of the newly reified space of the purely visual, have any more general intelligibility?

Today (but maybe only today), I am tempted to read it as follows: the brush gave us the strands of mingled color in a kind of streaked suspension. The palette-knife now enacts the Utopian dream of an effortless collapsing or compression of all matter back into itself, a relentless squeezed assimilation of all textures into a single homogeneous substance, of all the colored surfaces into some primal putty you can rework with your own fingers. Yet into the flat you can stare, seeing layers upon layers, ghosts of older surfaces of paint hanging for a moment beneath the surface, older colors swimming beneath the overwash of yellow or grey that presses them ever further down. It is a cruel process, as we can judge by the women's faces, those parrotty beak-like grinning caricatures, which, like the tiny features of an octopus, imperiously distract you from the otherwise swirling, non-figurative movement of colored paint. This remorseless minaturization of the faces of organic women, of the vestiges of Eros, makes of such "portraits" a veritable figure of the flat itself, betraying the last remnants of some necessary heterogeneity, some last obligatory differentiation of feature and painted trait, before the palette-knife relentlessly smooths it into a marbled surface into which you gaze, stirring with memories of a faded multiplicity now forever immobilized within the triumphant new homogeneous substance of glazed paint.

II

Well, you don't do things like that to Cézanne, whose institutionalization effectively discredits such irresponsibility and, like the novels of Henry James, say, demands a well-nigh compulsory respect for the unity of the individual work and the architectonic composition of the isolated canvas. For that very reason, on the other hand—because the value of Cézanne has become a functional component in the ideology of establishment modernism—I doubt whether anyone can have a direct or unmediated experience today of a Cézanne painting. It is a little like the role of print in present-day speech; we talk and listen, but subliminally we continue to see printed words. We explore a Cézanne landscape visually, but the underlying subliminal "text" remains the "idea" of Cézanne, and the feeling that we are engaging a full-blown cultural institution. How can we break out of this vicious circle?

Brecht (but also the Russian Formalists) taught us that we have to *estrange* things that have come to seem "natural" in order to recover some sense of their original historical function. Let's estrange Cézanne by supposing that all these very different paintings—which represent work in so many codified genres, from portraits, still lifes, and landscapes all the way to the occasional nudes, as in *The Bathers*—are "in reality" versions or variants of a single narrative, ways of reembodying with distinct visual content a single story that Cézanne's paintings tell over and over again. The "reader" is obviously going to be actively involved in the reconstruction of this "story," which the canvasses—inert collections of visual data—can scarcely "tell" all by themselves. So it is a kind of decision, from the outset: we decide that we will "read" our own eye-movements back and forth across these painted surfaces as a proto-narrative text.

But this is not an arbitrary decision: it corresponds to something objective in these paintings, and in particular to a peculiar stereoptic "double standard" familiar to anyone who has spent time looking at Cézannes. I'm talking about the distance from which you look at the painting, and in particular about the way it asks you to move in close and eyeball the segments of individual paint with which it is put together, only to lose all sense of the objects of representation—the houses and trees, rocks, tablecloths, and human faces—that you have to back away again to recognize. Unlike the classical constructions of Renaissance perspective—which determine a single ideal viewing position from which the whole composition comes into focus—Cézanne's paintings project two distinct "viewpoints"—nose-close and ten feet away—which are rigorously incommensurable and discontinuous, and which can never fold together in some single unified hierarchical visual experience.

There is a verbal or a literary equivalent to this peculiar structural discontinuity in our reception of Cézanne: you can reproduce it in your reading of Flaubert by replacing distance with reading speed. Flaubert's novels are still stories; and if you run your inner movie projector at the proper speed, you can still watch recognizable characters forming comprehensible desires and engaging in familiar activities within situations that are readily reimaginable for us as in Balzac, as in Dreiser or Zola, as in Dickens. What you can also do with Flaubert—and it is not possible with the other "realistic" novelists just mentioned—is to slow down your reading tempo to the point at which a different kind of intelligibility becomes visible: the intelligibility of the individual sentences, as they are blocked together with unequal phrases, and themselves discontinuously placed in such a way as to result in that unexpected formal unity, the finished paragraph. This kind of attention, if you like, still articulates a narrative: only it is the narrative of the adventures of Syntax, and its characters are not anthropomorphic figures, but rather tenses of verbs, pronouns on the point of becoming proper names, catalogues of nouns whose plurals amplify them into some microscopic or purely verbal equivalent of mass psychology or the behavior of collective groups. This microscopic dynamism of words is intelligible as music is intelligible, or painting: its narrative coherence cannot, unlike the more representational storytelling level of the text, be conveyed in everyday language. We would have to build a complicated and technical meta-language to do justice to the patterns our reading experience feels in the relationships between the individual words.

It is easier to show this in a negative way: there is always someone to come along and remind us that Balzac and Dickens, Zola and Dreiser, are also put together out of words; that we ought to be able to read their sentences as slowly as we can read Flaubert's, and with the same new "objects" (nouns, verbs, pronouns, phrases, syntax, paragraphs) slowly coming into view. All I can say is that on that enlarged micro-level the words of those writers do not project any distinct and autonomous intelligibility in their own right: they remain instrumental in the transmission of the larger narrative, and force us constantly to shift our gears back to the content level, in order to understand their relationship to each other. In Flaubert, however, you can remain on the micro-level, and live as fully in a single page as in the novel's "unity of action." Back to painting for a moment: the distinction between Flaubert and the other realists in this respect is not unlike that between Cézanne and the other impressionists. With the latter, also, you can experimentally approach the canvas, and watch your perceptions systematically disintegrate into atomic sensations, as the initial Gestalt returns to the sense-data that presumably made it up. The point is that on this level, the painted spots and specks which are the raw material of impressionism have no intelligibility of their own: nothing is going on here that has an intrinsic interest in its own right; this is sheer flux, whose organizational dynamics you can grasp only by stepping back and recognizing the representations of which it proves to be the support.

The moment of Flaubert, the moment of Cézanne, is a historically exemplary one in which "for the first time" the distinct dimensions of what Deleuze and Guattari (in their *Anti-Oedipus*) have usefully called the *molecular* and the *molar* (those larger empty formal unities in which the microscopic data of the molecular are "organized" and recontained) can be observed to move apart, to go their separate ways, and, as in some vast geological drift, to begin to lead distinct existences. It is the moment of the twin birth of modernism and mass culture, when as in some historically new "division of labor," the older molar storytelling or representational unities are now assigned to the "degraded" status of the best-seller or the film, while the molecular experience of language or sheer paint becomes the perceptual center of the new "high art" of the plotless novel or the modernistic lyric, or of abstract painting. In Cézanne, in Flaubert, for one long last unstable moment, both uneasily coexist in the double standard or discontinuous focus we have described above, before that definitive historical dissociation within which the aesthetic in our own time continues to dwell.

So we do no violence to Cézanne by trying to read this painting on its molecular level, as a coherent, well-nigh narrative dynamic which is quite distinct from the landscapes or furniture or human bodies that on its other, molar level it purports to represent. To try to rewrite the molecular level as a narrative has the methodological advantage of giving us something explicit to look for, and of making us ask ourselves who the "characters" of this estranged and microscopic action are and what they do to one another, what kind of plot or intrigue they can possibly be said to be involved in.

I will say that the "characters" of this story are colors, and that the principal protagonists, as you move about the museum and look at one painting after another, prove to be blue, green, and ochre. I will say that these characters are locked in combat with one another; and that, on this level, Cézanne's imagination is a melodramatic one, with "heroes" and "villains," with happy endings that can just as easily be reversed into the disasters which are perhaps the more characteristic outcome. Going all the way with this, I will finally assert that the principle of evil in this conflictual universe can be none other than ochre itself, that yellowish brown that so oppressively disengages itself as the ground tone of large collections of Cézanne's paintings; and that the triumph of ochre celebrated by these works is to be read as the triumph of instinctual repression.

Why is it, indeed, that no one has been willing publicly to acknowledge the dreariness that emanates from Cézanne's most characteristic color scheme, when you are exposed to room upon room of these canvasses? I have already mentioned the ideological status of Cézanne, which goes a long way towards explaining why people might hesitate to voice such impressions even where the latter nag insistently at their aesthetic reception. But perhaps such impressions meet other kinds of interference as well, and know censorship by other agencies. It seems to me just possible, for example, that inhabitants of the northern tier of industrialized nations (Parisians, New Yorkers, Londoners, Berliners) willingly read this peculiarly drab reach of the spectrum between yellowish orange and brown as a sign and a symbolic expression of the subtropics, of the Mediterranean and the Côte d'Azur, the landscape of Cézanne but also of the sun and of the tourist's mirage of that Other of the everyday routine of the city of industrial capitalism. It seems to me just possible that such viewers do their best to suppress the gap between the depressing visual immediacy of Cézanne's ochre and the conceptual or ideological coding of its subtropical content as the "promesse de bonheur" of its invitation to the Utopian voyage.

Nor are they wrong exactly, for ochre really is the ground tone of the subtropics, yet in a somewhat different fashion than they might be willing to entertain. In the real world, indeed, ochre is the color of drought and brown dust, of poverty and heat; it is the sub-text and underlying reality of Southern California which instantly reemerges when, leaving its appearance behind you, you cross the Mexican border. Ochre is that omnipresent element from which only the massive irrigation of expensive villas makes lush vegetation spring. Even the sea itself is less blue from within the dust bowl; and with these three colors, the "main characters" of Cézanne's visual microcosm are given.

This is so far, however, little more than the semantics of Cézanne's color scheme. It would be a mistake to ground our reading on the hypothesis of some universal system of perceptual meanings or color symbolism, whether of a sociological or a "natural" type. Whatever class content ochre may have for us must be historically acquired and symbolically reproduced by this otherwise neutral element; nor are "scientific" ideologies, such as the optical psychology in which Cézanne himself seemed to believe ("le vert étant une couleur des plus gaies et qui fait le plus de bien aux yeux"—letter of May 11, 1886 to Victor Chocquet) of much use in helping us understand how the painting reinvents and virtually produces the symbolic value attributed to it after the fact by this or that theory.

Ochre is in other words not to be seen as a static symbol but rather as the result of an operation performed by mechanisms within the painting itself. On our reading, it was a non-color, the place of repression in which the more genuine, positive, primary colors are somehow cancelled out. Yet even this process of cancellation is a dynamic which requires a certain number of preconditions, first and foremost among which is surely the very "positive" value of those primary colors which are the object of its repression in the first place. Green and blue are not, in other words, static symbols either; they must somehow initially be invested with their positive value in order to be able to take their symbolic places in what is essentially a process.

Libidinal analysis is not psychological or psychoanalytic explanation; but these dynamics can be clarified by a digression through depth psychology. It ought to be clear that repression is itself always a process: not some mere steady-state lack of affect, or windless absence of feeling, it is always a way of dealing with the anxieties aroused by some preexistent desire. To use the Sartrean formula, repression is always repression *of* something; and this, even in that terrifying emptiness of which the schizophrenic complains, or with that disturbing failure that motivates the hysteric's desperate "desire to desire." The problem is however compounded when we have to do, not with the first-degree situations of the subject's psychic life, but with those second-degree ones which are the realm of aesthetic experience. On some first-degree level, repression of the visual might range from simple sensory privation all the way to pathological disorders of the eye itself: it would in any case exclude in advance any entrance into the aesthetic experience of painting as such. In order for repression to be grasped as a mechanism immanent to the painting itself, and constitutive of a particular aesthetic and visual experience, such as that of Cézanne's works, we would have to show how the eye is first lured into this purely visual realm with promises of some heightened visual gratification, thereupon to learn its lesson of repression or visual renunciation the more surely. At the outside limit, we would have to posit a situation in which the visual experience of repression offers an aesthetic pleasure of some kind in its own right.

Such a situation suggests a "transgressive" structure, in which what is to be repressed—we will now call such "positive" instinctual expressions *intensities*—must first be generated by the libidinal apparatus of the painting before they are available to fill their ritual destinies as its ultimate victims. I believe that this mechanism by which intensities are generated can, in our present purely visual context, be understood in terms of a play of gradations that simulate intensification. (The idea is not mine, but Pierre Klossowski's, in his book on Nietzsche.) To oversimplify things, we may observe that the solid color, taken all by itself (but it never can be taken all by itself), is neither intensity nor its absence. It would be desirable to think intensity as a temporal progression that needs to inscribe itself on a material scale or system of gradation. The impressionists constructed their "libidinal apparatus," generated their characteristic intensities, by a lively interplay between the various colors: the originality of Cézanne, meanwhile, was to have resituated a dynamic of gradations within the individual colors themselves, each of which—blue, green, ochre—now knows a patch-by-patch intensification from faint to strong, by which its own specific intensity is virtually produced. To this heightened exaltation, in which libidinal energy invests the expanding gradations of blue or green, is then opposed the contracting counterforce of ochre, which winds this excitement down and effectively recontains its energies, diverting the emergence of color and intensity into the rather different construction of a pseudo-color in which they are extinguished.

This visual story or proto-narrative clarifies the ideology of *volume* as it informs Cézanne's thinking and that of his critics, and finds expression in that peculiar fragmentary genre of the watercolor sketch—Cézanne's version, perhaps, of the practice of the fragment and the aphorism among his contemporaries—in which the paper is seen to be the blank upon which the various intensities become inscribed, and on which and from which volume presumably emerges. Yet Cézanne's well-known account of the matter is in this respect ambiguous: "Only nature can help us progress, and the eye is educated by contact with it. It becomes concentric from looking and working. What I mean is that in an orange, an apple, a sphere, a head, there is a culminating point; and this point is always—despite the difficult effects of shadow and light, and colored sensations—what is closest to our eye; the periphery of objects flees towards a center situated on our horizon" (letter to Emile Bernard, July 25, 1904). Volume is thus invoked in terms of intensities; yet in our reading of these canvasses it can emerge only when we step away and leave the libidinal world of color for that, quite different, of molar forms. The ideology of volume is intended to generate something like a myth about ochre itself: that the latter is not negative, not a form of privation, but rather a color in its own right, a nascent intensity of the same type as blue or green, which knows its own specific density. That the emergence of volume always represents the triumph of ochre, however, suggests that this "event" is of a piece with that celebration of libidinal repression—the period word is "renunciation"—which Cézanne shares with so many other late-nineteenth-century artists, Henry James, Fontane, Mallarmé, Ibsen, the ageing Tolstoy or Mark Twain, being among those who come to mind.

This archetypal narrative then knows specific embodiment in the various genres in which Cézanne worked, of which the central one would seem to be landscape. Yet the term is too general for these varied pictures, which tend to organize themselves around village or countryside, houses or mountain: so many ochre-scapes, rather, enforcing the dominant of the brownish walls that line the street or village canvasses, the brownish buildings that surge up from an inhabited greenery, and to which from time to time the great bluescapes of the Mont Sainte-Victoire are opposed, in which mountain or sky presses outward in liberatory fashion, allowing the bluish air to circulate ever more freely ("la nature, pour nous hommes, est plus en profondeur qu'en surface, d'où la nécessité d'introduire dans nos vibrations de lumière, représentées par les rouges et les jaunes, une somme suffisante de bleutés, pour faire sentir l'air"—letter to Emile Bernard, April 15, 1904).

Yet such moments of liberation are provisory and unstable, and tend to be recuperated by their counter-forces: hence such a paradox as the great *Bibemus Quarry* painting of 1898, in which ochre explodes triumphantly from out of a repressive mass of greenery. Here an immense simulation takes place, in which what is genuinely repressive is coded in terms of the centrifugal, the explosive release of freedom—as though repression were some positive intensity in its own right—while the molar structure of the painting encourages us to read the green vegetation as that from which the eye struggles to emerge.

The still lifes represent a significant modification of this narrative scheme, owing to the unexpected role that white suddenly begins to play in them—the porcelain of a statue, above all, the folds of the tablecloth on which the colored shadows of fruit fall. White now marks the momentary suspension of the basic tensions of the repressive operation: it offers the serene *ataraxia* of a visual space which is neither intensity nor pseudo-color, and which, itself a positive visual experience, holds out the Utopia of a release from the peculiar infernal machine of intensification and its inevitable reversal.

We have not yet mentioned the ultimate genre in which Cézanne's libidinal apparatus finds expression, namely the portrait. We need to develop some sense of the peculiar unsuitability of the human body within this scheme of chromatic tensions: its scandalous heterogeneity is perhaps best sensed in the embarrassment we feel before the great nudes, and in particular the various *Bathers*.

Yet the body represents the supreme challenge to this narrative system, and its structural position better than anything else, perhaps, allows us to register the latter's ultimate value as a symbolic act. For flesh, the body, the very support of libidinal intensity in any conventional scheme of things, has in Cézanne become its opposite: the privileged locus of ochre itself, the ultimate field of expression of the repressive principle, or, if you prefer, of the death wish. The portrait, the rarer nude, complete the tendencies inherent in this libidinal machinery; turning back the momentary exaltation and enlargement of landscape or open space, they effectively seal off, drawing the whole now yellowing world of color compromises back into what is now a final repressive center, the human face, the human body. O terrible nineteenth century, whose *belle époque* is thus secretly peopled with so many emblems of renunciation, like the skeleton who gives her hand to the artist-child among the Sunday finery of Rivera's *Alameda*.

III

In the late twentieth century, it is best to come by accident upon the shock of painted surfaces for which everything in your own daily life and object world has unwittingly prepared you. You want to enter the permanent collection (in Berlin, it is housed on the lower level of the gallery) in a distracted state, like a Hoffmann character, working your way dutifully back through time, from Romantic interiors through the fateful monumental canvasses of the middle-class age, sniped at by a few eccentric symbolists and expressionists, with only a half-empty lobby and souvenir counter waiting for you at the end of your journey through history. Fatigue, boredom, overstimulated eyes, are the best weakened condition in which to receive, turning as though sensing something behind your back, an immense image on the lobby wall which by some great good fortune you had completely—so unaccountably!—overlooked on your way in. Titles and signatures—*Barbara und Gaby*, Franz Gertsch, March, 1974—have nothing to do with the ten-by-fifteen feet square hallucinatory surface that at once obliterates everything else around you.

Two women, seen from the back, the one standing in the doorway from which you watch this enlarged and floating space, extending a comb to the other, who hesitates between the cosmetics and perfume bottles on her bathroom sink. This photorealism evidently wants to compete with Vermeer, in all the variety of textures and surfaces produced by modern civilization, from the material of the towels and the velvet of one of the dressed figures all the way to denim and the plastic surface of the shower curtain. Among such a range of tactile solicitations, not skin, but rather the human *chevelure* stands out as the ultimate material reality; and the comb proffered to it across this bathroom space obscurely designates the painter's act itself, intervening in the tangled hair, carding its fibres, freeing it to shake and glisten in the air and the light, much as he will himself sort out the fingered memory traces of these now purely luminous objects.

Something invisible intervenes to silence the reference to Vermeer in the same breath we draw to stammer our impressions of this glossy, flawless surface: an absent presence, something we will never see and which we have no right to deduce, in short, the original *photograph* from which it was presumably painted and which in some sense thus constitutes the fundamental object of its representation. Why should this abstract knowledge insert itself into our visual field and, undermining the glorious immediacy of the eye, stamp this immense artifact as secretly degraded and commercial? Surely the photographic prop is no more determinant than Cézanne's landscapes or Vermeer's "real" rooms, or the sketches they may have made of them; nothing in it provides any short-cut or substitute for the dextrous hand and brush that had to produce the glow of these fabrics, or the metallic shine of the bottles, the dull white of the bathroom porcelain. The interference has nothing in common with those unfortunate lapses that reveal the mountainous sunset of a movie image to be nothing but a painted backdrop, or the houses of some filmic street to be little more than a studio set.

Here, where everything is "mechanical reproduction," there is no room for such humiliation of artificial techniques by the telltale remnant or tag-end of a once "natural," real-life situation. The painting, on the contrary, assures us that the "natural" has disappeared without a trace; and this is perhaps the ultimate source of our discomfort, confronted unexpectedly with a nostalgia for the "natural" which this image so triumphantly frustrates. Can it really be true that we would have preferred to keep up the pretenses of some "natural" referent, if only in the brush-strokes of some "real" De Kooning, or in the "knowledge" that Cézanne's landscapes, on a historical date, at that particular hour of the day, under unique local atmospheric conditions, really did exist?

And why does photography not intensify this reassurance, instead of undermining it? The photographic original, if it still exists, documents and forever suspends the instant in which a real comb changed hands within a real apartment. The photographic image, however, dislocates this sense of reality in an unexpected way, by underscoring the mortality of its human subjects. Not the comforting conviction of some ontological referent—not the reassuring illusion of a world of sheer being beyond artistic representation, which the being of the canvas itself reinforces—but rather History and time—the flux in which Cézanne, De Kooning, the landscape around Aix, the painters' studios, their reputation and their paintings themselves, are inexorably carried away—is the unpleasant "fact" this photorealistic interior so unexpectedly confronts us with.

Meanwhile, there is the sheer size of this representation, which, like a movie screen, has consequences of its own that are strangely disproportionate with its objects. This is no manageable easel-painting, that you hang, like a small mirror, within the room it represents; nor does this outsized clarity bring any of the minute order of the other end of the telescope. Space and bodies thus enlarged offer a glimpse into other dimensions, in which the humble and the banal, the trivial and the routine, have somehow been secretly, incomprehensibly, transfigured, as though in some mindless replication of consumer society in an alien universe.

If the household has one place, indeed, which is effectively beyond nature, it is the modern bathroom. Bloch has written eloquently on this artificial space, in which everything is abstract and non-representational (for even chairs, in other rooms, hold out their arms like human beings, tables "stand," and beds lie open and "invite"). Whoever wishes to flee anthropomorphism is driven into the bathroom; to the other places, as in Balzacian descriptions, too much human activity or idleness clings. Even the photographic infrastructure cannot complete this ultimate depersonalization, which needs a certain staging, certain angle-shots, to avoid the intrusion of those objects still too warm or redolent with human life: a photorealistic representation of human living irrevocably transforms the unnatural into the sentimental, Freud's "uncanny" turning out to be nothing but Andrew Wyeth.

Still, there are the bottles, the artificial flora and fauna of that most advanced achievement of commodity civilization, the modern drug-store shelf. Here the production process implicit elsewhere, in the fabrics, the plumbing, even the svelte bodies of these modern young women, is now foregrounded and packaged as such. This glass-and-plastic array supplies the icons of a religious, even mystical meditation, and throngs the altar towards which both women move and bend. Stoppered bottles distantly remind us of the magical containers and vessels of archaic, long-forgotten fairy tales. The word "commodity" should here be pronounced none too lightly: for these products have been disconnected from the advertising image-and-fantasy systems which offered them as so many insistent but unformulated wish-fulfillments: yet they are not for all that reduced to the shabby, pitiful materiality of a bathroom closet in which, after the decease of its owner, one comes upon the relics of a lifetime accumulation of prescription drugs and unfashionable cosmetics. Nor are they transformed into the strange and magical fetishes of the surrealists, into Magritte's immense razorblades or Breton's baleful and expressionless mannequins.

They continue to emit the Utopian promise of consumer society itself, transfigured and projected into some unimaginable post-human space.

We have already alluded to the mechanism by which the meretricious hints and pledges of the supermarkets and the advertising imagery of our society are thus transformed and visually "fulfilled." It is none other than that "return of the repressed" which Freud—describing its aesthetic manifestation—called the "uncanny": that peculiar effect whereby a represented event becomes intrinsically marked as the repetition of some older, archaic fantasy of which no independent traces remain in the text. This return of the repressed then makes its presence felt by the garish and Technicolor representation of what is known to have a sober black-and-white existence, figures as daubed and rouged as in a carnival, objects derealized by the very plenitude of their sensory being, by which, however, the merely perceptual is unmasked as sheer obsession. Ken Russell's *Tommy* gave a vivid illustration of this process, in which even the normal and well-nigh obligatory representational apparatus of the color film was reduplicated by a heightened, cartoon-like, second-degree artificial coloring system. But if this is so, then the paradoxical importance of the photographic original can now be explained, which must stand as the humdrum initial text, the prosaic everyday black-and-white still, which is to be transformed beyond recognition by the sensorium of photorealism.

Photorealism is thus the aesthetic ideology and the fullest living expression of that sterile thing which is consumer capitalism or the *société de consommation.* No doubt it projects the latter's view of itself and thereby legitimates it. Are we then ourselves implicitly condemned by the hallucinatory fascination it exercizes over us? Perhaps. And yet this gleaming depersonalization of the commodity vision is strangely silent about its own fundamental impulse, which it neither affirms nor denies, in all the icy neutrality of the reified eye.

(*1979*)

13

A Note on *A Vision*

If I want to say something today about *A Vision*, it is certainly not to encourage any renewed theoretical dabbling in the occult, and not even to use it—for Yeats his most ambitious philosophical project—in order to clarify the poetry or the other literary works. This last is a perfectly proper task for a certain kind of scholarship, but I have no qualifications to pursue it. As for the first possibility, I also resent the rising tide of mysticism in the current interest in Benjamin's early writings; but I acknowledge that anyone who likes to collect batches of opposites, contraries, contradictions and the like could not find a richer field of materials than the delirious structural typologies of Yeats's gyres and phases, whose multiplications and successive reelaborations are enough to disgust one with structuralism forever. The modernist bookshelf contains any number of these private systems, these idiosyncratic records of personal revelations and formulations universalized—what T.S. Eliot called Blake's home-made furniture; and sometimes we have to live in those furnishings for a time, for whatever reason. Sometimes—generally also just for a time—we get comfortable in them and pretend to adopt the system in question. Will Yeats's *A Vision* know a comeback of that kind in our own day? I doubt it and I rather hope not; but I do think there are new ways of reading it if we still care to.

I want to begin with the book that sent me back to all this, Brenda Maddox's new biography of either Yeats or his wife George—a work first entitled *Georgie's Ghosts* and now (maybe for obvious reasons) entitled *Yeats' Ghosts*.[1] But I also need to say a word about Brenda Maddox, who has given us a series of admirable biographies of the strong wives of certain writers. D.H. Lawrence was an obvious choice and a flowerbed already trampled by many feet. But it was the eponymous biography of Joyce's wife Nora that was the first great revelation: first, that there was so much to say about her, and second, that her very being was so inextricably tied into the work of the author of *Ulysses*. One cannot say that Brenda Maddox's work in this field supplants that of Ellman, although it certainly displaces it. What one can say is that no one can ever read Joyce the same way after reading Brenda

Maddox. I want precisely to avoid the obvious conclusion that Nora Joyce was in every possible way the model for Molly Bloom. It is precisely this notion of model, of the original, of the transposed life story and so forth, that one wants to get rid of: in this day and age of the death of the author—which is also an age of the resurrection of biography as a form—we need some new concepts to deal with phenomena like these. They are concepts that must also replace the tired notion of influence, and they are very much solicited by issues of plagiarism, as in the pseudo-scandal organized a few years ago around Brecht's female assistants, who really, or so it was claimed, wrote all the good plays. I want to propose that we rediscover in this situation a whole new conceptuality of the collective, and of collaborative work: one which does not depend on some private property of the individual imagination. Virtually everything in our minds, Goethe said, comes to us from the outside, except our own energies. This is then the sense in which *Ulysses* is henceforth to be regarded as collaboration, co-authored by the couple and not at all as the solitary product of Joyce's private subjectivity.

All the more so is this the case with Yeats, whose case will now more centrally concern us. For, despite some indiscreet revelations in a later version of *A Vision* (that of 1928), the prodigious role of Yeats's wife George in its inception and conception cannot fully have been clear to anyone before the publication of the *Vision* script in 1992. I quote Maddox:

> The Automatic Script ... covers 3,600 pages, produced in 450 sittings over 20 months. Some of the entries were written backwards, in mirror writing, by Mrs. Yeats' supposedly "grasped" hand, illustrated by sketchy diagrams and obscure symbols. When the Script petered out, more messages emerged through her speaking voice as she slept. Yeats recorded them all as best he could in his Sleep and Dream Notebooks. These too form part of the three volumes of newly transcribed material.[2]

Maddox's principal storyline (there are others) covers the years of the spirit dictation, "from the end of 1917 to 1922, with a close examination of the Automatic Script and its coincidence with the gestation and birth of the Yeats' two children."[3] Indeed, this last phrase gives Maddox's interpretation away, for she suggests, without I think absolutely coming out and saying so, that the dictation was Georgie's way of keeping Yeats's easily distracted attention focused on her during those years and in addition of imposing on him (by command of the spirits themselves) the two not necessarily passionately desired pregnancies. The spirits were indeed full of advice and instruction about these practical daily matters, not unlike those moments in the Koran (they are fairly frequent I believe) in which the Angel Gabriel tells Mohammed how to resolve this or that urgent or thorny political or familial problem.

My comparison is a deliberate one, and if we had time I would like in this context to pursue Norman O. Brown's argument[4] (in *Apocalypse and/or Metamorphosis*) about the coming to terms with great prophecy, about the line that connects the Koran to Blake and *Finnegans Wake* (I don't remember whether Brown anywhere took up the case of Yeats). This is an argument about poetics and not about the spirit world; about the political character of prophetic discourse; and, implicitly, about the end of the era of individualism and the centered subject. "We have come to give you metaphors for poetry," the spirits famously advised Yeats. But it is now clear that the prose of *A Vision* (and the poetry that emerged from it) is collaborative and collective; what kind of prophecy it yields remains to be seen.

I situate Yeats's book among several other, roughly contemporaneous efforts, which have, I think, comparable aims. But before I mention them, I have to dispel a rather different interpretation of Yeats's ideology. This one has to do with his politics, whose more symptomatic moments include a brief admiration for Mussolini, a growing distaste for the rabble or the mob (it being understood that for Yeats as an exemplar and indeed an ideologist of the declining Protestant Ascendency in Ireland that "rabble" is largely Catholic), and finally an enthusiasm for the most suspicious proposals in the area of eugenics (the biographers also hasten to assure us that at the very least Yeats had no trace of anti-Semitism unlike his close friend Ezra Pound). These ideological positions then determine a cyclical philosophy of history in which the great wheel revolves from civilization to barbarism and back, and from authoritarianism to democracy. Not only is it easy to read *A Vision* thus cyclically but the whole latter half of the book imposes such a reading on us, and can indeed be scarcely be read any other way. These pages—often very attractive evocations of moments of the past—can be ranged under what I will take as at least one of the possible meanings of that slippery term "historicism": that is, as an essentially aesthetic view of history which offers all the moments of the past and of other civilizations for an essentially aesthetic consumption and delectation. Yeats mentions one of the monuments to this kind of historicism, in Spengler's contemporaneous *Decline of the West*, whose musical pessimism echoes Yeats's own (both of them, Yeats notes, finding their ultimate source in Vice). A more modern and perhaps ideologically more satisfying version can be found in Malraux, particularly in the *Voices of Silence*. As we all do also consume the past aesthetically from time to time, I would want to insist on some of these works as poetic achievements, even though I think as a general rule we had better find something more satisfactory to do with the past.

But *A Vision* is more than that, I believe, even though its elaborate machinery certainly calls out for this kind of cyclical historical elaboration. I would prefer to range it among a different set of works, of which I will mention two: Carl Jung's *Psychological Types* and Gertrude Stein's *Making of Americans*. As different as these books are from each other (and from *A Vision*), I think they share one impossible ambition: namely to "describe really describe every kind of human being that ever was or is or would be living."[5]

Jung's interest in psychological types derives intellectually from Schiller's theory of so-called naïve and sentimental poetry—which might better be translated as spontaneous or natural on the one hand and reflexive or even modern on the other. Schiller worked his theory up in order to account to himself for his profound differences, in style, in working method, in formal construction, from his neighbor Goethe, whose genius intimidated him, as it did so many other people. Schiller's initial binary theory of psychological types, then—expanded by Jung into a fourfold system—reflected, not an anxiety of influence exactly, but rather an anxiety of rivalry and competition, and a sense of personal inferiority, which is addressed if not resolved by making a place for the subject alongside the form of the Other, or alongside a series of forms of the Other. It's not clear to me whether either Gertrude Stein or Yeats himself explicitly situates the presiding subjectivity anywhere within their series of forms. Insofar as Yeats's system involves a cycle or temporality within the so-called phases of the moon that govern these various personality constellations, one might imagine his willingness to position himself within a drift from one type to another. Nor should we rule out the possibility that for both of them inventing the system as a whole meant positioning themselves outside of it altogether.

In the case of Gertrude Stein, she tells us that the impetus for her personality-type research came from experiments in William James's laboratories; we can also take her title at its word and assume some attempt to order and to explore the immigrant America of an increasingly populist democracy; an attempt that could only have been heightened by her move to France in 1903—it is notorious that life in a foreign country encourages the feeling that everyone looks like someone you already know, and thus that there must be some system behind this multiplicity. In any case, if the Other is an initial ontological scandal, then the experience of the sheer demography of the Other is a heightened version, something both Gertrude Stein and Yeats must have felt in their very different ways and according to their very different historical experiences. That Yeats is attempting, with his character types, to organize the human chaos of Ireland's time of troubles and the Civil War cannot be doubted: but surely *A Vision* goes back further than that and attempts a picture of the immense and varied creative energies of modern Ireland in its formative period which coexisted with Yeats's youth. I would also add that it often seems to me that so-called Western individualism is greatly exaggerated, and that for various reasons, true individualism is sometimes far livelier in conditions of subalternity, as in Ireland during that period, or in India: the theory of character types then becomes a way of dealing with that kind of multiplicity, particularly for someone as profoundly political and indeed collective as Yeats, of whom his biographer has noted his "need to form organizations and to assert his authority within them."[6]

But now we have little enough time for the specifics of Yeats's classification machine itself, which may be seen, from one perspective, as a way of weighing politics and poetry against each other, or rather, for finding a common denominator for classifying political militants together with intellectuals (the two types of names and references that recur throughout *A Vision*). Then there is the dramatic, one may even say Shakespearean, tone of all the portraits (there are 28 of them, including the two full and as it were impossible moments of pure objectivity and pure subjectivity). The great leitmotif of Yeats's poetry after all is the word "passionate," which recurs fatefully throughout to characterize the absolute commitment of an individual desire to a specific historical and structural situation. If there are empty moments in this scheme, ideological hesitations and uncertainties, boredom, empty longing, that "desire to desire" as which Freudian "hysteria" has been characterized, these all assume strong or "passionate" forms as well. All the phases, as Yeats called his psychological or character types, are ontological choices or, better still (using his own language), combinations of destiny and fate (which is to say of subjectivity and objectivity).

The cyclical movement through the phases is fairly simple, which is why it is easily appropriated for the ideological historicisms I have mentioned; but the machinery is horrendously complicated, involving simultaneous clockwise and counterclockwise rotations through contraries and variables which themselves define each position.

There are six terms we need to elucidate (the choice of these terms sometimes remaining mysterious or arbitrary): primary versus antithetical; the Will and the Mask; the Creative Mind and the Body of Fate. Primary and antithetical seem to mean something as forthright as objective and subjective: they characterize "tinctures" (apparently a term of Jakob Boehme) or in other words each one covers half of the total cycle or some thirteen phases or possible positions. If we were reading the phases in a historicist fashion, we would say that the first phase begins in objectivity—something perhaps not utterly unlike Schiller's naïve or primitive or natural being—passes through subjectivity by conquering or constructing the personality (Schiller's sentimental or reflexive or self-conscious being)—only then to harden over into routine and character on its way back to objectivity as such. But that is the ideological way of grasping the phases: the diachronic way. I am suggesting that each phase deserves a synchronic reading, and that it is in this fashion that each phase becomes (in Ranke's famous phrase about moments of history) "immediate to God." Seen synchronically there is no ethical judgement on any of these positions or characterological constellations: each one is necessarily contradictory, in some Whitmanesque way none is better than the others, Yeats celebrates all of them in turn, whence the richness of this strange text which offers all the elements of narrative in some pre-narrative stage in which all the ontological possibilities coexist in a kind of extratemporal suspension.

But now we need to look at the other fundamental terms: I will translate Will into the more contemporary terminology of Desire; then in that case the Mask is something like the object of desire or even perhaps, as we shall see, Lacan's *objet petit a* (or small a).[7] As for the Creative Mind, it is simply reason or the intellect as such, provided we understand that for each of the positions the intellect is of a different type—here perhaps a mathematical intellect, there a strategic one, here reduced to the simplest and most brutal forms of apprehension, there so oversubtle and hyperintellectualized that it is constantly caught in its own spiderwebs. There will then naturally enough come into being a kind of dialectic between the forms of desire and the forms of intellect by which the world—or the Body of Fate—is perceived. For the outside world, the situation and its constraints, is real enough, but from each phase modelled and perceived differently: here organized as a painful stumbling block against which the personality collides, there organizable into problems the self of ingenuity can solve or resolve; here baleful, there a source of boundless opportunity. And now all these variables need to be combined in their multiple possibilities and according to some immensely complex *combinatoire.*

But in fact we have not yet grappled with the most remarkable feature of this scheme, which results from Yeats's stubborn insistence on conflict and contradiction. It is evident that all kinds of conflicts are inherent in a system like this, between the variables themselves: and they can no doubt be translated back into more banal terms, where the conflict between Will and Creative Mind simply becomes that between Desire and Reason; or that between the Mask and the Body of Fate, between destiny and fate, the internal Daimon and the external constraint.

But there is also something a great deal more interesting at work here, and it is the unexpected dependence of each structure on the Other and on Otherness as such. The positive descriptions of each phase are in other words, as it were, "for us," in Hegel's expression. Thus, to take an example, phase 17, Daimonic man, is characterized as innocence in terms of its Mask and as subjective truth in terms of Creative Mind, while its Body of Fate is described thus: "none except impersonal action."[8] We are still in a phase of subjectivity moving back towards objectivity; but now when we read the account of this phase, we discover that these qualifications—Mask, Creative Mind, Body of Fate—are all derived from their opposites on the wheel of the phases. The Mask is thus derived from phase 3, and is characterized as "simplification through intensity"; while Creative Mind is characterized as "creative imagination through antithetical emotion," and the Body of Fate is simply described as "Loss."[9] One can see how these three phenomena might modulate into what was ascribed earlier, so that the attempt at simplification restores a kind of innocence, while a profound loss in the area of the outside world might leave the actor of the phase with little more than impersonal action.

What seems to me more extraordinary here is the way in which the influence of the Other somehow dictates the terms and the limits of the solution. Despite their role in Yeats's own experience, parents do not figure here with any primordial force of the Freudian system, as in Lacan's big A or big Other;[10] still, the otherness of the opposing phases foreshadows much of the Lacanian emphasis, the force of gravity of the Other constantly precluding psychic unity and fomenting a creative unrest that leads to ever new structures and energies, as the self seeks to incorporate these features of otherness it lacks and envies, reproducing them in what turn out to be wholly new and original ways.

All of this makes for a remarkably subtle and articulated "construction of subjectivity"; it allows Yeats to forge a language which can model psychic structures with enormous suggestiveness. I can do no more here than quote briefly from one such development, which I take from this same phase 17 (under which Dante and Shelley are ranged):

> Because of the habit of synthesis, and of the growing complexity of the energy, which gives many interests, and the still faint perception of things in their weight and mass, men of this phase are almost always partisans, propagandists and gregarious; yet because of the Mask of simplification, which holds up before them the solitary life of hunters and of fishers and "the groves pale passion loves," they hate parties, crowds, propaganda. Shelley out of phase writes pamphlets and dreams of converting the world, or of turning man of affairs and upsetting governments, and yet returns again and again to these two images of solitude, a young man whose hair has grown white from the burden of his thoughts, an old man in some shell-strewn cave whom it is possible to call, when speaking to the Sultan, "as inaccessible as God or thou."[11]

It is a pointed yet complex psychic portrait, which clearly engages Yeats's intelligence to its fullest linguistic powers, at the same time that it overloads the reader who seeks to absorb too many of these phases in turn.

I need to go back now and qualify my observation that everything is positive here. The successive figures can for one thing be "in" or "out of" phase: that is to say, they can either fight against their psychic constellation and cripple themselves, or they can "enjoy their symptom" and choose their own destiny. Thus, a standard of judgement—a kind of psychoanalytic ethics—is here reintroduced. Meanwhile, Yeats is not always up to the demands of his own task: when confronted with the phase of a Shaw or a Wells, for example, he may become somewhat more sour in his characterization, something that generally strikes forms in which feeling is lacking or has been blocked. Thus, the figure of the Hunchback (number 26) seems to lack all positive virtue or energy (and also to owe something to Nietzsche's psychic portraits, which should also be mentioned as forerunners of Yeats's work here).

Finally, however, there is the unavoidable fact that the transitions are always more complicated and interesting than the positions or phases themselves. Yet in a transition, where the power of comparison comes to the fore as a stylistic instrument, unless emotional and ontological impartiality is preserved with enormous tension and delicacy, the lapse into judgement and the admission that one phase is after all somehow "better" or more "admirable" than another is a constant threat. This is why the synchronic must remain the center of gravity in these portraits, even though each is constructed out of diachronic elements and constantly threatens dissolution back into the diachronic again.

But what is the use for us, then, of this series of discontinuous synchronic portraits of equal ontological value? Are we then to recognize ourselves in one of them and act accordingly? And where does Yeats recognize and position himself? That would seem to be a perfectly permissible, if unresolvable, preliminary question. I'm afraid that this series of horoscopes—materialist horoscopes, if you like, without the stars (despite the phases of the moon) and very much bearing on the possibilities of a life in history, and on the role of intellectuals as well as of political praxis—nonetheless falls prey to the objection Adorno made long ago to their astrological counterparts, namely, that you can recognize yourself in all of them. The psyche is not in that sense a thing, but a language-learning force: it adopts the style and adapts itself to the description with the greatest suppleness, unless warned away by ethical signposts and the taboos and prescriptions of this or that binary system of good and evil. The structure of *A Vision* thus frustrates in and of itself: a fascination with history which wants to rise above it and identify with all of its active elements, it is also in that sense a suspension of action, whose concrete intervention perhaps it really does find only in the poems for which it was supposed to offer metaphors.

(*2004*)

Notes

1 Brenda Maddox, *Yeats' Ghosts* (New York, 1999). See also *D.H. Lawrence: The Story of a Marriage* (New York, 1994) and *Nora: The Real Life of Molly Bloom* (Boston, 1998).
2 Op. cit., p. xiv.
3 Ibid., p. xvi.
4 N.O. Brown, *Apocalypse and/or Metamorphosis* (Berkeley, 1991).
5 Gertrude Stein, *Lectures in America* (Boston, 1985), p. 142.
6 R.F. Foster, *W.B. Yeats: A Life*, vol. I (Oxford, 1997), p. 33.
7 Lacan's theory of the object of desire.
8 William Butler Yeats, *A Vision* (New York, 1965), p.98.
9 Ibid., pp. 96–9.
10 Lacan's theory of the authority figure or superego.
11 Op cit., p. 143.

FIVE

14

In the Mirror of Alternate Modernities: Introduction to Kojin Karatani's *The Origins of Japanese Literature*

I have high hopes that the publication of Kojin Karatani's book[1]—one of those infrequent moments in which a rare philosophical intelligence rises to the occasion of a full national and historical statement—will also have a fundamental impact on literary criticism in the West; and this in two ways, which are rather different from its effects in Japan itself. For *The Origins of Japanese Literature* has some lessons for us about critical pluralism, in addition to its principal message, which turns on that old and new topic of modernity itself.

I take it that any reflection on modernity—it is a little like the question about the self, or better still, about the nature of language, when you are inside it and cannot be expected to imagine anything which is outside—has known three renewals, three moments of an intense and speculative questioning. The first is presumably the moment in which the thing appears, which we call Enlightenment or Western science or industrialization, and which we might also call the last illness of God or the onset of the secular market, or capitalism and commodification. But in this first moment, the definition of science is at one with its defense, and the antediluvian Enlightenment heroes, like Auden's Voltaire, remain alert to the grim possibility of mythic regression:

> And still all over Europe stood the horrible nurses
> Itching to boil their children.

The philosophers are thus still bathed in the triumphalism of a conquest of nature that also promised to be a conquest of the self and a reconstruction of the social order in the human image and on a human scale.

Few statues to those heroes remained when the second period of a renewed interrogation of the nature of modernity rolled around: the *fin de siècle*, the period of positivism, of Simmel and Durkheim, the end of the *Gründerzeit* and of the heroic age of the establishment of the bourgeois republics, and the beginning of a long doubtful future constellated by immense working-class suburbs as well as the points of light of hysteria and neurosis, from the midst of which the more grimly stoic were able to "see how much they could bear" (Max Weber) as Freud and Nietzsche asked themselves unpleasant questions about the instinctual repressions and renunciations which "civilization" demanded in payment.

This second Enlightenment, or era of suspicion and demystification, was characterized both by imperialism and by a wave of technological innovation which signed itself as irrevocable: its theorists had to confront a fundamental change in their experience, about which they had begun to be able to doubt that it was to be called progress, but were otherwise quite unable to imagine that it might ever again disappear. In fact, of course, it was still about the future that they were thinking, since outside the big cities (of the "Western" or "advanced" countries), the new science-and-technology was socially in the minority: aristocratic governments and countrysides, precapitalist colonies, still largely surrounded these "modern" industrial islands or enclaves (the spaces of Baudelaire and Zola).

In a third moment, however—our own—those vestiges of different noncapitalist pasts, if they have not everywhere disappeared, have at least receded to the point where they are objects of nostalgia. Today, therefore, a fully "modernized" life-world can be experienced as well as imagined as a realized fact: we call this fact postmodernity, at least in part because of the radically new technology that has accompanied the new global standardization, but mainly, I think, because what had previously been thought of as modernity, with its various modernisms, has now been revealed to us as a peculiarly old-fashioned and outmoded historical stage compared to our own (modernism thus paradoxically proving to be the result of incomplete modernization). Yet that older modernity could be the object of avant-garde excitement and affirmation (as the first forms of Western science were for the Enlightenment *philosophes*): the Futurists dramatized that for us from within that industrial late-comer (Italy) which at the same time inspired the thought of Gramsci; while a profound *Kulturpessimismus* offered another option, another affective or libidinal investment, with respect to the modern fact and the modern self. Postmodernity has relegated its enthusiasms and affirmations to science and technology (that is to say, to the consumption of the new gadgetry of a communications age), but is equally innocent of any Wagnerian or metaphysical global pessimism, despite the precise information it has about atomic energy, endemic famine, AIDS, and global warming. Instead, the theorization of the postmodern has seemed to billow and eddy around a new project: namely, that "overcoming of the modern" which the Japanese were the first to conceive of and name in the early 1940s (when, to be sure, for some of them it meant something as simple as "overcoming" the United States and the West).

In Japan these three stages, separated in the West by two hundred years, have been compressed into a century. This is why Karatani's vision of the modern leaps out at us with such blinding force. It is indeed well known in the sciences how the "outsider principle" explains the capacity of non-card-carrying unprofessional tourists and visitors-to-a-given-discipline to deduce impending fundamental paradigm shifts; so also in the arts, where modernism is scarcely dreamed of in the British industrial core, but makes its claims in more recently "developed" areas and even more intensely in "semi-peripheral" ones such as Nicaragua and Uruguay, St Louis, Idaho, and Lisbon or Alexandria (where experience is focused and heightened by the burning glass of the metropolis).

Here, however, it is as though—even more paradoxically science-fictional than the "inversions" (*tentō*) with which Karatani will perform a whole series of theoretical prestidigitations—it is as though his book itself, written in the Japanese 1970s and 1980s, and, as it were, lost and forgotten, had somehow preceded all the other earlier theories of modernity that now look like so many commentaries on it. This is the first reason for its claims on us: it is not even an "alternate history" which is offered us by this "postmodern" analysis of the institutions of the modern self, writing, literature, and scientific objectivity that were constructed and imposed by the Meiji Revolution. Rather, it is as though that great laboratory experiment which was the modernization of Japan allows us to see the features of our own development in slow motion, in a new kind of form (which might be compared to an older traditional history or sociology as the cinema to the novel, for example, or animation to documentary).

Karatani's references are, to be sure, local and unfamiliar to many of us, although he makes it clear how immensely a figure like Natsume Sōseki (1867–1916) ought ideally (along with Rabindranath Tagore or Lu Xun) to loom on a truly global map of modern literary production. I find that, as with certain kinds of music criticism or theory, an account of the initial situation of production itself, with its raw materials and specific form problems, allows one to imagine the structure of the work more purely and abstractly than any distracted *ad hoc* audition might do; that is, certain kinds of analyses—like those of Karatani here—are analogous to creative works themselves, insofar as they propose a schema which it is the reader's task to construct and to project out onto the night sky of the mind's eye; and this is in fact, I believe, the way in which a good deal of contemporary theory is read by artists, who do not in fact use such books primarily for their perceptive contributions to the analysis of this or that familiar work of art, the way an older criticism was appealed to by readers of belles lettres. These younger "postmodern" readers, as I understand it, look at the theoretical abstractions of post-contemporary books in order to imagine the concrete referents to which those abstractions might possibly apply—whether those are artistic languages or experiences of daily life. Here, the analysis produces the absent text of what remains to be invented, rather than modestly following along behind the achieved masterpiece with a running commentary. It is—to use the expression again—science-fictional (as befits a culture like ours, just catching up with science fiction, not merely in its content, but in its form): the new abstractions model the forms of a reality that does not yet exist, but which it would be interesting to experience.

But in Japanese literature and culture we have just such a reality; and whether or not Soseki and the other names in Karatani's pages are as yet familiar to us even in the (translated) flesh-and-blood of their *écriture*, it can be a satisfying experience to imagine the literary situation and the multiple form-problems for which Soseki (as Karatani presents him) is the name.

Now let us take a closer look at Karatani's modernity, that is to say, at ourselves and those otherwise invisible scars of our modernization that here briefly light up like an infrared flare: subject and object, to be sure; the old "centered self" and the old "real" world of scientific objectivity; but also—wonder of wonders!—the novel (is it so modern, let alone socially so important?) and also landscape, and even disease (the kind you write about in the newspapers), children, and "depth"—for are not children a kind of depth?—but a depth rather different from Freud's unconscious or Marx's infrastructures, which Karatani will surprise us by locating at the very surface of our modernity.

None of these symptoms can be made visible to the naked eye without reckoning in the effects of Karatani's "inversion" (*tentō*), which as the Formalists, Brecht, Barthes, and so many others taught us, turns the historical into the natural, and generates an illusion of temporal depth and continuity—a past! the illusion of a past!—where there was none before. Here the Nietzsche/Foucault lesson of the genealogy can be misleading indeed, often seeming to reestablish this very past which its vocation was to have demystified. Thus, to take Karatani's central example, the sudden emergence, full-blown and aureoled with its own spurious history, of the "novel" in its Western sense, at once sends scholars not merely searching for its "genealogy," the larval forms that later on in the evolutionary tree will become retroactively identified as the novel as such, but also—what is in a sense much more serious—for pre-novelistic forms, for narratives that are utterly non-novelistic and can thus stand as the sign of "genres" that existed before Meiji (or, in Western terms, before capitalism). But perhaps there never were genres in this sense? And perhaps adding the fatal prefix somehow always irredeemably deformed the form identified as somehow "preceding" what thereby becomes the fulcrum of the definition? It is thus to transgress the fundamental law, the basic distinction between the synchronic and the diachronic, which in this sense forbids the mixing of the two realities: "inversion" is a synchronic drama, of no little magnitude and interest (origin, emergence, reshuffling of the deck, reorganization of the world); it can be witnessed only on the condition that we do not try to introduce any diachronic reflections or reference into the matter (which need to be pursued in some other place: like a tribal taboo, in which one group of magicians works on the plants, while another, wholly segregated from those, deals with the uncleanliness of blood and living organism).

The "novel" turns out to stand for a great many novelties, some familiar, some less so. Landscape is the first of these which Karatani will seize upon as a more suggestive way of conveying the strangeness and the freshness of an interest in "nature without people." It has the advantage of enforcing the analytic inseparability of experience and art or form, since the landscape in question is not a thing but a paradigm, called "Western landscape"; and the very example makes it clear that the experience of the natural earth spread out contemplatively before the eyes is necessarily mediated by categories of representation developed inside the mind by artistic (or, if you prefer, formal or generic) production. The emergence of that same unpeopled landscape in the West has long been one of the most interesting stories Western historians of art have had to tell (see, for example, John Barrell's work[2]), but here the movement is speeded up, and much more visibly coordinated with forms of narrative than its Western opposite number.

Meanwhile, "landscape" as an independent and autonomous reality—no longer a mere sign, as we shall see in a moment, but a wash of contingency—dialectically brings into being its unrelated correlative, namely the human face (it is an insight Gilles Deleuze and Félix Guattari will develop independently in their *Mille Plateaux*). Karatani explains: "I do not mean to say that landscapes and faces had not previously existed. But for them to be seen as 'simply landscape' or 'simply face' required, not a perceptual transformation, but an inversion of that topos which had privileged the conception landscape or face." The perceptual warning is a crucial one, for there is a strong diachronic temptation to rewrite all this in terms of the emergence of a new kind of body (I've done so myself). At Karatani's level of abstraction, however, this is unsatisfactory because it tends to attribute a kind of causality to the body as such and to the McLuhanite sensorium. The force of Karatani's analysis lies rather in the attribution of this new body and its perceptions and sensations to a more fundamental restructuration (or "inversion") which involves categories that take precedence over experience in this sense. To the degree to which Derrideanism has become a kind of method, or named philosophy, it might also be preferable, despite Karatani's careful indications, to remove the new synchronic event from the whole code of writing and *écriture* as well (which then tends to reform into a kind of "cause" in its own right): even though the primary factor in the pages that deal with literature here is a kind of scriptive aesthetic, the *genbun itchi*, or a Japanese version of that drive to break up rhetoric and to bring writing closer to popular speech and the vernacular, which one can observe in all the European languages in this same period. But owing to the intermediation of Chinese characters, this effort in Japanese is a far more visibly ideological matter, which at once (but as already in Wordsworth) implies some greater authenticity and sincerity, indeed, some more fundamental embodiment of expression and expressiveness, than is visible in the various Western realisms and naturalisms.

It is an ideal which now for the first time projects something like literature into a Japanese social space in full reorganization: to the degree to which causality is a formal and a narrative structure (which is to say, the degree to which we cannot really think without it, although we can try to cancel it after the fact), we can also tell the story that way, and suggest (as Karatani sometimes seems to do) that literature—the new institution of the literary as such—*causes* that reorganization called Meiji to fall into place around it. Or we can more modestly retain literature as a privileged object in which that reorganization can be analogically observed: the form of the narrative is at this point of self-consciousness not now very important (although we will return to its political consequences in a moment).

There are, to be sure, other versions of the narrative as well: Masao Miyoshi's classic *Accomplices of Silence* marks the gap between the raw material of Japanese social experience and these abstract formal patterns of Western novel construction that cannot always be welded together seamlessly. Meanwhile, a similar account—which tests the imported technology (the Western form of the novel) against the content or social experience of the non-Western importing country, thereby also allowing us to measure the systematic modifications, or *Umfunktionierung*, of the former in the context of the latter—can also be found in Menakshee Mukerjee's study of the origins of the Indian novel, *Realism and Reality*. Nor will the Western reader forget the lessons of Raymond Williams, in *Keywords*, about the slow emergence of the word "literature," or of Foucault about the slow formation of that related tiling he calls "humanism": slow is here the watchword for those related experiments, the measurement time is too long, the graphs in the laboratory oscillate idly over too many empty periods. The new experiment and the new laboratory equipment allow us to reproduce the same thing in a more compact set of equations, and as a more vivid event.

But there is a more basic reversal of causality at work in Karatani's *Darstellung* which is crucial insofar as it tries to strike at the most fundamental of our social and psychic illusions (at precisely those objective illusions for which literature in this sense is responsible): this is the notion of interiority, the centered subject, the psychological, indeed the self in its intolerably Western sense (Karatani has observed elsewhere that the Japanese never needed deconstruction because they never had a centered subject to begin with: here, at least, he documents a tendency and a kind of formation). What we call interiority, however, and think of in terms of psychological experience (and by way of a great deal of imagery) is, however "simply," the effect of the literary institution as such, which by inventing a new kind of "unspeakable sentence" (Ann Banfield's name for the related phenomenon of *style indirect libre*) slowly causes a new "experience" to come into being as what that kind of sentence "expresses" (or would express if it were possible to speak it in the first place). The pages on narrative in Japanese, and in particular about the drama of Soseki as he glimpses the radical difference of the Western novel and then produces a host of very different and unique generic experiments as a way of approximating that condition and avoiding it all at once—these pages have very little equivalent in Western criticism; only the remarkable density of Barthes's pages in *Writing Degree Zero* is comparable (and indeed, were those epigrammatic pronouncements of Barthes developed in the direction of the social and the psychoanalytic, the result would be a statement of the dimensions of Karatani's for the West).

Now, however, we can also move in two directions: if it is not romanticized as a pre-anything, or as a form of more authentically primitive and primal writing-cum-experience, a certain approximation to what literature destroys can be attempted—it is simply the *figure*, as Chinese characters (but also the related forms of Chinese and Japanese landscape, and also the fixed forms of narrative and poetry and the like) can dramatize:

> My own concern ... has been to consider the kind of inversion of semiotic constellation which makes transcription possible. In order for us to assume it to be natural that things exist and the artist merely observes them and copies them, "things" must first be discovered. But this requires the repression of the signification, or figurative language (Chinese characters), that precedes "things," as well as the existence of a language which is supposedly transparent. It is at this point that "interiority" is constituted.[3]

Once such interiority is constituted, however, we can begin to work in the other direction and trace out some of the more surprising consequences: that of "disease," for instance, and of the medical in general. Karatani's striking chapter on literary tuberculosis is in fact preceded by a very interesting series of reflections on the role of Christianity in Japan as the "ideology," so to speak, of a "repression of the diversity of polytheism," and thereby the production (or "discovery") of the "natural body"—a discovery which is at one with Western sexuality and Western sexual guilt.

Meanwhile, medicine builds on the production of that new body to achieve a host of new kinds of effects: it was indeed, in most non-Western countries, the first and primary form of Western science, an "agent of modernization" whose symbolic value cannot be underestimated. Any reader of Lu Xun, for example, will remember the simultaneously personal and national meaning of his decision to study medicine (in Japan), as well as the even more pointed meaning of his resolution to convert a practice of physical medicine into that of cultural production (see the preface to *Na Han* [A Call to Arms]). Medicine is thus all of Western science, as well as being *a* science: it is "thoroughly political, constituting one form of centralized power," and it also produces in this case, not only the medical body, but "disease" itself, in its various theories. Karatani proposes something like a medical version of the James–Lange theory of the emotions in which what we sometimes think of as disease is the production of disease theory (in this case, the theory of "germs"), such that the appropriation of diseases for social and ideological purposes (as in Susan Sontag's *Illness as Metaphor*) cannot properly be the object of an ideological critique, which would imply that there existed an objective, non-ideological reality of "disease" as such out there that the appropriation denatured and deformed. But for Karatani disease is always already "infected" with the literary: the illusion of an objective physical reality to which "science" and "medicine" were supposed to turn their nonideological attention is itself part of that ideology. The production of "childhood" and also of the "primitive" (or the object of anthropology and the ethnological gaze—here the inhabitants of the internally colonized Japanese "west" or the frontier of Hokkaido Island) is then an extension of this interiorizing process in a different direction.

We reach the analytic climax of this line of inquiry with Karatani's discussion of "depth" as the abstract pattern and paradigm of all these ideological productions or acts of constitution. The Western reader, already bombarded with any number of post-Marxisms and revisions of Freud, will find much to ponder in Karatani's reversals of the stereotypes of those figures:

> While the theories of Marx or Freud ... are often described as discoveries of a kind of substratum or base, what they actually accomplished was a dismantling of precisely that ideological and transcendental perspectival configuration that produces the concepts of substratum and stratification: it was the surface level, rather, that commanded their attention.[4]

The literary debate over plot versus surface provides the vehicle for this discussion, anchoring it back into the literary institution with which the book begins and recirculating its fundamental insights through the codes and thematics of nationalism and of aesthetic construction, bringing these issues down to the present of Karatani's writing (which corresponds to the postmodern self-consciousness of the rich and prosperous corporate Japan after the end of the postwar, and leaves open the fate of these structures and the questions about them in a future in which, among other things, Karatani's own book exists). I am reminded a little of Henri Lefebvre's call for a new spatial dialectic, a reconstruction of the dialectic in different terms from Hegel's old temporal ones, terms more consistent with the synchronic nature of contemporary thought.[5] Karatani's discussions also reflect these contemporary constraints (as must everyone's), and it is not always clear whether the choice of even that minimal figure of depth versus surface does not, in its last shred of content, plunge you back into the very episteme you sought to analyze (and above which you imagined yourself somehow at least momentarily to float). But by the time this is over a reversal has taken place in which the reader—having begun by observing Japan—now finds Japanese theory observing him, and waiting for his own drawing of the consequences: as those emerge from the vague questions as to how you would do something like this in a Western context and what "application" this kind of thinking and reading might have for our own (even more "modern," modernized, and modernist) texts. This is an excellent and healthy geopolitical reversal, in my view; but any discussion of it needs to be preceded with a remark about Karatani's own political agenda.

For now we need to complicate our discussion of the dilemmas of historical representation (*Darstellung*) in an analysis like this (causality as a form, etc.), and in particular revise our suggestion that the novel or literature was at one with Meiji, and that its choice as an allegorical resonator or condenser for the historical narrative was relatively optional. For Karatani also simultaneously projects a historical narrative which stands outside this one, and which has determinate political consequences: this is the notion that what we are here calling "Meiji"—that is to say, modernization and modernity, literature, interiority, "Westernization"—is itself the result of defeat and failure. There were on this view two Meiji revolutions, one that succeeded and one that failed. The successful one is the constitution of the Japanese modern state as we know it; the failed revolution was contemporaneous with the Paris Commune, the popular uprisings that arose in millenarian fashion at the "dawn smell" of a new era and at the collapse of the old structures (like Bakhtin's moment of Rabelais, at the end of the Middle Ages; or Imamura's apocalyptic and Utopian film *Eijanaika* [1981] about this same period). These needed to be repressed in order for power to be consolidated by the clique around the new emperor; but it is their repression and defeat which is accompanied by a massive popular disillusionment that can alone enable the setting in place of the new authoritarian structures: "[T]o speak in Freudian terms, the libido which was once directed towards the People's Rights Movement and the political novel lost its object and was redirected inward, at which point 'landscape' and 'the inner life' appeared."

We here fleetingly glimpse an alternate world alongside our own historical one: a world in which modernity in the current coinage did not occur, without our being able to discern clearly the outlines of what, equally supplanting precapitalist forms and relations, took its place. But this alternate world, outside our own history, also lies beyond the boundaries of our explanatory and narrative systems. It is at the least, however, a rather different vision from that of Lévi-Strauss, for whom the "West" (Greek philosophy, abstract reason, science) need never have happened. Lévi-Strauss's attractive nostalgia, rooted in the experience of and commitment to "cold" or tribal societies, evokes an aleatory moment, an effect of chance, of the recombination of historical molecules, which fatally leads, or not, to the infernal machine we know as modernity or capitalism; it is a peculiarly fatalist view of the inevitability of historical development as a roll of the dice or a chance lightning strike, and then the rigid stasis of the irremediable! (This is not to suggest that history might not really be like this ...)

In Karatani, however, a notion of popular struggle survives which is not nostalgic, since it eventuated in failure and does not seem to imply any particular optimism about current Japanese conditions, from which all radical initiative seems to have evaporated in the years since the onset of their *Wirtschaftswunder* (the economic miracle of the early 1970s). We must remember, also, that we are ourselves trying to think this notion of a collective creativity that preempts institutions during a period of national stasis and disillusionment in the United States today which is doubled by a virtually global one: our difficulty in imagining any other narrative paradigm than a deterministic one—the slow, fateful, irresistible Foucauldian encroachments of systems and institutions—may thus be a historical symptom as much as an epistemological problem.

But I want to add something about the relationship of thought and disillusionment, which seems consistent with this glacial backward look at an unfinished project that was also a missed opportunity. We are, indeed, more than familiar with the conception of an expressive relationship between a thought system and the social fate of its class fraction: Lucien Goldmann's picture, in *The Hidden God*, of the way in which Jansenism's Augustinian pessimism articulated the failure of the *noblesse de robe*, from which it issued, to become something like a mandarin ruling class, is suggestive for a range of other moments as well. But we need to kick this static notion of relationship into historical motion, if only in the past tense, and to restore to this litany of class failures the freshness of opportunities, even and particularly of the missed ones. It is a way of thinking that might even let us look differently at our own time, which so many people seem intent on reading as the triumph of the market, if not indeed of the nationalisms and religious fundamentalisms, over socialism. What if it were the other way around, however? What if it were the failures of socialism, better still, of socialists and communists, which left in their wake a universal disillusionment in which only consumption and narrow fanaticisms (market as well as confessional) seem possible, at least for the present?

The national question, then, brings me to my conclusion, which also has something to do with the lessons of Karatani's book for North American theory and criticism in the present conjuncture. I suggested that a formal and suggestive way of reading about unfamiliar literary works was possible, and sometimes, although surely not always and not even often, recommended. Now we need to see that something analogous can be said about unfamiliar criticism and theory, on the occasion of a book in which no little attention is paid to classic Japanese debates most of us have never suspected the existence of. There are also ways of reading the form, as well as the content, of theoretical debates and critical moves and countermoves: indeed, for anyone interested in the procedures called *mapping*, current scientific fashions show computers at use, not in solving substantive problems, but, by way of so-called "phase space," in matching up the abstract shapes and rhythms of a variety of different scientific hypotheses and results, as well as in measuring the abstract rhythms into which certain complex forms of movement seem to break down. We don't need to extrapolate the metaphysical slogans (the way humanists once did with Einsteinian relativities): it is the nature of this mapping procedure which is suggestive, and not for predictive purposes either, or with a view toward identifying recurrent paradigms. Rather, Karatani sets us the example of a criticism of criticism, a theorization about theory, which respects the passionate content of these interventions, while measuring, as it were, their velocity and reactive patterns, and in particular the fidelity with which so many ideologically different positions offer precise symptoms of the detectable absence of that unrepresentable cause he calls inversion.

This presupposes a double movement, a double reading, in which the critical text is apprehended simultaneously for what it is and for what it stands for, as statement and as symptom, or if you prefer my old-fashioned language, as content and as form. But it is only at this price that criticism and theory can today recover an urgency they seemed to have had even a few years ago. Then, it was a question of a struggle for a certain theoretical pluralism: a parliamentary struggle, so to speak, in which repressed and silenced or ignored critical tendencies spoke out for representation and swaggered in the broad daylight of a tumultuous popular forum. But it happened to critical theory as to the parliamentary struggle itself: the achievement of pluralism and of representation (however marginal) then gave way to the Hemingwayesque moment (it isn't fun anymore), any number of practitioners finding that once you were allowed a hearing for your product, it automatically became less interesting. This is of course what happened universally in Europe when social democracy (generally in alliance with the tiny remains of an old communist party) came to power and offered to run capitalism (as Stanley Aronowitz has put it) impartially in the interests of all of its factions. Nor was the experience unique to Europe: my Taiwanese friends paint a similar picture of the depoliticization that followed the legalization of the opposition parties (after a vibrant period of militancy and hope). This letdown (which does not even, in good Aristotelian fashion, *follow* on achieved coitus) is what was predicted under the name "the end of ideology" and characterized, when it finally arrived, as "the end of history." But it is not very interesting to attribute it, as Daniel Bell does, to that tired old bourgeois narrative paradigm, the disappearance of belief, the waning of "values," the end of commitment (otherwise known as "the death of God").

I would have us look in another direction, one we have necessarily already acknowledged when as North Americans we open *The Origins of Japanese Literature*, this remarkable achievement of contemporary Japanese theory. The center has a special kind of blindness, which the margins, for all their discomforts, do not have to cope with. I've described elsewhere the astonishment an intellectual from the superstate can feel, not about the nationalism of other countries and culture areas—that would be a superficial and self-serving view of it, given the nasty things people say about nationalism—but rather about their preoccupation with the national character and the national situation, the permanent and allegorical vocation of their intellectuals to denounce the national misery. This is very much a matter of structural possibilities: dependency arouses consciousness, however unwanted; but those who are not dependent—let's not call it independence or freedom, exactly—can scarcely have that same awareness, and can scarcely want to. One is dependent on one's own dependents in some other sense, to be sure: but masters have never paid the same kind of attention to slaves or servants as the latter have paid to their overseers (developing in the process those characterological traits of subalternity with which more recent Gramscian and Fanonian analysts have enriched the basic Hegelian paradigm). The American Jeremiad was a brief flash of cultural inferiority during the shaking off of English cultural tutelage; and the essential insecurity of a cultureless business-oriented superstate today is an unconscious one, whose repressed return only in the symptoms of jingoism, masculinist fantasy, and the imported fashions of the ancien régime (as in the Anglophilia of PBS or the Francophilia of high theory).

But if we are the first truly secular state, the first truly godless one, without any of the remnants of older class systems and cultural inheritances that weigh down other places with a certain dead splendor, then we need to embrace our insecurity as a special historical privilege, as a unique national gift. We need to cultivate a new kind of "national" inferiority complex—the inferiority complex of the superstate. We need to train ourselves to be vulnerable in some new and original sense, to be passive-receptive, weak, un-American, susceptible to boundless influence by currents from foreign countries and distant cultures (as indeed our mass culture already is with respect to its internal minorities). A long process of collective psychoanalysis, collective self-analysis, might well begin with this letting down of the barriers and with a decisive reveling in a new kind of geopolitical subalternity. If this becomes the task of American intellectuals, I think we can expect them to recover something of that same sense of mission and commitment which we find in these pages, in which Karatani so memorably sets out to remake the traditional historical and cultural image of Japan's modernization in the Meiji Era.

(*1993*)

Notes

1 This essay was first published as the foreword to Kojin Karatani's *The Origins of Japanese Literature* (Durham, NC 1993).

2 *The Dark Side of the Landscape: The Rural Poor in English Painting 1730–1840* (Cambridge, 1980).

3 Karatani, op. cit., p. 61.

4 Ibid., p. 143.

5 Henri Lefebvre, *La production de l'espace* (Paris, 1974), p. 382.

15

Sōseki and Western Modernism

Analyzing translations—even in the era of the misreading (strong or otherwise)—can lead one into the comical situation in which it is the translator (in this case, V.H. Viglielmo) whom one is, in reality, comparing to Henry James, all the while imagining oneself to be thinking about Sōseki. What has disappeared is not merely the resistance of the original language (its untranslatable sentence structure, or, the other way around, what it cannot, as one individual language among others, structurally do) but, above all, its historicity. Adorno is not the only one to have thought that the most immediate experience of history afforded by a literary work lies in the very texture of its language. But translations do not yield that sense of the passage of time any Japanese reader must feel on confronting a text written in 1916. Yet, whatever has become outmoded in Sōseki's last, unfinished novel, *Meian*,[1] is an index of its historical situation fully as much as those stylistic and linguistic things it was able to do that, for whatever reason, later users of the language could no longer achieve. Finally, however, the ridicule to which a critic of translations exposes himself is the milder one—more humdrum, and the least interesting of all—of simple gestural and contextual miscomprehension, about which native speakers shrug their shoulders, not even offended: that stars mean it's time for Christmas shopping (seasonal marker), that raising your hand in the classroom means you need to go to the bathroom (cultural code). Instead, the alien critic invents a whole cosmology for the former and reads a fundamental gesture of resistance and subversion into the classroom interruption. These often uninteresting discrepancies, however, are the obverse of a phenomenon in which literary critics have long been passionately interested, namely irony: the non-native speaker in the situation of translation seems the outside—unfamiliar—which inside familiarity utterly domesticates; modern irony, however, seems to involve the inverse situation: one of inner comfort and familiarity with which, on the inside, each is deeply comfortable; the self as the old clothes we wear around the home—which, however, looks different and unfamiliar, somehow shocking, from the outside. Sōseki's novel is about the structure of the ironic situation, and about it in its very novelistic form. Meanwhile, the whole cultural period to which this novel somehow corresponds—that of high modernism, which in East Asia seems peculiarly to coincide with the period of realism (and this belatedly, according to Western chronology), rather than to follow and to replace and discredit it—is itself equally deeply obsessed with irony as such, in which modernism thinks it glimpses a metaphysic and a philosophical and moral value, fully as much as this or that mere technique. Perhaps, therefore, mistakes that call for irony are less misplaced in a study of this particular novel than in texts from other corners of time and space.

Meanwhile, the very hermeneutic of this particular narrative—the concealment of Tsuda's complaint—evidently a venereal disease of some sort, if not hemorrhoids, and the euphemistic evocation of Kobayashi's adherence to the socialist movement—these reticences, and the complicity they demand from the reader, are something like the inscription, in reverse, of the kind of contextual blindness here anticipated.

The idea of familiarity, however—from Baudelaire on, one of the great obsessive themes of the modern generally—reminds us that translation tends to block out what makes up the most confusing and vivid feature of our experience of Otherness, namely, the unfamiliar itself—what is seemingly uninterpretable and doesn't compute, what seems to mark deep characterological and cultural difference. Most often, a little "familiarity" dissipates the illusion of difference and shows that the strangest locutions (or the simple-minded designations of the various pidgins) are perfectly ordinary thoughts and expressions that are familiar on the inside to any native speaker and need to be replaced by something equally familiar for the foreigner, as well. Not people but situations are radically different; on the other hand, nothing mars a translation more than the attempt to render an idiom idiomatically. But even that is an impossible situation, since the avoidance of the idiomatic causes an impassivity to rise upon the textual surface that is deeply neoclassical and becomes a textual connotation and a stylistic ideology (the absence of style as a style in its own right) that may be culturally and historically utterly inappropriate.

But the absence of difference then generates yet another kind of comedy, as the reader tries desperately to decide what this unknown but non-alien (*qua* translated) object is basically like: it is a psychological comedy, and you tend to laugh at the people who are unprepared for new experiences but must first assimilate them somehow to what is already known and long since inventoried and catalogued. Still, Proust himself described at great length this anxiety of the New, which we seek to assuage with comparisons until enough time has passed for a certain new familiarity to take its place among our habits, at which point Sōseki's once unfamiliar name becomes a word for an independent object, a thing in its own right, a style or work that no longer has to be like anything.

It may still, of course, be "related," but I must confess that I have always found Wittgenstein's overused concept of the family likeness oddly feeble and lacking in explanatory power, although it is refreshing to be able, henceforth, to forget about that even older chestnut, "influence." Is Sōseki's resemblance to the generation of Henry James and the ironists who followed him a genuine historical problem, and one that ought to summon forth a whole multidisciplinary research effort in order to avoid trivializing notions of influence, on the one hand, and metaphysical or cosmological notions of generational translation rhythms, on the other? Is modernization a useful clue, insofar as it designates a feature, a very dramatic feature indeed, that is common to the social situations of the writers on both sides of that particular globe-in-history? What seems certain to me is that the traits of similarity, the shared components, of these distant works are put together differently in each case, thereby facilitating identification, since we are no longer tempted to confuse the parts of the structure with the empirical qualities of the individual work.

Meanwhile, the nascent abstraction of both movements, of *Meian* fully as much as the works of the European ironists, seems to have left its trace in the critical methods that themselves emerged in the moment of nascent modernism and, in particular, in a focus on the form-problem, which can also be compared to the phenomenological bracketing or suspension of content. In a situation, in other words, in which the achievement or construction of form is the paramount interest of the critic and can eventually be marshaled in support of primary historical theses (as in the work of Lukács, most dramatically, but not exclusively, in *Theory of the Novel*)—in such a situation, content tends to be degraded to the status of a mere pretext for the achievement of the form; and I will not proceed otherwise here. I say so because the echoes I have retained from the Japanese critical debates on *Meian* turn essentially on what I consider to be matters of content, namely Tsuda's spiritual state and his putative regeneration, the whole (unfinished) novel coming to seem a psychodrama of archetypal proportions, about which it might be more accurate to say that it is the illusion or appearance of interpretable meaning thrown off by some initial psychological content.

Perhaps, indeed, the temptations of such moralizing and archetypal readings are generated by the very simplicity of the plot itself, which relates a series of interviews and conversations from the life of a man who has just undergone a minor surgical intervention and goes to recuperate in the countryside. His problems with his wife O-Nobu, with his sister, and with other more wealthy or distinctly less well-to-do acquaintances are conveyed in some detail by way of this occasion or narrative pretext: its slightness causes the more detached observer to return to the character of Tsuda himself with a view toward determining whether it holds some clue to the reason for showing us these interactions in the first place. Yet in the process of reading the novel line by line, larger questions of that kind tend to be eclipsed by a fascination with the sheer narrative present.

At any rate, my own experience of the novel had little in common with the kinds of interpretations just mentioned, as though the absence of significance, or the need to discover it or reinvent it, did not have much urgency. My reading is probably also an interpretation, essentially a Utopian one, but one that can be characterized as having to do with a formal experience of great purity (in the sense of specialization rather than moral qualities), of a registration of interpersonal relations of extraordinary exactitude, implying a narrative machinery of a unique kind, theorized long after the fact in discussions such as Nathalie Sarraute's about the *subconversation*,[2] and suggesting literary parallels that are at best anachronistic and at worst culturally and generically inappropriate. I think, for instance, of the plays of Racine, but only in the sense in which it can be affirmed, say, that of the fifteen hundred alexandrines of *Andromaque*, his first major tragedy, no more than a handful serve uniquely to convey information; every one of the rest can be shown to be overdetermined in such a way that whatever else the verse is meant to say, it also functions as an instrument in the mouth of the speaker designed to work the conversation partner over (most scenes involve no more than two actors, in an intense exchange whose deeper truth, if not its outer form, is stichomythic), whether to touch, to humiliate, to manipulate, to revile, or to fawn or grovel. The theatrical medium and the aesthetic of the unities become the vehicles as well as the cause, along with the condition of possibility, for a bravura organization in which the right speaker erupts on the stage at the right time, so that a plausible accident (which advances the plot) always motivates the copresence of the next and most appropriate partners. (The stage directions of another play, which house all these meetings in an anteroom, beyond the living space and the chambers of state alike, seem in a deeper sense to mark them all, lifting up the stage into a place beyond the world, in which purely interpersonal interaction at its most intense can alone happen.) The comings and goings of Sōseki's characters sometimes strike one like that (most take place in that space beyond the world that is Tsuda's peculiar upper-story "hospital room"); and their specific motivations (to tell so-and-so not to come today, the dispatching of endless messengers and telephone calls, the nonetheless unlikely and undesirable coincidence of two visits, etc.) are all as elegantly drawn back into the movement of the interpersonal dialogue as the analogous plot machinery in Racine. What is different, above and beyond the secular impurity of the bourgeois urban drama, is the obligatory presence of the object world in the novel; it can be removed from drama, as triumphantly in Racine himself, while elsewhere in the history of theater a too-insistent object turns back heavily into a symbol, as in Ibsen's duck or gun. In the novel, however, it is the absence of the object-world that attracts attention (as in the aesthetics of Woolf or Gide, which aimed at reducing external description to a minimum and thereby at once seemed mannered). The form itself leaves residual traces:

> He went out into the road, and slowly walked away from the Yoshikawa home. But this did not mean that his mind could withdraw as rapidly as his body from the parlour where he had just been. As he made his way through the relatively deserted evening streets, he could still clearly see the bright interior of the room.
>
> The coldly gleaming texture of the cloisonné vase, the colours of the brilliant pattern flowing on its smooth surface, the round, silver-plated tray which had been brought to the table, the cube sugar and cream containers of the same colour, the heavy curtains of bluish-black fabric with a brown arabesque design, the ornamental album with three of its corners set in gold leaf—these vivid images passed in a disorderly manner before his mind's eye even after he had gone out from under the bright light and was walking in the dark outside. (20)

Perhaps this cushioning layer of objects and residual furnishings explains the incomparable distance between the violence of Racine (aristocratic elegance is at one with such violence in its very origins, whereas bourgeois elegance has virtually the inverse function of repressing it) and the chamber music of Sōseki, which can, to be sure, reach moments of great intensity but which seems to offer the Utopian de-materialization and stylization of the outside world and whatever in it is sordid and marked by sheer need. But it does this by including passion, need, social class, and money rather than by leaving them out; by translating all those things into its own idiom—the interpersonal language exchange—just as there is some distance between a brute fact or event and the *récit* in which its occurrence is put into words. Kobayashi's lower-class shabbiness and willful psychic ugliness ("Mrs Tsuda, I live to be disliked. I purposely say and do things people don't like" [154]) enter the narrative relay in a way in which, for example, a Dostoyevskian character of his type could not be imagined within the country houses of a Henry James novel. As for money, it is a fundamental, although curiously eccentric, datum of the plot: Tsuda's father has suspended his monthly allowance, while on top of that he needs a medical absence from his job and a period of recuperation in the countryside (from whom is he to borrow money? or who can influence his father?). But in fact, money—so often, in any case, as canonically in Simmel, associated with abstraction as such—provides the pretext for the very rarefaction of narrative we have been discussing; giving the characters something to talk about, it opens the space for their interaction. Money is here in league with interpersonality rather than with what distracts from it or tears through its delicate web of relationships. Quite unexpectedly in a sense unmentioned by Simmel in his famous essay,[3] it provides the formal ground for abstraction in the ceaseless weaving of well-nigh decorative arabesques that are composed of dialogue sentences and replied: "a lace made up of rope," Cocteau described his plays (which he rather preciously termed "theatrical poetry"). Perhaps something similar might be observed about these scenes of Sōseki, than which nothing could be further from actual theater or from the dramatic in any conceivable generic sense. Still, as Gore Vidal once observed, dialogue is not prose, so that this novel offers us sheet upon sheet of an arrangement of writing that is not poetic at all but not subject, either, to the normal kind of story reading.

Still, a dialectic is generated by the extreme compression of this particular pole of the novel's language, so that one has the sense of endless murmured conversations, in quiet tones, linked or interrupted by the movement of the characters on peaceful trolley cars in that small town that is the Tokyo of the pre-earthquake period. The point, however, is that the urban transitions stand out and that, however muted, they designate the presence—not always perceptible as such—of a spatial dimension underpinning this extraordinarily de-materialized narrative seemingly tressed from interweaving human voices. The overemphasis on rarefied spoken language, however, calls up its dialectical opposite in the emergence of a spatial grid that links the various scenes of dialogue—houses and rooms—in a network presumably characteristic of some uniquely Japanese construction of urban space and landscape that erupts in the great concluding sequence in which we leave built space for the countryside and the inn and hot spring in which the novel presumably concludes. I will return to this remarkable and unexpected spatial experience in a moment.

But the construction of some absolute conversational element in the novel demands not only that it be limited by an external space of a different kind but also that it be enabled by an inner form, which would not merely "motivate the device," by providing an implicit philosophy of the sub-conversation, but which would also, by incorporating narrative expectations, allow these moments to function like stories.

In Sōseki, indeed, we seem to surprise the simultaneous existence of the two distinct and seemingly antithetical distortions of narrative raw material observable in the West. These were, on the one hand, a postulation of enormous length and distention, and, on the other hand, a minimalism tending toward a veritable instant without duration: continuity and discontinuity, respectively, of so peremptory a type that either extreme offers the radical stylization that modernism strove for in its flight from common-sense realism and the ratification of the status quo implicit in the various literary verisimilitudes. Thus, in music, we find the enormous movements of Mahler's symphonies, which play havoc with the memory and attention span of their listeners in order to incorporate an extraordinary range of intense styles or experiences of all sorts, from vulgarity to mystical ecstasy, from heroics to pastoral experiences of nature, from Italianate emotion and recitative to the Viennese bittersweet. But here the dialectic of length and instantaneity becomes clarified, since immoderate duration tends to impede the establishment of perspectival order, the positioning of any individual part or detail within a larger whole. In other words, beyond a certain point, length ceases to be monumental and returns the listener's punctual experience to a new kind of absolute present. The aesthetics of that absolute present, then—Schoenberg's expressionism, say, where the musical work is reduced to units of one to three minutes in length—perhaps only overtly disengages the inner truth of the aesthetics of infinite duration.

Still, in the West, these two ways (which thus, like Proust's, ultimately and dialectically rejoin each other) have been felt to be aesthetically and philosophically distinct, Beckett's breaks and silences seeming to share with the eternity of Proust's three-hundred-page-long receptions and dinners only a will to do violence to normal middle-class perception (and to the reading that accompanies that). This is why any speculation about Sōseki ought to include a discussion of whether in Japanese social life in this period there existed the same kinds of bourgeois stereotypes about everyday life that were constructed in the West during the realist period and which had in the modern already entered into crisis and become the object of satirical or Utopian contestation. I've suggested above that the sequence of stages implied here is purely ideal (and also local) and that one could imagine a situation, in the modernizing East, in which the construction of bourgeois everyday life (the realist moment) took place simultaneously with its modern moment. Indeed, the wondrous rhythms of the daily life of Sōseki's characters—what Genette called the iterative; what, in Proust, constructs the very idea of a routine and a daily life in the first place—are here seemingly at one with a virtually modernist distension of temporality, such that enormous conversations or interviews between the main characters swell to fill the entire novel. Read thus microscopically, held up close to the eyes, Sōseki does not seem much shorter or swifter than Proust himself, despite the fact that *Meian* is virtually all dialogue, in contrast to that single enormous explanatory Proustian paragraph into which bits of dialogue are inserted.

But in Sōseki, stylized length (the climactic central conversation lasts some fifty pages) is accompanied by a systematic fragmentation and autonomization more characteristic of the minimalists, if not of Brecht himself, who systematically broke his scenes up into complete miniature gestures, each one (a *gestus*) labeled with a title and a potential moral. The analysis of Sōseki's narrative flow into small numbered sections has a similar effect on perception, combining the minute with the infinite; that such an arrangement owed something to journalism and serialization is scarcely an alternative causal explanation, since the form of the newspaper ultimately loops back into the general determinations of bourgeois culture in its own right, while such seemingly external economic necessities are always overdetermined by being drawn within the work of art and transformed into the pretexts for its new formal innovations.

But where everything is dialogue, the traditional, non-dialogical components of narrative now tend to implode and to find their equivalents within the unidimensionality of the spoken exchange itself. Whence the extraordinary drama of these seemingly placid and desultory conversations that must now stand in for the larger struggles and adventures which once seemed to characterize life itself and its epic narratives. All of the excitement and the tension of these last will now be miniaturized and retranslated into the conversational exchange itself, whose predominant inner form now comes to be the *agon*, or the life-and-death struggle or duel, between two protagonists (these change and shift throughout the novel, but the deeper sense of all conversations being one ultimate agon persists throughout the scenes). Actually, in this novel, a more familiar local reference prevails: "In a certain sense, when [O-Nobu] and Tsuda privately viewed their relationship, very similar to that between *sumo* wrestlers facing each other in the ring every day, they felt that it was of a kind where she was always his opponent and occasionally even his enemy" (80–1). It is important not to overshoot the mark here and to conclude that this antagonistic relationship characterizes only the married couple itself; in fact, it organizes all the encounters in the novel in one way or another.

Inevitably, then, the account of such conversations will come to be framed in military terms, particularly since tactical or strategic winning or losing, advancing or falling back, need not be completed by the larger picture but can be read off the present like the score in a basketball game. The military agon is thus perfectly consistent with the perpetual present of the narrative, since finally in warfare only the present counts, while a variety of moves can be subsumed under it: "O-Nobu wondered how she should behave, now that she was being treated as a child by her uncle in this way, so as to provide an easy transition from the awkward situation" (123). What counts in a moment like this is not particularly any longer-term relationship with her uncle, nor any decisive revelation of O-Nobu's own character, nothing that would cause her to make a fundamental decision or a basic characterological change or life decision; rather, it is simply whether she wins or loses, whether she cuts her losses and decently escapes, or remains subjected to overwhelming superiority on the other side.

The formal simplification of complex and often traditional situations into simple winning or losing is a narratological variant of Weber's rationalization and is surely characteristic of a capitalist or money economy as such (it is first dramatically rehearsed in Balzac). It should be clear how such a zero-sum logic can coexist for a time with the demands of more traditional social interaction (as in the familial and hierarchical situation from which the previous notation was drawn) but will end up emptying this last of any meaningful content or value.

This is not, however, a matter of personal or collective psychology. The following strategic appreciation has, for example, nothing to do with either national aggressivity or some "argumentative character" that might be attributed to O-Nobu personally: "She boldly jumped ahead. She decided to break through all the round-about talk entwined with personal considerations and to meet O-Hide directly" (241). By the same token, a rather different dramatistic assessment at a different moment in the agon does not necessarily signify passivity:

> O-Nobu shortly came to a decision. It was quite simply that to make the problem meaningful she would have to sacrifice either O-Hide or herself, for if she did neither, the discussion would never amount to anything. It would not be difficult to sacrifice her opponent. If she only broke through somewhere at one of O-Hide's weak points, that would suffice. Whether that weak point was actual or hypothetical was not then O-Nobu's concern. By comparison with the effect she was attempting to obtain merely from O-Hide's natural reaction, the investigation of the truth or falsehood of O-Hide's weakness was an unnecessary consideration. But she still sensed a certain danger in her action. O-Hide would undoubtedly become angry. And to make her angry both was and was not O-Nobu's objective. Therefore O-Nobu was necessarily perplexed as to how to move. Finally she roused herself to seize a certain opportunity. And as she did so she had already decided on sacrificing herself. (238–9)

What this kind of structure does tend to produce, as a new kind of form-problem for the novelist, is some sense—hitherto absent from either reality or from the reader's narrative habits—of what it would mean to "win" or to "lose" these struggles: "It was as if Mrs Yoshikawa had already defeated Tsuda by showing him clear-cut evidence that he still was attached to Kiyoko. His attitude, equivalent to one a person might have after a confession, strengthened Mrs Yoshikawa, as she put an end to one phase of the contest between them" (264). Despite the thematization of "egotism" here and there in the novel and among its critics, events of this type do not signal a world of characters committed to the will to power, not even, as in Proust, the ineradicable force of some deeper ultimate selfishness of the individual subject. The satisfactions of amour propre are less significant here than the opening up of some well-nigh infinite chain of future manipulations, which only intensify our ultimate question as to where they lead and what they can possibly construct or produce as the ultimate "end" of this linked series of "means." Fortunately, the absent conclusion leaves this question permanently open; surely Sōseki could never himself have answered it in any satisfying way (and the plausibility of the surmises of his commentators, that the final meeting with Kiyoko would have marked some deeper regeneration in his character, strikes me as being aesthetically unsatisfactory—a sentimental way of finishing the novel off that would surely have diminished the power of the remarkable effects we are here describing).

On the other hand, the language of battle permits a larger absent form to arise from these present instants of confrontation in a way that no merely realistic account of the interchange—where form and pretext would remain indistinguishable—could have conveyed. So it is that we feel the great impending curve of the agon on its downward slope: "O-Nobu realized that she was more flurried than her husband. When she forsook the argument upon realizing that if it went on in this vein he could no longer be defeated, she turned aside adroitly before betraying her own weakness" (281). Still, a glimpse like this of the movement of the agon as a whole then raises the equally embarrassing question of what it would mean to be defeated in it, where answers having to do with vanity or subordination equally risk trivializing the event itself. Formal abstraction of this kind is possible only where the content of the drama, of these human relations themselves, can be suspended and questions of ultimate ends bracketed.

Meanwhile, the form—about which we remember that it no longer exactly involves prose as such—presses language itself up against its most extreme expressive limits, as though to invent, from out of itself and from the very material of a language that can no longer say anything, new and linguistic, yet material, modes of expression. This is most notably the case with the look or glance, which here acquires a heightened power, as though indeed the eye were able by some inner intensification literally to gleam more sharply and brightly: not only O-Nobu's looks, which continue to startle her husband as though she were always up very close to him, but in the various duels and encounters of social life, looking is like saying something. Indeed, in the following episode the look is uncharacteristically felt from the inside rather than seen by its destinatee or victim: "At the moment O-Nobu gave O-Hide this one glance she sensed that O-Hide already understood her present mood. But this was after the single glance had suddenly flashed from the deep spring of her artifice, which she could in no way control. Since she did not have the power to check this small act, which by chance had sprung from some unfathomable area of her being, she could do nothing but tamely await its effect" (233). We cannot accept the idea that looks are physiological events (if only because that would commit us to participate in a certain kind of scientistic-materialist ideology); rather, they must be seen as narrative constructs, the empty place of an exchange, from which words, sentences, and the very acts of language are constitutively lacking. The look then becomes a kind of narrative space that the novelist can cover with sheets of decoration of a functional kind, the most extreme example of which must surely remain this classical passage from Proust, which, preposterous on any literal reading, can stand as a microcosm and an emblem of at least one remarkable modernist linguistic strategy (it is a question of an acquaintance who, in Horatian fashion, denounces over and over again the city, high society, and social snobbery, but who is, in this episode, suddenly revealed to be a snob himself, since he is unwilling to introduce Marcel's bourgeois family to the aristocratic lady he happens to be accompanying):

> Near the church we met Legrandin coming towards us with the same lady, whom he was escorting to her carriage. He brushed past us, and did not interrupt what he was saying to her, but gave us, out of the corner of his blue eye, a little sign which began and ended, so to speak, inside his eyelids and which, as it did not involve the least movement of his facial muscles, managed to pass quite unperceived by the lady; but, striving to compensate by the intensity of his feelings for the somewhat restricted field in which they had to find expression, he made that blue chink which was set apart for us sparkle with all the zest of an affability that went far beyond mere playfulness, almost touched the border-line of roguery; he subtilised the refinements of good-fellowship into a wink of connivance, a hint, hidden meaning, a secret understanding, all the mysteries of complicity, and finally elevated his assurances of friendship to the level of protestations of affection, even of a declaration of love, lighting up for us alone, with a secret and languid flame invisible to the chatelaine, an enamoured pupil in a countenance of ice.[4]

Whatever the inner elasticity and limits of what we have been calling the agon-model, however, it is important to note that Sōseki disposes of other, more melodramatic inner forms with which to preserve the tension of his dialogues. The most obvious is that of the mystery, the withholding, the expectation of the secret or the revelation (which Barthes called the "hermeneutic code" in *S/Z*). To begin with, he has himself withheld the matter of Tsuda's earlier lover, Kiyoko, so that allusions to this earlier secret (by Kobayashi and Mrs Yoshikawa) remain suitably dark and mysterious. This also means that the agon between interlocutors can take the additional form of a struggle for the secret, the avowal, the mystery, the denunciation, or the confession, as though the plot of the mystery story had been interiorized, and attention to its larger movements now adapted to the parrying of observation and response in a miniature reproduction of its form within the limits of the verbal interchange.

Finally, one must note the emergence of a kind of rationalization of the form, which comes closer to something like a philosophy of human relations (or of language itself). At these moments, conversation—while remaining agonistic—no longer seems driven by the will to win a struggle, but rather by the need to express and to verbalize: "Both O-Hide and Tsuda were primarily bothered by how best to solve the practical problem, and yet neither had the courage to probe verbally to the depth of the matter" (176). Something even more fundamental than the intimacy and hostility between brother and sister seems at stake in a verbal grappling of this kind: "And yet they were both already inextricably involved with each other. They could not really be satisfied unless they extracted, by means of conversation, a certain something from the other's heart" (183). This is not, I think, the Hegelian struggle for recognition, which on the German philosopher's view marks the very nature of interpersonality ("each consciousness desires the death of the other"). Rather, in Sōseki's world, some larger network of forces seems to hold these individual subjects in its grasp and to determine convulsive efforts by each of them that are not individually desired:[5]

> The three had fallen into a strange predicament. Since by force of circumstances they were linked together in a special relationship, it had become increasingly difficult for them to change the subject of the conversation; and of course they could not leave. Thus, while remaining where they were, they had to resolve their problem one way or another.
>
> And yet, seen objectively, it certainly was not an important one. In the eyes of anyone able to view their situation from a distance dispassionately, it could not but appear insignificant. They knew this very well without needing to have it brought to their attention. They were, however, forced to quarrel. Some controlling power extended its hand from an unfathomable, remote past, and manipulated them at will. (197)

Indeed, a final remark of the novelist would seem to project all this out into the metaphysical itself:

> From the context of the situation she was forced to adhere to that one point with the force of her entire being and to the limit of her powers of thought and judgment. It was her nature to do so. Unfortunately, however, the entirety of nature, which included her own, was greater than she. Extending far above and beyond her, it did not hesitate to cast an impartial light on the young couple and even to attempt to destroy her in her pitiable state. (283)

But from the formal standpoint that is ours here, the philosophical implications of such a passage, which suggest a worldview of Sōseki's own and a kind of vision of life to be rhetorically conveyed by the construction of the novel, are beyond our reach. We must say, on the one hand, that such philosophical views are of significance here only insofar as they ultimately enable the formal development we have been examining and, on the other hand, that a philosophical consideration of them in their own right would have to give place to a consideration of the period ideologies and the social context in which such a metaphysic could be entertained in the first place and which could alone suggest its ultimate personal and social functionality. In the dialectical analysis of literary form, then, such questions of philosophical content or message are either too much or too little; either they overshoot the formal mark by raising illicit questions about the meaning of life, or else they have not been sufficiently pursued to the point at which they become part of a more general social and historical inquiry into the period.

Surely this rather austere view of metaphysics is consistent with Sōseki's own narrative procedures. The latter are, for example, utterly resistant to questions of psychology, something worth stressing in a residual situation in which conventional views of modernism still see this last as an essentially subjectivistic movement, whose innovations lay in introspection and in the discovery of deeper psychological quirks or pathologies. In fact, however, what can be witnessed in all the moderns is rather a distancing from psychology in this sense and a reification of the feelings or emotions that names them in new ways and allows us to walk around them and to contemplate them like so many objects. Surely Lawrence's canonical attack on traditional characters and on the ego itself ("it is the inhuman will ... that fascinates me" [letter to Edward Garnett, June 5, 1914]) is also an attack on psychology and subjectivity in the name of objectifying modes of figuration. In Sōseki, also, feelings stand out sharply and vividly, but only because they are so rare as to constitute virtually meteorological events:

> The spectators were indeed strange, for they did not in the least complain about the long intermission during which there was nothing at all to do. Without showing a trace of their previous boredom, they were tranquilly absorbing desultory sensations in their vacant minds, and were being swept along frivolously with the passing moment. They appeared drunk from the very breath which they breathed on one another, and when they had recovered a bit from it, they would immediately turn their eyes and observe someone's face; they then would just as quickly discover therein a certain intoxicating substance. They appeared to be able to acclimatize themselves instantly to their companion's feelings. (84)

The fact that this peculiar intensity of feeling is associated with the theater and its spaces distances it still further and frames the affect, estranging it and suggesting that the very feelings that materialize so vividly against the blankness and impersonality of the narrative have some deeper constitutive relationship to the aesthetic and to representation itself.

Even irony itself can be seen as the intrusion of an outside into this seemingly sealed inside that is conversational impersonality, for irony can essentially be described as a brusque movement in which the inside becomes aware (in pride or shame, as Sartre might have said) that it has an outside in the first place. In this sense, O-Nobu's thoughts about Tsuda ("It suddenly occurred to O-Nobu that Tsuda was extremely egotistical") are as ironic as anything he might suddenly think about himself, since by way of their conversational intimacy his own "character" belongs to her as well. It is indeed as the discovery of something like a "character," an external being that other people see and that is radically distinct from that intimate consciousness that cannot be characterized in such characterological language, that irony is to be understood, as both a psychological and a social, or aesthetic, matter. The unfurling of a wave of modern irony over late nineteenth-century European culture—beginning with Flaubert and Baudelaire, and then becoming the explicit program of a host of novelists from Henry James to Gide, not to speak of the relativism of newer playwrights like Pirandello or of the point-of-view poets like Fernando Pessoa, with their multitudinous personae—is a sociological event, as well, and signals the porosity of the middle classes to their Others, whether within the nation state, in the form of hostile subaltern classes, or outside it, in the form of the colonized. That this drama should play itself out in the limited symbolic forms of the moral or ethical, where a single sovereign consciousness is suddenly made to feel its degradation, as archetypally in Kafka's "The Judgment," is an index of the complexity of the differentiations of modern culture and society and also a warning against the literal reading of aesthetic appearance. Nowhere are hermeneutic and interpretive operations, or, indeed, dialectical modes of comprehension, more urgently demanded by the content of the cultural text itself than in these symptomatic structures (which have been deformed and canonized in the academic versions of the modernist "classics"). Here, too, then, Sōseki displays a significant variant form of this trans-modern phenomenon, which we have learned mainly from Europe, but about which this remarkable non-European text can be expected to have new lessons.

I would be tempted to argue that the themes of "egotism" (sounded in the previous quote), along with those—dear to the critics—of moral degeneracy and regeneration are something like "motivations of the device": Paul de Man was using an essentially Russian Formalist logic when he argued that guilt and the content of the moral fall derive from the form of the confession, rather than the other way around (the peculiarities of the James–Lange theory of emotion also come to mind, in which the "feeling" follows on the physiological symptoms, anger deriving from bodily heat and tension, etc.). In this particular instance, however, since we do not possess the essentials of Tsuda's ironic unmasking and indictment (which the ending alone would have disclosed, although dark mutterings from Kobayashi and Mrs Yoshikawa enforce the sense that there will eventually be such a revelation), the form is, as in a laboratory experiment, disclosed to us in a virtually pure, self-bracketed way, mapping out an immense interior space about which we can only say, from within, that it has an outside, without knowing what that outside might be. This space is intolerable, but it is also what I am here characterizing as Utopian.

Before we reach that point, however, we must lay in place the final and most momentous effect of this conversational interiorization, which is the convulsive emergence, in the final section, of what I hesitate to call "nature," for fear that concept plays a different role in the equivalent Japanese ideological construction. Yet when Tsuda leaves the city, a radical shift in narrative can be observed, as well as existential experience, in which the provincial inn plays a fundamental role, not so much because of its relationship to the countryside and the peasantry, as within itself, where a virtual labyrinth is opened up. I have already commented on the distinctiveness of the urban map offered by *Meian*: a network of nodal points and characteristic inner spaces, rather than a set of relationships, or the geometry of avenues, or the profile of a city, with its staggered monuments and facades. When the content of the conversations has faded from the memory, the reader retains these spaces—the peculiar upper room in the clinic, the shabby wine shop in which Tsuda and Kobayashi discuss the lower classes, the bourgeois living quarters of more or less affluence and of the more prosperous protagonists, as well as the petty-bourgeois households of the less so: these are valuable experiences indeed, which it is not the least triumph of the novel to have conveyed and so economically and as it were laterally and in passing, without any commitment to a heavy-handed aesthetic of description or of place.

But now, in the inn, interior space as such becomes immensely involuted, its multitudinous articulations turned within, so that Tsuda wanders up and down its split levels and uneven staircases as in a maze, not omitting at a climactic moment to see someone unfamiliar coming toward him who is, in reality, his own self in the mirror (345). But this peculiar experience, which now makes up the adventures of the narrative at some length and provides a very different kind of reading experience than the dialogues (the rest of the novel) is perhaps itself only the exfoliation and outer skeleton, made thing-like and built into compartments and rooms and corridors, of the truth of the earlier narrative itself. Here, too, the sense of an outside, beyond which other people mysteriously and unfathomably exist, is the dominant. Voices from beyond walls or outside windows, and anxieties felt on rounding a corner or hearing a footstep, all make the experience of a labyrinthine inner house into the perpetual surmise of the existence of the Other, just beyond the partition. Yet this is now intensified dialectically to the point of taking on a new linguistic mode from the preceding form in which the intimation of the Other was conveyed: from intersubjectivity to place, from language to things and the visual, from speech to ambulation. It is an extraordinary shift, which then breaks off before any official meaning (presumably derivable from the now vanished and eternally silenced "authorial intention") becomes clear or gives a clue.

I call what happens in this work Utopian not because it is pleasant or gratifying. Indeed, the conversational element *Meian* gradually constructs —like so many of the ironies of the European modernist "point of view"— is likely to grow constricting for the reader, and even stifling, if only because an existence of unbroken subjectivities is established from which we never have any relief. To be sure, we never think much of Tsuda himself (although we may never be quite sure why not), but even the noblest subjectivity or conscious point of view would here at length become intolerable. Yet pure intersubjectivity—which is wrong and ideological as a philosophical "system," since it suppresses the facts of life of omnipresent alienation and reification—becomes Utopian again precisely to the degree to which it does more than imagine, but in fact symbolically constructs and projects, a world from which alienation and reification have been, however violently or by fiat, excluded. This is the approach to the human age, to a condition in which matter is transformed by human praxis, such that it can never be encountered directly, in its contingent and antihuman state: something here, to be sure, realized only ironically, as when money becomes "humanized" and "spiritualized" by passing into the conversations of people still bedeviled by it. Yet it is enough: the Utopian dimension of the literary or cultural work can never be separated from its ideological existence and its complicity within a production system necessarily based on misery and blood guilt. Yet something has been gained when, for an instant, like a mirage, it can be projected and glimpsed beyond that. The dimensions of the Utopian achievement, however, must then be measured by replacing the text in everything it thereby had to overcome and returning this remarkable narrative music to the social material that had to be refined and transformed into sound in order to compose it.

(*1990*)

Notes

1 Natsume Sōseki, *Meian* (Light and Darkness), trans. V.H. Viglielmo (London, 1971); hereafter cited in my text by page number only. Besides the extensive and valuable translator's introduction to this volume, I have consulted Kathryn Sparling, "*Meian*: Another Reading," *Harvard Journal of Asiatic Studies* 42 (June 1982): 139–76; and Masao Miyoshi's chapter on Sōseki in his *Accomplices of Silence: The Modern Japanese Novel* (Berkeley, 1974). In addition, I have been privileged to hear Oe Kenzaburo's interpretation of this unfinished text and have profited from the perceptive reactions and helpful advice of Ted Fowler.

2 See my *Fables of Aggression: Wyndham Lewis, the Modernist as Fascist* (Berkeley, 1979), pp. 50–61.

3 The reference is to Simmel's classic "Metropolis and Mental Life" (translated in *On Individuality and Social Forms* [Chicago, 1971]) in which the nervous specificity of big city life and the urban mentality is linked to money and its abstractions. In his rather different, and more socially critical, reading of the novel, Miyoshi underscores the theme of money, particularly in relationship to Mrs Yoshikawa (see Miyoshi, *Accomplices of Silence*, 90).

4 Marcel Proust, *The Guermantes Way*, trans. C. K. Scott-Moncrieff, in *Remembrance of Things Past*, vol. II (New York, 1983), pp. 136–7.

5 In a different kind of overtone or afterimage, this sense of a larger determination can also take a more personal form: "But O-Nobu was even more greatly concerned with another problem. She even went so far as to think that a plot had been hatched against her and was secretly progressing somewhere" (273). Even the mildest forms of paranoia are, however, also distorted projections of cognitive mapping and secular degradations of a religious conception of Providence.

SIX

16

Mallarmé Materialist

il n'existe d'ouvert à la recherche mentale que deux voies, en tout, où bifurque notre besoin, à savoir l'esthétique d'une part et aussi l'économie politique ...

two paths into which our needs divide are alone open to mental research, namely aesthetics, and also political economy...

The characterization should come as no surprise, from a writer[1] whose one (carefully structured) book of essays (*Divagations*) begins with class struggle and concludes with an ironic appeal to the Académie française to rescue the physical book from its financial crises. Those were however always, for Mallarmé, allegories of the deeper social crisis, the so-called "crise du Vers"—the breakup of the "national cadence" (362), the alexandrian or hexameter (now, like the flag, to be reserved only for the appropriate national holidays), and the emergence of *vers libre*, a more serious symptom of democratic and egalitarian individualism in French than what is called free verse in English.[2] Alongside "le Vers," however (which we will now and throughout translate as Poetry), there exists another more collective form in which Mallarmé took a keen lifelong interest, and this is theater-going or the concert. Such rituals are to be contrasted to the Book as such, and yet related to it, in that ultimate aesthetic of *le Livre*, to which we will come later on (nor do they exactly correspond to the dualism of verse and prose, both however equally subsumed under Poetry or *le Vers*, as we shall also see). At any rate, the "two ways" from which we take our point of departure also know some strange anticipatory convergence in alchemy, the "glorious, premature and louche precursor" of political economy (400), just as its magic procedures also mark a "parité secrète" with Poetry as such: "évoquer, dans une ombre exprès, l'objet tu, par des mots allusifs, jamais directs, se réduisant à du silence égal, comporte tentative proche de créer" (400), "evoking in deliberate obscurity a mute object, by way of allusive, never immediate words which are themselves reduced to an equivalent silence, involves an attempt close to creation as such" (and Mallarmé is proud of having insisted on the economic dimension "dans une mesure qui a outrepassé l'aptitude à en jouir consentie par mes contemporains," who don't want to hear about such extrinsic, extra-aesthetic matters). So many dualisms, however, which make up the "dialectique du Vers" (332), and which turn out to be somewhat more complicated than that "physical vibration of language in the air" to which traditional Marxist materialism has prided itself on assimilating literature.

More promising, perhaps, but seemingly equally apolitical, is the physical dynamic of the printed book as such, whose very deployment as a "spiritual instrument" is dependent on typography and the folding of the pages (the fan, let alone, in an older France, the knife—"comme le cuisinier égorgeur de volailles"—381). The insistence on print and printing, however, becomes sociological only with the emergence onto the formerly literary scene of the newspaper, great rival of Poetry, and the Thousand-and-one-Nights (376) of the contemporary republican capitalist world, in which Mallarmé is the first secular aesthetician and theorist.

> A desire my own historical period cannot deny is directed towards separating the dual condition of speech, raw or immediate here, there essential, with a view to attributing different functions to each.
>
> Storytelling, teaching, even describing, no problem there, even though for the exchange of human thoughts it might be sufficient wordlessly to pass from one hand to the other a simple coin, the elementary function of speech consists in servicing that universal *journalism* in which all genres of contemporary writing participate, excepting literature. (368)

So it is that "communication" (about which Mallarmé has even deeper metaphysical reservations, as we shall see) returns us to political economy, in that figure of the coin which like all Mallarmé's figures is scarcely figurative at all in the trivial sense (or perhaps one wants to rephrase the matter by insisting that figuration is for Mallarmé a far more essential process than the merely literal-communicative). Perhaps this is the moment to raise the other issue of our title, namely the question of idealism: a philosophical matter even more political than the social question of aestheticism (or "art-for-art's sake"), at least since Leninism. For Hegel, idealism was a matter of the theoretical: thus the primacy of mathematics is already a demonstration of the necessity of idealism, unless it simply proves that all genuine philosophy is idealist. In Mallarmé, it would be preferable to grasp idealism in terms of absence and of the latter's dialectical function: the diaphanous veils of symbolist suggestion are period pieces, the mannerisms of *belle-époque* bourgeois taste, which it is best to ignore or to reinterpret, just as it would be preferable to differentiate their ritual function from the high-Anglican connotations of T.S. Eliot's conservative version which has become canonical with us.

Mallarmé deserves a post-contemporary reinvention which the interesting opposition between the physical book ("reading I grasp as a practice of desperation," he once famously said—647) and the spectacles on offer in the *rentrée* may well provide. Nothing indeed is quite so Parisian as the role of the fall season in Mallarmé's thought, a role at first literally seasonal: the great spectacle of the death of Nature and the holocaust of the vegetal world—"that background, ever-renewed flame in which woods and sky are sacrificed" ... "a pyre, days evaporating in majestic suspense, lit by nature itself..." (402)—this season of nature's agony and death, which will have a deeper meaning later on, is characteristically socialized by the French, "social and pragmatic rather than aesthetically inclined" (390), and absorbed into the *rentrée* as such, where it seems to be the conductor's baton which lights the first fires of the dying season.

Here, then, we meet the other, more collective arts: theater, mime, ballet, and the symphony orchestra, rituals of the crowd rather than the individual, which predictably lead us back to religion and to T.S. Eliot's mass. But we must be careful and judicious in our handling of what Mallarmé calls "le vieux vice religieux" (397). That art today should somehow draw again on these archaic sources is a carefully qualified prescription: Wagner is himself criticized for relying on a naïve belief (and behind it a primitive nationalism): "a theater that can be called old-fashioned insofar as its appeal is direct and peremptory, ordering us to believe in the existence of character and adventure—and simply to believe and nothing else" (542). As for the Catholic Church and its "intrusion into future fêtes" (392), its immediacy is cancelled by the logic of history, namely, that "everything is effectively interrupted in history, there is little enough transfusion; or else the relationship consists in this that the two states will have existed separately, for any confrontation with spirit. The eternal, or whatever seems that way, is not rejuvenated but sinks into the caves and becomes stagnant: nothing will henceforth, nothing new, be born except from its own source and spring" (394). Mallarmé does not, in his view of history, even admit the explosive Benjaminian reopening of some new and reenergizing affinity with the past; yet he must hold passionately to a conviction that the New is possible and that the Novum is imminent, already prepared by the crisis of modernity and of "le Vers" itself.

This may be the place to quote his most famous pronouncement about the post-Wagnerian "artwork of the future" or work to come, something his own premature death prevented him from achieving, if indeed you think it could ever have been achieved. I quote it now, however, in order to reinterpret it in the light of the new context to be supplied. It is a confession to Verlaine, one of the few contemporaries to whom he will have been inclined to make this admission or avowal. He speaks first of his marriage and his onerous daily routine as a lycée professor of English:

> Today, twenty years later and despite the waste of so many hours, I believe, sadly, that I did the right thing. The reason is that apart from the juvenilia in prose and verse and the sequel that echoed it, published everywhere when some first issue of a new literary review appeared, I always dreamt of something else and attempted it, with the patience of an alchemist, ready to sacrifice vanity and even satisfaction itself, as they used to burn the very furniture and beams of the roof to feed the furnace of the Grand Oeuvre. What was it to be? Hard to say: a book, to be perfectly frank, a book in many volumes, a book which was to be a real book, premeditated and architectonic and not some collection of chance inspirations no matter how marvelous those might be ... I will go even further and say, the Book, le Livre, convinced as I am that there only exists one, unknowingly sought after by everyone who writes, even the Geniuses themselves. The orphic explanation of the Earth, which is the sole duty of the poet and the game of literature *par excellence*: for the very rhythm of the book, both impersonal and alive down to its very pagination, is conjoined with the equations of this dream, or Ode. (662–3)

Of this tantalizing vision, which prefigures all the modernist visions of the Book of the World, and of which only the floor plans survive and the depressingly arid mythic fragments,[3] we will here retain only one or two features. It is to be sure another version of the famous dictum, "everything in the world exists to end up in a book" (378); and also embodies the longing to overcome contingency (or chance, *le hazard*—366)—more forcefully expressed in Flaubert's famous letter about a book without content[4] (precisely because any conceivable form of content is also a mark of contingency). What may be less apparent, however, is the insistence on impersonality and the disappearance of the self or the poet ("disparition élocutoire du poète"—366[5]), and also on the multiplicity of creators all writing this same book at the same time, so that the Book—the "ideal" of poetic idealism—is itself in another way the public sphere or culture as such.

But now we must return to the image of collective ritual which persists in Mallarmé's imagination alongside this individual book (which will itself be evoked as a kind of ritual, officiated by a public reader, and recombined in a variety of possible combinations of its pages in order to generate multiple mythic narrative strings that might have been the envy of Lévi-Strauss himself). The mass, he tells us, has three main features: the space of the nave, the absent hero (not to be confused with the priestly officiant), and the organ, which, "relegated to the portals, expresses the outside, an enormous stuttering of shadows or their exclusion from the refuge, before they are poured down extasiated and pacified, thereby deepening it with the entire universe and lending the inhabitants a plenitude of pride and security" (396).

The various collective arts will now all express aspects of these fundamental features, of which ballet (or modern dance) is perhaps the most dramatic incarnation: "Floor, chandelier, obnubilation of tissues and liquefaction of mirrors in the order of the real, all the way to the excessive leaps of our form, gauzed around a pause, erect, of our virile stature, a Place is presented, a scene, the intensification before everyone's eyes of the spectacle of Self" (370). The irony ("virile" stature) lies in the male claim to presence, when it is the danseuse who more surely expresses the absence at the heart of this spectacle: "When the curtain rises on a gala soiree or any more local venue, there appears—like a snowflake driven in the furious storm but from where?—the dancer: the floorboards avoided by her leaps or hardened by her slippered tiptoes, acquires an undreamed of virginity, which the figure isolates and will construct and flower. The decor lies buried, latent in the orchestra, that treasure of imaginations; in order, by bursts, to emerge, according to the vision dispensed, here and there, by the officiant from idea, here and there, to the platform" (308). Loïe Fuller, he tells us, "institutes the place itself," "instituant un lieu" (309); and our poetic memory supplies the rhyme: "nothing takes place but the place"—"rien n'aura eu lieu que le Lieu," the final chord that terminates that great epic in a single long sentence which is *Un Coup de dés.*

For this is indeed for Mallarmé the lesson and the experience of spectacle as such: it is the production and the celebration of the empty place or what Kenneth Burke would have called the Scene as such, the space of the event that never happens, or did once happen, or is to come. Space of the present of time as well: "not an effective action, in the vicious yet sacred hymen of desire and fulfillment: here anticipating, there rememorating, in the future and the past, under the false appearance of a present" (310). One is reminded, in this evocation of pantomime, of the enigmatic feeling of Gertrude Stein that the time of theater is always "syncopated," always "either behind or ahead of the play at which you are looking."[6] It is the very existence of the present which is in doubt, as we shall see, and which it is the most august function of spectacle to convey, along with our own correlative nothingness as spectators.

For the non-existence of the hero is the other face of this primacy of scene and space: or perhaps, more dialectically, we should speak of his essential *absence.* But the poetic argument for this absence includes a number of levels of relevance: it says something, clearly, about the nature of the human subject, but also about the nature of literary characters and their narratives; about representation as such, as well, and that "elocutionary disappearance" of the poet of which we have already spoken; and finally about myth or its absence, about death as myth and the failure or shipwreck of the one great Mallarmean hero, notable only in his disappearance between the waves (in an image strongly recalling the catastrophe at the end of *Moby Dick*).

As far as metapsychology is concerned, Mallarmé clearly anticipates the great themes of existentialism and later on of Lacanianism: the split subject, the gap between consciousness and the self, Gombrowiczian "immaturity," the not-being at the very heart of our apparent being ... So it is that Mallarmé gently consoles an activist colleague—no doubt another self—for longing "to produce on many people a movement which retrospectively offers you the exciting feeling that you exist: something none of us can really be sure of in advance" (369).

But this conviction of the "néant" of the self and the person will clearly have the most immediate consequences for genres which stage people in the form of characters, for the various stage and novelistic realisms about which Mallarmé is prudent but watchful. The respect for Zola's innovations in both media is as apparent as the unshakable conviction that modernity poses impossible problems for the staging of characters (his interest in popular theater has other sources, as we shall see in a moment). The violence of naturalism is acceptable as the sign of the unrepresentability of this new impersonal life of drives and instincts;[7] and thereby rejoins the general absence of the Event on stage. As for the characters, however, modern individuality makes the older formulaic idioms very difficult indeed, in a situation in which "everyone has but one preoccupation day and night, replacing all the codes of the past, which is never to do or say anything which can be copied with exactitude in the theater" (343). Thereby verisimilitude is reduced to the cry: the passage from naturalism to expressionism will later on bear out this prognosis. We may then here detect a curious play of mirror reflections: the book of stories

> contradictorily avoids the weariness caused by the direct frequentation of other people at the same time that it multiplies the precautions to prevent our finding ourselves in face of or nearby the self as such: a double danger. The genre expressly combines disengagement and confusion, and by an adroit oscillation between promiscuity and the void, furnishes "verisimilitude." Such novels offer the remarkable artifice of presenting circumstances filled with fictive contemporaries which at the outer limit offer nothing foreign to the reader; but only a recourse to life in its uniformity. In other words, there exist nothing but people like us, even among beings that it is a matter, in our reading, of imagining. With the basic letters of the alphabet, whose subtle combinations always correspond to this or that attitude of Mystery, this cunning practice will certainly always evoke people: without that compensation that making them into characters or borrowing for them on the meditative properties of the mind they do not have the power to bother us. These annoying persons (to whom from time to time we will open the

> door of our dearest innermost hearts) from out of their opened books walk in, emerge, and ingratiate themselves; *and we suddenly understand that they are ourselves.* (374–5)

This unexpectedly Sartrean dénouement[8] nonetheless leaves the question of narrative in full doubt: a word I prefer to crisis in this case inasmuch as the latter—having to do with Poetry—implies for Mallarmé a solution evidently lacking here in the story form.

Except, perhaps, for his notion of myth, which in its archaic and future connotations is omnipresent: no doubt, the myth of the shipwreck, the catastrophic failure and mortal disappearance of the hero who was never present in the first place and never representable or realizable as such—this particular and unique Mallarmean myth offers the allegory of the disappearance of the poet behind his impersonal words and the non-personal dynamics of Language as such. It allows us to grasp the way in which allegory comes as the solution to the dilemma of content and the peril of contingency and chance. Modern individuality offers materials which are only that, only this particular here-and-now, the non-universalizable, the brute facts which can never offer a meaning or a law, a truth or any collective belief or conviction. Its representation can therefore only frustrate (and exasperate the Flaubertian dream of a literature "pure" of any content whatsoever) unless the mythic solution of allegory is embraced, which offers to make of this very and inevitable failure a dramatic success, in which the problem becomes its own solution and the secular finitude and meaninglessness of individual death is miraculously transformed into the figure of the effacement of the poet ("le Maître est allé au Styx" ...) behind the triumphant existence of Language itself.

But this is not the only value of the concept of myth in Mallarmé: its other meaning and the other source of its anxious fascination lies in the collectivity it evokes at the same time that the latter is itself defined by its longing for myth as such. Such is then the sense in which "ritual" must be used in this context: it can only mean the longing for a ritual which does not (yet) exist, just as Deleuze, in much the same spirit, taught us that "the people" was an energizing concept only when a people is yet to be forged and brought into existence.[9] Whence also the prudence of Mallarmé with these collective substantives—we have already witnessed a refusal of the term "society" which is matched only by the ironies of the word "nation." "La Foule"—his most customary term for the public and the collective—is neither the revolutionary mob nor the citizenry of the modern secular Republic: more like the crowd of strollers and flaneurs on the grands boulevards, a bourgeois public, in coats and hats, capable of the finery of concert halls as we shall see ("mainte aigrette luit divinatoire"—390): neither masses nor multitude, "the crowd, which begins to astonish us as some virgin element or ourselves, *par excellence* fulfills the function towards music's sonorities of the guardian of mystery! its own! it confronts the orchestra with its own rich silence, in which collective grandeur lies buried. This is the price, without our knowing it and in this context, of the mediocre exterior presently undergone and accepted by the individual" (390).

Leaving the concert aside for the moment, this fascination of the bourgeois and popular spectacles alike then makes up Mallarmé's status as a forerunner of present-day cultural studies. His was a cultural populism not in conflict but in deepest complicity with his literary elitism, and with that ideology of "art for art's sake" which Gautier only projected in the crudest dandyism and which Baudelaire more profoundly yet unconsciously symptomatized. For the very secret of the hermetic poet, or better still of the meaning of Poetry itself, *le Vers*, in the secular democratic age is somehow also to be found in what we might today call the Utopian impulses of the mass-cultural public, whether it knows it or not.

"Une époque sait, d'office, l'existence du Poéte" (377): "every age carries routinely within itself knowledge of the Poet and of the place of his existence". The poet is thus something like the absent center or axis around which the social order revolves, and that order must somehow obscurely grasp itself, however degraded it may be, through that inner sense of equilibrium, even where it has never heard of the poet or his activity in the first place. It is a familiar proto-political position, elaborated by Yeats and Pound each in their own fashion, and in another way by Stefan George, if not already by Schiller: and the vanishing of this fantasy altogether from postmodernity and its cultures defines the latter more reliably than almost any other feature. We can here identify the source of the avant-gardes as well, who sought to put it into practice in impatient and peremptory ways (and perhaps, even beyond that, of the modernist political avant-gardes as well). In this sad historical perspective, Mallarmé's fantasy of the Book as a collective ritual may be at best embarrassing; and his great social poetics—

> donner un sens plus pur aux mots de la tribu

—have become a commonplace or aesthetic stereotype of an earlier state of language as of society itself. But none of the "geniuses" or movements referred to above lived the tension between solitude and collectivity in quite so intense and productive, original a way as this one, and it is to that secret tension in music that we must now turn.

I have already suggested in passing that Mallarmé was no Wagnerian (in his own period's crazed sense of the word), even though references are everywhere, as befits a rather different practitioner of the "total art work of the future." That it is the Symphony (unidentified by composer) which is central to Mallarmé's experience the repeated evocations make clear enough, along with the striking periodization the poet attributes to music in general (La Musique, à sa date, est venue balayer cela [384]) where it is less a question of periodization (although a close friend of Manet, for example, Mallarmé never seems tempted to associate the revolution in poetic language with the much more dramatic contemporaneous one in oil painting), than of the tolerance for obscurity (music being non-verbal) as well as the possibilities of typographic innovation to follow the lead of music's rhythmic alternations and heterogeneities and even to imitate the play of intensities and silences in the blank spaces on the page. Thus, the mediation seems to remain that of collective reception, which by way of the institutionalization of the concert hall makes new and more abstract forms available to the public, and thus eventually to the practice of Verse itself.

The description of music then becomes the privileged place for the evocation of poetic form as such: "yesterday's well-formed melodies are succeeded by an infinity of broken ones that enrich the texture without such strongly marked cadences" (867). The variable openings, for example the "éclat triomphal" which gives way to unexpected echoes and aftereffects (384), or the initial massed doubts whose formlessness allows some "simple definitive splendor" to emerge with force (385). Already these multiple possibilities, which direct our attention to the variability of the sentence as form, encourage the otherwise arbitrary freedoms of the newly liberated "vers libre"; while the multiplicities of orchestral instrumentation also stimulate the poet's envy and intensify a search for the equivalent in the words themselves "by way of the clash of the inequalities their very multiplicity mobilizes; they light up with reciprocal reflexions like a virtual trail of fire on precious stones, thereby replacing the rhythms of the breath perceptible in an older lyric voice or the enthusiastic personal direction of the phrase" (366).

Yet paradoxically it is by way of the very weaknesses of the verbal when evaluated against their sonorous competition in orchestration that the superiority of Poetry as such can be defended: even a poetry whose modernist possibilities are to be found in a gradual effacement of content as such, a reduction of language's well-known "double inscription" (dear to the linguists) to the play of the signifier alone. Yet language's natural lack turns out to be the deeper meaning of the poet's vocation, as a famous passage makes clear:

> Languages being imperfect owing to their very multiplicity, the supreme one is lacking: if to think is to write without accessories, no whispering but the immortal word still tacit, that very diversity of idioms on earth prevents anyone from proferring words which otherwise, owing to their unique stamp or coinage, would materially turn out to be the truth. This prohibition expressly remains in force, namely that in nature (but as a stumbling block it merits but a passing smile) there is no reason to consider yourself God; yet just now, my mind turned towards the

> aesthetic finds itself regretting the swoon of discourse as it attempts to express objects by traits or touches that might correspond to their coloration or allure, brushstrokes which exist in the instrument of the voice, among the languages, and sometimes even in a single individual. Side by side with *ombre* and its opacity, *ténèbres* is scarcely dark; and what a disappointment to find the perverse conferral on *jour* and on *nuit* the contradictory timbres, obscure here and a clear one there. A longing for a term of brilliant splendor, or that it be extinguished, inversely; and as for simple luminous alternatives—*yet know but this, that otherwise Verse would not exist*: for it philosophically compensates that defect of natural languages, completely superior to them. (363–4)

The famous passage marks a first approach to the inner circle of Mallarmé's aesthetic convictions, which will however need to be probed from a variety of directions, according to these reciprocal glints and reflexions celebrated in the very play of words they seek to formalize. But this particular text fails to underscore the complementary value of closure in "le vers which from out of a number of vocables remakes a total word, a new word, foreign to the language and as though incantatory" (368). This closure will be, we shall see shortly, the closure of the sentence itself: Mallarmé's identification of the sentence as absolute form is as revolutionary and irrevocable as Joyce's sealing of the blooming, buzzing confusion of the world into a single temporal day.

But the musical analogy reminds us that such closure will need to contain powerful breaks and heterogeneities: "the supreme instrumental rifts, in the consequence of transitory spirals, burst forth on a plane of immanence more veridical, in their argumentation by way of light, than any reasoning ever conducted" (385). We here approach the notion of some deep underlying system of categories whose interplay defines a level of abstraction realer than the surface meanings themselves: thus, slowly, philosophical analogies begin to displace the musical ones.

Still, the nature of this "system" remains to be designated, which is to say, the mechanisms of its systematicity, the laws which govern its choices and its limits: it is an even more fundamental question for Mallarmé, and one whose answer will take us to the very heart of the matter:

> What is the pivot I grasp as maintaining the intelligibility of these contrasts? for some guarantee is needful—
>
> Syntax as such—
>
> Not its fresh and springlike phrasings alone, as those are included in conversation's facilities; although such artifice excels in compelling conviction. Indeed, one spoken idiom, French, retains its native elegance even in négligé; the past bears witness to this quality, which established itself from the outset as a fundamentally exquisite trait of our race: yet our literature transcends "genre," whether

> memoirs or correspondence. Yet the most abrupt and skyward wing-beats will also gaze across at each other: and whoever controls them will perceive an extraordinary appropriation of limpid structure by the most primitive lightning bolts of logic. The seeming stuttering of the sentence, repressed in the service of subordinate clauses, multiplies, concentrates itself and rises up in some higher equilibrium, with the foreseeable rocking to and fro of inversions. (385–6)

The word itself now verifies our allusion to logic, which we may more openly identify with Mallarmé's master Hegel, whose self-generating categories bear no little resemblance to the internal "dialectique du Vers" (332), with its late-nineteenth-century version of Hegel's more Spinozan definition of philosophy as the demonstration of necessity (Adorno identified an analogous demonstration at work in Beethoven and in the symphony form). The difference is that in the years of the triumph of the bourgeois revolution this process was sealed by the attempt to include everything: in its late and disabused decadence, it is by leaving out and by the gaps and blanks that the trick is turned:

> To apply one's own ingenuity to the blank space which variously inaugurates the page, forgetful even of its title that talks too loud: and when chance, overcome word by word and one at a time, is aligned with the slightest break or disseminated fissure, the blank space, hitherto gratuitous, now marked by certainty, returns, to convince us that nothing exists beyond itself and to authenticate silence as such. (387)

Still, the laborious conquest of "le hasard" in each individual word at a time offers some heroic echo of Hegel's "labor and suffering of the negative."

In terms of metaphysics, what is now to be underscored is the relationality of all this, the stress not so much on the individual object—the old-fashioned Aristotelian substance, with its solid presence and its unambiguous name, lending itself candidly and confidently to representation—as rather the multiplicity of overdetermined relationships into which the name of the object enters not merely with all the other words of its language but with all its internal connotations as well, the former thing now dissolving into a complex process which must somehow be modelled as such in all its heterogeneities and reversals, and yet ultimately brought to its own closure as though biting its own tail. Closure, then, and relationality make up this poetic totality which is also a total name as well as a fundamental absence—the famous rose: "I say: a flower! and beyond the oblivion to which my voice relegates every real contour, as something other than the calyx known from the here-and-now, there musically rises, suave, a pure idea, the absent from all bouquets" (368). It can be the last glowing flower of a world vanishing into nothingness; but in our present context it is rather the apparatus that produces this ephemeral Platonic image, hallucinogenic among the smudged and fading black-and-white surfaces that must be emphasized.

> Surgi de la croupe et du bond
> D'une verrerie éphémère
> Sans fleurir la veillée amère
> Le col ignoré s'interrompt. (74)

> Reared from rump and jump of a glass bauble, the hour no sweeter by a flower, the unknown neck breaks off.[10]

Language is precisely this empty vase whose graceful dramatically interrupted opening onto empty space traces and prolongs the absent flower it so eloquently announces: "une rose dans les ténèbres." Like the empty room that produces its absent Master, or the empty stage that produces the hero himself, even with his own actors and counterfeiters (Hamlet: "le seigneur latent qui ne peut devenir"—300), a whole battery of mechanisms, a whole spiritual instrumentation, is here deployed, in its national imperfections and idiosyncrasies, to release the central ritual mystery, which as what Mallarmé is pleased to call *l'Idée* or *l'idéal* is at one and the same time not real and not nothing either. For "we know, prisoners of an absolute formula, that there is nothing but what there is … Nature has already taken place, it is not to be added to …" (647). Yet "in view of some superior attraction as powerful as the void, we do have the right, finding it in ourselves in the boredom of things when they have established their solidity and preponderance, passionately to detach and appropriate them, and also to endow them with splendor, through empty space, in wilful and solitary festivals" (647). If you wish for a metaphysics to complete this poetics, then, it will be the atheist splendor of life in the dead space of an inanimate and mechanical universe:

> L'espace a soi pareil qu'il s'accroisse ou se nie
> Roule dans cet ennui des feux vils pour témoins
> Que s'est d'un astre en fête allumé le génie. (67)

> Space like itself increasing or forswearing spins in that apathy base fires to witness the Genius of a festive star is flaring.[11]

This mortal human idealism is the gesture of defiance in a meaningless Newtonian system; but if one wants something a little less heroic (Mallarmé is always ironically aware of the gap between these grand and mythic heroic gestures and the sober bourgeois uniform, to which "à tel égard et de ce côté," a tipping of the hat is respectfully, if ironically required: "with all correctnesss to raise, by way of greeting—the thing to do, however faintly, in favor of whatever is the so black egalitarian ceiling fallen on all the bald spots where it now dwells"—416)—if more modesty is appropriate, then it may well be this: "the equal of creation: the notion of an object slipping away from us and now lacking" (647).

This "simplification" of the world into two registers—that higher dialectic of failure and the lower ban on immediacy—which preempts all direct attempts on objects such as the sea ("dont mieux vaudrait se taire"—403) or "l'horreur de la forêt, ou le tonnerre muet épars au feuillage" (365) unless it is a matter of the real wood that goes into making paper; or unless—even more interesting—the refusal of the photographic moves directly towards the cinema[12] (only too nascent at the very moment of Mallarmé's premature death)—this dual simplification has not yet touched upon an opposition which must be central for us here, inasmuch as so much of the preceding essay not only speaks in Mallarmé's own words, but primarily in those of his prose as well. Are there then another "two ways," is there another more fundamental dualism we have failed to respect, even as the modernity of *vers libre* begins to efface the boundary between poetry and prose?

It's by no means clear: "at first, in the reign of language, it had to be tuned to its origin in order for an august meaning to appear: in Verse itself, in the line, dispensing and ordering the play of pages, master of the book as such. Its integrality visibly appears in the margins and the blanks: or else it dissimulates itself—and then you can call it Prose—but this is still Poetry if there remains within it some secret pursuit of music without the reserves of Discourse" (375). I think that "origin" here stands for genre and its identification, which necessarily precedes the reading operation and enables it, orienting it properly, in a situation which is slowly dissolved today ("la Musique est venue balayer cela"—384), leaving the pure play of relationalities behind it in both of the former types of discourse.

What we can assert and establish is that for Mallarmé poetry and prose—both of them "obscure" in both the Mallarmean and the journalistic sense, where obscurity is musicality, and where even the interviewee must detain his impatient journalistic colleague with the pitiful plea, "Attendez, par pudeur, que j'y verse, du moins, un peu d'obscurité!"—that the two are at the very least obscure in very different ways, which define them.

Both involve a more basic linguistic situation, which is that of the ellipse and which can be characterized as the omission of some central phenomenon of which only bits and pieces, aspects, symptoms, are given, and which then demands reconstruction. It would be desirable to ground this situation in the social reality of the period itself and the state of its language, for it seems more plausible to trace the suspicion of immediacy and the critique of immediacy in a reaction to historical developments rather than to grasp them as some otherwise inexplicable (or timeless) ethical imperative. What "the age demanded," however, must itself be reconstructed from Mallarmé's own diagnoses (which we will examine in conclusion) rather than in general impression and conjecture.

We thus confront a linguistic content which requires new representational strategies and therefore new reading processes. It is indeed to these that the word "reconstruction," which I have repeatedly used here, corresponds: it conveys a kind of elliptical constructivism, or, to use a contemporary term, an interactive situation, in which the reader reassembles a new totality on the basis of hints and directions, and out of the isolated parts, "significantly" positioned and on tactical offer from the poet. We must be careful, however, not to reach for the old romantic catch-all of the "fragment" in this context, for these parts are not really given as fragments: they are so many isolated objects, floating in a void and without background or context. The camera panning around the empty salon in the *ptyx* sonnet, for example, merely registers a collection of knickknacks and Victorian curiosities—the statue in the form of a lamp, the ashes in their tray, the credenzas, the missing ptyx (presumably a vial of some kind), the window and the windowframe, glints of a constellation, the mirror in which the statue of the nude is reflected.

Ses purs ongles très haut dédiant leur onyx,
L'Angoisse, ce minuit, soutient, lampadophore,
Maint rêve vespéral brûlé par le Phénix
Que ne recueille pas de cinéraire amphore.

Sur les crédences, au salon vide: nul ptyx,
Aboli bibelot d'inanité sonore,
(Car le Maître est allé puiser des pleurs au Styx
Avec ce seul objet dont le Néant s'honore).

Mais proche la croisée au nord vacante, un or
Agonise selon peut-être le décor
Des licornes ruant du feu contre une nixe,

Elle, défunte nue en le miroir, encor
Que, dans l'oubli fermé par le cadre, se fixe
De scintillations sitôt le septuor.

Her pure nails raised high dedicating their onyx, Anguish, this midnight, sustains, torch-bearing, many an evening dream burned by the Phoenix that no cinerary amphora gathers.

On the sideboards, in the empty parlour: no ptyx, abolished trinkets of sonorous vacuity (for the Master has gone to draw tears from the Styx with this sole object with which the Void honours itself).

> But near the empty north window, a golden light is dying in accordance perhaps with the scene of unicorns lashing fire against a water nymph.
>
> She, dead and naked in the mirror, and yet in the oblivion enclosed by the frame, is fixed instantaneously the septet of scintillations.[13]

One cannot say that these odds and ends are parts or fragments of the room, which is itself, although empty, named and identified only by its inhabitant, the Master, who is not or no longer there, if he ever has been. Indeed, we leave the room (and the sonnet) behind us as soon as the glints in the window are identified as the form of the Big Dipper beyond it in the sky (and the Big Dipper is itself made up of separate objects, which are certainly not fragments and perhaps not even "parts" in any meaningful organic sense). The complete object—the named constellation—reflects the closure of the "total" new word of the poem which ends as soon as its allegory becomes visible.

This inorganic collection of distinct objects is by no means uncharacteristic of the phenomenological world of Mallarmean verse: the single vase, the single rose, the curtain, the lone window, all of which return upon the very phenomenological notion of a "world" to call it into question as some pre-existing totality.

The totality is rather a constructed one, of the poem, or better still, the sentence itself, which is the most powerful reunifier of these individual objects, otherwise a random selection of kitsch from a flea-market. Indeed, so strong is the power of the sentence and the attention it compels to the momentum and inevitability of its own unifying force that we fail in the process to notice the heterogeneity of its contents or the arbitrariness with which they are placed in relationship. It would be tempting to describe the whole as a kind of collage, in which so many separate items (a term that might be more appropriate here than that of object, and certainly more satisfactory than the semiotic vocabulary of signs and the like) float side by side in a void; save that the collage generally works with bits and pieces and by way of at least an appearance of visual simultaneity (another reason, perhaps, why Mallarmé seems to evade the languages of painting in the construction of his aesthetic). "Items," however, tend to suggest the list, that other great form of nineteenth-century poetic language: but Whitman's great enumerations, better theorized by Deleuzian "conjunctive synthesis" (and ... and ... and ...),[14] have an energy that opens up the work, as well as an interminability that celebrates infinite possibilities of further names and their objects (the finiteness of these small collections is comparable, rather, to Emily Dickinson, who also traffics in isolated items rather than whole groups):

Oui, dans une île que l'air charge
De vue et non de visions
Toute fleur s'étalait plus large
Sans que nous en devisions.

Telles, immenses, que chacune
Ordinairement se para
D'un lucide contour, lacune,
Qui des jardins la sépara.
(from "Prose pour des Esseintes" [56])

Yes, on an island charged by air not with visions but with sight every flower showed off, freer though we never spoke of it.

Such, immense, that every one usually adorned itself with a lucid edge, lacuna which from the gardens set it off.[15]

But it is equally important to sense the imperfections of such reunifications: to entrust this preeminently active process to reading—that "pratique désesperée"—is to leave open the possibility that it may fail to be fulfilled or completed, that the gaps and breaks between the items will show, that relationality and its resultant totalization will remain a dead letter. Indeed, totality must remain in at least some faint sense a dead letter, in order for the poem to stand as a collection of signals to be unified in the first place. Reading must subsist on this razor's edge between the signals and their activation: the poem must fail at the same time that it succeeds and must always offer itself as a heterogeneity on the point of becoming a single total word, a room identified as one only when we are on the point of leaving it.

What are then the operators of this strange internally contradictory process? A fresh glance at the sonnet in question makes them glaringly visible: in the octave we have to do with the famous "incidentes" or dependent clauses, and even here the appositions for the most part replace the missing relative pronouns. "La Syntaxe"! here we find syntactical relationships operating at the highest form of rarefaction and abstraction, yet powerful enough to keep the clauses together like an invisible force of gravity. In the sestet, then, conjunctions seem to take over this task: "encor que", while attempting to remain as inconspicuous as possible (that is to say, to remain relatively undetected as a familiar conjunction), begins to betray the logic of sheer juxtaposition in its most visible nullity—here is one thing, the reflexion, but here is another one alongside it; and the hint of a reservation, an "although", betrays syntax working on empty and is utterly unmotivated, if not even to say meaningless—as syntax is itself meaningless without content.

But now we can see that conjunction is but the weaker form of a different part of speech, the preposition as such, for which it is a mere stand-in.

"Proche" is to be sure passed over as rapidly as possible: its literal meaning of spatial juxtaposition tends to efface its figurative operation as what juxtaposes and ranges things side by side. At length, then, we come to the Mallarmean part of speech *par excellence*, supreme preposition and operator of his most characteristic poetic and linguistic effects, namely the strange word "selon," which virtually designates the purest form of relationality without any content whatsoever. If it is taken to mean "according to," then it is clear that in this verse line that meaning can scarcely be honored, it is not even a promissory note, its very signal designates no operation to be carried out, like undecipherable messages from outer space.

It would be tempting to make an inventory of these empty Mallarmean prepositions,[16] of which "avec" is another characteristic though less striking example, along with "parmi," and even some unidentifiable uses of "à." These are the instruments of the Mallarmean sentence, which it might now be better to call his false syntax, his fictive or imitation sentences, which (like Ashbery's versions today) unfold, in a perfectly grammatical way and offer the syntactical part of the mind a set of operations which has no other identifiable motivation and which thus unexpectedly simply designates itself as pure operation, as pure syntactical process to be completed.

I note a final result of this process before moving on: it is the effect of such a pastiche of syntax on the negative, which is, of all grammatical functions, the most unsettled by this mirage of the sentence, whose phrases and clauses float alongside each other in such a way as to weaken decisive judgement in the logical sense. This is all the more pronounced in French whose act of negation generally comes in two parts, which open and close the negative judgement firmly—the annunciatory "ne" and the concluding "pas" (or "guère" or "point" or "que," or whatever other qualification, attenuation or reinforcement, seems to be called for). This language also has a free-standing "ne" (termed the pleonastic "ne") which is called for by certain constructions, where it remains unclear whether it is not purely formal (having no negative results) or simply a negational shorthand. Mallarmé's language multiplies these indeterminable negative particles in such a way as to leave us uncertain as to their force and immediate meaning—something more serious in prose, which is evidently supposed to make its decision one way or another, than in verse, which can clearly support the latter's indefinite suspension. Verse in general, but in particular Mallarmé's, is more concerned with phanopeia, with the projection of the poetic idea or image as such, than with its ontological affirmation or denial: and in any case, Mallarmean absence is precisely this state in which negation is affirmed and denied all at once, and in which the ambiguity of the "ne," far from signaling indecisiveness, is a fundamental and active dimension of the poetic process. This weakened and ambiguated negation then further underscores the kinship between Mallarmé's aesthetics and the Hegelian dialectic, which does not so much call the negative function or act of judgement into question, as it seeks to look deeply into the very heart of negation and to find the object affirmed there by virtue of its very denial. The dialectic then expresses this process in its content, as that very identity of success and failure that has already been touched on, and which is quite the opposite of defeatism or pessimism. Its effect is indeed, given the failure inevitably inscribed in mortality, finitude, time, and the very extinction of the species, to convert this inevitability into a new kind of dialectical success or victory which has nothing of the smugness and individualistic egoism of the traditional anthropomorphic or ethical kind. There is a kinship here with Spinozan stoicism as well which cannot be explored here: but it is certain that Mallarmean negation also expresses something of this Hegelian spirit, in which we cannot tell whether a thing is being affirmed or denied and take up a place at the very vanishing point of meaning as such, which the poet dramatizes as the empty stage, or else the scene which breathlessly awaits its Event to come.

Yet, as has been observed in passing, the transfer of this system to prose brings some new problems with it, inasmuch as these parts of speech, which operate poetic juxtaposition, thereby effectuating the poetic totality, the prepositions and conjunctions, the negations themselves—are called upon in prose to function more unequivocally. The solution or method, for Mallarmean prose, will then be simply to leave them out: and to substitute typographical blanks, the spacing between what used to be paragraphs, or simply the comma itself. For the comma, in this often exasperatingly mannered discourse, is no longer the pause for breathing that would inscribe the human reading subject back into the text: it is the imperative to construct the larger text in the first place and calls for a more forceful cognitive projection than the poetry, even though the operation is different more in degree than in kind (being after all always self-descriptive).

These are features which can also be brought out by some remarks on the problems such structure poses for translation, which thus merit a brief "divagation." The reader will already have understood that the present essay is less an exposition than a kind of *florilège* and anthology of the choicest quotations from the prose, to be made available in both languages. Still, the translations remain an unhappy mixture of literality and explanation which can hopefully offer the occasion for grasping Mallarmé's poetics insofar as it is found at the site of the bifurcation between poetry and prose. I will only say now that the awkwardness of an English version can be explained: it is not worth wasting time over the notion of the "untranslatable" unless it can lead somewhere productive. First of all, Benjamin's idea (borrowed from the forgotten Rudolf Pannwitz), that a translation should be non-fluent in order to convey the difference of the other language and its capacities,[17] is less relevant here, where the French is already deliberately so deformed and idiosyncratic: only if the deformations are themselves somehow profoundly French would their translation as such be capable of conveying the distinctiveness of the French language.

Still, there are two kinds of deformations at work in Mallarmé's prose, which account for the alternating literality and explanation indicated above. On the one hand, he has attempted to break ordinary French syntax down into a series of isolated substantives, separated by the numerous commas any inspection of the original will reveal. Insofar as spoken French is distinguished from the high or written form by a frequent use of appositives[18] this kind of separation remains true to the "genius of the language" and may be considered to be characteristic, but also very difficult to render in English: yet its ultimate effect—and its secret intentionality—is to isolate each element of the sentence—not so much to destroy the syntax so much as to make it visible in its absence, by way of the blank spaces between the words or substantives—a typographical figure dear to Mallarmé and embodied in *Un coup de dés*. Commas are then here the minor form of the peculiar and very ostentatious paragraph breaks in these essays; and my literality tries to express the isolation of the individual words, most often cognates of the English. These islands, then, are from time to time related by the syntax of a recognizable and flowing sentence: and the relationship to music is also dramatized by this alternation between the vertical and the horizontal, the effects of great chords and the more recognizable thematic developments: it will be seen that Mallarmé greatly valued this asymmetry and rhythmic heterogeneity which is, however, meant to incite to the reconstruction of relationship and Syntax as such.

Yet every so often, within this interplay, there opens up a parenthetical phrase of a different type: more concentrated and elliptic, and often colloquial in a mannered sense, that is to say, in the annoying insertion of the spoken into the written, or the conversational into the abstract-conceptual (annoying because it will later on designate the intellectual and his self-defense). These conversational bits I have found it necessary to replace with extended paraphrases, meant to explain the phrased allusion and inevitably to interpret it for the puzzled reader. Thus, if my literality provokes the hostile reaction so often aroused in readers who know enough of the French to take the English cognates as a sign of unimaginative and pedestrian misreading, the interpretive interpolations can also stimulate the dissent of readers ingenious enough to prefer their own commentary. Yet insofar as these are the twin reefs and dangers of translation in general—overliterality and excessive and arbitrary paraphrase—the versions offered here risk pleasing no one, as any proper translation should do (a Mallarmean negative which can be disambiguated by explaining it as the proposition that "no proper translation should please").

Now that we have at least pulled back into our own time in order to look at all this from the vantage point of another language (that language Mallarmé taught in high school, and that he wrote a grammar for, about which it would be worth speculating the role it played as a kind of internal foreign body in his own speech,[19] as Latin did for Flaubert, French for Henry James, and the dead sacred languages of the Middle East in their religious rituals), it will be a matter of interest, and not merely curiosity, to ask how characteristic this unique experience of language was for the period: later on, to be sure, there were "disciples," those who frequented his "mardis"; there were certainly also peers whom he respected, like Villiers or Verlaine (and the others he memorialized, but who have so little in common with him): forebears, as well, above all Poe and Baudelaire. None of which—not even his poetic "tombeaux" or his prose portraits—tells us much about aesthetic ideology, which is in this context chiefly discussed in terms of verse form, and its modifications.

It is therefore from his views of language as such that we must work our way back to Mallarmé's relationship to other people, and then to these other people in particular—the poets—and finally to "la Foule" or the larger collectivity, Republic, public, readers of newspapers and of newspaper interviews, etc., etc. But we know that the communicational function of Mallarmé is easily identified: it is silence, at least when it comes to speech: placing a coin in the hand of the other, token of meaning and exchange,—"encor qu'à chacun suffirait peut-être pour échanger la pensée humaine, de prendre ou de mettre dans la main d'autrui en silence une pièce de monnaie" (368). The suggestions are multiple, particularly when we begin with Mallarmé's diatribes about the various contemporary financial scandals, and his dismissal of the nullity of gold—"élire un dieu n'est pas pour le confiner à l'ombre des coffres en fer et des poches" (398) ... "en raison du défault de la monnaie à briller abstraitement ... d'amonceler la clarté radieuse avec des mots qu'il profère [le poète] comme ceux de Vérité et de Beauté" (399) ... Language, and in particular poetic language, is thus in competition with this other substance with which in archaic times its destinies were entwined (in alchemy and the *Grand Oeuvre*); the economic reference is thus maintained throughout, now on the level of high finance and business (Zola's *L'Argent*) and of scandals transmitted through poetry's other competitor, the daily newspaper.

It should also be noted that the silence to which communication is likened is not at all the same as the silence that follows the sentence or the symphony, the "total word," which in fact "authenticates" such silence of a different sort, in which chance has been reduced word by word and sound by sound: this new silence is henceforth a silence of necessity, reclaimed from contingency, an essential blank space rather than an accidental one—yet, it would seem, one from which communication and meaning have been triumphantly erased.

Such a conception bodes ill for individual contacts: Mallarmé allows a fitful contact between the poetic generations, which is more of a ritual or a courtesy than an exchange of ideas, techniques or recipes: "une approche contient l'hommage; et la sécurité de hanter même région naît de mots évasifs dans une promenade à pas égal que persiste, entre ans différents, l'abord" (406).

But there is really no talking about art: the poet would do best to follow "une règle, souveraine—qu'on ne doit s'attarder même à l'eternel plus que l'occasion d'y puiser" (406). You can send your poems to your contemporaries, but it is by way of offering "sa carte de visite, stances ou sonnet, pour n'être point lapidé d'eux, s'ils le soupçonnaient de savoir qu'ils n'ont pas lieu" (664). The arrogance is ironic only, inasmuch as we have seen how the poet himself, in the very act of "ceding the initiative" to his words, disappears into a nothing which in any case corresponds to the universal not-being of human beings and their consciousness. In that case, what is there to talk about? Mallarmé's views here very much concur with Deleuze's scandalous remarks about the impossibility of communication and the absurdity of conversation as a form in the first place.[20]

It is ultimately the stupidity of content, the stupidity of ideas and opinions and of the very fact of expressing them, that leads to the final disabused and stoic position on conversation in the first place:

> I attribute to the awareness of this case, in a time when two people have perhaps never, despite the grimaces suggesting the act of speaking to each other, exactly discussed the same object for even a few words at a time—I attribute to this awareness the restriction that keeps interlocutors from really revealing anything and keeps them vigilant; but persuades them—mutual ruse, bravado, relic of outmoded and generous baroque intellectual battles or in conformity with a social world for which letters and literature are the ultimate refinement—to withdraw their thought as much as they reveal it, first of all and second, obstinately to understand something other than what has been meant—in order to retain their own integrity when a cordial need entices them into a meeting with each other. (408–9)

The social is not to be found there, in these accidental encounters between individuals who are so many hollow men: the social totality does not lie in the individual nor even in his chance encounters, but in the social order as a whole whose opposite number is the poem or *Grand Oeuvre* as a total word. One may alternately see the one as the expression of the other ("il s'agit que vos pensées exigent du sol un simulacre"—654—for example, which suggests that the relationality of the state should itself imitate that of the poem), but they are in every case, materialist or idealist, whichever one comes first, decidedly allegories of each other:

> Serious damage has been done to terrestrial association down through the centuries by failing to make citizens understand that this brutal mirage of the *cité* or the polis, its governments, its legal system, is in fact the mere emblem, or in our own case what cemeteries are to the paradise they evaporate: earthworks, almost not vile. Tolls and elections, everything which seems to sum up the reference—these down here are not really where the formalities of the popular cult take place as representatives of the Law housed in all its transparency, nudity and miracle. Dig into these substructures when obscurity offends our perspective on them, no better still: align them with lanterns, to mark their outlines: for your thoughts require a simulacrum from the soil itself. (653–4)

This is then the sense in which he quietly repeats in a footnote the fundamental conviction ("tout se résume dans l'Esthetique et L'Économie politique"—656) at the same time that he breaks his lecture off (it is the famous public lecture at Oxford) with the feeling that he may already have said too much, and that either the content of this allegorical lesson or its very lack of obscurity have been too forthright, too close for comfort.

But it will be more appropriate to close with the grand meditation on contemporaneity, which more even than his poetics or his projects, and more than his biographical relations to others as well as his intellectual and artistic life in the Paris of his day, articulates the situation of the intellectual most forcefully and pertinently, replacing Mallarmé in his own experience of history in such a way that that and himself again become available to us:

> Externalized as the very cry of space itself, the traveller perceives the whistle's distress. "Doubtless," he convinces himself, "we are passing through a tunnel—the age itself—the last long stretch beneath the city before the all-powerful station of the virginal central palace that crowns it." The underground, oh impatient one! will last as long as your meditative preparation of the tall glass tower subjected to Justice's flight.
>
> Suicide or abstention, doing nothing at all, why?—Uniquely in the history of the world, because of an event I will explain there is no Present, no—the present does not exist ... in the absence of a collective self-affirmation, in the absence—of everything. Poorly informed he who claims to be his own contemporary, a deserter and a usurper of equal impudence, when this or that past breaks off and the future is late in coming, or the two are perplexedly recombined with a view towards masking the gap between them. Except for the newspapers' page one whose mission lies in confessing their belief in the daily nothingness, inexpert as they are if the scourge measures its period according to a fragment of the century, important or not." (371–2)

(*1963–2006*)

Notes

1 I here mainly draw on the 1895 essays Mallarmé first entitled "Variations sur un sujet," and later (partially) collected in the volume called *Divagations* (1897). Page numbers in the text reference the old one-volume Pleiade *Œuvres complètes*, ed. H. Mondor and G. Jean-Aubry (Paris, 1945). The texts themselves are reproduced after these notes, the numeral in parentheses designating the page of their appearance in the present essay, the second their place in the 1945 French edition (or providing their translation, as the case may be).

2 "Le remarquable est que, pour la première fois, au cours de l'histoire littéraire d'aucun peuple, concurremment aux grandes orgues générales et séculaires, où s'exalte, d'après un latent clavier, l'orthodoxie, quiconque avec son jeu et son ouïe individuels se peut composer un instrument, dès qu'il souffle, le frôle ou frappe avec science: en user à part et le dédier aussi à la Langue." (363)

3 See Jacques Scherer, *Le "Livre" de Mallarmé* (Paris, 1957). More fragments are collected in the new two-volume Mallarmé edition (Paris, 2003).

4 See note 7 to the Introduction, above.

5 And see also pp. 370, 372.

6 Gertrude Stein, *Lectures in America* (Boston, 1985), p. 93; and see also Essay 17.

7 Gilles Deleuze, *Cinéma I* (Paris, 1983), pp. 173ff. And also Mallarmé's interesting note on *La Curée* (op. cit., p. 321).

8 "The ideal in Brecht's drama would be for the audience to be like a team of ethnographers suddenly coming across a savage tribe and, after they approached them, finding out they were in fact exactly like themselves." Jean-Paul Sartre, *Sartre on Theater* (New York, 1976), p. 74.

9 Gilles Deleuze, *Cinéma II* (Paris, 1985), pp. 281–3.

10 Mallarmé, *The Poems*, trans. Keith Bosley (Harmondsworth, 1977), p. 185.

11 Ibid., p. 167.

12 "Si vous remplacez la photographie, que n'allez-vous droit au cinématographe, dont le déroulement remplacera, images et texte, maint volume, avantageusement" (878).

13 Translation by William Rees, ed., in *Penguin Book of French Poetry* (London, 1990), p. 212.

14 Gilles Deleuze and Felix Guattari, *L'Anti-Œdipe* (Paris, 1972) pp. 80ff.

15 Mallarmé, *Selected Poems*, trans. C.F. MacIntyre (Berkeley, 1957), p. 63.

16 In fact, Jacques Scherer has already done so, in *L'Expression littéraire dans l'œuvre de Mallarmé* (Paris, 1947).

17 Walter Benjamin, "The Task of the Translator", in *Illuminations* (New York, 1969), pp. 69–82.

18 The first sentence of Raymond Queneau's *Dimanche de la vie* offers a virtual textbook illustration: "Il ne se doutait pas que chaque fois qu'il passait devant sa boutique, elle le regardait, la commerçante, le soldat Bru." (Paris, 1952), p. 15.

19 V.N. Voloshinov (Bakhtin), *Marxism and the Philosophy of Language*, (New York, 1973).

20 Deleuze, *Cinéma II*, p. 299.

The Texts:

(313) 400: le glorieux, hâtif et trouble précurseur …

(314) 368: Un désir indéniable à mon temps est de séparer comme en vue d'attributions différentes le double état de la parole, brut ou immédiat ici, là essentiel.

Narrer, enseigner, même décrire, cela va et encore qu'à chacun suffirait peut-être pour échanger la pensée humaine, de prendre ou de mettre dans la main d'autrui en silence une pièce de monnaie, l'emploi élémentaire du discours dessert l'universel *reportage* dont, la littérature exceptée, participe tout entre les genres d'écrits contemporains.

(315) 647: strictement j'envisage … la lecture comme une pratique désespérée.

(315) 402: son bûcher, les jours évaporés en majestueux suspens, elle l'allume … l'arrière mais renaissante flamme, où se sacrifient les bosquets et les cieux …

(315) 542: un théâtre, le seul qu'on peut appeler caduc, tant la Fiction en est fabriquée d'un élément grossier: puisqu'elle s'impose à même et tout d'un coup, commandant de croire à l'existence du personnage et de l'aventure de croire, simplement, rien de plus …

(315) 394: Tout s'interrompt, effectif, dans l'histoire, peu de transfusion: ou le rapport consiste en ceci que les deux états auront existé, séparément, pour une confrontation par l'esprit. L'éternel, ce qui le parut, ne rajeunit, enfoncé aux cavernes et se tasse: ni rien dorénavant, neuf, ne naîtra que de source …

(316) 662–3 Aujourd'hui, voilà plus de vingt ans et malgré la perte de tant d'heures, je crois, avec tristesse, que j'ai bien fait. C'est que, à part les morceaux de prose et les vers de ma jeunesse et la suite, qui y faisait écho, publiée un peu partout, chaque fois que paraissaient les premiers numéros d'une Revue Littéraire, j'ai toujours rêvé et tenté autre chose, avec une patience d'alchimiste, prêt à y sacrifier toute vanité et toute satisfaction, comme on brûlait jadis son mobilier et les poutres de son toit, pour alimenter le fourneau du Grand Oeuvre. Quoi? c'est difficile à dire: un livre, tout bonnement, en maints tomes, un livre qui soit un livre, architectural et prémédité et non un recueil des inspirations de hasard fussent-elles merveilleuses … J'irai plus loin, je dirai: le Livre, persuadé qu'au fond il n'y en a qu'un, tenté à son insu par quiconque a écrit, même les Génies.

L'explication orphique de la Terre, qui est le seul devoir du poëte et le jeu littéraire par excellence: car le rythme même du livre, alors impersonnel et vivant, jusque dans sa pagination, se juxtapose aux équations de ce rêve, ou Ode.

(316) 378: tout, au monde, existe pour aboutir à un livre ...

(316) 366: Une ordonnance du livre de vers poind innée ou partout, élimine le hasard ...

(316–17) 396: Je finirai par l'orgue, relégué aux portes, il exprime le dehors, un balbutiement de ténèbres énorme, ou leur exclusion du refuge, avant de s'y déverser extasiées et pacifiées. l'approfondissant ainsi de l'univers entier et causant aux hôtes une plénitude de fierté et de sécurité ...

(317) 370: Plancher, lustre, obnubilation des tissus et liquéfaction de miroirs, en l'ordre réel, jusqu'aux bonds excessifs de notre forme gazée autour d'un arrêt, sur pied, de la virile stature, un Lieu se présente, scène, majoration devant tous du spectacle de Soi ...

(317) 308: Quand, au lever du rideau dans une salle de gala et tout local, apparaît ainsi qu'un flocon d'où soufflé? Furieux, la danseuse: le plancher évité par bonds ou dur aux pointes, acquiert une virginité de site pas songé, qu'isole, bâtira, fleurira la figure. Le décor gît, latent dans l'orchestre, trésor des imaginations; pour en sortir, par éclat, selon la vue que dispense la répresentante ça et là de l'idée à la rampe.

(318) 369: produire sur beaucoup un mouvement qui te donne en retour l'émoi que tu en fus le principe, donc existes: dont aucun ne se croit, au préalable, sûr ...

(318) 343: dans la modernité où personne ne nourrit qu'une préoccupation, pendant ses heures de la nuit et du jour, remplaçant tous les codes passés, c'est de ne jamais accomplir ou proférer qui puisse exactement se copier au théâtre ...

(318) 374–5: contradictoirement il évite la lassitude donnée par une fréquentation directe d'autrui et multiplie le soin qu'on ne se trouve vis-à-vis ou près de soi-même: attentif au danger double. Expressément, ne nous dégage, ne nous confond et, par oscillation adroite entre cette promiscuité et du vide, fournit notre vraisemblance. Artifice, tel roman, comme quoi toute circonstance où se ruent de fictifs contemporains, pour extrême celle-ci ne présente rien, quant au lecteur, d'étranger; mais recourt à l'uniforme vie.

Ou, l'on ne possède que des semblables, aussi parmi les êtres qu'il y a lieu, en lisant, d'imaginer. Avec les caractères initiaux de l'alphabet, dont chaque comme touche subtile correspond à une attitude de Mystère, la rusée pratique évoquera certes des gens, toujours: sans la compensation qu'en les faisant tels ou empruntés aux moyens méditatifs de l'esprit, ils n'importunent. Ces fâcheux (à qui, la porte tantôt du réduit cher, nous ne l'ouvririons) par le fait de feuillets entre-bâillés pénètrent, émanent, s'insinuent; *et nous comprenons que c'est nous.*

(319–20) 390: La foule qui commence à tant nous surprendre comme élément vierge, ou nous-mêmes, remplit envers les sons, sa fonction par excellence de gardienne de mystère! Le sien! elle confronte son riche mutisme à l'orchestre, où gît la collective grandeur. Prix, à notre insu, ici de quelque extérieur médiocre subi présentement et accepté par l'individu ...

(321) 867: aux mélodies d'autrefois très dessinées succède une infinité de mélodies brisées qui enrichissent le tissu sans qu'on sente la cadence aussi fortement marquée ...

(321) 366: par le heurt de leur inegalité mobilisés: ils s'allument de reflets réciproques comme une virtuelle traînée de feux sur les pierreries, remplaçant la réspiration perceptible en l'ancien souffle lyrique ou la direction personnelle enthousiaste de la phrase ...

(321–22) 363–4: Les langues imparfaites en cela que plusieurs, manque la suprême: penser étant écrire sans accessoires, ni chuchotement mais tacite encore l'immortelle parole, la diversité, sur terre, des idiomes empêche personne de proférer les mots qui, sinon se trouveraient, par une frappe unique, elle-même matériellement la vérité. Cette prohibition sévit expresse, dans la nature (on s'y bute avec un sourire) que ne vaille de raison pour se considérer Dieu; mais, sur l'heure, tourné à de l'esthétique, mon sens regrette que le discours défaille à exprimer les objets par des touches y répondant en coloris ou en allure, lesquelles existent dans l'instrument de la voix, parmi les langages et quelquefois chez un. A côté d'*ombre*, opaque, *ténèbres* se fonce peu; quelle déception, devant la perversité conférant à *jour* comme à *nuit*, contradictoirement, des timbres obscur ici, là clair. Le souhait d'un terme de splendeur brillant, ou qu'il s'éteigne, inverse; quant à des alternatives lumineuses simples—*Seulement,* sachons *n'existerait pas le vers*: lui, philosophiquement rémunère le défaut des langues, complément supérieur.

368: Le vers qui de plusieurs vocables refait un mot total, neuf, étranger à la langue et comme incantatoire ...

(322) 385: Les déchirures suprêmes instrumentales, conséquence d'enroulements transitoires, éclatent plus véridiques, à même, en argumentation de lumière, qu'aucun raisonnement tenu jamais ...

(322–3) 385–6: Quel pivot, j'entends, dans ces contrastes, à l'intelligibilité? il faut une garantie—

La Syntaxe—

Pas ses tours primesautiers, seuls, inclus aux facilités de la conversation; quoique l'artifice excelle pour convaincre. Un parler, le français, retient une élégance à paraître en négligé et le passé témoigne de cette qualité, qui s'établit d'abord, comme don de race foncièrement exquis: mais notre littérature dépasse le "genre", correspondance ou mémoires. Les abrupts, hauts jeux d'aile, se mireront, aussi: qui les méne, perçoit une extraordinaire appropriation de la structure, limpide, aux primitives foudres de la logique. Un balbutiement, que semble la phrase, ici refoulé dans l'emploi d'incidentes multiplie, se compose et s'enlève en quelque équilibre supérieur, à balancement prévu d'inversions.

(323) 387: Appuyer, selon la page, au blanc, qui l'inaugure son ingénuité, à soi, oublieuse même du titre qui parlerait trop haut: et, quand s'aligna, dans une brisure, la moindre, disséminée, le hasard vaincu mot par mot, indéfectiblement le blanc revient, tout à l'heure gratuit, certain maintenant, pour conclure que rien au-delà et authentiquer le silence—

(324) 368: Je dis: une fleur! et, hors de l'oubli où ma voix relègue aucun contour, en tant que quelque chose d'autre que les calices sus, musicalement se lève, idée même et suave, l'absente de tous bouquets ...

(324) 647: Nous savons, captifs d'une formule absolue que, certes, n'est que ce qui est ... La Nature a lieu, on n'y ajoutera pas ...

(324–5) 416: ... convient—avec correction, de soulever, par un salut—qu'il y ait à faire, légèrement, en faveur de quoi que ce soit—la si noire plate-forme égalitaire chue sur les calvities, qui y séjourne ...

(325) 647: A l'égal de créer: la notion d'un objet, échappant, qui fait défaut ...

(325) 375: Tandis qu'il y avait, le langage régnant, d'abord à l'accorder selon son origine, pour qu'un sens auguste se produisît: en le Vers, dispensateur, ordonnateur du jeu des pages, maître du livre. Visiblement soit qu'apparaisse son intégralité, parmi les marges et du blanc: ou qu'il se dissimule, nommez-le Prose, néanmoins c'est lui si demeure quelque sècrete poursuite de musique, dans la réserve du Discours.

(332) 368: even though, to exchange human thought, it would perhaps be enough in silence to remove a coin or place one in the other's hand ...

(332) 398: you do not select a god in order to confine him in the darkness of iron strongboxes or pockets ...

(332) 399: owing to money's failure to gleam abstractly ... to accumulate the radiant clarity of words like Truth and Beauty with those the poet proffers ...

(333) 406: the approach is itself a tribute; while along with the security that comes with a mutual hantation of the same region there emerge evasive words in a stroll of equal gaits which remains the contact between generations ...

(333) 406: one supreme rule: to tarry even with the eternal but the time to draw from it ...

(333) 664: his visiting card, stanzas or sonnet, to avoid being stoned by them if they suspect him of knowing that they don't exist ...

(333) 408–9: J'attribue à la conscience de ce cas, dans un temps que deux hommes ne se sont, peut-être, malgré la grimace à le faire, entretenus, plusieurs mots durant, du même objet exactement, la restriction qui garde des interlocuteurs de rien livrer à fond et de prêter souci; mais les persuade, par ruse mutuelle avec de la bravade, reliquat des surannés combats d'esprit généreux et baroques ou conformément au monde dont les lettres sont le direct affinement—de soustraire autant que révéler sa pensée, le premier; le second, de saisir, obstinément, autre chose—pour réserver leur integrité, quand un besoin cordial les leurre à se rencontrer.

(334) 653–4: *Un grand dommage a été causé* à l'association terrestre, séculairement, de lui indiquer le mirage brutal, la cité, ses gouvernements, le code autrement que comme emblèmes ou, quant à notre état, ce que des nécropoles sont au paradis qu'elles évaporent: un terre-plein, presque pas vil. Péage, élections, ce n'est ici-bas, où semble s'en résumer l'application, que se passent, augustement, les formalités édictant un culte populaire, comme représentatives—de la Loi, sise en toute transparence, nudité et merveille.

Minez ces substructions, quand l'obscurité en offense la perspective, non—alignez-y des lampions, pour voir: il s'agit que vos pensées exigent du sol un simulacre.

(333) 654: the point being that your thoughts require a simulacrum of earth's ground itself ...

(334) 371–2: Extérieurement, comme le cri de l'étendue, le voyageur perçoit la détresse du sifflet. "Sans doute" il se convainc: "on traverse un tunnel—*l'époque*—celui, long le dernier, rampant sous la cité avant la gare toute-puissante du virginal palais central, qui couronne." Le souterrain durera, ô impatient, ton recueillement à préparer l'édifice de haut verre essuyé d'un vol de la Justice.

Le suicide ou l'abstention, ne rien faire, pourquoi? Unique fois au monde, parce qu'en raison d'un événement toujours que j'expliquerai, il n'est pas de Présent, non—un présent n'existe pas ... Faute que se déclare la Foule, faute—de tout. Mal informé celui qui se crierait son propre contemporain, désertant, usurpant, avec impudence égale, quand du passé cessa et que tarde un futur ou que les deux se remmêlent perplexement en vue de masquer l'écart. Hors des premier-Paris chargés de divulguer une foi en le quotidien néant et inexperte si le fléau se mesure sa periode à un fragment, important ou pas, de siecle.

17

Gertrude Stein and Parts of Speech

When speaking of Gertrude Stein, one has first to begin with the question of trust. It precedes and determines all the other views and impressions one wishes to convey, and is in her case particularly urgent. Do we trust her or is she a charlatan? And if we do agree to trust her, do we take her at her own evaluation as a "genius"? Or to use a different language, do we agree to acknowledge her wisdom? In her own language, do we admit what she says she knows, do we adequately appreciate what she calls knowledge? She herself insists on the question, and indeed insists on the answer:

> Oh yes you do see.
> You do see that.[1] (34)

You see what I mean when I tell you what I know, insists her vernacular:

> as I have said knowledge is what I know, as I do so very essentially believe in knowledge. (10)

> And in asking a question one is not answering but one is as one may say deciding about knowing. Knowing is what you know and in asking questions although there is no one who answers these questions there is in them that there is knowledge. Knowledge is what you know. (102)

The reader/listener is initially tempted to take this knowledge as what must be radically distinguished from it, namely opinion; is tempted to hear Stein's insistent questions as another form of the question, do you agree? do you agree with this opinion of mine?

And to be sure, on the superficial or story-telling, anecdotal level, the assimilation of this evidently charged and private word knowledge to the more general sense of opinion confirms the stereotype of the speaker as opinionated and a dictatorial, a hectoring rather than a lecturing figure, whose own wry assimilation of listening to speaking ("I always as I admit seem to be talking but talking can be a way of listening that is if one has the profound need of hearing and seeing what every one is telling"—135) can only confirm the hostile reader in this "opinion."

But if we decide to trust Gertrude Stein we must begin by rejecting this view and by understanding "knowledge" as some deeper impersonal matter more on the order of Plato's *episteme* (rather than *doxa* or opinion): something the very first sentence of the *Lectures* warns in advance ("one cannot come back too often to the question what is knowledge and to the answer knowledge is what one knows"—1). This is a trip down the mine-shaft to the place, if not of the Ideas, then at least of the categories: what one finds there is not personal, and yet experience comes into it somehow. Gertrude Stein's observations about her first play, her first oil painting, her earliest readings, are only apparently interesting biographical and anecdotal data. In fact, they mark out that part of the space of "knowledge" (or the episteme) which her own personal trajectory has allowed her to know. Thus, opening a discussion of "the real question of punctuation, periods, commas, colons, semi-colons and capitals and small letters," she tells us characteristically:

> I have had a long and complicated life with all these. (216)

Her authority, her "knowledge," derives from just this long and complicated life-with (to frame a neologism); nor does it claim omniscience:

> I often wonder how I am ever to come to know all that I am to know about narrative. Narrative is a problem to me. I worry about it a good deal these days and I will not write or lecture about it yet, because I am still too worried about it worried about knowing what it is and how it is and where it is and how it is and how it will be what it is. (232)

Still, she knows enough about it to know that in the three great twentieth-century novels, "there is, in none of them a story" (184). So the pacing about the underground space of knowledge, its measurement by pacing, what has been lit up by your own experience as a precondition of that particular and specific knowledge, can also be productive by way of negation or of absence. Yet Stein is not at all dialectical, indeed there is a sense in which her modernism or her aesthetic (the very subject of the knowledge of *Lectures in America*) is positively anti-dialectical: a topic that brings us to the writing itself, or in other words, to Stein as unreadable.

Well at least you have to read it aloud, and the absence of punctuation (save for the special case of periods; see pp. 217-18) has the effect of excluding skimming or speed reading, reading for the "ideas" rather than the words, or if you like, reading for content. It is certain that other works of Stein are far more unreadable than this (one may consult Wendy Steiner's extraordinary readings of the truly unreadable portraits for a demonstration of what truly complete and thoroughgoing readings of these texts demand and entail).

But there is more to it than her own efforts to substitute another set of words for the first, obvious ones: "that unintelligible surface," as Steiner puts it, "which is ... militantly unintelligible through striking disruptions of syntax, time–space reference, and sense, through the rhyming of words devoid of semantic relation, the multiplication of negatives, and the use of circumlocutions so disjointed as seldom to suggest their real meaning."[2] Put this way, the procedures suggest cockney rhyming slang, or secret in-group code languages; but we here do not here have to deal with Stein's work as a whole but only with the more readable *Lectures* (and only in the sense in which the latter may well afford significant clues and hints towards an understanding of the former).

One of these hints and clues is inserted at the midpoint of *Lectures in America* in the form of a reference to another text:

> The business of art as I tried to explain in Composition as Explanation is to live in the actual present that is the complete actual present and to completely express that actual present. (104–5)

On the face of it, this aesthetic does not seem particularly concrete, until we begin to collect a host of secondary consequences it entails in the course of this very lecture series (the reference text is none too helpful). Thus, an understanding of what is involved in living in the actual present is focused in an unexpected direction by the various attacks on remembering (as well as by the insistence that there is no such thing as repetition). Meanwhile, the confusions attributed to memory are now generalized by the analysis of the "syncopated time" of the theater, and also by the problem of "reference" in painting; while the identification of a different form of the underlying issue in terms of the contemporary distinction between the diachronic and the synchronic is imposed by her discussion of the problem of the portrait, both in *The Making of Americans*, with its ambitious typological program ("to make charts of all the people I had ever known or seen, or met or remembered"—141), and in her account of that archaic genre, the portrait, which she reinvented and made uniquely her own.

Living in the actual present then little by little becomes something more than a mere formal strategy (if it does not, indeed, take on the philosophical and ethical dimensions of Deleuze's related notion of the "ideal schizophrenic");[3] it begins to clarify her problems with narrative, which we have already designated in passing; but also to raise some fundamental questions about language as such and in particular about the need for any speaker to remember the meaning of the words he uses. Would not the effort to do without remembering leave a speaker in a peculiarly disadvantageous situation of aphasia if not of silence?

But it is precisely this kind of question that Stein poses for herself and for which, at the level of language, she develops some extraordinary answers, which at once forestall the stereotypical popular satisfaction at finally understanding why she writes in such an incomprehensible way. For these answers at once plunge deeply into the structure of language itself and as such, into the question of syntax and parts of speech; while on another (diachronic) level a whole history of the relationship of a specific language (our own) to those deeper structures is elaborated, a history which the allegedly apolitical Gertrude Stein will ultimately link to imperialism itself, as well as to American exceptionalism.

Lectures in America is thus as much a history lesson as it is a treatise on language, and it is worth reiterating our initial warning about opinion and the categories of personality that go with it by stressing the differences between the psychological and culturalist approach of a D.H. Lawrence[4] and this "knowledge," which is impersonal to the point of excluding any psychoanalytical dimensions, and for which it is the concrete socio-economic structure—for England what she calls an "island daily life"—which explains a nation's literature and its language practices and possibilities, and which opens up the more general perspective of an aesthetic geopolitics. Even though the situation of imperialism and its colonies at the end of the nineteenth century is radically different from that of present-day globalization, it becomes clear that Stein's perspective has a good deal more in common with contemporary needs than with the psychologism or formalism which dominated the interwar and, also the Cold War years.

We may very briefly summarize the rich historical periodization of the first lecture by a brief excerpt:

> One century has words, another century chooses words, another century uses words, and then another century using the words no longer has them. (27)

These "centuries" or periods can be identified as follows: the first, which simply "has" the words, is that of Chaucer, of which she claims that it is a literature of nouns and names:

> Nouns are the name of anything. Think of all that early poetry, think of Homer, think of Chaucer, think of the Bible and you will see what I mean you will really realize that they were drunk with nouns, to name was to know how to name earth sea and sky and all that was in them was enough to make them live and love in names … (233)

We will later on retroactively feel some astonishment at this aesthetic promotion of the noun (her own theory of poetry in Lecture Six is based not only on a stylistic refusal of the noun but an attempt to substitute a specific language elaboration for such stigmatized "parts of speech"); at the same time something of a cloud begins to gather over this early moment when we understand that it is also the first form of what will under imperialism not merely constitute an exercise of private property but also a ritual of colonial possession as well. Here is the nineteenth century, characterized in its "life of things":

> They have shut in with them in their daily life but completely shut in with them all the things that just in enumeration make poetry, and they can and do enumerate and they can and do make poetry, this enumeration. (18)

But at this point the apparently simple reiteration of this idea—as in some child's history of English literature—has in fact been complicated by two or three other thematic concerns. The intervening centuries (that of the Elizabethans, that of the eighteenth century) are marked by the possibility of choosing meanings (and also "making mistakes," as we shall see): the richness of the Elizabethans lies in that of the choices, the clarity of the eighteenth century in a refusal of the multiple meanings which first differentiates meaning from words and points ahead to the nineteenth century imperial dissociation.

Yet it is important not to confuse this train of thought, in which words reenact possession, with the brief evocation of "god and Mammon" in literature, which turns out to distinguish a new (modernist) use of language which is not indebted to the past, from a traditionalist language in which "you write the way it has already been written" (54)—a sin which is less that of private property than it is precisely that commitment to remembering which has already been denounced.

But there is another matter to be dealt with in this expository chapter (and which she already rehearses in her still enigmatic remarks about knowing: having all of English literature "right in you right inside you"—11); and this is the dialectic of the inside and the outside which resurfaces in the discussion of the British Empire—the daily life inside the island, and owning everything outside the island—as well as in the worries about texts and in particular portraits: how to have everything inside them all at once, when the personality traits being represented can only be discovered or appreciated over time. "Inside" thus here designates a new form of the present, albeit a problematical one; and poses the dilemma of what we will later on come to call the synchronic (as opposed to the diachronic or narrative forms of experience or text).

It should also be noted that the dialectic of inside and outside is closely related to that of completion, which very much engages Stein throughout the work and is already evident in the conviction that *The Making of Americans* (supposed to describe every kind of person alive) could actually be completed. Yet the two sets of oppositions can play off against each other, combining in unexpected ways: thus England is somehow complete in itself as an island, and yet owns everything *outside* itself. Meanwhile the literary crisis determined by this structural dissonance or contradiction—described as using the words and yet no longer having them—takes the form of the writing of "phrases" rather than "sentences"(43–4), making us aware that a sentence is also something that can be complete or incomplete, and also that can include or exclude. This crisis will be solved by the radically new space of America as we will ultimately see, in a situation in which the quite distinct possibilities of American language become for Stein the very epitome of modernism itself.

But first we need to recover the thread of the aesthetic of an "actual present," and follow its privileged negation in remembering and memory through a series of other genres or forms of art, beginning with Gertrude Stein's central passion for painting ("I like to look at it. That was my real answer because I do, I do like to look at it, that is at the picture part of modern art. The other parts of it interest me much less."—59)

This is the beginning of two autobiographical accounts of her aesthetic education, the other one telling the story of her earliest experiences in the theater. Her "long and complicated life" with painting and with theater are scarcely gratuitous or self-indulgent; they make a productive use of memory as a phenomenological inquiry into the very structure of these arts, whose idiosyncratic evocations are anything but personal in their significance. Still, they record features we do not often pause to interrogate—the specification of painting as oil painting for example ("anything painted in oil anywhere on a flat surface holds my attention and I can always look at it"—60)—or the syncopated nature of her temporal experience in the theater.

She does not explain the well-nigh visceral relationship between her own personal looking, her own unique physical specularity, and the requirement of oil paint as such: but we may conjecture that oil calls attention to itself as a medium distinct from whatever is painted in it (even if those subjects themselves are non-figurative or as in Malevich consist in pure color as such). A possibility of a kind of secondary aesthetic autonomy is thus reserved for oil paint that cannot so well be imagined for watercolors or silverpoint or whatever.

Stein herself approaches this familiar modernist formulation in a different language, by insisting on the "relation between anything that is painted and the painting of it" (79), a relationship which is also the source of a profound annoyance. People think this annoyance comes from the representational problem and the judgements about resemblance:

> But I myself do not think so. I think the annoyance comes from the fact that the oil painting exists by reason of these things the oil painting represents in the oil painting, and profoundly it should not do so, so thinks the oil painting, so instinctively feels the person looking at the oil painting. Really in everybody's heart there is a feeling of annoyance at the inevitable existence of an oil painting in relation to what it has painted. (84)

This is more complicated than the standard defense of the non-figurative in modern painting; than the mere repudiation of the "other parts" of the painting (its narratives, its objects) in favor of the "picture part." I believe that Gertrude Stein did not at this time know or at least reflect on an absolutely non-figurative art, such as that of Malevich or Kandinsky, or later on the abstract expressionists; but I am convinced that even in those (very different) instances she would have identified a "subject" of the painting—whether geometry, pure color, or the movement inherent in so-called action painting—which would "annoy" by virtue of its coexistence with the oil paint itself, the aforesaid "picture part." The point to be made is that these two levels, the oil paint and what it "represents," are always present.

> I wonder if I have at all given you an idea of what an oil painting is. I hope I have even if it does seem confused. But the confusion is essential in the idea of an oil painting. (87)

This is a momentous assertion, which would seem to cancel any facile account of modern art in terms of non-figurality or a turn away from representation. The confusion is the permanent existence of these two planes, of the oil paint as medium and the "subject" which it cannot but bring with it no matter how much the medium thinks "it should not do so." There can thereby never exist any pure reception of this art, any really successful viewing and aesthetic apprehension of it: the act of attempting the latter will always entail a "confusion," it will require a permanent tension between the two failures of reading for resemblance and the mere staring at an inert object. The permanence of this tension sets to be sure a certain test for the right kind of viewing, but it is a peculiar test which asks us to fail as much as we succeed. The consequences for criticism and aesthetics are then also evident: any attempt to define art as a pure practice, and to offer a method in which the viewer ultimately succeeds in her engagement with the art object—all such positive and affirmative models of aesthetics are utterly misguided; not only are they positivistic and empiricist, they are also naïve and dare I say academic, and they unconsciously struggle to escape everything uncomfortable about a dialectic which tries to keep faith with the present as over against a mere theory (on her use of this word see p. 180).

Yet this return to temporality reminds us that we have not yet resituated this discussion of the visual arts within that aesthetic of the "actual present" that has been our topic here. If memory and remembering are bad, what role can they possibly play here? The context of the question immediately suggests its own specific answer, for it can only be the recognition of the objects painted, that "confusing" subject of the painting, which mobilized memory and remembering by way of the identification of the thing painted, its recognition, its name or noun, previous to any attempt to separate that level of representation from the looking which attempts to concentrate on the pure oil paint itself. The theme of remembering is thus another way of designating the intrinsic or representational in painting, at the same time that it warns us of the impossibility of doing without it altogether (any more, one would think, than one could do without memory, familiarity, identification, and the past of temporality, in any other kind of experience).

All of which will be redramatized for the theatrical medium in terms of that temporal syncopation whereby we as spectators are always a little ahead or a little behind the action on stage. But this is to be contrasted with the way we might live this same action "in real life": "In the real thing it is a completion of the excitement, in the theater it is a relief from the excitement, and, in that difference the difference between completion and relief is the difference between emotion concerning a thing seen on stage and the emotion concerning a real presentation that is really something happening" (96–7). The telltale appearance of the theme of completion alerts us to the relationship of this problem to the other discussions we have been following in *Lectures in America*; and it also suggests the imminence of a different outcome in this particular version, inasmuch as Gertrude Stein neither painted nor did she write English literature. But not only could she write plays, she did so; and we may thus understand why the resolution of this particular dilemma between the thing represented (the real action, which gives completion) and the representation (which only gives relief); or between the medium and its represented "subject," will take a different form and result in an invention or an innovation.

Memory can of course itself take a novel and unexpected form in plays, namely in the necessity of identifying the characters: in real life you know them already, they are familiar (yet that very familiarity in time may determine a transformation in form when it comes to making portraits of them); in reading a play she reminds us of "the necessity of going forward and back to the list of characters to find out which was which and then insensibly to know" (110); while on stage (leaving aside the added complication that we may already know the actors playing an unfamiliar character), we have to earn our familiarity with the people and characters we see before us, that is to say, we have to develop a very keen and intensified memory-sense as the play's exposition is going on. (One can imagine analogous exercises in remembering which are demanded by the reading of a novel, a reading and a form she will pronounce "soothing" (181) but not exciting.) All of which ends up implicating and indicting the form of storytelling itself as complicitous with remembering rather than with some "actual present."

The solution to these formal contradictions in drama can be rapidly indicated, but will move us one step forward towards the full form of Stein's two privileged genres, portraits and poetry. The actual present of the theater can be retrieved by considering the play as pure Scene, that is to say as landscape; and the troublesome features of remembering in traditional theater can be avoided, first by allowing the characters to be absorbed in the landscape, and second by the substitution for a recognizable, identifiable action of something which could not simply be named in that sense:

> So naturally what I wanted to do in my play was what everybody did not always know nor always tell ... I wanted to tell what could be told if one did not tell anything ... And the idea in What Happened, a Play was to express this without telling what happened, in short to make a play the essence of what happened. (119)

Here too then, we find the same logic of substitution at work in Stein's other aesthetic projects: but here we can note a shift in emphasis. It is no longer the autonomy of the medium which is being stressed, as over against the extrinsic position and intrusion of the content or "subject." Now, rather, it is something in that subject itself which calls out for substitution, without our yet quite knowing why it is necessary or at least needful. It is this shift which will be explored in the final essays, where a first approach stresses the greater intensity or liveliness of the substitution over the original (that is to say, the reality, the real action or object).

We may suppose, then, that, as in a host of other modernist aesthetics, from the "making strange" of the Russian Formalists to Proust's art of metaphor, the rationale for the program lies in the sense that modern life has become habituated and numb to perception, for which the defamiliarizations of modern art are designed to act as a stimulus. And something of the sort was certainly implicit in Stein's "history of English literature" as well as in her notion of "liveliness." Like a painter, she works from the scenes and still lives, the people, of everyday life; and these occasions offer the material for finger exercises and for workshop or studio experiments in technique and in perceptual renewal.

But particularly as we approach that very special genre called the portrait—which will eventually become Stein's privileged medium (including portraits of things) and which marks a distinctive generic revolution and a modernist restructuration of this ancient form, one which is uniquely Stein's contribution to modernist literature—the dynamics of the object, that is to say, of the people sitting for the portrait, of the individuals and those differences peculiar to each which allow them to be subjects for portraiture in the first place, begin to come into view. This is a shift signaled by the word "intensity," and it directs us almost at once to one of Stein's most idiosyncratic convictions, and no doubt one of the greatest stumbling blocks to any initial trust to be placed in her, no matter how winningly self-deprecatory and absurd this tenet of belief may seem. But it is a complicated matter: we start with an affirmation which is not necessarily absurd, namely that individuality—"the rhythm of anybody's personality" (174) as she calls it—consists in saying the same thing over and over again. This is the discovery of "just how everybody was always telling everything that was inside them that made them that one" (136). "I then began again to think about the bottom nature in people, I began to get enormously interested in hearing how everybody said the same thing over and over again with infinite variations but over and over again until finally if you listened with great intensity you could hear it rise and fall and tell all that there was inside them ..." (138) What is this same thing? I think it is the answer to her extraordinary question: "how do you like what you have?" (171). It is a question which combines the Lacanian question, "où en es-tu avec ton désir?" with the Steinian fascination with possession and ownership, with the objects that surround one and are included in one's daily life. Desire and private property—perhaps this is what everyone is reiterating; and the formula will become less banal if we add in the inevitable dissatisfaction—I don't like what I have, I like what you have, I only partially like what I have, which is to say, myself; and so on. Yes, no doubt our sense of the personality of another derives in part from our well-nigh subliminal sense of the satisfaction or dissatisfaction with self of the other, of their joyous or resentful mode of existence, which they cannot help but convey in this constant repetition which Stein insists we call insistence.

The portraitist listens to this insistence and the registration of it becomes the portrait itself. But there is a problem with this listening: it is presumably in danger of being drowned out by our own insistence, that is to say, by our own talking. How do we then combine these two seemingly incompatible and yet unavoidable and simultaneous modes of talking and listening? And what are we to make of a situation—this is then what is most immediately comic in Stein's explanation—of a listener who is herself a big talker? She is well aware of the problem: "To begin with, I seem always to do the talking when I am anywhere ... I always as I admit seem to be talking ... And I began very early in life to talk all the time ..." (135–6).

How to square this circle? As Sherlock Holmes put it, even if the only remaining explanation seems utterly fantastic, it must be the correct one: "talking can be a way of listening that is if one has the profound need of hearing and seeing what everyone is telling" (135). But this is not only the most fantastic but correct solution, it also explains something else, something also a deeply held and yet startling if not necessarily absurd conviction of Gertrude Stein:

> If the same person does the talking and the listening why so much the better there is by so much the greater concentration. One may really indeed say that that is the essence of genius, of being most intensely alive, that is being one who is at the same time talking and listening. It is really that that makes one a genius, And it is necessary if you are to be really and truly alive it is necessary to be at once talking and listening ... (170)

Later on seeing will come to complicate this interesting picture. Yet even granting its premises—especially granting its premises—the question of representation returns with a vengeance to transform the two subcategories into a problem in their own right. There is the matter of intensity—the insistence of each speaker on what is not repeated but insisted on over and over again—and then there is the matter of inside and outside: how does this content remain inside the completed portrait, rather than becoming diachronic and turning into something like a narrative? The problem is only intensified further by the issue of movement, for the insistence is already in itself a movement, and it is a movement in which each new movement is just slightly different from the last: how then to hold it together within a single form or frame:

> And so I am trying to tell you what doing portraits meant to me, I had to find out what it was inside any one, and by any one I mean every one I had to find out inside every one what was in them that was intrinsically exciting and I had to find out not by what they said not by what they did not by how much or how little they resembled any other one but I had to find it out by the intensity of movement that there was inside in any one of them. (183)

As for repetition, however, it entails the past and the memory of the same, the identification of a person through time and thereby that remembering which is "repetition and confusion," unlike the actual present insisted on by insistence:

> slowly I realized this confusion, a real confusion, that in writing a story one had to be remembering, and that novels are soothing because so many people one may say everybody can remember almost anything ... But and this was the thing that I was gradually finding out listening and talking at the same time that is realizing the existence of living being actually existing did not have in it any element of remembering and so the time of existing was not the same as in the novels that were soothing. (181)

And this is why the portrait (like the painting) is not to be recognizable or to represent the already familiar and the identifiable: it is to seize the essence of each one in that "actual present" which we have found to be the unalterable demand of Stein's aesthetic. (How movement can be seized within this complete thing and within this actual present will be explained by another condition of possibility which we will come to at the end of this essay.)

So now once again we return to language and substitution, and at the same time we reach our ultimate topic which is the matter of parts of speech. For the final lecture will coordinate the matter of parts of speech with a definition of poetry that completes the generic system and the two as yet unfinished cycles—the one of prose versus poetry, the other of the various arts or media, from painting and the novel through portraits all the way to poetry itself.

In order to do so we must naturally enough pass in review all the different parts of speech and pass judgement on them with respect to their liveliness. The opposition between nouns and verbs is not particularly novel or surprising, indeed in the historic transitional period between an Aristotelian substantialism and the modern process-oriented set towards relationality and meaning-production it is an inevitable bias: Stein gives it her own twist by slighting verbs and adverbs as such, turning them into gerundives, and directing our attention to the most hitherto neglected and subaltern parts of speech as we shall see shortly.

But the noun is just a name, and as we learned from the history of English literature there is a time—a dawn of language—in which the name is still exciting because we are the first to use it and to make up the name or noun that governs a thing or person. This capacity, this experience, is not at all negligible; but we have lost the language with which to realize it and we will find that if you like names or nouns you must today have recourse to something else, which will shortly be identified as poetry: "a noun is a name of a thing and therefore slowly if you feel what is inside that thing you do not call it by the name by which it is known" (210), and this substitution is very precisely the definition of poetry. But it can govern other kinds of strategies, and it is appropriate to mention here that unknown masterpiece at the very heart of Stein's work which is *Four in America*, and which consists in a historical experiment by which four Americans are seized in their essence and yet transformed by the substitution of different names for their original ones: it is an unexpected way to answer the question that specifies poetry as such: "was there not a way of naming things that would not invent names, but mean names without naming them" (236). The name change ("Ulysses" to "Hiram") is the experimental variation which allows us to grasp history as such:

> If Ulysses S. Grant had been a religious leader who was to become a saint what would he have done.

> If the Wright brothers had been artists that is painters what would they have done.
>
> If Henry James had been a general what would he have had to do.
>
> If General Washington had been a writer that is a novelist what would he do.[5]

This experimental variation will in *Lectures in America* be called the mistake. The noun makes no mistakes and must therefore be dealt with by the more radical means of substitutions or modifications of its attributes. But "verbs and adverbs are more interesting. In the first place they have one very nice quality and that is that they can be so mistaken. It is wonderful the number of mistakes a verb can make and that is equally true of its adverb" (211). Mistakes presumably designate what theoretical critics have called ambiguities, polysemia or simply the "suggestiveness" called for by the Symbolists. Mallarmean is also the identification of that part of speech "that can of all things be most mistaken and they are prepositions. Prepositions can live one long life being really being nothing but absolutely nothing but mistaken" (212).

Why? and what does this unexpected centrality of the preposition tell us about the Stein aesthetic? In Mallarmé, the preposition was virtually the privileged part of speech, being that empty operator which linked the diverse items together in a purely formal way, acting as a pure imperative to make connections, or better still, to register the montage of the separate objects. Thus, "selon," "according to," becomes strictly meaningless as you try to translate its syntactical function into any sort of conceptual paraphrase. Still, it acted in the service of an overall strategy of unification, in order to yield the complete sentence (the sentence of the world, so to speak, in *Un coup de dés*); it linked the parts of speech of the sentence together in a closed and formal continuity that no longer signified anything but Syntax.

In Stein, however, the preposition is endowed with its mission in a situation in which language has broken down into phrases: her nineteenth century, which it was the vocation of her modernism (just like all the others) to discredit and to displace. I think that the preposition (and its related formerly secondary parts of speech) serves the function of reconstructing the sentence from all those dispersed phrases (which are analogous to the dispersal of Britain's colonies throughout the world). But as we have already seen, the sentence itself belongs to the past, to the history of English literature: it will not be enough, in and of itself, to reconstruct a living (or to use her word, a lively) language. But it would seem that we have run out of possibilities, having already run through all of them: first words (or nouns), then choices between words, then the words and meanings of the eighteenth century (which I interpret to mean their sentences), and finally the nineteenth-century phrases. We cannot go back to any of these. What we can do, however, and what I believe she does, is to endow our linguistic practice with not one but two absolutes, whose coordination yields a historically new kind of text.

One of these absolutes will be the reconstructed sentence: the other, however, will be the paragraph, the absent unity of all the concrete sentences within it: the actual present of a sequence of sentences, which holds them together without remembering. This combination yields an unexpected corollary: "Sentences and paragraphs. Sentences are not emotional but paragraphs are. I can say that as often as I like and it always remains as it is, something that is" (223). This opposition is a virtually metaphysical one, with all the amplitude and consequences for literature of Frege's distinction between *Sinn* and *Bedeutung* in the conceptual realm.

It is not diminished by the peculiar autobiographical testimony that follows: "I found this out first in listening to Basket my dog drinking. And anybody listening to any dog's drinking will see what I mean." It is not a senseless nor maybe even a trivial way of conveying rhythm in the abstract.

"Paragraphs are emotional not because they express an emotion but because they register or limit an emotion" (48). We are thereby instructed to add back in the question of completion, of a new kind of inside and outside: not the frame exactly (always for her decorative and badly elegant, as in the Louvre) but an inner cohesion quite different from the dispersal of empire to which we have already referred:

> As I say as daily living was no longer being so positively lived every day and they were not all of them so certainly owning everything outside them, explaining and expressing their feeling was not any longer an inevitable thing and so the phrase no longer sufficiently held what a phrase had to hold and they no longer said what they thought and they were beginning not to think about what they thought.
>
> This brought about something that made neither words exist for themselves, nor sentences, nor choosing, it created the need of paragraphing, and the whole paragraph having been made the whole paragraph had rising off of it its meaning. (47–8)

With this new arrangement (and it is a dualism that can expand and contract, a single sentence can sometimes expand to become a paragraph in its own right, a paragraph can contract into a single sentence: but both must remain present and active in the text—223–4) we emerge not only into the historically new, that is to say into what we now call modernism, but also into the latter's geopolitical condition of possibility.

This can no longer, clearly, be the British Empire; and it comes as no surprise that it is for Stein the new condition of American reality and American space. To be sure, her initial awakening to this new possibility comes at the very moment in which America is really entering the era of its own empire, as opposed to the British one: the Philippines *de jure* and Cuba *de facto*—

something her teacher William James was deeply aware of (and which Conrad also registers in *Nostromo*). But perhaps one can insist that it is an empire of a different type, founded on a space of a different type.

At any rate it is certain that for Gertrude Stein (as for so many others) modernism is an American thing, and it is able to be brought into being by the peculiarities of American spatiality: its actual present is spatial, it is the "sense of a space of time" (160). But this is something at first to be approached negatively:

> In America as I was saying the daily everything was not the daily living and generally speaking there is not a daily everything. They do not live every day. And as they do not live every day they do not have the daily living and so they do not have this as something that they are telling. (50)

So far so good: but how to go a little farther with this account of what is not a daily life: "that anything is not connected with what would be a daily living if they had it" (50), and this is to identify the action and the effect of a *separation* in American reality:

> Think about all persistent American writing. There is inside it as separation, a separation from what is chosen to what is that from which it has been chosen ... a separation a quite separation between what is chosen and from what there is the choosing ... This makes what American literature is, something that in its way is quite alone. As it has to be, because in its choosing it has to be, that it has not to be, it has to be without any connection with that from which it is choosing. (51)

(If you doubted the significance of prepositions, the "in," "from," "between," "without" of this passage ought to drive the point home.) But we need a few more elements to grasp the implications of this separation, which can be conjectured to be some essential distance from whatever we call a context, or roots, or the land itself, or even, if we want to reduce it to a banality, from tradition.

But this can now be said positively: the abstraction from a context allows one to refocus whatever context as something you can fill up, something you can use as a frame to work in. And now that space becomes time:

> besides this there is the important thing and the very American thing that everybody knows who is an American just how many seconds minutes or hours it is going to take to do a whole thing. It is singularly a sense for combination within a conception of the existence of a given space of time that makes the American thing the American thing, and the sense of this space of time must be within the whole thing as well as in the completed whole thing. (160)

I believe that the "space of time" is what she means by "composition" in the earlier lecture called "Composition as Explanation" (where it also means generational time or period as well as our common or cultural context). But this is still a relatively formal account, which needs at least a specification of the content of this form (or in other words of the form of its content). We have already observed that a third term came to complicate the two dimensions of the painting and of the "subject" of the painting, and that is the possibility of movement. Something about modern painting seems to have called into being the possibility of movement within the picture, or at least the interest of the painters in trying to capture this new element ("the trouble is always, is it the people in it who move or does the picture move and if so should it"—86).

In literature, it would seem that movement offers a useful distinction with the older European writing, inasmuch as the movement registered there is always movement against something, movement against an obstacle: one which can be that of tradition or that of social class and class antagonism. For Stein, however—and it seems possible that in her moment of history there is the temptation to deny either an oppressive tradition in America or the kinds of rigid class distinctions preserved in England—the American space of time seems to allow for a movement without such friction or obstacles. The movement within the American context, or separated from the American context, does not know the same kind of resistance: "this thing is a thing to know, if and we in American have tried to make this thing a real thing, if the movement, that is any movement, is lively enough, perhaps it is possible to know that it is moving even if it is not moving against anything" (165). "This generation has conceived an intensity of movement so great that it has not to be seen against something else to be known, and therefore, this generation does not connect itself with anything, that is what makes this generation what it is and that is why it is American ..." (166) Finally, the description resumed: "An American can fill up a space in having his movement of time by adding unexpectedly anything and yet getting within the included space everything he had intended getting" (224).

This could be an account of American space (or at least of American space as Stein and her generation felt it in the early years of the twentieth century). It could be an account of modernism as abstraction and separation in those early years in which modernism had no name and was coming into being and alive. It could also be an account of the rootlessness of the exile, who has no context and no social friction to deal with, as well as an income which permits just such a separation from the working life. But perhaps it is that very separation which allows the new and the American to be named and conceptualized and to find its requisite and idiosyncratic language. Or perhaps not. We may end with a different and a grimmer reflexion: "I am certain that what makes American success is American failure. I am certain about that." (172)

(*2005*)

Notes

1 All page references in the text are to Gertrude Stein, *Lectures in America* (Boston, 1985 [1935]).

2 Wendy Steiner, *Exact Resemblance to Exact Resemblance* (New Haven, 1978), p. 101.

3 Gilles Deleuze and Félix Guattari, *L'Anti-Oedipe* (Paris, 1972).

4 D.H. Lawrence, *Studies in Classic American Literature*, (London, 1923).

5 Gertrude Stein, *Four in America* (New Haven, 1947).

SEVEN

18

"Madmen Like Kings"

> It is necessary to study precisely how permanent collective wills are formed, and how such wills set themselves concrete short and long term ends—i.e., a line of collective action.
>
> —Gramsci

Nobel-prizewinners seem to fall into two categories: those whom the prize honors, and those who honor the prize. And then there are those assumed to be in the first, who turn out to have been in the second category all along. Such was, for example, "the author of a dirty book called *Sanctuary*" who proved unexpectedly to be the greatest novelist in the world. Such is also, I believe, the case of Oe Kenzaburo, whose latest novel shows how mistaken his American stereotypes were (and perhaps how mistaken his own stereotype of himself was as well).

At least two things were thought to have been known about this writer when Grove Press gradually began to introduce his works into English in the late 1960s (Oe was born in 1935). The first is that he was a passionate anti-nuclear activist (the West probably not knowing enough about Japanese politics to grasp the complexities of the AMPO movement of 1960). The second is that he is the father of a handicapped son, born with a strange protuberance on the head, who has grown up to be a musician and a composer. Anyone unaware of the first of these features, is much less likely to have been able to remain unaware of the second, since it reappears in virtually every book Oe has written.

But it reappears with variations, as do all of Oe's themes or obsessions. Even the most interesting writer only rewrites the same book over and over again, someone once said; but in Oe's case this is not to be understood psychologically, as pretext for deducing the primal fantasy or archetype repeating itself like the eternal return of some endless murmur. I prefer to think of the process as some never-ending construction and reconstruction with a finite number of building blocks, which you put together in all kinds of different ways, tragically, comically, mythically; and in the case of *Somersault*,[1] with a kind of "late-style" simplicity, like the architectonics of a Bruckner symphony. Still, it would seem that something is new here (the very "somersault" of the title suggests renunciation and rebirth). Oe has himself announced that what he calls the "idiot son" cycle of his narratives is over. That is not quite true; but the father–son motif, withdrawing into the background, does seem here transformed almost beyond recognition, giving way to an urgent preoccupation with group formation which was always present in Oe's earlier work, but never posed so directly as this. *Somersault* (*Chugaeri*, published in Japan in 1999) indeed tells the story of the attempt by its founder to resurrect a religious cult he has himself discredited and virtually destroyed. It is an oddly formalistic exercise, in which the sheer mechanics of group formation—assembling mailing lists, scheduling meetings, renting meeting places and deciding the order of business—seems to take precedence over the content of this particular religion. Not that such a focus would be altogether without interest: one imagines the naturalist novelists taking this social phenomenon apart like a machine, and describing all the steps and all the pitfalls with gusto, while disregarding the spirituality altogether. Oe's novel has little in common with naturalism, but is also resolutely non-spiritual and non-psychological; what he does have in common with Dostoyevsky (a comparison often made in the literary press) are the endless philosophical conversations which allowed the latter's novels to escape the "monologic" perspective of that ideology or set of opinions or beliefs the author may have held in real life. With Oe too, it might be preferable to dissociate the author from ideas he merely seems to endorse (we will touch on the "sacrificial" and indeed on religion itself later on); and where the naturalists might have offered us a sociologically rich cast of character types—organizers and bureaucrats, fanatics, groupies, secretaries, fellow travellers, etc.—the supporting cast here are larger than life, and both formulaic (the building block system I've already mentioned) and existential or unique all at once.

But we should not neglect the shadow presence of *The Devils* behind all this; nor the equally Dostoyevskian abjection, in which grotesque characters wallow in their shame and inferiority (Oe's greatest novel begins with the narrator squatting in a muddy pit destined for a new septic system, and holding a stinking dog in his arms as he evacuates). Victorianism, to be sure, did not permit the Russian novelist to indulge in the outbursts of obscenity recurrent in Oe's work (Judge Woolsey might have pronounced them "emetic" rather than "aphrodisiac") and very much in evidence in *Somersault* as well; I doubt whether they reflect the hatred of the body often implicit in such passages, but I also very much wish to exclude culturalism and its myths (such as the idea of some "Japanese" sexuality).

Contingency seems to me a better way of understanding all this: it presides over the grotesque detail fully as much as the various bodily functions;

and replaces Oe squarely in the existential tradition, to which, as a French scholar, he remains indebted (the Japanese critics, however, also make much of his American-style narratives, including the "Americanisms" of his Japanese sentences). Thus, if Oe is not exactly a realist, he is not really a modernist either (despite the fireworks of his earlier writing: "his woolen jacket striped with light and dark brown was worn with an air of reverent care, though the odds were that it would soon deteriorate into a crumpled, baggy heap like a large dead cat" [*The Silent Cry*, 1974, p. 24]). These works avoid standard modernist structures such as autoreferentiality; and, although it is often a question of art here—the great Jonah triptych here, the Tantra Buddhist painting of hell in *The Silent Cry*—my sense is that, as in Hegel, the center of gravity of aesthetics for Oe knows an imperceptible displacement towards ritual rather than in the direction of the autonomous work of art as such. Postmodern, however, is only the content of *Somersault*, the interest in small groups which parallels a Western ethnic or identity politics.

Indeed, it now seems best to grasp the "idiot son" motif as being itself a first attempt at group formation. It is a failed attempt, although it is not "a personal matter" (the title of Oe's most famous version of the subject) and is thus not to be interpreted according to the usual humanist misreadings, such as guilt, nor even the existential ones, such as the "life sore" of Paule Marshall[2] or Sartre's ineradicable past act. Rather, the multiple permutations of this relationship end up disclosing it as that sad and comic dramatic structure Beckett called the pseudo-couple, a vaudeville-laden system of neurotic dependency in which two differentially maimed and underdeveloped subjectivities provisionally complete each other. Nor is this a family structure exactly: sometimes a wife is introduced into the situation—vengeful and aggressive (as in *The Pinch Runner Memorandum* [1994: *Pinchi ranna chosho*, 1976]) or alcoholic, lachrymose, and catatonic (as in his greatest novel, *The Silent Cry* [*Man'en Gannen no Futtoboro*, 1967]) but we could equally well see this pseudo-couple as a fraternal pair, and indeed in *The Silent Cry*, the deformed baby is very much upstaged by the central struggle between the two enemy brothers; while in *The Pinch Runner Memorandum*, in a galloping and comic oneiric nightmare more reminiscent of Lem's *Futurological Congress* than of anything in Philip K. Dick, the father and son actually change places (this novel might have been called *The Switchover*), the former becoming a teenager while the latter assumes the advanced old age of the father himself (thirty-eight), the whole being projected onto an analogous father–handicapped son pair whose "story" the narrator (presumably Oe himself) relates in the voice of the alternate progenitor, who has become the son and teenage buddy of his wiser son–father.

The pseudo-couple has not disappeared altogether from *Somersault*, where the handicapped boy (who has, like Oe's own son, become a musician and begun to compose in his own right) is a minor character, accompanied by a "normal" sister; but it can be reidentified in the central narrative frame itself, where it is remotivated by outright homoeroticism in the person of the cancer-ridden arts teacher (Kizu) fascinated by the "dog-faced boy" (Ikuo), a taciturn and stubborn youth he had once observed long ago as a small child awkwardly carrying an enormous model building (they will years later be unexpectedly united around the reorganization of the sect). Yet even this idiosyncratic adolescent figure was already foreshadowed in a completely different narrative context in *The Silent Cry*, where he turns out to be the leader of a children's group in Oe's native Shikoku forest valley (a role Ikuo reassumes in *Somersault* when the sect moves to that same valley, itself a constant throughout Oe's works).

What to do with these multiple permutations, in which the return of the same is always different? The pseudo-couple, to be sure, traces an august (if ridiculous) lineage all the way back (via Flaubert) to the *Quixote* itself; but Beckett, who was the first to name this structure (in *Mercier and Camier*, I believe) gives us what is perhaps a more productive clue in *Waiting for Godot*. The Beckett play, indeed, involves not one but two pseudo-couples, the relatively egalitarian team of the two *clochards* (differentiated only by their physical ailments) being episodically juxtaposed with a very different and decidedly unegalitarian pair in the persons of Pozzo—the master, presumably signifying England—and Lucky—the slave, presumably signifying Ireland and its intellectuals. The first pseudo-couple offer the interminable repetitions of everyday life and existential experience and boredom, the second bring power and history into the matter (nor does the conflation of both pairs into one in *Endgame* overcome this mysterious incommensurability, even though we are told that Beckett came to loathe his first, allegorical and world-historical effort).

We have not yet observed that this kind of doubling is also to be found in *Somersault*, where the first pseudo-couple of the sickly painter and the adolescent rebel (itself harboring, as we have said, echoes of the primal pseudo-couple of father and handicapped son) is confronted with what may be called a political pseudo-couple, in the twin direction of the sect and the persons of the peculiarly named Patron and Guide. But these nicknames (invented by a journalist) are modest euphemisms for their fundamental roles as Savior and Prophet respectively. And we may note in passing that such spiritual division of labor is not uncommon in the history of religious movements: Moses and Aaron, Jesus and Saint Paul, Sabbatai Zevi and Nathan of Gaza, are only a few of the joint religious leaderships that come to mind. (Meanwhile, in an article in the *London Review of Books*, Perry Anderson has suggested that, at least for Latin American politics, something of the reverse is frequent, the public leader being shadowed by his decidedly unpublicized *éminence grise*: perhaps a theory is to be concocted on the basis of this interesting inversion?)

At any rate, something of the catastrophic reversal of *Waiting for Godot* is also to be found here in *Somersault*: for early in the revival Guide is murdered by the so-called radical faction of the older followers. His disappearance serves to lay Patron's fundamental helplessness bare: not only has the "Savior" had no new visions since the end of the older cult, the public interpretations of those visions turn out to have been fabrications on Guide's part, flights of fancy very much engineered according to Guide's own personal view of the direction the movement is to take (indeed, the sub-faction of scientists and technicians responsible, as we shall see shortly, for the group's dissolution, and later on for Guide's own death, was very much his own operation).

The disappearance of Guide then also clarifies Patron's decision to start the group up again: *Somersault* is very centrally concerned with the possibility of forming a group—a political movement, an active collectivity, a return to the communal in some new form after the ravages of modern or modernist individualism—which does not posit violence as a necessary accompaniment or outcome. This is a fundamental dilemma in what is, despite appearances, a political novel rather than a religious one: religion being, in an apolitical age like our own, the privileged form of the Ruse of History of politics. But politics or political theory is here not a matter of empirical interests or even ideologies and parties, class struggle as such: it constitutes an ontological inquiry into the very possibility for biologically isolated human beings to form groups which can function as historical agencies. Nor is Patron's preoccupation with violence to be grasped as a merely pacifist or humanist "value," as Oe's early history as an anti-nuclear activist has been considered in the West: rather, it addresses a fundamental dilemma in the very being of groups as such. The philosophical confrontation with these issues has been at best sporadic; in modern times one thinks of Carl Schmitt or the Sartre of the *Critique*, while in the rest of human history it is mainly around the founding of religions (and their subsequent schisms) that group formation has been produced as a problem, one that escapes the field of vision of liberalism or humanism and their various forms of repressive tolerance. For the conceptualization of the group or collective always comes up short against the unhappy fact (if it has to be a fact) that in order to differentiate itself and to achieve that mode of collective praxis which is today loosely and ideologically called its "identity," the nascent collectivity seems necessarily to have to define itself by way of frontiers and borders, by way of a kind of secession: it must always, in other words, following Schmitt's remarkable formulation, posit an enemy. Thus, in order for humanity as a whole to know the perpetual peace and harmony fantasized by the humanists, or in other words, to enjoy one great collective identity all across the globe, we would need, as Sartre observed, the unifying intervention of an enemy in outer space (it is a logical corollary beautifully imagined by Ursula LeGuin in her novel *The Lathe of Heaven*, precisely at the moment of universal peace on earth).

But the issue is not only a philosophical or ontological one, and the recent history of Japan is there to account for the way Oe stages it, and also for the relative formalism of that staging, in *Somersault*. For Japan—that simultaneously violent and very well-behaved place—having had, to be sure, its own experience of the great mass movements of communism and fascism, came to the contemporary forms of collective action somewhat earlier than Europe or the US, in the great AMPO or New Left, anti-treaty demonstrations of 1960, from which both an anti-nuclear mobilization and the Narita Airport movement emerged, the latter knowing perhaps the longest life-span (some twenty years) of any radical action of the post-war period.[3] The displacement and supercession of the Communist Party by New Left or extraparliamentary Left movements—what the France of 1968 called groupuscules—meant not merely a draining away of the central ideological conflict of the Cold War (particularly since most of these small groups were more passionately anti-communist than anti-capitalist in the first place); it also meant the emergence of a new political dynamic, one epitomized by the fraternal conflicts of Oe's *Pinch Runner Memorandum*, where it is difficult to distinguish between the revolutionary group and the counterrevolutionary group attacking it.

This is not to suggest that Oe, himself the target of right-wing and nationalist, pro-Emperor violence, believes in some hypothetical convergence between Left and Right today, let alone to compare skinheads with multiple Left groupuscules, perfectly capable, to be sure, of killing each other off without the help of the Right. Oe is indeed fiercely anti-nationalist, but as we shall see shortly, he may also be seen as a kind of political regionalist, substituting the problematic of space for the reprehensible rhetoric of the nation and of patriotism. In *Somersault*, indeed, warring factions coexist uneasily within the overarching religious framework of the movement. Here too, however, it would seem important not overhastily or automatically to characterize this kind of religious politics as conservative or reactionary, as one would for the most part be entitled to do for similar movements in the US or Europe. Oe's religion could probably be described as Blakean (see above all *Rouse Up, O Young Men of the New Age*; *Atarashii hito yo mezameyo*, 1983), Blake being, along with Sartre and Dostoyevsky, the central literary reference of his work (always accompanied by a host of minor allusions, such as the lengthy appreciation of the poetry of R.S. Thomas and his doctrine of "quiet emergence" in the present novel).

We have indeed in recent times learned that religion emerges (quietly or not) as the ideological form of political content whenever the openly political or socio-economic has been discredited or withdrawn: as it was by the long history of Stalinism, or, in the Middle East, by the wholesale massacre of one national Communist Party after another, which left only Islam as an available framework for revolt and resistance.

But all this is complicated by a peculiar turn in recent Japanese history which must also be taken into account for proper intelligence of *Somersault*. In Japan, indeed, the September 11 experience, the shattering of a First World complacency with political results as yet incompletely known, took place on a different fateful date which will not generally be recognized in the West, namely on June 27, 1994. This was the date on which a "religious sect" called Aum Shinrikyo spread sarin gas in the Tokyo subway system, killing seven persons and injuring hundreds.[4] It is only after Al Qaeda that the West has been able to appreciate the collective trauma thus inflicted on Japan, one different in kind from its earlier political violence. For the long-lasting experience of the Narita Airport movement was not only geographically contained, confined to the "solidarity huts" ringing the airport then under construction; it was also repressed by the Japanese public sphere, which ceased to report or to discuss it, and at the same time antiquated by the multiple Left ideological slogans which still decorated its banners. The invasive power of Aum's intervention could not, however, be thus muffled or disguised. This is how *Somersault* summarizes this historical movement, on which its narrative is a more than implicit commentary:

> The founder of the group called Aum Shinrikyo was trained in India, and at the point where he first declared himself to be the Final Liberated One he had only thirty-five followers. By the next year this had grown to fifteen hundred. Later, a core leadership joined that committed several terrorist acts. The following year, the year their Mount Fuji headquarters was completed, they reached thirty-five hundred followers and became a religious corporation. Two years later they ran candidates in a national election, and even the one billion yen they spent in the effort didn't seem to faze them, so great were their financial resources by this time. Finally, they made contacts with sources in the collapsing Soviet Union and purchased some large helicopters, all the while developing the capability to produce seventy tons of sarin.
>
> So they started with thirty-five people and got to this point in less than ten years. If they'd really been able to carry out their Armageddon battle, the four thousand people killed and injured in the sarin attack on the subway would have been nothing in comparison. (173)

Patron's Church of the New Man in fact also preached the end of the world, the dystopian collapse of late capitalism in ecological disaster, mass starvation and internecine violence of all kinds. Predictably, it also included a "radical faction" bent on Aum-style violence, a strategy to which *Somersault*, and Patron in his second or revised movement, propose an alternative.

Both movements, however, the real one as well as its fictive analogue, will necessarily startle the Western political observer in one respect: namely the presence in them of highly educated scientists and technicians (as attested by Aum's formidable arsenal). We are to be sure accustomed to learning that militia sympathizers study the Internet for their technological recipes, but not that such fringe groups include a significant population of trained doctors and university researchers attracted to their aims and beliefs. But Patron's church includes scientists (among them the "radical faction" which killed Guide); along with many other kinds of social combinations—a feminist collective, for example (the Quiet Women) who meditate a Jonestown-style solution at the end of the novel; a group of teenage or pre-teen boys, the so-called Young Fireflies, ultimately led by Ikuo (but already foreshadowed in Oe's first novel, *Nip the Buds Shoot the Kids* [*Memushiri kouchi*, 1958], a Solzehnitsyn-like novel about juvenile delinquents); the significantly named Moosbrugger Committee (after the eponymous serial killer in Musil's *Man without Qualities*, one of the most remarkable portraits of psychopathic consciousness in all of literature); various groups of surviving followers from the earlier Church, who had turned away from Patron after his "somersault" and gone their own independent way; and not excluding the various oddball, handicapped or misfit protagonists in the foreground. This multiplicity of social backgrounds serves in my opinion to displace standard Western diagnoses of alienation and anomie with the more positive appeal of collective practice and group participation; the novel thus encourages an attention to the construction of the group at the expense of psycho-social theories about its motivations.

That same ignorant liberal Western reader who has been so convenient a strawman throughout these remarks will also provide yet another misreading for instructive denunciation, namely the impression that Patron's "somersault" is designed to avoid the pitfalls of tyranny and totalitarianism, the cult of the personality and charismatic authority of all kinds; but I think that such liberal or anarchist preoccupations with egalitarian or radical democracy are not much of an issue here. Both Patron and Guide are to be sure flawed characters with seriously doubtful pasts (although neither quite so horrendous as the 1976 anticipation of Patron in *The Pinch Runner Memorandum*, where he is the very caricature of corrupt power, pulling all possible strings behind all possible scenes and worthy of every imaginable political protest, including assassination). The novel faithfully lays the facts before us, without debunking the mission or vocation to which these not very successful people have suddenly found themselves called: perhaps psychoanalysis has defused the critical impact of such psychological revelations (or perhaps the current regime of cynical reason takes them for granted). At any rate, Patron's qualifications as a prospective savior seem to lie exclusively in his vaguely schizophrenic visions, to which I prefer those of *The Pinch Runner Memorandum*:

> My personal speculation is this: Earth is part of a gigantic cosmic construct, and it is being pulled along, like on a conveyor belt, toward its proper place in that construct! And our Milky Way is the conveyor belt carrying Earth to its designated point on the blueprint; at the last stage of this journey, the Milky Way functions both as the launch pad, and as the energy source providing the correct vector and thrust for Earth's liftoff. This near-perfect spherical unit, humankind's abode for so long, will fit into place with a snap, and complete the preplanned cosmic construct! However, back in the preparatory stages, when all the units for assembling *were first being created*, a minute defect was found on the sphere called Earth. In the end, to correct that defect, beasts, birds, fish, and insects, as well as humans—all infinitesimal on the cosmic scale—had to be introduced ... I think those nuclear explosions that have occurred—on deserts or coral atolls—are Earth's finishing touches, the polishing up or corrections of the defect—whatever you want to call it. The next targets are big cities, excluding of course the two already devastated. When Earth is a perfectly sized sphere meeting cosmic specs, it will blast off from the Milky Way launch pad, and snap into its proper place in the ultimate structure! (141)

But Patron's visions are perhaps little more than the necessary but not sufficient qualifications for group formation: Guide was always there to give them the appropriate content. Indeed, one has the sense that in this novel it would be enough for someone publicly to announce the intent to form a new group or sect for people to flock to it. But poor Fourier advertised in vain (he remained at home faithfully, at eleven a.m. every Tuesday, waiting for a Maecenas who never appeared); and Americans will be more familiar with the process whereby an already existing group fragments into smaller and smaller ones, in never-ending schism and sectarianism, than with the process by which new ones are formed.

But what was the "somersault" in the first place if not just such a schism in which (as with Mao or Lacan) the former devotees and believers are invited to "bombard the headquarters"? In this radical act, indeed, Patron moved to disarm his militant faction (intent on bringing about the long-prophesied end of the world by nothing less than the nuclear destruction of Tokyo itself) by publicly renouncing his own doctrine and confessing that he and Guide were both charlatans who had never had any authentic visions and whose prophecies were little more than an elaborate hoax. With this, the movement for the most part collapses, the radical scientists are rounded up by the police, and Patron and Guide "enter hell," where they remain for ten years until reemerging (at the beginning of this novel) to found a new movement on the ashes and rubble of the old one. This somersault was thus already a form of self-destruction, which anticipates the suicide whereby Patron removes himself from his own regenerated movement at the novel's conclusion. But I would rather not characterize it as sacrificial, any more than I would like to lapse into culturalism in suggesting something quintessentially Japanese about the suicides which run through Oe's work and culminate in this one. Sacrifice is here seen as the momentum of history and of the repetitions of revolt, but we cannot understand that properly without coming (in conclusion) to the "power of place," the "power of the land."

I have not yet confronted the return, in almost all of Oe's novels, to his native valley in Shikoku (predictably Patron moves his church there in the present book). This new regionalism is no surprise in the era of globalization, where the local tends to constitute an inevitable protest against urban standardization and the destruction of nature and the peasantry (or farmers) by agribusiness: it also tends to organize itself into an ideology and a compensatory fantasy rather than a political program. *The Silent Cry*, however, teaches us that we must grasp "the power of the land" as the recovery of history; and even Patron's last and sacrificial act is explicitly linked to a similar episode on the same spot a generation earlier (an incident then celebrated in the as yet untranslated *Burning Green Tree* trilogy of 1993). But Oe's work contains many more historical levels than this: and *Somersault* merely adds a new post-Aum layer to a series of historical strata which reach all the way back to a pre-Meiji Shikoku peasant uprising, proceeding then through the new imperial dispensation down to the village turmoil at the end of World War Two. The 1960s looting of the new capitalist supermarket (in *The Silent Cry*) once again recapitulates the cycle of revolt that resonates through Oe's novels, now in mythical form (in *M/T and the Marvels of the Forest*; *M/T to mori no fushigi no monogatari*, 1986) and now in the grim and bloody desperation of *The Silent Cry*. *Somersault*, in yet a new way, continues to make accessible to us "these madmen, who like kings, come one at a time" (SC, 54).

(*2003*)

Notes

1 Kenzaburo Oe, *Somersault*, trans. Philip Gabriel, (New York, 2003).
2 See Susan Willis, *Specifying* (Wisconsin, 1987), Chapter 3.
3 See on this remarkable political phenomenon David Apter and Sawa Nagayo, *Against the State* (Cambridge MA, 1984).
4 On the Aum, see Haruki Murakami, *Underground* (New York, 2001).

19

Euphorias of Substitution

Shooting as writing, writing as shooting (in both homicidal and sexual senses): such are the symbolic conflations which enable the construction and the narrative slippages, the unfoldings and refoldings of Hubert Aquin's *Prochain episode* (1965), a novel which, although far from being the inaugural text of the new Québecois literature (and even from being in any way characteristic of it), seems to have burst on the radical Québecois intelligentsia of the Quiet Revolution like a bombshell. Aquin quickly became his own legend, having been arrested during the period of the "first" FLQ (Front de libération du Québec) for carrying firearms (1964), at which time he was briefly interned in a psychiatric prison before his acquittal by the court. Aptly described as a "revolutionary dandy," Aquin continued to agitate as a separatist militant during the end of the decade, while working and writing for Canadian radio and television (notoriously a stronghold of Québécois intellectuals), and sealed the mystery of his existence by his suicide long after the close of the sixties, during the year following the victory of the Parti Québécois in 1976.

The temptation must be resisted to assimilate his four novels to the new formal "experimentation" of the French *nouveau roman* (Gérard Bessette's later work has far more kinship with that aesthetic, despite his more Sartrean origins). The search for influences and similarities is indeed in general a rather sterile academic pastime or habit: yet we have the testimony of Proust that, faced with something radically new, with a style or language we are not yet equipped to read, the earliest witnesses of such work normally tend to protect themselves by multiple comparisons with already familiar languages until in time the new text becomes transformed into itself.[1]

This will in any case be my excuse for beginning these reflections with a few remarks on the history of my own relationship to these novels, something that may have some usefulness for American readers to whom, despite the existence of English translations of *Prochain épisode* and *Trou de mémoire* (1968), they remain as unfamiliar as the overwhelming body of the nascent, yet already rich and vibrant, literary production of the new

Québec. As a matter of fact, *Prochain épisode* was the first Québécois novel I ever read (thanks to the prompting of a Canadian-American friend), and almost the last I cared to read for a considerable period of time. I found it amateurish and repulsive, indulgent, narcissistic, and distressingly thin from any novelistic point of view. I mention this principally because today this novel, and its three successors, have come to seem inexhaustibly fascinating to me, texts I now find myself able to read and reread on virtually any occasion with ever greater delight. How such an astonishing and unexpected transformation was possible (although perhaps mainly of interest to myself) may stand as something of a case history in support of the Proustian theory of discovery.

In fact, it was not Aquin's text that changed, but my own distance from it: by which I mean to say that all the unpleasant adjectives I have used above, and which characterized my first assessment of this peculiar textual object, remain for me in force; only I now feel differently about all those "objective" defects. And as it is a writer's style which tends first to strike or to distract us, I will begin by complaining about that feature of Aquin's sentences that immediately distinguishes him from the impersonal sobriety of the *nouveau roman*, namely the obsessive and intolerable celebration of the first person, the grimacing and posturing of an in any case hollow subjectivity, the mimicry of an aesthetics of subjective expression whose paradigm, reduced to something as elementary as a cry or an outburst, seems to betray its own poverty by a repeated series of exclamation points. Very different this from the "egotistical sublime" of a Proust or a Claude Simon, whose meditative sentences slowly explore the contours of a complex and objective world, using sensations and perceptions as a means to leave mere subjectivity—their starting point—behind themselves. But we learned from Flaubert that a first-person sentence can rarely have aesthetic density, and that spontaneous "lyricism" is to be systematically expunged in order for the massive solidity of an achieved and modern style to rise, slowly, in its place. I have elsewhere associated the grotesqueries of this intolerable flexing of the first person with a certain Russian tradition and with "an endemic ego-deficiency or identity failure which … resulted from the backwardness of the Russian bourgeoisie."[2] The diagnosis, perhaps applicable in a very different way to the Québecois situation, has at least the merit of putting us on the track of Aquin's one identifiable forebear and literary alter ego: Nabokov, whose exile literature, peopled with doubles and indulgent autoreflexivity, presents many instructive parallels with Aquin's own books, as we shall see shortly.

I have not changed my mind about the "first-person self-indulgent," nor about the ugliness of this language: what I have found (having had a similar experience many years previously with Mailer's *American Dream*) is that when this garish surface is approached ever more closely, as with the smears and lips of an open wound, suddenly microscopic hues appear, a whole oil-slick rainbow of the most delicate and unusual subcutaneous perception, swarming, marbled, a whole minute molecular life of language beneath the words. Even the exclamations now seem to me to have an inner tension, to speak their pent-up "emotion" with all the tautness of a drawn bow: "Je veux vivre foudroyé, sans répit et sans une seule minute de silence!"[3] ("I want to live thunderstruck, without respite, and without a single moment of silence.") It is a sentence that has something of Breton's characterization of beauty as an "explosion-fixe." (In any case, as with Gide's *Paludes*, Aquin's books, and Nabokov's seem constantly on the point of urging us to make up a private list of our own favorite sentences from them ...) If writing is shooting, then, at least a few of these sentences strike the reader square in the heart, with all the wide-eyed ideal transparency of instantaneous death.

Nor have I changed my mind about the "emplotment" of *Prochain épisode*: a clumsy, shoddy, homemade thing indeed when measured against the elaborate architectonics of any Robbe-Grillet novel (as are Nabokov's "ingenuities" when compared with those of any professional detective-story novelist). The obligatory doubles and their mirror multiplications in effect reduce this text to a score for three voices: the nameless first-person narrator, his victim, and his lover and co-conspirator, K. The alter ego is a counter-revolutionary agent whose banking connections allow him to follow the transfer of funds organized by the hero's worldwide conspiratorial network and to block them at will; he must therefore be suppressed, provided he can be identified, and in fact he possesses at least *two* known identities, a historian of Roman history, H. de Heutz, and a banker, Carl von Ryndt. In one of the more stunning sequences, then, the narrator urges his vehicle desperately over half the place names in Switzerland, only to find that the bank is closed, the coop is flown, and the putative target is lecturing, under his other name, on Swiss resistance to Caesar's armies virtually at the other geographical tip of the confederation: the same frantic unfolding of place names now takes place in the other direction. There is however some curious reality principle at work in this passage, as though you were free to multiply these imaginary doubles only at a certain price, namely, having laboriously and materially (whether in the text or on the road itself) to live through every unit of real space and time that separated the two fantasmatic entities.

The predictable encounter then takes place in a sumptuous chateau, with reversals and hesitations (first, it is de Heutz who holds the weapon, then the narrator, who in spite of his lyric celebrations of assassination curiously postpones and thereby misses his chance) whose narrative curves and arabesques gradually begin to organize themselves around the carved figure of a naked warrior, narcissistic imago of all the tripartite adventurers in this book (lovers, writers, combatants), from the Gallic Wars down to mid-

1960s Québec. It would, however, be wrong to read this figure as anything more than decorative closure; wrong to search for stable symbolism in what is rather staged as a delirium of symbolic dissemination, of perpetual symbolic displacement.

The conventional climax of such plays of doubles—the moment in which the universe of matter touches its mirror image in the universe of antimatter with a cataclysmic shudder in which both worlds are abruptly erased, in which the hero lodging a bullet in his double's heart finds himself bleeding and dying (or, as in Nabokov's second-degree variant, *Despair*, discovers that his "double," successfully executed, looks nothing like him at all)—this moment is indefinitely postponed, traversed and immobilized by Aquin's own arrest, in July, 1964, for illegal possession of firearms (an event, as we shall see, inscribed within the text itself).

Only the slow approach of this predictable resolution is developed, when, at the end of the text the narrator begins to become aware that his alter ego has also been seen with a blond woman who can be no other than K. herself, and whose multiple rendezvous begin to overlap and cancel each other out. Doubles have been a staple of literary criticism at least since Rank, and of literature at least since E.T.A. Hoffmann; yet Lacan's distinction between the Imaginary and the Symbolic (which I will not rehearse here[4]) suggests that the logic of an infinite proliferation of such mirror images is not itself meaningful in any significant way, not itself "symbolically" interpretable, but only an infinitely empty purely formal movement.

I will therefore suggest that the interpretive temptation here is that of a mirage, the mirage of the ultimate building block of narrative, the simplest primal plot—self and other, with the object of desire shared by both. The mirage is a Cartesian one, in which the mind, searching for the ultimate "key" to all narrative, imagines that the complex novels in which the latter has been most richly developed bear somehow within themselves this "smallest minimal unity," this stark and final situation of conflict and desire, which is their inner "truth" and "secret." But this is very precisely to confound the Symbolic and the Imaginary (the latter being little more than the raw materials worked over by the former in the production of a dialectically very different kind of text indeed).

We must, rather, Aquin's novel has convinced me, take this play of three primal figures and positions as the impossible attempt to generate *narrative* itself out of the radical solitude and imprisonment of the individual ego or subject. This play of doubles is not narrative, then, and never could be; but it is the desperate effort in a radically nonnarrative situation—absence of other people and of the outside world—to fantasize narrative into being by an effort of the will, to produce a whole concrete universe of the contingency of encounters with other people and the irreversibility of events and destinies out of the impoverishment of the individual body in isolation.

Such a body, such a literally walled monad, can easily project an alter ego over against itself; as for K., even the impoverishment of the seemingly distinct and sexually differentiated erotic object is betrayed by her dissolution into national allegory. K. is thus immediately Québec (*Kébec*), and the flesh celebrated in the erotic moments of the text is at once explicitly transmuted into the absent geography of the homeland or the nation, the primal landscape and language for whose political cause Aquin (and his first-person narrator) will be incarcerated within the four walls of the psychiatric institute Albert-Prévost in Montréal, beyond which, absent and invisible, the abstract totality of the province stretches like a fantasy in the prisoner's mind.

The mark of the failure to produce genuine narrative is then here detectable, in the compulsive repetitions of neurosis, in the failure to reach the new, the unforeseen, the event, the contingent, and the fatal return of a pseudonarrative fantasy into aimless circular rhythms that reproduce the initial impulse. There is thus some deeper kinship with pornography itself, which seeks to achieve some genuine object satisfaction out of the individual reading body, only to end up in masturbation (and pornography also, as Sartre shows us in his study of Jean Genet's novels, has some privileged relationship to the space of imprisonment). Aquin's own work, particularly in the delirious erotic-homicidal mysticism of *Neige noire* (1974) (with its overtones of Balzac's *Séraphita*), betrays such affinities by its development of a pornographic register of high quality, by the production of pornographic sentences and a pornographic style of no little originality; and the same movement can be found in Nabokov's own work, particularly as it relaxes into the language pools of *Ada*.

But *Prochain épisode* is not, finally, pornography, but something distinct, a structural variant on the pornographic impulse which has its own textual specificity. Not the wish fulfillment, but its failure; not the mesmerization of the image, but the drab walls against which it fades—this is the resistant infrastructure across which a sequence of decorative, optically fascinating surfaces play and annul one another. The novel is the story of a *room*: the same, from the ornate hotel room in Lausanne (or Montréal) in which a delirious love is celebrated, to the monumental chamber of the isolated chateau in which the hero pursues or is alternately pursued by his enemy, and behind both of them the confinement cell in which this novel is written, while even further back than that, there continues to exist, for us, the real room in which this text is being read. The return, the elaborate snare devised by the protagonist, who waits again in the silence of the chateau for the reappearance of his former hunter, now his putative victim, can be taken not as some mere setting for suspense, but rather, in a Gestalt reversal, as the empty form through which, little by little, the stunning fixity and blankness of space comes to inscribe itself on eyes functioning in the void. Rooms are both the external manifestation of the isolated ego or monad, the bourgeois psychic subject, and the latter's material determination; they also entertain curious historical relations with that most specialized and artificial of modern activities, reading and writing, which, unlike oral storytelling, seem inextricably bound up, not merely with the printing press, nascent industrial machinery and the technological reproduction of production, but also, in some more littered and extrinsic, scandalous sense, with furniture itself.

Yet this primal room is never given to us directly, but always, as we have just seen, through what Aquin, in a revealing phrase, calls a very "euphoria of substitutions"; and this is the moment to develop the most structurally original feature of Aquin's book, one which compensates the failure of the Imaginary text to loop itself into the appropriate Nabokovian spatial twists and closures by displacing that kind of horizontal attention (waiting for the return of identity, the moment of equation in which hero and double suddenly fuse and coincide) to a rather different, and properly infinite, sense of vertical superposition.

We will describe these "substitutions" as so many provisional allegorical frameworks, which emerge and vanish in a seemingly random or aleatory way, never hardening over into the monumental or dogmatic, but opening the text up to multiple interpretative temptations which have all the transitory insubstantiality of fantasy or daydream. Dates and chronology, seemingly the most stubborn and undecomposable foreign bodies within the literary text, are perhaps the most dramatic locus for these unsettling transformations—"between the 26th of July and the 4th of August, 1792": a fusion in which the attack on the Moncada barracks, which gave its name to the Cuban revolutionary movement itself, and the inaugural year of the Quiet Revolution in Québec, and the night in which, in the voluntary surrender of feudal privileges, the middle ages at last came to an end in revolutionary France (1789), mingled with that other fateful year, 1792, in which the battle of Valmy will mark the beginnings of a whole new people's age[5] and is retroactively designated as the beginning of Year I of the new revolutionary calendar—these references or interpretative frameworks, articulated in difference or even in dissonance, then begin to proliferate and to generate other, related, yet distinct temporal systems: July, 1964, for instance, in which Aquin himself will be arrested and confined; in which *Prochain épisode* will begin to be elaborated; or June 24, feastday of Saint-Jean-le-Baptiste, the patron saint of the province of Québec, which has since the victory of the Parti Québécois officially been designated as the national holiday of the newly emergent political entity.

Yet not merely temporal but also geographical coordinates are unfixed by a similar logic and movement: "Cuba sinking in flames in the midst of Lake Geneva"—the opening phrase of *Prochain épisode* is only the most dramatic of a host of geographical substitutions, of which the imperceptible contamination of Swiss place names by those of Québec itself is perhaps the more fundamental. The waxing and waning of these optional allegorical frameworks then allows the significance of the official Swiss setting to be suggested: Swiss neutrality comes to figure as one possible Utopian image of an independent Québec—with its hydroelectric riches—ideally distanced from the struggle of the world system all around it. Yet this ideal image is problematized by the Cuban framework: will Québécois independence be a respected enclave within protective mountain ranges, or the embattled blockade of a revolutionary island? The allegorical hesitation dramatizes the struggle of political interpretations of the Québec of the 1960s: the last of the First World states, or the most prosperous of Third World colonized entities? Or, as one Québécois political and cultural leader put it, is Montreal to conceive its identity in terms of Havana or of Vienna? This play of what I have called elsewhere "national allegory"[6] will remain central in Aquin's work: opening up to the colonial relationship to British Canada in *Trou de mémoire* (where the love object and victim is explicitly allegorical of the Anglophone "partner"), to the United States itself in *L'Antiphonaire*, which takes place in San Diego, until national allegory proper becomes rarefied and metaphysical in the dazzling Norwegian snow of *Neige noire* (in which, however, something of the wintry landscape of Switzerland—and of the Saint Lawrence basin— makes a symbolic return).

One must, finally, note a whole range of literary allusions of the same provisional and allegorical type: so Byron fitfully enters and leaves these pages, having composed the *Prisoner of Chillon* within them (in echo of Aquin's own composition of *Prochain épisode*), at the same time emitting the other distinct overtone of the revolutionary commitment to the Greek struggle for independence; while Balzac, who met Madame Hanska on the shores of this same lake, emits the strong afterimage of the author of the *Histoire des treize*, of the epic poet of conspiracy and terrorism.

For *Prochain épisode* is also, and most immediately, the aesthetic expression of a certain 1960s "terrorism" and the most enduring literary monument of the first FLQ (with which Aquin was said to have been associated).[7] We can therefore not omit, in conclusion, some remarks on this phenomenon, of which one would want to insist first of all that as such it is an *idéologème*, an ideological vision generated and propagated by the Right, for purposes which the feeble revival of this slogan under Reagan and by publicists like Claire Sterling[8] can give some sense. This is not to say that the realities to which the *idéologème* called "terrorism" corresponds did not exist, that there were no bombings or assassinations, nor that at a certain moment certain political militants, in many national or colonial situations, did not attempt explicitly to theorize political action in terms of "terrorist" strategies and tactics of the type which Marx, Lenin, Trotsky and the Marxist tradition has always denounced. But if you use that word and call it *that*, you are fatally playing into the hands of a whole elaborate right-wing cultural and ideological offensive, whose immediate successes can be detected in the omnipresent role of the "terrorist" in mass culture, who, like the homicidal maniac of an older social moment, is called upon to figure sheer Evil and to clinch the plot by explaining the inexplicable, producing an illusion of formal totality by way of the conventionalized illusion of motive and meaning. (One should also posit some relationship between such "terrorism" and international media society: often the political activity so designated refers to the attempt of desperate and powerless groups to stage their version of their cause before a vaster world public, from which monopoly of the media has excluded them. This "pedagogical function" of so-called terrorism thus has its kinship with the very different left strategy of provocation pioneered by the "Provos" in Holland.)

In that sense, however, Aquin's novel demystifies the "terrorist" impulse and unmasks the poverty of the conspiratorial small group as so many fantasies of solitary confinement, and of an isolation which is that of the class isolation of even revolutionary intellectuals fully as much as that of the locked prison cell. If writing is shooting (in both homicidal and sexual senses), then in the last desolate reversal of *Prochain épisode*, it turns out that shooting is little more than mere writing after all, albeit a writing that, fortunately, has left the sentences of this text in being behind it.

(*1982*)

Notes

1 See for example the remarks on Claudel in *Le Côté de Guermantes* (*A la recherche du temps perdu* [Paris, 1954] vol. II, pp. 325ff.)

2 *Fables of Aggression: Wyndham Lewis, The Modernist as Fascist* (Berkeley, 1979), p. 40.

3 Hubert Aquin, *Prochain épisode* (Montréal, 1965), p. 138. An English translation of the novel by Penny Williams was published under the same title by McClelland and Stewart (Toronto) in 1967.

4 But see my "Imaginary and Symbolic in Lacan," in *The Ideologies of Theory: Essays, 1971–1986* (Minnesota, 1988), vol. I.

5 Valmy, however, the *levée en masse*, the extraordinary superiority of the first people's army over the mercenaries of the *ancien régime*—that battle of which Goethe is supposed to have said that from that time and place a new era in the history of humankind began—Valmy is evidently a singularly ironic and problematical reference for a novel whose politics is that of the Blanquiste small conspiratorial group.

6 *Fables of Aggression*, op. cit., chapter 5.

7 It has become conventional to distinguish "two" *Fronts de libération du Québec*: the first centered around the period in the early 1960s when Aquin was himself arrested;

the second, emerging at the end of the decade, and culminating in the still suspicious assassination of the minister Pierre Laporte and in the October Crisis of 1970, during which Trudeau's army occupied the province. There exists a far more extensive literature on this last, including novels such as Brian Moore's *The Revolution Script.* On the first FLQ, see the interesting materials on the personal histories and formations of the participants contained in Gustav Morf, *Terror in Quebec; Case Studies of the FLQ* (Toronto, 1970). The links Morf shows between the first FLQ and resistance movements in Europe during World War Two, and also the first (or French) phase of the Vietnam war are very suggestive; the psychoanalytic conclusions are to my mind much less so.

8 And its far more successful deployment today (2007)!

20

"A Monument to Radical Instants"

I

The Aesthetics of Resistance, Peter Weiss's three-volume historical novel about the struggles of the German communist anti-Hitlerian networks from 1937 to the end of World War Two, marks a powerful intervention in German historiography, or more precisely into the sense of history and the construction of the past in which Germans and leftists of the last decade of the Cold War still lived: an intervention felt both in the German West and East (it was published in both countries) and cutting across, while acknowledging, the sterile polemics about Stalinism still current in that period. Posthumously (Weiss died six months after the publication of the final volume in 1981), it now has a significant role to play in the historicity a united Germany must construct in order to incorporate the experience of the German Democratic Republic (DDR)—a problem distantly comparable to the intellectual and historiographic appropriation of the complex and varied life world of the conquered South after the American Civil War. The new Germany is necessarily in search of a new vision of its own past, at the very moment when History, which will not stop for that effort of Hegelian *Erinnerung* and reconstruction of collective identity, is about to absorb Germany and its neighbors into some new and larger, transnational unity (at the same time that it threatens to annul even the autonomy of that new unity into the even larger networks of an all-subsuming late capitalist globalization).

But this is not merely a local German agenda: such dilemmas also confront the Left in general in the world today; and the modification of Germany's sense of its own radicalisms and revolutionary impulses must necessarily contribute to the reconstruction of a worldwide Left vision of its vocation and its possibilities in a seemingly post-revolutionary world situation in which capitalism and the ever-expanding penetration of the free market are commonly felt to be henceforth unchallenged. But the failure of the reconstruction of the former DDR means that some future German radicalism will emerge in unexpected forms from those conquered provinces, and emerge without warning, like all great revolutionary moments, very much according to Benjamin's messianic figures: "Every second of time is the strait gate through which Messiah may enter."[1] Thus here too the messianic preparation for a rebirth of the Left in Germany, and out of its older revolutionary traditions, stands as an allegory for the Left in general: Stalin, the cultures and strategies of Soviet communism, the Leninist dimension itself, will never be reborn, nor is such a rebirth even desirable for revolutionary impulses (such as those depicted in Peter Weiss's novel) which deplored, feared and loathed so many of the things associated with the old Soviet Union; but it will only be out of an unflinching contemplation of the past, an *acknowledgement* of it (to use Stanley Cavell's keyword), that the radical Novum of some new political and revolutionary movement can surge, unrecognizable, and seemingly without warning. But this contemplation is not required "in order to learn from the past and avoid its mistakes"—a silly notion at best; nor either to "make amends" and confess the guilt of the Stalinist period—for guilt is both a paralyzing impulse and a task in which, if properly considered, virtually everyone in the world might well be involved. Rather, just as in the familiar dialectic of the Communist period (reflected over and over again in the endless discussions and debates throughout the *Aesthetics of Resistance*), for which the defense of the Soviet Union was both impossible and unavoidable, so now the idea of the Soviet period, the memory of that immense historical experience, brooks no detour, even though there can be no reassuring way of "coming to terms with it." Such a confrontation with the past must also necessarily include the resistance to it and the disgust with which (West) German readers today greet the older political literature of the West German Gruppe 47 pre-unification writers,[2] as well as that which postmodern readers in general bring to the now dead past of the interwar years and of World War Two—a boredom sometimes mingled with curious stabs of nostalgia, and strengthened by consumerist habits for which the outmoded and the old-fashioned are somehow more intolerable than the palpable shoddiness of much of what is truly contemporary. There is no right way of dealing with the past—forgetfulness is no more therapeutic than a mesmerization by persistent trauma; but history is not made up of passing fashions which you are free to discard or replace. Still, the afterlife of Peter Weiss's novel can be explained by the historically modified role it is called upon to play in this new post-Cold War period, so different from the still feverishly political situation of the early German 1980s. This is the excuse (along with the unfamiliarity of the work to readers outside Germany or Sweden) for adding a contemporary confrontation with this text to the already voluminous critical work on Peter Weiss.[3]

Yet the active intervention in the past, the return to the only too familiar dilemmas of a worldwide Left politics in the Hitler era—but this time beyond the sterile alternative of apologia or strident anti-communism—this is not the only vocation of this "novel," nor the only intellectual context in which its originality and power can be felt. The unavoidable references that have already been made to memory, collective and individual alike, remind us that for good or ill the last few years have known a feverish preoccupation with historical memory (and also autobiography), with mourning and melancholia, and finally with the Holocaust itself.[4] *The Aesthetics of Resistance* commemorates political failure and defeat, but scarcely overlooks the physical suffering and martyrdom that accompanied such defeat; and to this also it wishes to provide, not a monument of some sort (the question of monuments is also one of the burning issues of our period), but rather a machine for reliving that sheerly corporeal agony. This is not a testimony either,[5] that witnesses might piously record and preserve: but rather an immediacy of the body and the anguished mind which we are ourselves called upon to retraverse by way of reading. It is a peculiarly juxtaposed set of materials: sparsely selected yet vivid landscapes along with interiors and rooms which have a different function; the visual lessons of many paintings; and finally the sheer suffering of bodies whose primary sexuality (chastely absent from these pages) is replaced by pain. Peter Weiss has his contribution to make to current theories of the body as well as to the varied figural or intellectual, or sometimes wordless or impossible, modes of approaching something like the Holocaust. Yet this is not a book about the Holocaust, I think, although a place is made for that within it. Still, it would be enough to remember the critiques addressed to his Auschwitz play, *The Investigation*—that in it Jews were assimilated unacceptably to the other victims, most notably to communists; that the event was thereby stripped of its uniquely Jewish meaning[6]—a reproach which can be prolonged to the *Aesthetics* as well (despite Peter Weiss's own half-Jewish origins)—to realize that the work cannot be reclaimed for Holocaust literature and the Holocaust tradition. But it certainly remains central to all the themes and theoretical questions raised by the debate over that literature, from that of the impossibility of representation all the way to that of the uses of memory.

The reconstruction of the past and of some future Left; the commemoration of the suffering of the dead—to these projects must be added another, already registered in the title: yet *The Aesthetics of Resistance* is not so much a contribution to aesthetic theory as rather the working out of an aesthetic pedagogy. For this is also a *Bildungsroman*, in which a young German worker learns a politics of resistance in the vicissitudes of history, but also appropriates a whole aesthetic culture, which is meant to complete that first and political education and which may in many ways even precede it and prepare the cultural (and dare one even say, in keeping with the German context, "spiritual" [*geistig*]) receptivity for those more pragmatic lessons and dilemmas. Famously, it is with a visit to the Pergamum altar by three schoolfriends that the novel begins: the first form of physical suffering in these pages is that of tortured statuary—the agony of the giants crushed by the Olympians; the first political lesson is a mythological and aesthetic, an imaginary one—the vision of defeat, the triumph of the Olympian rulers over the rebellious demi-gods. The first step in this aesthetic pedagogy, in this aesthetic formation of the subject, is thus one of "a massacre impenetrable to the thought of liberation":[7] a seemingly frustrating and paralyzing first step.

Yet this is a proletarian *Bildungsroman*, a pedagogy of the subaltern: and it is worth remembering that, of the hundreds of characters who people this vast novel, only three are fictional: the unnamed narrator and his parents. All the rest are real historical figures on whom Weiss did voluminous research. Nor should we forget that these three central fictive characters are only objects of autobiographical identification in a severely mediated way: for Peter Weiss was a bourgeois and his father a business manager. It would be abusive to suppose that the novelist was free to transpose his own experiences effortlessly into those of a fictive youth, who just happened to be a working-class subject growing up in a working-class neighborhood. The debates that have swirled around Proust's fictional description of heterosexual love from a supposedly homosexual standpoint[8] ought to find their resonance and their analogy here, if we assume that this representation is also simply the description of an already existing experiential state of things or state of mind.

But the pedagogical framework, if it means anything at all, means that we have to do here not with a state of things but with an emergence and the modification of all such previous "states": this is a self-fashioning, a construction of subjectivity, in which the subject attempts to master and reappropriate even those blows from outside that might ordinarily be thought to be beyond his control. He is to do this through art and culture; and collectively, with his fellows and a few teachers (Brecht as well as the psychiatrist Hodann), to construct a new education for himself and for them. Politically and theoretically, of course, this pedagogical framework takes a philosophical position, which is recognizably that of certain new or oppositional Marxisms which have asserted the indispensability of consciousness and culture over against the reductions by a mainstream of praxis to the economistic and the narrowly political-ideological.

Yet this is not merely a philosophical or an intellectual position: it has its symbolic working-through in the concrete process of reading itself. For whatever the value of such pedagogical demonstrations for a properly working-class or subaltern public itself (and it may be safely assumed that today the afterlife of *The Aesthetics of Resistance* is more secure in the former East Germany than in the old Bundesländer)—and whatever the implications for a socialist state in these new proposals for an *Erbe* and a new cultural tradition, and in particular for the hotly debated question of the appropriation or not of the bourgeois artistic tradition, not to speak of the precapitalist ones—it must also be remembered that we—the new current readership—are ourselves mainly middle-class people, formed under capitalism. Peter Weiss's personal effort of an imaginative self-projection into the *Bildung*-situation of a working-class protagonist from the 1930s is thus itself an allegory of our own possibilities of imaginative sympathy as readers of this text: it is his mediation that can alone make our own reading possible; even though one also wishes to reassert Sartre's famous insistence on the incomparable richness imposed on texts and narratives that cannot avoid addressing two distinct publics, two distinct readerships.[9]

2

Yet to all these programs must be added a final one, a formal project this time, quite different in its problems and obstacles from any which have been mentioned thus far. For this is also a historical novel, and it must somehow confront and solve in new ways all the dilemmas with which the newly emergent genre of the historical novel has had to grapple at least since its first codification by Sir Walter Scott. Yet despite this respectable generic cover, apologists for the work have been remarkably defensive. Thus it has become conventional to begin discussion of the *Aesthetik* by acknowledging its formal peculiarities: Manfred Haiduk calls it a "Monstrum"; Robert Cohen suggests that, of the three volumes, only the last is really a novel; etc.[10] Formal innovations no doubt always make for problems and difficulties in reading: but it can happen, more rarely, that the formal innovation lies far more centrally in the demand for a new reading practice. This was the case with the proponents of *nouveau roman*,[11] whose experiments with what in the media is called "real time" will be suggestive here; and it is also and preeminently the case with Peter Weiss, even though the innovation his book proposes is utterly different in meaning and spirit from theirs.

On completing his violin concerto, Schoenberg is said to have exclaimed, "Now they will have to invent a completely different way of playing the violin." But I believe that a true avant-garde is characterized, not merely by a modification in the way a work is constructed or executed, but also by a program of changes for its reception (it is true that the performing of an already written musical score lies somewhere in between these poles, which are often thought of as active and passive, respectively). New kinds of perception, new forms of listening attention, are explicitly demanded, along with the new material or content, the new formal structures, of the "text" in question. These programs then allegorically project the vision of a new community organized around them, so that while the essentially collective production of a given avant-garde is necessary in order to mark a given aesthetic moment as such, it is not sufficient. In this spirit, the *nouveau roman*, whose collective character as a "school" is in any case relatively dubious, is at best a borderline case.

Peter Weiss, to be sure, reflected throughout his life and work on the possibility of an avant-garde, both artistic and political; but one may say, following the Deleuze of the film books (for whom political films are defined as such precisely by the absence of community and praxis), that that work, relatively solitary in its emergence, even though it is marked by collaboration and collective performance, mourns the loss of the possibility of an avant-garde more than it manages to reinstate one.[12] Comparable in that perhaps only to COBRA, Weiss's essentially late modernism attempts to repeat one of the earlier, now classical forms of the modern, but where the great majority of this production finds its coordinates in the "great moderns"—non-avant-gardists, writers of a solitary book of the world,[13] like Joyce or Mallarmé—Weiss still thinks in terms of movements, like surrealism and experimental film. In that, it is worth underscoring the analogies between Weiss and another immense yet unclassifiable figure of the postwar, who also tried to "reconcile" art and politics, Marx and Freud, sexual revolution and social revolution. Pasolini was if anything even more of a loner than Peter Weiss, projecting his vision of the collectivity back into the myths and rituals of premodern villages and tribes, as supremely in the *Medea* (1970), with its cannibalism and magic, and its lament for the modern "desacralization" of the world (the centaur teacher Chiron first appearing as centaur, then in modern-dress clothes on two legs—because we moderns have lost the framework in which we believe in centaurs). But I want to underscore a more basic analogy between Pasolini and Weiss—both otherwise incomparable, and Weiss virtually without any national tradition of his own—contemporaneous with the Beats, but here too without any genuine similarities, nor can I think of any other figures to compare them with. What they shared formally, besides the themes I have mentioned, is that crude hacking simplicity of the pedagogue who initiates forms; who feels no particular respect for a series of formal exercises or innovations, but chops into the medium in order to convey a point which would be unsophisticated and programmatic in the form of a philosophical position[14]—as for example the juxtaposition of Marat and Sade themselves, or the thesis on magic I have just alluded to in Pasolini's *Medea.* Add to this the reliance on preexisting texts—most often documents, in the case of Weiss, rather than myths or the tales of the *Decameron* or *The Arabian Nights*, in that of Pasolini.

I have indulged this comparison in order to position Weiss in the postwar period, in a framework a little wider than the merely German one. The politics of both figures—essentially men of the 1950s—would merit attention, but for our purposes it suffices that alongside a lifelong commitment to politics and to the reinvention of a kind of avant-garde art, both were passionately nostalgic for a vanguard politics as well, and both keenly attentive to the sexual liberation of the 1960s and 1970s. Pasolini's work is, however, drenched in sexuality from the very beginning, in contrast to the restraint of *The Aesthetics of Resistance* (which would have to be juxtaposed to the sexual themes of Weiss's earlier works, along with the emblematic figure of Sade himself).

Yet in Pasolini, as with COBRA, a preoccupation with history takes the form of the archaic and the mythic, and expresses the conviction that collective life can only be glimpsed, let alone recaptured, by a return to precapitalist societies, from the astonishing rituals of Medea's tribal society all the way up to Boccaccio or *The Arabian Nights*. Contemporary works, such as *Theorema* (1968), are framed politically—the factory owner's gift of the factory—but in programmatic or Utopian ways; even the early images of Roman low life and Pasolini's favorite *Lumpens* exclude the perspective of a historical interpretation and causal analysis of the recent past.

Weiss is thus alone, among the late modern writers (not to speak of overtly postmodern ones) in confronting the dilemmas of the historical novel as a form; and this in so uncompromising a fashion as to demand a thoroughgoing (and, as has been seen with the critics, often also perplexing) revision of conventional narrative and representational techniques. This is not to ignore the moments of narrative bravura of an older modernist style: as for example the great cross-cutting montage at the end of Volume I, in which the show trials and the execution of Bukharin alternate in dramatic Sartrean fashion with Hitler's occupation of Austria, the Anschluss, and the feverish discussion of the foreign militants on the rapidly deteriorating Republican front of the Spanish Civil War (I, 270–286/288–304). Nor must we forget Brecht's flight from Sweden at the end of Volume II, during which, "collapsing on the gangplank, between the German embassy building, on the left, and the German freighters flying the swastika, on the right, he had to be virtually carried on board" (II, 331): all this preceded by an extraordinary comic sequence in which, visited by the Swedish secret police, who examine his library, Brecht celebrates their departure by pelting them with Edgar Wallace and Agatha Christie paperbacks from a second-storey window. Yet such narrative set-pieces are inevitably affairs of beginnings and endings, whose unique tempos call forth the architectonic as such, that grand arabesque which is construction fully as much as decoration.

Otherwise this ostensible story of the teeming and dramatic events of the onset of World War Two is conveyed by way of endless conversations and debates about political positions and strategy, housed in a strangely abstract space, whose very lyrical openings—onto the orange groves of Valencia, for example—at once turn into historical and economic disquisitions on the region and its agricultural characteristics. This is decidedly not the kind of vivid representation of the experience of history we have been trained to expect from fiction. With signal exceptions—the rather painterly account of the Bremen uprising of 1919, not to speak of the grisly step-by-step description of the executions of the last of the resistance network in Plötzensee, about which one could to be sure argue that such corporeal vividness is achieved primarily by way of its contrast with the time of discussions and debates, a time of waiting and of enforced passivity, in which history can only arrive in the form of news and rumor—historical events are here for the most part mediated, and at best "represented" secondhand, by way of a weighing of the conflicting evidence and a sifting of detail. Still, and particularly since the *nouveau roman* has been fleetingly evoked above, it is worth registering a similarity between the passage of historical time in this novel of Peter Weiss, and the scoring and unregistering of reading time I have elsewhere described for a (non-historical) novel by Claude Simon[15] (a novelist to be sure equally obsessed with history, but in a far more experiential way, and through deep memory and repetition). There, a narrative apparatus is constructed, in such a way that the time of reading has been dissociated into two distinct registers: on the one hand the time of the individual sentences and words, the microscopic fragmented perceptions we receive one after the other, up very close, in proximate vision and magnified reception; and the time of the pages and of the book itself, which slowly runs out, irreversibly and surely, irrespective of the minute content of the present of the words themselves. The clock is ticking, one wants to say, or better still, the meter is running: the page numbers are still changing, piling up, no matter how intolerably paralyzed or suspended we seem to be in an endless reading present. So in Weiss also: the time of history continues, despite these endlessly suspended arguments and exchanges out of time. Spain is slowly but irrevocably lost; the German armies inexorably colonize Europe; the war itself at length draws to a close—despite the agonized fixation of the characters upon their positions and perplexities, their ideological clashes, and their interrogation of the demands of the concrete situation itself, an interrogation which must remain abstract and a matter of thinking and argument, however urgent and particular the dilemma, which is in any case bound to be overtaken by events and transformed into a new and utterly different one. What can account for such a radical and seemingly perverse choice of narrative strategies, whose massive preponderance throughout these nine hundred pages goes well beyond any reasonable intention to bring out and articulate the ideological and philosophical issues at stake in the war itself?

To be sure, *Marat/Sade* is there to remind us, if need be, of the dichotomous nature of Peter Weiss's conceptual imagination: everywhere in his work, forces and positions are defined by way of oppositions, from which the great political divergences of the "third period" and the Popular Front can scarcely be expected to be exempt. One imagines serious historians attempting to be even-handed, and to do justice even to the reasonings and motivations of those on the "wrong" side (here primarily the Stalinists and the orthodox party members, since, as in Malraux, the fascists and the Nazis are rigorously excluded from this cast of characters). Still, the discourse of the historians is fatally monological, as Bakhtin might have said; and any empathetic reconstruction of Stalinism is bound to be a set-up, in which the foreknowledge of historical failure and revelation to come cannot but influence the drift and the outcome. Nor is Weiss above the fray himself: as has been said, the pedagogical focus secures an option for cultural politics which will be incorporated in the doomed yet larger-than-life figure of Willi Münzenberg—supreme genius of communist agitation and world propaganda in the Popular Front period, hunted pariah in the first years of the war, when his body will be found hanged from a tree in a French forest during the exodus. Hodann, the Reichian psychiatrist, who insists on the place of sexuality and the transformation of daily life in the midst of any committed politics, offers a realist and approachable analogue in the personal experience of the narrator. Yet even these passionate commitments (which are unmistakably those of Peter Weiss himself) cannot be expressed, let alone validated, without an argument with the opposite side; they have to emerge in struggle with persuasive adversaries, who sensibly and reasonably insist that the revolution must first be defended and secured against a frightening array of dangers and enemies, before the luxury of full personal and social liberation can be indulged. Finally, neither side wins these ideological battles; but each needs the other to achieve full expression and historical representation.

We may enumerate some of these oppositions, which are related but not identical. Clearly the great schism and opposition between German Social Democracy and the communist movement (inside and outside Germany) will be a central preoccupation: in a scene on a bench in Paris during the 1930s, the narrator's father takes the position of disillusioned socialists, while Herbert Wehner argues a communist one (the narrator must himself reenact the argument with his father as he draws closer to the party). In Spain, to be sure, it is anarchism which becomes communism's ideological adversary, and whose leaders and spokespersons are one by one physically eliminated.

Yet in a work whose palpable aesthetic preoccupations have not yet sufficiently been outlined, there will also be artistic oppositions, which are argued out fully as much in aesthetic as in political terms: most obviously that between modernism and realism, in an immense movement in which the deciphering of the Utopian and social impulses at work in modern art will be matched by a faithfulness to the most neglected monuments of a genuine social or socialist realism. We will return to this, the narrator's aesthetic education, in more detail later on.

Yet this opposition inevitably generates that other one of which we have already spoken, which is related but not the same: the Münzenberg position on cultural politics, as it confronts the more military or sheerly political, resolutely non-aesthetic, strategies of others in the communist movement. Hodann is meanwhile there to secure the modulation of this theme into the Reichian one of sexual politics as over against the conventional Left.

Finally, in a very different register there is the opposition of the father to the mother: the first a locus of historical working-class memory (the Bremen uprising), now withdrawn from current struggles; the mother, sinking into a visionary and nightmarish schizophrenia, into a stubborn silence and mutism born of the trauma of the collective agony and displacement by the Nazi armies and finally of the rumors of the death camps themselves; the father in contrast obsessed by the "machine" of this society. Both are thus locked in the past, but in active and passive registers respectively; the one brooding over the failures of praxis, the other immobilized by intense and vivid physical suffering relived over and over again. The narrator will unite these two registers, but overcome them in some new and future-oriented way, offering the promise—if not yet the image or representation—of the possibility of productively combining agency and mourning.

Yet to all these we must finally add that opposition in which we ourselves share as readers: namely that between bourgeois and proletarian experience, in which the whole notion of subalternity is necessarily relevant; the lack of access to this or that mainstream culture, the way in which mainstream (or bourgeois) culture is marked as belonging to others and to some inaccessible upper-class or privileged elite; the sheer physical obstacles, finally, to the acquisition of culture by working people who have no leisure for its acquisition, or even for the acquisition of its preconditions. All of this is given to us in the account of the narrator's *Bildung*, and in the harsher reactions of his family and fellows to an alien culture whose overt ideologies are often either privatized or aestheticized, if not openly those committed to oppression or repression—as at the very outset the glorification of the conquering Olympians in the Pergamum altar. This is an issue which, as we shall see, will lead to a hermeneutic deciphering far more complex than anything deployed in an exclusively bourgeois context.

It would flatten out the specificity of all these issues and oppositions to resume them under the great antithesis of politics and art, which is nonetheless inscribed in its fashion in the very title of the work, and which is certainly one of the fundamental themes under which this work was composed. Yet it is always worth remembering Adorno's remark—it being understood that in the twentieth century art itself is bound up with the problem of the avant-garde—that people today cannot imagine the degree to which, before the break of Stalin's socialist realism in the early 1930s, the two avant-gardes were absolutely linked, and the fortunes of avant-garde art were never felt to be dissociated from those of vanguard politics (something Perry Anderson also points out for artistic modernity in a famous essay).[16] For us, or at least until very recently, when it is vanguard politics that has seemed to vanish, it was the other way round; and the various Western traditions (and in particular the Anglo-American one) have all seemed to insist on the way in which vanguard art—mostly conceived as modernist poetry—finds its precondition in an absolute separation from the political or from "social issues." But Peter Weiss was one of the rare late-modern artists who refused this separation; and who tried, virtually by fiat and by an effort of the will, to put the two vanguards back together (as early as *Marat/Sade*), his originality consisting in the sense that dilemmas and contradictions relate fully as much as they separate, and that to impose the problem of the two avant-gardes is also at least partially to overcome it.

3

But we have not yet replaced these forms and materials within the problematic of the historical novel as such, whose dilemmas—duly registered at the birth of this form of genre, and belatedly codified by Lukács in his *The Historical Novel*[17]—can only be intensified in modernity with its demographic increase and its technological innovations. Even the "traditional" historical novel, however, was inscribed at the center of two irresolvable oppositions or contradictions, which only palliatives (like Lukács's "average hero" or observer) could weaken in such a way as to allow the novel to be written in the first place.

The first of these axes, unsurprisingly, is the opposition between the individual and the collective, or, better still, that between individual or existential experience and that dimension of collective reality inscribed in institutions, as what Sartre calls the practico-inert; inscribed in economics and the market as well, and which finally transcends all individual categories.[18] It is important to disjoin this problem from the act of witnessing as such,[19] even though the same impossibilities reign in that more restricted and specialized form of experience as well: for who has ever seen the depression, or the market system, or the nation state? who has ever seen war as such?—something not to be restricted to the witnessing of a battle (even though Stendhal famously, and very early in the career of the historical novel as a form, inscribed even that impossibility in his historical narrative of the "experience" of the battle of Waterloo[20]). One is tempted to suggest that this is something of a spatial dilemma, with its temporal analogy in the individual biological life span equally out of synchrony with the great waves and rhythms of properly historical change.

Yet in modern history there have been rare moments in which the antithesis between the existential and the collective seems to have been transcended, if not overcome. These are not battle scenes, although for the bourgeois reader the battle offers their most accessible analogy, other versions being ideologically subsumed under the stereotype of mob violence. The strong moment, however, clearly remains the experience of revolution, with its lower-order forms in the general strike and the mass rally or demonstration. Were we speaking ontologically here, I would want to argue that precisely in such moments the isolated being of the individual subject is heightened and dissolved, lifted up and transfigured, into a kind of collective being of a fleeting or ephemeral type, which nonetheless Left political theory has always attempted to recreate in the concept and to prolong in new institutional arrangements (the "construction" of socialism as a temporal process, for example, rather than the actual institutions of some achieved socialism). Certainly Peter Weiss was fascinated by such moments, as the father's narratives of the Bremen uprising testify (I, 92–97/100–106), and as is shown by the two emblematic novels on which the narrator meditates at some length: Kafka's *The Castle* and the less well-known *Barricades in Wedding* by Klaus Neukrantz, a proletarian work from the 1920s which tells the story of an ill-fated Berlin uprising. These two works—for the bourgeois reader clearly of unequal value—dramatize the classic philosophical opposition between making and what is made in the realm of history: reified structure from the outside, the dynamic historical process of struggle and collective resistance from the inside.

But they also problematize any contemporary effort to reinvent the great collective scenes through which a Scott or a Manzoni, and later on a Victor Hugo or a Flaubert, attempted to dramatize history and make it visible to the individual reader/witness. Such scenes, rare and precious enough in literary history, and generally (as has been observed above) subsumed under this or that ideology of the mob famously codified by LeBon and Freud, wager their stakes on the possibility of a kind of collective narration, one which is not exactly impersonal or omniscient, but rather somehow extrapolated from extinct or nonexistent grammatical and verbal categories such as the dual: a kind of "man" or "on" (to appropriate Heidegger in his German and French versions, English having no equivalent) which, far from being the realm of the inauthentic, would offer a glimpse of the truly collective itself as it is momentarily revealed to be the demiurge of what we call history.

But demography and globalization mean that today this fiction of a truly collective narrative—or at least of a truly collective narrative moment—can no longer be sustained: it would be the worst sort of allegory to imply that this or that local street fight can truly stand in for the collective process (or if you prefer, can in the present situation convince us that genuine revolution is still conceivable, let alone possible). It is therefore not on the level of a linguistic innovation or a language experiment that Peter Weiss can resolve the formal problem of collective representation: the opposition between the isolated individual and collective history will certainly be inscribed here, over and over again, in the physical separation and loneliness of the individual militants and in the great collective forces at work beyond them, in Moscow or Berlin. But it is the form of the work as a whole that tries to convey the dilemma (and thereby negatively to offer its very representation).

The formal contradictions of the historical novel can, however, also be registered in a different way, in the opposition between power and its effects: but this is already a system which implies a frame, an extreme situation, such as war or revolution, since normally the locus of power is less visible and more difficult to anthropomorphize. Kings and queens, presidents, leaders and bosses, continue to exist in peacetime, but their real control over events, and above all their relationship to the functioning of a given social system itself, with its inequities and uneven privileges, its chances and its sacrifices, is less plausible, and certainly harder to dramatize. Even Hegel's concept of the "world-historical individual" is an intermittent one, its appearance dependent on the capacities for change inherent in a given moment of the system itself. Still, the aporias of such peacetime representations of power persist over into the crisis situations themselves, when these are interrogated with sufficient formal intensity.

If we look, indeed, more closely at the existential reality of decision making, or of what is today loosely called power, it becomes evident that it is a diminished or impoverished situation which at its outer limit resolves into a room or a communications center with banks of telephones and the entrance and exit of innumerable messenger-bureaucrats. The dictator, at the center of this web, experiences very little in immediacy; everything is mediated to him (for example, it is said that in his early years of power, Stalin depended on his first wife, still a student, to tell him what was going on in the outside world and what his subjects were thinking and saying[21]). Far from being a full center on the order of Hobbes's sovereign, made up of innumerable little human beings, let alone Borges's aleph or Dante's ingathered Book, the center of power is existentially empty, and the attempt to represent it must at best fall back on conjectural psychology: as witness the innumerable debates about Hitler's real motives or intentions—debates which either move in the direction of psychosis or childhood trauma or on the other hand (as most memorably in A.J.P. Taylor[22]) decide to reduce this figure to a conventional German statesman, with fully rational plans, projects and war aims. Thus, for Lukács, the "world-historical individual" must never be the protagonist of the historical novel, but only viewed from afar, by the average or mediocre witness (that such a figure can on the other hand be the center of historical drama, for Lukács, is explained by the fact that in that case it is we, the spectators, who are the witnesses, and who continue to observe the world-historical gestures and utterances from the outside).

It was the originality of Solzhenitsyn to have grasped this, in *The First Circle*, and in a memorable scene to have given us an unaccustomed portrait of the dictator in his solitude:

> And he was only a little old man with a desiccated double chin which was never shown in his portraits, a mouth permeated with the smell of Turkish leaf tobacco, and fat fingers which left their traces on books. He had not been feeling too well yesterday or today. Even in the warm air he felt a chill on his back and shoulders, and he had covered himself with a brown camel's-hair shawl.
>
> He was in no hurry to go anywhere, and he leafed with satisfaction through a small book in a brown binding. He looked at the photographs with interest and here and there read the text, which he knew almost by heart, then went on turning the pages. The little book was all the more convenient because it could fit into an overcoat pocket. It could accompany people everywhere in their lives. It contained two hundred and fifty pages, but it was printed in large stout type so that even a person who was old or only partly literate could read it without strain. Its title was stamped on the binding in gold: *Iosif Vissarionovich Stalin: A Short Biography.*
>
> The elemental honest words of this book acted on the human heart with serene inevitability. His strategic genius. His wise foresight. His powerful will. His iron will. From 1918 on he had for all practical purposes become Lenin's deputy. (Yes, yes, that was the way it had been.) The Commander of the Revolution found at the front a rout, confusion; Stalin's instructions were the basis for Frunze's plan of operations. (True, true.) It was our great good fortune that in the difficult days of the Great War of the Fatherland we were led by a wise and experienced leader—the Great Stalin. (Indeed, the people were fortunate.) All know the crushing might of Stalin's logic, the crystal clarity of his mind. (Without false modesty, it was all true.) His love for the people. His sensitivity to others. His surprising modesty. (Modesty—yes, that was very true.)[23]

Here, then, the final form of this approach to the center brings us up short against a play of mirrors, and reality oscillates between its own reflections in some final static movement. It is as though Stalin himself became the reader in search of the ultimate representation; as though the emptiness of his own consciousness, his own *pour-soi* (an emptiness shared by all other human reality), incited him as well to substitute his own image for the missing self. The ultimate book within the book thus proves to be a children's biography, in which Stalin has turned into his own stereotype, power feebly and toothlessly attempting to find its own delectation in all that can be represented of itself. This extraordinary moment marks a kind of climax in the approach of the historical novel as a form towards its own limits and the impossibility of its representational aesthetic. After this the classical historical novel is at an end, and its world-historical individual must become an anti-hero.

This is the sense in which the most thoroughgoing and productive recodification of the larger form has been the new genre of the Great Dictator novel, most widely practiced in Latin America. Here what comes to the surface is the profound ambivalence of the figure, who fascinates at the same time that he repels. But it is a constitutive ambivalence which now reflects the geopolitical structure of the forms of power available for representation in the Latin American countries. For here the great dictator is still a monster, but one whose very inhumanity is required by the nature of the situation of sovereignty itself, that is to say, by the equally monstrous and overpowering presence of that force such a dictator can alone resist: namely, the United States. Whence the mixture of admiration and loathing that these figures call up in the reader. From a structural point of view, however, this is the equivalent of saying that this particular center of power is ultimately not really the center, since its very power is reactive, and the true center lies elsewhere, to the North, remaining itself unrepresented.

We must thus appreciate in this light and context the wisdom of Malraux's choice, in his novel of the Spanish Civil War, *L'Espoir*, not to represent the enemy and not even to show fascist figures and protagonists as such, since the reader can have no real access to the Otherness of their evil, and thus at best risks a kind of mesmerized external fascination. (Camus's decision, in *La Peste*, to dramatize the Nazi Occupation in terms of disease is clearly a more doubtful matter.) This is also, as we have said, the case with the *Aesthetik des Widerstandes*, whose immense cast of (real, historical) characters remains limited to the Left, or to the various lefts within the antifascist movements.

Still, if the pole of power can finally not be represented, why should the same be true for the other pole of ordinary people, the subjects of power and the recipients of its effects? Why should some genuinely historical representation of daily life in a given crisis not be achievable? I think that this perfectly proper question also takes us to the heart of what is unsatisfactory in Lukács's more general notion of "typicality." But let me anticipate, and jump rapidly ahead in time to our own period, in order, by way of a form I have discussed in some detail elsewhere,[24] to show a kind of final formal outcome and a structural dilemma already implicit in the earliest version of the historical genre.

For what "nostalgia film" shows us is that at the same time that history, the historicity of the various distinct historical pasts and periods, degenerates into visual images of itself—styles, pop music, appliances, clothing, hairdos, the furnishings of a given era—so also does the "knowledge" of historical events and the contents of historicity become degraded into the stereotypes of the simplified history manuals taught in the schools (or later on recycled through various television "instant replays"). This means that what we now take to be "typical" of a given historical period—its ideological preoccupations and struggles, characteristic events, the very kinds of people who populate its social space—are little more than stereotypes drawn from just such childhood reading as we found Stalin absorbed in. This is why "nostalgia films" fail to solve the older as well as the newer problems of historical representation (that they necessarily deal with historical materials is however constitutive of the "genre," if it may be called that). There is no novelty in the invention; we never encounter the contingent or the unexpected in such representations; and in that sense they fail to offer one of the basic pleasures of narrative form as such. And this is because we already know their content: their characters and events are always-already examples of a preexistent historical knowledge (or pseudo-knowledge). They must necessarily come before us as already familiar, since their validation as such depends on precisely such recognition by the spectator that, yes, that was what was happening in that particular period (the Roaring Twenties or the Great Depression)—I acknowledge that I recognize those "types" of characters, those "types" of events.

And this is the deeper reason why, at the pole of collective representation (as opposed to that of power or the state), the classic genre of the historical novel also confronts a fundamental dilemma: it must (insofar as it is also a novel) offer a narrative of individual lives and stories. But insofar as these stories are those of really individualized (that is to say, privatized) characters, there opens up here a realm of complete arbitrariness where the novelist's imagination reigns supreme. Yet this is to say that those private stories can be stories about anything, they are completely disengaged from their putative historical context, they could just as well furnish a contemporary novel as anything set in the past (once one removes the historical trappings, the costumes, the spatial layout and the like). But insofar as those stories purport to entertain organic or constitutive links with a genuine historical situation, their motivation and their content will always reflect just that precooked stereotypical knowledge of a given past we have found to operate so close to the surface in postmodernity. "Typicality" in this sense is an unholy synthesis between a narrative particular and a conceptual (historiographic) universal; the latter tends fatally to transform the former into sheer example, thereby divesting it of its narrative immediacy.

Contemporary historical fiction will be authentic only if it confronts these contradictions and formal dilemmas in some energetic fashion that originates a formally innovative (if only provisional) solution. *The Aesthetics of Resistance* will never serve as a model for future historical representation; but nothing can do that anyway. Yet its structural novelties (so often, as has been seen, perceived as awkwardnesses or formal flaws or transgressions) can only be appreciated and evaluated in that light.

4

Peter Weiss's "solution" to these dilemmas—which is to say his intensified articulation of them—takes the form of a depersonalized collective voice which I will call a dialogical agon. It is a concept I want to model on that of a depersonalized individual subject whose forms one finds throughout contemporary literature, committed as it is to the theory and practice of a radically depersonalized consciousness beyond all individual identity and subjectivity: the famous "decentered subject" or "consciousness without the me" (Blanchot), sometimes illicitly celebrated in a rhetoric of the "death of the subject" or as an ideal schizophrenia (Deleuze), and to be found in all those enigmatic third persons of modern literature, more mysterious, as has so often been remarked, than any of its first-person characters, inasmuch as we can see and observe them, but must ourselves be confined to looking out through the gaze of this narrative one, which then takes on something of the unknowability of Kant's noumenal subject, always adding "the I to all its acts of consciousness," while itself remaining unknowable and inaccessible. Yet these approaches to some anonymous individual subjectivity—which has become depersonalized and inaccessible, owing to the movement of history, and about which it is never clear whether modern philosophy's varied efforts to do away with its illusions of subjectivity simply replicate the tendencies in late capitalist society or on the other hand propose energetic reactions to it—remain locked in the "philosophy of consciousness." They are so many descriptions of the monad, which variously attack Descartes or enlist new interpretations of him with a view towards undermining his subjectivist and idealist heritage. Nor is it surprising that this should be so: one does not break out of monadic isolation by the simple act of taking thought; one does not produce collective forms and experiences by fiat.

In any case, and for the very same reasons, we find it difficult to think the collective except as modeled on the individual: the much-decried slogan of "collective consciousness" remains in place, however much we wish to analyze collective dynamics in a fashion rigorously distinct from those of the individual. Greek choruses, depersonalized historical narrative, "subjects of history," myths and archetypes, banal allegorical "representatives" of group forces—such are the traps and failures that lie in wait for any narrative commitment to collectivity (nor are their traces absent from this novel either).

This is why it seems desirable to resurrect the program of a post-structuralist onslaught on individual consciousness—itself finally yet another avatar of an old individualist bourgeois subjectivity—and in particular to attempt to transfer its essential themes—decentering, depersonalizing, the notion that "identity" is an object for consciousness rather than its "subject," the materiality of a language which now "speaks us" rather than the other way around, the objectification of intention, the analytic dissolution of subjectivity into so many layers of stereotypes and of the inauthentic voices of a public sphere saturated with transpersonal information and images—to the new collective program.

Peter Weiss's conversations and debates—which take up so enormous a part of this three-volume novel—mark just such a new formal innovation. If we read them as the interference of extraneous types of discourse—political commentary, philosophical argument, historical information—and if we see the various interlocutors simply as so many mouthpieces for the author, or for the various ideological positions he means to represent—then we have let a constitutive tension go out of the reading, and it slackens into mere retrieval. Yet a new text cannot really impose its new form of reading on us (as Plato says, when its father is gone, it cannot reply, it merely offers mute silence to our questions and conjectures); the reader must somehow restore the impossible aesthetic imperative of this experiment in collectivity and must grasp every moment of the irresolvable conflicts as a movement of absolutes. This is to say that in these obsessive rehearsals of the past—mistakes, missed opportunities, necessary crimes or accidental miscalculations—and in the anxiety-laden, fearful and hopeful prognoses of the future that accompany them in the form of strategies and tactics, assessments and the helplessness of sheer lack of knowledge or information, throughout these exchanges in which language itself seems discredited by the facts of the past and the unpredictability of the future, the reader must at every point reconstitute a present.

I observed above that one of the temporal peculiarities of the text lay in an irreversible movement of history beyond the sterile opposition of fixed antitheses that never seemed to get off the mark: now we must add to that temporality the other related one, that history never exists in a past that preceded the current dilemmas or in a future in which they would be once and for all surmounted: it exists as sheer present in the heated disagreements of what may otherwise seem contingent circumstances and a merely particular content. Thus what is intolerable in these conversations is their very truth, aesthetic as well as historical: an eternity of debate and discord, a perpetual present of ideological passion and politicized consciousness. The reader is being trained to live within that present, already a modification of the traditional temporality of the novel and its readerly expectations. It will be interesting, therefore, to see how Peter Weiss can end his narrative (which began conventionally enough with the biological youth of his protagonist). History ends it, to be sure, but in some other, external way, which we know, but which is outside the text—as it is outside of and external to the characters and their debates about it.

Yet in another sense, such narrative resolution—or the illusion of such an impossible narrative resolution, as that generally presides over what is called fiction—has itself been drawn within the text, within the very content of the debates and arguments among its characters. For it is what is called *unity*, and all these verbal and ideological struggles turn on it in one way or another: since unity—or unification—is necessarily the most burning issue in all political theory which aims at action or praxis, rather than at simple rules for power or the analysis of power's mode of functioning in the status quo. It is this concentration on collective action (whether on the Right, as with Carl Schmitt or Hobbes, or on the Left, as with Machiavelli or Lenin) which distinguishes the new science of politics that emerged in the twentieth century from the traditional bourgeois political philosophy into which it seems once more in the process of disappearing without a trace. And it is clear enough that its premise or fundamental starting point must be the question of unification—of which here the debates between socialists and communists offer only one empirical "example" and dramatization. This is because the end or aim can only emerge in the process of action itself; but action cannot begin until a unified agency is constituted: Gramsci's meditations on the "historic bloc," Laclau and Mouffe's theorization of a kind of momentary hegemonic constellation—so many diverse contemporary reflections on the unavoidable first step or principle of unity itself.

So it is that the urgency of the dialogical, about which I've argued elsewhere that it has to be conflictual and antagonistic, is fuelled by a passion for a unity that can never come into being. Yet Bakhtin's supreme example was in any case Dostoyevsky, whose feverish debates between irreconcilable Weltanschauungen surely offer the model of a narrative pitched on this level beyond the individual or the monadic. We have to invent a way of reading this text and in particular these endless dialogues as though politics had taken the place of Dostoyevsky's metaphysical passions, and as though each of these interlocutors had become a kind of vehicle for the absolute on the order of Dostoyevsky's figures.

5

But there is a dialectic at work in the raw materials themselves: such a radical formal modification in the role of dialogue and in the way in which conversation advances narrative events cannot leave the rest of the novelistic apparatus intact. If here conversation as such tends to become an event in its own right, and a unique historical event at that—some mixture of feverish waiting and frustration, of rationalization and hope—we would expect the other conventional features of the traditional novel to be modified accordingly. This is preeminently the case with space itself whose new role in Peter Weiss we must now characterize.

The nature of this space will naturally enough be determined by the nature of the event—the ideological debate-discussion—that it houses and of which it then stands as a kind of abstract container. This space has already been alluded to metaphorically: it is none other than the room itself which for the most part bounds the events of this novel. Where the room is replaced—the museum island in which the initial viewing and discussion of the Pergamum frieze is conducted, the park bench in Paris on which the narrator's father explores future political possibilities with Herbert Wehner—these relatively more open, or at least opening spaces mark a move towards the larger world which will be identified in a moment.

Otherwise the room itself becomes a kind of absolute here: and that its essential form is abstract and utterly denuded is underscored for us in the opening section of the novel, where the kitchen takes on the traditional role of the place in which working-class families talk, assess their crises, and make their decisions. Yet in this opening section (in which the narrator prepares to leave for Spain and the civil war) an even more fundamental process of stripping away and of abstraction down to an almost geometrical figure of extension is imitated, as it were, by the emptiness of the narrator's apartment, from which the parents have already left in flight to Czechoslovakia, taking all their furniture and belongings with them. Indeed, this moment of empty waiting, in that anxiety and impatience in which one life is finished and another has yet to begin, proves to be an even more revealing form, an even more receptive vessel for the specific potentialities of the novel's categories of experience: for in this last night in Hitlerian Germany, the narrator dreams of an abolition of the room as such—the moldering corpse of his father (in reality still alive) shatters the floorboards, and the dreamer is allowed to float in oneiric suspension, like some of Chagall's flying figures, across the nightscape of Berlin. We will return to the significance of the oneiric in Peter Weiss later on: suffice it to say that if the sheerly dialogical agon is the strong form or category of experience here (with the abstract room as its correlative space of possibility), then there is a sense in which the oneiric is its other term, its opposite and its complement.

It may then be asked whether the oneiric in its turn has any specific spatial vehicle or vessel that is characteristic of its narrative operations, or whether in fact it is not precisely characterized by the utter absence of any such spatial container, being the radical opening up of all space. Yet there is such an alternate space within Peter Weiss's production in general, and that is painting as such, or at least painting as he conceived and practiced it. It would be a mistake to characterize these large figurative and nightmarish works as surrealist inasmuch as Peter Weiss, coming out of the German expressionist tradition, was for a long time suspicious of the French movement and only began to appreciate it after World War Two, at a time when he had virtually completed his work as a painter: still, the Max Ernst-style collages which he constructed later on are certainly in that second modernist tradition, at the same time that they offer a second mode of representation of the oneiric which is much closer to the collages of documentary raw materials which make up most of the plays as such (and whose research certainly underpins the *Aesthetik*, even if it is not visible there). Peter Weiss himself associated the first figurative painting with Kafka, but we will see later on that this seemingly conventional reference has an unexpected specificity which tends to remove it from the stereotypically nightmarish.

This is obviously not the place to speak of Peter Weiss's considerable achievement as a visual artist: yet one further feature does demand mention in this particular context. It is the fact that he painted or drew virtually every room he dwelt in over the course of his life (and most of these representations have been preserved). The portrait of the room thus becomes a virtual genre in the framework of a work whose originality was, among other things, to have modified any number of traditional genres in idiosyncratic and profoundly meaningful ways. To memorialize your daily life in the form of the room is certainly to say something significant about that daily life; as I have suggested above, it is to produce a new category—and this Novum greatly outweighs the more conventional suggestion of an autobiographical sketch or note *pour mémoire*. Not to amass materials in view of some future account of a life, then, so much as to underscore some new conception of a life as the story of a movement from room to room; and this is precisely the conception—heightened by historical crisis and the convulsions of war—that we find in *The Aesthetics of Resistance*.

Once the new spatial category is set in place, its empty or abstract frame begins to evolve and to submit to all kinds of variations and developments in its content. It is as though the movement of the novel across space and through history offered some secondary and as it were philosophical advantage: to permit the interrogation of the category of the room from a variety of perspectives, to draw out its possibilities and dramatize the limits which, not only inherent in it, also stand as its content. If indeed we follow Deleuze in thinking that a filmmaker or a painter also produces concepts as the philosopher does, yet in the distinctive and different non-conceptual form of their own media,[25] then indeed this series of rooms can be thought to be philosophical in its implications as well. The narrator himself directly reflects on these possibilities at the moment of leaving the last space he might have called "his": "Ownership molded the attitude that was taken towards things [in the bourgeois novel and its descriptions], while for us, to whom the living room never belonged and for whom the place of residence was a matter of chance, the only elements that carried weight were absence, deficiency, lack of property" (I, 124–5/133–4; the whole passage is of the greatest interest).

So the very nature of the room will be modified in clandestinity: or better still, a deeper feature of the room not normally accessible to legal or bourgeois or peacetime perception will in the new crisis situation be brought out. One thinks, for example, of Rosner's room in Stockholm (in Book II, 176): the gnome-like militant becomes virtually a prisoner in a back room sealed off from the official "apartment" of his hosts (an illegal, he must avoid any notice by the Swedish authorities). Yet in this room (to which we will return) paradoxically his political task is the diffusion of information to communist movements all over the world—his clandestine journal is the recipient and the source of worldwide knowledge in strict correlation to his own lack of mobility.

When one thinks of clandestinity in Nazi Germany itself, however, the figure of imprisonment becomes even more intense. Thus the spaces through which Bischoff arrives back in Germany from Sweden: she spends three days and nights in the hold of the ship, and this new spatial modulation of room-like concealment has an unexpected result, a strange new ontological enhancement of her perception:

> She perceived the whole ship, distinguished the directions of the footsteps, and whether a door had been opened or shut, when something was scraped or dragged, she recognized the movement of the lever of the mechanical telegraph, and adjusted to every manoever of the ship itself. She rose through the ship, became it herself, heard its pulse and its shuddering in her ear, in her fingertips, her skin was at one with the vibrating metal plates. (III, 73)

This is in a sense an aesthetic apologia for the novel as a whole: how can one claim a generalized aesthetic interest for a work thus imprisoned in sensory privation as well as in the enforced lack of knowledge imposed by clandestinity? Yet in such a situation the signals from the outside become magnified, and their receivers undergo an unusual training in the decipherment of signs along with the apprehension of dangers. This is the perceptual world of *The Aesthetics of Resistance*; and we will have to see to what degree this simultaneous impoverishment and heightened sensibility figure in the larger picture of *Bildung* and proletarian cultural formation the novel means to propose.

Yet the final form of the room will clearly enough be the cell itself, and in this instance the death cell, from which the only spatial opening out is onto that covered inner courtyard in which the prisoners are hanged or guillotined: the novel itself wishes to be a different kind of opening in which their resistance and suffering finds memorialization and an active potential for energizing posterity.

These enclosed spaces, however, have their own specific dialectic: for a perception and a groping reading of the outside of them can itself—a kind of blind cognitive mapping—only be organized by and projected onto some larger grid; just as the very movement of the clandestines from one room to another demands advanced planning and spatial foresight. The other pole of the closed room therefore turns out to be the urban map: mapped by foot by the clandestines as they move through Berlin (I, 80/87–8), as they remember the topology of Bremen (I, 89/97), or are treated exceptionally to an outside tour of Stockholm, like Bischoff during her provisional imprisonment (II, 78–87). The narrator is able to juxtapose larger pieces of geographical space in his movement from Spain to Paris and then on to Sweden; but it is essentially the underground figure of Bischoff whom we accompany across the urban grid as such, returning with her first to Bremen and then to Berlin itself in wartime in the third volume of the novel (III, 64, 158).

We therefore confront a veritable system, which may be represented diagrammatically:

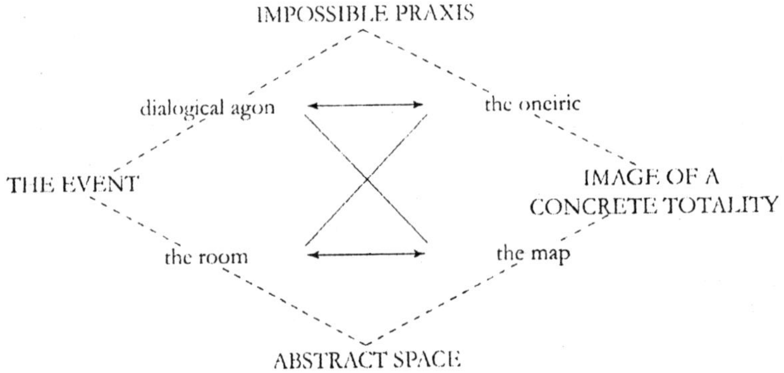

But we must not leave the matter of space without recording a further potentiality, and it is a rare moment of aesthetic flowering in the midst of the paralysis of collective action and the asphyxia of existential experience. We are in a room again, it is Rosner's, and one of the rare moments in which, besides the visits of the narrator (whose clandestine task it is to deliver information and remove copy from this frustrating "communications center"), two other important militants—Stahlmann and Arndt/Funk—join him for a truly conspiratorial discussion on the fate of the underground in Germany and the possibilities of action, at a time when the first rumor about the Holocaust and the fate of the Jews is beginning to trickle out of the continent:

> This room, three and a half meters long and two meters wide, as high as a shaft, with dusk gradually darkening the green lampshades (the shutters could no longer be opened)—this tomb was the headquarters of the Party in the underground, a

> provisional headquarters, only for a few hours, to be struck again as the various participants scatter to their own individual "tombs". (III, 114)

As the impossible conversation disintegrates without agreement or prospects, each of the three drifts off into his own private musings, Stahlmann to his experiences at Angkor Wat (to which a long chapter has already been dedicated), Arndt to his hobby of gardening, while Rosner loses himself in the Italian opera still quietly murmuring over the radio:

> So, as I moved through the dawn to the train station, I took with me the picture of the three comrades, from out of their other existences, the unshakable spokesman of the Comintern paying homage to the art of song, the grim party organizer caring for his fragrant and decorative flowers, the man of war surrendering himself to a stone dancer on a frieze. (III, 127)

Nor should we forget the aesthetic fulfillment of the narrator as well, the would-be future writer, who has himself transformed this frustrating argument and fetid airspace for once into an aesthetic image—the very image of imaging itself.

6

Still, in the midst of these abstractions, characters remain and continue strongly to exist: that they are historical, and bear the names of real people, is no more relevant to their poetic or novelistic representation than the provenance of the names in Dante's *Divina Commedia*. But no less relevant either: both works (Dante being in a certain sense one of the models for this one) are prophetic investigations of History, which nonetheless rely on narrative techniques not greatly differing from what one finds in ordinary fiction. Yet as in Dante as well, these are not merely historical figures, who are present in the work on account of the purely empirical fact of their having existed in real history. Both works develop on the premise that empirical history also vehiculates transcendent meanings: and the characters thus somehow embody those meanings in what I hesitate (owing either to the frequency or infrequency of the uses of this term) to call allegorical. In *The Aesthetics of Resistance*, which also wishes to chart the *Bildung* of the proletarian student, militant and author-to-be, they all have a function, which I want to outline briefly with respect to three of these supporting figures or characters.

Hodann begins the work and ends it: he summons the narrator to Spain to work in his clinic at the front, and the work closes, not so much with his death in Norway in 1946, after his break with the Communist Party, as with his great speech at the end of the war, calling for unity once again and projecting a new kind of cultural politics (III, 258), for which the term "cultural revolution" is perhaps not misplaced. For it is an essentially cultural politics that Hodann "represents" in this novel: behind him the dead figure of Münzenberg looms, the only truly world-historical figure celebrated in this novel, whose achievements in the enlargement of merely political propaganda to a Popular Front program of culture and the unification of Left intellectuals and writers generally are nonetheless philosophically more restricted than what Hodann's program embodies.

As a doctor and a psychiatrist, Hodann allows the fundamental concern with healing to be introduced into the twin dynamics of civil war and class struggle. Following Reich, he insists on the ideologically baleful effects of sexual repression and the necessity to link political commitment with sexual liberation. More modestly, in the context of the Spanish Civil War, he underscores again and again the constitutive relationship between political melancholy—the crippling discouragement of the losers with their embattled positions both in Spain and in the larger international situation—and sexual deprivation. (Not coincidentally, the political work of the war's end and of the new postwar situation also begins with the soldiers: the German prisoners of war in Sweden will become the first new space in which a properly German radical political reeducation must begin [III, 254, 262].)

Sexuality as a constitutive part of culture or of a revolution in consciousness: just as the narrower elements of the Party disregard and postpone genuine cultural questions, so in a context of Left Puritanism generally (the revolutionaries themselves did not have the benefit of an already achieved cultural revolution), so also this emphasis on sexuality is even more scandalous and threatens a significant break: Stahlmann "brought along a copy of *La Voz de la Sanidad*, in which Hodann had an article on the sexual problems of soldiers in wartime. To propose a discussion of this kind, he said, would be petty bourgeois, in a liberation struggle such as was being waged in Spain, sexual needs had to be put last, and in a time like this it was not part of a physician's duties to deal with private matters" (I, 243/260). But what Stahlmann calls private matters ("*die Privatsphaere*") are in fact public ones, or such is the argument of Hodann himself. It is a discussion framed by anxieties and arguments around Stalin's trials, as well as around the execution of the POUM leaders: and in particular by an impassioned denunciation of what we would today call the sexism and patriarchal prejudices of the Politburo itself, by a woman militant, Marcauer, who will later also be arrested (I, 274/293).

Hodann is also to be sure a father figure for the narrator, who cannot be said to have had bad fathers but only insufficient ones; his own illness and chronic fatigue reinscribes the body in the form of political weakness and strategic lucidity ("pessimism of the intellect"): "Although Hodann stakes everything on the bringing into reality of that democracy whose seeds had been laid in the German underground, he was also a seer, and an adept of human weaknesses and confusions, and it was this that suddenly brought him up short" (III, 256)—not a fit of coughing, however, but a sobering sense of the postwar political program of the Party members returning from the East, and its continuity with the mistakes of the past he had so often denounced. The Hodann figure thus sets in place a profound materiality or physicality of culture, at the same time as a premonition of the impossible dilemmas of this postwar Left future (which is now our own past).

I have said that the framework of Peter Weiss's novel excludes fascism and the Nazi "point of view"; now I must correct this assertion by identifying a major figure who had her moment of sympathy with the Nazi mass movement: for the task of an intelligent and thoroughgoing cultural-political strategy will be to seek to grasp the mass appeal of fascism with a view towards reappropriating its energies and its Utopian impulse. But the Swedish writer Karin Boye also sets in place another dimension of sexual politics with the fact of lesbian desire, at that time irreconcilable with Left politics and unthinkable in its context. Her suicide in 1942 then poses yet a different kind of scandal for the political movement: namely that of an overdetermination by political discouragement and the then impossible world situation, as well as by sexual misery and by personal guilt: this overdetermination itself poses a dilemma for the narrow political psychology of the time, whose horizons the novel cannot itself transcend:

> It may be the case [Hodann said] that some people are dominated by the idea of an unbridgeable gap between art and political life, while for others art is precisely inseparable from politics. Maybe these were only different conceptions of the same basic matter, and those who thought that she did not fail on account of the pressure of external realities on art, but rather because of the damaged and diminished power to bring art, that is autonomous thought, to bear on and to change a seemingly unshakable external reality itself—those people had perhaps thereby only made themselves a life preserver, in order to stay on the surface, whereas Boye could not stop herself from diving as deep as possible. (III, 48)

Is this only to say that unlike Hodann, who constitutes a whole program for the future and for politics, whatever its immediate fate in the postwar period and the communist movement as such, Boye is laid in place as an unresolvable contradiction, on some future agenda? To be sure, Peter Weiss's own program overtly calls for some new unification of art and politics, as has been said above: but the status of such a program or cultural politics within the work of art itself can equally well be served by failure as by success. To have shown the antagonism between these practices and axiological domains, to have articulated that tension in the form of a contradiction, this is also in some sense to solve it artistically: one recalls Hegel's doctrine about limits (he's thinking of Kant's rationally unknowable noumena and the alleged limits of Reason), that whoever traces a boundary line is already beyond it and has already begun to incorporate it. Here too, under certain circumstances, difference can unify or relate fully as much as sheer identification. All of which is to neglect Karin Boye's art itself, which is equally reappropriated by the process of *Bildung* of the novel: *Kallocain* is a kind of *1984* to be sure, or perhaps less anachronistically a kind of *We*, a political dystopia. But it is one of the rare modern dystopias to have been based on the Nazi rather than the communist movement. This work (less well-known outside of Sweden) clearly marks the psychic liquidation of her 1930s fascination with Nazism (the search for a lost father, Hodann diagnoses it—III, 41). The novel is a science-fictional depiction of a scientist who invents a truth serum in order to help the absolute state abolish truth altogether. Yet this is a leap ahead into nightmare, which confronts Boye with a vision of a post-ideological conflict between two instances of state terror. As with the schizophrenic nightmares of the narrator's own mother, there is here set in place yet another vision of the future, along with another distinct discourse or mode of representation of such a future: the question of culture cannot be properly raised unless we mention both things, both dimensions—the form or language of the vision and its content. In any case, this ending, along with Boye's art, can provoke the same stupid and realistic, unavoidable question that Hodann's therapies aroused: are such cultural productions energizing now, in the midst of crisis and struggle; where is the place for the negative in an embattled political culture?

These are questions then equally appropriate in the case of our final figure, Brecht himself, whose relationships to his own doubts and discouragements were notoriously far more tactical and Machiavellian than for either of the other figures. There is no doubt for many of us some great historical and literary satisfaction in this lengthy encounter with Brecht (whom Peter Weiss himself can only have glimpsed from afar during the former's brief stay in Sweden); whatever the accuracy of the portrayal, this is the section of the novel that comes the closest to the traditional pleasures afforded by the historical novel as a genre. The portrait has been described as a hostile one: besides Brecht's evasiveness about the Moscow trials, the presence of the various women is underscored, along with the rumors about them; and the narrator's own fictive role as a helper makes it clear enough how Brecht, to adopt a naïve American idiom, "uses people." Meanwhile, we have already observed his well-known physical cowardice and his disgrace at the end of this volume, on his flight out of a Sweden now menaced by Nazi armies. No one would want to minimize these defects of character, for they are in fact precisely what fascinate us about Brecht and indeed, to be a little more provocative about it, what endear the personage to us. The

Brecht we are shown here is not, however, the object of a satiric portrait but rather the space of literary and theatrical production itself. Peter Weiss uses this pretext to write or at least to imagine a project conceived by Brecht himself but never realized: an opportunistic project no doubt, for as an attempt to get his works performed in exile, Brecht always planned new works on the basis of national traditions (some were completed: *Herr Puntila* for Finland, for example; some left unfinished, as with *Der Brotladen* for the US). The Swedish stay suggested a revolutionary episode from what we cannot too hastily call Sweden's middle ages (since alone of all the European countries Sweden never knew feudalism): rather a kind of first bourgeois uprising against the nobility in 1434, led by the serendipitously named Engelbrekt. The resultant sketch often sounds more like a Peter Weiss play than a Brecht one: tableaux, static speeches of ideological position, a seeming absence of those intricate and paradoxical exchanges in which Brecht inverts folk wisdom and common sense, cynically reifying the resultant maxim in a song placard or silent-filmic overtitle. Yet even for Brecht himself we can draw some aesthetic consequences from the results (while Brecht's questions to his collective research staff are often more Brechtian than the narrator's summary of what in any case never gets written).

But it takes us some time to get to Engelbrekt himself: for a whole prehistory of the Swedish political situation, going back some eighty years, must first be set in place: the story of the struggle against the Danes for the accession to the throne of the Infanta Margareta. This is all sketched out in the style of the medieval theater, with levels for the classes, pageants and the like: but it seems to me that its lesson for us is the drive of Peter Weiss—in that compulsive archival scouring of the past for suggestive details and empirical inspiration which he shared with Brecht himself—to begin before the beginning, ever to seek out the seeds of time in the prehistory of their own flourishing germination. It is in fact this impulse generally which accounts for what seem to be lengthy historical essays and factual narratives interpolated throughout the novel: the history of the coast of Valencia for example, stretching all the way back to the Phoenicians (and not coincidentally to the builders of the Pergamum altar); the history of Swedish social democracy in modern times (including the brief contact of one of its founders with Lenin as he passed through on his way to Petersburg and October—II, 277); the story of Angkor Wat. These seeming digressions in another ("non-fictive") type of discourse will find their deeper justification in Peter Weiss's conception of the aesthetic and of *Bildung* when we get to it: suffice it to say now that they mark a refusal of the distinction between form and content which is also a refusal of that between art and its non-artistic or historical pretexts. The material of the work of art has its own semi-autonomous history: but that history is itself part of the material, and one must seek it out just as one must appreciate the physical and chemical properties of the stone—quartz or granite, marble or porphyry—which makes up the building or the statue. This is an appreciation that must be achieved through knowledge itself: a knowledge which in this situation is not distinct from the aesthetic that henceforth includes it.

Yet Engelbrekt's appearance—surging suddenly out of nowhere when history demands him (II, 214)—presents the work-to-be with the formal problem of the revolutionary break with the past, which can thus no longer be incorporated except as what is repudiated. Is the preliminary work then useless and a waste of precious time? In any case it has been frequently broken off, not only by Brecht's own illnesses but by the heavy mood and confusions with which the collaborators receive the news, first of the German invasion of Poland, and then, in the East, of the Soviet one (yet another cross-cutting section). Perhaps not altogether labor lost, however: and it is at least partly clear that what has been laid in place here is a conception of the production of the work of art as a process fully satisfying in itself, and a collective process at that. Such a view of the work as process has surfaced any number of times in the modern period, from Valéry to *Tel quel*: but the collective constitution of the process has less often (which is a polite way of saying hardly at all) been added to the formulation, save in the various avant-gardes, most notably among the surrealists. The name Brecht is thus relatively unique in signifying, not an individual artist, but a group, thereby incarnating not only what is necessarily and implicitly collective about any theatrical production, but also what is central for any Marxian view of production and praxis. (It is not inappropriate at this point to mention the unmarked collaboration, from *Marat/Sade* on, in all his works, between Peter Weiss and his spouse Gunilla Palmstierna-Weiss.)

Still, the unfinished play is as valuable for its formal dilemmas as for its achieved historical glimpses: the dramatization of revolution is the foremost of these, for not only is its temporal structure problematic, as we have seen; its "representational" system must also raise doubts and problems from any Left perspective, insofar as Engelbrekt's moment is that of sharp popular unrest, and his very essence as "world-historical figure" consists in the hopes invested in him by a collectivity which cannot itself really be represented on stage (II, 222). As with all Left works (see above) Engelbrekt's political problem is the achievement of unity between the various dissatisfied classes who have very different agendas; his downfall and assassination are the result of a situation in which he has been able to serve the interests of one party (the great nobles), who now no longer need him and can throw him aside: a vanishing mediator, who embodies the truth of a revolutionary and a populist rhetoric that was little more than an ideological mask for the more privileged component of this "popular front". Here is, then, the central formal problem, which is also a political one: what Brecht and his co-workers took for a genuinely revolutionary moment turns out to have been a mere bourgeois revolution. There has been a good deal of interesting debate over whether a so-called bourgeois revolution is really a revolution at all in the Marxian sense; nor does the term particularly matter provided we separate the two kinds of historical events sharply from each other. In that case, the first or bourgeois variety, with its necessary end in failure, can be the object of various kinds of representations, from Marx's ironic-satiric one in *The Eighteenth Brumaire of Louis Bonaparte*, to Michelet's tragic narrative of the Great Revolution. The question would then be whether a socialist or proletarian revolution can be represented at all, since it precisely aims at challenging the political as well as the aesthetic sense of "representation" itself.

It is thus extraordinarily telling that Brecht's greatest moment of enthusiasm for this material comes at the moment when Engelbrekt, to threaten the royal city of Stockholm, finds himself obliged to dig a considerable canal in order to reinforce the siege. "The building of the canal, Brecht opined, would almost be worth an entire play in its own right. Here we could separate the principle of collective work from the power of egotism and profit ... A dragging and a hauling, a slave labor, yet voluntarily performed, as meaningful as after a triumphant revolution" (II, 250). (This is, after all, the epic moment of Magnitogorsk, the Dnieper hydroelectric project, and the White Sea–Baltic Canal.) So the representation of production itself is at length laid in place, an impossible representation no doubt, as so many socialist realist novels testify, and yet here—in *The Aesthetics of Resistance*—inscribed as what cannot be represented, yet as the necessary and absent center of all work and value.

7

Such labor is first and foremost physical, to be sure, and the current theoretical celebration of the individual body as the very locus of materialism rarely enough includes labor alongside its privileged themes of desire and suffering. It may seem paradoxical to discuss suffering, trauma and the body alongside Weiss's oneiric discourse, and yet the latter is the dialectical complement of the former, just as it constitutes a strange reversal and fulfillment of that "caverned" perception we attributed to the figures in the room or the cell, those "overwakened" senses that the condemned Heilmann evokes again on the eve of his death and in the content of a long final letter precisely devoted to dreaming: "There would be much to say about the abyss into which each of us has sunk, about the stone we taste and which seems through the outer efforts of our consciousness to have become as porous as dough in which our fingers can plunge and penetrate and yet our hands feel its hardness, so confusing is this new feeling" (III, 211).

The Aesthetics of Resistance thus in fundamental ways calls out precisely for this "theory of dreaming" which Heilmann only tentatively elaborates on the eve of his execution, and which draws its ultimate poignancy from the fact that he will never dream again, "will never again fall asleep" (III, 216). The lifelong significance of the oneiric for Peter Weiss himself can be documented by the paintings as well as by the extensive role of dream protocols in his earlier fiction, all this theoretically reinforced by that appreciation for Jung that he derived from his youthful frequentation of Hermann Hesse (we may also suppose a certain distance from that side of Freud intent precisely on the analytic destruction of the "charm" and fascination of the dream experience). Yet we may at the same time detect a certain tension in Peter Weiss's relationship to this material, a refusal to abandon himself to the facile mythographies of a Jung or to the equally facile "automatic writing" of the surrealists either.

It is this tension—rather than any final conceptual "position" on dreams —which we must retrace in *The Aesthetics of Resistance.* "In the dream, I am a body that refuses to learn Thought" (III, 214). At the same time, the dream is that space of infinite possibility before the world itself, as the youthful comrades once speculated, in their discussions of Rimbaud or Hölderlin:

> We spoke about seeing in dreams. Asked ourselves how within such absolute darkness this intensity of colors could develop inside us. They are produced by our knowledge of light. Knowledge sees. Illumination stimuli are no longer present, but only remembered. We observed that the dream contained these earliest images, sharp and exact in every detail. Then in an immense variety reflections superimposed themselves on each other, ordered intuitively as they belonged to specific groups of experiences; they cluster together, or rather they swim, they float around the various emotional centers, they search each other out as sperm to the egg, lead to continuous insemination, each cell of feeling seems to be receptive, releasing ever newer apparitions generated by the ever changing thrusts, similarities and identities never occur, can owing to the perpetual flow itself never take place, yet always related images in this or that region, according to the goal-oriented intensity of the impulse towards its basic form, and sometimes it can even happen that the original image itself suddenly emerges, everything that concealed it washed away in a flash. (III, 211)

In this earliest version of a kind of youthful "interpretation of dreams," then, the immense and demiurgic, generative productivity of the dream is somehow challenged by the real object of desire and the impatience of the Freudian "wish" that imperiously seeks fulfillment. But now Heilmann wonders about a different problem, a different tension, namely "why we do not in dreams experience the suffering of which we are observers" (III, 215). He juxtaposes with the oneiric that different and wakeful, yet equally intense, imagination with which he relives in sympathy that pathway of experiences, humiliation and pain, which his comrade Libertas must have traversed on her way to a neighboring cell. This is a different mode of image perception, in which the visionary suffers as much from his own helplessness and paralysis to change her destiny as from Libertas's own suffering.

I think that it is also here that we must position the mother's schizophrenic hallucinations, which, alongside the executions, constitute the other affective pole of Book III. Here clearly Peter Weiss faced a technical problem: how to incorporate the experience of Eastern Europe and the Nazi concentration and then death camps, in a narrative whose trajectory takes us from Berlin in 1937 to Spain, and after Spain to Paris and Sweden, only to reinfiltrate wartime Germany (Bremen and Berlin) in the person of the clandestine Bischoff at the same time that the narrator is able to piece together at a distance the executions of his old comrades on the Plötzensee. The (relatively awkward) solution lies in the flight of the parents from Czechoslovakia in the first days of the war: they are only able to make their way across Poland in the throes of the Blitzkrieg, accompany the exodus of populations in flight, including considerable groups of Polish Jews and passing near the significant railroad crossing of Oswiecim on an immense detour through White Russia and Lithuania, until they reach Riga, the Swedish consulate, and safety. Even this laborious journey is interrupted, however, when the mother, separated from her husband, identifies herself as Jewish and follows the refugees on their own path, huddling together with them in an act of wordless solidarity:

> She felt the thick warmth, she belonged to these sweating bodies, seized one of the feverish hands and gripped its fingers together, and as the hands reached to grasp each other, she pressed her face against a moist cheek. Arms, breasts, hips, straggly beards, a crowd made out of limbs, beating hearts, hoarse breathing, that she was in their midst gave her strength. The foul air was a blossoming for her, she breathed it in deep, she lived within this organism, never would she wish to emerge from out of this closed space, separation would be her own destruction. her downfall. (III, 12)

And so it proves: her rescue precipitates her into a psychic withdrawal and a silence from which she never reemerges (only breaking it once, when she has been present at a discussion of the first rumors of the actual death camps themselves—III, 134). Thematically, this solidarity stands in dialectical opposition to the father's paranoid fantasies about machinery, and in particular about the universal war machine itself: it is an opposition which completes the image of the death camps in their two dimensions—the Eichmann-organized functioning of the logistics, the suffering of the victims. Yet two other features of the mother's fate seem more significant.

For one thing, the mother's sympathy and solidarity, like Heilmann's impossible attempt to imagine and to feel in the place of his beloved, are failures: she has, according to Boye who becomes close to her in the final months, "passed beyond the limits of our power to imagine" (III, 25). In her last moment of speech she tells of the grave in which she lay with the still warm and twitching bodies of the dead and dying (III, 128): yet her unspoken and unspeakable hallucinations show that even solidarity as extreme as this cannot come to terms with the absolute of other people's physical suffering. This is not however, at least on my view, a portrait of trauma, even though the narrator associates the mother with Dürer's great image of Melencolia, the angel paralyzed in silence and an almost catatonic inaction and incapacity to produce or create (III, 136–7).

It is no doubt this association which leads Hodann to suggest the other path of artistic expression: this is one of the moments in which the narrator's vocation comes to the surface in the form of that future conditional which will dominate the last pages of the novel itself ("someday it would be possible to describe what my mother experienced"—III, 139). For it is on that level of linguistic recreation that the real problem of trauma (or what Shoshana Felman would call "testimony") is to be located: in the failures of language and the impossibility of expression—this, rather than the failure of sheer imagination, is the real problem of the relationship with the past, which is not so much that of reliving it as that of doing something with it:

> Our incapacity to follow my mother was not conditioned by anything metaphysical or mystical, it was just that as yet we possessed no register for what transcended the ordinary, our helplessness was merely provisional, had not our whole development proved that concrete judgements were gradually constructed first out of dawning approximations and groping experiments ...? I thought that what now came upon us could be expressed only with some new language. But Hodann replied that for our purposes there would never be another language than the one known to everybody, and that what was to be expressed, in order to make it incomprehensible would have to be transmitted by way of the same old used-up words. (III, 139–40)

The relationship of all these materials to each other can now be suggested by a chart:

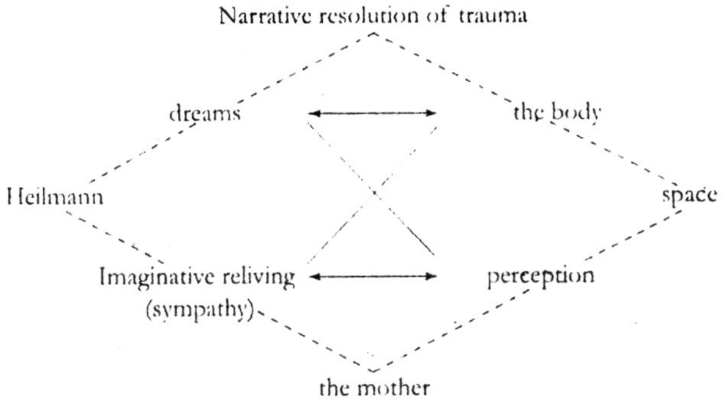

8

And thus at length we come to the ultimate theme, the most important and central one, of pedagogy. In reality, with what has been termed above "the narrative resolution of trauma" we had already arrived there. For if the new cultural revolution, the new proletarian pedagogy, as it is the novel's vocation to describe and to embody it, is a kind of aesthetic education, it is also very much an effacement of subalternity and a transcendence of the trauma of historical defeat, class oppression, alienated labor and the paralyzing humiliations of ignorance. The great works—those "monuments to radical instants"—are no doubt memorials of pain and suffering: the butchering of the giants in the Pergamum frieze, the starvation, debility and cannibalism of the survivors on Géricault's raft, the mute screams of *Guernica* as well, along with the minute daily fears and anxieties of Kafka's characters; but the question is rather how to draw energy from such endless images of horror, how to enhance praxis and production by the spectacle of this charnel-house, the "nightmare of history"?

The famous opening sequence on the Pergamum altar remains the fullest statement of this aesthetic, which it may be usefully initially to frame in the reduced terms of a "critical method," supplementing it with other set pieces from the later pages—on Picasso, but also on Menzel and Kohler—and with the equally monumental discussion of Géricault in the next volume (significantly enough, Volume III contains none of these aesthetic exhibits or readings).

The proliferation of themes and digressions around the Pergamum frieze makes it clear that any simple opposition between form and content needs to make way for a far more complex movement of multiple reversals and inversions. So it is, for example, that in the midst of the slow agony of the Spanish Republic, the narrator and Hodann, amid the orange groves of the landscape, begin to speak "about events that took place two millennia earlier on this same coast" (I, 302/321). The classical world of the Pergamum altar is now discovered to have had its outpost here in Valencia, and a history of the Spanish peasantry and that Spanish agricultural labor whose story will at length find its climax in the Civil War reveals its immemorial continuities with the public work of art contemplated in the first pages. An emphasis on violence and death, on the failure of a thousand mortal generations to overcome their misery, is enough to secure this view of history from the idealistic illusions otherwise almost always implicit or explicit in theses about cultural continuities over time. But this materialism is also reinforced by the sharp mental reversal administered by such a view: we do not normally connect the Spanish Civil War with the classical past, and even more fundamentally, we do not often see the history of oppressed classes as a continuity: continuities are always on the side of "culture," that is to say on the side of the modes of living of the dominant classes. To invert these ideological priorities is thus not necessarily to revive an idealist conception of history, so much as to administer a materialist shock to just such categories and stereotypes. Thus Walter Benjamin recommends a dual procedure: "For the materialist dialectician discontinuity must be the regulative idea of the tradition of the ruling classes (essentially the bourgeoisie), continuity that of the oppressed classes (the proletariat)."[26] The figure of Hercules, whose mythic travels afford a different kind of link between the eastern and western shores of the Mediterranean, will be discussed in a moment.

In fact, it is precisely the idea of the methodological reversal which will provide the key to so many bewildering twists and turns in Peter Weiss's aesthetic analyses here: nor, given the agon-organized structure of his dialectical thought generally, should there be any surprise in the way in which the sympathetic contemplation of a given aesthetic position suddenly and without warning generates the emergence of a not always predictable opposite.

Yet the first moves are logical enough: the bloody triumph of the Olympians over the giants is a celebration and a warning, and transposes and expresses the power of the Attalid dynasty who commissioned the frieze. And just as this translation of human rulers into divine ones effaces history with a vision of the sheer eternity of power, so also the sculptors must make of the frieze itself a superhuman artifact, from which all traces of production have been removed: stylistic perfection then here also serves the ideology of the masters. Yet this shift of attention towards the production of the work reminds us that class struggle can also be identified there, in the pulling and hauling of unskilled labor under the direction of the builders and master sculptors. Nor is the monitory effect of the frieze some merely "historical" one, which present-day viewers can abstract in the name of pure aesthetic reception: "We heard the thuds of the clubs, the shrilling whistles, the moans, the splashing of blood. We looked back at a prehistoric past, and for an instant the prospect of the future likewise filled up with a massacre impenetrable to the thought of liberation" (I, 9/14). But this reactivation of historical memory opens an access to the Alexandrian period generally, and in particular to Pergamum's own failed revolution, the uprising of Aristonikos (I, 43/49), and even, ironically, all the way back up to the nineteenth century and the ideological reasons for the newly united German Empire to "buy" the newly excavated altar and transport it to Berlin (I, 45/51). These seemingly extraneous historical footnotes are not only part and parcel of our reinterpretations: "After a lengthy silence, Heilmann said that works like those stemming from Pergamum had to be constantly reinterpreted until a reversal was gained and the earth-born awoke from darkness and slavery to show themselves in their true appearance" (I, 47/53). More than that, I think we have to conclude that, for such analyses from below, the split between form and content, between the intrinsic and the extrinsic, the aesthetic and its context, has not yet taken place. It is only for the bourgeois spectator or reader that it exists, only there that at best it has to be struggled against and overcome. It is the structure of bourgeois daily life and subjectivity, and the collective division of labor and privileges of power which tacitly underpin that structure and which exclude the social unity of the work of art as something that can no longer be perceived or conceived, that escapes bourgeois categories of perception and reception, let alone analysis. A true "aesthetics" of resistance therefore will not seek to "correct" bourgeois aesthetics or to resolve its antinomies and dilemmas: it will rather search out that other social position from which those dilemmas do not emerge in the first place. The difficulties under which that other, proletarian aesthetic education labor, however, are of a different kind: not the philosophical or conceptual antinomies of form and content, but rather those of subalternity: fatigue after work, lack of access to knowledge and information, repudiation of the aesthetic as class privilege, underdevelopment, finally, of a stubborn will to appropriate the achievements of the dominant class—aesthetic as well as scientific and technological—in the interests of building a new social order. In the present instance one may say that the very existence of the project of a proletarian aesthetic education is a sign that this will already exists.

This is also to say that from the standpoint of suffering and defeat, aesthetic experience is not devalued but rather able to emerge with a new kind of unity, transcendent as well as immanent: the problem of suffering adds urgency to the purely formal side of art, that is to say to the dilemmas of representation and the sign-systems deployed, otherwise so refractory to this ultimate mute and inexpressible experience. The nature of class subordination, meanwhile, by revealing the solidarity between the "extrinsic" situation of the classes in the historical context and the "intrinsic" labor presupposed by the work of art itself, volatilize the old (bourgeois) critical problems, endlessly and unproductively turning around the sticking point of some "specificity," some unique poeticity or literariness, of the aesthetic object itself. The commitment to suffering in the novel itself can thus be grasped not as some morbid fascination and intention of memorializing this past and these dead; but rather as the keeping open of a historical perspective—very precisely that of subordination and resistance—which enables praxis as such. Contemporary discussions of melancholy and mourning, which begin with the latter's paralysis in muteness and inaction (as with the narrator's mother), are only gradually moving towards an understanding of the ways in which such experience (politically termed "the experience of defeat") can also constitute an energizing precondition for action. At the very least, and to reverse the argument, Peter Weiss's novel can only be adequately read and grasped if this perspective is conceivable.

Now there is very little time to rehearse the other aesthetic demonstrations contained in this novel: one would want to single out the extraordinary concentration which replaces Géricault's *Raft of the Medusa* in the position it deserves, between Dante and the Isenheim crucifixion, by restoring a situation of truly subaltern French colonization—the African destination as a sop thrown by the English to the losers of Waterloo—to the derisory and gratuitous conditions underlying the catastrophe (II, 7–34). In *Guernica*, on the other hand, it is the bizarre presence of a winged Pegasus in Picasso's earliest sketches which allows us to reidentify the Utopian moment of this bleakly archetypal work (I, 312–17/332–6). The juxtaposition of Menzel's great factory painting with Kohler's *Strike* (1868—the first North American socialist realism!) allows the reader to identify the inescapable links between the painter's inevitable class position and his technical and representational capacities (I, 332–9/352–60). The reading, finally, of Kafka's *Castle* as a proletarian novel (I, 168/179) itself powerfully reverses canonical stereotypes and offers a new way into this nightmarish magic realism whose gestural strangeness is the result of the paralysis of a disempowered and subaltern population.

There remains the question of the figure of Hercules, a leitmotif which runs from the absence of the legendary figure from the Pergamum fragments to its reemergence on the very last page of the novel. Hercules, I believe, is meant to figure a heroic temptation by the symbolic or the mythic: the hero, the "world-historical individual," destined to fulfill the hopes of a whole people: none of the real historical figures is a hero in this sense (even though the agony of Lenin's final illness is characterized as a "shirt of Nessus"). Is Hercules, then, meant to figure the illicit longing for positive heroes, or, worse yet, for charismatic leaders? Is he not also a locus for the old dilemmas of a ruling-class leadership in underclass political movements? For after all, on the frieze itself, his empty place stands among the Olympians rather than the giants; while in an extraordinarily tortuous speculation, Heilmann attempts to reread the mythic labors as a covert form of resistance and of encouragement to the lower classes (I, 17–20/23–5).

I think we must see Hercules as an allegorical rather than a symbolic motif: that is, a place marker for problems of representation, rather than an inscription of ideological content. Scherpe has characterized this function admirably:

> Missing from the fragments preserved of the frieze is its most important symbol: the lion's paw of Heracles—according to the novel's symbolism the final and perfect historical act of liberation of the oppressed. The novel's last sentence cannot be in the historical indicative ... Peter Weiss' *Aesthetics of Resistance* wishes to be an indication, a sign of this historical work of liberation that has not yet become history. The empty space in the frieze, at the spot where the lion's paw of Heracles would hang, designates precisely something absent, unrealized. Literature cannot and should not fill this space by way of compensation, but rather render its contours sharp and visible.[27]

One final bourgeois opposition is displaced and cancelled by the perspective of *The Aesthetics of Resistance*: it is that between critic and writer. For the narrator's aesthetic education, the pedagogical training in the appropriation of a different class culture, is also the preparation for his vocation as a writer whose observation of history as a witness is also at one and the same time an intervention in it. The circularity of such narrative forms—the *Bildungsroman* which ends up in its own production—is familiar; the conclusion of this one in the future conditional is not. Anticipations of the failure of postwar hopes—the Cold War, the loss of unity in the revival of the Socialist–Communist split, the Stalinization of the East—are somehow destabilized by a tense which robs them of their sheer empiricity and allows something like an alternate future perfect to rise alongside them. Here factual history, seemingly as unshakable as being itself, is transformed—to use Habermas's glorious expression—into an unfinished project: what seemed over and done with is thus opened up for a new beginning, a new continuation. This is surely the ultimate and fundamental lesson of Peter Weiss's novel, a lesson about the productive uses of a past and a history that is not simply represented or commemorated but also reappropriated by some new future of our own present:

> Again and again, when I would try to convey something of the time that ended with May 1945, its consequences would impose themselves on me. Across the experiences already soaked with death, there would superimpose itself a future colored garishly, and once again filled with torture, destruction and murder. It would again and again seem as though all earlier hopes would be brought to nothing by lost or forgotten intentions. And even if it did not turn out as we hoped, nothing would be changed about those hopes themselves. The hopes would remain. Utopia would be necessary. Even later on those hopes would flame up again countless times, smothered by the superior enemy and ever newly

reawakened. And the realm of hopes would become greater than it was in our time, and would be extended to all the continents of the globe. The poorly repressed discontent would grow and the drive to contradict and to resist would not be lamed. Just as the past was unchangeable, so those hopes would remain unchangeable, and they—which we once, when young, burningly experienced—would be honored by our rememoration of them. (III, 274–5)

(2003)

Notes

1 Walter Benjamin, "Theses on the Philosophy of History," in *Illuminations*, trans. H. Zohn (New York, 1969), p. 264.
2 See the by now notorious "Friedenspreis speech of Martin Walser, reprinted in *Erfahrungen beim Verfassen einer Sonntagsrede* (Frankfurt, 1998).
3 I have drawn heavily here on the indispensable work of Robert Cohen: see *Understanding Peter Weiss* (S. Carolina, 1993), which includes extensive bibliographical references, including his other works in this area.
4 See Dominic LaCapra, *History and Memory after Auschwitz* (Cornell, 1998) for extensive bibliographical information.
5 See Shoshona Felman and Mori Laub, *Testimony* (New York, 1992).
6 See James E. Young, *Writing and Rewriting the Holocaust* (Bloomington, 1988); and for a more balanced general study of the matter, Robert Cohen, "The Political Aesthetics of Holocaust Literature", in *History and Memory*, X, 2 (1998) pp. 43–67.
7 References will henceforth be given in the text to the three-volume East German edition of *Aesthetik des Widerstands*, published by Henschelverlag, Kunst und Gesellschaft (Berlin, 1987); and for the first volume to the English translation published by Duke, 2005. The volume number is indicated by Roman numerals, and in the case of Volume One, the English reference will be given first. (I have occasionally revised this translation without explicit indication; translations from the last two volumes are my own.) Thus, the present reference is I, 9/14.
8 But see on this Peter Weiss's denial, in Klaus R. Scherpe, "Reading the Aesthetics of Resistance: Ten Working Theses", in *New German Critique*, 30 (Fall, 1983). Scherpe's collection, "*Aesthetik des Widerstands" Lesen* (Argument, 1981) is still very useful.
9 Sartre, "Qu'est-ce que la littérature?," pp. 143–150, in *Situations II*, (Paris, 1948).
10 "A difficult book." Critic Heinrich Vormweg called *The Aesthetics of Resistance* "monstrous ..."—Cohen, op. cit., p. 160. "Ein unbequemes Buch ..."—Manfred Haiduk, "Nachwort", *Aesthetik des Widerstands*, Vol. III, p. 278. "this uncooperative work ..."—Scherpe, op. cit., p. 100. Etc.
11 See note 18.
12 Gilles Deleuze, *Cinéma II* (Paris, 1985), pp. 281–91. Deleuze thus takes a quite different position from that of Jean-Luc Nancy, whose *Inoperative Community*

(Minnesota, 1991) argues for the impossibility of *any* group solidarity after the end of the regimes of actually existing socialism.

13 See the work of Franco Moretti translated as *The Modern Epic* (London, 1998).

14 "For that very reason he has to start immediately, and whatever the circumstances, without further scruples about beginning, means or End, proceed to action." Hegel, *Phenomenology of Spirit*, trans. A.V. Miller (Oxford, 1977), p. 240.

15 See *Postmodernism, or, The Cultural Logic of Late Capitalism* (Durham & London, 1991), Chapter 5.

16 T.W. Adorno, *Aesthetische Theorie* (Frankfurt, 1970), pp. 376–7; and Perry Anderson, "Modernity and Revolution", *New Left Review* 144 (March/April 1984) pp. 96–113.

17 Georg Lukács, *The Historical Novel*, (Lincoln, NE, 1983).

18 Sartre, *Critique of Dialectical Reason*, two volumes (London, 2002).

19 See note 6.

20 *The Charterhouse of Parma*, Chapter 3.

21 N.S. Khrushchev, *Khrushchev Remembers*, trans. Strobe Talbott (Boston, 1970), pp. 42–4.

22 A.J.P. Taylor, *Origins of the Second World War* (London, 1961).

23 Alexander Solzhenitsyn, *The First Circle*, translated by Thomas P. Whitney (New York, 1968), pp. 86–7.

24 Fredric Jameson, *The Cultural Turn* (London, 1998) pp. 7–8, 82.

25 Gilles Deleuze, *Cinéma I* (Paris, 1983).

26 Walter Benjamin, *Gesammelte Schriften* (Frankfurt, 1982), Vol. V, pp. 459–60.

27 Scherpe, op. cit., p. 105.

Acknowledgments

The author and publishers would like to thank the journals and publishers listed below for granting permission to reproduce certain essays in this volume. Original publication details as follows:

"Céline and Innocence," *South Atlantic Quarterly*, 93:2, 1994, pp. 311–19.

"*Ulysses* in History," *James Joyce and Modern Literature*, eds W.J. McCormack and Alistair Stead, Routledge and Kegan Paul, 1982, pp. 126–41.

"Modernism and Imperialism," *Nationalism, Colonialism and Literature*, ed. Seamus Deane, Field Day Press, 1990, pp. 43–66.

"Exoticism and Structuralism in Wallace Stevens," *New Orleans Review*, V:11, No. 1, 1984, pp. 10–19.

"Baudelaire as Modernist and Postmodernist," *Lyric Poetry: Beyond the New Criticism*, eds C. Hosek and P. Barker, Cornell University Press, 1985, pp. 247–63.

"Rimbaud and the Spatial Text," *Rewriting Literary History*, eds Tak-Wai Wong and M.A. Abbas, Hong Kong University Press, 1984, pp. 66–88.

"Towards a Libidinal Economy of Three Modern Painters," *Social Text*, No. 1, 1979, pp. 189–99.

"In the Mirror of Alternate Modernities: Introductions to Kojin Karatani's *The Origins of Japanese Literature*," *South Atlantic Quarterly*, 92:2, 1993, pp. 295–310.

"Sōseki and Western Modernism," *boundary 2*, 18:3, 1991, pp. 123–41.

"Madmen Like Kings," *London Review of Books*, 25:22, November 20, 2003, pp. 21–3.

"Euphorias of Substitution," *Yale French Studies*, No.65, 1983, pp. 214–23.

"A Monument to Radical Instants," Introduction to *The Aesthetics of Resistance*, Peter Weiss, Duke University Press, 2005.

Index of Names

Index of Names

India's Trade With Japan

India's Trade With Japan

Badar Alam Iqbal

Academic Foundation

DELHI

First Published 1990
Academic Foundation
24 - A, Sriram Road, Civil Lines, Delhi - 110054.
Phone : 232966, 2520037, 233730.

INDIA'S TRADE WITH JAPAN
by Badar Alam Iqbal
ISBN-81-7188-001-0

Laser-typeset by Comprint India

CONTENTS

Publisher's Note

The two-way trade between India and Japan is now showing positive trends. India's trade deficit with Japan is also declining year by year. According to the latest analysis made by the Indian Section of Indo-Japan Business Cooperation Committee (IJBCC), India's trade deficit with Japan in 1989 is likely to decline to $ 130 million as against more than double the figure of the previous year's trade deficit of $ 278 million in 1988. During the eight-month period of January-August 1989, the trade deficit was only $ 63 million as against the figure of $ 162 million in the corresponding period of the previous year 1988. According to IJBCC, a welcome feature of India's exports to Japan during the period April-August, 1989, is the substantial increase in the share of non-traditional items. (Engineering goods registered a growth of 104.4 per cent, basic chemicals and pharmaceuticals 37.7 per cent, sports goods 131.2 per cent, ready-made garments 36 per cent, tea 50.5 per cent, coffee 230.8 per cent, non-ferrous 30 per cent and raw-cotton 47.1 per cent).

The appreciation of Dollar in terms of Yen, has been a significant factor in reversing the trend in Indo-Japan bilateral trade. The Indo-Japan Business Cooperation

Committee points out that for the first time trade trends in Yen were higher than in Dollars. The Indo-Japan two-way trade increased by 10.9 per cent in terms of Yen and only 6 per cent in terms of dollar. Exports from India increased by 16 per cent in terms of yen and 10.6 per cent in terms of dollar. Imports from Japan increased by 6.4 per cent in terms of yen and 2.1 per cent in terms of dollar.

— ***Ed.***

FOREWORD

I would like to congratulate Dr. Badar A. Iqbal for his painstaking study *India's Trade With Japan : Performance and Prospects,* which covers practically all aspects of the growing trade relations between India and Japan. Japan, in recent years, has emerged as one of India's largest trade partners as well as aid doners; as such, Dr. Iqbal's study, by providing practioners and scholars in the subject with a very timely analysis of factors influencing Indo-Japan trade, should be a valuable addition to the literature on the subject.

Exports have a critical role to play in our development as accelerated growth of interaction with our major trading partners will facilitate the process of opening up our economy to the forces of modernisation and international competition. In this regard, Dr. Iqbal, in his book, has provided a comprehensive analysis of Japan being one of the foremost industrial powers in the world, offers vast scope for Indian industry and commerce to take advantage of India's proximity to that country for keeping abreast of the world in sophisticated technological developments. The present study of India's trade with Japan, therefore, acquires much significance.

I am sure all concerned individuals and institutions will find the book very useful and Dr. Iqbal deserves our compliments for making his scholarship easily accessible to all.

I wish the book every success.

ABID HUSSAIN

Member,
Planning Commission,
(Government of India).

October, 1989.

PREFACE

Japan's trade relations with India are traditional, strategic and of vital importance. The trade relations are in the upswing and poised for a new turn. What turn and twist they will take will depend a great deal on factors affecting global trade pattern in general, and Japan exercising her considered own policy options in particular.

Japan is India's third biggest trading partner after the USSR and the USA. It accounts for nearly 10 per cent of India's total trade. But the share of India in Japan's total trade is barely 0.9 per cent. Although Japan's trade with India has been increasing over the years, it has had a trade surplus with India in the current decade so far. This means that imports from India have not fared better as compared to Japan's exports to India. Hence, the need of the hour is to increase exports to Japan? This study is an attempt to expose the nature, problems and potentialities of Japan's trade with India. It is the outcome of my research work done at the Institute of Developing Economies, Tokyo, (Japan) as a Visiting Research Fellow from February 10, 1988 to 1st September 1988.

Objectives of the Study

The following are the objectives of the study :

1. It seeks to review Japan's trade relations with India since 1960.
2. It studies the major constraints standing in the way of increasing the total trade turnover.
3. It endeavours to identify the main items of imports and exports offering trade prospects between Japan and India, and
4. It suggests suitable strategies for increasing exports from India to Japan.

Scope of the Study

This study attempts to analyze the rationale of Japan's trade relations with India. It covers a fairly long period of 26 years i.e., from 1960 to 1986.

At the beginning of Indian Planning era i.e., 1951, trade relations between India and Japan were at the low ebb. The real momentum started when India's first Prime Minister, Late Pandit Jawahar Lal Nehru visited Tokyo in 1956 and showed his keen interest in increasing bilateral trade between the two nations. That visit opened a new chapter in the history of Japan's trade relations with India. An agreement on commerce between Japan and India which came into force on April 8, 1958 provided for the grant of the most favoured-nation-treatment by both the countries. Thereafter, Japan gave financial aid to India for the first time in the form of Yen credits, deferred payments, Government grants for special projects and Japan's private investments. Hence, these are the basic and fundamental reasons to start study from 1960. The study is both descriptive and analytical. This study also tries to identify some possible areas for future studies relating to trade relations between India and Japan.

Framework of the Study

The study contains eight chapters. Chapter 1 deals with the evolution of Japan's trade relations with India. Chapter 2 depicts Japan and India in world trade setting. Chapter 3 analyzes the trends in India's trade with Japan. Chapter 4 highlights the trends in India's major imports from Japan. Chapter 5 analyzes the trends in India's major exports to Japan. Chapter 6 examines the major constraints in exporting to Japan. Chapter 7 questions : What to export to Japan? Chapter 8 suggests a suitable strategy for increasing exports to Japan.

Research Methodology Adopted

The methods for conducting research are both documentary and discussion with experts on the subject within the Institute of Developing Economies and outside of the Institute. The data and work published in journals and papers* of repute is used extensively.

1. Secondary data was collected from various international sources namely : IMF Financial Statistics, Direction of Trade of the World Bank and Asian Development Bank Statistics.

2. Secondary data was also gathered from the various sources in Japan such as JETRO publications, The Japan Economic Journal Publications and Economic Planning

---

* Data and work published in the following journals have been used extensively.

1. *Foreign Trade Review*, New Delhi, July-September 1986, October-December 1986 and January and March 1987.

Agency, Government of Japan.

3. Interviews with some importers were made so that first-hand knowledge on the problems relating to imports from India could be ascertained, and

4. Discussion with area development experts of the IDE was also held so that a broad based policy could be evolved for increasing trade relations between Japan and India.

In an endeavour of this type of research, it is imperative to solicit academic cooperation from various sources. It is my privilege to acknowledge the needed cooperation I got from such institutions and persons whose help was immense in the present research project. The core of this work was written as a Visiting Fellow, at the Institute of Developing Economies, Tokyo (Japan) from February 10 to 1st September 1988. I am very much grateful to the Institute for awarding me a fellowship to undertake such study.

At the very outset, I have to record my debt of gratitude to Mr. Syed Hashim Ali, the Vice-Chancellor, Aligarh Muslim University, Aligarh (India) for sanctioning me leave for academic pursuits without which the present study would not have been completed.

First and foremost, I must acknowledge my great debt of gratitude to my teacher and well wisher Prof. Ishart H. Farooqi, the then Chairman, Department of Commerce, Aligarh Muslim University, Aligarh (India), who has been a source of inspiration and encouragement to me at all times. He was also instru-

2. *Indian Foreign Review*, New Delhi, July 31, 1987.
3. *Commerce, Weekly*, September 5-11, 1987, and September 12-18, 1987.
4. *Margin*, New Delhi, July-September 1987.
5. *The Financial Express*, New Delhi, October 13, 1987 and
6. All issues of *Foreign Trade Bulletin*, New Delhi, 1986 and 1987.

mental in getting me leave for academic pursuits. Prof. Habib ur-Rehman, Chairman, Department of Commerce, Aligarh Muslim University, Aligarh (India) and the Coordinator, Department of Special Assistance (DSA), had been kind enough not only to give necessary encouragement but also for offering useful and constructive suggestions. I am greatly beholden to him. I am also very much grateful to Prof. Nafees Baig under whom I did my Ph.D.; he took keen interest in my present endeavour. I am also grateful to Prof. Sammiuddin and Prof. Najmul Hasan and Prof. Mehmood A. Raz for extending every possible help to bring this effort to fruition.

I am also thankful to my friends inside and outside the Department for needy help, encouragement and support in my academic endeavour without which this study would not have been possible.

I am very much obliged to Mr. Abid Hussan, Member, Planning Commission, Government of India, for writing foreword to this book.

I have to thank my wife Tehmina not only for sustaining me through this tedious job but also for helping in computational work which would have otherwise meant extra time and effort for me.

Lastly, I am very much thankful to Mr. Raj Kapila, Director, Academic Foundation, New Delhi, for making all out efforts in giving an excellent shape to my manuscript in the form of a book in the shortest possible time.

February, 1990. Badar A. Iqbal

THE AUTHOR :

Born in 1951 (Aligarh, India), Badar Alam Iqbal got his Doctorate in 1977 from Aligarh Muslim University (India). He had earlier obtained Post-graduate Diploma in Bank Administration and Post-graduate Diploma in Secretarial Works. During his research tennure he got UGC's Faculty Research Fellowship, Junior Research Fellowship and Senior Research Fellowship. He was later awarded Post-Doctoral Research Fellowship and UGC Research Associateship.

Prof. Iqbal has, to his credit, 4 books and 105 papers in Indian and foreign journals. He has reviewed 80 books in India and 40 books in foreign journals of U.K., U.S.A., Switzerland, Canada, Hong Kong, Belgium, Japan, France and the Federal Republic of Germany. Dr. Iqbal has participated in 12 national and international symposia and conferences. In 1988 he was invited by the Institute of Developing Economies, Tokyo, Japan as a Visiting Research Fellow to undertake the research project "Japan's Trade Relations with India".

Prof. Iqbal has been invited by the Kiel Institute of World Economics, Germany, to undertake a research project on "Indo-FRG Trade and Economic Cooperation".

List of Tables

CHAPTER ONE

Evolution of India's Trade with Japan

Japan's relations with India were established in old times. "The teaching of Buddha which contributed much to shape India's social and cultural attitudes reached Japan in the middle of the sixth century".[1] Indian textiles were first introduced into Japan with Buddhism around the 7th century.[2] The modern commerce, however, began much later when Japan came out of isolation at the end of Tokugawa era. During the seventh decade of the nineteenth century, trade relations between India and Japan were confined to exports of cotton, twist and yarn from India to Japan and imports were limited to copper from Japan to India. But thereafter, composition of Indo-Japanese trade underwent a sea-change. Exports of cotton yarn were gradually substituted by raw cotton which Japan began to import due to the removal of export duties in India in 1896 following an overall free trade policy.[3] Trade between 1887 and

1. Coelho, V.H., "Indo-Japanese Relations", *Commerce*, Vol. 123, No. 3161, December 4, 1971, p. 30.

2. Maki, M., "Indo-Japanese Economic Ties", *The Economic Times*, Bombay, May 31, 1966, Col. 2.

3. Lockwood writes, "With the removal of the Duty on Cotton in 1896

1898 showed ups and downs in quantitative terms and can be seen from Table 1.1. The change in composition of Indo-Japanese trade was the direct result of the growth of Japanese industries during the Restoration era.[4]

Trade between India and Japan continued to grow since the beginning of the twentieth century. Since 1902 and till 1919 the most important commodities, which constituted the total value of trade, were raw cotton, cotton manufactures and silk manufactures. Table 1.2 indicates trends in relative share of Japan in the value of imports and exports of selected commodities between 1901 and 1919.

Indian textile industry was growing fast during this period. It was a period of growth of textile industry in India and Japan. According to Helen Lamb, "textile industry, being a light industry dependent on cheap labour of which India has abundance - did survive government neglect and discrimination though it never grew and flourished as the dynamic Japanese textile industry."[5] Indian trade during the said period largely reflects this development. Japan purchased increasing quantities of raw cotton from India and supplied small quantities of cotton manufactures.

The period between 1902 and 1919 was more productive. During this period Indo-Japanese trade recorded regular growth and Japan was sharing gains of trade with India and other countries of the world. There was a much spurt in this upward movement during the First World War period.[6] Not being in-

---

Japan accepted dependence on imports of Indian cotton." *The Economic Development of Japan*, 1896-1938, London, 1954.

4. Ibid., p. 29.

5. Lamb, H.B., 'The State and Economic Development in India", in Kuznets, Simon et. al, p. 481.

6. Anstey, V., "The Economic Development of India", London, 1952, pp. 340-341.

volved in the war, Japan had an opportunity to fill the gap created by cessation of imports into India of manufactured goods from the UK, Germany and many other European countries.[7] Table 1.3 shows the rising trend in the share of Japan in India's foreign trade between 1901 and 1919. It is seen that the relative share of Japan in India's total imports and exports went up from one per cent and two per cent respectively in 1901 to 19.8 per cent and 12.1 per cent respectively in 1919. Not only Japan's share in India's foreign trade increased, the composition of Indo-Japanese trade also underwent a radical change and new items namely, jute, rice, iron ore, lac, oilcakes etc. had emerged on the scene of major imports from India. On the export horizon new items such as rubber manufactures, paper, glass and glasswares etc. were added. During this period not only did Japan become an important supplier and customer of India, India's role in Japan's trade also became significant. In 1893 India's relative share in Japan's imports and exports amounted to 9 million Yen and 2 million Yen out of total of 86 million Yen and 88 million Yen respectively. Whereas in 1913, India accounted for 173 million Yen in imports and 30 million Yen in exports out of the total value of trade of 795 million Yen and 716 million Yen respectively.[8] Between 1910 and 1913, sixty per cent of Japan's imports of raw cotton were supplied by India.[9] On the other side, India was an important buyer of Japanese raw silk and manufactures and cotton yarn and cloth.

Post War Period

On the resumption of normal trade relations (after termination of the First World War) with continental and empire

7. Ibid., p. 343.

8. Lockwood, W.W., The Economic Development of Japan; Growth and Structural Change, 1868-1938, London, 1954, p. 3.

9. Ibid., p. 32.

countries, the rising trend in Indo-Japanese trade was halted. In relative terms, India's imports from Japan had gone down to 9.2 per cent in 1920 from 19.8 per cent in 1919. Whereas her exports to Japan showed a slight increase of 2.1 per cent i.e., from 12.1 per cent in 1919 to 14.8 per cent in 1920. Trade between India and Japan during the period from 1920 to 1940 showed an erratic trend and wide fluctuations as evident from Table 1.4. In the third decade of this century Japan's share in India's total trade declined and continued to do so till 1940 except for a period of seven years i.e., from 1931 to 1937, when it recorded an upward trend.

It is important to note here that Indo-Japanese trade during the period under review has been a reflection of continuous industrialisation of Japan. India imported a number of manufactured goods from Japan. Japan penetrated into the Indian market of miscellaneous manufactured items at the expense of empire countries.

Apart from cotton and silk manufactures, which constituted more than 60 per cent of total imports from Japan, shoes, chemicals, hosiery, woollen fabrics, paints soap, glassware, cast iron pipes, umbrellas etc. were the other items of imports from Japan. During this period India had been second to the USA as a market for Japanese camphor. It absorbed 25 per cent of Japanese silk. It consumed 60 per cent of woollen piecegoods in 1925 and 13 per cent in 1933. India alongwith Manchuria had been the major market for Japanese iron manufactures and consumed 14 to 19 per cent of her output. India has also been the second largest market for Japanese pottery and her share each year ranged from 8 to 10 per cent. So far glass manufactures were concerned, India ranked first and her relative share went from 19 per cent to 31 per cent in 1929 over 1925. It went up further to 37 per cent in 1935. India had also been the third biggest market for Japanese toys after the USA and the UK. India's share had been ranging from 8 to 10 per cent in the said items. India was the second most important market for Japan after the UK so far as buttons were concerned and constituted 8 to 13 per cent of Japan's total output of the same. Similarly, India's relative share in gem and jewellery had been 30 per cent. Likewise, India also absorbed 9 per cent of boots and shoes in 1929, 13 per cent in 1934 and 9.1 per cent in 1935.[10]

On the export horizon, major items consisted of raw cotton, raw jute and jute manufactures, manures, rice, iron and steel (mainly pig iron), oilcakes, ores and lead ingots and slabs, etc. Raw cotton was the largest item constituting more than 50 per cent of the total exports from India to Japan. "In the decade 1921-32 India had supplied 50 per cent of Japanese requirements of raw cotton... In 1925 India supplied nearly 18 per cent of rubber... In pig iron, lead and zinc India's position was comparatively strong. India held the third place in the order of importance as an exporter of lead to Japan. India and Australia supplied 65 per cent of Japanese requirements of zinc in 1935."[11] India also supplied nearly 41 per cent of the total requirements of rice and paddy to Japan in 1925 and 6.0 per cent in 1935.

Table 1.5 indicates trends in relative share of Japan in the value of India's imports and exports of selected commodities from 1920 to 1940.

From Table 1.5 it may be seen that during the period 1920 to 1940 Indo-Japanese trade confined only to cotton and silk manufactures and the raw cotton. This appears as a story of cotton and silk as well as the story of the triangular struggle among the UK, Japan and the domestic cotton textile industry for capturing the Indian market.[12] An analysis of Table 1.5 would reveal that out of the total exports of raw cotton from

---

10. Ganguly, B.N., "Reconstruction of India's Foreign Trade", Delhi, 1946, p. 45.
11. Ibid., p. 47.
12. Agarwal, B.M., "Indo-Japanese Trade Relations - A Diagnosis"; Aalekh Publishers, Jaipur-New Delhi, 1974; p. 56.

India, Japan purchased 70 per cent in 1920 and remained the biggest buyer during the period. However Japan's share went down to nearly 36 per cent in 1940. Similarly Japan has been the biggest supplier of manufactures to India and these items accounted for 56 per cent of the total imports of silk manufactures in 1920 and this figure touched the all time high of 78.5 per cent in 1938. Thereafter, her share started looking down.

However, the trend in regard to supply of cotton manufactures to India is quite different. Starting from 10 per cent of the total supplies to India, Japan continuously increased her share and reached upto 55 per cent in 1940. Quantitatively speaking, "India annually imported on an average 3.1 million yards of cotton piecegoods from Japan. During the war period the average increased to 54 million yards per year. In the following years they continued to increase pace and attained the peak of 561 million yards in 1929-30.[13]

Indo-Japanese Trade Agreement of 1934

Due to certain protection measures initiated by the Indian Government on raw cotton, Japan boycotted the purchase of Indian raw cotton. But both the parties agreed to talk and negotiate to find out the suitable way for increasing trade between themselves. A Japanese delegation visited India in October 1933. After several months of talk and negotiations, an agreement was signed on July 12, 1934 which had become operative with retrospective effect from January 8, 1934.

The Agreement contained two parts. Part I, known as the convention, defined the broad principles governing trade relations between India and Japan. Both the nations agreed to accord most-favoured-nation treatment to each other. There had been a provision for imposing import duties for economic

13. Sovani, V.N., "Economic Relations of India with SouthEast Asia and Far East", New Delhi, 1949; p. 24.

balancing. But each nation would revise her tariff policy at the request of the other and would enter into negotiations. Part II concentrated on the Protocol, specified the conditions relating to the import of Japanese cotton piecegoods into India as also the export of Indian raw cotton to Japan. The Agreement was to expire on March 31, 1937.[14]

"Though the Agreement secured a stable market for Indian cotton, it worked more to the advantage of Japan than that of India."[15] As Japan purchased much larger quantities of cotton, Indian cultivators reaped the greatest advantage. But the reduction of duties from 75 per cent to 53 per cent and securing the most-favoured-nation treatment brought about more monetary gains to Japan. Moreover, Japan did not fail to take advantage of the loopholes remaining in the quota system. The most interesting aspect of 1937 Agreement was that ready-made garments, silk goods were not included under the quota. This all worked against the interest of Indian exporters and the environment for newly established industries in India remained shaky.[16]

Indo-Japanese Trade Agreement of 1937

As Indo-Japanese Trade Agreement of 1934 had favoured more the interest of Japanese exporters, Indian business community felt the need for re-orientation of the Agreement. The negotiations for a new Indo-Japanese agreement began in July 1936. During negotiations the loopholes of 1934 Agreement were brought to the notice of officials. As a result, the new agreement came into force on April 1, 1937 for a period of three years, to expire on March 31, 1940.

---

14. For detailed study go through 1934 Agreement contents.

15. Arkaiswamy, M. "A Textbook of Indian Economic History"; Tiruchirapalli, 1954, p. 346-347.

16. Agarwal, B.M., op. cit., p. 62.

In the Agreement of 1937, the convention remained same. However, the second part, i.e., protocol, was modified keeping in mind the balanced approach in the interest of both the nations. The revised quota of piecegoods in different categories was as follows :

		Quota in	
		1937 Agreement	*1934 Agreement*
1.	Plan Grey	40%	45%
2.	Bordered Grey	13%	13%
3.	Bleached White	10%	8%
4.	Coloured and Printed	37%	34%

After the expiry of 1937 Agreement, a provisional agreement was concluded that no nation will take such measures as to prejudice the other's trade. But this agreement did not see the light of the day due to Second World War.

Balance of Trade

It was interesting to note that India had been enjoying a favourable trade with Japan till 1936-37. But it is surprising to note that since the inception of the Indo-Japanese Trade Agreement of 1937, India began to have an unfavourable balance of trade with Japan which continued till her trade with Japan came to a halt during the Second World War period. Table 1.6 shows trends in India's balance of trade with Japan from 1913 to 1943.

Post Independence

After the Second World War, India's trade with Japan revived at a gradual pace. In the early fifties trade between India and Japan was small but it began to pickup since the end of the First Five Year Plan i.e., 1956.

Re-emergence of Japan as a dominating trading nation of the world during the sixties and onwards has been phenomenal. But India's trade with Japan has not been able to take advantage from this situation and as a result the flow and volume of trade between the two nations have been at the low ebb. In 1960, India accounted for 2.7 per cent of Japan's total exports. Similarly, India accounted for nearly 3 per cent of Japan's total imports. But in 1986 the relative share of India in Japan's total exports and imports went down to 0.8 per cent and 0.9 per cent respectively. This means that right from 1937-38 India's relative position in Japan's total exports and imports have been looking down.

In recent years, it is observed that despite the advantage of low labour cost which India has been enjoying as compared to East Asian and South East Asian economies, Japan's total value of trade with India has not increased much as compared to other important trading nations of Asia and she has been at the bottom (Table 1.7). Similarly, in terms of annual average compound growth rate, India has been lagging far behind the major trading nations of Asia as evident from Table 1.7.

Table 1.8 show that while relative share of South Korea, Taiwan, Hong Kong, Singapore and Indonesia in Japan's total value of trade has gone up, the relative share of India has come down. The most striking feature as seen from Table 1.9 is that India, which had second place in 1960, has become seventh in 1986. This means between 1960 and 1986 India has lost much in relative share and this is due to low trade turn over between India and Japan.

TABLE 1.1

Exports to Japan from India 1887 to 1898

Year	Cotton (Raw) Lbs (000)	Cotton Yarn Lbs (000)
1887-88	14.0	17391
1888-89	43.7	23143
1889-90	6809.6	22686
1890-91	8713.6	11876
1891-92	44800.0	6682
1892-93	49728.0	7351
1893-94	41216.0	5768
1894-95	52080.0	2613
1895-96	95872.0	635
1896-97	167888.0	1208
1897-98	146832.0	354

Source : Adapted from Sovani, N.V., Economic Relations of India with South East Asia and Far East, New Delhi, 1949, p. 24.

TABLE 1.2

Percentage Share of Japan in the Value of Imports and Exports of Selected Commodities 1901 to 1919

Year	Exports to Japan	Imports from Japan	
	Cotton - Raw	Cotton Manufactures	Silk Manufactures
1901	-	-	30.0
1902	46.6	-	19.4
1903	27.0	-	27.0
1904	21.2	0.3	37.2
1905	33.7	0.3	24.2
1906	32.2	0.5	31.6
1907	25.3	0.5	40.4
1908	28.2	0.8	42.0
1909	33.8	1.0	43.4
1910	38.2	1.2	45.3
1911	34.3	1.5	43.0
1912	48.1	1.5	51.2
1913	51.1	1.3	50.6
1914	47.2	1.8	46.1
1915	42.7	2.2	48.3
1916	68.3	3.3	53.8
1917	71.9	8.6	50.5
1918	72.1	9.1	56.1
1919	75.4	27.9	55.0

Sources : As Table 1.1.

TABLE 1.3

Percentage Share of Japan in India's Imports and Exports from 1901 to 1919

Year	*Imports*	*Exports*
1901	1.0	2.0
1902	0.9	5.8
1903	1.1	4.6
1904	1.5	5.6
1905	1.2	6.3
1906	1.2	6.3
1907	1.4	4.1
1908	1.7	5.1
1909	1.7	4.8
1910	2.1	6.8
1911	2.6	6.6
1912	2.5	7.5
1913	2.5	7.7
1914	2.6	9.2
1915	3.2	8.8
1916	5.6	9.5
1917	8.9	11.8
1918	12.1	14.6
1919	19.8	12.1

Source : Same as Table 1.1.

TABLE 1.4

Percentage Share of Japan in India's Foreign Trade from 1920 to 1940

Year	*Imports*	*Exports*
1920	9.2	14.8
1921	9.2	10.0
1922	7.8	16.8
1923	6.2	13.4
1924	6.0	14.3
1925	6.9	14.3
1926	8.0	15.1
1927	7.1	13.6
1928	7.1	9.0
1929	6.9	10.4
1930	9.8	10.3
1931	8.8	10.7
1932	10.5	8.9
1933	15.4	10.5
1934	14.2	8.9
1935	15.7	15.7
1936	16.2	13.6
1937	17.0	15.3
1938	12.8	10.0
1939	10.1	9.0
1940	11.6	6.8

Source : Venkatsubbiah, H., Foreign Trade of India 1900 - 1940, New Delhi, 1946.

TABLE 1.5

Relative Share of Japan in the Value of India's Imports and Exports of Selected Commodities from 1920 to 1940

Year	*Imports*		*Exports*
	Cotton Manufactures	*Silk Manufactures*	*Raw Cotton*
1920	10.0	55.7	70.3
1921	14.6	53.0	49.5
1922	11.4	47.1	60.3
1923	11.7	51.1	48.6
1924	12.4	40.9	43.2
1925	13.8	47.7	50.3
1926	19.0	46.1	50.0
1927	17.2	40.0	58.7
1928	18.1	43.9	46.1
1929	18.3	44.3	43.8
1930	26.4	47.4	41.9
1931	30.4	42.0	45.3
1932	35.4	46.9	47.1
1933	38.0	63.9	54.6
1934	35.0	73.5	39.6
1935	32.5	74.6	61.1
1936	41.6	74.4	53.1
1937	43.2	73.4	57.2
1938	43.5	78.5	50.9
1939	50.2	64.0	47.2
1940	55.0	47.3	35.8

Source : Indo-Japanese Trade Relations - A Dianosis, Aalekh Publishers, Jaipur - Delhi, 1974, p. 56.

TABLE 1.6

India's Balance of Trade with Japan from 1913 to 1943

(Rs. in Crores)

Year	Exports	Imports	Balance
1913-14	23	5	+ 18
1934-35	24	21	+ 3
1935-36	22	22	---
1936-37	28	19	+ 9
1937-38	19	22	- 3
1938-39	15	15	---
1939-40	14	19	- 5
1940-41	9	22	- 13
1941-42	5	12	- 7
1942-43	-	3	- 3

Source : Agarwal, B.M., Op. Cit., p. 64.

TABLE 1.7

Trends in Total Value of Trade of Selected Asian Countries with Japan from 1960 to 1986

Name of the country	1960 (Million US $)	1986	Over all rise in no. of times	Annual average growth rate	Annual compound growth rate
South Korea	118.7	15766	132	507	20.6
Taiwan	165.7	12542	75	287	18.1
Hong Kong	178.9	8234	45	173	15.8
Singapore	100.4	6040	59	227	17.0
Thailand	189.8	3421	17	65	11.7
Malaysia	225.3	5553.9	24	90	13.1
Indonesia	180.5	9972	54	208	16.6
India	208.2	3396	16	63	11.3
Japan	8727.0	338310	39	149	

Source : Compiled and calculated from various issues of Year books of IMF and White Paper on International Trade of Japan, JETRO.

TABLE 1.8

Relative Share of Selected Countries in Japan's Total Value of Trade in 1960 and 1986

Name of the Country	*1960*	*% to total*	*1986*	*% to total*
South Korea	118.7	1.4	15766.4	4.7
Taiwan	165.7	1.9	12542.2	3.7
Hong Kong	178.9	2.1	8234.1	2.4
Singapore	100.4	1.2	6040.0	1.8
Thailand	189.8	2.2	3420.6	1.0
Malaysia	225.3	2.6	5553.9	1.6
Indonesia	180.5	2.1	9972.4	2.9
India	208.2	2.4	3396.4	1.0
Total Volume of trade of Japan	8727.0	100.0	338310.0	100.0

Source : Same as Table 1.7.

TABLE 1.9

Trends in Ranking of Selected Asian Countries in Japan's Total Value of Trade in 1960 and 1986

Name of the Country	*Ranking in 1960*	*Ranking in 1986*
Malaysia	I	VI
India	II	VII
Thailand	III	VII
Indonesia	IV	III
Hong Kong	IV	IV
Taiwan	V	II
South Korea	VI	I
Singapore	VII	V

Source : Compiled and calculated from Table 1.7 and Table 1.8.

This page is intentionally left blank.

CHAPTER TWO

India and Japan in World Trade Setting

Rapid expansion in global trade after mid-twentieth century had been due to much improvement in international competitiveness. Increased supply capacity and expanded demand was possible through increasing technological innovations. Technological innovations had boosted the needed higher productivity resulting in increased supply capacity, improved quality and reduced costs, thus leading to improved international competitive ability.[1] Indirectly, it had helped the demands cross national frontiers by reducing distances and pushing up communications.[2] Hence, the international trade of nations had grown in degree to the extent of technological innovations or developments. Developed nations (industrialised) had much greater share in the growth of world trade than the developing nations.[3] In India, a technological revolution

1. Indo-Japanese Trade Relations - A Diagnosis, op. cit., p. 62.
2. Ibid.
3. See, The Industrial Bank of Japan Ltd., Research Department, Quarterly Survey of Japanese Finances and Industry, Vol. XIX, No. 1, Jan-March 1967, p. 1.

was brought with the introduction of planning in 1951. In Japan, rejuvenated technological development set in under the impact of American technology around the said period. It is in this context that the period under review (1960 to 1986) of this study has been taken to analyse India's and Japan's trade in world perspective.

The prospects for global trade are both highly promising and acutely disturbing.[4] The volume of trade is now increasing at a steep pace, but the rate of growth may be halted if trade warfare increases between the nation-states. It is true that the recovery from recession of 1981 is still moving forward. The only worry is that it is not moving as fast and as sturdily as had been expected.[5]

Trends in Global Value of Trade

In 1960 total volume of trade stood at 63,000 million US $ and this figure went up to 4,055,000 million US $ in 1986 showing an over all rise of more than 15.4 times or 1442 per cent. Table 2.1 shows trends in global value of trade and the relative share of India and Japan in global trade. Table 2.1 also indicates that during the period under review India's share in global trade has gone down from 1.4 to 0.6 per cent. The declining trend was set in 1960 and the same is still continuing. But India's absolute value of trade went up by nearly 6 times or 568 per cent. Japan's total value of trade showed an over all increase of 3859 per cent or nearly 39 times between 1960 and 1986 and her relative share in total world volume of trade went up by 5.1 per cent. This has been a remarkable performance for Japan from all angles and Japan has contributed significantly in the

4. Goldstein, W., Trade, Jobs and Technology in the World Market : The Demands of Change; Foreign Trade Review, New Delhi; Oct.-Dec. 1986; p. 277.

5. Ibid.

growth and development of world volume of trade or flow of trade.

Trends in Annual Average Growth and Annual Average Compound Rates

Annual average growth rates and annual average compound growth rates are shown in Table 2.2. It is seen from the Table 2.2 that the period between 1970-75 was most productive for the global trade in which period the annual average growth rate and the annual average compound growth rate were highest i.e., 39.5 and 24.3 per cent respectively. Period from 1975 to 1980 was also comparatively better in which period annual average growth rate and annual average compound growth rate stood at 23.4 per cent and nearly 17 per cent respectively. The worst period for the global trade was between 1980 and 1986 when the annual average growth rate and annual average compound growth rates were the lowest i.e., 0.9 per cent and 0.8 per cent respectively. The period between 1970 and 1975 was also very productive for India. During this period India recorded 31.7 per cent and nearly 21 per cent annual average growth rate and annual average compound growth rate respectively. In case of India, the period from 1965 to 1970 was most unfortunate when she recorded negative annual average growth rate and annual average compound growth rate i.e., (-) 1.5 per cent and (-) 1.2 per cent respectively. In regard to Japan, the period between 1970 and 1975 was boom period. She recorded 39.5 per cent and 24.3 per cent annual average growth rate and annual average compound growth rate. Here, it is important to note that during this period Japan equated annual average growth rate and annual average compound growth rate to global annual average growth rate and annual average compound growth rate. This is really a remarkable achievement from all angles for Japan and other developing nations must get lesson from her progress. Periods between 1965 and 1970 and 1975 and 1980 were also fairly good for her. The most striking feature is that the period 1980-86, which was least productive for world and India, was comparatively more unproductive for Japan in the sense that she recorded (-) 2.1 per cent and (-) 2.0 per cent, i.e., negative annual average growth rate and annual average compound growth rate respectively as against 0.9 and 0.8 and 1.1 and 1.0 per cent of world and India respectively. It is also interesting to note that the period between 1960-65 was also more productive for Japan and world as compared to India. This all shows that world trade mechanism has proved "engine of growth" for Japan while India has failed to make use of the same. Japan has used world trade mechanism to a maximum possible extent and through this she has boosted her standard of living, the employment and the strength of her currency. But India did not use the same for her economic problems and as a result, standard of living, the employment of workforce and the strength of the currency have not been achieved.

Trends in Imports: World, India and Japan

The value of world's total imports went up from 126,000 million US $ to 2,065,900 million US $ showing an over all increase of 1537 per cent or more than 16 times between 1960 and 1986. The value of India's total imports showed an over all rise of nearly 566 per cent or nearly 6 times during the period under review. Total value of Japan's imports recorded an over all increase of 2740 per cent or more than 28 times during the period under reference and have also outpaced the rise in case of world imports and India's imports. India's relative share in world imports has been continuously decreasing and went down from 1.7 per cent to 0.7 per cent in 1986 over 1960 (see Table 2.3). Her rank among the importing countries of the world has also gone down from 13th to 22nd after being 29th rank in 1980. Japan's total imports have been growing regularly. Her relative share in global imports went up from 3.3 per cent in 1960 to 6.2 per cent in 1986. Her rank in the global importing countries has gone down from 6 to 4 (see Table 2.3).

Trends in Exports : World, India and Japan

Total world exports went up from 128,000 million US $ in 1960 to 1,989,400 million US $ in 1986 indicating an over all rise of more than 1454 per cent or more than 15 times. India's total exports showed an overall increase of more than 584 per cent or nearly 6.8 times between 1960 and 1986. In 1960 India's total exports stood at 1,367 million US $ and the same figure went up to 9,352 million US $ in 1986. Japan's total exports increased from 4,055 million US $ to 2,10,757 million US $ during the period 1960 to 1986. The exports of Japan recorded an over all increase of more than 5097 per cent or more than 51.8 times during the same period. This means that the rate of increase in the exports of Japan is remarkable and is many times higher than the rate of increase in global and India's total exports.

Table 2.4 shows trends in World, India and Japan's total exports and their relative share in global exports. Table 2.4 also indicates the ranking of India and Japan in total world exports between 1960 and 1986. Not much different is the story of India's share in global exports which has been declining faster. From 1.1 per cent in 1960, her share in the global exports went down to 0.4 per cent in 1986 and her rank also fell from 18th to 31st during the period under review.

Japan's total exports have been rising faster and with great degree of consistency and diversity. This is indicated by the fact that her share in global exports went up from 3.2 per cent to 10.6 per cent in 1986 over 1960 and her rank has also improved considerably i.e., from 7th to 3rd after USA and the Federal Republic of Germany during the period under reference.

From the above analysis it is clear that India's foreign trade has not been able to keep pace with world trade and her exports are particularly lagging far behind in providing cover to her imports which are rising at much faster pace and keeping trade balance negative for the last so many years. Whereas Japan has recorded phenomenal growth in her exports and the rate of increase has outpaced the rate of increase in global exports during the period 1960 to 1986.

Annual Average Growth Rates and Annual Average Compound Growth Rates

Table 2.5 indicates trends in annual average growth rates and annual average compound growth rates of world, India and Japan's total imports between 1960 and 1988. It shows that the period between 1970 and 1975 was most productive and fortunate for world imports. This is because the highest growth rates were recorded. Period between 1975 and 1980 was also better as compared to other periods (1960-65 and 1980-86). The worst period for the global imports was 1980-85 in which period global imports recorded negative growth rates. In regard to India the period between 1970-75 was most unproductive. Period between 1975-80 was also less unproductive. But period from 1965 to 1970 was the best period for her in which she recorded negative growth rates in total imports. Japan recorded highest growth rates between 1970 and 1975. Periods between 1965-70 and 1975-80 were less unproductive as compared to the period of 1970-75. During these periods the annual compound growth rates were around 19 per cent. The most fortunate period for Japan's imports was the period between 1980 and 1986 in which she also recorded negative growth rates. In comparative terms, Japan did fairly well as compared to India and the World. The most surprising feature of this analysis is that India has recorded positive growth rates during 1980-86 though marginal. Japan and world imports showed negative trends in growth rates during the same period. Another noteworthy feature of the period 1970-75 is that India recorded much higher growth rates as compared to world imports. However, India's figures were slightly lower than the figures of Japan during the same period.

Table 2.6 indicates trends in annual average growth rates and annual average compound growth rates of World, India and Japan's total exports. From the Table 2.6 it appears that the period 1970-75 was most productive for World, India and Japan's total exports. During this period growth rates were highest. Similarly, period between 1975-80 was also productive for world, India and Japan's total exports. But for Japan's total exports, the periods 1960-65, 1965-70 and 1975-80 were also fairly result oriented. For world exports, the period 1975-80 was also fairly productive. For India, the period 1975-80 was also result oriented. The most unfortunate period for world exports was 1980-85 in which she witnessed negative growth rates. Similarly, for India the said period was also unproductive and during this period she also recorded negative growth rates. But for Japan's total exports the entire period (1960-86) remained productive as Japan's total exports rose continuously. For world exports the lowest growth rates were recorded during 1960-65. But India recorded lowest growth rates during the period 1965-70. This analysis indicates that there has not been any uniform trend for world, India and Japan. They had different growth rates in different times.

The phenomenal growth in Japan's total exports has been responsible for ending the Japanese trade deficit and converting it into a surplus in 1965, 1970 and again in 1985 and 1986 (Table 2.7) which also shows balance of trade of India and Japan between 1960 and 1986. Thus Japan's trade deficit amounting to 962 million US $ in 1960 was converted into a surplus amounting to 46676 million US $ in 1985. This figure went up further amounting to 83204 million US $ in 1986. India's trade deficit shot up from 436 million US $ to 5979 US $ during the period 1960 and 1986. The most revealing feature of this analysis is that India's balance of trade has been negative throughout the period and the same also rising continuously during the period under review. In case of Japan, the negative trade balance was recorded in 1960, 1975 and 1980. The most surprising feature that emerges if we throw a glance on Table 2.6 and 2.7, is that despite recording highest growth rates in total exports, Japan's balance of trade during the period 1975-80 remained negative. This may be due to higher rate of growth in Japan's total imports (due to higher oil prices).

The annual average compound rate of growth of world trade has been 11.2 per cent during 1960-1986 (Table 2.8). But the annual average compound growth rate of India's foreign trade (a developing country) has been only 7.6 per cent. The annual average compound growth rate of Japanese foreign trade (a developed country) has been 15.1 per cent even much higher than the world growth rate. During the period 1960 to 1986, India's imports have grown annually at a rate of 7.5 per cent and exports grew at a rate of 7.6 per cent i.e., 0.1 per cent higher than the imports. Japanese imports have grown at the rate of 13.7 per cent and exports grew at a faster rate of 16.4 per cent keeping Japan's foreign trade more strong. This too shows that India's exports are lagging far behind in financing her imports.

While considering the overall growth rates it is worthwhile here to analyse trends in the variations in growth rates of foreign trade of World, India and Japan during the period 1960 to 1986. A look at Table 2.9 showing index number (base 1960, 1970 and 1980) of imports of World, India and Japan it appears that while taking 1960 as a base year for measuring the variations in imports of World, India and Japan, the variations in world imports, India's imports and Japan's imports were gradual and the rate of variations is not the same for the entire period. The rate of variations during 1975 and 1986 were higher as compared to the period between 1960 and 1975. Japan's imports have taken a big leap during the last 11 years as compared to India's and world imports. But if we take 1970 as a base year then the story is much different. The variations were not as high as they were during 1960 and 1986 when the base year taken was 1960. But when we take 1980 as a base year the variations' trend is most disturbing and erratic and in case of Japan variation trend in imports was considerable. In case of India the variations were also marginal and erratic. Variations in world imports were also showing ups and downs.

Table 2.10 shows trends in variations in World, India and Japan's total exports from 1960 to 1986 taking into account the three different base years (1960, 1970 and 1980). If we take 1960 as the base year, the variations in regard to India's exports were erratic and variations in world exports were by and large gradual and steady. Japan's total exports showed gradual and steady variations during the period. If we take 1970 as the base year then variations in regard to India's exports were fairly steady except in 1985 and variations were also not prominent as compared to world exports. The most revealing fact is that variations in regard to Japan's exports were not as prominent as compared to variations recorded during the period when the base year was 1960. When we take 1980 as the base year then the variations in regard to world and India's exports were erratic. Variations in regard to Japan's exports were prominent.

Direction of India's Trade

To analyse the flows of trade, the normal practice in recent times is to divide the whole world into three major groups namely, industrialised nations, developing nations and centrally planned nations. Now we will analyse the direction of India's foreign trade with these three groups between 1960 and 1986.

In 1960 more than two-thirds of India's trade was with the industrialised nations. These nations accounted for nearly 80 per cent and 70 per cent of India's total imports and exports respectively (Table 2.11). India's trade with developing nations accounted for nearly 18 per cent and 22 per cent of India's total imports and exports respectively. Centrally planned economies were having very low share i.e., 3.4 per cent and 8.1 per cent respectively in India's total imports and exports.

1970 showed a slightly different picture. In 1970 the share of industrialised nations in India's total imports and exports declined by 19.5 and 5.0 per cent respectively. Whereas the share of developing nations in India's total imports and exports went up by 26.3 per cent and nearly 4 per cent respectively. The share of centrally planned economies also went up during the period under review.

In 1980 the share of industrialised nations in India's total imports and exports went down further and they constituted less than 50 per cent of the total imports and exports of India whereas share of developing and centrally planned nations increased further during the said period.

In 1986 the most surprising feature was that the share of industrialised nations in India's total imports and exports again went up considerably and they accounted for 62 per cent and 58.4 per cent of India's total imports and exports respectively. The share of developing economies went down considerably during the said period. However, the share of centrally planned nations in India's total imports showed a decline of 1 per cent whereas the share of centrally planned nations in India's total exports went up considerably.

In 1960 India's major trade partners were the USA, the UK, the Federal Republic of Germany, the USSR and Japan whereas in 1986 the major trade partners were the USA, the USSR, Japan, the EEC and the OPEC. This all shows that India's trade is getting diversified year after year.

Direction of Japan's Trade

In 1960 it was surprising to note that Japan, an industrialised country, had not much large trade relations with other industrialised nations of the world as compared to India. These nations accounted for 62 per cent and 48 per cent of Japan's total imports and exports respectively. Developing nations constituted 36.4 and 51 per cent of Japan's total imports and exports respectively. Japan's trade with centrally planned economies was at the low ebb.

In 1970 the share of industrialised nations in Japan's total imports showed a decline of 11.6 per cent (Table 2.11 and 2.12). But the share in exports showed a marginal rise of 0.4 per cent during the same period. The share of developing nations in Japan's total imports showed a rise of 13.8 per cent. But their share in Japan's total exports went down by 2.3 per cent. Trade with centrally planned economies was, by and large, stagnant.

In 1980 the share of industrialised nations in Japan's total imports and exports showed a declining trend. The share of developing nations in Japan's total imports went up. But their share in Japan's total exports went down marginally. The relative share of centrally planned economies in Japan's total imports and exports remained, by and large, on the same level.

In 1986 Japan's share in total imports and exports of industrialised nations showed an upward trend and the share in total imports and exports of developing nations went down considerably. This all shows that direction of Japan's trade has been erratic and there has been least trade with centrally planned economies.

Since the late 1920's one global trend related to trade development is that the world production has increased more rapidly than world trade.[6] Rise in the volume of trade, in fact, has followed the increase in production but its growth has been slower. But the trend has been reversed since the 1960's and now world trade has increased more than world production.[7]

---

6. World Economic Survey 1958 onwards, UN, New York, 1959 onwards, p. 17.

7. World Development Report 1987.

India, however, could not participate in such upward movements in world trade. Japan has, on the other side, participated with dynamism. Another pattern noticed in trade variations by Prof. Gunner Myrdal[8] is that the larger a country, the greater the amount of international trade and *vice versa*. This is but natural. But in case of India (larger country) ratio of exports and imports to GDP are low. More developing economies have low volume of trade ratios and India being among them exports much less than Japan. The genesis of this state of affairs has been the reason that India selected domestic development method (development of domestic resources leading to self-sufficiency) for restructuring her alien-plundered economy. But Japan adopted foreign trade as a mode of reconstructing war-shattered economy.

Trends in 1987

In 1987 world trade recorded 4 per cent growth in volume and 15.6 per cent in dollar-value terms. Industrialised nations are still facing the problem of sustainable levels. However in 1987 the situation improved in volume terms when Japan and West Germany, the two largest surplus economies, increased their imports at a faster rate than exports. The existing world trade imbalances are responsible for foreign exchange rates, high degree of protectionism in trade and the moves among some nations toward making regional economic block.

In 1987 Japan's total imports showed an increase of 18.3 per cent, outpacing the growth of exports which increased by nearly 10 per cent. This indicates that Japan's trade and industrial structure is changing for providing necessary help in correcting world imbalances.

In 1987 India's exports showed a rise of 14 per cent whereas

8. Myrdal G., Asian Drama, Vol. 1, London, 1968, p. 584.

imports showed a marginal rise of nearly 2 per cent. As a result, India's negative balance of trade declined marginally.

Conclusion

From the foregoing analysis it has been brought out that growth of Japan's trade has been much faster and that of India slower than the growth of global trade. Japanese exports have grown much faster than her imports and as a result her adverse balance of trade has vanished and got converted into a favourable one. India's total exports have increased at a much lower rate and imports have increased regularly at a much faster pace. Hence, India's adverse balance of trade has consequently grown in magnitude year after year.

The main reason for India's lingering trade deficit is, in part, its "lack of export mentality". The country's exports stood at only 6 per cent of her GDP in 1986, which is still below the 7 per cent figure recorded in 1977. This calls for increasing the production capabilities which is a key to correct her huge trade deficit. Japan is sustaining her economic growth by opening a new frontier through new product and technology innovations. In this regard, Japan should help India by opening her market more to Indian products and should also extend more economic and technological cooperation, including the transfer of management resources.

Suggestions

India should adopt a multi-pronged strategy for promoting exports. The strategy should identify sectors, industries and products having good export potential and provide for a policy framework conducive to growth of exports. For a coordinated approach on matters concerning exports and for speedy decision making, institutional arrangements up to the highest level must be established.

Very recently it was pointed out that "with countries becoming interdependent, Japan cannot continue to prosper unless further development of the world is ensured". The present situation calls for Japan's positive approach to this effect. Japan has all potentials for contributing much in the shortest time for solving huge world imbalances.

Japan must help the Asian nations in achieving a balanced expansion of their economies so that they could contribute much for solving world trade imbalances. It is believed that in years to come the "Asian Continent" will become the centre of economic power.

TABLE 2.1

Trends in Total World Trade and the Relative Share of India and Japan in Total World Trade between 1960 to 1986

(Million US $)

Year	*Total World Trade*	*Total Trade of India*	*% in Total*	*Total Trade of Japan*	*% in Total*
1960	263,000	3,696	1.4	8,564	3.2
1965	383,000	4,499	1.2	16,622	4.3
1970	594,900	4,150	0.7	38,199	6.4
1975	1,770,600	10,736	0.6	113,679	6.4
1980	3,843,100	23,159	0.6	271,737	7.1
1985	3,690,100	22,882	0.6	307,652	8.3
1986	5,055,300	24,682	0.6	238,310	8.3
Total Increase	1441.9	567.8		3858.7	

Source : Compiled and computed from I.M.F. Year Book 1987

TABLE 2.2

Trends in Annual Average Growth Rates and Annual Average Compound Growth Rates of World Trade, India's and Japan's Total Trade between 1960 - 1986

Year	*World*		*India*		*Japan*	
	AAGR	*AACGR*	*AAGR*	*AACGR*	*AAGR*	*AACGR*
1960 - 65	9.5	7.8	4.3	4.0	8.9	14.2
1965 - 70	11.1	9.2	- 1.5	- 1.3	25.9	18.1
1970 - 75	39.5	24.3	31.7	20.9	39.5	24.3
1975 - 80	23.4	16.7	23.1	16.6	23.2	19.0
1980 - 86	0.9	0.8	1.1	1.0	- 2.1	- 2.0

Note : AAGR - Stands for Annual Average Growth Rate.
AACGR - Stands for Annual Average Compound Growth Rates.

Source : Same as Table 2.1.

TABLE 2.3

Trends in Imports : World, India and Japan and Their Relative Share in the Total World Imports from 1960 to 1986

(Million US $)

Year	World	India			Japan		
	Value	Value	% to Total	Rank	Value	% to Total	Rank
1960	126,200	2,303	1.7	13	4,491	3.3	6
1965	182,100	2,838	1.4	16	8,169	4.2	5
1970	304,500	2,124	0.7	25	18,881	6.2	4
1975	837,800	6,381	0.7	27	57,860	6.9	3
1980	1,946,400	14,864	0.7	29	141,296	7.3	3
1985	1,894,700	14,879	0.8	21	130,488	6.9	3
1986	2,065,900	15,330	0.7	22	127,553	6.2	4

Note : Rank among the importing countries of the world.
Source : Same as Table 2.1.

TABLE 2.4

Trends in Exports : World, India and Japan and Their Relative Share in the Total World Exports from 1960 to 1986

(Million US $)

Year	World	India			Japan		
	Value	Value	% to Total	Rank	Value	% to Total	Rank
1960	128,000	1,367	1.1	18	4,055	3.2	7
1965	186,200	1,688	1.0	19	8,452	4.5	5
1970	290,400	2,026	0.7	27	19,318	6.7	4
1975	932,800	4,355	0.5	38	55,819	6.0	3
1980	1,896,700	8,295	0.4	40	130,441	6.9	3
1985	1,795,400	9,003	0.4	38	177,164	9.9	3
1986	1,989,400	9,352	0.4	31	210,757	10.6	3

Source : Same as Table 2.1.

TABLE 2.5

Trends in Annual Average Growth Rates and Annual Average Compound Growth Rates of World, India and Japan

Total Imports 1960 - 86

Period	*% Rise in 5 Years*	*Annual Average Growth Rates*	*Annual Average Compound Growth Rates*
		WORLD	
1960 - 65	44.3	8.9	7.6
1965 - 70	67.2	13.4	10.8
1970 - 75	175.2	35.1	22.4
1975 - 80	132.0	26.4	18.3
1980 - 85	- 2.7	- 0.6	- 0.5
1985 - 86	9.1	9.1	9.0
		INDIA	
1960 - 65	23.2	4.7	4.2
1965 - 70	- 25.2	- 5.1	- 5.9
1970 - 75	200.4	40.8	24.6
1975 - 80	132.9	26.6	18.4
1980 - 85	0.1	Neg	Neg
1985 - 86	3.0	0.6	0.3
		JAPAN	
1960 - 65	81.9	16.4	12.7
1965 - 70	131.1	26.2	18.2
1970 - 75	206.5	41.3	25.1
1975 - 80	144.2	28.8	19.5
1980 - 85	- 7.7	- 1.5	1.5
1985 - 86	- 2.3	- 0.5	- 2.3

Source : Compiled and computed from I.M.F. Years Book 1987 and Direction of Trade, UN, 1987.

TABLE 2.6

Trends in Annual Average Growth Rates and Annual Average Compound Growth Rates of World, India and Japan

Total Exports 1960 - 86

Period	*% Rise in 5 Years*	*Annual Average Growth Rates*	*Annual Average Compound Growth Rates*
		WORLD	
1960 - 65	45.5	9.1	7.7
1965 - 70	55.9	11.2	9.2
1970 - 75	221.2	44.4	26.2
1975 - 80	103.3	20.7	15.2
1980 - 85	- 5.3	- 1.1	- 1.1
1985 - 86	10.8	10.8	10.8
		INDIA	
1960 - 65	23.5	4.7	4.3
1965 - 70	20.0	4.0	3.7
1970 - 75	114.9	22.9	16.5
1975 - 80	90.5	18.1	13.7
1980 - 85	- 3.5	- 0.7	- 0.7
1985 - 86	16.9	16.9	16.9
		JAPAN	
1960 - 65	108.4	21.7	15.8
1965 - 70	128.6	25.7	17.9
1970 - 75	188 9	37.8	23.6
1975 - 80	133.7	27.7	18.5
1980 - 85	35.8	7.2	6.3
1985 - 86	18.9	18.9	18.9

Source : Same as Table 2.5.

TABLE 2.7

Trends in Balance of Trade : India and Japan 1960 - 1986

(US $ in Millions)

Year	*India*	*Japan*
1960	- 436	- 962
1965	- 1123	+ 282
1970	- 98	+ 437
1975	- 2026	- 2041
1980	- 6569	- 10855
1985	- 6876	+ 46676
1986	- 5978	+ 83204

Source : Compiled from Table 2.3 and Table 2.4.

TABLE 2.8

Trends in Rates of Annual Growth * of World Trade 1960 - 1986

	Total Trade	*Imports*	*Exports*
World	11.2	11.3	11.1
India	7.6	7.5	7.6
Japan	15.1	13.7	16.4

* Rates refer to annual average compound rates of growth between 1960 and 1986 defined by the expression :

$$(1+r)^t = \frac{Yt}{Yo}$$

where Yo and Yt are variables, whose growth is being measured in initial and final years respectively of the period under consideration. r annual average compound growth rate to be calculated and t is the time period taken into consideration.

Source : Compiled and computed from the statistics given in I.M.F. Year Book 1987.

TABLE 2.9

% Variations in Imports : World, India and Japan 1960 - 1986

Year	World	India	Japan
		1960 = 100	
1960	100.0	100.0	100.0
1965	144.3	123.2	181.9
1970	241.3	92.3	420.4
1975	663.8	277.1	1288.4
1980	1542.2	645.4	3146.2
1985	1501.3	646.1	2905.6
1986	1637.0	665.7	2840.2
		1970 = 100	
1970	100.0	100.0	100.0
1975	275.0	291.0	306.4
1980	639.2	699.8	798.4
1985	622.3	700.5	691.1
1986	678.5	721.8	675.6
		1980 = 100	
1980	100.0	100.0	100.0
1985	97.3	100.1	92.3
1986	106.1	103.1	90.3

Source : Compiled from Table 2.3.

TABLE 2.10

% Variations in Exports : World, India and Japan 1960 - 1986

Year	*World*	*India*	*Japan*
		1960 = 100	
1960	100.0	100.0	100.0
1965	145.5	123.5	208.4
1970	226.9	148.2	476.4
1975	728.8	318.6	1376.5
1980	1481.2	606.8	3216.8
1985	1402.7	585.4	4369.0
1986	1554.2	684.1	5197.5
		1970 = 100	
1970	100.0	100.0	100.0
1975	321.2	214.9	288.9
1980	653.1	409.4	675.2
1985	618.3	395.0	917.1
1986	685.0	461.6	1090.9
		1980 = 100	
1980	100.0	100.0	100.0
1985	95.7	96.3	135.8
1986	104.8	112.7	161.6

Source : Compiled from Table 2.4.

TABLE 2.11

Trends in flow of Imports from 1960 to 1986

(in %)

Country	Industrialised Nations				Developing Nations				Centrally planned Nations			
	1960	*1970*	*1980*	*1986*	*1960*	*1970*	*1980*	*1986*	*1960*	*1970*	*1980*	*1986*
Japan	61.6	50.0	33.6	47.3	36.4	50.0	63.1	47.1	2.0		2.7	1.9
India	79.8	60.3	46.2	62.0	16.7	43.0	43.9	28.9	3.4	5.2	9.6	8.5

Source : Compiled and computed from IMF and Direction of Trade Statistics, 1987.

TABLE 2.12

Trends in flow of Exports from 1960 to 1986

Country	Industrialised Nations				Developing Nations				Centrally planned Nations			
	1960	*1970*	*1980*	*1986*	*1960*	*1970*	*1980*	*1986*	*1960*	*1970*	*1980*	*1986*
Japan.	47.6	48.0	45.3	61.8	50.6	48.3	46.9	32.4	1.8	2.0	2.8	1.9
India	70.0	65.0	48.7	58.4	21.9	25.6	31.9	22.9	8.1	10.2	18.8	18.2

Source : Same as Table 2.11.

CHAPTER THREE

Trends in India's Trade with Japan

Foreign trade has steadily become of great importance to India's economic policies and plans. However, the same has not been accorded much significance as it receives in Japan and Korea. But in the present economic environment, exports will have to provide an increasing proportion of India's foreign exchange needs which are mounting very fast as the new economic policies begin to take effect.

In the field of foreign trade, India's progress has been none too small. India's total value of trade has increased substantially since the beginning of the planning era (Table 3.2). However, the trend and pattern of growth of India's foreign trade has been largely in favour of developed countries of the West, the centrally planned economies of East Europe, Australia, New Zealand and Japan (Table 2.11). But it is important to note that the volume of trade with Japan, though crucial and important, is small and the rise has not been in proportion to her overall rate of growth (Table 3.2). This is no doubt a strange phenomenon. Vigorous efforts therefore, have to be made to reverse this trend. The vast economic potential of Japan provides promising scope for the growth of bilateral trade. In the light of the above observations, the present chapter seeks to examine the past, the present position and the future prospects of India's trade relations with Japan.

The Indo-Japan trade, which has been experiencing an upswing in recent years, is expected to get a further boost with the trade liberalisation measures taken by India recently and the high-level dialogues (IJBCC) initiated between the two nations. Japan is the third biggest trading partner after the USSR and the USA. It accounts for nearly 14 per cent of India's total value of trade (Table 3.2). But India's relative share in Japan's total value of trade is barely 1.0 per cent. This means there has been by and large, one way trade between India and Japan; this is rather surprising.

Indo-Japan Trade in World Perspective

In 1960 the global value of trade stood at 263,000 million US $ and this figure went up to 4,055,300 million US $ in 1986 recording an overall rise of 1441 per cent or more than 14 times during the period. Indo-Japan trade witnessed an overall increase of nearly 1533 per cent or more than 15 times between 1960 and 1986 (Table 3.1). This shows that the rate of increase in Indo-Japan trade is slightly higher than the rate of increase in the global value of trade during the same period. This has led to an increase in the relative share of Indo-Japan trade in global trade between 1960 and 1986. However, increase is very marginal i.e., 0.01 per cent. The lowest share was witnessed in 1980 and since then the share has been looking up. All this indicates that Indo-Japan trade has done fairly well in world trade perspective during the period under review.

Trends in Total Value of Trade of India and Japan and of Indo-Japan Trade

Total value of trade between India and Japan went up from

208 million US $ in 1960 to 3396 million US $ in 1986 showing an overall increase of more than 15 times during the period under reference. Similarly, India's total value of trade recorded an overall increase of nearly 6 times i.e., from 3696 million US $ to 24682 million US $ between 1960 and 1986. Japan's total value of trade witnessed an overall increase of nearly 39 times i.e., from 8546 million US $ in 1960 to 338310 million US $ in 1986. This means that the rate of increase in Japan's total value of trade is many times higher than the rate of increase in India's total value of trade. Similarly, it is also higher than the rate of increase in Indo-Japan value of trade. In 1960 the Indo-Japan trade accounted for nearly 6 per cent of India's total value of trade. But by 1986 the share of Indo-Japan trade in India's total value of trade increased to nearly 14 per cent i.e., a net increase of 8.2 per cent (Table 3.2) during the period. From 1960 to 1970 Indo-Japan trade showed an upward trend. Thereafter i.e., from 1975 to 1980 the trend was looking down. Again in 1985 it went up. However, Indo-Japan total value of trade has a declining trend in Japan's total value of trade. In 1960 Indo-Japan total value of trade accounted for 2.4 per cent and was on its peak. Thereafter the declining trend set in and in 1986 it constituted only 1 per cent of Japan's total value of trade. The most disturbing trend has been a continuous decline in the relative share till 1980. Since then there has been a slight improvement in the relative share of Indo-Japan trade in Japan's total value of trade. However, the present share in the light of expanding Japanese foreign trade is negligible and requires immediate strategy to boost it up in years to come. This analysis also indicates one way trade between India and Japan.

If we throw a glance on the annual average growth rates and annual average compound growth rates of India's total value of trade, Japan's total value of trade and Indo-Japan total value of trade, it appears that Japan's total value of trade and Indo-Japan value of trade have done fairly well and the growth rates are fairly high as compared to India's total value of trade (Table 3.3). The most interesting aspect is that during 1965-70 when India's total value of trade recorded negative annual average growth rates and annual average compound growth rates, Indo-Japan value of trade witnessed fairly high annual average growth rates and annual average compound growth rates i.e., nearly 9 per cent and 8 per cent respectively (Table 3.3). Another note-worthy feature of the analysis is that during 1980-86 the total value of Indo-Japan trade recorded much higher growth rates as compared to Japan's total value of trade and India's total value of trade. The figures are 15.2 per cent and nearly 10 per cent for Indo-Japan total value of trade, 4.1 per cent and 3.7 per cent for Japan's total value of trade and 6.6 per cent and 1.0 per cent for India's total value of trade respectively. Similarly, during the period 1980-86 India's annual average compound growth rate is lagging far behind the annual average compound growth rate of Indo-Japan total volume of trade which showed the highest increase i.e., 9.8 per cent as compared to 3.7 per cent of Japan and the lowest 1.2 per cent of India. This all indicates that Indo-Japan trade had done fairly well between 1980 and 1986 so far as growth rates are concerned.

Trends in Japan's Imports from India

The pattern of Japan's imports from India has remained more or less unchanged over the years. India's present share in Japan's imports of manufactured goods, for which there is an expanding market, is by and large negligible. At present nearly 80 per cent of India's exports to Japan consist of iron ore, shrimps and prawns, diamonds, leather and textile goods.

In 1960 Japan's total imports from India stood at 100 million US $ and the same went up to 1297 million US $ in 1986 indicating an overall increase of nearly 1197 per cent or a rise of nearly 13 times. Similarly, Japan's total imports showed an overall rise of 2740 per cent or more than 28 times i.e., from 4491 million US $ to 127553 million US $ during the period under review. Likewise, India's total exports went up from 1367 million US $ to 9352 million US $ indicating an overall increase of more than 584 per cent or nearly 7 times between 1960 and 1986. This trend shows that Japan's imports from India have done comparatively well and as a result Japan's share in India's total exports went up by 6.6 per cent (Table 3.4). But the share of Japan's imports from India in Japan's total imports has declined by 1.2 per cent during the same period. This is due to the fact that the rate of increase in Japan's total imports is much higher than the rate of increase in Japan's imports from India.

Comparison in Growth Rates

During the period 1960-65, India recorded lowest annual average growth rates and annual average compound growth rates as compared to the growth rates recorded by Japan's total imports and Japan's total imports from India (Table 3.5). But during the period 1970-75, India's total exports recorded much higher growth rates as compared to growth rates witnessed by Japan's total imports from India. Similarly, during 1975-80, India's total exports witnessed much higher growth rates as compared to Japan's total imports from India. But during 1980-86 the trend was reverse and Japan's total imports showed much better growth rates as compared to Japan's total imports and India's total exports. It is surprising to note that during 1980-86 Japan's total imports showed negative growth rates and India too recorded lowest growth rates. The best period for Japan's total imports and India's total exports was 1970-75 when the growth rates stood at 41.3, 25.1, 22.9 and 16.5 per cent respectively. For Japan's total imports from India the best period was 1965-70 when it witnessed the highest growth rates i.e., 36.1 per cent and nearly 23 per cent. Similarly, the period 1975-80 was also better period for Japan's total imports and India's total exports as during this period Japan and India recorded much higher growth rates as compared to growth rates witnessed by Japan's total imports from India. As a whole,

Japan's total imports from India did fairly well during the period under review.

Table 3.6 gives a comparison in compound growth rates recorded by World imports, Japan's total imports, India's total imports and Japan's total imports from India.

During the period 1960 to 1986 Japan recorded much better compound growth rate as compared to others and her growth rate was even higher than the growth rate of world imports. Japan's total imports from India also showed much better compound growth rate and the same is slightly lower than the compound growth rate of world imports. However, the lowest compound growth was recorded by India's total imports and they were lagging far behind others.

Trends in Japan's Exports to India

In recent years nearly 70 to 80 per cent of the imports from Japan consist of finished products namely, machinery, transportation equipments, handling equipments, metal goods, chemical goods and telecommunication equipments. A survey conducted by India-Japan Study Committee indicated that there has been increased outflow of foreign exchange on account of technology imports from Japan which has not been matched by an increase in export earnings. The Indian engineering industry accounted for the bulk of technology imports. Hence, diversification of trade is vital not only for the expansion of bilateral trade but even to maintain the current level of trade flows.

In 1960 Japan's total exports stood at 109 million US $ and they went up to 2099 million US $ in 1986 showing an overall increase of more than 1825 per cent or more than 19 times during the same period. Japan's total exports have increased by 5097 per cent or by nearly 52 times i.e., from 4055 million US $ to 210757 million US $ during the period under review. India's total imports recorded an overall increase of nearly 566 per cent or nearly 7 times, (from 2303 million US$ to 15330 million US$) during the period under reference. This means Japan's total exports outpaced Japan's total exports to India and the rate of increase is many times higher than the rate of increase in Japan's total exports to India. In 1960 the relative share of Japan's exports to India in Japan's total exports accounted for 2.6 per cent. But since then, till 1980 the same has been decreasing (Table 3.7) and the decline was 1.9 per cent. But thereafter the same improved slightly and reached to a level of 1 per cent in 1986. However, it is still at the low ebb. In 1960 the relative share of Japan's total exports to India in India's total imports stood at 4.7 per cent and the same went up to nearly 14 per cent (Table 3.7). In 1965 the share stood at 7.2 per cent and then it came down to 4.8 per cent in 1970. In 1975 it went up again to 7.4 per cent and again came down to 6.2 per cent in 1980. But thereafter, there is gradual and steady rise in the relative share of Japan's total exports to India in India's total imports. However, increase has not been gradual and steady during the period 1960 to 1986. It is important to note that the rate of decrease in the share in Japan's total exports is much less as compared to the rate of increase in the share in India's total imports.

Comparison in Growth Rates

During 1960-65 annual average growth rates and annual average compound growth rates in regard to Japan's total exports and Japan's total exports to India were fairly high. But during the period 1965-70 Japan's total exports to India recorded negative growth rates and the rates were fairly high (Table 3.8). It is surprising to note that during this period Japan's total exports witnessed much higher growth rates. Similarly, another surprising feature was that during 1970-75 Japan's total exports to India showed very high growth rates and they were much higher than the growth rates recorded by

Japan's total exports during the same period. However, the period 1970-75 was also the best for Japan's total exports. During 1975-80 the trend became reverse and during the same period Japan's growth rates of total exports outpaced the growth rates recorded by Japan's total exports to India. But during 1980-86 again, Japan's total exports to India showed much higher growth rates as compared to growth rates witnessed by Japan's total exports and the growth rates are as high as 26 per cent and 15 per cent as against 10.3 per cent and 8.3 per cent respectively. However, it is important to note that Japan's growth rates of total exports are gradual and steady as compared to the growth rates of Japan's total exports to India.

Trends in annual average compound growth rates reveal that total exports to India from Japan have done well during the period 1960 and 1986 (Table 3.9). The growth rate is even higher than the total world exports growth rate during the same period. It is also reasonable if we compare the same with the growth rate of Japan's total exports. It is further higher than the growth rate of India's total exports. This means that exports from Japan to India have fared much better than exports from India to Japan.

Balance of Trade

Although India's trade with Japan has been increasing in absolute terms over the years, she has had a negative balance of trade with Japan since 1981 (Table 3.10). The liberal trade policy adopted by India coupled with large purchases of iron and steel, industrial machinery and equipments required for infrastructure and industrial sector were conducive to the growth of Japan's exports to India and led to higher rate of growth in trade deficit. One of the major reasons for the growing deficit is the narrow base of India's exports to Japan.

If we throw a glance on compound growth rates of world trade, Japan's trade, India's trade and Indo-Japanese trade

(Table 3.11), we see that Indo-Japan trade has done well in world's and Japan's trade perspective and her growth rates are far ahead of India's total trade. This all shows that India has failed in improving her base in world trade perspective but done fairly well in Japan's trade perspective though the volume of trade has been low.

Conclusion

The very fact that India has a large trade deficit with Japan and that India's exports to Japan continue to consist of raw materials and primary products, it has become of paramount significance for India to diversify its trade and promote her exports on an increasing scale. In recent times, it is noticed that there is a decline in the market for raw materials in Japan. The major reason for this state of affairs, as pointed out by India-Japan Study Committee, is the relative shift from raw material intensive industries such as iron and steel to electronics which uses less raw materials. Economies in the use of raw materials due to change in the manufacturing methods and recycling of materials has been another factor in weakening demand for raw materials. Taking these factors into consideration, India must take such steps as to change her image as a supplier of primary goods to manufactured goods.

Suggestions

According to the latest study concluded by the Indian Committee of the India-Japan Study Committee, there has been a huge increase in foreign exchange outgo on account of the rising trend in technology imports from Japan. But, there has not been matching rise in export earnings from that country. This could be one of the reasons for India's large trade deficit with Japan.

The Standing Committee of India-Japan Business Cooperation Committee which had meaningful deliberations at Srinagar (Jammu and Kashmir) on June 15, 1987 had decided upon certain measures to bring down India's trade deficit with Japan. Both the sides agreed to cooperate in the areas of trade promotion and joint ventures which would facilitate diversification of trade. It was also decided to increase the level of bilateral trade to 6 billion US $ by 1990 and bring to 400 million US $ in the next two years. This is possible since new opportunities have emerged for export of engineering goods, electronic software, leather and leather goods, jewellery, besides exporting goods such as paper from bagasse, aluminium, meat and meat products. It was also agreed to bring down the deficit by half in the next two years. The Japanese delegation stressed the need for positive efforts by Indian manufacturers and exporters for increasing exports to Japan by taking advantage of the appreciation of Yen as well as Japan's need to increase imports to deal with the big trade balance.

TABLE 3.1

Trends in Total World Trade, Total Japan's Trade with India and their Relative Share in the Total World Trade from 1960 to 1986

(Million US $)

Year	*Total World Trade*	*Japan's Total Trade with India*	*% to Total World Trade*
1960	263,000	208	0.07
1965	383,000	342	0.08
1970	594,900	493	0.08
1975	1,770,600	1,129	0.06
1980	3,843,100	1,929	0.05
1985	3,690,100	2,785	0.07
1986	4,055,300	3,396	0.08

Source : Compiled and computed from I.M.F. Year Book, Direction of Trade Year Book and various issues of White paper on International Trade, JETRO.

TABLE 3.2

Trends in Total Value of Trade between Japan and India and its Relative Share in Japan's and India's Total Value of Trade 1960 and 1986

(Million US $)

Year	*Total Value of Trade between Japan and India*	*India's Total Value of Trade*	*Japan's Total Value of Trade*	*% in India's Total Trade*	*% in Japan's Total Trade*
1960	208	3696	8546	5.6	2.4
1965	342	4499	16622	7.6	2.0
1970	493	4150	38199	11.9	1.2
1975	1129	10736	113679	10.5	0.9
1980	1929	23159	271737	8.3	0.7
1985	2785	22882	307652	12.2	0.9
1986	3396	24682	338310	13.8	1.0

Source : Samė as Table 3.1.

TABLE 3.3

Trends in Annual Average Growth Rates and Annual Average Compound Growth Rates of India and Japan's Total Trade and Indo-Japanese Total Trade between 1960 and 1986

Year	India		Japan		Indo-Japan	
	Annual Average Growth Rates	*Annual Average Compound Growth Rates*	*Annual Average Growth Rates*	*Annual Average Compound Growth Rates*	*Annual Average Growth Rates*	*Annual Average Compound Growth Rates*
1960-65	4.3	4.0	18.9	14.2	12.9	10.4
1965-70	- 1.6	- 1.3	25.9	18.1	8.8	7.5
1970-75	31.7	20.9	39.5	24.3	25.8	18.5
1975-80	23.2	16.6	27.8	19.0	14.2	11.3
1980-86	6.6	1.2	4.1	3.7	15.2	9.8

Source : Compiled and computed from IMF and JETRO Year Books.

TABLE 3.4

Trends in Japan's Total Imports from India and their Relative Share in Japan's Total Imports and India's Total Exports between 1960 and 1986

(Million US $)

Year	*Total Imports from India*	*Japan's Total Imports*	*India's Total Exports*	*% to Japan's Total Imports*	*% to India's Total Exports*
1960	100	4491	1367	2.2	7.3
1965	139	8169	1688	1.7	8.2
1970	390	18881	2026	2.0	19.2
1975	658	57860	4355	1.1	15.0
1980	1014	141296	8295	0.7	12.0
1985	1187	130488	8003	0.9	14.0
1986	1297	127553	9352	1.0	13.9

Source : As Table 3.1.

TABLE 3.5

Trends in Average Annual Growth Rates and Annual Average Compound Growth Rates of Indo-Japan Imports, Japan's Total Imports and India's Total Exports 1960 - 1986

Year	*Japan's Total Imports from India*		*Japan's Total Imports*		*India's Total Exports*	
	AAGR	*AACGR*	*AAGR*	*AACGR*	*AAGR*	*AACGR*
1960-65	7.8	6.8	16.4	12.7	4.7	4.3
1965-70	36.1	22.9	26.2	18.2	4.0	3.7
1970-75	13.7	11.0	41.3	25.1	22.9	16.5
1975-80	10.8	9.0	28.8	19.5	18.1	13.7
1980-86	5.6	4.1	- 1.6	- 0.3	2.1	2.0

Note : AAGR stands for annual average growth rates.
AACGR stands for annual average compound growth rates.

Source : Same as Table 3.1.

TABLE 3.6

Trends in Compound Growth Rates of Total Imports of Japan, Total Imports of India, World Imports and Japan's Total Imports from India 1960 - 86

Particulars	*Annual Average Compound Growth Rates*
Total World Imports	11.3
Japan's total Imports	13.7
India's total Imports	7.5
Japan's total Imports from India	10.3

Source : Compiled and computed from Table 3.4.

Method of Computation :

$$(1+r)^t = \frac{Yt}{Yo}$$

where Yo and Yt are variables, whose growth is being measured in initial and final years. r is annual average compound growth rate to be found out and t is time period taken into consideration.

TABLE 3.7

Trends in Japan's Total Exports to India, Japan's Total Exports, India's Total Imports and the Relative of Japan's Total Exports to India in Japan's Total Exports and India's Total Imports between 1960 - 1986

(Million US $)

Year	*Japan's Total Exports to India*	*Japan's Total Exports*	*India's Total Imports*	*% Share in Japan's Total Exports*	*% Share in India's Total Imports*
1960	109	4055	2303	2.6	4.7
1965	203	8452	2838	2.4	7.2
1970	103	19318	2124	0.5	4.8
1975	471	55819	6381	0.8	7.4
1980	915	130441	14864	0.7	6.2
1985	1596	177164	14879	0.9	10.7
1986	2099	210757	15330	1.0	13.7

Source : Same as Table 3.4.

TABLE 3.8

Trends in Annual Average Growth Rates and Annual Average Compound Growth Rates of Japan's total Exports to India, Japan's Total Exports and India's Total Imports between 1960 - 1986

Period	*Japan's Total Exports to India*		*Japan's Total Exports*		*India's Total Imports*	
	AAGR	*AACGR*	*AAGR*	*AACGR*	*AAGR*	*AACGR*
1960-65	17.2	13.12	21.7	15.8	4.7	4.2
1965-70	- 9.8	- 14.5	25.7	17.9	- 5.1	- 5.9
1970-75	71.4	35.5	37.8	23.6	40.8	24.6
1975-80	18.9	14.2	27.7	18.5	26.6	18.4
1980-86	25.8	14.8	10.3	8.3	0.5	0.5

Source : Same as Table 3.5.

TABLE 3.9

Trends in Compound Growth Rates of Japan's Total Exports to India, Japan's Total Exports, India's Total Exports and World Exports 1960 to 1986

Particulars	*Annual Average Compound Growth Rates*
Total World Exports	11.1
Total Exports to India from Japan	12.0
Total Japan's Exports	16.4
Total India's Exports	7.6

Source : Same as Table 3.6.

TABLE 3.10

Trends in Japan's Balance of Trade with India 1960 - 1986

(Million US $)

Year	*Japan's Exports to India*	*Japan's Imports from India*	*Balance of Trade*
1960	109	100	- 9.0
1965	203	139	- 64.0
1970	103	390	+ 287.0
1975	471	658	+ 187.0
1980	915	1014	+ 99.0
1985	1596	1187	- 409.0
1986	2099	1297	- 802.0

Source : As Table 3.4 and Table 3.6.

TABLE 3.11

Trends in Annual Average Compound Growth Rates of Indo-Japanese Trade 1960 - 1986

	Total Trade	*Imports*	*Exports*
World	11.2	11.3	11.1
Japan's Total Trade	15.1	13.7	16.4
India's Total Trade	7.6	7.5	7.6
Indo-Japanese Trade	11.3	10.3	12.0

Source : As Table 3.1, Table 3.4 and Table 3.6.

Method of Computation : Same as Table 3.6.

CHAPTER FOUR

Trends in India's Major Imports from Japan

India is on the way to development and hence requires more imports of technology and capital goods. India's imports are to be guided by her needs for capital and intermediate products. With the introduction of programmes and policies for economic reconstruction, the pattern of India's imports was bound to change in nature and in volume. In 1950, cotton textile manufactures and other consumer goods were dominating the scene of India's imports from Japan. But during the last 15 years i.e., from 1950 to 1965, these items have gone out of the scene. However, silk manufactures and raw silk were imported in small quantity. Gradually and steadily, these items were replaced by machinery and equipments. In recent years, it is observed that nearly 70 to 80 per cent of the imports from Japan consist of finished products namely, machinery (general and electrical), transportation and handling equipment, iron and steel and telecommunication equipment. In the light of the above observations, the present chapter deals with the trends in Japan's major exports to India.

Major items of importance which figure in the import schedule are : light industry goods, chemical goods, metal goods, general machinery, electric machinery, transport equipment, textile goods, non-metallic mineral goods and other light industry goods. Table 4.1 shows trends in major exports of Japan to India between 1960 and 1986.

It is seen from the Table 4.1 that the trend in Japan's major exports to India has been erratic. Fluctuations in the value are of high magnitude. Japan's exports to India of light industry goods showed an overall increase of nearly 20 times. Chemical goods recorded nearly 18 times increase. Metal goods witnessed a small rise of nearly 8.5 times. General machinery recorded an over all rise of more than 38 times. Electrical machinery witnessed an overall increase of nearly 39.7 times. Transport equipment showed the highest increase of nearly 41.5 times. However, textile goods recorded the lowest increase of nearly 38.5 times, and other light industry goods recorded an overall rise of nearly 23.6 times (between 1965 and 1986). The most revealing fact is that rise has been more prominent after 1970. However, during the period between 1980 and 1986 the rise has been huge and sudden.

So far annual rate of change in Japan's major exports to India is concerned, it showed ups and downs (Table 4.2). During the period 1960-65, transport equipment showed highest increase followed by electric machinery, general machinery, chemical goods, non-metallic mineral goods and light industrial goods. But metal goods and textile goods recorded negative rate of change i.e., nearly (-) 12 per cent and more than (-) 22 per cent. It is surprising to note that during the period 1965-70, all the items except other light industrial goods recorded negative rate of change. Transport equipment recorded highest decline of 82 per cent followed by electric machinery, textile goods, general machinery, chemical goods, metal goods, light industry goods and non-metallic mineral goods. However, other industrial goods recorded an overall rise of 34 per cent. The decline has been more alarming in case of chemical goods, general machinery, electric machinery and transport equipment. This has been the worst period for Japan's major exports to India. Period between 1970-75 has been more productive for Japan in the sense that during the said period all items recorded positive change in value. The positive change was more revealing and sudden in case of chemical goods and transport equipment. The highest increase was recorded in regard to transport equipment i.e., as high as 867 per cent. The rate of change in regard to chemical goods was also as high as 816 per cent. The other items also recorded increase in value. The lowest increase was recorded in respect of non-metallic mineral products i.e., nearly 58 per cent. During the period 1975-80, the rate of change in regard to light industry goods, general machinery, electric machinery, textile goods and non-metallic mineral products, the lowest rate of change was recorded in respect of transport equipment i.e., as low as 3 per cent only. However, chemical goods which had recorded highest increase during 1970-75 witnessed negative rate of change i.e., more than 45 per cent. During the period 1980-86, some items namely, transport equipment, electric machinery, general machinery and non-metallic mineral products recorded positive rates of change with high degree of variation as compared to other items. But the rate of variation has not been as high as during 1975-80. The other items such as light industry goods, chemical goods, metal goods and other industrial goods have also recorded modest rate of change. However, textile goods witnessed negative rate of change and the decline has been considerable. Overall, the rate of change has been very erratic and fluctuations were very frequent and sharp in nature. The period between 1970 and 1975 has been the most productive from Japan's point of view as during this period all items showed positive rate of change with high magnitude.

Annual average compound growth rate of major exports of Japan to India showed the same trend. However, the trend is more clear and understandable. Table 4.3 indicates trends in annual average compound growth rate of Japan's major exports to India from 1960 to 1986. The most revealing fact is that textile goods have been recording negative annual average compound growth rate between 1960 and 1970 and again during the period 1980-86. Thereafter, chemical goods and metal goods had recorded negative annual average compound growth rates. Other items had recorded negative annual average compound growth rates only during 1965-70 when all the major items witnessed negative annual average growth rates. This all indicates that during the period under review trend had been erratic and ups and downs were frequent.

An analysis of the relative share of Japan's major exports to India in Japan's total exports, reveals that during the period 1960 to 1986 all major items showed a declining trend (Table 4.4). In regard to light industry goods, the relative share had started looking down from 1965 till 1970. Thereafter, it showed a slight improvement. However, in 1986 it went down again. Chemical goods showed a gradual rise from 1960 to 1965. In 1970 the share went down. In 1975 it went up again and in 1980 it declined and in 1986 the relative share further went down. The relative share of metal goods by and large, started looking down since 1965. It is interesting to note here that the relative share of machinery and equipments recorded marginal decline as compared to other items during the period under review. The relative share of non-metallic mineral goods and other light industrial goods have been stagnant. However, the decline in the relative share has been more alarming in respect to metal goods and textile goods.

Table 4.5 indicates trends in the relative share of Japan's major exports to India in India's total imports from 1960 to 1986. The most revealing aspect of the analysis has been that the relative share of textile goods in India's total imports showed a declining trend during the period under review, whereas, all other major items showed a rise in their share in India's total imports. The relative share of general machinery in India's total imports recorded highest rise, followed by metal goods (see Table 4.5), transport equipment, electric machinery and light industry goods. This all means that Japan's major exports have gained considerably in India's total imports.

Trends in the relative share of Japan's major exports to India in Japan's total exports to India are also showing a disturbing picture (Table 4.6). Between 1960 and 1986 so many items have recorded a decline in their relative share in Japan's total exports to India. Chemical goods showed marginal decline over 1960 though it has got maximum share of 35.17 per cent in 1975. Metal goods have witnessed considerable decline in their share during the period under review and their decline has been as high as 33.28 per cent. Textile goods have also recorded considerable decline in their relative share in Japan's total exports to India. But items like general machinery, electrical machinery, transport equipment, other light industry goods, light industry goods and non-metallic mineral goods have recorded increase in their relative share in Japan's total exports to India. The lowest increase in the relative share has been witnessed by light industry goods i.e., 0.26 per cent whereas highest increase in the relative share has been recorded in regard to general machinery i.e., 12.92 per cent.

From the above discussion it appears that the three items namely, general machinery, electrical machinery and transport equipment have dominated Japan's exports' scene. In 1960 these three items accounted for nearly 29 per cent whereas, in 1986 these three items constituted more than 59 per cent of the total exports to India from Japan. This means these items have replaced other items such as metal goods, chemical goods and textile goods. This also means Japan's exports to India have not diversified during the period under review. There has been an increase in value and in the relative share at the cost of other items.

After analysing the commodity structure of exports from Japan to India, it would be worthwhile to analyse the major items exported to India.

Light Industry Goods

Light industry goods are one of the major items which Japan has been exporting to India during the last more than three decades. These items have gained much in Japan's total export. In 1960, these items constituted 0.63 per cent of the total exports whereas in 1986 these items accounted for 2.26 per cent of the total exports of Japan in these items (Table 4.7). However, the trend has been erratic. The relative share of these items in Japan's total exports showed increase till 1965. In 1970 the relative share of these items went down considerably. In 1975 these items improved their relative share marginally. In 1980 the relative share of these items went up considerably and in 1986 their relative share went up further. This all indicates that since 1975 these items have shown gradual and steady increase. These items have also improved their share in India's major imports from Japan. (Table 4.6).

Chemical Goods

Chemical goods have witnessed marginal decline in their relative share in Japan's total exports to India (Table 4.6). Similarly, the relative share of these items in Japan's total exports of these items between 1960 and 1986 have gone down considerably. In 1960 these items constituted more than 4 per cent of the total exports of these items by Japan whereas in 1986 these items accounted for 1.32 per cent. In 1960 the share of these items in Japan's total exports of these items stood at 4.17 per cent. This figure went up to 4.32 per cent in 1965. In 1970 the share went down to 1.46 per cent. In 1975 it went up sharply to 4.26 per cent which was the maximum these items ever recorded. Since then they have started looking down gradually and steadily (Table 4.8).

Metal Goods

Metal goods have lost much ground in India's total imports during the period under review. In 1960 these items accounted for as high as 56 per cent of Japan's total exports to India. In 1986 the relative share of these items went down considerably and stood at more than 22 per cent. As a matter of fact right from 1965 the figures for relative share in Japan's total exports had started looking down. However, these items are still the second largest in Japan's total exports to India (Table 4.6).

Metal goods have also lost their share in Japan's total exports of these items. In 1960, these items accounted for more than 37 per cent of the total exports of these items whereas in 1986 these items constituted nearly 12 per cent of Japan's total exports of these items. The relative share of these items started looking down from 1965. Ups and downs have been frequent in the relative share during the period under review (Table 4.9).

General Machinery

This item has gained a lot in India's total imports and in India's major imports from Japan. Import of this item in India has been continuously increasing. The relative share of general machinery in India's total imports went up by nearly 2 per cent (Table 4.5). Similarly, the relative share of this item in Japan's total exports to India also increased considerably i.e., more than 12 per cent (Table 4.6). General machinery ranks first in Japan's major exports to India and Japan's total exports to India.

General machinery's share in Japan's total exports of general machinery however, went down considerably. In 1960, this item accounted for nearly 6.4 per cent of the total exports of general machinery by Japan. This figure went up to nearly 8 per cent in 1965. However, the relative share of this item in Japan's total exports went down at the low level of nearly 1 per cent (Table 4.10). This figure went down to the lowest ebb of 0.55 per cent in 1975. Thereafter, it has started looking up. In 1986, this item constituted 1.42 per cent.

Looking at the increasing import needs of the country (India), growing Indo-Japanese trade and the predominant share of this item, the imports of machinery from Japan are likely to have more than the present share. However, the future of such imports will be largely determined by the degree of import substitution which India has to achieve and by the extent of aid which Japan might give.

Electric Machinery

This is the fourth largest export item in Japan's major exports to India (Table 4.6) and in Japan's total exports to India (Table 4.5) and comes after general machinery, metal goods and transport equipments. Electric machinery accounts for more than 2 per cent of India's total imports whereas in 1960 this item constituted only 0.34 per cent (Table 4.5). Similarly, the relative share of electric machinery in Japan's major exports to India also went up considerably i.e., by nearly 8 per cent. In 1960 the relative share of this item in Japan's total exports to India stood at more than 7 per cent and in 1986 this figure went up to more than 15 per cent.

However, the relative share of this item in Japan's total exports of electric machinery has decreased during the period 1960 to 1986. In 1960 this item accounted for nearly 3 per cent of the total exports of Japan in this item whereas in 1986 the relative share of this item in the total exports of electric machinery stood at 0.67 per cent. The relative share of this item in Japan's total exports was maximum in 1965 i.e., nearly 3.5 per cent of the total. Thereafter, declining trend set in and contin ued till 1970. Since, 1975 the relative share of this item in Japan's total exports of this item has started looking up (Table 4.11). In years to come there will be more imports of this item and there are indications that due to the recent liberalisation of imports the share of this item may go up.

Transport Equipment

This is the third (see Tables 4.5 and 4.6) biggest item among the major exports of Japan to India and India's total imports (Table 4.5 and 4.6). Japan became a real and regular supplier of this item in a big way since 1955-56. In 1960 this item accounted for 0.39 per cent of the total imports of India whereas in 1986, the relative share of this item went up to 2.46 per cent i.e., an overall rise of 2.7 per cent. Similarly, the relative share of this item in Japan's total exports to India in 1960 stood at more than 8 per cent. This figure went up to 18 per cent in 1986 and this item has emerged as the third largest item among the major exports of Japan to India (Table 4.6).

However, the relative share of transport equipment in Japan's total exports of this item went down during the period under review. In 1960 this item accounted for more than 2 per cent of the total whereas, in 1986, the share stood at 0.63 per cent. In 1965, this item had the maximum share i.e., more than 3 per cent (Table 4.12). But in 1970 the share had gone down to a low level of 0.20 per cent. In 1975, it improved much and the figure was 0.46 per cent. But again in 1980 the relative share of this item went down to the lowest ebb i.e., 0.19 per cent. However, in 1986 the relative share of the same stood at 0.63 per cent.

Conclusion

From the foregoing discussion, it is seen that Japan's exports to India has an erratic trend. Ups and downs are very frequent. There has been a concentration of few items. Traditional items such as light industry goods, textile goods and metal goods have been replaced by general machinery, electric machinery and transport equipments.

TABLE 4.1

Trends in Japan's Major Exports to India from 1960 to 1986

(Million US $)

Items	*1960*	*1965*	*1970*	*1975*	*1980*	*1986*
Light Industry Goods	7.8	11.2	9.6	29.3	125.7	155.7
Chemical Goods	7.0	23.6	18.1	165.8	90.9	125.3
Metal Goods	55.0	48.9	40.0	145.9	359.7	468.4
General Machinery	14.2	48.3	18.7	37.4	156.9	545.6
Electric Machinery	8.0	30.0	6.3	19.0	76.2	317.6
Transport Equipment	9.1	38.5	6.9	66.7	68.5	378.0
Textile Goods	8.1	6.3	3.6	10.2	76.6	56.5
Non-Metallic Mineral Products	0.8	2.0	1.0	3.0	10.5	30.8
Other Light Industrial Goods	-	2.9	3.9	16.0	38.0	68.4

Source : Various issues of White Paper on International Trade - JETRO.

TABLE 4.2

Trends in Annual Rate of Change (Per cent) in Japan's Total Exports to India from 1960 to 1986

Items	*1960-65*	*1965-70*	*1970-75*	*1975-80*	*1980-86*
Light Industrial Goods	43.6	- 14.3	205.2	329.0	23.9
Chemical Goods	237.1	- 23.3	816.0	- 45.2	37.8
Metal Goods	- 11.8	- 18.0	264.8	146.5	30.2
General Machinery	240.1	- 61.3	100.0	319.5	247.7
Electric Machinery	275.0	- 79.3	201.6	301.1	316.8
Transport Equipment	323.1	- 82.0	866.7	2.7	451.8
Textile Goods	- 22.2	- 75.0	183.3	650.9	- 26.2
Non-Metallic Mineral Products	150.0	- 10.0	57.9	250.0	193.0
Other Industrial Goods	-	34.0	310.3	137.5	80.0

Source : Computed from Table 4.1.

TABLE 4.3

Trends in Annual Average Compound Growth Rates of Japan's Total Exports to India from 1960 to 1986

Items	*1960-65*	*1965-70*	*1970-75*	*1975-80*	*1980-86*
Light Industrial Goods	7.5	- 3.1	25.0	33.8	3.6
Chemical Goods	27.5	- 4.9	55.7	- 12.7	6.6
Metal Goods	- 2.3	- 4.0	29.5	19.8	4.4
General Machinery	27.7	- 20.8	14.8	33.2	78.5
Electric Machinery	30.2	- 36.6	24.7	32.0	26.8
Transport Equipment	33.4	- 41.0	57.4	00.5	32.9
Textile Goods	- 5.1	- 11.8	23.1	49.6	- 5.2
Non-Metallic Mineral Goods	20.1	- 14.8	24.5	28.4	19.2
Other Light Industrial Goods	-	6.1	32.6	18.8	10.2

Source : Computed from Table 4.1.

TABLE 4.4

Trends in Relative Share of Japan's Major Exports to India in Japan's total Exports from 1960 to 1986

(*In %)*

Items	*1960*	*1965*	*1970*	*1975*	*1980*	*1986*
Light Industrial Goods	0.19	0.13	0.04	0.05	0.09	0.07
Chemical Goods	0.17	0.28	0.09	0.29	0.07	0.06
Metal Goods	1.35	0.57	0.20	0.26	0.27	0.22
General Machinery	0.35	0.57	0.09	0.06	0.12	0.25
Electric Machinery	0.19	0.35	0.03	0.03	0.05	0.15
Transport Equipment	0.22	0.45	0.03	0.11	0.05	0.17
Textile Goods	0.22	0.07	0.01	0.01	0.05	0.02
Non-Metallic Mineral Goods	0.01	0.02	Neg.	Neg.	Neg.	0.01
Other Light Industrial Goods	-	0.03	0.02	0.02	0.02	0.03
Japan's Total Exports	4055	8452	19318	55819	130441	210757

Source : As Table 4.1.

TABLE 4.5

Trends in Relative Share of Japan's Major Exports to India in India's Total Imports from 1960 to 1986

(In %)

Items	*1960*	*1965*	*1970*	*1975*	*1980*	*1986*
Light Industrial Goods	0.33	0.39	0.45	0.45	0.84	1.01
Chemical Goods	0.30	0.83	0.85	2.59	0.61	0.81
Metal Goods	2.38	1.72	1.88	2.28	2.41	3.05
General Machinery	0.61	1.70	0.88	0.58	1.05	3.55
Electric Machinery	0.34	1.05	0.29	0.29	0.51	2.07
Transport Equipment	0.39	1.36	0.32	1.04	0.46	2.46
Textile Goods	0.39	0.23	0.16	0.15	0.51	0.36
Non-Metallic Mineral Goods	0.03	0.07	0.04	0.04	0.07	0.20
Other Light Industrial Goods	-	0.10	0.18	0.25	0.25	0.44
Total Imports of India	2303	2838	2124	6381	14864	15330

Source : As Table 4.1.

TABLE 4.6

Trends in Japan's Major Exports to India in Japan's Total Exports to India from 1960 to 1986

(In %)

Items	*1960*	*1965*	*1970*	*1975*	*1980*	*1986*
Light Industrial Goods	7.17	5.50	9.31	6.21	13.78	7.43
Chemical Goods	6.43	11.60	17.55	35.17	9.93	5.96
Metal Goods	55.59	24.04	38.79	30.95	39.32	22.31
General Machinery	13.06	23.74	18.13	7.93	17.15	25.98
Electric Machinery	7.53	14.74	6.11	4.03	8.36	15.12
Transport Equipment	8.37	18.92	6.69	14.14	7.48	18.00
Textile Goods	7.45	3.09	3.49	2.16	8.37	2.69
Non-Metallic Mineral Goods	0.73	0.98	0.96	0.63	1.14	1.46
Other Light Industrial Goods		1.42	3.78	3.39	4.15	3.25
Total Exports to India	108.76	203.48	103.17	471.43	914.80	2099.40

Source : As Table 4.1.

TABLE 4.7

Trends in Relative Share of Light Industrial Goods in Japan's Total Exports of Light Industrial Goods from 1960 to 1986

Year	*Japan's Total Exports (Million US $)*	*Japan's Total Exports to India (Million US $)*	*% to Total*
1960	1223.3	7.8	0.63
1965	1581.7	11.2	0.70
1970	2407.5	9.6	0.39
1975	7220.4	29.3	0.40
1980	6295.3	125.7	1.99
1986	6873.8	155.7	2.26

Source : As Table 4.1.

TABLE 4.8

Trends in Relative Share of Chemical Goods in Japan's Total Exports of Chemical Goods from 1960 to 1986

Year	*Japan's Total Exports (Million US $)*	*Japan's Total Exports to India (Million US $)*	*% to Total*
1960	169.2	7.0	4.17
1965	546.9	23.6	4.32
1970	1234.5	18.1	1.46
1975	3888.7	165.8	4.26
1980	6766.7	90.9	1.34
1986	9483.8	125.3	1.32

Source : As Table 4.1.

TABLE 4.9

Trends in Relative Share of Metal Goods in Japan's Total Exports of Metal Goods from 1960 to 1986

(Million US $)

Year	*Japan's Total Exports*	*Japan's Total Exports to India*	*% to Total*
1960	147.8	55.0	37.23
1965	304.6	48.9	16.05
1970	713.6	40.0	5.60
1975	1801.1	145.9	8.10
1980	3946.9	359.7	9.11
1986	3912.8	468.4	11.97

Source : As Table 4.1.

TABLE 4.10

Trends in Relative Share of General Machinery in Japan's Total Exports of General Machinery from 1960 to 1986

Year	*Japan's Total Exports (Million US $)*	*Japan's Total Exports to India (Million US $)*	*% to Total*
1960	221.7	14.2	6.40
1965	624.3	48.3	7.73
1970	2006.0	18.7	0.93
1975	6729.0	37.4	0.55
1980	18088.5	156.9	0.86
1986	38380.7	545.6	1.42

Source : As Table 4.1.

TABLE 4.11

Trends in Relative Share of Electric Machinery in Japan's Total Exports of Electric Machinery from 1960 to 1986

Year	*Japan's Total Exports (Million US $)*	*Japan's Total Exports to India (Million US $)*	*% to Total*
1960	273.9	8.0	2.92
1965	865.4	30.0	3.46
1970	2864.7	6.3	0.21
1975	6920.6	19.0	0.27
1980	22760.4	76.2	0.33
1986	46747.1	317.6	0.67

Source : As Table 4.1.

TABLE 4.12

Trends in Relative Share of Transport Equipment in Japan's Total Exports of Transport Equipment from 1960 to 1986

Year	*Japan's Total Exports (Million US $)*	*Japan's Total Exports to India (Million US $)*	*% to Total*
1960	432.7	9.1	2.10
1965	1243.1	38.5	3.09
1970	3442.5	6.9	0.20
1975	14528.3	66.7	0.46
1980	34372.5	68.5	0.19
1986	58426.4	378.0	0.63

Source : As Table 4.1.

This page is intentionally left blank.

CHAPTER FIVE

Trends in India's Major Exports to Japan

After the Second War, in the resumed trade relationship between India and Japan, the commodity structure of India's exports to Japan underwent vast changes. As against a single commodity viz., raw cotton which overwhelmingly dominated the exports to Japan during the pre-war period, the post-war era witnessed considerable diversification of exports. Yet commodity concentration of exports remained higher. Bulk of India's exports to Japan consist of raw cotton, iron ore, steel scraps, manganese ore and non-ferrous metals. They comprised nearly 57 per cent of exports in 1951-52, 82 per cent in 1955-56, and 75 per cent in 1960-61. New items entering this list of exports recently are shrimps, prawns, lobster, leather and leather goods, textile goods, non-metallic mineral products (precious and semi-precious stones, glass and glassware and worked stones) and diamonds. In 1986, 80 per cent of India's exports to Japan consisted of iron ore, shrimps and prawns, diamonds, leather and textile products.

Between 1960 and 1986 raw cotton exports from India to Japan showed an overall increase of more than two-and-a-half times. Iron ore exports from India to Japan witnessed an over all rise of 11 times. Manganese ore exports to Japan recorded 2.2 times increase during the period. Leather and leather products witnessed an increase of more than 6 times. Non-ferrous metals recorded an over all rise of more than 2 times. Shrimps, prawns and lobster witnessed an overall increase of more than 10 times between 1970 and 1986. Textile goods recorded an over all rise of 54 times between 1965 and 1986. Non-metallic mineral goods showed a rise of about 9 times between 1975 and 1986 and diamonds recorded an over all rise of more than 35 times between 1970 and 1986. This means that textile goods showed the highest increase followed by diamonds, shrimps and prawns, iron ore, non-metallic mineral products and leather goods. Table 5.1 show trends in value of Japan's major imports from India between 1960 and 1986. The most striking feature of the table is that after 1980 the value of exports in regard to manganese ore, leather and leather goods, non-ferrous metal and textile goods showed a decline whereas the value of exports in regard to raw cotton, iron ore, shrimps, prawns and lobster, non-metallic mineral products and diamonds recorded an upward trend.

So far, annual rate of change of major exports from India to Japan is concerned, it showed an erratic trend (Table 5.2). During the period 1960-65 manganese ore showed highest increase, followed by raw cotton, non-ferrous metals, iron ore and leather and leather goods whereas during 1965-70 iron ore recorded highest increase followed by non-ferrous metals, manganese ore and leather and leather goods. But raw cotton witnessed a decline. During 1970-75, shrimps, prawns and lobster showed a high rate of change i.e., an increase of nearly 54 per cent followed by leather and leather goods, non-ferrous metals, textile goods, iron ore and the lowest change was witnessed by manganese ore. But raw cotton showed negative variation. However, the rate of negative variation came down. The period 1975-80 has been more erratic. Except textile goods, non-metallic mineral goods and raw cotton, all the major items showed a declining trend and the variation rate has been quite alarming. Similarly, such items as manganese ore, leather and leather goods and non-ferrous metals recorded negative rate of change. Period 1980-86 was also more erratic in the sense that those items which showed positive rate of change during 1975-80 recorded a substantial decline and in case of textile goods the rate of change became negative during 1980-86. Non-metallic mineral goods and diamonds also showed a considerable decrease. Items showing negative rate of change during 1975-80 showed negative rate of change during 1980-86 also with the addition of textile goods in the list. The only item which recorded gradual positive rate of change was raw cotton. This all indicates that Japan's major imports from India showed ups and downs during the period under review.

Annual average growth rate of Japan's major imports from India also tells the same story i.e., an erratic trend. Table 5.3 shows trends in annual average compound growth rates of Japan's major imports from India from 1960 and 1986. The most surprising thing is that despite the yearly negotiations between the delegations of India and Japan, the trend between 1975 and 1986 has been deteriorating with the annual average compound growth rates being more negative as compared to the growth rates recorded between 1960 and 1975. If we throw a glance on Table 4.3 it is evident that only raw cotton recorded negative growth rate between 1960 and 1975. But thereafter many major items recorded negative annual average compound growth rate. This means the yearly deliberations between the two countries have failed in improving the persisting trend and they proved to be only a forum of discussion and not bearing any fruitful results.

The relative share of India's raw cotton in Japan's total imports went down considerably between 1960 and 1986. Iron ore's share in Japan's total imports also went down during the same period (Table 5.4). The relative share of manganese ore, leather and leather goods and non-ferrous metals have become negligible in 1986 over 1960. The most satisfactory thing is that the relative share of shrimps, prawns and lobster, non-metallic mineral products and diamonds have gone up between 1970 and 1986. It is important to note that the relative share of non-metallic mineral products and diamonds have increased gradually and steadily. This indicates that these two items have great potential in Japan's market and India should capitalise the situation and make all out efforts to increase their exports to a maximum possible extent.

Table 5.5 shows trends in the relative share of Japan's major imports from India in India's total exports from 1960 to 1986. The most revealing fact is that raw cotton, manganese ore, leather and leather goods and non-ferrous metals have recorded a decline in their relative share in India's total exports during the period under review whereas items such as iron ore, textile products, non-metallic mineral goods and diamonds witnessed considerable rise in their share in India's total exports. Their increase in share has been gradual and steady one. If efforts are made, the relative share of these items in India's total exports and in Japan's total imports could be increased in years to come.

Trends in the relative share of Japan's major imports from India in Japan's total imports from India also show a declining trend in so many items. The most revealing trend has been in the case of raw cotton. The share of iron ore has also been declining during the period under review. Iron and steel has no place in Japan's total imports from India after 1965. Manganese ore has also been on the same footing and its share has become negligible in 1986 over 1960 (Table 5.6). Leather and leather goods have also lost ground in Japanese market. But the decline during the period 1960 and 1986 has been marginal. Non-ferrous metals have also lost considerable share during the period under review. This means all the traditional items have lost their ground in Japanese market during the period under reference. However, new items such as shrimps, prawns and lobster, textile goods, non-metallic mineral goods and diamonds have gained their share in Japan's total imports from India. Shrimps, prawns and lobster are on the top. Their relative share in Japan's total imports from India have increased substantially. Thereafter, non-metallic mineral goods have emerged on Japan's import scene from India. They have also done well during 1975 and 1986. Their share has also gone up considerably. Then comes diamonds. Their relative share has also increased substantially. Another item i.e., textile goods have also come up and they are also gaining share in Japan's total imports from India. This all gives the impression that India's traditional items are being replaced by non-traditional items during the period under review.

Having analysed the broad commodity structure from India to Japan, it would be desirable to analyse the major commodities that were exported to Japan. Each commodity contains data for not only the major exporting countries, but also the total imports of Japan in that particular item so that relative position becomes comparable and more meaningful.

Cotton Raw

Notwithstanding its little importance in total exports, raw cotton has been one of the major commodities imported by Japan from India. Of Japan's total imports of raw cotton, India had 3.1 per cent share in 1960. It went up by 1.6 per cent in 1965 and went down by 0.6 per cent in 1970. Thereafter, it has been looking down till 1985. In 1986 it went up considerably i.e., by 2.2 per cent over the figure of 1980. However, it showed a marginal increase of 0.8 per cent over the figure of 1960. It means raw cotton has an erratic trend. This marginal rise of 0.8 per cent has been due to the fall in the share of the USA in Japan's total imports of raw cotton. During the period under review the relative share of the USSR, Australia and Pakistan has gone up considerably (Table 5.7).

According to a study published in The Economic Trends,* Indian raw cotton may have greater demand in future. This is due to the fact that Japanese firms have claimed to have developed a very high quality fabric from Indian cotton and are prepared to transfer technology as also invest financially in Indian companies for this purpose. In 1987 a Japanese team of representatives of textile mills and trading houses importing cotton from India visited the country as also held an exhibition of fabrics in Bombay showing textiles made of Indian cotton. The Japanese are considering lifting a large quantity of cotton from India with emphasis on best quality. This is a healthy sign and India should not miss the opportunity. This trend indicates that in years to come Indian cotton may have great potential in Japanese major importing items from India.

Iron Ore

Gaining gradually in importance, iron ore ranks high among the exports of India to Japan. Japan's rapidly expanding steel industry in 60s and 70s needed iron ore as a raw material for producing pig iron and, therefore, Japanese iron and steel industry created an excellent market for the consumption of Indian iron ore together with other Asian and Latin American countries. Japan's contribution in the growth of iron ore exports of India was substantial till 1965 (71.4 per cent of the total). After that declining trend set in. In 1970 the relative share of iron ore in India's total exports to Japan went down further to 53 per cent. Figure for 1975 stood at 50 per cent. In 1980 the share was nearly 42 per cent. In 1986 the share stood at 35 per cent. These figures are indicating a continuous decline in the relative share over the years. This state of affairs has been due to the emergence of Brazil, Australia and Chile as the major exporters of iron ore to Japan. Table 5.8 gives trends in relative share of

* The Economic Trends, New Delhi, (India), "Japan Keen on Cotton Tie-ups", Vol. XVI; No. 10, May 16, 1987.

major exporting countries in Japan's total imports of iron ore between 1960 and 1986.

If we throw a glance on the figures of major exporting countries of iron ore to Japan it is certain that India has been loosing her grip on Japan's iron ore market. Between 1960 and 1986 however, India lost share by 2.7 per cent whereas the relative share of Brazil and Australia showed a rise of 16.2 per cent and 38.1 per cent respectively. But Chile gained only 3.4 per cent. India had lost her share due to poor quality and higher cost. If India wants to remain as one of the leading exporters of iron ore to Japan in particular and other countries in general, she has to make all out efforts to improve the quality and competitive prices in the international market. Therefore, the application of modern technology is the need of the hour.

It is heartening to note that a new strategy for stepping up the exports of iron ore is being worked out by the Government of India. The strategy covers the development of new mines, improvement and expansion of mining operations as well as port facilities, exploring of new markets, increase in exports to the traditional markets (Japan) and making long-term arrangements with the importers. This may go a long way in gaining India's lost ground in Japanese market in particular and other markets in general.

Leather and Leather Goods

Leather and leather goods are one of the traditional items which Japan has been importing from India. But their relative share in Japan's total imports from India has been looking down gradually and steadily (Table 5.9). During 1960 and 1986 their share in Japan's total imports from India went down by 1.2 per cent. Similarly, their share in Japan's total imports of leather and leather goods have also declined enormously i.e., by 13.8 per cent. It is interesting to note that the relative share of other major exporting countries in Japan's total imports of leather and leather goods has also decreased between 1970 and 1986. Share of the Republic of Korea went down by 8.8 per cent. Share of Pakistan also decreased by 10.1 per cent. It is only the USA whose share showed a very marginal decline i.e., by 1.5 per cent during the period under review. This indicates that small countries are gaining share in Japan's total imports of leather and leather goods. However, India may explore the possibilities of increasing exports to Japan specially in the light of increase in cost of production in Republic of Korea and the USA. Being a labour-intensive industry, India can capitalise the advantage and may increase exports to Japan.

Shrimps, Prawns and Lobster

Shrimps, prawns and lobster have emerged as most potential items for export to Japan. Year after year they are gaining importance in Japan's total imports from India. That Japan's contribution in the growth of shrimps, prawns and lobsters exports of India is large is manifest from her percentage share in India's exports. During the span of nearly 17 years, their share in India's total exports went up nearly 21 per cent (Table 5.6). They have also gained share in India's total exports during the period under review (Table 4.5). Their relative share in Japan's total imports have also increased over the years (Table 5.4). These trends show that these items have good prospects in Japanese market and India should increase her share further in years to come. This fact may also be born out from the Table 5.10 which indicates that these items have gained share by nearly 2 per cent during 1970 and 1986. This increase in the relative share has been due to declining trend in the relative share of these items in some major exporting countries namely China and Thailand. This means India has taken out share of these countries during the period under review. However, the share of other major countries namely Australia and Indonesia have also increased during the period under reference. But it is important to note that Taiwan has also emerged as the biggest exporter of these items in 1986. In 1986 Taiwan accounted for more than 17 per cent of Japan's total imports from these countries. This may prove a threat to India. Hence, India should make all out efforts to develop new technology of fish culture as Taiwan has also developed the same with the help of Japan. India may also learn the same technology from Japan. If she fails in doing so then there is possibility of loosing her grip on Japan's market in the years to come.

Textile Goods

Textile goods have emerged as an important item in Japan's total imports from India. These items have gained share in Japan's total imports between 1960 and 1986 (Table 5.5). They also gained share in India's total exports (Table 5.6) during the period under review. Their relative share in Japan's total imports from India have increased during the period under reference (Table 5.6). These trends show that Indian textile goods have promising future in Japanese market. India should not give up this opportunity.

India, China, Republic of Korea and Italy are the major exporting countries of textile goods to Japan. Table 5.11 gives a relative picture in regard to the percentage share of India, China, Republic of Korea and Italy in Japan's total imports of textile goods from 1975 and 1986.

It is heartening to note that India's relative share in Japan's total imports of textile goods has shown a very marginal rise. This is due to decline in the relative share of Republic of Korea in Japan's total textile goods imports. The relative share of China and Italy in Japan's total imports of textile goods have also increased during the same period. However, China gained highest share during the same period. Italy improved her share slightly. India may increase her share further if she makes research in Japanese needs and taste and produce goods accordingly. Here too India has an edge over other producing countries due to low wages.

Non-Metallic Mineral Products

Non-metallic mineral items which consist of precious and semi-precious stones, glass and glassware and worked stones have come up as vital items in Japan's imports from India. These items have gained percentage share in Japan's total imports (Table 5.4). They have also increased their relative share in India's total exports (Table 5.5). Their relative share in Japan's total imports from India have increased enormously during the period of 1975 and 1986 (Table 5.6). These trends, therefore, indicate that these items have promising future in Japanese market. These items are also very much in demand due to quality and reasonable unit value as compared to other major producing countries. Table 5.12 indicate trends in major exporting countries of non-metallic mineral products in Japan's total imports of these items from 1975 to 1986.

It is heartening to note that India has taken out from the share of Israel and the USA in these items in Japan's total imports of these items. The relative share of Israel and the USA have come down by 3 and 2.2 per cent respectively. However, the share of other major producing nations namely the Belgium and the Republic of Korea have increased during the same period. As these items are labour intensive in nature, India can increase her share in Japan's total imports of these items in years to come. But she has to be very careful and cautious on quality and price horizons.

Diamonds

India has emerged as one of the leading exporters of diamonds in the world. India has also been exporting larger quantity of diamonds to Japan and this item has also come up as one of the leading items in Japan's total imports from India.

This may be seen from the fact that diamonds are the third biggest item of Japan's imports from India after shrimps, prawns and lobster and non-metallic mineral products. This item accounts for nearly 17 per cent of Japan's total imports from India. It also constitutes 2.3 per cent of India's total exports (Table 5.5). Diamonds share in Japan's total imports have also improved during the period under review. Table 5.13 shows trends in relative share of major exporting countries in Japan's total imports of diamonds.

In 1970 Belgium was the biggest supplier of diamonds to Japan. The USA came next to Belgium. Israel was the third largest exporter of diamonds to Japan and India was the fourth biggest supplier of diamonds to Japan. Whereas in 1986 Belgium maintained her rank, the USA lost her second rank and in her place Israel became the second largest country exporting diamonds to Japan. India remained the fourth largest supplier of diamonds to Japan. But it is heartening to note that India has gained a lot in relative share in Japan's total imports of diamonds. This has been due to a fall in the share of Belgium as well as the USA. It is also important to note here that Israel gained very marginal share (0.8 per cent) as compared to India (15.1 per cent) during the period under review. There are indications that in the years to come Indian diamonds may gain share further provided she upgrades her quality, keeps export unit value competitive, and ensures credibility and reliability which are missing linkings these days.

Conclusion

From the foregoing analysis it is brought out that the trend in Japan's imports from India has been erratic. Traditional items have been loosing their share in Japan's total imports, Japan's total imports from India and India's total exports. On the other hand non-traditional items gained share in Japan's total imports, Japan's total imports from India and India's total exports. These trends indicate a sort of replacement of traditional items by non-traditional items. This is one of the major contributing factors in keeping India's trade deficit with Japan. India should make all out efforts to stabilize the exports of traditional items alongwith an expansion in the export of non-traditional items. India has to widen her existing narrow base of exports to Japan.

TABLE 5.1

Trends in Japan's Major Imports from India between 1960 to 1986

Items	*1960*	*1965*	*1970*	*1975*	*1980*	*1986*
			(Million US $)			
Raw Cotton	12.9	21.5	20.4	20.1	24.1	32.5
Iron Ore	40.5	60.2	205.2	329.8	424.5	448.5
Iron & Steel Scrap	15.3	17.6	-	3.2	-	-
Maganese Ore	4.0	9.4	19.8	24.2	22.2	8.9
Leather & Leather Products	2.1	2.9	5.1	15.1	13.7	12.7
Non-ferrous metal	7.2	11.1	27.8	64.6	45.7	15.7
Shrimps, Prawns & Lobsters	-	-	24.7	91.2	193.9	269.6
Textile Products	-	1.0	6.2	13.7	59.9	53.5
Non-Metallic Mineral Products	-	-	-	25.8	78.5	222.3
Diamonds	-	-	6.0	25.0	73.4	213.8

Source : Various issues of White Paper on International Trade, JETRO, Japan.

TABLE 5.2

Trends in Annual Rate of Change (Per Cent) in Japan's Major Imports from India 1960 - 1986

Items	*1960-65*	*1965-70*	*1970-75*	*1975-80*	*1980-86*
Raw Cotton	13.3	- 1.0	- 0.3	3.9	5.8
Iron Ore	9.7	48.2	12.1	5.7	0.9
Maganese Ore	27.0	22.1	4.1	- 1.8	- 9.9
Leather & Leather Products	7.6	15.2	39.2	- 1.9	- 1.2
Non-ferrous metal	10.8	30.1	26.4	- 5.8	- 10.9
Shrimps, Prawns & Lobsters	-	-	53.8	22.2	6.5
Textile Products	-	-	24.2	67.4	- 1.7
Non-Metallic Mineral Products	-	-	-	40.9	30.5
Diamonds	-	-	63.3	38.7	31.9

Source : Compiled and computed from Table 5.1.

TABLE 5.3

Trends in Annual Average Compound Growth Rates of Japan's Major Imports from India 1960 - 1986

Items	*1960-65*	*1965-70*	*1970-75*	*1975-80*	*1980-86*
Raw Cotton	10.7	- 1.0	- 0.2	3.6	5.1
Iron Ore	8.2	27.8	9.9	5.2	0.9
Maganese Ore	18.6	16.0	4.0	- 1.7	- 16.4
Leather & Leather Products	6.6	11.9	24.2	- 1.9	- 1.3
Non-ferrous metal	9.0	20.1	18.3	- 7.1	- 19.5
Shrimps, Prawns & Lobsters	-	-	29.8	16.2	5.6
Textile Products	-	-	17.1	34.3	- 1.9
Non-Metallic Mineral Products	-	-	-	24.9	18.9
Diamonds	-	-	33.0	24.0	19.5

Source : Same as Table 5.1.

TABLE 5.4

Trends in Relative Share of Japan's Major Imports from India in Japan's Total Imports 1960 to 1986

(In %)

Items	*1960*	*1965*	*1970*	*1975*	*1980*	*1986*
Raw Cotton	0.30	0.30	0.10	0.03	0.02.	0.03
Iron Ore	0.90	0.73	1.08	0.60	0.30	0.40
Maganese Ore	0.34	0.21	0.10	0.04	0.01	Neg.
Leather & Leather Products	0.04	0.03	0.02	0.02	Neg.	Neg.
Non-ferrous metal	0.22	0.13	0.14	0.11	0.03	Neg.
Shrimps, Prawns & Lobsters	-	-	0.13	0.15	0.14	0.21
Textile Products	Neg.	Neg.	0.03	0.02	0.04	0.04
Non-Metallic Mineral Products	-	-	-	0.04	0.06	0.17
Diamonds	-	-	0.03	0.04	0.05	0.16

Source : Same as Table 5.1.

TABLE 5.5

Trends in Relative Share of Japan's Major Imports from India in Japan's Total Exports 1960 to 1986

(In %)

Items	*1960*	*1965*	*1970*	*1975*	*1980*	*1986*
Raw Cotton	0.9	1.3	1.0	0.5	0.3	0.3
Iron Ore	2.9	3.6	10.1	7.5	5.1	4.8
Maganese Ore	0.3	0.6	0.9	0.6	0.3	0.1
Leather & Leather Products	0.2	0.2	0.3	0.3	0.2	0.1
Non-ferrous metal	0.5	0.7	1.4	1.5	0.6	0.2
Shrimps, Prawns & Lobsters	-	-	1.2	2.1	2.3	2.9
Textile Products	-	-	0.3	0.3	0.7	0.6
Non-Metallic Mineral Products	-	-	-	0.6	0.9	2.4
Diamonds	-	-	0.3	0.6	0.9	2.3

Source : Same as Table 5.1.

TABLE 5.6

Trends in Relative Share of Japan's Major Imports from India in the Total Imports from India from 1960 to 1986

(In %)

Items	*1960*	*1965*	*1970*	*1975*	*1980*	*1986*
Raw Cotton	12.9	15.5	5.2	3.1	2.4	2.5
Iron Ore	40.5	43.3	52.6	50.1	41.9	34.6
Iron & Steel Scrap	15.3	12.7	-	-	-	-
Maganese Ore	4.0	6.8	5.1	3.7	2.2	0.7
Leather & Leather Goods	2.1	2.1	1.3	2.3	1.4	0.9
Non-ferrous metals	7.2	8.0	7.1	9.8	4.5	1.2
Shrimps, Prawns & Lobsters	-	-	6.3	13.8	19.1	20.8
Textile Goods	-	0.7	1.6	2.1	5.9	4.1
Non-Metallic Mineral Goods	-	-	-	3.9	7.7	17.7
Diamonds	-	-	1.5	3.8	7.2	16.5

Source : Same as Table 5.1.

TABLE 5.7

Trends in the Relative Share of Major Exporting Nations in Japan's Total Imports of Raw Cotton 1960 - 1986

Year	*Japan's Total Imports*	*Japan's Total from India*		*Japan's Total from USA*		*Japan's Total from USSR*		*Japan's Total from Australia*		*Japan's Total from Pakistan*	
		In Value	*In %*	*In Value*	*In %*	*In Value*	*In %*	*In Value*	*In %*	*In Value*	*In %*
1960	420.0	12.9	3.1	215.1	51.2	6.6	1.6	-	-	17.1	4.1
1965	435.0	21.5	4.9	132.9	30.6	7.1	1.6	-	-	11.3	2.6
1970	470.7	20.4	4.3	76.7	16.3	24.3	5.2	-	-	-	-
1975	846.8	20.1	2.3	270.3	32.0	171.1	20.2	10.3	1.2	37.9	4.5
1980	1359.2	24.0	1.7	583.0	42.9	108.0	7.9	87.5	6.4	114.5	8.4
1986	817.0	32.8	3.9	215.9	26.4	56.7	6.9	101.5	12.4	102.9	12.6

Source : Same as Table 5.1.

TABLE 5.8

Trends in the Relative Share of Major Exporting Countries in Japan's Total Imports of Iron Ore 1960 - 1986

Year	Japan's Total Imports		Imports from India		Imports from Brazil		Imports from Australia		Imports from Chile	
	In Value	In %	In Value	In %	In Value	In %	In Value	In %	In Value	In %
1960	213.7	100.0	40.5	18.9	-	-	1.0	0.5	4.1	1.9
1965	523.6	100.0	60.2	11.5	-	-	-	-	103.2	19.7
1970	1208.0	100.0	205.2	16.9	99.3	8.2	514.9	42.6	112.2	9.3
1975	2197.7	100.0	329.8	15.0	393.5	17.9	1001.9	45.6	135.8	6.2
1980	3448.7	100.0	424.5	12.3	800.2	23.2	1374.4	39.9	247.0	7.1
1986	2759.3	100.0	448.3	16.2	672.9	24.4	1064.3	38.6	148.3	5.3

Source : Same as Table 5.1.

TABLE 5.9

Trends in the Relative Share of Major Exporting Countries of Leather and Leather Goods in Japan's Total Imports of Leather and Leather Goods 1970 - 1986

Year	*Japan's Total Imports*		*Imports from India*		*Imports from R. of Korea*		*Imports from Pakistan*		*Imports from USA*	
	In Value	*In %*	*In Value*	*In %*	*In Value*	*In %*	*In Value*	*In %*	*In Value*	*In %*
1970	22.6	100.0	5.1	22.6	3.4	15.0	4.6	20.4	5.6	24.8
1975	82.9	100.0	15.1	18.2	6.5	7.8	7.6	9.2	5.0	6.0
1980	144.1	100.0	13.7	9.5	12.4	8.6	18.7	12.9	14.7	10.3
1986	144.9	100.0	12.7	8.8	9.1	6.2	14.9	10.3	33.7	23.3

Source : Same as Table 5.1.

TABLE 5.10

Trends in Relative Share of Major Exporting Countries in Japan's Total Imports of Shrimps, Prawns and Lobster 1970 - 1986

Years	*Japan's Total of Japan*		*Imports from India*		*Imports from China*		*Imports from Thailand*		*Imports from Australia*		*Imports from Indonesia*	
	In Value	*in %*	*In Value*	*In %*	*In Value*	*In %*	*In Value*	*In %*	*In Value*	*In %*	*In Value*	*In %*
1970	212.3	100.0	247.0	11.6	18.5	8.7	18.5	8.7	-	-	22.1	10.4
1975	461.9	100.0	91.2	19.7	47.2	10.2	36.8	7.9	27.4	5.9	92.2	19.9
1980	1105.7	100.0	193.9	17.5	136.8	12.3	66.8	6.0	88.5	8.0	217.5	19.6
1986	1966.3	100.0	269.6	13.7	173.4	8.8	-	-	150.3	7.6	268.1	13.6

Source : Same as Table 5.1.

TABLE 5.11

Trends in the Relative Share of Major Exporting Countries in Japan's Total Imports of Textile Goods 1975 - 1986

Year	Japan's Total Imports		Imports from India		Imports from China		Imports from R. of Korea		Imports from Italy	
	In Value	In %	In Value	In %	In Value	In %	In Value	In %	In Value	In %
1975	1310.4	100.0	13.7	1.0	198.9	15.2	418.7	31.9	117.5	8.9
1980	3179.8	100.0	59.9	1.8	551.3	17.3	1025.5	32.2	292.4	9.1
1986	5026.6	100.0	53.5	1.1	1132.5	22.5	1291.6	25.7	458.4	9.1

Source : Same as Table 5.1.

TABLE 5.12

Trends in Relative Share of Major Exporting Countries In Japan's Total Imports of Non-Metallic Mineral Products 1975 - 1986

Years	Japan's Total Imports		Imports from India		Imports from Belgium		Imports from Isreal		Imports from USA		Imports from R. of Korea	
	In Value	in %	In Value	In %	In Value	In %	In Value	In %	In Value	In %	In Value	In %
1975	466.7	100.0	25.8	5.5	61.4	13.2	67.6	14.5	69.8	14.9	15.4	3.3
1980	1136.1	100.0	78.5	6.9	138.9	12.2	182.3	16.0	154.9	13.6	57.2	5.0
1986	1926.9	100.0	222.3	11.5	312.7	16.2	237.7	12.3	235.2	12.2	224.6	11.6

Source : Same as Table 5.1.

TABLE 5.13

Trends in the Relative Share of Major Exporting Countries In Japan's Total Imports of Diamonds 1970 - 1986

Year	Japan's Total Imports		Imports from India		Imports from Israel		Imports from Belgium		Imports from USA	
	In Value	*In %*	*In Value*	*In %*	*In Value*	*In %*	*In Value*	*In %*	*In Value*	*In %*
1970	77.0	100.0	6.0	7.7	18.9	24.5	28.0	36.4	20.2	26.2
1975	227.8	100.0	25.8	10.9	67.2	29.5	60.0	26.3	33.8	14.8
1980	564.5	100.0	73.4	13.0	181.5	32.2	135.0	23.9	73.7	13.0
1986	939.3	100.0	213.8	22.8	237.6	25.3	312.7	33.3	235.2	25.0

Source : Same as Table 5.1.

CHAPTER SIX

Major Constraints Affecting Exports to Japan

Japan is India's third largest trade partner after the USSR and the USA. She accounts for nearly 10 per cent of India's total trade. There has been diversification with products such as textiles, leather and leather goods, shrimps, prawns and lobster, non-metallic mineral goods and diamonds partly replacing an export-mix mainly of agricultural commodities. However, more sophisticated goods such as engineering goods, electronics and chemicals, which seemed to have had a promising start, have not really made progress. In the light of the above observations, the present chapter analyses, in brief, the major factors affecting the flow of exports to the Japanese market.

Short-Sighted Trade Policy

A trade policy is ultimately concerned with exports. However, some regulations have a more immediate effect. Hence, bilateral matters should be given much attention as compared to multi-lateral issues. One of the major defects in our approach is that we do not use the linkage available from our big purchases abroad to promote exports. This aspect should be tackled effectively and a suitable machinery should be set up for the purpose. India has done well with Japan under GSP arrangements in the past. It is important to note here that further deepening of the existing GSP concessions is not likely to make much difference. But values, volumes and quotas require regular revision keeping in mind the long-term perspective. There is also a need to study the availability of GSP for new exports entering into Japanese market. For instance, a case can now be made for reduced tariffs or GSP quota for certain tropical agricultural products namely shrimps, where the ACP get reduced duty and where there is no history of their being traditional exporters. India also needs to get reductions in the tariff on processed agricultural commodities or supplied in consumer packs. This area has got lesser attention in trade policies. Hence, trade policy should be dynamic and result oriented in the long-term perspective.

Export Promotion Organisation

Export promotion is a broader term divided into three parts namely, product development, marketing, and infrastructure improvement. There are a number of organisations dealing with promotion and project development, which do not involve individual producers. Similarly, there are inadequate incentives for producers to undertake exports themselves and these producers do not have necessary resources at their command to get involved the needed expertise. This trend leads to speculative sales resulting in defaults, price instability, commercial disputes and eventually a setback to the entire export promotion effort. Hence, the need of the day is to give more emphasis on the participation of individual producers and they should get all sorts of encouragements by the Government. There is an urgent need for decentralisation of promotion efforts. The present export promotion organisations should be gradually democratised and permitted to develop so that they can undertake the major effort in export promotion. These organisations should have a capacity for self-policing. Government paternalistic approach may not go a long way in export promotion. If resources are pooled by the exporters (producers) for export promotion, only then will they feel really involved. It is also observed that there are too many export promotion councils and organisations with much overlapping of jurisdiction and effort. There should be a self-sustaining and self-governing export community for each major export commodity.

Fluctuations in Exchange Rates

Fluctuations in exchange rates have also hampered India's exports to Japan during the last 15 years. From 1971 to 1975 Indian rupee was depreciated in real terms mainly because of sharp depreciation of the Nominal Exchange Rate (NER), which resulted from the fact that the rupee was, for most of the time, pegged to pound sterling which was itself falling very sharply. Between 1973 and 1974, inflation in India was quite rapid and somewhat faster than inflation abroad. During the 70s Indian exports grew at a remarkable rate of 8 points per year in real terms, largely due to depreciation of the real exchange rate. The period beginning from 1979 tells an entirely different story. This period began with the world oil-price increase. The need to increase non-oil exports and the adverse international trade and the aid climate suggested that our Real Exchange Rate (RER) be brought down. In fact, it rose. In the third quarter of 1985 the RER was higher than in 1979 by 15 per cent. Only in the last quarter of 1985 it came down sharply. It was, however, still higher than in 1979 level. Table 6.1 indicates the trends in Nominal and Real Effective Exchange Rate of the Rupee from 1971 to 1985.

Infrastructure

Infrastructure problems namely, transport, freight costs and packaging, have hampered the flow of goods from India to Japan. Hence, they require much more attention. Not only are freight rates often more expensive than that of competitors, but transport arrangements are also more primitive, cumbersome and slower. Shipping and ports are the backbone of exports to foreign markets. Indian shipping services are inadequate and, wherever available, are infrequent. Indian ports are also ill-equipped to handle the large-sized ships effectively and efficiently. It is essential that we stay up-to-date and compete in our ports, airports and all types of handling facilities. Regrettably, even the State Corporations, such as the Shipping Corporation and Air India, sometimes utilise their monopoly positions to increase export freight rates. The port charges are also disproportionately high, being 3 / 4 times of those prevailing in Asian ports such as Colombo, Hong Kong, Singapore and South Korea. What is urgently needed is to provide for efficient container vessels at least for most of our identified destinations. These services must be competitive in quality, cost and frequency.

Packaging is getting better, but improvement is slow, particularly on packaging for retail distribution, which is where there is most value additions. Serious consideration needs to be given to allowing exporters to do this in India or Japan depending upon where it can be done better and economically.

Cost and Quality

Despite India's relatively cheap manpower and endowment of large resources, India is rated as one of the highest cost nations in the world. This trend has done irrepairable damage to India's export structure. India has also lost so much share in world trade and the trend is still persisting. The high cost trend is persisting due to heavy burden of taxes, direct and indirect, and their cascading effect, the high cost of finance, inputs and raw materials. These factors keep the quality at a low ebb. Hence, the need of the hour is to overcome these impediments at all costs. Commodity taxes should be so rationalised as to make Indian exports competitive. Despite the recent reduction in the interest rate on export credit (pre and post-shipment) India is still no where near the major exporting countries such as Switzerland where export credit is available at 7 per cent and Japan where it is available at 6 per cent. Malaysia provides export credit at 5 per cent and Pakistan, the neighbouring nation, provides export credit at the lowest i.e., 3 per cent. But in India the rate of interest on export credit is as high as 9.5 per cent. How can Indian exporters keep the cost and quality constraints at a low ebb and make themselves competitive? Prices of raw materials and inputs are also on the high side as compared to other major exporting countries such as South Korea, Japan and Taiwan. This aspect also needs rethinking so that raw materials should be made available to exporters on internationally competitive rates. Excise and customs duties must be reduced and exemption on machinery and equipment required for export must be made so that expansion, modernisation and technological upgradation could be possible because these are the only alternatives for keeping cost and quality at a competitive level.

Power

Erratic power supply and sudden cuts as well as high cost of power have far reaching adverse effects on Indian goods' competitiveness in Japanese market. By and large, units are not able to have optimum utilisation of their capacity on account of these constraints thereby raising their overhead costs. Labour remains idle leading to increase in the wage bill without contribution to production. In fact, the exporting units should be insulated against power cuts and power shedding. Power tariffs for export units should also be rationalised. Some sort of rebate on the consumption of power should be made available.

Marketing

Indian exports to Japan are also lacking in marketing infrastructure and marketing techniques. Indian exporters are not able to either negotiate or offer competitive terms, invest in creation of distribution channels, keep constant track of business opportunities in Japan and provide needed after-sales service. Counter-trade and barter deals are assuming significance as effective trading techniques. But India has not made such dealings so far. However, there is an urgent need to adopt these techniques of marketing so that flow of trade could be increased. The private export and trading houses, which account for bulk of the export trade, are not allowed to enter into such trade transactions. This is coming in the way of export expansion to Japanese market. Hence, the need of the hour is that both governmental agencies as well as private sector exporting organisations should have access to this modern method of export promotion. To start with, a few sectors should be identified for the purpose. There is also an urgent need for entering into marketing collaborations with Japanese firms and setting up joint trading companies specially for promoting exports of Indian traditional goods in particular and non-traditional goods in general.

Lack of Risks

It is rightly said "no risk no gain". Indian exporters are not taking risk of entering into Japanese market with their new products. They are having fear of losing their capital due to the sensitivity of the Japanese market. They know that nothing dies faster than a newly launched product. They also know that more than 80 per cent of the new products develop leakages at an early stage of their development, meeting a pre-mature death in their marketing adventure. Such a high mortality rate of new products is shocking, for it involves a tremendous wastage of human effort and materials. This fear keeps Indian exporters away from exporting their goods to Japanese market. But for increasing exports to Japan risk has to be taken at all costs. Governmental agencies and other export promotion agencies should come forward and motivate the new entrants to export goods to the Japanese market. They should extend moral support and should make efforts to take out the fear from the minds of the new exporters. They should provide all possible information on the movement and consumers' trend to these exporters.

Government Red Tape

While Government of India's intentions to boost exports by grant of various incentives to exporters are to be lauded, the implementation of the incentives leaves much to be desired. This situation also hampers the flow of goods from India to the Japanese market. It is often observed that the incentives meant for genuine exporters either do not reach them at all or reach them so late that their advantage is nullified. There are numerous occasions when these incentives have gone to wrong hands (The Hindustan Times, May 8, 1987) while genuine exporters have faced harassment. This situation should be avoided and the incentives must go to the needed exporters so that they could contribute much for the promotion of exports.

Nature of Delays

Sometimes it happens that Indian exporters face unnecessary delays in getting incentives for the promotion of exports to Japanese market. They lose their precious time, money and energy in getting the incentives. In case of cash assistance scheme, it is often found that in the last two months of the financial year the applications from the exporters for cash assistance are not accepted in certain number, at the counter of the joint CCI & E for some reason or the other (Commerce, May 30 - June 5, 1987). If at all the application is found complete in all respects the authorities say that they do not have cash to pay and thus ask the exporters to submit the same at a later date. This means exporters do not get the assistance in time. Hence, it may be said that "assistance delayed in effect is assistance denied".

The similar is the of International Price Replenishment Scheme (IPRS). The benefit under the said scheme to exporters is also frequently delayed. Once it is done, though with great difficulty and inconvenience, the export promotion council might not have the money to make the payments of IRPS. Hence, the hardship in securing incentives and other benefits must be minimised. They could be minimised with some flexibility in the procedures and gearing the administrative machinery. If these trends continue then whatever efforts are made all will become infructuous.

Lack of Selective Approach

All goods in general and engineering goods in particular, require selective approach for exports. This is due to the fact that there is severe competition in Japanese market. The time has come to think in terms of not only creating the right type of "winner" but also ensuring that resources are not spread too thinly. It is thus high time to be selective in strategy and approach. Looking at engineering exports, the concept of selectivity becomes all the more important. Those items which are gaining market in Japan must get all sorts of help and encouragement so that they could attain "economies of scale" and emerge as the leading items in India's engineering exports.

Lack of Image as an Industrial Country

In Japanese market there has not been the image of India as an industrial country, though India has been 10th among the industrialised countries of the world. As a result, there is an impression that Indian goods are not qualitative and hence, have not penetrated in Japanese market. India is also the producer of quality goods and has the ability to compete in Japanese market. Therefore, there is need for projecting India's image as an industrial country, capable of producing the sophisticated industrial goods, having good and excellent technology in several lines of industrial output comparable with the best available anywhere. Government of India should encourage and sponsor trade fairs and exhibitions in major cities of Japan in which industrial goods, including machinery and various descriptions of engineering goods, figure prominently. Japanese importers still believe that Indian engineering goods lack quality. Building up capabilities in this behalf will make it possible for Indian companies to face international competition and exposure of various sorts. Such exposure may have far-reaching effect on the product (its design, specification, performance, operational life and productivity); supply schedule (maintenance of regular supply, assembly in foreign countries, installation of machinery, etc.); quality, pricing, packaging, etc.

Exporters' strategies and policies as also tactics matching those of competitors and, to some extent, substitutes; specifications and technical quality requiring high technical excellence and responsiveness; pricing aimed at long term interest of customer rather than immediate profit, even though the market can bear higher prices in the short run; and packaging with all its variety and sophistication in conditions where the packages seem to sell the contents etc., are very important for Indian exporters for the purpose of expanding exports to Japan.

Exposure would be a real test of strength which many organisations would like to face. There are other rewards that go a long way with exporting and which may be big enough compensation, as for instance, protection from recession in the domestic market causing large scale under-utilisation of capacity, acquaintance with foreign markets (Japan), knowledge of competitor and its way of handling issues, improvements in designs and more up-to-date know-how, all of which would have high costs if procured from other channels. Hence, all out efforts should be made to boost the image of India in general and Indian goods in particular.

Lack of Export Obligation

The promotion of the Government for exploring new channels instead of concentrating and consolidating knows pastures has given rather poor results because wrong commodities, wrong countries, wrong organisations have all created an unnecessary rush of activities in different circles. Not only that, the quantitative results have been poor, the returns have not been quite economical considering the cost of promotional activities involved (Commerce, Bombay, May 30 - June 5, 1987). The major factors standing in the way of developing export obligation concept are (a) cumbersome procedures creating credibility gaps; (b) delay in getting clearance from the Government at the Centre and the States as also various agencies controlled by them; (c) restriction of their freedom to sell in the domestic market even when the export markets have remained subject to recessionary forces, and (d) non-availability of other incentives. Similarly, the requirements of market promotion and market maintenance are different in the sense that once a market has been developed, it requires sustained efforts to keep it. This is not easy in conditions dictated by the other competitors and substitutes.

Dismal Performance of EOUs

Although launched with laudable aims and objectives in

December 1980, their export performance has been dismal. Out of the 609 units approved by the end of 1985, only 94 units have become operative. Against the original target of earning foreign exchange worth Rs. 5,000 crores in five years, the actual cumulative earning of these units has amounted to a meagre sum of 380 crores by the end of 1985 i.e., far behind the set target. The surprising aspect is that many units have shown interest in de-bonding or in other words opting out of the scheme. Hence, it is necessary to review and restructure the entire scheme so that it could become more productive and economically viable.

Non-Effectiveness of FERA

The Foreign Exchange Regulation Act (FERA) enforced in 1973 has outlived its utility. Therefore, it must be recast to promote exports and to enable Indian business to compete in Japanese market. This is of paramount significance in the sense that the conditions in which business operates now, are entirely different from what they were when the original legislation was framed. Time changes very fast and is of vital importance for the expansion of international business. Decision making at times, have to be done quickly and on the spot. But the existing procedure is time-consuming and delay in getting clearance from the RBI makes the decision unproductive. This situation has affected Indian goods export in foreign markets in general and Japanese market in particular. Hence, the need of the day is to make the same more effective, flexible and productive so that the entrepreneurs have the freedom to operate according to the circumstances of the business.

Lower Unit Value Realisation

This is another major constraint affecting the flow of goods from India to Japan. There are many commodities in which although physical targets have been achieved, the unit value realisation has declined as in case of tea, raw cotton, iron ore, jute, cashew nuts and tobacco. This has been due to the demand squeeze and intense competition which India has been facing from major exporting countries of the said items in Japanese market.

The Pull of Domestic Demand

A major factor for India's poor export performance in relation to Japan is the heavy pressure on exportable surplus from domestic demand and supply constraints. This makes our export promotion yet more formidable and challenging. In recent years, this pressure has become more alarming due to the drought conditions in India.

Lack of Value Addition

Notwithstanding the inroads made by Indian traditional and non-traditional items in Japanese market, it is surprising to note that Indian exporters have not been able to add value to their product lines. There are a number of cases in which India fails to obtain value-added realisation in regard to specific goods. Such goods range from agro-based items such as cashew, marine products, spices, tea and coffee to clothing and engineering goods. The Government of India has also laid stress on technology upgradation in several key export sectors which is reflected in adequate measures in our recent import policy. It is high time for Indian exporters to capitalise the situation and they must develop higher-value realisation in specific goods such as engineering goods, leather manufactures and ready-made garments, in Japanese market.

Lack of Warehousing Facilities

Apart from the value addition problem, there is need for the establishment of warehousing / storage facilities at important commercial centres such as Tokyo, Osaka, Hiroshima and Kyoto in Japan. Such warehouses can be set up jointly with some of the leading processors, packers or the distributors in Japan for joining marketing arrangements. The most advantageous aspect of warehousing in Japan's commercial cities is that, apart from ensuring prompt deliveries, it establishes a strong market presence in Japan. This may serve as a key of capturing Japanese market. But unfortunately, none of the major commercial cities of Japan has warehousing facility for Indian goods and this is why Indian non-traditional items such as engineering goods, textiles, gems and jewellery and carpets have failed in making any dent in Japanese market.

Lack of Long-Term Promotion Efforts

One of the reasons responsible for the narrow base of Indian goods is that India's export promotion efforts are too short-term in nature and are also spread too thin over too many goods at one and the same time. The essence of marketing in Japan is that competition requires a concentrated campaign possibly over years, to establish a market for a particular product or even a brand of product. The campaign has to be directed at wholesalers, distributors or consumers, possibly varying the projection and technique. One launched, it should not be subject to sudden variations even for financial reasons. Added to this, there has to be constant follow-up, which itself will cause adjustments in the campaign and development of the product. One big promotion by itself is often wasteful and ineffective. The time-frame within which we expect to develop a market is usually too short and we try to sell too much at the same time.

Lack of Knowledge of How to Export to Japan

This is another important constraint standing in the way of

widening export base of Indian goods in Japanese market. The exporters do not have adequate knowledge about exporting to Japanese market or how to enter into the Japanese market. Every Indian exporter should know the basic regulations and procedures to be followed while exporting goods to Japanese market. They must know currency requirements and exchange regulations, trade policy and trade regulations, structure of duties and taxes on exports and imports, documentation, trading channels, etc. The knowledge of these basic requirements may go a long way in expanding India's exports to the Japanese market.

Conclusion

From the foregoing analysis it becomes clear that there have been so many major factors which have hampered India's exports to Japan and due to these factors India has failed in widening her export base in the Japanese market. These factors have to be tackled on war-footing so that India can capitalise on the opportunity of liberal import policy recently announced by Japan.

TABLE 6.1

Trends in Nominal and Real Effective Exchange Rate of the Rupee between 1971 and 1985

Year	*Ner (1975 = 100)*	*Rer*
1971	125.42	113.24
1975	100.00	100.00
1979	91.81	82.66
1980	94.19	90.32
1981	94.50	94.44
1982	94.81	92.34
1983	92.88	95.15
1984	87.36	93.82
1985 (Quarter I)	85.91	92.35
1985 (Quarter II)	84.94	93.93
1985 (Quarter III)	83.63	87.64
1985 (Quarter IV)	77.58	87.64
1985 (Annual)	82.99	94.44

Note : A decline denotes depreciation.

Source : Reverse Bank of India Bulletin, Bombay.

This page is intentionally left blank.

CHAPTER SEVEN

What to Export to Japan

From the foregoing analysis it is concluded that India's exports to Japan have been looking down in real and relative terms and keeping the balance of trade negative during the current decade. As there has been increased outflow of foreign exchange on account of technology imports from Japan, diversification of trade is very vital and crucial not only for the expansion of bilateral trade but even to maintain the current level of trade flows. If past trends were any indication, export earnings from primary goods are not likely to witness appreciable increase in future. In the long run, increased export earnings can be brought about only through manufactured goods. It could be said that India should export those products in which she has a definite comparative advantage and certain degree of sophistication since India has attained industrial and technological competence over the years. In the light of the said observations, the present chapter seeks to identify what to export to Japan so that the volume of trade could be increased substantially in the years to come.

It is an undisputed fact that exports are vital for a developing country like India to attain rapid progress. The export activity not only enables a country to earn precious international currency with which to buy scarce raw materials but it also has a far-reaching influence on the ethos of the people. The reasons for India to expand exports are very clear. First, being a developing country India needs foreign inputs continuously to meet the developmental needs. Since India aims at accelerating her economic growth, the need for increased foreign exchange is of paramount significance. As a result, estimated deficit in the current account of India's balance of payments during the Seventh Plan period stood at 20,000 crores. This estimate does not take into consideration the purchasing power of exports resulting from increased prices of imports. Secondly, the official development assistance to finance the foreign inputs over the last three decades, is not expected to play any major role in the coming years on account of a number of factors, the most important one being aid dis-enchantment. In the Sixth Plan, 75 per cent of foreign capital inflow was contributed by official development assistance. Thirdly, a very compelling need is to repay the overseas loans. In fact the period from 1985 to 1990 is the period of pressure for repayment of loans as the loans and interest will become due. These circumstances have compelled India to make all out efforts to increase her exports enormously so that the said needs could be met effectively and efficiently. As Japan is liberalising her import policy India must make a dent in this direction so that it could increase her exports substantially.

Vast Potential

Japan has vast potential for absorbing goods from developing countries in general and India in particular. She has come up as a land of opportunities for exporters. Since the appreciation of Yen and Japan's policy of liberalisation of imports, a chain of goods have been surging into Japan at a rapidly accelerating rate since early 1986. According to the Annual Economic White Paper, in 1986, there was a substantial rise in Japan's imports of manufactured goods and they constituted more than 44 per cent of Japan's total imports. The rate is likely to expand and there are indications that this percentage may cross 50 in the current year. This means that Japan's traditional import structure has been transforming into industrial goods. Hence, this is the high time for bolstering the two-way trade between India and Japan. The various liberalisation steps taken by the Government of India in recent years has transformed the face of Indian economy. India has already entered into the high-tech era and her very technological competence should enable her to cater to the sophisticated and diversified needs of the Japanese market.

The Standing Committee of India-Japan Business Cooperation Committee at its various deliberations have identified a number of items for exporting to Japan's Market. These items include cuttle fish, cashew nuts, pepper, tea, coffee, spices, curry powder, shrimps and prawns and mangoes among food stuffs. Consumer items consist of leather (chrome tanned), jute fabric, carpets, wigs and other articles made from human hair wastes, gems and jewellery, handicrafts, furnishing fabrics, ready-made garments, etc. There are certain other items which have also been identified by the Committee in the recent negotiations. They are electronic software, paper from bagasse, aluminium and meat products. The major items identified by the Committee are discussed in the following pages.

Engineering Products

It is rather astonishing to see that Japan does not import those commodities from India which are her major export items such as engineering goods, tea, cashew, chemicals and ready-made garments. As a result, these items have not made any dent in Japanese market. Engineering goods which are much in demand in world market, have hardly made any impact on the Japanese market. India's share in Japan's total imports has been negligible. It is very surprising that engineering goods, which are now qualitative, have no more expanding demand in Japanese market though there has been a great potential of this. India must make all out efforts to penetrate the Japanese market in this important and leading export item. The Engineering Export Promotion Council (EEPC) is now taking interest in the matter and have identified certain qualitative items of this sector which may have good market potential in Japan. The identified items include hosiery needles, air-conditioning machines, electrical capacitors, heating and cooling machines, electrical machinery, hand tools, pumps, integrated circuits, medical instruments, textile sewing machines, etc

But it is important to note here that in increasing the export of these items in Japanese market, India has to face a formidable task of facing stiff competition from highly developed nations such as the USA, the Federal Republic of Germany, the UK, Italy and Switzerland who are leading exporters to Japan. For this, India has to develop a comprehensive as well as well-knit action plan to face the challenge of these countries on the one hand and on the other hand to penetrate the Japanese market. This may require an effective and efficient managerial and professional marketing approach.

In view of the growing complexities of marketing engineering goods in Japanese market, new and different marketing mechanism and strategies must be formulated and implemented. The mechanism and the strategy should include the following steps. Firstly, there is need for trade-creating joint ventures (manufacturing and / or trading) with buy-back arrangements to be located not only in India but also in Japan. Secondly, there is need for long term marketing arrangements and establishing a strong marketing presence conjointly with other exporters in Japan with warehousing and after-sales servicing facilities. Thirdly, there is need to undertake detailed market surveys to identify goods which may have potential for export. Fourthly, the need to make efficient use of low-technology and energy intensive industries which have been vacated by the Japanese firms and to take them to India with Japanese technology and capital commitment. Fifthly, India must have tie-ups with Japanese trading houses for selling Indian goods in Japan and other connected nations and lastly, the need for increasing participation in trade fairs and exhibitions in Japan. These measures may go a long way in increasing exports of engineering goods to Japanese market.

Electronic Software

This is another item which may have potential for export to Japan as identified by the Standing Committee of India-Japan Business Cooperation. Japan may be one of the major markets for a variety of electronic softwares. Since Indian capabilities in this sector are being reinforced through liberal import policies, a major breakthrough is anticipated in the electronic software export by the end of the Seventh Plan, and Japan would naturally feature as a prime target market. But there must be need for a strong marketing presence in Japan. Such a presence could be ensured by a combination of marketing strategies including selling through a Japanese manufacturer who is keen to supplement his own-product lines or operating through a manufacturer's representative or distribution agency to promote the exporter's product lines. This particular mode of marketing has many advantages. Firstly, they not only sell the components but also keep clients informed of new products in the market, variations in prices, delivery period and the like. Secondly, the establishment of warehouses will create a strong base which is one of the pre-requisites for penetrating into the market. Thirdly, by having a Japanese address, the manufacturer's foreign identity will be known to the buyer which is vital for establishing initial credibility which is presently a missing link in regard to Indian goods in Japanese market.

Chemicals

Indian chemical goods have reached a stage where they can

match production and quality standards in international market. In recent years the export of these goods to Japan is rising. In view of the emphasis of the Governments of the major developed nations (the USA, the USSR, the UK, the FRG, Sweden and Japan), to keep price-rise under check through competitive imports from developing countries like India and to tackle problems of pollution, there are favourable indications for Indian manufacturers to gear up the production and export marketing efforts with a view to capturing the emerging opportunities. Joint ventures, linkages and bulk sales through large private trading houses may prove useful in expanding Indian exports to Japanese market.

Textiles

Textile goods in general and ready-made garments in particular, have promising future in Japanese market. These items have also gained in relative share in Japan's total imports and major imports from India over the years. Another item which is also an important items of textile goods exported to Japan is handloom fabrics. The handlooms with unique originality must be given priority. A wide range of goods should be produced and exported on a small lots basis and attention must be paid to younger generation fashion goods of ethnic pattern, colour and style. There is also an urgent need to advertise the special characteristics of Indian garments. In this direction India must seek the services of renowned Japanese designers and consultants and try to cater to the Japanese tastes and fashions. Japan is also a vast market for various other home furnishing items. Hence, the need of the hour is that Apparel Export Promotion Council and the State Trading Corporation must make all out efforts to increase exports to Japan of the said items. They must send teams of experts to study the trend of designing and finishing. Tie-ups with the leading importers and departmental stores must be made. A well planned strategy on a long-term basis must be evolved. Continuous vigil must be kept on the rapidly changing demands of the ultimate consumer.

Leather and Leather Goods

Japan is an important market for a wide variety of leather and leather goods. However, the Indian leather manufacturers have not been able to take advantage of the growing market opportunities in Japan, notwithstanding the fact that overall exports of these items looked up. Keeping in view our resource base of the largest cattle population in the world and the liberalisation affected in the import policy for modernisation the production activity, the performance of this sector can by no means be termed as encouraging.

To take advantage of Japan's growing import demand for semi-finished and finished leather, Indian manufacturers have to gear up their production to suit the requirements of this highly quality-conscious and intensely competitive market. Indian exporters will have to consolidate their strength and mobilise their resources to get bulk orders from transitional corporations, departmental stores and leading importers. Joint ventures, development of linkages with the leading Japanese importers and creation of export production bases in those countries which have easy access to the Japanese market may go a long way in increasing exports to Japan. The export of these items can be expanded provided an in-depth study is also made of the Japanese market, followed by regular exchange of sales-cum-study and buying missions. Technical collaboration with Japanese counter-parts needs to be explored.

Gem and Jewellery

Gem and Jewellery is one of the items which has gained in Japanese market. Their exports have been steadily rising with diamonds constituting the major share. Most of the diamonds exported to Japan are of small size, though demand for medium and large size are also increasing in Japanese market. Japan is a potential market for diamond studded jewellery. But design and finish are very crucial and vital for success which would be possible only if machine made jewellery is exported. There is an urgent need to develop facilities for machine made jewellery and in this area Japanese investment and technical know-how is of great importance. Recently, Indian Embassy in Tokyo has done some basic study of demand for gold jewellery. A strategy is being worked out to step up the export of this item to Japan on an increasing scale. Indian strategy for expanding her share in Japan's total imports of gem and jewellery is of crucial and vital importance. She has to face tough competition with Belgium and Israel. She has to keep the cost down without tampering with the quality of the items. The production end of the strategy for export expansion of gem and jewellery in general and diamonds in particular, has to encompass : (a) systematic and scientific organisation of the gem and jewellery industry; (b) enlargement of the production base; (c) qualitative improvements; (d) greater emphasis on value added products and (e) production diversification.

Handicrafts

Handicrafts are one of the items which may have promising future in Japanese market. Handicrafts with unique originality of India should get priority for Japanese market. The new generation of Japanese society may like them very much if proper advertisement is made. Although India's exports of handicrafts to Japan are not very encouraging, the scope for expanding their market is immense. Some of the items that may be popular are incense burners, tapestries, tableware and pottery, ceramic materials, handmade paintings, knives for cutting papers and imitation jewellery. Exports can be made on an increasing scale, provided appropriate marketing efforts are made with Japanese assistance in product development including packaging. In this direction development of linkages with leading sales outlets and dealers and the acquisition of entities in the Japanese market for instant sale success are of vital importance.

Carpets

Carpets may create their potential in Japanese market provided an aggressive sales strategy is adopted. Though Indian carpets are comparable to the best in the world, exports of these items constitute just 0.7 per cent of Japan's total imports from India. The rank was seventh among the carpet exporting countries. Pakistan is one of the leading exporter of carpets in the world and her share in Japan's total imports is much higher than India. To expand exports to Japan, India should start supplying small size carpets also. Consumers prefer small sized carpets instead of wall to wall. Light shades are always preferred. There is an urgent need for Indian exporters to establish contact with wholesalers and department stores in Japan.

Conclusion

From the foregoing discussion it has been brought out that there is an urgent need to increase exports in general and exports to Japan in particular. Japan is an expanding market and India must capitalise the existing situation on an increasing scale. In this direction exports of finished products is of great importance as there is vast potential of these items in Japan's market. India should endeavour to sell products in which she has a definite comparative advantage and certain degree of sophistication since India has achieved industrial and technological competence over the years. India should take steps to change her image from a supplier of primary goods to a supplier of manufactured goods. The items identified in preceding pages may go a long way to widen the narrow base of India's exports to Japan which is the need of the hour.

CHAPTER EIGHT

How to Increase Exports to Japan

Recently a Seminar on "India's Exports — Challenges of the Nineties" organised by the International Marketing Forum was held in New Delhi. Mr. Abid Hussain, Member, Planning Commission, had rightly pointed out that "in coming years ruthless competition and intelligent application of novelties in the manufacturing process will be the corner-stone of successful survival in foreign trade". He further stressed the need for adopting "an aggressive marketing strategy" and full utilisation of the versatile manpower in the country in order to capture a sizeable chunk of the international markets in future. In order to face the challenges in the international markets, India has to make all out efforts to intensify export promotion.

As Japan has emerged a land of opportunities for importers, India must make all out efforts in capitalising the opportunities offered by Japanese market. Japan is a highly sophisticated buyers' market. However, penetrating Japanese market is not an easy job. It requires skill and professional approach. In the light of the above observations, the present chapter suggests some measures for trade promotion.

Uncompetitive Export Prices

This is one of the most important factor affecting India's exports to Japan. India is basically a high cost economy. This trend is due to a number of factors namely - (a) high cost of inputs such as steel, power and oil; (b) low productivity due to low efficiency of labour and outdated technology; (c) high incidence of commodity taxation; (d) uneconomic size of production and (e) high cost of credit. These factors lead to higher prices for Indian goods entering into Japanese market. As a result, Indian goods become uncompetitive and lose their position. Hence, the need of the hour is to reduce cost without tampering with quality. Only then could India survive in the savagely competitive Japanese market. In this particular issue Japan can play an increasing role by transferring such technology to India as will enable her to reduce cost to a minimum possible extent.

Poor Quality

It is important to note that the Japanese consumers are very sensitive to quality. They want quality goods at reasonable prices. Indian exporters should not risk compromising on quality if they want to have a major share of Japanese market. It is also essential for Indian exporters to study very carefully the characteristics of the Japanese market and particularly the needs of Japanese consumers. Hence, it is of paramount significance to apply innovative elements in the manufacturing process so that a new dimension could be given to the consumer goods. Indian manufacturers and exporters must keep themselves abreast of the latest developments in technical knowledge in their respective fields and should also endeavour to implement the "marketing game" of international trade. Tampering with quality should be avoided at all costs.

Non-Fulfilment of Delivery Schedules

This is the third biggest issue to be looked into when an export strategy is to be formulated. Indian export performance in regard to Japan is affected very much due to non-supply of goods in time to the main outlets. Major organisations dealing with the Indian goods have complained about the said problem. Strict adherence to time schedule is an important factor in marketing goods particularly in Japan. In the absence of time schedule, exporters may loose their credibility and reliability. These two factors are missing in India's exports to Japan. Too often, goods fail, because they reach market at off timings. It is generally said that delays make the product lose 80 per cent of its sale. This sort of loss of sales could conveniently be averted by offsetting the delays through prompt acceleration of various programmes by timely appraisal of the production and market situation. Exporters should keep some time gap so that goods could be delivered in time.

Commercial Feasibility

It is another vital factor for the marketing success of Indian products in Japanese market. Products are exported for earning larger profits. If a product cannot be manufactured on a large scale and sold at profit, it has little commercial value. Certain industrial and consumer goods which involve highly advanced engineering technology and specialised skills in their production do not, at times, qualify the test of commercial feasibility and therefore seldom succeed in the market. In regard to certain items namely, carpets, engineering goods and non-metallic goods, assessment of commercial feasibility is of vital importance in Japanese market. Indian exporters of these goods should carefully assess the commercial feasibility before evolving export strategy to Japanese market.

Sales Promotion

Japan is an open and highly competitive market where the consumer can be won over through publicity media like TV, radio, newspapers, specialised trade journals, bill boards etc. The Japanese Government has been very active in encouraging imports through various promotion schemes and using booklets providing details on how the market has become more open. Indian exporters should capitalise on these schemes for expanding exports of their items. The Japan External Trading Organisation is one of the organisations, which help importers to get all sorts of trade information. Indian exporters should establish effective and efficient link with such organisations so that they could know what and how to export to Japan.

Lobbying

Lobbying is a powerful medium through which necessary influence can be exerted on high-ranking decision makers in Tokyo. Lobbyists offer a wide range of services, utilising their contacts, influence and rapport with Government officials, which goes a long way in expanding trade and economic relations between India and Japan. Since it is an accepted act of intervention and plays a vital role in not only promoting trade interest but also averting undesirable decisions hampering imports of the country. Hence, it is desirable to create a special fund in India for lobbying in Japan. This could be done by earmarking a nominal portion of export earnings from the amount earned from Japan. Some matching grant should be provided by the Government. This may prove as an effective tool for expanding trade and economic relations between India and Japan.

Institutional Support

As Japan is the third largest trade partner of India after the

USSR and the USA, it needs a special treatment and thrust. It immediately requires an institution for (a) supplying information on Japan's trade policy changes and changes in practices for effective and efficient marketing in Japanese market; (b) analysing the far-reaching impact on India's exports and imports due to changes in trade policy and providing necessary feedback; (c) identifying export opportunities; and (d) giving specific recommendations to Government on changes needed for export promotion policies and incentives to respond to the marketing opportunities. These tasks must be assigned to a Special Task Force created for the purpose. It may work in collaboration with India-Japan Committee for Business Cooperation, Institute of Foreign Trade of India and Indian Council for Research on International Economic Relations. The said institutional support is the need of the hour and may go a long way in expanding trade relations between India and Japan.

Strengthening of Territorial Division and Creation of Japan Division

As India's trade relations with Japan are traditional, strategic and vital for both the countries, it is of paramount significance to establish a territorial division for Japan's trade in the Ministry of Commerce or if desirable to make it a separate division. But the division must be headed by a senior official who has vast knowledge of Japan's economy. The main thrust of this would be to provide necessary help to manufacturers and exporters to capitalise on the identified opportunities and also to provide protection against the perceived threats. These divisions are also of vital importance as they may be very useful in translating the huge potential of this market into actual reality which is the need of the day. So far India has failed in capitalising on the identified opportunities and as a result India has a narrow base in Japan's imports.

Empowered Committee

Keeping in mind the growing importance of India's trade and economic cooperation with Japan, it is of vital significance to give additional emphasis to these relations. Viewed from any angle, Japanese market will remain a very important trading destination for India in years to come. Hence, it is desirable to appoint or form an empowered committee under the control of Cabinet Secretary. The main purpose of this committee would be to give guidance on the working of territorial / Japan division in the Ministry of Commerce. It would monitor the export expansion policies, plans and programmes for various products meant for Japanese market. It would also adopt selectivity criteria and will evolve the concept of strategic targeting at micro-level in collaboration with India-Japan Committee for Business Cooperation. The feedback will be the responsibility of the territorial / Japan division. This Committee may also serve as a coordinating agency for avoiding duplication of various organisations working on India and Japan trade relations.

Development of Export Culture

The recent trends in Indo-Japan trade are undoubtedly causing concern to Indian exporters in general and all concerned in particular. A balance between imports and exports should be brought as early as possible. This may be possible if necessary thrust is given to promote exports on the one hand and on the other hand to attain a high growth in the economy. We should take a lesson from Republic of Korea who has secured a trade surplus in 1985. For this an effective export culture should be developed. This may be attained by creating "an export mentality". It is correct to say that India's lingering trade deficit is due to "lack of an export mentality" on the part of the Government as well as the exporters. Their policies are half-hearted. In all nations of the world, export is not the responsibility of exporters alone. It is the result of "group activity" involving Government on the one hand, and industry and trade on the other. In Indian economic setting this link is missing. Unless and until group activity is not created, export culture which is the need of the day cannot be developed. India must take lesson in this regard from South Korea, Taiwan, Singapore and Hong Kong, which are the best examples of excellent export performers. These nations have developed export culture and there has been the closest possible coordination between the Government, industry and trade. It is hereby suggested that Export has to be made "a national effort" in the interest of the country. Export culture may serve a very useful purpose in expanding trade with Japan. India can develop export culture easily as she has abundant natural resources, cheap labour and entrepreneurship which are essential for the same. Export promotion also needs an effective structure of its own. Japan has set up Japan External Trade Organisation (JETRO) and Korea has established Korea Trade Promotion Corporation (KOTRA), which are serving great cause for their respective economies by providing infrastructural facilities which export trade requires. India has no such organisation which can outflow the required information on JETRO and KOTRA pattern. India does have IFTI and TDAI but there purpose and functions are different. India should also get a lesson in this regard and should set up an organisation on JETRO and KOTRA pattern. This organisation may go a long way in developing export culture which is badly needed.

Production for Export

In India the question of achieving stability in production and improvement in productivity are of vital importance specially in the context of export development. India's major traditional exports have been showing ups and downs. This state of affairs has been due to the fluctuations in the domestic production of traditional items. In these situations, exporting countries give up their share for the home market in favour of other importing countries. In India stability has been lacking on the production horizon. Expanding exports cannot be sustained on fluctuating production and low productivity. India, therefore, needs a sound production base to undertake export development activities. But this should not be a long drawn out process as India cannot afford delay.

Inductive Targets

Inductive targets may serve useful purpose in expanding exports to Japan. Product-by-product targets may also be set in regard to items being exported to Japan. They will facilitate and encourage the development in a planned manner.

Sector-by-Sector Approach

A sector-by-sector approach may also serve a useful purpose in trade expansion with Japan. It may also be a strategy for wider economic cooperation between India and Japan. This approach may lead to consistent economic development of India.

Need for Exchange of Information

There is also a need for regular exchange of information among trading organisations of India and Japan. This flow of information would promote trade effectively and will also evolve various forms of cooperation such as counter-trading and trade-oriented joint ventures. This aspect should be given top priority as India and Japan have shown their interest in the promotion of joint ventures.

Basic Principles for Negotiations

In future negotiations between India and Japan for trade expansion and diversification, the basic principles of mutuality of interest, limited or full reciprocity, equivalence in burden sharing and flexibility regarding participation, have to be applied. Detailed negotiations should follow a product-by-product or sector-by-sector approach. The guiding principle should lay emphasis on the increasing flow of goods and services consistent with the development plans of India and Japan. Concessions to be negotiated are to be perceived from the point of view of enabling and inducing flows of inputs required to develop and / or to maintain individual economies. The main criterion to be adopted, specially in regard to commodities, raw materials and agro-products, is of comparative advantage and not of domestic availability at whatever cost.

Trade Fairs and Exhibitions

It is said that Japan does not know what India can offer. It is also pointed out that importers in Japan do not have a clear idea what items India is in a position to offer and whom they should contact. A prominent businessman of Japan has observed that "thousands of Japanese importers are seeking good import items from India, but in vain". This is the most surprising aspect of Indo-Japan trade and requires immediate action thereon. In this direction the role of Trade Fair Authority of India is of paramount significance. The blame of the said ignorance goes to TFAI which is the principal organisation for boosting the image of Indian goods among the trading partners.

Participation in fairs and exhibitions is an important aspect of image-making abroad and also an integral part of export promotion effort. India has not done much in this direction in relation to Japanese market. Trade Fair Authority of India should formulate an aggressive plan of boosting Indian goods' image in Japanese market. It is suggested that trade fairs and exhibitions should be held in Tokyo and other important cities of Japan on yearly basis. As India-Japan Committee for Business Cooperation has identified new items such as handicrafts, handlooms, carpets and gem and jewellery for expanding exports, trade fairs and exhibitions will go a long way in building a promising image of these items in the public in general and importers in particular. In recent years, many Japanese importers have introduced new items of brassware in Japanese market. But the introduction of these new items requires some sort of exhibitions in various shopping centres so that Japanese people should know much about the same and this will increase the exports of these items to Japan. TFAI should undertake such plans and programmes with zeal and dedication. For example, Engineering Export Promotion Council should undertake an aggressive plan for fairs and exhibitions of those items which have potential in Japanese market so that the feeling that Indian engineering goods are of poor quality could be erased from the minds of Japanese importers. Similarly, items like carpets, handlooms and handicrafts should also get priority in fairs and exhibitions so that the export of these items could be expanded. It is to be kept in mind that trade fairs and exhibitions are sina-qua-non for Japanese market.

Constant Vigilance

Japanese market is a dynamic one. Changes in the fashion, taste and likeness are very frequent. Hence, constant vigilance of market conditions and changing needs of the people is another aspect of marketing goods in Japanese market. It is generally observed that Indian exporters do not keep in mind the consumers' needs once the market development of a product gets a start. This is an error. For the successful marketing of a product, continuous watch over the market developments and their impact on the consumers is essential. In expanding the export of many identified items, Indian exporters have to put in more efforts in researching the Japanese market and make an in-depth study of consumer tastes and requirements. Constant vigilance will be of great help to accurately grasp market movements and consumer trends in order to improve the competitive edge in terms of expanding exports. Constant vigilance is also essential on department stores, supermarkets, family run stores and other distribution outlets.

Professional Approach

Apart from the constant vigilance on the movements of Japanese market and consumer trends, an overall professional approach on the part of the Indian exporters is a sina-qua-non for efficient marketing of Indian goods. Non-professional approach of the exporters often lets them down in marketing goods in foreign markets. Japanese market is a sophisticated buyers' market and requires more skilled and professional approach. Non-profession approach can make compromises on quality horizon. But a professional approach will never make any compromise on quality horizon at any cost. Non-professional approach lacks in experience in and / adaptability to the requirements of marketing a product.

Marketing a new product in Japanese market is a challenging job with more pitfalls than promises of success. The risk of failure can, however, be eliminated by means of proper planning and product development, based on a realistic view of the consumers' irrational behaviour and uncertain marketing conditions. An adhoc approach, which would seek to unload surpluses, as and when available, is not conducive to healthy export trade with Japan. On the other hand, it may do irreparable damage to efforts to build up export markets. Hence, more conscious and sustained efforts (professional approach) are needed to build capacities to ensure continuity in the supply of the required goods to the Japanese market at a comparative price. All this underscores the need for a professional approach.

Professional approach, by and large, is a missing link in India's exports to Japan.

Need for Long-Term Strategy

In addition to the reliability of the product, mutual understanding of the business conditions of the corporate partners is indispensable in order to become established in the Japanese market. This is a long process and takes a long time. Japanese manufacturers and distributors (wholesalers and retailers also) are linked together by a strong awareness of their common goal. The manufacturers frequently emphasise the theme of the common goals to the wholesalers and retailers chosen to handle the products. In the past, imported goods in general had a high-quality image. Today, however, in many product fields the image of domestic items has been rising greatly. Consequently, considerable efforts have to be made in order to convey the high quality image of a brand.

If Indian goods are to succeed in the Japanese market, an indispensable pre-requisite for the Indian exporters is to execute a comprehensive marketing strategy, on long-term basis, which can equal that of the Japanese manufacturers. The essential measures for Indian exporters who want successful entry into the Japanese market are : (a) plan on a long-term policy; (b) have perseverance; (c) don't be discouraged by initial cost of entering into the market; (d) make an effort to discover the taste of the Japanese people; (e) be prepared to adapt your good to the changing tastes of the consumer; (f) listen to the real desires of the consumers; and (g) attract the attention of the Japanese consumer. If something really attracts the attention of the Japanese consumer, it will have assured success.

Publicity

Japan is experiencing today an information explosion, the

channels of information being myriad, multi-dimensional and quick. In this milieu of information explosion, product promotion in the context of different distribution systems, consumer tastes and preferences, buying systems and methods of promotion assumes more significance than ever before. Indian goods are lacking publicity and, as a result, they remain ignored. Hence, Indian exporters must make an all out effort to inform Japanese consumers about the availability and attributes of products and services and also to convince consumers to purchase the product offered. They should bring to light their products on collective basis. In Japan publicity and advertisement is a part and parcel of marketing goods in domestic market. Japanese manufacturers are spending millions of yens in publicity and advertisement and are also successful in penetrating into Japanese market. Indian exporters have to follow their path.

It is certain that if the said measures are taken in true spirit, India can widen her export base in the Japanese market. This could lead to an appreciable increase in the value and flow of Indo-Japanese trade in years to come. According to a study entitled "Markets for Export 1989-90" conducted by the Federation of Indian Chambers of Commerce and Industry (FICCI) a small increase in India's share in the total intake of 10 major countries, which have so far accounted for nearly 3 / 5 of our exports mean a lot in terms of foreign exchange earnings. According to the said study, between 1985 and 1990 i.e., during the period of five years, compound growth rate of India's exports to Japan would be nearly 18 per cent which certainly is a fairly high figure as well as encouraging one. Hence, the need of the day is that the Indian Government and various chambers and organisations in the field of exports, should develop a "Group Activity" and direct their pooled efforts for increasing exports to Japan which is a land of opportunities.

Table 8.1 indicates trends in India's projected exports to major importing countries between 1985 and 1990.

TABLE 8.1

India's Projected Exports

Country	Estimates Based on Proportionate Increase in Growth of Exports to Different Countries		Estimates Based on Constant Shares	
	Exports (Target) 1989 - 90	Compound Growth Rate 1985 - 90	Exports (Target) 1989 - 90	Compound Growth Rate 1985 - 90
USA	4,981	21.0	3,150	10.4
USSR	4,474	22.0	4,480	22.0
Japan	1,791	12.5	2,250	17.8
West Germany	1,374	22.5	1,040	15.8
UK	1,254	12.5	1,390	14.5
Saudi Arabia	967	29.1	630	18.5
South Korea	622	36.1	680	11.9
Belgium	480	18.8	570	23.0
France	473	18.0	440	16.6
Sri Lanka	447	30.4	240	15.7

Source : Foreign Trade Bulletin (IIFT), New Delhi, October 1985.

Select Bibliography

Books

Agarwal, B.M., Indo-Japanese Trade Relations - A Diagnosis; Aalekh Publishers, New Delhi, 1974.

Agarwal, M.R., Regional Economic Cooperation in South Asia; S. Chand and Company, New Delhi, 1979.

Albert, F., Rich and Poor Nations in the World Economy; New York, 1978.

Allen, G.C., A Short Economic History of Modern Japan; London, 1962.

Allen, R.G.D., International Trade Statistics; New York, 1953.

Anesty, V., The Economic Development of India; London, 1952.

Blass, B., The Theory of Economic Integration; Illinois, 1961.

Balogh, T., Unequal Partners; Oxford, 1963.

Baran, P.A., Monopoly Capitalism; Penguin Books, 1968.

Battra, R.N., Studies in the Pure Theory of International Trade; Macmillan, 1973.

Behari, B., Imports in a Developing Economy; Bombay, 1968.

Bettlehem, Studies in the Theory of Planning; 1959.

Bhagwati, J., The Economics of Underdeveloped Countries; 1966.

Bhararadwaj, R., The Structural Basis of India's Foreign Trade; Allied Publishers, Bombay, 1962.

Boltho, A., Economics of the Third World; London, 1975.

Buchanin & E., Approaches to Economic Development; 1965.

Caves, R.E., Trade and Economic Structure; 1963.

Cohen, J.B., Japan's Postwar Economy; Bloomington, 1958.

Cordon, W.M., Recent Development in the Theory of International Trade; 1965.

Currie, L., Accelerating Development - The Necessity and the Means; 1966.

Curzon, V., The Essentials of Economic Integration; London, 1974.

Datta, B., Economic Development and Exports; 1962.

Dutta, R.C., Indian Trade, Manufactures and Finance; Calcutta, 1905.

Eco, Plan-Agency, New Long Range Economic Plan of Japan; Tokyo, 1957.

Emmanuel, A., Unequal Exchange; London, 1972.

Enke, S., International Economics; New York, 1957.

FICCI, Our Export Trade; 1959.

FICCI, India's Trade With Some Asian Countries; New Delhi, 1969.

Floystad, G., Foreign Trade, Aid and Economic Growth in Less Developed Economies; Stockholm, 1968.

Frank, I., The European Common Market; New York, 1961.

Friedberg, A.S., The UNCTAD of 1964; Rotterdam, 1969.

Friedrich, K., International Economics; New York, 1974.

Frumkin, A., Modern Theories of International Economic Relations; Moscow, 1969.

Ganguli, B.N., India's Economic Relations With Far Eastern and Pacific Countries; Bombay, 1945.

Ganguli, B.N., India's Economic Relations; Madras, 1956.

Ganguli, B.N., Reconstruction of India's Foreign Trade; Delhi, 1946.

Ganguli, B.N., Devaluation of the Rupee; Delhi, 1966.

Ghate, B.G., Asia's Trade; Bombay, 1947.

Gill, K.K., An Analysis of Forces of Neo-colonialism in India; Patiala, 1980.

Gill, K.S., Evolution of Indian Economy; New Delhi, 1977.

Gill, S.S., Political Economy of Indo-Soviet Relations, New Delhi, 1983.

Gupta, A.K.D., Planning and Growth in Developing Economies; 1964.

Gupta, A.K.D., Trade Theory and Commercial Policy in Relation to Under-Developed Countries; 1965.

Gupta, K.R., A Study of General Agreement on Tariffs and Trade; New Delhi, 1967.

Gurtoo, D.N., India's Balance of Payments, 1920-1960; New Delhi, 1961.

Habereler, G., The Theory of International Trade; New York, 1937.

Habereler, G., A Survey of International Trade Theory; 1955.

Harrod, R., International Trade Theory in a Developing World; 1964.

Harrod, R.F., Towards Dynamic Economics; London, 1948.

Harris, S.E., International and Interregional Trade; New York, 1957.

Hirschman, A.O., National Power and the Structure of Foreign Trade; Berkeley, 1945.

Hirschman, A.O., The Strategy of Economic Development; Yale, 1958.

Ho, K.A., Japan's Trade Liberalisation in the 1960s; New York, 1973.

Hollerman, L., Japan's Dependence on the World Economy; Princeton, 1967.

Hunsberger, W.S., Japan and the United States in World Trade; New York, 1964.

Hussain, S.A., Politics of US Foreign Aid; Michigan, 1968.

ICSSR, The New International Economic Order; New Delhi, 1983.

IIFT, International Trade and Development; New Delhi, 1972.

IIFT, Trading with the World; New Delhi, 1968.

IASE, Asia's Economic Growth and International Cooperation; Tokyo, 1967.

IIFT, India's Trade and Economic Cooperation with Asia; New Delhi, 1974.

Iuh, K.M., Japan's Trade in Asia; London, 1966.

Jain, O.P., Regional Cooperation for Trade in Asia; New Delhi, 1973.

Jayraman, T.K., Economic Cooperation in the Indian Sub-continent; Bombay, 1978.

Johonson, H.G., International Trade and Economic Growth; 1958.

Johonson, H.G., Money, Trade and Economic Growth; 1962.

Johonson, H.G., Economic Policies Towards Less-Developed Countries; 1967.

Johonson, H.G., New Trade Strategy for the World Economy; 1968.

Johonson, H.G., Trade Strategy for Rich and Poor Nations; 1971.

Joshi, R.M., Indian Export Trade; 1962.

Kahnert, F., Economic Integration among Developing Countries; Paris, 1969.

Kapuria, K.S., The Indian Rupee; Bombay, 1967.

Kemp, K.C., The Pure Theory of International Trade; New Jersey, 1964.

Khan, K.S., Gains from International Trade; Bombay, 1971.

Kindlegerger, C.P., Economic Development; New York, 1958.

Kindlegerger, C.P., International Economics; Bombay, 1976.

Klein, L., Economic Growth : The Japanese Experience since the Meji Era; Illinois, 1968.

Kojima, K., Japan and a New World Economic Order; London, 1977.

Kostyukhin, D., The World Market Today; Moscow; 1979.

Kuznets, S., Economic Growth : Brazil, India, Japan, London; 1958.

Koyoshi, K., Economic Development and Import Dependence in Japan; Tokyo, 1960.

Lakdawala, D.T., International Aspects of Indian Economic Development; Bombay, 1951.

Lall, G.S., Finance of Foreign Trade; Delhi, 1968.

Leibenstein, H., Economic Backwardness and Economic Growth; New York, 1957.

Lenin, V.I., Collected Works, Moscow; 1972.

Lenin, V.I., Imperialism the Highest Stage of Capitalism; Moscow, 1975.

Levin, J.V., The Export Economics; Cambridge, 1960.

Lewis, A.W., Development Planning; 1966.

Lockwood, W.W., The Economic Development of Japan, growth and Structural Change; London, 1954.

Lo, F., Asian and Pacific Economy towards the Year 2000; Malaysia, 1988.

Maddison, A., Economic Growth in Japan and the USSR; London, 1969.

Maizels, A., Industrial Growth and World Trade; Cambridge, 1963.

Maizels, A., Exports and Economic Growth of Developing Countries; London, 1968.

Meade, J.E., The Theory of International Trade Policy; Oxford University Press, 1951-55.

Meade, J.E., A Geometry of International Trade; New York, 1952.

Meade, J.E., The Theory of Customs Unions; Amsterdam, 1956.

Meir, G.M., International Trade and Development; London, 1964.

Modigiliani, H., National Incomes and International Trade; Urbana, 1963.

Mohammad, K., United States Foreign Policy; Michigan, 1962.

Mookerjee, S., Factor Endowments and International Trade; Bombay, 1958.

Myint, H., The Economics of Developing Countries; London, 1964.

Myrdal, G., Against the Stream; Macmillan, 1977.

Myrdal, G., Asian Drama, Vol. 1; London, 1970.

Myrdal, G., The Challenge of World Poverty; London, 1968.

Myrdal, G., An International Economy; 1956.

Nandwani, S.C., Outlook for a South Asian Common Market; Chandigarh, 1970.

Naoroji, D., Poverty and Un-British Rule in India; 1901.

NCAER, India's Export Potential in Selected Countries; New Delhi, 1970.

NCAER, Looking Ahead - Prospects of India's Economy and Trade; New Delhi, 1962.

Nayar, D., India's Exports and Export Policies in the 1960s; Cambridge, 1976.

Norman, S., Crisis in Economic Relations between North and South; Essex, 1984.

Nukse, R., Pattern of Trade and Development; Stockholm, 1959.

Nukse, R., Equilibrium and Growth in the World Economy; Cambridge, 1961.

Ohlin, B., Inter-Regional and International Trade; Harward, 1952.

Owen, S.B., Studies in the Theory of Imperialism; London, 1972.

Patel, I.G., Foreign Aid; 1968.

Palekar, S.A., Trade of India; Bombay, 1946.

Pandit, Y.S., India's Balance of Indebtedness; London, 1937.

Paul, A., Economic Development; 1963.

Paul, S., Trade Strategies for Development; London, 1973.

Poduval, R.N., Recent Trends in India's Foreign Trade; Delhi, 1950.

Praiger, F.A., Japan's Trade in Asia; New York, 1966.

Robertson, D., International Trade Policy; London, 1983.

Robertson, P., Towards a New Trade Policy for Development; New York, 1960.

Robinson, J., Exercises in Economic Analysis; London, 1964.

Rostow, W.W., Economics of Take-Off into Self-Sustained Growth; 1964.

Rummel, F.J., Research Methodology in Business; New York, 1963.

Rix, A., Japan's Economic Aid; London 1980.

Sachs, I., Foreign Trade and Economic Development of Under-developed Economies; 1966.

Salvi, P.G., New Directions in India's Trade Policy; Bombay, 1964.

Sau, R.K., Indian Economic Growth : Constraints and Prospects; Calcutta, 1973.

Schleicher, C.P., International Relations - Cooperation and Conflict; Prentice Hall, 1962.

Satayanarayan, India's Trade With Asia and the Far East Countries; New Delhi, 1986.

Sen, S., India's Bilateral Payments and Trade Agreements; Calcutta, 1965.

Shonfield, A., International Economic Relations of the Western World; London, 1976.

Simkin, C.G.F., The Traditional Trade of Asia; London, 1968.

Singer, H.W., International Development, Growth and Change; New York, 1964.

Singh, M., India's Export Trends and the Prospects for Self-Sustained Growth; London, 1964.

Singh, V.B., Economic History of India; New Delhi, 1965.

Singh, R.K., Prosperity Through Export; Calcutta, 1965.

Sodersten, B.O., International Economics; London, 1970.

Sovani, N.V., Economic Relations of India with South-East Asia and the Far East; New Delhi, 1949.

Spero, J.E., The Politics of International Economic Relations; London, 1982.

Sraffa, P., Production of Commodities by Means of Commodities; Bombay, 1960.

Srivastava, S.K., Trade of India; Delhi, 1956.

Streeten, P., Trade Strategies for Development; London, 1973.

Takahashi, M., Mercantilism and East India Trade; London; 1926.

Taussig, F.W., International Trade; New York, 1936.

Thomas, R.K., Japanese Foreign Trade; London, 1975.

Thompson, U.H., Product Strategy; 1962.

Tsunoyama, S., A Concise Economic History of Modern Japan; Bombay, 1965.

Tauru, S., Essay on Japanese Economy; Tokyo, 1958.

Uri, P., Development without Dependence; New York, 1976.

Vakil, C.N., Economic Consequences of Divided India; Bombay, 1950.

Vakil, C.N., Economic Relations between India and Pakistan; Bombay, 1949.

Varsheny, R.L., India's Foreign Trade; Allahabad, 1954.

Verghese, S.K., India's Foreign Trade; Bombay, 1964.

Venkatsubbiah, H., Foreign Trade of India : 1900-1940; New Delhi, 1946.

Venkatsubbiah, H., Indian Economy Since Independence; Bombay, 1958.

Vinner, J., Studies in the Theory of International Trade; New York, 1937.

Vinner, J., International Trade and Economic Development; Oxford, 1953.

Wadia, P.T., Our Economic Problems; Bombay, 1959.

Weissman, S., The Trojan Horse; San Francisco, 1974.

White, E.W., Commercial Policies for the Nineteen Sixties; GATT, Geneva, 1960.

Wightman, D., Toward Economic Cooperation in Asia; ECAFE, Yale, 1963.

Wiles, P.J., Communist International Economics; Oxford, 1968.

Williamson, International Trade Theory Reconsidered : In Readings in International Trade; London, 1982.

Willy Brandt, A Programme for Survival; London, 1980.

Yates, P.L., Forty Years of Foreign Trade; London, 1959.

Yoshino, M.Y., Japan's Managerial System; Massachusetts, 1968.

Unpublished Ph.D. Theses

Mathur, A.B.L., Indo-US Trade Relations since 1947;University of Rajasthan, 1971.

Piparsania, L.N., Economic Aspects of Indo-Pakistan Relations; University of Jabalpur, 1964.

Satyanarayan, S., India's Trade with Asia and the Far East Countries; Osmania University, Hyderabad, 1971.

Singh, R.G., Indo-Pakistan Trade Relations; Punjabi University; Patiala, 1986.

Singh, R.N., Indo-Soviet Trade Relations 1947-67; University of Rajasthan, 1970.

Monographs

Agbi, S.O., Japan's Attitudes and Policies Towards African Issues Since 1945 : A Historical Perspective; 1982.

Librero, A.R., Philippine Trade with Japan : Pattern and Prospects; 1974.

Ogunremi, G.O., Nigeria-Japan Trade Relations : 1914, 1979; 1980.

Sirikrai, S., Japan-ASEAN Relations; The Pacific Basin Corporation, 1985.

Wanigaratne, Economic Relations between South Asia and ASEAN; 1985.

Articles

Bhatt, P.R., India's Trade Relations with Japan : A Quantitative Analysis; Margian, New Delhi, July-September 1987, p. 29.

Chakraborty, New Strategy to Step up Iron Ore Exports; Commerce, Bombay, Sept. 12-18, 1987, p. 34.

Champbell, B., Trade Between Asian Developing Economies : Record and Prospects; Asian Development Review, Maniala, No. 2, 1986, p. 57.

Goldstein, N., Trare, Jobs and Technology in the World Market; The Demand of Change, Foreign Trade Review, New Delhi, Oct-Dec. 1986, p. 277.

Gonsalves, E., Some thoughts on India's Export Strategy; Foreign Trade Review, New Delhi, July-Sept. 1986, p. 111.

Joseph, M., Spurt in Two-Way Trade; The Financial Express, Bombay, Oct. 13, 1987, p. 11.

Joseph, M., Role of Economic Cooperation Council; The Financial Express, Bombay, Oct. 13, 1987, p. 11.

Kanojia & Lal, What Indian Exporters Should Know? Foreign Trade Bulletin, New Delhi, Feb. 1986, p. 6.

Kumar, S.V., Imports : A Viable Policy; The Economic and Political Weekly, Bombay, July 27 - August 9, 1987, p. 95.

Mehta, S.S., Industrial Cóoperation in Regional Economic Grouping among Developed Countries and Lesson for SAARC; Foreign Trade Review, New Delhi, Jan.-March 1986, p. 343.

Model & Pandey, South Asian-ASEAN : Trade Possibilities of Expansion and Development; Foreign Trade Review, New Delhi, Jan-March 1986, p. 422.

Pareshnath, Export Obligation : A Cat and Mouse Game; Commerce, Bombay, Sept. 12-18, 1987, p. 11.

Prabhu, A.N., Indo-Japan Economic Relation : New Turn in Offing; Indian Foreign Review, New Delhi, July 31, 1987, p. 4.

Vinod, A., Indo-Japanese Cooperation : How Stable is it? Commerce, Bombay, Sept. 5-11, 1987, p. 5.

Periodical Publications

Annual Reports of International Monetary Funds, Washington, D.C.

Annual Development Reports of the World Bank, Washington, D.C.

Annual Reports of Ministry of Commerce, New Delhi.

Annual Reports of the Foreign Trade of Japan, Tokyo.

Economic Survey of Japan from 1975 to 1987, Tokyo.

Economic Bulletin for Asia and Far East. UN. New York.

Economic Survey of Asia and the Far East, UN, Bangkok.

Foreign Trade of Japan, Tokyo, from 1950 to 1965.

Foreign Trade of India, Ministry of Commerce. New Delhi.

Fuji Bank Bulletins, Tokyo.

India's Trade Agreements With Other Countries, Ministry of Commerce, New Delhi.

India's Trade with ECAFE Countries, ICC. Calcutta.

India's Foreign Trade Statistics, New Delhi.

International Financial Statistics, I.M.F., Washington, D.C.

International Trade, GATT, Geneva.

Japan Economic Almanac, Tokyo from 1970 to 1987.

Monthly Statistics of the Foreign Trade, DGCIS, Calcutta.

Quarterly Survey of Japanese Finance and Industry, Bank of Japan, Tokyo.

Report on Currency and Finance, RBI, Bombay.

Reserve Bank of India's Publications, Bombay.

Reviews of the Trade of India, Ministry of Commerce, New Delhi.

Statistical Handbook of Japan, Tokyo.

Statistical Year Book of United Nations, New York.

Statistical Survey of Japan's Economy, Tokyo.

Statistics on Japanese Industries, MITI, Tokyo.

Survey of India's Foreign Trade, ICC, Calcutta.

The Summary Report of Trade of Japan, JTA, Tokyo.

Yearbook of International Trade Statistics, United Nations, New York.

White Papers of Japan, (JIIA), Tokyo.

White Paper on International Trade of Japan, JETRO, Tokyo.

World Economic Survey, United Nations, New York.

World Trade News, ICC, Calcutta.

Working Papers of RBI, Bombay.

Working Papers of IMF, Washington.

Working Papers of FICCI, New Delhi.

Working Papers of IIFT, New Delhi.

Yearbook of Asia, Hong Kong.

Journals

Asian Development Review, ADB-Manila, Philippines.

Business India, Bombay.

Capital, Calcutta, India.

Commerce, Bombay, India.

Economic and Political Weekly, Bombay, India.

Economic Trends, FICCI, New Delhi, India.

Foreign Affairs Record, New Delhi, India.

Foreign Trade Bulletin, IIFT, New Delhi, India.

Foreign Trade Review, IIFT, New Delhi, India.

Hitotsubashi Journal of Economics, Tokyo, Japan.

Japan Eco, Toyko, Japan.

Journal of Japanese Trade and Industry, Tokyo, Japan.

Indian Foreign Review, New Delhi, India.

Margin, NCAER, New Delhi, India.

Tokyo Business Today, Tokyo, Japan.

The Developing Economies, IDE, Tokyo, Japan.

The Japan Economic Journal, Tokyo, Japan.

The Economist, New Delhi, India.

The Pacific Friend, Tokyo, Japan.

State Bank of India, Monthly Review, Bombay, India.

Papers

The Business Standard, Calcutta, India.

The Economic Times, Bombay, India.

The Financial Express, New Delhi, India.

The Japan Times, Tokyo, Japan.

The Wall Street Journal, Hong Kong.

The Telegraph, London.

The Telegraph, Calcutta, India.

The Financial Times, London.

Index

J

K

L

M

N

O

P

R

S

T

U

W